Lecture Notes in Artificial Int

Subseries of Lecture Notes in Computer Science
Edited by J. G. Carbonell and J. Siekmann

Lecture Notes in Computer Science

Edited by G. Goos, J. Hartmanis and J. van Leeuwen

Springer

Berlin
Heidelberg
New York
Barcelona
Hong Kong
London
Milan
Paris
Singapore
Tokyo

Neil V. Murray (Ed.)

Automated Reasoning with Analytic Tableaux and Related Methods

International Conference, TABLEAUX'99
Saratoga Springs, NY, USA, June 7-11, 1999
Proceedings

Springer

Series Editors

Jaime G. Carbonell, Carnegie Mellon University, Pittsburgh, PA, USA
Jörg Siekmann, University of Saarland, Saarbrücken, Germany

Volume Editor

Neil V. Murray
University at Albany - SUNY
Department of Computer Science, Institute for Programming and Logics
Albany, NY 12222, USA
E-mail: nvm@cs.albany.edu

Cataloging-in-Publication data applied for

Die Deutsche Bibliothek - CIP-Einheitsaufnahme

Automated reasoning with analytic tableaux and related methods : international conference ; tableaux '99, Saratoga Springs, NY, USA, June 7 - 11, 1999 ; proceedings / Niel V. Murray (ed.). - Berlin ; Heidelberg ; New York ; Barcelona ; Hong Kong ; London ; Milan ; Paris ; Singapore ; Tokyo : Springer, 1999
(Lecture notes in computer science ; Vol. 1617 : Lecture notes in artificial intelligence)
ISBN 3-540-66086-0

CR Subject Classification (1998): F.4.1, I.2.3

ISBN 3-540-66086-0 Springer-Verlag Berlin Heidelberg New York

Typesetting: Camera-ready by author
SPIN 10705220 06/3142 – 5 4 3 2 1 0 Printed on acid-free paper

Foreword

This volume contains a selection of papers presented at the International Conference on Analytic Tableaux and Related Methods (TABLEAUX'99) held on June 7-11, 1999 at the Inn at Saratoga, Saratoga Springs, NY, USA. This conference was the continuation of international meetings on Theorem Proving with Analytic Tableaux and Related Methods held in Lautenbach near Karlsruhe (1992), Marseille (1993), Abingdon near Oxford (1994), St. Goar near Koblenz (1995), Terrasini near Palermo (1996), Pont-à-Mousson near Nancy (1997), and Oisterwijk near Tilburg (1998). TABLEAUX'99 marks the first time the conference has been held in North America.

Tableau and related methods have been found to be convenient and effective for automating deduction in various non-standard logics as well as in classical logic. Examples taken from this meeting alone include temporal, description, tense, quantum, modal, projective, hybrid, intuitionistic, and linear logics. Areas of application include verification of software and computer systems, deductive databases, knowledge representation and its required inference engines, and system diagnosis. The conference brought together researchers interested in all aspects – theoretical foundations, implementation techniques, systems development and applications – of the mechanization of reasoning with tableaux and related methods.

The members of the program committee worked diligently in selecting the presented papers. Each research paper was given a formal evaluation by three referees – to whom we are indeed grateful. From the 41 submissions received, 18 original *research papers* and 3 original *system descriptions* were chosen by the program committee for presentation at the conference and for inclusion in these proceedings, together with the invited lectures. Also included are the abstracts of 2 *tutorials*, a summary of the non classical systems comparison conducted for TABLEAUX'99, descriptions of the comparison entries, and the titles and authors of *position papers*, which were also presented at the conference.

Acknowledgements First, I would like to thank the local arrangements chair, Joan Nellhaus, who helped with virtually all aspects of organizing the conference. I also thank Fabio Massacci, who organized the comparison. Ron Goebel put much time and effort into installing the web software that facilitated secure discussions amongst program committee members.

I also thank the authors of all submissions, the speakers, the tutorial organizers, the comparison entrants, program committee members, and, last but not least, the sponsors, who made it possible to organize this conference in Sartoga Springs, NY.

March 1999 Neil V. Murray

Previous Tableaux Workshops/Conferences

1992	Lautenbach, Germany	1993	Marseille, France
1994	Abingdon, England	1995	St. Goar, Germany
1996	Terrasini, Italy	1997	Pont-à-Mousson, France
1998	Oisterwijk, The Netherlands		

Invited speakers

Randal Bryant	Carnegie Mellon Univ., Pittsburgh, U.S.A.
David S. Warren	Univ. at Stony Brook – SUNY, Stony Brook, U.S.A.

Program Chair

Neil V. Murray
University at Albany - SUNY

Local Arrangements

Joan Nellhaus
Inst. for Programming & Logics (SUNY)

Program Committee

P. Baumgartner	University of Koblenz, Germany
B. Beckert	University of Karlsruhe, Germany
K. Broda	Imperial College, London, U.K.
R. Dyckhoff	St. Andrews University, U.K.
A. Felty	Bell Labs, U.S.A.
C. Fermueller	TU Wien, Austria
M. Fitting	CUNY, New York City, U.S.A.
U. Furbach	University of Koblenz, Germany
D. Galmiche	LORIA, Nancy, France
R. Goré	Australian National University, Australia
J. Goubault-Larrecq	GIE Dyade, France
R. Hähnle	University of Karlsruhe, Germany
J. Hodas	Harvey Mudd College, California, U.S.A.
C. Kreitz	Cornell University, U.S.A.
R. Letz	Technical University of Munich, Germany
D. Miller	Pennsylvania State University, U.S.A.
U. Moscato	University of Milan, Italy
N. Murray	University at Albany - SUNY, U.S.A.
N. Olivetti	Torino University, Italy
J. Pitt	Imperial College, London, U.K.
E. Rosenthal	University of New Haven, U.S.A.
P. Schmitt	University of Karlsruhe, Germany
H. de Swart	Tilburg University, The Netherlands

Referees

Each submitted paper was refereed by three members of the program committee. In some cases, they consulted specialists who were not on the committee. We gratefully mention their names.

Wolfgang Ahrendt
Alessandro Avellone
Matthias Baaz
Matteo Baldoni
Felice Cardone
A. Cichon
Ingo Dahn
C. Faggian
Mauro Ferrari
Camillo Fiorentini
Andreas Goerdt
Guido Governatori
M. Kuehn
D. Larchey-Wendling
Alexander Leitsch
Donald Loveland
James Lu
Ornaghi Mario
Fabio Massacci
Georg Moser
Christian Pape
Uwe Petermann
Torsten Schaub
Gernot Stenz
Mark Stickel
L. Vigneron

Sponsors

University at Albany

Research Council
College of Arts and Sciences
Department of Computer Science
Institute for Programming & Logics

Position Papers

The regular conference program included the presentation of nine (of eleven accepted) position papers. Informal proceedings containing these papers appeared as the internal scientific report "Position Papers, TABLEAUX'99", TR 99-1, Department of Computer Science, University at Albany - SUNY, Albany, NY, U.S.A.

Sequent Decomposition: A Sequent Calculus as Efficient as Resolution.
Noriko H. Arai, Shinji Inoue, and Ryuji Masukawa

Tactics for Translation of Tableau in Natural Deduction.
Alessandro Avellone, Marco Benini, and Ugo Moscato

Depth-First Proof Search without Backtracking for Free Variable Semantic Tableaux.
Bernhard Beckert

Gentzen-Like Methods in Quantum Logic.
Uwe Egly and Hans Tompits

Unification-Based Proof Method for Modal Logic with Well-Founded Frames.
Shigeki Hagihara and Naoki Yonezaki

Model Generation for Natural-Language Semantic Analysis.
Karsten Konrad

A Proof of Completeness for Non-Horn Magic Sets and Its Application to Proof Condensation.
Miyuki Koshimura and Ryuzo Hasegawa

An Application of Labelled Tableaux to Parsing.
Karl-Michael Schneider

COLOSSEUM An Automated Theorem Prover for Intuitionistic Predicate Logic Based on Dialogue Games.
Claus Zinn

Goal Lift-Up: A Technique for Improving Proof Search in Connection Tableau Calculi.
Dirk Fuchs and Marc Fuchs

Simultaneous Sorted Unification for Free Variable Tableaux: An Elegant Calculus.
Pedro J. Martín de la Calle and Antonio Gavilanes Franco

Table of Contents

Extended Abstracts of Invited Lectures

Comparison

Abstracts of Tutorials

Contributed Research Papers

Contributed System Descriptions

Microprocessor Verification Using Efficient Decision Procedures for a Logic of Equality with Uninterpreted Functions*

Randal E. Bryant[1], Steven German[2], and Miroslav N. Velev[3]

[1] Computer Science, Carnegie Mellon University, Pittsburgh, PA
Randy.Bryant@cs.cmu.edu
[2] IBM Watson Research Center, Yorktown Hts., NY
german@watson.ibm.com
[3] Electrical and Computer Engineering, Carnegie Mellon University, Pittsburgh, PA
mvelev@ece.cmu.edu

Abstract. Modern processors have relatively simple specifications based on their instruction set architectures. Their implementations, however, are very complex, especially with the advent of performance-enhancing techniques such as pipelining, superscalar operation, and speculative execution. Formal techniques to verify that a processor implements its instruction set specification could yield more reliable results at a lower cost than the current simulation-based verification techniques used in industry.

The logic of equality with uninterpreted functions (EUF) provides a means of abstracting the manipulation of data by a processor when verifying the correctness of its control logic. Using a method devised by Burch and Dill [BD94], the correctness of a processor can be inferred by deciding the validity of a formula in EUF describing the comparative effect of running one clock cycle of processor operation to that of executing a small number (based on the processor issue rate) of machine instructions.

This paper describes recent advances in reducing formulas in EUF to propositional logic. We can then use either Binary Decision Diagrams (BDDs) or satisfiability procedures to determine whether this propositional formula is a tautology. We can exploit characteristics of the formulas generated when modeling processors to significantly reduce the number of propositional variables, and consequently the complexity, of the verification task.

1 Introduction

Microprocessors are among the most complex electronic systems created today. High performance processors require millions of transistors and employ exotic techniques such as pipelining, multiple instruction issue, branch prediction, speculative and/or out-of-order execution, register renaming, and many forms of caching [HP96]. When correctly implemented, these implementation artifacts should be invisible to the user. The

* This research was supported at Carnegie Mellon University by SRC Contract 98-DC-068 and by grants from Fujitsu, Motorola, and Intel.

processor should produce the same results as if it had executed the machine code in strict, sequential order.

Design errors can often lead to violations of the sequential semantics. For example, an update to a register or memory location by one instruction may not be detected by an instruction following too closely in the pipeline. An instruction following a conditional branch may be executed prematurely, modifying a register even though the processor later determines that the branch is taken. Such *hazard* possibilities increase dramatically as the instruction pipelines increase in both depth and width.

Historically, microprocessor designs have been validated by extensive simulation. Instruction sequences are executed, in simulation, on two different models: a high-level model describing the desired effect of each instruction and a low-level model capturing the detailed pipeline structure. The results from these simulations are then compared for discrepancies. The instruction sequences may be taken from actual programs or synthetically generated to exercise different aspects of the pipeline structure [KN96].

Validation by simulation becomes increasingly costly and unreliable as processors increase in complexity. The number of tests required to cover all possible pipeline interactions becomes overwhelming. Furthermore, simulation test generators suffer from a fundamental limitation due to their use of information about the pipeline structure in determining the possible interactions in an instruction sequence that need to be simulated. A single conceptual design error can yield both an improperly-designed pipeline and a failure to test for a particular instruction combination.

As an alternative to simulation, a number of researchers have investigated using formal verification techniques to prove that a pipelined processor preserves the semantics of the instruction set model. Formal verification has the advantage that it demonstrates correct execution for all possible instruction sequences. Given the large amount of resources currently spent simulating processors, formal verification tools hold the promise of producing more reliable results at a lower cost.

Most of the complexity in modern processors comes from their control logic. The processing of data is localized to a few subsystems such as the arithmetic logic unit and the floating point unit. These can be formally verified separately. We can therefore create an abstract model of the processor that captures the complexities of the control logic while ignoring the details of the data processing. We view program data and addresses as symbolic "terms" having no specified mathematical properties other than the ability to compare two values for equality. We abstract the functionality of data processing blocks as *uninterpreted functions*, with no specified properties other than "functional consistency," i.e., that applications of a function to equal arguments yield equal results: $x = y \Rightarrow f(x) = f(y)$.

Earlier work on formal verification of processors requires detailed analysis of the pipelined structure, e.g., using automated theorem provers [SB90]. Our interest is in developing automated techniques that apply powerful symbolic evaluation techniques to analyze the behavior of the processor over all possible operating conditions. We believe that high degrees of automation are essential to gaining acceptance by chip designers.

Burch and Dill [BD94] were the first to demonstrate that automated decision procedures for a logic of equality with uninterpreted functions (EUF) could be used to verify pipelined processors. They assume there are two abstract models of the processor—

a "program" model providing a direct implementation of the instruction set, and a "pipeline" model that captures the complexities of the actual implementation. Verifying that the pipelined processor has behavior matching that of the program model can be performed by constructing a formula in EUF that compares for equality the terms describing the modifications to the programmer-visible state (i.e., the registers, data memory, and program counter) produced by the two models and then proving the validity of this formula.

In their 1994 paper, Burch and Dill also described the implementation of a decision procedure for this logic based on theorem proving search methods. Their procedure builds on ones originally described by Shostak [Sho79] and by Nelson and Oppen [NO80], using combinatorial search coupled with algorithms for maintaining a partitioning of the terms into equivalence classes based on the equalities that hold at a given step of the search. More details of their decision procedure are given in [BDL96].

This paper describes some of our recent results in reducing formulas in EUF to propositional logic in the context of verifying pipelined processors. We show that characteristics of the formulas generated can be exploited to significantly reduce the number of propositional variables and consequently the complexity of proving that the formula is a tautology. By reducing the validity condition to propositional logic, we can apply powerful Boolean methods such as Binary Decision Diagrams (BDDs) [Bry86] as well as highly-optimized satisfiability checkers. By this approach we have achieved much better performance than more classical decision procedures for formulas with uninterpreted functions. More of the technical details are presented in [BGV99b,BGV99a].

2 Verification Methodology

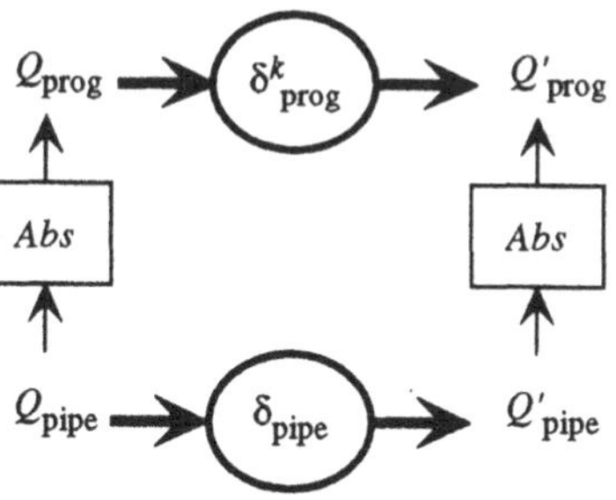

Fig. 1. Correctness criterion for verifying that pipelined processor "pipe" preserves the sequential semantics of the machine-level language program "prog".

Our task is to verify that a processor will execute all possible instruction sequences properly. Since there is an infinite number of possible sequences, this condition cannot be proved directly. Instead, we show that each possible individual instruction will be executed correctly, regardless of the preceding and following instruction sequences. The correct execution of a complete sequence then follows by induction on its length.

One approach to proving the correctness of individual instructions is based on proving the invariance of an abstraction function between processor and program states by each instruction execution. A similar method was proposed by Hoare for proving the correctness of each operation in the implementation of an abstract data type [Hoa72].

We model the processor as having states in the set $\mathcal{Q}_{\text{pipe}}$, and the behavior of the processor for each clock cycle of operation by a next-state function $\delta_{\text{pipe}}: \mathcal{Q}_{\text{pipe}} \rightarrow \mathcal{Q}_{\text{pipe}}$. Similarly, the state visible to the assembly language programmer (typically the main memory, integer and floating point registers, program counter, and other status registers) is modeled by a state set $\mathcal{Q}_{\text{prog}}$ and the execution of a single program instruction by a next-state function $\delta_{\text{prog}}: \mathcal{Q}_{\text{prog}} \rightarrow \mathcal{Q}_{\text{prog}}$. In our simplified formulation, we we do not consider the input or output to the processor, but rather that the action taken on each step is determined by the program or pipeline state.

Our task is to show a correspondence between the transformations on the pipeline state by the processor and on the program state by the instruction execution model. This correspondence can be described by an *abstraction function* $Abs: \mathcal{Q}_{\text{pipe}} \rightarrow \mathcal{Q}_{\text{prog}}$ identifying which program state is represented by a given pipeline state. Typically, this corresponds to the effect of completing any instructions in the pipeline without fetching any new instructions. For each pipeline state, there must be a value k indicating the number of program instructions fetched in a given cycle that are ultimately executed. For example, classical RISC pipelines have $k \leq 1$, while superscalar pipelines have k bounded by their "issue rate," typically between 2 and 8. In some pipeline states, we will have a value of k less than its maximum (including possibly $k = 0$). This can occur when instructions must be stalled due to resource conflicts or data dependencies. It also occurs when instructions are fetched and partially executed, but their results are discarded, e.g., due to a mispredicted branch.

The first verification condition [Bur96], is the "correspondence" property illustrated in Figure 1:

$$\forall Q_{\text{pipe}} \in \mathcal{Q}_{\text{pipe}} \exists k \left[\delta^k_{\text{prog}}(Abs(Q_{\text{pipe}})) \;=\; Abs(\delta_{\text{pipe}}(Q_{\text{pipe}}))\right] \qquad (1)$$

where δ^k_{prog} denotes the k-fold composition of δ_{prog}. Since k is bounded by a small integer, we can eliminate the existential quantification in this equation by forming a disjunction over the possible values of k. For example, a dual-issue pipeline would have the verification condition:

$$\forall Q_{\text{pipe}} \in \mathcal{Q}_{\text{pipe}} \begin{bmatrix} Abs(Q_{\text{pipe}}) = Abs(\delta_{\text{pipe}}(Q_{\text{pipe}})) & \vee \\ \delta_{\text{prog}}(Abs(Q_{\text{pipe}})) = Abs(\delta_{\text{pipe}}(Q_{\text{pipe}})) & \vee \\ \delta_{\text{prog}}(\delta_{\text{prog}}(Abs(Q_{\text{pipe}}))) = Abs(\delta_{\text{pipe}}(Q_{\text{pipe}})) & \end{bmatrix} \qquad (2)$$

We require as a second verification condition that Abs be surjective to guarantee that all program behaviors can be realized. That is, for every program state Q_{prog}, there must be a state Q_{pipe} such that $Abs(Q_{\text{pipe}}) = Q_{\text{prog}}$.

We require as a third verification condition a "liveness" property that guarantees the processor can always make forward progress. Otherwise we could successfully "verify" a processor that never changes state, giving $k = 0$. This can be expressed by the verification condition:

$$\forall Q_{\text{pipe}} \in \mathcal{Q}_{\text{pipe}} \begin{bmatrix} [\delta_{\text{prog}}(Abs(Q_{\text{pipe}})) \neq Abs(Q_{\text{pipe}})] \\ \Rightarrow \\ \exists k[Abs(Q_{\text{pipe}}) \neq Abs(\delta^k_{\text{pipe}}(Q_{\text{pipe}}))] \end{bmatrix} \quad (3)$$

That is, as long as the corresponding program state is one in which the program makes forward progress (e.g., it is not repeatedly executing an instruction that jumps to itself), the pipeline will make forward progress within k cycles for some value of k. In this paper, as with most of the research on processor verification, we will focus on the correspondence property given by Equation 1.

Observe that the abstraction function can be arbitrary, as long as it satisfies the three properties listed above. The soundness of the verification is not compromised by an incorrect abstraction function. That is, an invalid abstraction function will not cause the verifier yield a "false positive" result, declaring a faulty pipeline to be correct. We can let the user provide us with the abstraction function [BF89,NJB97], but this becomes very cumbersome with increased pipeline complexity. Alternatively, we can attempt to derive the abstraction function directly from the pipeline structure [BD94]. Unlike simulation-based test generation, using information about the pipeline structure does not diminish the integrity of the verification.

Burch and Dill [BD94] first proposed using the pipeline description to automatically derive its own abstraction function. They do this by exploiting two properties found in many pipeline designs. First, the programmer-visible state is usually embedded within the overall processor state. That is, there are specific register and memory arrays for the program registers, the main memory, and the program counter. Second, the hardware has some mechanism for "flushing" the pipeline, i.e., to complete all instructions in the pipeline without fetching any new ones. For example, this would occur when the instruction cache misses and hence no new instructions could be fetched. A symbolic simulator, which computes the behavior of the circuit over symbolically-represented states, can automatically derive the abstraction function. First, we initialize the circuit to an arbitrary, symbolic state, covering all the states in $\mathcal{Q}_{\text{pipe}}$. We then symbolically simulate the behavior of a processor flush. We then examine the state in the program visible register and memory elements and declare these symbolic values to represent the mapping Abs. Using similar symbolic simulation techniques, we can also compute the effect of the processor on an arbitrary pipeline state δ_{pipe} and the effect of executing an arbitrary program instruction δ_{prog}. Thus, a symbolic simulator can solve the key problems related to verifying pipeline processors.

3 Logic of Equality with Uninterpreted Functions (EUF)

The logic of Equality with Uninterpreted Functions (EUF) presented by Burch and Dill [BD94] can be expressed by the following syntax:

$$\begin{aligned} \mathit{term} &::= \mathit{ITE}(\mathit{formula}, \mathit{term}, \mathit{term}) \\ &\quad\;\; \mid \mathit{function\text{-}symbol}(\mathit{term}, \ldots, \mathit{term}) \\ \mathit{formula} &::= \mathbf{true} \mid \mathbf{false} \mid (\mathit{term} = \mathit{term}) \end{aligned}$$

$\mid$ (*formula* $\wedge$ *formula*) $\mid$ (*formula* $\vee$ *formula*) $\mid$ $\neg$*formula*
$\mid$ *predicate-symbol*(*term*, ..., *term*)

In this logic, *formulas* have truth values while *terms* have values from some arbitrary domain. Terms are formed by application of uninterpreted function symbols and by applications of the *ITE* (for "if-then-else") operator. The *ITE* operator chooses between two terms based on a Boolean control value, i.e., *ITE*$(\mathbf{true}, x_1, x_2)$ yields x_1 while *ITE*$(\mathbf{false}, x_1, x_2)$ yields x_2. Formulas are formed by comparing two terms for equality, by applying an uninterpreted predicate symbol to a list of terms, and by combining formulas using Boolean connectives. A formula expressing equality between two terms is called an *equation*.

The *ITE* operator distinguishes this logic from other logics of uninterpreted functions, e.g., that used by Shostak [Sho79]. It can be used to model the behavior of "multiplexors" in hardware as well as the effect of a conditional operation in a program. Observe also that this operation has a formula as an argument. We use truth values to represent control values rather than introducing a separate Boolean data type. As a consequence, our logic allows terms to contain formulas, and vice-versa. Although this nesting of operations can be "flattened" into a more conventional form such as conjunctive normal form, this process can cause the formula to grow exponentially. Instead, we prefer to devise decision procedures that can operate directly on our logic.

Every function symbol f has an associated *order*, denoted $ord(f)$, indicating the number of terms it takes as arguments. Function symbols of order zero are referred to as *domain variables*. We use the shortened form v rather than $v()$ to denote an instance of a domain variable. Similarly, every predicate p has an associated order $ord(p)$. Predicates of order zero are referred to as *propositional variables*.

The truth of a formula is defined relative to a nonempty domain $\mathcal{D}$ of values and an interpretation I of the function and predicate symbols. Interpretation I assigns to each function symbol of order k a function from $\mathcal{D}^k$ to $\mathcal{D}$, and to each predicate symbol of order k a function from $\mathcal{D}^k$ to $\{\mathbf{true}, \mathbf{false}\}$. Given an interpretation I of the function and predicate symbols and an expression E, we can define the *valuation* of E under I, denoted $I[E]$, according to its syntactic structure. $I[E]$ will be an element of the domain when E is a term, and a truth value when E is a formula.

A formula F is said to be *true under interpretation* I when $I[F]$ equals $\mathbf{true}$. It is said to be *valid over domain* $\mathcal{D}$ when it is true for all interpretations over domain $\mathcal{D}$. F is said to be *universally valid* when it is valid over all domains.

4 Reducing EUF to Propositional Logic

Ackermann has shown [Ack54] that the universal validity of any EUF formula F can be decided by considering only interpretations over a finite domain. In particular, it suffices to have a domain as large as the number of syntactically distinct function application terms occurring in F. Such a domain provides enough distinct values to capture all possible combinations of equalities and inequalities between terms—the only property of terms that our logic considers.

Ackermann also described a technique for eliminating all applications of function and predicate symbols having nonzero order. Each function application is replaced by a domain variable and then constraints are added to enforce functional consistency. For example, if formula F includes terms $f(x_1)$ and $f(x_2)$, we would introduce domain variables fx_1 and fx_2. We would modify F to use these domain variables rather than their respective function application terms, giving formula F'. The verification condition would then be expressed as $[x_1 = x_2 \Rightarrow fx_1 = fx_2] \Rightarrow F'$. Observe how the antecedent enforces functional consistency. By this method, any EUF formula F can be transformed into a formula F^* containing only domain and propositional variables.

In principle we can therefore reduce any EUF formula F having n distinct function application terms to a propositional logic formula by considering as domain the set of all bit vectors of length m, for some value $m \geq \log_2 n$. Each term is then represented as a vector of n formulas, with each domain variable encoded as a vector of m propositional variables. We implemented a variation on this scheme using ordered Binary Decision Diagrams (BDDs) [Bry86] to represent the Boolean functions encoding the terms and formulas symbolically [VB98]. We were able to verify a simple RISC processor implementing only arithmetic instructions. Unfortunately, we found that the BDDs became too complex as we added memory load and store instructions or branch instructions. The interactions between the terms representing successive instructions created circular constraints on the variable ordering that precluded having a good variable ordering. More recent work by Pnueli *et al* [PRSS99] has shown that by examining the detailed structure of the equations in a formula, much tighter bounds can be obtained on the size of the domain associated with each domain variable.

Goel *et al* [GSZAS98] describe an alternate approach to reducing formulas in a logic of equality with uninterpreted functions to propositional logic. They first use Ackermann's method to replace all function applications with domain variables coupled with constraints to impose functional consistency. They then introduce a propositional variable $e_{i,j}$ for each pair of domain variables x_i and x_j in the formula, encoding whether or not the two variables are equal. Based on these variables they generate a propositional formula for each equation encoding the conditions under which the two argument terms will have equal valuations. From this they can generate a propositional formula describing the conditions under which the original formula evaluates to **true**. This formula must include constraints to enforce the transitivity of equality among the terms. Their BDD-based implementation of this approach was able to verifying only relatively simple pipelines.

5 Positive Equality

We have recently shown that major improvements can be obtained by exploiting the polarity of the equations in the original formula F before replacing any function applications with domain variables. Let us introduce some notation regarding the polarity of equations and their dependent function symbols. For a formula F of the form $T_1 = T_2$, we say this equation is a *positive equation* of F. For formula F of the form $\neg F_1$, any positive equation of F_1 is a *negative equation* of F, and any negative equation of F_1 is a positive equation of F. For formula F of the form $F_1 \wedge F_2$ or $F_1 \vee F_2$, any positive (respectively, negative) equation of either F_1 or F_2 is a positive (resp., negative) equation of F as well. As we consider all of the equations occurring in F, we will also have those that appear as part of the formulas controlling *ITE* operations. We label these to be both positive and negative.

For term T of the form $f(T_1, \ldots, T_k)$, function symbol f is said to be a *data symbol* of T. For term T of the form $ITE(F, T_1, T_2)$, any function symbol that is a data symbol of either T_1 or T_2 is a data symbol of T.

A function symbol f is said to be a *p-function* symbol of formula F if there are no negative equations occurring in F for which f is a data symbol of one of the argument terms. Typically these will be symbols that either are not data symbols of any equation or are data symbols only of the top-level verification conditions. For verifying the correspondence property given by Equation 1, we will see that we can represent all operations involving program data and addresses with p-function symbols. The only function symbols that do not qualify as p-function symbols in our application are those representing register identifiers.

We can exploit the presence of p-function symbols to greatly reduce the number of interpretations that must be considered to determine universal validity. Let Σ denote a subset of the function symbols occurring in F. We say that interpretation I is diverse with respect to Σ for F when for any function application term $f(S_1, \ldots, S_k)$ where $f \in \Sigma$ and any other function application term $g(U_1, \ldots, U_l)$ we have $I[f(S_1, \ldots, S_k)] = I[g(U_1, \ldots, U_l)]$ iff $f = g$ and $I[S_i] = I[U_i]$ for $1 \leq i \leq k$. Interpretation I is said to be "maximally diverse" if it is diverse with respect to the set of all p-function symbols in F.

Theorem 1. *P-formula F is universally valid if and only if it is true in all maximally diverse interpretations.*

The essential idea behind this theorem is that a maximally diverse interpretation forms a worst case as far as determining the validity of a formula. For any less diverse interpretation I, we can systematically derive a maximally diverse I' such that among the equations, only the positive ones can change their valuations under I', and these can only change from **true** to **false**. Therefore the valuation of F under the two interpretations must either be equal or have $I[F] = \mathbf{true}$ and $I'[F] = \mathbf{false}$.

6 Eliminating Function Applications

We have devised a method of eliminating function application terms from a formula that differs from that of Ackermann [Ack54]. Our method uses a nested *ITE* structure to capture the functional consistency constraints rather than imposing these as antecedents to the formula. Our method has the advantage that it leads to a direct method to exploit positive equality.

We illustrate our technique for replacing function applications by domain variables with a small example. Let F be an EUF formula containing three terms applying function symbol f: $f(x_1)$, $f(x_2)$, and $f(x_3)$, which we identify as terms T_1, T_2, and T_3, respectively. Let vf_1, vf_2, and vf_3 be domain variables that do not occur in F. We generate new terms U_1, U_2, and U_3 as follows:

$$U_1 \doteq vf_1 \tag{4}$$

$$U_2 \doteq ITE(x_2 = x_1, vf_1, vf_2)$$
$$U_3 \doteq ITE(x_3 = x_1, vf_1, ITE(x_3 = x_2, vf_2, vf_3))$$

We then eliminate the function applications by replacing each instance of T_i in F by U_i for $1 \leq i \leq 3$. Observe that as we consider interpretations with different values for variables vf_1, vf_2, and vf_3, we implicitly cover all values that an interpretation of function symbol f may yield for the three arguments. The nested *ITE* structure shown in Equation 4 enforces functional consistency.

The general method for eliminating function applications follows that of our example formula. For a function symbol f of nonzero order and having n instances, we generate domain variables $vf_1, vf_2, \ldots, vf_n$. Rather than directly replacing function application term T_i with a domain variable, we generate a nested *ITE* structure comparing the arguments of this application to those of each application term T_j for $j < i$. As we consider different interpretations for the newly-generated domain variables, these nested *ITE* structures implicitly cover all possible interpretations of the function application terms while preserving functional consistency. A similar technique can be used to eliminate all instances of a predicate symbol p, using newly-generated propositional variables $ap_1, ap_2, \ldots$. This process is repeated for all function and predicate symbols yielding a formula F^* that contains only domain and propositional variables.

Our method can exploit positive equality by considering only distinct interpretations of the domain variables that are generated when eliminating the p-function symbols. Define Σ_p to be the set of domain variables occurring in F that are p-function symbols, plus the set of all domain variables of the form vf_i generated when eliminating the applications of each p-function symbol f.

Theorem 2. *EUF formula F is universally valid if and only if its translation F^* is true under all interpretations I^* that are diverse over Σ_p.*

This theorem follows by an inductive application of the following argument. Suppose f is in the set of function symbols Σ, that I is diverse over Σ for formula F, and that we replace all instances of f with nested *ITE* structures involving newly-generated domain variables $vf_1, \ldots, vf_n$ to give a formula F'. Then we can construct an interpretation I' for F' that is diverse over $\Sigma - \{f\} \cup \{vf_1, \ldots, vf_n\}$ such that $I'[F'] = I[F]$. Conversely, for any interpretation I' of F', we can extend it to an interpretation I including an interpretation of function symbol f such that $I[F] = I'[F']$.

We can further simplify the task of determining universal validity by choosing particular domains of sufficient size and assigning fixed interpretations to the variables in Σ_p. Let Σ_g be the set of variables occurring in F^* that are not in Σ_p. Let $\mathcal{D}_p$ and $\mathcal{D}_g$ be disjoint subsets of domain $\mathcal{D}$ such that $|\mathcal{D}_p| \geq |\Sigma_p|$ and $|\mathcal{D}_g| \geq |\Sigma_g|$. Let α be any 1–1 mapping $\alpha\colon \Sigma_p \to \mathcal{D}_p$.

Corollary 1. *Formula F is universally valid if and only if its translation F^* is true for every interpretation I^* such that $I^*(v_p) = \alpha(v_p)$ for every variable v_p in Σ_p, and $I^*(v_g)$ is in $\mathcal{D}_g$ for every variable v_g in Σ_g.*

This property follows because any interpretation I^* that is diverse with respect to Σ_p must provide a 1–1 mapping from the variables in Σ_p to domain values. It must therefore be isomorphic to some interpretation where $I^*(v_p) = \alpha(v_p)$ for every $v_p \in \Sigma_p$.

7 Generating a Propositional Formula

We have reduced the problem of deciding the universal validity of an arbitrary formula to one of determining whether a translated formula F^* containing only domain and propositional variables is true under all interpretations that are diverse with respect to some subset Σ_p of the domain variables in F^*. Our method borrows from [GSZAS98] the idea of introducing propositional variables to encode the equalities between domain variables. In our case, however, we only introduce propositional variables for a subset of the domain variable pairs.

For each pair of domain variables, u and v occurring in F^*, we only need to generate a propositional variable $e_{u,v}$ when both u and v are in Σ_g, and there is some equation $T_1 = T_2$ in F^* such that u appears as a data symbol of T_1 while v appears as a data symbol of T_2, or *vice-versa*. This encoding exploits the property that if either u or v is in Σ_p, we can assume they have distinct interpretations. It also exploits the sparse structure of the equations—we need only consider the relation between pairs of variables that appear as data symbols of terms being compared for equality. We can then construct a propositional formula $\hat{F}$ that is a tautology if and only if formula F^*, and consequently our original EUF formula F, is universally valid.

As with [GSZAS98], formula $\hat{F}$ should include constraints of the form $e_{u,v} \wedge e_{v,w} \Rightarrow e_{u,w}$ to consider only interpretations of these variables that satisfy the transitivity of equality. We have found in verifying microprocessor designs that these constraints can often be omitted—hardware designs do not seem to make use of any principles as mathematically deep as transitivity.

8 Modeling Microprocessors in EUF

Our verifier starts with a "term-level" model of both the pipeline and the program version of the processor. That is, we have already abstracted away details of the datapath, replacing functional units with uninterpreted functions. We represent control signals as formulas and multi-bit signals such as operation codes, register identifiers, memory addresses and data as terms. Each instruction is coded as a collection of formulas and terms based on an instruction format having a 3-bit instruction type field, an opcode, two source and one destination register identifiers, and an immediate data value. The task of proving a formal correspondence between such a model and a more detailed register-transfer level model remains a challenging research problem.

To model the register file, we use the memory model described by Burch and Dill [BD94], creating a nested *ITE* structure to encode the effect of a read operation based on the history of writes to the memory. That is, suppose at some point we have performed k write operations with addresses given by terms $A_1, \ldots, A_k$ and data given by terms $D_1, \ldots, D_k$. Then the effect of a read with address given by the term A is given by the term:

$$ITE(A = A_k, D_k, ITE(A = A_{k-1}, D_{k-1}, \cdots ITE(A = A_1, D_1, f_I(A)) \cdots)) \quad (5)$$

where f_I is an uninterpreted function expressing the initial memory state.

By careful design of the term-level model, we are able to treat all symbols representing opcodes, program data, and memory addresses as p-function symbols and hence the domain variables encoding such values are in Σ_p. The symbols representing register identifiers, on the other hand, do not satisfy the restrictions we impose on p-function symbols. In particular, the pipeline control must compare the register identifierss of successive instructions to determine when stall or register forwarding conditions arise. The memory model described by Equation 5 involves equations over address terms that control the outcome of *ITE* operations, and hence any data symbols occurring in such terms are not p-function symbols. This causes no problems for the register file, since the addresses are register identifiers. We cannot use such a memory model to represent the main data memory, however, or we would be unable to use p-function symbols to represent instruction and data addresses. Instead, we use a more abstracted memory model in which the effect of a write operation is to cause an arbitrary change of state (represented by an uninterpreted "memory update" function) for the entire memory. Such a model is a conservative abstraction of a true memory, but it suffices for modeling processors that perform their memory operations in program order.

9 Experimental Results

We have verified a variety of pipelined processor designs ranging from a single-issue, 5-stage pipeline similar to the DLX processor [HP96] to a variety of superscalar dual-issue pipelines. The most complex of these can handle all instruction types in either side of the pipeline. Our verification times range from less than 1 second for the single-issue case up to 50 seconds for the superscalar cases. The memory requirement (often the limiting factor for BDD-based applications) ranges from 1.5 to 80 Megabytes. The number of propositional variables ranges from 47 to 189, with between 17 and 129 comprising the $e_{u,v}$ variables encoding the relations between register identifiers.

By contrast, Burch [Bur96] verified a somewhat simpler dual-issue processor only after devising 3 different commutative diagrams, providing 28 manual case splits, and using around 30 minutes of CPU time. We have particularly found that our BDD-based approach can handle the disjunctive verification condition of Equation 2. Methods based on combinatorial search have unacceptably long run times, unless the disjunction is split into separate cases.

We have also experimented with using several different Boolean satisfiability (SAT) packages to prove that the complement of our generated propositional formula is not satisfiable. We have found these packages perform very well for the single-issue model, and they can often find counterexamples in complex designs containing errors. However they do not complete even after running for many hours when attempting to verify a correct dual-issue design.

10 Conclusions

When verifying pipelined microprocessors using abstracted data paths, we have found that the properties of the EUF formulas to be proved valid can be exploited to greatly simplify the propositional formulas we generate. As a consequence we have been able to verify complex superscalar pipelines with a high degree of automation.

Binary Decision Diagrams provide a powerful mechanism for verifying complex systems. Compared to methods based on combinatorial search, including both decision procedures for EUF as well as SAT solvers for the propositional translation of the verification condition, BDDs capture the full structure of a problem as a single data structure, rather than repeatedly enumerating and disproving possible counterexamples. Our experience has been that BDDs consistently outperform search-based methods when verifying complex designs.

BDDs can only be applied to tasks that are reducible to either propositional logic or to quantified Boolean formulas. An important area of research is to see what other classes of logic can be efficiently reduced to one of these forms.

References

[Ack54] W. Ackermann, *Solvable Cases of the Decision Problem*, North-Holland, Amsterdam, 1954.

[BDL96] C. Barrett, D. Dill, and J. Levitt, "Validity checking for combinations of theories with equality," *Formal Methods in Computer-Aided Design (FMCAD '96)*, M. Srivas and A. Camilleri, *eds.*, LNCS 1166, Springer-Verlag, November, 1996, pp. 187–201.

[BF89] S. Bose, and A. L. Fisher, "Verifying Pipelined Hardware Using Symbolic Logic Simulation," *International Conference on Computer Design (ICCD '89)*, 1989, pp. 217–221.

[Bry86] R. E. Bryant, "Graph-based algorithms for Boolean function manipulation", *IEEE Transactions on Computers*, Vol. C-35, No. 8 (August, 1986), pp. 677–691.

[BGV99a] R. E. Bryant, S. German, and M. N. Velev, "Processor verification using efficient reductions of the logic of uninterpreted functions to propositional logic," Technical report CMU-CS-99-115, Carnegie Mellon University, 1999. Available electronically as: `http://www.cs.cmu.edu/~bryant/pubdir/cmu-cs-99-115.ps`.

[BGV99b] R. E. Bryant, S. German, and M. N. Velev, "Exploiting positive equality in a logic of uninterpreted functions with equality," *Computer-Aided Verification (CAV '99)*, 1999.

[BD94] J. R. Burch, and D. L. Dill, "Automated verification of pipelined microprocessor control," *Computer-Aided Verification (CAV '94)*, D. L. Dill, *ed.*, LNCS 818, Springer-Verlag, June, 1994, pp. 68–80.

[Bur96] J. R. Burch, "Techniques for verifying superscalar microprocessors," *33rd Design Automation Conference (DAC '96)*, June, 1996, pp. 552–557.

[GSZAS98] A. Goel, K. Sajid, H. Zhou, A. Aziz, and V. Singhal, "BDD based procedures for a theory of equality with uninterpreted functions," *Computer-Aided Verification (CAV '98)*, A. J. Hu and M. Y. Vardi, *eds.*, LNCS 1427, Springer-Verlag, June, 1998, pp. 244–255.

[HP96] J. L. Hennessy, and D. A. Patterson, *Computer Architecture: A Quantitative Approach*, 2nd edition Morgan-Kaufmann, San Francisco, 1996.

[Hoa72] C. A. R. Hoare, "Proof of Correctness of Data Representations," *Acta Informatica* Vol. 1, 1972, pp. 271–281.

[KN96] M. Kantrowitz, and L. M. Noack, "I'm Done Simulating; Now What? Verification Coverage Analysis and Correctness Checking of the DECchip 21164 Alpha Microprocessor," *33rd Design Automation Conference (DAC '96)*, 1996, pp. 325–330.

[NO80] G. Nelson, and D. C. Oppen, "Fast decision procedures based on the congruence closure," *J. ACM*, Vol. 27, No. 2 (1980), pp. 356–364.

[NJB97] K. L. Nelson, A. Jain, and R. E. Bryant, "Formal Verification of a Superscalar Execution Unit," *34th Design Automation Conference (DAC '97)*, June, 1997.

[PRSS99] A. Pnueli, Y. Rodeh, O. Shtrichman, and M. Siegel, "Deciding equality formulas by small-domain instantiations," *Computer-Aided Verification (CAV '99)*, 1999.

[Sho79] R. E. Shostak, "A practical decision procedure for arithmetic with function symbols," *J. ACM*, Vol. 26, No. 2 (1979), pp. 351–360.

[SB90] M. Srivas and M. Bickford, "Formal Verification of a Pipelined Microprocessor," *IEEE Software*, Vol. 7, No. 5 (Sept., 1990), pp. 52–64.

[VB98] M. N. Velev, and R. E. Bryant, "Bit-level abstraction in the verification of pipelined microprocessors by correspondence checking." *Formal Methods in Computer-Aided Design (FMCAD '98)*, G. Gopalakrishnan and P. Windley, *eds.*, LNCS 1522, Springer-Verlag, November, 1998, pp. 18–35.

Design and Results of the Tableaux-99 Non-classical (Modal) Systems Comparison*

Fabio Massacci**

Dip. di Informatica e Sistemistica - Univ. di Roma I "La Sapienza"
via Salaria 113, I-00198 Roma - Italy
email: massacci@dis.uniroma1.it

Abstract. This paper reports the main ideas behind the design, the benchmarks, the organization, and the rating of the ATP systems of the TABLEAUX-99 Non-Classical (Modal) System Comparisons (TANCS).

1 Introduction

In order to stimulate automatic theorem proving (ATP) development in non-classical logic, and to expose ATP systems to researchers, the TABLEAUX conference has decided to promote a Non-Classical Systems comparison (TANCS).

Its aim is to provide a set of benchmarks and a standardized methodology for the assessment and comparison of ATP systems in non-classical logics, as it is done for first-order logic with the CADE System Competition [18]. At first, this should promote the competition among ATP systems and yield novel solutions. Second, a scientific approach to benchmarking non-classical ATP systems is needed to avoid that experimental "results" claimed at a conference are rebutted at the next[1]. TANCS is a step in the this direction.

The first comparison has been held in 98 [1] on modal and related (e.g. $\mathcal{ALC}$) logics [4, 9, 3] and this continues the series.

2 Design and Organization of the Comparison

The first problem of a comparison is how to rate two systems. Since the aim of ATP is solving problems, two natural measures are *effectiveness* and *usability*.

Effectiveness can be measured on the basis of the type and number of problems solved, the average runtime for successful solutions, the scaling of the prover as problems gets bigger. Usability can be assessed on the basis of availability via web or other sources, portability to various platforms, need for additional software besides the prover itself, ease of installation and use (eg visual interfaces), possibility of customizing the search heuristics, etc.

* More details are at htpp://www.dis.uniroma1.it/~massacci/TANCS.

** I would like to thank F. Donini, R. Goré, P. Liberatore, N. Murray, and A. Voronkov. This work has been supported by a CNR fellowship and by CNR and MURST grants.

[1] See for instance the claims by Giunchiglia & Sebastiani [7], rebutted by Hustadt & Schmidt [10] and then the (final?) reply by Giunchiglia et al. in [6].

The second decision regards the *choice of benchmark problems*[2] which offer the possibility to generate enough different samples so that "benchmark-tailored" techniques will not work, and which are either representative of the difficulties of the underlying satisfiability decision problem or representative of some real-world case. Third, the *rating of the systems* may not be based only on raw running times nor on internal aspects of the algorithm (e.g. Davis-Putnam calls) as we may end up with the impossibility of comparing in any fair way the performance of ATP using different hardware, operating systems and calculi.

For TANCS-99, we used benchmarks based on randomly generable formulae, as first suggested in [17] for SAT and applied to modal logic in [7]. Unfortunately, just taking a standard 3-SAT benchmark and "generalizing it" to modal logic may lead to many pitfalls [10]. We may even end up with too easy a benchmark which does not capture the complexity class of the underlying decision problem. Moreover, the use of randomly generated formulae implies that care is needed to use a good "random" number generator [16].

The TANCS-99 benchmarks were grouped into main divisions and categories, as in the CADE System Competition [18], according the complexity of the underlying decision problem and certain properties of the input formulae.

The following divisions were envisaged: a modal PSPACE division, a multi-modal PSPACE division, a global PSPACE division, a modal EXPTIME division. We recall that deciding modal logic satisfiability is PSPACE complete [14] and EXPTIME-complete if one uses global axioms Fitting-style [9], although not necessarily every benchmark set is able to capture this complexity class. For an introduction to modal or description logics see also [3, 4, 9].

3 Benchmark Problems

The basic idea behind each benchmark is that for each category within a division there are few *reference problems* which every entrant of the comparison has to try. Then a *C program* can generate all random instances of one's size and choice.

Besides parameters such as numbers of clauses and variables, the C program makes it possible to choose between a "plain" version of the benchmark and "modalized" one. With the modalized version we may try to analyze one of the interesting question of modal theorem proving: how can we tell that a prover is lousy on modal reasoning but makes up its speed just by a very efficient propositional Davis-Putnam implementation?

This check can be done by *encoding propositional variables as modal formulae* [8]: in the (satisfiability preserving) encoded problem there is only one variable and thus propositional reasoning is encoded as modal reasoning. Two encodings were possible: a simple encoding based on logic K and an harder one based on the logic S4. Modalized problems turned out to be harder than their plain version.

Below we sketch the generation procedure only for the submitted problems.

[2] The format of the benchmarks was a variant of the TPTP benchmark format for first-order logic [18]. See also TPTP's web page `http://www.cs.jcu.edu.au/~tptp`.

The Bounded Modal CNF benchmark has been proposed in [7] and later on corrected in [10]. As for the Random 3-SAT benchmark for propositional satisfiability [17], a set of modal clauses is generated in a random way with modal depth bounded by d (default 2). Each clause at depth 0 has k propositional literals (def. 3), which are obtained by randomly generating k different variables, each negated with probability 0.5. For clauses at depth x a literal is, with equal probability, either a modal clause $\Box c$ of depth $x-1$ or a propositional literal.

Setting $d = 0$ will generate the 3CNF random SAT problems according the fixed length clause model [17], a good representative of the hardness of the NP complexity class. Unfortunately, setting $d \geq 1$ does not yield problems in Σ_d^P of the polynomial hierarchy up to PSPACE [13]. As shown in [8], we are stuck at NP, no matter how big or hard[3] our instances are. Thus, *this benchmark is a problem in* NP crafted into a modal language.

The next benchmark, Unbounded Modal QBF, aims at solving this problem. It has been first proposed here for TANCS and the main intuition is to encode Quantified Boolean Formulae (QBF) into modal logic, using a clever variant of Ladner's original translation [14] so that auxiliary variables are not introduced.

In practice, we generate a quantified boolean formula with c clauses, alternation depth equal to d, and for each alternation at most v variables are used. A formula like $\forall v_{32} v_{31}.\exists v_{22} v_{21}.\forall v_{12} v_{11}.\exists v_{02} v_{01}.cnf_{c-\text{clauses}}(v01 \ldots v_{32})$ can be generated with $d = 3$ and $v = 2$.

For each clause we randomly generate k different variables (default 4) and each is negated with probability 0.5. The first and the third variable (if it exists) are existentially quantified. The second and fourth variable are universally quantified. This aims at eliminating trivially unsatisfiable formulae as reported in [2]. Other literals are either universal or existentially quantified variables with probability 0.5. The depth of each literal is randomly chosen from 1 to d.

The resulting formula is translated into modal logic with a variant of Ladner's encoding and the addition of formulae to guarantee the alternation of quantifiers in a tree-like form. For every fixed valued of d we can capture the problems in Σ_d^P in the polynomial hierarchy. That's better (we move upward in the complexity chain), yet PSPACE can only be reached by an unbounded value of d.

Finally, the benchmark Periodic Modal CNF can capture PSPACE. It encodes periodic satisfiability problems [15] with global axioms Fitting-style [4].

Periodic satisfiability has been introduced by Orlin [15]. The intuition is that propositional variables are indexed by time instants, so that a clause may refer to a constraint spanning over different time instants. A periodic satisfiability problem is a problem in which the time instants of the literals of the same clauses are distant at most d, where d is a prefixed constant. This problem has been proved by Orlin himself to be PSPACE-complete when $d \geq 1$. The embedding of periodic satisfiability into modal logic has been proposed here for the first time and is a faithful translation of the problem from both a semantical (a set of clauses is periodically satisfiable iff the translation is modally satisfiable) and computational perspective.

[3] Expensive checks are also necessary to avoid the generation of trivial instances.

In practice, a modal periodic formula has c clauses, and in each clause a (modal) literal may refer to the current instant of time, and be a propositional literal l, or to a future time randomly chosen from 1 to depth d, and thus have the form $\Box^d l$. For each instant of time, at most v variables are used and for each clauses we generate k (default 4) different variables and each is negated with probability 0.5. The first literal is always from the present instant of time and the second literal (if it exists) alway refers to a future instant of time. Other literals are chosen among present or future instants of time at random.

4 Performance Analysis and Conclusions

The running time on reference problems is the yardstick used to compare provers as the problems get harder and, above all, to give a reasonably fair comparison of different provers run on different machine, operating systems etc. as done for the DIMACS challenge [12].

In a nutshell, for every prover we compute the geometric mean time on the reference problems and then normalize the run time of each problem with respect to (i.e. divide by) this reference mean time. Then we obtain a relative ranking which makes it possible to abstract away, at least to a certain extent, machine and run dependent characteristics [5]. Notice that the geometric mean time must be used, otherwise we may draw meaningless conclusions [5]. Scaling, ability of handling large instance, and asymptotic behavior emerge more clearly [11,12].

A compacted report of the comparision is described in table 1 (more details are in the web pages). Note that the totals include timeouts and that numbers are *not* absolute value but relative performance wrt the benchmark Bounded Modal CNF with 8 clauses and 4 variables. Timeouts were only obtained by KtSeqC on "NP problems" and by DLP on the harder Periodic Modal CNF. The dash means that the ATP system has not entered any result in that category.

We may see that DLP is the most effective system (KtSeqC scaled slightly better but had timeouts and submitted less test results). It is worth mentioning that KtSeqC is the most portable, since it just require a C compiler, whereas DLP requires ML and HAM-ALC requires Lisp. More details on the ATP systems can be found in the corresponding system descriptions in these proceedings.

We may conclude as in [1]: systems and benchmarks of this comparison can be considered a main reference point for provers in modal and description logics.

References

1. P. Balsinger & A. Heuerding. Comparison of theorem provers for modal logics. In *Proc. of TABLEAUX-98*, *LNAI* 1397, p. 25–27, Springer Verlag 1998.
2. M. Cadoli, A. Giovanardi, & M. Schaerf. An algorithm to evaluate quantified boolean formulae. In *Proc. of AAAI-98*, 1998.
3. F. Donini, M. Lenzerini, D. Nardi, & A. Schaerf. Reasoning in description logics. In *Foundation of Knowledge Representation*, p. 191–236. CSLI-Publications, 1996.
4. M. Fitting. Basic modal logic. In *Handbook of Logic in AI and Logic Programming*, vol. 1, p. 365–448. Oxford Univ. Press, 1993.

Table 1. DLP, HAM, and KTS Timings

Sample			Total			Sat				Unsat			Tout
Sample	C	V	DLP	HAM	KTS	%	DLP	HAM	KTS	%	DLP	HAM	
BoundCnf	8	4	1.00	1.00	1.00	100%	1.00	1.00	1.00				
BoundCnf	16	4	3.89	2.00	0.96	100%	3.89	2.00	0.96				
BoundCnf	32	4	7.84	4.53	1.70	100%	7.84	4.53	0.96				14%KTS
BoundModK	8	4	2.96	1.95	0.96	100%	2.96	1.95	0.96				
BoundModK	16	4	5.44	4.00	1.04	100%	5.44	4.00	1.04				
BoundModK	32	4	10.59	10.62	5.13	100%	10.59	10.62	1.93				25%KTS
UnbndQbfCnf	8	2	9.00	19.54	-	94%	9.28	20.27		6%	5.71	11.32	
UnbndQbfCnf	16	2	10.05	24.33	-	19%	12.96	31.90		81%	9.47	22.86	
UnbndQbfCnf	32	2	12.26	38.33	-					100%	12.26	38.33	
UnbndQbfModK	8	2	12.88	17.85	-					100%	12.88	17.85	
UnbndQbfModK	16	2	17.61	26.09	-					100%	17.61	26.09	
UnbndQbfModK	32	2	26.27	44.55	-					100%	26.27	44.55	
PersatCnf	8	4	1.08	-	-	100%	1.08						
PersatCnf	16	4	2.12	-	-	100%	2.12						
PersatCnf	32	4	7.99	-	-	100%	7.99						
PersatModK	8	4	1060.95	-	-	63%	397.78						37%DLP
PersatModK	16	4	3789.22	-	-	6%	16.60						94%DLP
PersatModK	32	4	1898.29	-	-	19%	49.03			19%	2195.47		62%DLP

5. P. Fleming & J. Wallace. How not to lie with statistics: the correct way to summarize benchmark results. *CACM*, 29(3):218–221, 1986.
6. E. Giunchiglia, F. Giunchiglia, R. Sebastiani, & A. Tacchella. More evaluation of decision procedures for modal logics. In *Proc. of KR-96*, p. 626–635. 1998.
7. F. Giunchiglia and R. Sebastiani. Building decision procedures for modal logics from propositional decision procedures - the case study of modal k. In *Proc. of CADE-96*, *LNAI* 1104, p. 583–597. Springer-Verlag, 1996.
8. J. Halpern. The effect of bounding the number of primitive propositions and the depth of nesting on the complexity of modal logic. *AIJ*, 75(2):361–372, 1995.
9. J. Y. Halpern & Y. Moses. A guide to completeness and complexity for modal logics of knowledge and belief. *AIJ*, 54:319–379, 1992.
10. U. Hustadt & R. Schmidt. On evaluating decision procedure for modal logic. In *Proc. of IJCAI-97*, p. 202–207, 1997.
11. D. Johnson. A theoretician's guide to the experimental analysis of algorithms. Invited talk at AAAI-96. See `http://www.research.att.com/~dsj`, Aug. 1996.
12. D. Johnson & M. Trick, editors. *Cliques, Coloring, Satisfiability: the second DIMACS implementation challenge*, vol. 26 of *AMS Series in Discr. Math. and Theor. Comp. Sci.*. Am. Math. Soc., 1996.
13. D. Johnson. A catalog of complexity classes. In *Handbook of Theoretical Computer Science*, p. 67–162. Elsevier Science, 1990.
14. R. Ladner. The computational complexity of provability in systems of modal propositional logic. *SIAM JoC*, 6(3):467–480, 1977.
15. J. Orlin. The complexity of dynamic languages and dynamic optimization problems. In *Proc. of STOC-81*, p. 218–227, 1981.
16. W. Press, B. Flannery, S. Teukolsky, & W. Vetterling. *Numerical Recipes in C: The Art of Scientific Computing.* Cambridge Univ. Press, 1990.
17. B. Selman, D. Mitchell, & H. Levesque. Generating hard satisfiability problems. *AIJ*, 81(1-2):17–29, 1996.
18. C. Suttner & G. Sutcliffe. The CADE-14 ATP system competition. *JAR*, 21(1):99–134, 1998.

DLP and FaCT

Peter F. Patel-Schneider[1] and Ian Horrocks[2]

[1] Bell Labs Research, Murray Hill, NJ, U.S.A.
pfps@research.bell-labs.com
[2] University of Manchester, Manchester, UK
horrocks@cs.man.ac.uk

DLP [Patel-Schneider(1998)] and FaCT [Horrocks(1998)] are two recent description logic systems that contain sound and complete reasoners for expressive description logics. Due to the equivalences between expressive description logics and propositional modal logics, both DLP and FaCT can be used as satisfiability checkers for propositional modal logics.

FaCT is a full-featured system that contains a highly-optimized satisfiability checker for a superset of $\mathbf{K4}_{(\mathbf{m})}$. FaCT has an interface to allow the direct satisfiability checking of propositional modal formulae. FaCT is available for research purposes from *http://www.cs.man.ac.uk/~horrocks*.

DLP is an experimental system, designed to investigate various optimization techniques for description logic systems, including many of the optimizations pioneered in FaCT. DLP is available for research purposes from *http://www.bell-labs.com/user/pfps /dlp*. DLP contains a highly-optimized satisfiability checker for a superset of Propositional Dynamic Logic ($\mathbf{PDL}$), and includes a simple interface for the direct checking of the satisfiability of formulae in $\mathbf{PDL}$ as well as the modal logics $\mathbf{K}_{(\mathbf{m})}$, $\mathbf{KT}_{(\mathbf{m})}$, $\mathbf{K4}_{(\mathbf{m})}$, and $\mathbf{S4}_{(\mathbf{m})}$.

Both DLP and FaCT have performed very well on several comparisons of modal provers [Horrocks and Patel-Schneider(1998a),Horrocks and Patel-Schneider(1998b)]. The remainder of this submission will concentrate on DLP, as it is somewhat faster than FaCT. Significant differences from FaCT will be noted.

Architecture and Algorithm

At the heart of the DLP system is its highly-optimized tableaux satisfiability engine. DLP first performs a lexical normalization phase, which uniquely stores sub-formulae; eliminates repeated conjuncts and disjuncts; replaces local tautologies and contradictions with true and false, respectively; and performs several other normalization steps. It then attempts to construct a model of the normalized formulae; if it can construct the model then the formulae is satisfiable, if not, the formula is unsatisfiable.

DLP deals with non-determinism in the model construction algorithm by performing a semantic branching search, as in the Davis-Putnam-Logemann-Loveland procedure (DPLL), instead of the syntactic branching search used by most earlier tableaux based implementations [Giunchiglia and Sebastiani(1996)]. DLP deterministically expands disjunctions that present only one expansion possibility and detects a clash when a disjunction has no expansion possibilities.

DLP performs a form of dependency directed backtracking called *backjumping*, backtracking to the most-recent choice point that participates in a clash instead of to the most-recent choice point. To support backjumping, DLP keeps associated with each formula the set of choice points that gave rise to that formula.

DLP (but not FaCT, which has a different caching mechanism) caches the satisfiability status of all modal nodes that it encounters, and uses this status when a node with the same formula is seen again. DLP uses a combination of heuristics to determine the next disjunct on which to branch: it tries to maximize backjumping by first selecting disjunctions that do not depend on recent choice points, and it tries to maximize deterministic expansion by using the MOMS heuristic [Freeman(1996)] to select a disjunct from amongst these disjunctions. DLP defers modal processing until all propositional processing is complete at a node, again using a backjumping maximization heuristic to determine the order in which modal successors are explored.

To handle transitive modalities, and modality constructs in **PDL**, DLP checks for loops in the model it is constructing. If a loop is detected, it must be classified as either as a loop that leads to satisfiability or a loop that is unsatisfiable. This loop checking allows DLP to handle the S4 problem classes.

Implementation

DLP is implemented in Standard ML of New Jersey, and uses many of the features of the standard libraries of this language. DLP is a mostly-functional program in that the core of the engine has no side-effects. In fact, the only side effects in the satisfiability engine involve the unique storage of sub-formulae and node caching. (FaCT has a more traditional implementation in LISP.)

The unique storage of sub-formula and node caching are handled in DLP by a formula cache. When a formula is encountered, it is looked up in the cache. If the formula is in the cache, it is reused; if not, a new formula is created and added to the cache. Each formula has a satisfiability status; when a new node is created, the formulae for the node are conjoined and this formula is looked up in the formula cache; when a node's status is determined, the satisfiability status of its formula is updated.

Special Features

Full **PDL** loop checking can be replaced in DLP by a simpler (and much less costly) loop checking mechanism for transitive modalities. An optimization that is valid for transitive modalities but not for transitive closure can also be enabled. These changes turn DLP into a satisfiability checker for a multi-modal logic where some or all of the modalities may be transitive. The standard embedding can also be used to allow DLP to reason with reflexive modalities. DLP is therefore able to handle many modal logics, including $\mathbf{K}_{(\mathbf{m})}$, $\mathbf{KT}_{(\mathbf{m})}$, $\mathbf{K4}_{(\mathbf{m})}$, and $\mathbf{S4}_{(\mathbf{m})}$. DLP was recently extended to allow global axioms.

DLP has many options, including options to turn off all the above non-heuristic optimizations and options to vary the heuristic optimizations. The version of DLP used in the tests employs the simpler transitive modality loop checking, has all optimizations enabled, and uses the backjumping maximization and MOMS heuristics as described above.

Problem	Num	Sat	Time Outs	Time	(sat)
p-bound-cnf-K3-C8-V4-D2	16	16	0	0.016	0.003
p-bound-cnf-K3-C16-V4-D2	16	16	0	0.032	0.006
p-bound-cnf-K3-C32-V4-D2	16	16	0	0.064	0.014
p-bound-modK-K3-C8-V4-D2	16	16	0	0.050	0.007
p-bound-modK-K3-C16-V4-D2	16	16	0	0.096	0.013
p-bound-modK-K3-C32-V4-D2	16	16	0	0.190	0.027
p-bound-modS4-K3-C8-V4-D2	16	8	7	57.349	57.116
p-bound-modS4-K3-C16-V4-D2	16	1	15	93.910	93.861
p-bound-modS4-K3-C32-V4-D2	16	0	16	100.000	100.000
p-unbound-qbf-cnf-K4-C8-V2-D3	16	15	0	0.162	0.094
p-unbound-qbf-cnf-K4-C16-V2-D3	16	3	0	0.183	0.094
p-unbound-qbf-cnf-K4-C32-V2-D3	16	0	0	0.229	0.093
p-unbound-qbf-modK-K4-C8-V2-D3	16	0	0	0.232	0.053
p-unbound-qbf-modK-K4-C16-V2-D3	16	0	0	0.319	0.058
p-unbound-qbf-modK-K4-C32-V2-D3	16	0	0	0.478	0.064
p-unbound-qbf-modS4-K4-C8-V2-D3	16	0	0	2.496	0.018
p-unbound-qbf-modS4-K4-C16-V2-D3	16	0	0	3.659	0.026
p-unbound-qbf-modS4-K4-C32-V2-D3	16	0	0	6.463	0.049
persat-cnf-K4-C8-V4-D2	16	16	0	0.016	0.009
persat-cnf-K4-C16-V4-D2	16	16	0	0.038	0.025
persat-cnf-K4-C32-V4-D2	16	16	0	0.207	0.185
persat-modK-K4-C8-V4-D2	16	11	5	56.245	56.234
persat-modK-K4-C16-V4-D2	16	1	15	93.769	93.766
persat-modK-K4-C32-V4-D2	16	3	9	74.895	74.869
persat-modS4-K4-C8-V4-D2	16	7	0	10.833	10.666
persat-modS4-K4-C16-V4-D2	16	4	0	7.039	6.714
persat-modS4-K4-C32-V4-D2	16	2	0	3.041	2.395

Table 1. Reference Problems Results

DLP is also a complete description logic system. It has an interface that can be used to define a collection of concepts and roles. DLP automatically computes the subsumption hierarchy of these concepts and provides facilities for querying this hierarchy.

Performance Analysis

DLP was only tested on the problems that used logics $\mathbf{K}_{(\mathbf{m})}$ and $\mathbf{S4}_{(\mathbf{m})}$, possibly including global axioms. Testing was done on a machine with roughly the power of a Sparc Ultra 1. A time limit of 100 seconds was imposed for each problem instance. A special parser was written for DLP to input the problems. (Due to the fact that the problems were not in a format that FaCT could easily handle, FaCT was not run on the problems.)

There are two times reported for each problem class in Table 1. The first times are for an entire run, including inputing the file and normalizing the resulting formula. The second times are for just the satisfiability checker itself.

V	D	C/V									
		2	3	4	5	6	7	8	16	32	64
4	1	0.012	0.014	0.019	0.022	0.026	0.030	0.036	0.087	0.123	0.236
8	1	0.020	0.031	0.039	0.056	0.065	0.078	0.090	0.947	*29.581	0.739
16	1	0.047	0.075	0.105	0.142	0.180	0.214	0.264	0.992	*87.599	* 3.711
4	2	0.016	0.023	0.031	0.040	0.046	0.055	0.064	0.136	0.359	*7.701
8	2	0.034	0.049	0.067	0.084	0.106	0.129	0.154	0.402	1.235	2.269
16	2	0.016	0.023	0.031	0.040	0.046	0.055	0.064	0.136	0.359	*7.701

Table 2. Generated Problems Results—bound-cnf-K3 (average time)

Many of the reference problems were easy for DLP. The problems that were hard for DLP were the bound-modS4 problems and the persat-modK-K4 problems. They were *much* harder than the other problems. For the S4 problems this is probably because DLP uses an equality test to cut off modal loops. A subset test would probably be more effective We do not know why DLP is slow on the persat-modK-K4 problems.

DLP was run on some larger bound-cnf-K3 problems. The results are shown in Table 2. Times marked with a '*' indicate that some problem instances in the particular test exceeded the time bound.

DLP has also been run on a number of other test suites. It did very well on the Tableaux'98 test suite. It also performs well on random formulae generated by other generators. A plot of its performance on random bound-cnf-K3 formulae with a modal depth of 2 and and 9 variables is given Figure 1. The plot shows the 50th, 60th, 70th, 80th, 90th, and 100th percentiles of run time in seconds for various values of C/V (the ratio of clauses to variables). These results are competitive with the fastest propositional modal provers.

Future Work

We are in the process of designing and implementing a successor to DLP. This successor will have a different algorithmic base, and incorporate a newer backtracking optimization called dynamic backtracking [Ginsberg(1993)]. This will allow the optimized handling of nominals, or description logic individuals.

References

[Freeman(1996)] J. W. Freeman. Hard random 3-SAT problems and the Davis-Putnam procedure. *Artificial Intelligence*, 81:183–198, 1996.

[Ginsberg(1993)] M. L. Ginsberg. Dynamic backtracking. *Journal of Artificial Intelligence Research*, 1:25–46, 1993.

[Giunchiglia and Sebastiani(1996)] F. Giunchiglia and R. Sebastiani. Building decision procedures for modal logics from propositional decision procedures—the case study of modal K. In M. McRobbie and J. Slaney, editors, *Proceedings of the Thirteenth International Conference*

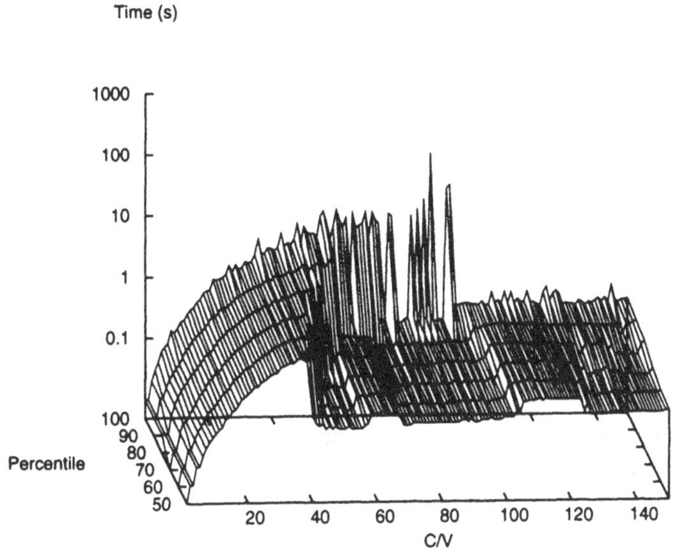

Fig. 1. Percentile times for formulae with 9–1350 clauses (C) and 9 variables (V)

on Automated Deduction (CADE-13), number 1104 in Lecture Notes in Artificial Intelligence, pages 583–597. Springer-Verlag, 1996.

[Horrocks(1998)] I. Horrocks. Using an expressive description logic: FaCT or fiction? In A. G. Cohn, L. Schubert, and S. C. Shapiro, editors, *Principles of Knowledge Representation and Reasoning: Proceedings of the Sixth International Conference (KR'98)*, pages 636–647. Morgan Kaufmann Publishers, San Francisco, CA, 1998.

[Horrocks and Patel-Schneider(1998a)] I. Horrocks and P. F. Patel-Schneider. FaCT and DLP. In H. de Swart, editor, *Automated Reasoning with Analytic Tableaux and Related Methods: International Conference Tableaux'98*, number 1397 in Lecture Notes in Artificial Intelligence, pages 27–30. Springer-Verlag, 1998a.

[Horrocks and Patel-Schneider(1998b)] I. Horrocks and P. F. Patel-Schneider. Optimising propositional modal satisfiability for description logic subsumption. In *International Conference AISC'98*, Lecture Notes in Artificial Intelligence. Springer-Verlag, 1998b.

[Patel-Schneider(1998)] Peter F. Patel-Schneider. DLP system description. In E. Franconi, G. De Giacomo, R. M. MacGregor, W. Nutt, C. A. Welty, and F. Sebastiani, editors, *Collected Papers from the International Description Logics Workshop (DL'98)*, pages 87–89, 1998.

Applying an $\mathcal{ALC}$ ABox Consistency Tester to Modal Logic SAT Problems

Volker Haarslev and Ralf Möller

University of Hamburg, Computer Science Department
Vogt-Koelln-Str. 30, 22527 Hamburg, Germany
{haarslev,moeller}@informatik.uni-hamburg.de
http://kogs-www.informatik.uni-hamburg.de/~{haarslev,moeller}

Abstract. In this paper we present the results of applying HAM-ALC, a description logic system for $\mathcal{ALCNR}$, to modal logic SAT problems.

1 Introduction

Research on description logics and modal logics tackles related problems from different viewpoints. One of the recent advances in the development of "fast" description logic systems was the FaCT architecture [4] which focuses on TBox reasoning. Besides optimizations for computing the subsumption hierarchy (e.g. taxonomic encoding and other techniques), the FaCT system is based on optimized algorithms with appropriate data structures for speeding up the basic concept consistency test (dependency-directed backtracking, semantic branching [2] and caching of models). FaCT supports the logic $\mathcal{ALC}$ plus transitive roles, features and role hierarchies. In addition, generalized concept inclusions (GCIs, [1]) as well as cyclic terminologies are handled by preprocessing techniques and specific blocking strategies being used in the concept satisfiability algorithm [4]. Among other improvements for concept satisfiability checking, the importance of extensive model caching for concept terms and appropriate data structures for models is demonstrated by the evaluation results of the DLP system, a reimplementation of the algorithms used in the FaCT architecture [5]. One of the main results of the research on FaCT and DLP is that a well-designed combination of different techniques and strategies is necessary in order to dramatically increase system performance in the average case. However, neither FaCT nor DLP deals with ABoxes.

In the following we discuss the optimized description logic system HAM-ALC, which has been developed to extend the facilities offered by FaCT. In addition, HAM-ALC supports ABox reasoning for the language $\mathcal{ALCNR}$ which is presented in [1] ($\mathcal{ALC}$ with number restrictions, role conjunction or role hierarchies as well as GCIs but without transitive roles). Besides optimizations for TBoxes, it provides optimized implementations for the well-known inference problems ABox consistency checking, instance checking, realization, instance retrieval [1].

In the following we briefly sketch how known optimization techniques for concept consistency checking can be exploited for building efficient *ABox consistency checking* architectures. Afterwards, we demonstrate that this architecture can also be used for effectively solving average-case modal logic SAT problems. These first tests indicate that the implementation overhead inherent in a system for expressive description logics supporting ABoxes can be reduced to a minimum compared to a concept consistency checking architecture provided by, for instance, DLP.

2 Basic Architecture of HAM-ALC

Similar to the techniques used in FACT a preprocessing phase transforms concept expressions into negation normal form, removes duplicates, performs obvious simplifications, detects obvious clashes, flattens nested and/or expressions, normalizes the order of disjuncts and conjuncts, and provides a unique identification for all concepts which are structurally equal. For each concept, its negated counterpart is precomputed in order to support a fast access to negations of concepts (required for clash detection, see below).

ABox constraints consist of individual assertions (i : C) as well as role assertions ($(\langle i_1, i_2\rangle$: R). The ABox consistency checker has to deal with (possibly cyclic) graph structures at least in a finite part of the ABox. Thus, HAM-ALC has to explicitly represent role assertions as well as individuals. For an individual assertion HAM-ALC represents its name and non-negated preprocessed concept expression with a separated negation sign and a set of dependency ABox constraints documenting the origin of this assertion. The dependency constraints are required for dependency-directed backtracking (see below). In order to facilitate extensibility HAM-ALC does not use special "encoding tricks" for representing concepts but uses record structures to store relevant information. It normalizes or-, all-, and number restriction concepts of constraints into their equivalent negated form (e.g. $(C_1 \sqcup C_2) \rightarrow \neg(\neg C_1 \sqcap \neg C_2)$, $(\forall\ R\ C) \rightarrow \neg(\exists\ R\ \neg C)$, and $(\exists_{\leq n}\ R) \rightarrow \neg(\exists_{\geq n+1}\ R)$) while representing the negation sign of the concept as part of the constraint itself. This architectural decision helps to speed up the usual clash checks that test whether two constraints $i : C_1$ and $i : C_2$ exist such that $C_1 \sqcap C_2$ is equal to $\bot$).

Constraints are considered as deterministic if their concept term is either atomic, an and-concept, or an or-concept with exactly one open disjunct (with an unknown truth value). The optimized algorithm treats the consistency test of ABox constraints generated by some- and at-least constraints as isolated subproblems if value and at-most restrictions are carefully handled (see the calculus presented in [1]).

2.1 Optimization Techniques

Or-constraints are a major source of complexity in tableaux expansion. Two major optimization strategies are embedded into the architecture of HAM-ALC that deal with this complexity. The first technique is called *semantic branching*, the second one is *dependency-directed backtracking*. A third strategy tries to avoid the recomputation of identical or similar subtableau by using a so-called "model caching and merging technique" that possibly replaces the tableau satisfiablity test by operating on cached models for concepts. We briefly review these techniques and explain their integration into HAM-ALC.

Semantic Branching In contrast to syntactic branching, where redundant search spaces may be repeatedly explored, semantic branching uses a *splitting rule* which divides the original problem into two smaller disjoint subproblems (see [2] for a discussion). Semantic branching is usually supported by various techniques intended to speed up the search.

A *lookahead algorithm* or *constraint propagator* is applied to reduce the order of magnitude of the open search space. Thus, after every tableau expansion step HAM-ALC propagates the truth value of the newly added constraint into all open disjuncts of all or-constraints with an unknown truth value. As a result of this step, or-constraints might be recognized as satisfied (i.e. one disjunct is satisfied), deterministic (i.e. exactly one disjunct remains open), or might even clash (all disjuncts are unsatisfied).

Various *heuristics* are used to select the next or-constraint and one of its disjuncts for processing. HAM-ALC employs a dynamic selection scheme. The oldest-first nesting strategy is used for selecting one or-constraint with at least two open disjuncts. The selection of a disjunct from this or-constraint is achieved by counting the negated and non-negated occurrences for each open disjunct in all other open or-constraints. These numbers are used as input for a priority function that selects the disjunct. The priority function is adopted from FaCT and achieves the following goals. It prefers disjuncts that occur frequently in unexpanded binary constraints and balanced or-constraints (i.e. containing a similar number of negated and non-negated occurrences of the same disjunct) but discriminates between unbalanced or-constraints. In order to perform individual-specific counting very quickly, HAM-ALC precomputes data structures for cross-referencing open or-constraints that contain this concept in negated and/or non-negated form. Once a disjunct is selected, the priority function is also used to determine which branch of the search tree is tried first by the splitting rule.

Dependency-directed Backtracking Naive backtracking algorithms often explore regions of the search space rediscovering the same contradictions repeatedly. An integral part of the HAM-ALC architecture is a dependency management system. It records the dependencies of every constraint, i.e. whenever a constraint is created, its precondition constraints are saved as a dependency set. This set is employed by the dependency-directed backtracking technique of HAM-ALC in order to reduce the search space.

Whenever a clash occurs, the union of the dependency sets of the clash culprits (referred to as clash dependency set) is recorded and backtracking is started.

When a semantic branching point is encountered during backtracking, HAM-ALC checks whether this or-constraint is responsible for a clash culprit (i.e. is a member of the clash dependency set). If the or-constraint is not found, this branching point can be safely bypassed. In case the or-constraint is found, either the remaining semantic alternative is tried or this disjunct is considered as unsatisfiable in the current subtree. The backtracking continues but removes the current or-constraint from the clash dependency set and adds the saved clash dependency set of the first clashed alternative. This technique was first realized in the FACT [4] system and is extended in the HAM-ALC architecture for dealing with different individuals.

Model-based Satisfiability Tests The third major strategy tries to avoid the recomputation of identical or similar subtableaux (caused by a some- or an at-least constraint and the corresponding all- and at-most constraints) by using operations on cached "models" for concepts. The test whether a concept C subsumes a concept D is preceded or may be even replaced by a merging test for the models of ¬C and D. This technique was first developed for the FACT system for $\mathcal{ALC}$. HAM-ALC extends this technique for $\mathcal{ALCNR}$ and refines it in several ways: (1) In contrast to FACT it deals with *deep* models and introduces and exploits *deterministic* models. (2) Every satisfiability test of a subtableau is preceded by a model merging test working with either deep or flat models. (3) The concept subsumption test is devised as a two-level procedure first trying a novel structural subsumption test (see below) that is optionally followed by a regular tableaux satisfiability test.

A model of a concept is computed by applying the standard satisfiability test. In case of a failure this incoherent concept is associated with the $\bot$-model. Otherwise HAM-ALC constructs and caches a model from the final tableau. A *model* consists of a *concept set* containing every (negated) atomic, some-, at-least, all-, and at-most concept occurring in the final constraint set of the tableau. And- and or-concepts may be safely ignored due to their decomposition by the tableaux rules. A model is marked as *deterministic* if the constraint set contains no or-constraint and no at-most constraint that caused fork elimination.

The standard *flat model merging test* (due to FACT) for a set of models $\mathcal{M} = \{M_1, \ldots, M_n\}$ works as follows. The concept sets of every pair $\langle M_i, M_j \rangle$ (with $M_i, M_j \in \mathcal{M}$ and $i \neq j$, $1 \leq i, j \leq n$) are mutually checked for a potential clash. If either a pair $\langle C_i, C_j \rangle$ (with $C_i \in M_i$, $C_j \in M_j$) of clashing atomic concepts or of potentially interacting some- and all-concepts via a common role R is found, the test returns *unmergable*. Otherwise it returns *mergable*. The flat model merging test is sound but *not* complete. Thus, it precedes every concept subsumption and subtableau satisfiability test and replaces it if the answer is *mergable*. HAM-ALC extends this technique for $\mathcal{ALCNR}$ in two ways. Its model merging test correctly deals with number restriction concepts and keeps track of deterministic models and becomes sound *and* complete if only deterministic models are involved. It realizes a *deep* model merging test that recursively checks the models of potentially interacting some- and all-concepts. HAM-ALC tries to maximize the use of deterministic models for concept subsumption tests.

Table 1. TANCS'99 selected reference problems of the modal pspace division.

Problem	Clauses	Variables	Depth	Runtime (10ms)
bounded CNF	8	4	2	0
	16	4	2	2
	32	4	2	6
bounded CNF modK	8	4	2	2
	16	4	2	5
	32	4	2	14
unbounded QBF	8	2	3	27
	16	2	3	33
	32	2	3	53
unbounded QBF modK	8	2	3	24
	16	2	3	36
	32	2	3	61

3 Implementation Language and Special Features

HAM-ALC is implemented in Common Lisp and has been tested with Macintosh Common Lisp, Allegro Common Lisp (SunOS, Windows, Linux). HAM-ALC provides a Web-based interface [3].

4 First Results on a Performance Analysis

For TANCS-99 we have tested HAM-ALC on the modal PSPACE division reference problems (see Table 1). The runtimes (in 10ms) are computed based on the files provided by TANCS-99. For each parameter setting (see Table 1) the computation results of the 16 problem instances are averaged (geometric mean). We have run the system on a Sun Ultra Sparc 2 (300 MHz) with Allegro CL 5.0.

References

1. M. Buchheit, F.M. Donini, and A. Schaerf. Decidable reasoning in terminological knowledge representation systems. *Journal of Artificial Intelligence Research*, 1:109–138, 1993.
2. J.W. Freeman. *Improvements to propositional satisfiability search algorithms*. PhD thesis, University of Pennsylvania, Computer and Information Science, 1995.
3. V. Haarslev, R. Möller, and A.-Y. Turhan. Implementing an $\mathcal{ALCRP}(\mathcal{D})$ ABox reasoner: Progress report. In E. Franconi et al., editor, *Proceedings of the International Workshop on Description Logics (DL'98), June 6-8, 1998, Trento, Italy*, pages 82–86, June 1998.
4. I. Horrocks. *Optimising Tableaux Decision Procedures for Description Logics*. PhD thesis, University of Manchester, 1997.
5. I. Horrocks and P.F. Patel-Schneider. FaCT and DLP: Automated reasoning with analytic tableaux and related methods. In *Proceedings International Conference Tableaux'98*, pages 27–30, 1998.

KtSeqC : System Description

Vijay Boyapati and Rajeev Goré*

Automated Reasoning Project and Dept. of Computer Science
Australian National University
ACT 0200 Canberra, Australia
{vijay,rpg}@arp.anu.edu.au

Architecture and Algorithm: **KtSeqC** is based upon the right sided labelled sequent system for tense logic **Kt** described in [BG98] which itself is based upon the work of [BP95, Mas94, HSZ96]. The work of Pitt [PC96] is closely related but Pitt uses the calculus KE incorporating an analytical cut-rule. We have also incorporated simplification as reported in [Mas98, HS98].

The system converts a given formula to implication-free negated normal form and performs some optimisations that handle the commutativity of the binary connectives. The search strategy picks a formula on the right hand side of the sequent and then applies the inference rule appropriate to the main connective of the formula. Since every inference rule in KtSeq is invertible the choice of the formula, from the right hand side of the sequent, does not affect completeness. This allows for various search strategies such as leaving formulae whose main connective is a conjunction until last. Special mechanisms for loop detection need to be added to handle transitive extensions of **Kt** and to handle global logical consequence.

Implementation: **KtSeqC** is implemented in roughly 1800 lines of C (which we expect to halve by using C++ and inheritance), using the flex and yacc libraries for parsing purposes. Each time a subformula A (of the principal formula) is parsed, the program determines, using a hash table of pointers to previously parsed formulae, whether the subformula has previously been parsed. If the subformula has previously been parsed, then the internal representation of the subformula (which can be located using the hash table) is returned to the next level of parsing. If the subformula had not previously been parsed, then an internal representation is created for A and $nnf(\neg A)$, with a "negation" pointer to connect them; both are then inserted into the hash table. This implements structure sharing. That is, if two different formulae A and B have a subformula C in common then the two occurrences of C are represented by the same location of the hash table.

The hash value of a subformula is computed recursively - an ascii value is given to literals, while complex subformulae receive a hash value based on the main connective and the sum of the hash values of their children. The resultant commutativity of the hash function allows $A \vee B$ to be recognised as equivalent to $B \vee A$ while parsing, but retains the difference between $A \vee B$ and $A \wedge B$. No

* Supported by an Australian Research Council Queen Elizabeth II Fellowship.

attempt is made to handle the associativity of the boolean connectives. That is, the two formulae $(A \vee B) \vee C$ and $A \vee (B \vee C)$ are parsed as different formulae.

The method of parsing the formula has proved useful since it allows us to negate arbitrary subformulae and compare subformulae for syntactic identity in constant time. This means that when parsing a formula A, we obtain the nnf of every subformula of A while increasing the parsing time for A by only a constant factor. Storage of sets of formulae is efficient since the formulae are represented as pointers.

Special Features: **KtSeqC** is still a prototype and handles local logical consequence in the minimal tense logic **Kt** (including the minimal normal modal logic **K**). It is trivially extendible to the multimodal logic **K**(m) but the necessary extensions have not been included so far. The current system **does not** handle global logical consequence. A proof trace of the sequents in the derivation can be obtained but it is not structured into an actual sequent tree proof. Printing the labelled literals associated with an open branch trivially gives a counter-model as required.

An advantage of **KtSeqC** is that it requires only a C compiler equipped with the lex and yacc libraries, making it quite portable. It has been tested using SunOS 5.6 and Redhat Linux 5.1.

Performance Analysis: We tested **KtSeqC** successfully on Heuerding's benchmarks [Heu98] to test for soundness, these results are not shown, but are available on request. The following results are for the benchmarks of the current comparison. Our results indicate that our prover is fast for satisfiable formulae but slow for valid formulae. We have not pinpointed the cause of this but suspect that our prover is simply being swamped by the large number of branches which must be closed when testing a valid formula. Clearly, further optimisations are required.

KtSeqC can be found at: `http://arp.anu.edu.au/~rpg/KtSeqC.html`

Category	Subsection	Problem Number	time (sec)	result
p-persat-cnf-K4	8	1-16	$> 100,000$	?
p-persat-cnf-K4	16	1-10	$> 100,000$	?
p-persat-cnf-K4	16	11	1000	not valid
p-persat-cnf-K4	16	12-16	$> 100,000$	?
p-persat-cnf-K4	32	1-16	$> 100,000$	?
p-persat-cnf-K4	32	1-2	$> 100,000$	?
p-persat-cnf-K4	32	3	1000	not valid
p-persat-cnf-K4	32	4	$> 100,000$	?
p-persat-cnf-K4	32	5	2000	not valid
p-persat-cnf-K4	32	6	$> 100,000$	?
p-persat-cnf-K4	32	7	2000	not valid
p-persat-cnf-K4	32	8-11	$> 100,000$	?
p-persat-cnf-K4	32	12	2000	not valid
p-persat-cnf-K4	32	13-14	$> 100,000$	?
p-persat-cnf-K4	32	15-16	1000	not valid

Category	Subsection	Problem Number	time (msec)	result
bound-cnf	8	1-6	1000	not valid
bound-cnf	8	7	2000	not valid
bound-cnf	8	8-16	1000	not valid
bound-cnf	16	1-16	1000	not valid
bound-cnf	32	1-5	1000	not valid
bound-cnf	32	5	> 100,000	?
bound-cnf	32	6-15	1000	not valid
bound-cnf	32	16	> 100,000	?
bound-modK	8	1-16	1000	not valid
bound-modK	16	1	2000	not valid
bound-modK	16	2-4	1000	not valid
bound-modK	16	5	2000	not valid
bound-modK	16	6-16	1000	not valid
bound-modK	32	1	> 100,000	?
bound-modK	32	2	4000	not valid
bound-modK	32	3-4	1000	not valid
bound-modK	32	5	> 100,000	?
bound-modK	32	6	1000	not valid
bound-modK	32	7	6000	not valid
bound-modK	32	8	1000	not valid
bound-modK	32	9	3000	not valid
bound-modK	32	10-11	> 100,000	?
bound-modK	32	12-15	2000	not valid
bound-modK	32	16	8000	not valid

References

[BG98] N. Bonnette and R. Goré. A labelled sequent system for tense logic Kt. In AI98, LNAI 1502:71-82. Springer, 1998.

[BP95] B. Beckert and J. Posegga. leanTAP: Lean tableau-based deduction. *Journal of Automated Reasoning*, 15(3):339–358, 1995.

[Heu98] A. Heuerding. A comparison of theorem provers for modal logics. In Tableaux98, LNCS 1397:25-26. Springer, 1998.

[HS98] U. Hustadt and R. Schmidt. Simplification and backjumping in modal tableau. In Tableaux98 LNAI 1397:187-201. Springer, 1998.

[HSZ96] A. Heuerding, M. Seyfried, and H. Zimmermann. Efficient loop-check for backward proof search in some non-classical logics. In Tableaux96, LNAI 1071:210-225, Springer, 1996.

[Mas94] F. Massacci. Strongly analytic tableaux for normal modal logics. In CADE-12, LNAI 814:723–737, Springer, 1994.

[Mas98] F. Massacci. Simplification: a general constraint propagation technique for propositional and modal tableaux. In Tableaux98, LNAI 1397:187-201. Springer, 1998.

[PC96] J. Pitt and J. Cunningham. Distributed modal theorem proving with KE. Tableaux96, LNAI 1071:160–176, Springer, 1996.

Automated Reasoning and the Verification of Security Protocols

Fabio Massacci

Dip. di Informatica e Sistemistica - Univ. di Roma I "La Sapienza"
via Salaria 113, 00198 ROMA - ITALY
email massacci@dis.uniroma1.it

Abstract. The formal verification of security protocols is one of the successful applications of automated reasoning[1]. Techniques based on belief logics, model checking, and theorem proving have been successful in determining strengths and weaknesses of many protocols, some of which have been even fielded before being discovered badly wrong.
This tutorial presents the problems to the "security illiterate", explaining aims, objectives and tools of this application of automated reasoning.

1 Scientific Contents

The tutorial will run through three modules, and a fourth one, if time allows.

At first, there is an *introduction to security protocols*. This module sets the terminology, the basic things we need to know about security and cryptography [1,7,12], and introduce the running examples for the rest of the tutorial: two simple protocols for challenge-response of the ISO standard [8] with few hints to either the well-known Needham-Schroeder public-key protocol [13,9] or the mechanized version of the Kerberos protocol [2].

The second module focuses on the *BAN Logics and the goals of security protocols*. It explains few of the main properties that a security protocol should provide, such as secrecy, integrity, freshness, authentication, proof of identity, non repudiation [5,7,15]. We use the original simple and intuitive BAN logic by Burrows, Abadi and Needham [5], and just point to more sophisticated logics [10,15]. Then, we can see some properties, with tableau-like proofs as in [10], which characterize the protocols we have seen in the first part.

We do not deal with automatic proof systems for belief logics (e.g. [4]) because their main feature is indeed being an high level formalism for proofs by hand (and, as such, also a bit semantically inaccurate [10,15]).

The third module focuses on *first order logic (with induction) and theorem proving*, going to the (interactive) theorem proving realm. The theory becomes complex (we need at least first order logic with sets or variants thereof) and the mechanization of the reasoning becomes imperative. The module presents the main ideas behind this approach: model the execution of a security protocol as a trace of atomic actions and then use first order logic [3], or eventually first order

[1] Indeed, the proposal to use tableaux for security verification dates back to 1983 [11].

logic with induction [14, 2], to prove properties about traces. The formalizations we present are those by Bolignano [3] and Paulson [14, 2], for which we give few examples in the modeling of the properties of messages (asymmetric encryption, hashing etc.), the simple challenge-response protocols we have seen, and the actions of a potential attacker.

Some desirable security properties, that we might like to prove with a theorem prover, will be shown and discussed. We will see how the properties we have sketched in the module on the BAN logic can be recaptured in this framework.

Last but not least, the main ideas behind *process algebras and model checking approaches*, such as those using CSP [9] or CCS [6], will be sketched. The last module shows how model checkers [9], together with state exploration tools [12], can be used to find attacks to security protocols, a nice complement to the theorem proving work.

References

1. R. Anderson and R. Needham. Programming Satan's computer. In *Computer Science Today*, LNCS 1000, pp. 426–440. Springer-Verlag, 1996.
2. G. Bella and L. Paulson. Kerberos version IV: inductive analysis of the secrecy goals. In *Proc. of ESORICS-98*, LNCS 1485. Springer-Verlag, 1998.
3. D. Bolignano. An approach to the formal verification of cryptographic protocols. In *Proc. of the 3th ACM Conf. on Comm. and Comp. Security*, pp. 106–118, 1996.
4. S. Brackin. A HOL extension of GNY for automatically cryptographic protocols. In *Proc. of the 9th IEEE Comp. Sec. Found. Workshop*. IEEE Press, 1996.
5. M. Burrows, M. Abadi, and R. Needham. A logic for authentication. *ACM TOCS*, 8(1):18–36, 1990.
6. R. Focardi and R. Gorrieri. The compositional security checker: A tool for the verification of information flow security properties. *IEEE TOSE*, 23(9):550–571, 1997.
7. D. Gollmann. What do we mean by entity authentication. In *Proc. of the 15th IEEE Symp. on Sec. and Privacy*, pp. 46–54. IEEE Press, 1996.
8. International Organization for Standardization. *ISO/IEC Draft Int. Std. 10181-2.2 IT - Open System Interconnection - Security Framework for Open Systems: Authentication Framework*, 1993. Section 8.1.5.
9. G. Lowe. Breaking and fixing the Needham-Schroeder public-key protocol using CSP and FDR. In *Proc. of TACAS*, LNCS 1055, pp. 147–166. Springer-Verlag, 1996.
10. W. Mao and C. Boyd. Towards formal analysis of security protocols. In *Proc. of the 6th IEEE Comp. Sec. Foundations Workshop*, pp. 147–158. IEEE Press, 1993.
11. B. Marick. The VERUS design verification system. In *Proc. of the 2nd IEEE Symp. on Sec. and Privacy*, pp. 150–157. IEEE Press, 1983.
12. C. Meadows. Formal verification of cryptographic protocols: A survey. In *Proc. of ASIACRYPT-94*, LNCS 917, pp. 133–150. Springer-Verlag, 1995.
13. R. Needham and M. Schroeder. Using encryption for authentication in large networks of computers. *CACM*, 21(12):993–999, 1978.
14. L. Paulson. The inductive approach to verifying cryptographic protocols. *J. of Computer Security*, 1998.
15. P. Syverson, and P. van Oorschot. On Unifying Some Cryptographic Protocols Logics. In *Proc. of the 13th IEEE Symp. on Sec. and Privacy*. IEEE Press, 1994.

Proof Confluent Tableau Calculi

Reiner Hähnle and Bernhard Beckert

Dept. of Computer Science, University of Karlsruhe
76128 Karlsruhe, Germany, {reiner,beckert}@ira.uka.de

1 Introduction

A tableau calculus is proof confluent if every partial tableau proof for an unsatisfiable formula can be extended to a closed tableau. A rule application may be redundant but it can never prevent the construction of a proof; there are no "dead ends" in the proof search. Proof confluence is a prerequisite of (a) backtracking-free proof search and (b) the generation of counter examples to non-theorems.

In this tutorial we discuss the rôle and perspectives of proof confluent calculi in tableau-based theorem proving. For the sake of simplicity the discussion focuses on clause tableaux.

2 Tableaux with Selection Function

Among the more effective resolution refinements are those based on selection functions such as hyperresolution and semantic resolution. A number of calculi related to these concepts were also introduced into the world of semantic tableaux in form of various proof confluent refinements.

The emphasis so far were tableau calculi corresponding to positive hyperresolution and binary resolution with selection function. In this tutorial, more general calculi based on arbitrary selection functions with hyper extension steps are discussed. For those selection functions that correspond to Herbrand interpretations one obtains a semantic tableau analogue of semantic resolution. All introduced calculi are based on a simple, generic saturation principle leading to brief and schematic completeness proofs.

It is shown that just as model generation theorem proving (MGTP) is an instance of hyper tableaux, constraint MGTP turns out to be an instance of hyper tableaux with selection function. This gives a formal justification why constraint MGTP is a complete procedure for many applications such as quasigroup problems.

3 Proof Confluence and Strong Completeness

For practical purposes, a completeness theorem merely stating the existence of a tableau proof is not sufficient. A stronger result is needed giving the guarantee that a concrete tableau proof *search procedure* will find a closed tableau if there exists one. Let us call this (as usual) the *strong completeness* problem.

This problem can easily be solved if the calculus is *non-destructive*, i.e., if all tableaux that can be constructed from a given tableau contain that tableau as an initial subtree. In that case, one can simply arrange input clauses in a queue (on each branch) and thus ensure that enough instances of each clause are used on each branch to obtain a proof. Examples of non-destructive tableau calculi are Smullyan tableaux and Fitting's delayed instantiation rule.

Unfortunately, the standard version of clause tableaux is a *destructive* calculus. The culprit is the closure rule, which allows to instantiate free variables.

The standard solution for proof search in all destructive calculi is *depth-first iterative deepening* search, it was pioneered by Stickel, and is used, for example, in the provers Setheo, $_3T^AP$, and KoMeT. One enumerates all tableaux up to a fixed size via backtracking over possible closure rule applications. Completeness is achieved by iterative increase of the bound on tableau size.

But how, besides backtracking, can be dealt with the strong completeness problem in case the calculus is destructive but proof confluent? A strongly complete procedure performing a depth-first proof search has several advantages. The information represented by the constructed tableaux increases at each proof step; no information is lost since there is no backtracking. In addition, considering similar tableaux or sequences of tableaux in different paths of the search tree is avoided.

The problem of constructing a strongly complete proof procedure without backtracking is discussed in the last part of the tutorial. A possible solution is presented that is based on a notion of *regularity* to make sure that there are no "cycles" in the search (it is not possible to deduce the same literals, clauses, or sub-tableau again and again). In addition, each literal is assigned a "weight" in such a way that there are only finitely many different literals (up to variable renaming) of a certain weight; thus, since literals with lesser weight are deduced first, sooner or later each possible conclusion is added to all branches containing its premiss, i.e., the strategy is *fair*. To handle the destructiveness of clause tableaux, the strategy employs *reconstruction steps*. Immediately after a rule application that instantiates free variables, the expansion steps that are needed to recreate the destroyed part of the tableau are executed.

Further Information

There is a Web page for this tutorial, where slides, references, and related papers are available; the URL is `i12www.ira.uka.de/tab99-tutorial`.

Analytic Calculi for Projective Logics*

Matthias Baaz and Christian G. Fermüller

Technische Universität Wien
A-1040 Vienna, Austria
[chrisf,baaz]@logic.at

Abstract. The class of projective propositional logics is defined by a certain format of the definition of truth functions for their connectives with respect to a semantic theory. All finite valued logics, but also infinite valued Gödel logic are shown to be projective. Analytic Gentzen type calculi are uniformly derived for all projective logics. Admissibility of cut rules and other structural rules is investigated. The special case of Gödel logics is exemplified in detail and compared with the previous approach of Avron (based on hypersequents).

1 Introduction

The construction of an analytic calculus is a key to a profound understanding of the relation between the syntax and semantics of a logic. In particular, it is the basis for the amenability of feasible proof search. However, typical application scenarios hardly allow to single out in advance a *particular* logic as the most adequate basis for formal reasoning. We are rather urged to investigate broad *families* of logics, and – if possible – provide *uniform* calculi that facilitate the switch from one logic to another and deepen the understanding of the relations between them.

A good example of successful research along this line is the development of uniform, proof search oriented calculi for the family of all finite valued logics (see, e.g., [3], [9]). Here we present a uniform approach to Gentzen systems for an even broader class of propositional logics. We define the class of *projective logics*, characterized by the form of the truth functions for its connectives and show how to translate a given specification of such a logic into a new type of analytic sequent calculus in a systematic, even mechanizable way. We also investigate, already at this general level, admissible forms of cut rules and other types of rules that may help to speed up proof search.

The most important example of projective logics are – finite as well as infinite valued – *Gödel logics* [8]. (In contrast, infinite valued Łukasiewicz logic and Product logic are not projective.) The significance of Gödel logics for reasoning in fuzzy contexts and other applications is well documented e.g., in [10, 12]. Since our framework covers *all* Gödel logics it provides insights into the relation between these logics beyond the horizon of previous approaches. An important

* Partly supported by COST-Action No. 15 and FWF grant P-12652-MAT.

and widely known alternative to our analytic calculus for infinite-valued Gödel logic is Avron's hypersequent system **G***LC* [1,2]. We provide an analysis of the connection between Avron's calculus and ours.

The significance of this work for Automated Reasoning appears at two levels:

1. We provide a framework that – in principle – allows the automated generation of cut-free calculi for a class of logics from given specifications of their semantics. This is very much in the spirit of 'logic engineering' as, e.g., propagated successfully by H.J. Ohlbach for modal logics (see, e.g., [11]). A system for automated reasoning of this type – for finite valued first-order logics – is MULTLOG [5]. Indeed, one can view this paper as a first step towards a sophisticated extension of MULTLOG.
2. It turns out that tableau style proof search algorithms based on our derived calculi seem to be computationally more adequate than other methods that have been proposed for particular projective logics. In particular, the central rule ('communication rule') of Avron's above-mentioned hypersequent **G***LC* for infinite valued Gödel logic poses a serious problem for efficient proof search. In our calculus this critical rule is not needed. We instead build on an extended syntax and additional axioms (i.e., tableau closure rules).[1]

2 Projective logics

The syntax of the propositional logics considered here is completely general. Thus, an *(object) language* for a logic consists of an infinite supply of *propositional variables*, a finite set of *connectives* (with fixed arity), and a finite number of *truth constants*. (Truth constants will also be considered as 0-ary connectives.) The *formulæ* of such a language are build up from its variables, constants, and connectives as usual.

The logics under investigation are characterized by a special format of the definitions of their semantics. Again, we take a very general approach. To specify a semantics we refer to some (classical, first order) theory **T** – called *semantic theory* – whose intended range of discourse is the set of truth values. **T** can, e.g., be the theory of linear orders or lattices or any other class of relational structures. It can also be the (first order) specification of single structure. The only requirements we put on **T** are as follows:

(F) **T** is based on a function free language with finite signature. I.e., the atomic formulæ are of form $R(t_1, \ldots, t_k)$, where the t_i are variables or constants.
(D) The set of Π_1-formulæ that are valid in **T** is decidable.

We use the notation "$\mathcal{M} \models A[\sigma]$" to denote that the formula A is satisfied in a model $\mathcal{M}$ (of **T**) under the assignment σ of elements of the domain of $\mathcal{M}$ to the free variables of A. The domain of $\mathcal{M}$ is called *set of truth values*. By

[1] A quite different approach to efficient theorem proving for infinite valued Gödel logic consists in translating formulæ to strict linear equalities over reals as R. Hähnle has pointed out.

"$\mathbf{T} \models A$" we mean that A is valid in $\mathbf{T}$, i.e. $A[\sigma]$ is satisfied in *all* models of $\mathbf{T}$ for all assignments σ.

Constants of $\mathbf{T}$ denote truth values and are identified with truth constants of the object language.

Quantifier and negation free formulæ of $\mathbf{T}$, i.e., formulæ built up from atomic formulæ using conjunction and disjunction only, will play a special rôle. Let us call such formulæ *simple.*

We call an n-ary connective $\Box$ *projective* if its *truth function* $\tilde{\Box}$ (i.e., the definition of its semantics with respect to $\mathbf{T}$) can be written in the following form:

$$\tilde{\Box}(x_1, \ldots, x_n) = \begin{cases} t_1 & \text{if } A_1 \\ \vdots & \vdots \\ t_m & \text{if } A_m \end{cases}$$

where each t_i is either a truth constant or in $\{x_1, \ldots, x_n\}$. The conditions A_i are simple formulæ of the underlying semantic theory $\mathbf{T}$ whose free variables are among $\{x_1, \ldots, x_n\}$. Since $\tilde{\Box}$ is a total function they have to satisfy the following properties:

Totality: $\mathbf{T} \models \forall x_1 \cdots \forall x_n \bigvee_{1 \leq i \leq m} A_i$

Functionality: For all models $\mathcal{M}$ of $\mathbf{T}$: $\mathcal{M} \models A_i[\sigma]$ and $\mathcal{M} \models A_j[\sigma]$ implies that $\sigma(t_i) = \sigma(t_j)$.

To specify a *logic* we also need a *notion of designated truth values* or, shorter, *designating predicate.* Any simple formula $Des(x)$ of $\mathbf{T}$ with exactly one free variable x may be chosen for this purpose.

An *interpretation* $\mathcal{I}$ (of any propositional many-valued logic) is a mapping from the set of propositional variables $\mathcal{PV}$ into the set of truth values V. Given projective truth functions for all connectives of the language, an interpretation $\mathcal{I}$ extends to an *evaluation function* $val_{\mathcal{I}}$, that maps all formulæ into truth values, as follows:

$$val_{\mathcal{I}}(F) = \mathcal{I}(F) \quad \text{if } F \in \mathcal{PV}$$

$$val_{\mathcal{I}}(\Box(F_1, \ldots, F_n)) = \tilde{\Box}(val_{\mathcal{I}}(F_1), \ldots, val_{\mathcal{I}}(F_n))$$

Observe that the semantics depends on an interpretation of the conditions A_i of the truth functions. These A_i are formulæ of the semantic theory $\mathbf{T}$. Therefore any model $\mathcal{M}$ of $\mathbf{T}$ determines a logic $\mathcal{L}_{\mathcal{M}}$: the *projective logic* of $\mathcal{M}$ (with respect to given projective truth functions for all connectives of the language). We call a formula F *valid* in $\mathcal{L}_{\mathcal{M}}$ if for all interpretations $\mathcal{I}$: $\mathcal{M} \models Des[val_{\mathcal{I}}(F)/x]$. (That is: if for all interpretations the assignment of the value of F to the only free variable of the designating predicate is satisfied in $\mathcal{M}$.) $\mathcal{L}_{\mathcal{M}}$ is identified with the set of formulæ that are valid in it.

There is another useful interpretation of this semantic machinery under which the semantic theory itself determines a logic. Namely, instead of evaluating the conditions A_i in a particular model of $\mathbf{T}$, we may check whether the relevant instances A_i' of A_i and Des' of Des are satisfied in *all models* of $\mathbf{T}$. This way we don't have to fix the set of truth values in speaking of the *projective logic* $\mathcal{L}_\mathbf{T}$ associated with $\mathbf{T}$ and some projective connectives (possibly including truth constants). This allows us to speak, e.g., of *the* projective logic of, say, partial orders (with respect to a fixed set of projective connectives). Formally,

$$\mathcal{L}_\mathbf{T} = \{F \mid \mathcal{M} \models Des[val_\mathcal{I}(F)/x] \text{ for all } \mathcal{I} \text{ and } \mathcal{M} \text{ of } \mathbf{T}\}$$

Example 1. To see that every finite valued propositional logic is projective we only have to consider *monadic* semantic theories.

Let the language of $\mathbf{T}$ contain a monadic predicate symbol C_i for each truth value c_i. In addition, assume that we have a constant for each truth value. Then any entry

$$\tilde{\Box}(c_{i_1}, \ldots, c_{i_n}) = c_j$$

in the truth table for the n-ary connective $\Box$ translates into the part

$$\tilde{\Box}(x_1, \ldots, x_n) = c_j \quad \text{if } C_{i_1}(x_1) \wedge \ldots \wedge C_{i_n}(x_n)$$

of the definition of the truth function as above.

Alternatively, we can base the semantics on a theory containing only the equality predicate and all truth constants: just replace $C_i(t)$ by $c_i = t$.

As we shall see below, even in the case of finite valued logics, it may be advantageous to choose a more expressive semantic theory to define the truth functions for its connectives.

2.1 Gödel logics

Our main example of projective logics is the family of Gödel logics. To formulate their semantics, we assume the set of truth values to be linearly ordered and equipped with a minimal element 0 and a maximal element 1 (distinct from 0). A standard axiomatization of the corresponding semantic theory is given by:

$\forall x : \neg(x < x)$	(Irrefl$_<$)	$\forall x : x = 0 \vee 0 < x$	(Min$_<$)
$\forall x \forall y \forall z : (x < y \wedge y < z) \supset x < z$	(Trans$_<$)	$\forall x : x = 1 \vee x < 1$	(Max$_<$)
$\forall x \forall y : x = y \vee x < y \vee y < x$	(Linear$_<$)	$0 < 1$	(Distinct)

Although one could derive a "sequent calculus of relations" (see Section 3) directly from this theory we prefer an alternative formulation of it. We do not want to have to consider "=" as a basic relation, but rather base $\mathbf{T}$ on the relation symbols "$\leq$" and "$<$" by adding the following to the axioms Irrefl$_<$, Trans$_<$, and Distinct:

$\forall x : x \leq x$	(Refl$_\leq$)	$\forall x : 0 \leq x$	(Min$_\leq$)
$\forall x \forall y \forall z : (x \leq y \wedge y \leq z) \supset x \leq z$	(Trans$_\leq$)	$\forall x : x \leq 1$	(Max$_\leq$)
$\forall x \forall y : x \leq y \vee y \leq x$	(Linear$_\leq$)	$\forall x \forall y : x < y \vee y \leq x$	(Connect)

We can now state the truth functions for disjunction ($\vee$ – maximum), conjunction ($\wedge$ – minimum), implication ($\supset$), and negation ($\neg$) in such a way that it gets clear that these connectives are projective with respect to $\mathbf{T}$.

$$\tilde{\vee}(x,y) = \begin{cases} x & \text{if } y \leq x, \\ y & \text{if } x \leq y \end{cases} \qquad \tilde{\wedge}(x,y) = \begin{cases} x & \text{if } x \leq y, \\ y & \text{if } y \leq x \end{cases}$$

$$\tilde{\supset}(x,y) = \begin{cases} 1 & \text{if } x \leq y, \\ y & \text{if } y < x \end{cases} \qquad \tilde{\neg} = \begin{cases} 1 & \text{if } x \leq 0, \\ 0 & \text{if } 0 < x \end{cases}$$

Negation can be treated as derived connective by defining $\neg A := A \supset 0$.

"1" is intended to be the only designated truth value. Therefore we take "$1 \leq x$" as designating predicate.

Infinite valued Gödel logic G_∞[2] is the logic of infinite models of $\mathbf{T}$. Infinity of the domain $\mathcal{M}$ of a model of $\mathbf{T}$ is enforced by adding the density axiom

$$\forall x \forall y \exists z : x < y \supset (x < z \wedge z < y) \qquad \text{(Dense)}$$

However, G_∞ is not only the logic[3] of the theory axiomatized by $\mathbf{T}$ + (Dense) or the logic $\mathcal{L}_\mathcal{M}$ for any infinite model $\mathcal{M}$ of $\mathbf{T}$, but also the logic $\mathcal{L}_\mathbf{T}$ itself.

If we restrict attention to finite models of $\mathbf{T}$ we obtain the family of finite valued Gödel logics G_n. Let, e.g., $\mathcal{M}$ be the (up to isomorphism) unique model of $\mathbf{T}$ with 5 elements, then $\mathcal{L}_\mathcal{M}$ is the 5-valued Gödel logic G_5. Instead of focusing on particular models $\mathcal{M}$ one may equivalently augment $\mathbf{T}$ to become the unique (first order) theory of $\mathcal{M}$. If we add the following axiom to $\mathbf{T}$:

$$\exists x_1 \cdots \exists x_n \forall y : y \equiv x_1 \vee \ldots \vee y \equiv x_n \qquad (\text{Finite}_n)$$

where $x \equiv y$ abbreviates $(x \leq y \wedge y \leq x)$, then $\mathcal{L}_\mathbf{T}$ becomes G_n.

2.2 A relation between finite and infinite valued logics

It is well known that G_∞ is the intersection of all finite valued Gödel logics. The concept of projective connectives allows us to grasp the connection between logics corresponding to finite and arbitrary models of a semantic theory, respectively, at a more general level.

Proposition 1. *Let* $\mathbf{T}$ *be a universal theory (i.e., axiomatized by* Π_1*-formulæ only) and* F *be any formula of a projective logic over* $\mathbf{T}$. *If a formula* F *is valid in* $\mathcal{L}_\mathcal{M}$ *for all finite models* $\mathcal{M}$ *of* $\mathbf{T}$ *then* F *is valid in* $\mathcal{L}_\mathcal{M}$ *for* all *models* $\mathcal{M}$ *of* $\mathbf{T}$. *More concisely:*

$$\Big(\bigcap_{\mathcal{M}\ \textit{finite}} \mathcal{L}_\mathcal{M}\Big) = \mathcal{L}_\mathbf{T}.$$

[2] Sometimes also called *LC* or Dummet logic, since Dummet presented its first axiomatization [6].

[3] There is only one infinite valued *propositional* Gödel logic. On the first order level different topologies on the set of truth values induce different logics.

Proof. Let $\mathcal{M}$ be an arbitrary model of $\mathbf{T}$ such that $\mathcal{M} \not\models Des[val_{\mathcal{I}}(F)/x]$ for some interpretation $\mathcal{I}$. Since the connectives of F are projective its evaluation only depends on the elements of $\mathcal{M}$ assigned by $\mathcal{I}$ to the propositional variables of F and the constants of $\mathbf{T}$. That is: we can filtrate $\mathcal{M}$ into a model $\mathcal{M}'$ with domain $\{\mathcal{I}(p) \mid p \text{ occurs in } F\} \cup \{c \mid c \text{ is the value of some constant of } \mathbf{T}\}$. Therefore, if F is valid in all finite models it must be valid in arbitrary models, i.e. in $\mathcal{L}_{\mathbf{T}}$.

Observe that the proof provides a bound for the size of models (i.e. number of truth values) that we have to consider if we want to check whether a formula is valid in $\mathcal{L}_{\mathbf{T}}$. In the case of G_∞ we obtain: $F \in \mathrm{G}_{|F|+2}$ implies $F \in \mathrm{G}_\infty$ where $|F|$ is the number of (distinct) propositional variables occurring in F.

3 Sequent calculi of relations

There are quite different ways to interpret Gentzen's classical sequent calculus **LK** [7]. These lead to different types of generalizations of Gentzen's calculus. One – very useful – interpretation of a sequent

$$F_1, \ldots, F_n \longrightarrow G_1, \ldots, G_m$$

is to understand it as expressing the assertion that either one of the F_i $(1 \leq i \leq n)$ is false or one of the G_j $(1 \leq j \leq m)$ is true. In this view a classical sequent can be identified with a sequence

$$False(F_1), \ldots, False(F_n), True(G_1), \ldots, True(G_m)$$

of (monadic) atomic formulæ referring to the usual semantic theory. It is well known how this leads to the formulation of sequent calculi for all finite valued logics (see, e.g., [13, 15, 4]).

However, one may prefer to think of the sequent arrow in

$$F \longrightarrow G$$

as associated with the *binary* semantic predicate "F implies G". In the context of a many valued logic with an ordered set of truth value this can, e.g., be understood as

$$val_{\mathcal{I}}(F) \leq val_{\mathcal{I}}(G)$$

for all interpretations $\mathcal{I}$.

The concept of "hypersequents" (as investigated extensively by A. Avron in, e.g., [1, 2]) extends the range of logics for which analytic Gentzen style systems can be given. Hypersquents are sequences of sequents understood as disjunctively connected (at the external level). If external contraction and external weakening are present and if a "splitting rule" (which is an instance of Avron's communication rule) is admissible, then the hypersequent

$$\ldots \mid F_1, \ldots, F_n \longrightarrow G \mid \ldots$$

is equivalent to the hypersequent

$$\ldots \mid F_1 \longrightarrow G \mid \ldots \mid F_n \longrightarrow G \mid \ldots$$

This hypersequent can again be viewed as a sequence of (binary) atomic formulæ referring to a semantic theory. (For this one needs truth constants that correspond to an empty left or right hand sight of the sequents.)

The connection to the semantic framework described in Section 2 is manifested in the following definition:

Let $R_1, \ldots, R_n$ be the predicate symbols of a semantic theory $\mathbf{T}$, then a *sequent of relations* is a finite sequence of form

$$R_{i_1}(F_1^1, \ldots, F_{r_1}^1) \mid \ldots \mid R_{i_k}(F_1^k, \ldots, F_{r_k}^k)$$

where for all $1 \leq j \leq k$: $i_j \in \{1, \ldots, n\}$, r_ℓ is the arity of R_{i_ℓ} and all F_j^i are formulæ of a logic. (Strictly speaking, the relational symbols R_j just *correspond* to symbols of the language of $\mathbf{T}$, since the terms of $\mathbf{T}$ are not formulæ but variables and constants for truth values.)

We are now going to define the *sequent calculus of relations* $\mathbf{R}\mathcal{L}_\mathbf{T}$ for a projective logic $\mathcal{L}_\mathbf{T}$ defined with respect to a semantic theory $\mathbf{T}$.

Axiom sequents

Let $\mathbf{T} \models \forall\bar{x} \bigvee_{1 \leq j \leq n} B_j$ where the B_j are atomic formulæ and $\bar{x}$ are the free variables in $\bigvee_{1 \leq j \leq n} B_j$. Let θ be any substitution of formulæ for the variables $\bar{x}$. Then

$$B_1\theta \mid \ldots \mid B_n\theta$$

is an axiom of $\mathbf{R}\mathcal{L}_\mathbf{T}$.

Remarks. (1) Since $\mathbf{T}$ decides all Π_1-formulæ the set of axioms is recursive. (2) Instead of taking all valid disjunctions of atomic formulæ to define axioms one may just consider *minimal* valid disjunctions. I.e., one reduces the set of axioms modulo the (provability) equivalence relation induced by the structural rules described below.

Structural rules

As already mentioned above, the structural rules for relational sequents should capture the intended interpretation of "|" as disjunction. Thus we have the following rules in $\mathbf{R}\mathcal{L}_\mathbf{T}$.

$$\frac{\mathcal{H} \mid A \mid B \mid \mathcal{H}'}{\mathcal{H} \mid B \mid A \mid \mathcal{H}'} \text{ permutation} \qquad \frac{\mathcal{H}}{A \mid \mathcal{H}} \text{ weakening} \qquad \frac{A \mid A \mid \mathcal{H}}{A \mid \mathcal{H}} \text{ contraction}$$

where A, B are arbitrary atomic relations on formulæ and $\mathcal{H}$, $\mathcal{H}'$ are arbitrary (possible empty) *side sequents.*

Remark. The intended interpretation of sequents is that of disjunctions of atomic relations between formulæ. Permutation and contraction reflect the commutativity and idempotency of (classical) disjunction, respectively. Weakening, of course, corresponds to "$\mathcal{H}$ implies (A or $\mathcal{H}$)".

Logical rules

Let $\Box$ be an n-ary projective connective with the following truth function:

$$\widetilde{\Box}(x_1,\ldots,x_n)=\begin{cases} t_1 & \text{if } A_1(x_1,\ldots,x_n)\\ \vdots & \vdots\\ t_m & \text{if } A_m(x_1,\ldots,x_n)\end{cases}$$

For each predicate symbol R of arity r and each position p, where $1 \leq p \leq r$, we obtain a rule ($\Box$: R: p) for introducing $\Box$ at position p into an R-component of a relational sequent. For this one considers the formula

$$\alpha_{\Box:R:p} = \bigvee_{1\leq \ell \leq m} A_\ell(x_1,\ldots,x_n) \wedge R(z_1,\ldots,z_r)\{t_\ell/z_p\}$$

Take any conjunction of disjunctions of atomic formulæ $\bigwedge_{1\leq j\leq s}\bigvee_{1\leq k\leq u_j} B_{j,k}$ that is equivalent in $\mathbf{T}$ to $\alpha_{\Box:R:p}$. Then we have the rule

$$\frac{B_{1,1}\theta \mid \ldots \mid B_{1,u_1}\theta \mid \mathcal{H} \quad \ldots \quad B_{s,1}\theta \mid \ldots \mid B_{s,u_s}\theta \mid \mathcal{H}}{R(z_1,\ldots,z_r)\{\Box(x_1,\ldots,x_n)/z_p\}\theta \mid \mathcal{H}}\ (\Box\colon R\colon p)$$

where θ is a substitution of formulæ for the variables $\{x_1,\ldots,x_n\}\cup\{z_1,\ldots,z_r\}-\{z_p\}$, and $\mathcal{H}$ is the side sequent of the rule.

Remarks. (1) We make use of the fact that the conditions A_i are simple, i.e. negation and quantifier free. (2) In general there are *many* conjunctive normal forms that are equivalent to $\alpha_{\Box:R:p}$. To obtain compact rules it is often essential to apply simplifications justified by $\mathbf{T}$-valid formulæ. (3) The $\alpha_{\Box:R:p}$ are Π_1-formulæ of $\mathbf{T}$. Since $\mathbf{T}$ decides all Π_1-formulæ, the transformation of the specification of a truth function into a logical rule for relational sequents can – in principle – be automatized.

Example 2. Continuing Example 1 we arrive at a sequent calculus of (monadic) relations for each finite valued logic if we follow the above definitions. In fact, because of the presence of the standard structural rules, these calculi are just notational variants of the many-placed sequent calculi or signed calculi as described, e.g., in [13, 4]. (The special case of classical logic – **LK** [7] – was already sketched at the beginning of the section.) We can even get rid of the truth constants in the formulation of the calculi. The reason for this is that, obviously, any atomic formula of $\mathbf{T}$ that contains a constant can only be of form $C_i(c_j)$, and thus is either simply true or false. For the axioms and rules this means that formulas $C_i(c_j)$ where $i \neq j$ are deleted from the sequents, and sequents containing $C_i(c_j)$ where $i = j$ are discarded, altogether.

3.1 Correctness, completeness, decidability

A sequent (of relations) $\mathcal{S}$ is called *provable* in $\mathbf{R}\mathcal{L}_\mathbf{T}$ if there is an upward tree of sequents rooted in $\mathcal{S}$, such that every leaf (topmost sequent) is an axiom and ever other sequent is obtained from the ones standing immediately above it by application of one of the rules of $\mathbf{R}\mathcal{L}_{\mathbf{T}}$.

For any sequent

$$\mathcal{S} = R_1(F_{1,1},...,F_{1,r_1}) \mid \ldots \mid R_n(F_{n,1},...,F_{n,r_n})$$

let

$$\beta_{\mathcal{S}} = \bigvee_{1\leq i\leq n} R_i(t_{i,1},...,t_{i,r_i})$$

be the **T**-*formula corresponding to* $\mathcal{S}$, where $t_{i,j}$ is identical to $F_{i,j}$ if $F_{i,j}$ is a truth constant[4] and is a new variable $x_{i,j}$ otherwise ($x_{i,j} = x_{k,\ell}$ iff $F_{i,j} = F_{k,\ell}$).

Since the designating predicate *Des* is a simple formula it is equivalent to a formula *Des*$'$ of form $\bigwedge_{1\leq i\leq p} \bigvee_{1\leq j\leq q_i} A_{i,j}$ where the $A_{i,j}$ are atomic formulæ with at most one free variable x. By

$$\mathcal{D}_1\{x/F\},\ldots,\mathcal{D}_p\{x/F\}$$

we denote the sequence of sequents that correspond to the conjuncts of *Des*$'$ if x is replaced by the formula F.

For the following statements let **T** be any semantic theory and $\mathcal{L}_{\mathbf{T}}$ be the logic determined by **T**, an object language, projective truth functions for this language and a designating predicate *Des*. $\mathbf{R}\mathcal{L}_{\mathbf{T}}$ is the corresponding sequent calculus of relations as defined above.

Theorem 1 (Correctness). *If all sequents* $\mathcal{D}_1\{x/F\},\ldots,\mathcal{D}_p\{x/F\}$ *are provable in* $\mathbf{R}\mathcal{L}_{\mathbf{T}}$ *then* F *is valid in* $\mathcal{L}_{\mathbf{T}}$.

Proof. We show by induction on the length of proofs that for all models $\mathcal{M}$ of **T** and all interpretations $\mathcal{I}$: $\mathcal{M} \models \beta_{\mathcal{S}}[\sigma_{\mathcal{I}}]$ if $\mathcal{S}$ is provable, where $\sigma_{\mathcal{I}}$ assigns $val_{\mathcal{I}}(F_{i,j})$ to the corresponding variable $x_{i,j}$. From this the theorem follows by the definition of $\mathcal{D}_1\{x/F\},\ldots,\mathcal{D}_p\{x/F\}$ and the fact that F is valid if for all $\mathcal{M}$ and $\mathcal{I}$: $\mathcal{M} \models Des[val_{\mathcal{I}}(F)/x]$.

For axioms the claim immediately follows from their definition.

For applications of structural rules with premiss $\mathcal{S}$ and conclusion $\mathcal{S}'$ we have $\beta_{\mathcal{S}}$ implies $\beta_{\mathcal{S}'}$ by the fact that the **T**-formulæ corresponding to sequents are classical disjunctions.

For the application of a logical rule $(\Box\colon R\colon p)$ it suffices to observe that, by definition, for any σ: $\mathcal{M} \models \alpha_{\Box:R:p}[\sigma]$ implies that $\mathcal{M} \models R(z_1,\ldots,z_r)[\sigma']$, where σ' is as σ except for assigning $\widetilde{\Box}(\sigma(x_1),\ldots,\sigma(x_n))$ to the only variable z_p that does not already occur in $\alpha_{\Box:R:p}$.

Theorem 2 (Completeness). *If* F *is valid in* $\mathcal{L}_{\mathbf{T}}$ *then all sequents* $\mathcal{D}_1\{x/F\}$, $\ldots,\mathcal{D}_p\{x/F\}$ *are provable.*

Proof. (Sketch) We employ Schütte's method of reduction trees [14]. That is, we construct a reduction tree *RT* for every sequent $\mathcal{S}$ such that either a proof of $\mathcal{S}$ or a model in which $\beta_{\mathcal{S}}$ is not valid can be extracted from *RT*.

[4] Remember that we identify the constants of **T** with truth constants of the object language.

The construction of the upward tree of sequents RT for the sequent $\mathcal{S}$ is in stages as follows:

Stage 0: Write $\mathcal{S}$ at the root of RT.

Stage k: If the topmost sequent $\mathcal{S}'$ of a branch contains only propositional variables (as arguments of its relations) then stop the reduction for this branch. Otherwise $\mathcal{S}'$ contains a relation $R(F_1, \ldots, F_r)$ where $F_p \equiv \Box(G_1, \ldots, G_n)$ for some $1 \leq p \leq r$. If the indicated occurrence of $\Box(G_1, \ldots, G_n)$ is not the result of a reduction at this stage and has not yet been reduced on this branch then replace $\mathcal{S}'$ by

$$\frac{B_{1,1}\theta \mid \ldots \mid B_{1,t_1}\theta \mid \mathcal{S}' \quad \ldots \quad B_{s,1}\theta \mid \ldots \mid B_{s,t_s}\theta \mid \mathcal{S}'}{\mathcal{S}'}$$

where the $B_{i,j}$ are as in the definition of rule $(\Box\colon R\colon p)$ and θ is given by $R(z_1, \ldots, z_r)\{\Box(x_1, \ldots, x_n)/z_p\}\theta = R(F_1, \ldots, F_r)$.

Since every occurrence of a formula is only reduced once in a branch the construction of RT stops after finitely many steps.

We say that a sequent $\mathcal{S}'$ *contains* an axiom if it can be derived from an axiom using structural rules only. If each leaf of RT contains an axiom of $\mathbf{R}\mathcal{L}_\mathbf{T}$ then a proof of $\mathcal{S}$ is easily constructed from RT by inserting weakenings, permutations, and contractions.

Otherwise there is a leaf sequent $\mathcal{R}$ that does not contain an axiom. Let $\beta_\mathcal{R}$ be the $\mathbf{T}$-formula corresponding to $\mathcal{R}$ (by replacing the propositional variables f_i occurring in $\mathcal{R}$ by variables x_i of the language of $\mathbf{T}$). By definition of the set of axioms, there is a model $\mathcal{M}$ of $\mathbf{T}$ and an assignment σ such that $\mathcal{M} \not\models \beta_\mathcal{R}[\sigma]$. The assignment σ of truth values to the x_i induces an interpretation $\mathcal{I}$ of the corresponding propositional variables f_i. By going down the branch from $\mathcal{R}$ to the root $\mathcal{S}$ one can augment $\mathcal{I}$ to an interpretation of all propositional variables occurring in $\mathcal{S}$ such that $\mathcal{M} \not\models \beta_\mathcal{S}[val_\mathcal{I}(H_1)/x_1, \ldots, val_\mathcal{I}(H_k)/x_k]$, where the H_i are the formulæ in $\mathcal{S}$. (For this one, of course, has to check the corresponding truth functions as interpreted in $\mathcal{M}$.)

F is valid in $\mathcal{L}_\mathbf{T}$ iff for all $\mathcal{M}$ and $\mathcal{I}$, $\mathcal{M} \models \forall x\, Des[val_\mathcal{I}(F)/x]$. Since $\mathbf{T} \models \forall x\, Des \Leftrightarrow \bigwedge_{1\leq i\leq p} \mathcal{D}_i$ it follows that all leaves of a reduction tree RT_i for a sequent $\mathcal{D}_i\{x/F\}$ contain axioms. Therefore all sequents $\mathcal{D}_1\{x/F\}, \ldots, \mathcal{D}_p\{x/F\}$ are provable in $\mathbf{R}\mathcal{L}_\mathbf{T}$ if F is valid.

Since the construction of the reduction trees is effective we obtain:

Corollary 1. *All projective logics $\mathcal{L}_\mathbf{T}$ are decidable.*

Remark. The construction of the reduction tree can be seen as the search for a proof in tableau format. Here, the atomic elements of the tableau are not just formulæ but (atomic) relations between formulæ. The reduction of compound formulæ corresponds to the introduction rules of the sequent calculus. The tableau closure rules correspond to the axioms. The close relationship between reduction trees (i.e., tableaux) and sequent proofs relies on the fact that, like in classical logic, we can view sequents as sets (i.e., modulo permutation and construction) and can move all weakenings up to the axioms.

3.2 Derivation of calculi for Gödel logics

We already saw in Section 2 that all Gödel logics are projective. As an illustration of the proof theoretic framework of the last section we derive a calculus $\mathbf{RG}_\infty$ of relational sequents for infinite valued Gödel logic G_∞ by considering the semantic theory $\mathbf{T}$ described in Section 2.1.

Axioms of $\mathbf{RG}_\infty$ are all sequents that contain a sequent

$$A_1 \lhd A_2 \mid A_2 \lhd A_3 \mid \ldots \mid A_k \lhd A_1$$

for $k \geq 1$, where $\lhd$ is to be replaced either by $<$ or by $\leq$, but at least one occurrence of $\lhd$ stands for $\leq$.

In addition, all sequents that are obtained from the above ones by deleting relations of form

$$A < 0, \qquad 1 < A, \qquad \text{or} \qquad 1 \leq 0$$

are axioms.

Proposition 2. *All valid closed disjunctions of atomic formulæ in* $\mathbf{T}$ *correspond to one of the above axioms modulo applications of structural rules.*

We derive the logical rules of $\mathbf{RG}_\infty$ as described in Section 3 above by manipulating the rule-defining formulæ $\alpha_{\Box:R:p}$ in $\mathbf{T}$. Here $R \in \{<, \leq\}$; $p \in \{l, r\}$ for the left and right argument position of the binary relations, respectively, and $\Box \in \{\supset, \wedge, \vee\}$. (As already remarked, $\neg$ can treated as defined connective.)

$$\begin{aligned} \alpha_{(\supset:<:r)} &\equiv (x \leq y \wedge z < 1) \vee (y < x \wedge z < y) \\ &\Longleftrightarrow (x \leq y \vee y < x) \wedge (x \leq y \vee z < y) \wedge \\ &\qquad (z < 1 \vee y < x) \wedge (z < 1 \vee z < y) \\ &\Longleftrightarrow (x \leq y \vee z < y) \wedge (z < 1) \end{aligned}$$

The rule for introducing implication at the right argument place of "$<$" in a relational sequent can therefore be stated as:

$$\frac{A \leq B \mid C < B \mid \mathcal{H} \qquad C < 1 \mid \mathcal{H}}{C < (A \supset B) \mid \mathcal{H}}\ (\supset:<:r)$$

Similarly we have in $\mathbf{T}$

$$\begin{aligned} \alpha_{(\supset:<:l)} &\equiv (x \leq y \wedge 1 < z) \vee (y < x \wedge y < z) \\ &\Longleftrightarrow y < x \wedge y < z \end{aligned}$$

Thus a rule for introducing implication at the left argument place of "$<$" is:

$$\frac{B \leq A \mid \mathcal{H} \qquad B < C \mid \mathcal{H}}{(A \supset B) < C \mid \mathcal{H}}\ (\supset:<:l)$$

For implication at the right hand side of the $\leq$-relations we obtain:

$$\begin{aligned} \alpha_{(\supset:\leq:r)} &\equiv (x \leq y \wedge z \leq 1) \vee (y < x \wedge z \leq y) \\ &\Longleftrightarrow (x \leq y \vee y < x) \wedge (x \leq y \vee z \leq y) \\ &\Longleftrightarrow x \leq y \vee z \leq y \end{aligned}$$

This induces the rule

$$\frac{A \leq B \mid C \leq B \mid \mathcal{H}}{C \leq (A \supset B) \mid \mathcal{H}} \ (\supset : \leq : r)$$

A compact rule for introducing implication at the left hand side of the $\leq$-relations is obtained by the following derivation in **T**:

$$\begin{aligned}
\alpha_{(\supset:\leq:l)} &\equiv (x \leq y \wedge 1 \leq z) \vee (y < x \wedge y \leq z) \\
&\Longleftrightarrow (x \leq y \vee y < x) \wedge (x \leq y \vee y \leq z) \wedge \\
&\quad\;\; (1 \leq z \vee y < x) \wedge (1 \leq z \vee y \leq z) \\
&\Longleftrightarrow (1 \leq z \vee y < x) \wedge (y \leq z)
\end{aligned}$$

This induces the rule

$$\frac{1 \leq C \mid B < A \mid \mathcal{H} \qquad B \leq C \mid \mathcal{H}}{(A \supset B) \leq C \mid \mathcal{H}} \ (\supset : \leq : l)$$

Observe that this is the only $\leq$-rule exhibiting "$<$" in the premisses. (This is of importance for the connection to Avron's **G**LC; see Section 3.4 below.)

Computing the rules for disjunction and conjunction is easy. They take the same form for both relations. We therefore let $\lhd$ stand for either $<$ or $\leq$ (uniformly in each rule):

$$\frac{C \lhd A \mid \mathcal{H} \qquad C \lhd B \mid \mathcal{H}}{C \lhd (A \wedge B) \mid \mathcal{H}} \ (\wedge : \lhd : r) \qquad \frac{A \lhd C \mid B \lhd C \mid \mathcal{H}}{(A \wedge B) \lhd C \mid \mathcal{H}} \ (\wedge : \lhd : l)$$

$$\frac{C \lhd A \mid C \lhd B \mid \mathcal{H}}{C \lhd (A \vee B) \mid \mathcal{H}} \ (\vee : \lhd : r) \qquad \frac{A \lhd C \mid \mathcal{H} \qquad B \lhd C \mid \mathcal{H}}{(A \vee B) \lhd C \mid \mathcal{H}} \ (\vee : \lhd : l)$$

To obtain a calculus $\mathbf{RG}_n$ for n-valued Gödel logic G_n one only has to add the axiom

$$A_1 \leq A_2 \mid A_2 \leq A_3 \mid \ldots \mid A_n \leq A_{n+1}$$

3.3 Extended structural rules

So far we only considered (analytic) rules for introducing connectives and traditional forms of structural rules. Let us now investigate which types of cut rules or more general forms of structural rules (that possibly allow to exchange formulæ from different relations in sequents) are admissible in our calculi. Although we know – by completeness – that such rules are not needed for proof search, one should keep in mind that vast speedups (at least with respect to proof length) can be gained by applying such rules. (This is already well known for the "simplest" case of a projective logic, namely classical logic.)

We call a rule *extended structural rule* if it is of the form:

$$\frac{\mathcal{H} \mid \Gamma_1\theta \qquad \ldots \qquad \mathcal{H} \mid \Gamma_n\theta}{\mathcal{H} \mid \Gamma\theta}$$

where $\Gamma_1, \ldots, \Gamma_n, \Gamma$ are sequences of atomic formulæ of $\mathbf{T}$ (separated by "|"), θ is a substitution of variables by formulæ and $\mathcal{H}$ a side sequent.

Remark. Because of the presence of weakening, contraction and permutation there is no loss of generality in considering only identical side sequents in the premisses. Indeed this "additive" version of rules is more suitable in the context of tableau style proof search.

An extended structural rule is *admissible* in $\mathbf{R}\mathcal{L}_\mathbf{T}$ if

$$\mathbf{T} \models \forall \bar{x}(\widehat{\Gamma_1} \wedge \ldots \wedge \widehat{\Gamma_n}) \supset \widehat{\Gamma}$$

where $\bar{x}$ is the vector of all variables occurring in $\Gamma_1, \ldots, \Gamma_n, \Gamma$ and $\widehat{\Delta}$ is the disjunction of the atomic formulæ Δ consists of. ($\widehat{\Delta} \equiv True$ for empty Δ.)

It follows from this definition that, indeed, all sequents provable in $\mathbf{R}\mathcal{L}_\mathbf{T}$ augmented by admissible extended structural rules are already provable in $\mathbf{R}\mathcal{L}_\mathbf{T}$ without these rules.

It is important to notice that admissibility is a decidable property of rules, because we required all Π_1-sentences to be decidable in $\mathbf{T}$.

Let $vars(\Delta)$ denote the set of variables occurring in the sequent Δ. We call an extended structural rule *cut rule* if $vars(\Gamma) \subsetneq \bigcup_{1 \leq i \leq n} vars(\Gamma_i)$. (That is at least one formula of the formulæ is "cut out" from the premisses.) If $vars(\Gamma) \supseteq \bigcup_{1 \leq i \leq n} vars(\Gamma_i)$ we speak of an *analytic structural rule.*

Remark. In general, *many* different extended structural rules are admissible. They constitute on open list of (by admissibility:) possible but (by completeness:) not necessary extensions of the analytic calculi defined in Section 3.

Example 3. If $\mathbf{T}$ contains a transitive relation "$\prec$" – e.g., "$<$" and "$\leq$" in the semantic theory of Gödel logics – then

$$\frac{F \prec G \mid \mathcal{H} \qquad G \prec H \mid \mathcal{H}}{F \prec H \mid \mathcal{H}} \text{ (tr-cut)}$$

is an admissible cut rule, called *transitivity cut.*

If the partial ordering $\prec$ has a minimal element 0 and a maximal element 1 distinct from 0 – again Gödel logics are concrete examples – then

$$\frac{F \prec 0 \mid \mathcal{H} \qquad 1 \prec F \mid \mathcal{H}}{\mathcal{H}}$$

is another admissible cut rule.

If $\prec$ is irreflexive – as "$<$" for Gödel logics – also the unary cut rules

$$\frac{1 \prec F \mid \mathcal{H}}{\mathcal{H}} \quad \text{and} \quad \frac{F \prec 0 \mid \mathcal{H}}{\mathcal{H}}$$

are admissible.

Example 4. Let "$\leq$" and 0, 1 be as in the semantic theory for Gödel logics. Then

$$\frac{1 \leq F \mid \mathcal{H}}{G \leq F \mid \mathcal{H}} \ (w{:}\leq{:}l) \quad , \quad \frac{G \leq 0 \mid \mathcal{H}}{G \leq F \mid \mathcal{H}} \ (w{:}\leq{:}r) \quad \text{and} \quad \frac{1 \leq 0 \mid \mathcal{H}}{\mathcal{H}}$$

are examples of admissible analytic structural rules. The first two correspond to (internal) weakening in standard sequent calculi.

An important analytic structural rule, admissible for Gödel logics, is:

$$\frac{F \le G \mid H \le I \mid \mathcal{H}}{H \le G \mid F \le I \mid \mathcal{H}}$$

It corresponds to an instance of Avron's communication rule as we shall see in the next section.

3.4 The connection to Avron's hypersequent calculus

We want to consider Avron's calculus **G***LC* [1] as a calculus of relations and therefore use an equivalent formulation, where the hypersequents are fully split (see Section 3). This version of Avron's calculus consequently consists of:

- axioms $A \le A$
- (external) structural rules
- internal weakening rules $(w{:}\le{:}l)$ and $(w{:}\le{:}r)$ (see Example 4, above)
- all $\le$-rules of $\mathbf{RG}_\infty$ with the exception of $(\supset{:}\le{:}l)$, which is replaced by

$$\frac{D \le A \mid \mathcal{H} \qquad B \le C \mid \mathcal{H}}{(A \supset B) \le C \mid D \le C \mid \mathcal{H}}\ (\supset{:}\le{:}l)^*$$

- the communication rule:

$$\frac{A_1 \le U \mid \ldots \mid A_n \le U \mid \mathcal{H} \qquad B_1 \le V \mid \ldots \mid B_m \le V \mid \mathcal{H}}{A_1 \le V \mid \ldots \mid A_n \le V \mid B_1 \le U \mid \ldots \mid B_m \le U \mid \mathcal{H}}\ \text{(comm.)}$$

$(\supset{:}\le{:}l)^*$ is derivable from $(\supset{:}\le{:}l)$ in our $\mathbf{RG}_\infty$ using transitivity cuts (see Example 3), which can be eliminated from proofs:

$$\dfrac{\dfrac{\dfrac{\dfrac{\dfrac{D \le A \mid \mathcal{H} \qquad A \le B \mid B < A}{D \le B \mid B < A \mid \mathcal{H}}\ \text{(tr-cut)} \qquad B \le C \mid \mathcal{H}}{D \le C \mid B < A \mid \mathcal{H}}\ \text{(tr-cut)}}{B < A \mid D \le C \mid \mathcal{H}}\ \text{(perm.)}}{1 \le C \mid B < A \mid D \le C \mid \mathcal{H}}\ \text{(weak.)} \qquad B \le C \mid \mathcal{H}}{A \supset B \le C \mid D \le C \mid \mathcal{H}}\ (\supset{:}\le{:}l)$$

Consequently, $\mathbf{RG}_\infty$ simulates Avron's **G***LC*. In the other direction, it easy to show that pure $\le$-sequents derivable in $\mathbf{RG}_\infty$ are also derivable in (the given version of) Avron's calculus: Let $(A < B)^d \equiv 1 \le ((B \supset A) \supset A) \wedge (A \supset B)$ and $(A \le B)^d \equiv 1 \le A \supset B$. Then all ^{d}-translations of derivable $\mathbf{RG}_\infty$-sequents of are derivable in **G***LC*, since the translations of $\mathbf{RG}_\infty$-rules are derivable in **G***LC*.

Concerning efficient proof search, the most important feature of $\mathbf{RG}_\infty$ is the fact that we do not have to use the communication rule (or any similar rule destroying the "locality" of tableau style proof search.) On the other hand, even if we enrich **G***LC* by the (more general) axioms of $\mathbf{RG}_\infty$ the valid sequent

$$A \supset B \le C \mid A \le B \mid C \le B$$

is *not* cut-free provable *without* using the communication rule. In other words: the communication rule cannot be avoided if "<" is eliminated from the signature.

4 Future research

An obvious open problem is the extension of sequent calculi of relations to first order logics. The subtlety of this task is highlighted by the fact that natural versions of quantifier rules for infinite valued Gödel logics are locally incorrect in our calculi. However, global correctness for sequents based on $\leq$-relations only can still be ensured. We plan to elaborate on this and related matters in future work.

Acknowledgement. We thank the referees for their friendly, helpful and stimulating remarks. Limitations of space and time did not allow us to take up all of their suggestions already in this (version of the) paper.

References

1. Arnon Avron. Hypersequents, logical consequence and intermediate logics for concurrency. *Annals of Mathematics and Artificial Intelligence*, 4(199):225–248, 1991.
2. Arnon Avron. The method of hypersequents in proof theory of propositional nonclassical logics. In *Logic: from foundations to applications. European logic colloquium, Keele, UK, July 20–29, 1993*, pages 1–32, Oxford, 1996. Clarendon Press.
3. Matthias Baaz and Christian G. Fermüller. Resolution-based theorem proving for many-valued logics. *Journal of Symbolic Computation*, 19:353–391, 1995.
4. Matthias Baaz, Christian G. Fermüller, and Richard Zach. Elimination of cuts in first-order finite-valued logics. *J. Inform. Process. Cybernet.* **EIK**, 29(6):333–355, 1994.
5. Matthias Baaz, Gernot Salzer, Christian G. Fermüller, and Richard Zach. MUltlog 1.0: Towards an expert system for many-valued logics. In *13th Int. Conf. on Automated Deduction (CADE'96)*, volume 1104 of *Lecture Notes in Artificial Intelligence*, pages 226–230. Springer, 1996.
6. Michael Dummett. A propositional logic with denumerable matrix. *Journal of Symbolic Logic*, 24:96–107, 1959.
7. Gerhard Gentzen. Untersuchungen über das logische Schließen I-II. *Mathematische Zeitschrift*, 39:176–210 and 405–431, 1934-35.
8. Kurt Gödel. Zum intuitionistischen Aussagenkalkül. *Anzeiger der Akademie der Wissenschaften in Wien*, 69:65–66, 1932.
9. Reiner Hähnle. *Automated Deduction in Multiple-valued Logics.* Clarendon Press, Oxford, 1993.
10. Petr Hajek. *Metamathematics of Fuzzy Logic.* Kluwer, 1998.
11. Hans Jürgen Ohlbach. Computer support for the development and investigation of logics. Technical Report MPI-I-94-228, Max-Planck-Institut für Informatik, Saarbrücken, Germany, 1994.
12. Nicholas Rescher. *Many-valued Logic.* McGraw-Hill, New York, 1969.
13. G. Rousseau. Sequents in many valued logic I. *Fundamenta Mathematicae*, 60:23–33, 1967.
14. Kurt Schütte. *Proof Theory.* Springer, Berlin and New York, 1977.
15. Moto-o Takahashi. Many-valued logics of extended Gentzen style I. *Sci. Rep. Tokyo Kyoiku Daigaku Sect. A*, 9(271):95–110, 1968.

Merge Path Improvements for Minimal Model Hyper Tableaux

Peter Baumgartner, J.D. Horton, and Bruce Spencer

University of New Brunswick Fredericton, New Brunswick E3B 5A3, Canada
{baumgart,jdh,bspencer}@unb.ca

Abstract. We combine techniques originally developed for refutational first-order theorem proving within the clause tree framework with techniques for minimal model computation developed within the hyper tableau framework. This combination generalizes well-known tableaux techniques like complement splitting and folding-up/down. We argue that this combination allows for efficiency improvements over previous, related methods. It is motivated by application to diagnosis tasks; in particular the problem of avoiding redundancies in the diagnoses of electrical circuits with reconvergent fanouts is addressed by the new technique. In the paper we develop as our main contribution in a more general way a sound and complete calculus for propositional circumscriptive reasoning in the presence of minimized and varying predicates.

1 Introduction

Recently clause trees [7], a data structure and calculus for automated theorem proving, introduced a general method to close branches based on so-called *merge paths*. In this paper we bring these merge paths to tableaux for minimal model reasoning (e.g. [5, 12–14]) by extending our framework of *hyper tableau* [3, 1, 2].

The paper [7] is devoted to *refutational* theorem proving. Merge paths allow branches to close earlier than it would be possible without them or when using merge paths to simulate known instances such as folding-down [9]. Expressed from the viewpoint of complement splitting [10], one advantage is that the splitting of literals can be *deferred*.

In this paper we advocate to use merge paths for *model computation* calculi. In addition to the advantages in the refutational framework, merge path allow one to partially re-use previously computed models instead of computing them again. To achieve this, new inference rules dealing with merge paths for minimal model computation are defined. In contrast to the purely refutational setting, these inference rules have to be applied with care, as termination is no longer a trivial property. Therefore, we give conditions for termination such that the central properties of minimal model soundness and minimal model completeness hold. More precisely, as our main result we develop such a calculus for the more general case of circumscriptive reasoning for minimized and varying predicates (Section 4). The minimal model completeness proof is given by a simulation of merge paths by atomic cuts (cf. Lemma 1 in Section 4). Viewed from this point, our approach can thus be seen as a more and generalized approach for a *controlled* integration of the cut rule for the purpose of minimal model computation.

The rest of this paper is structured as follows: first we briefly give the idea of *merge paths* as defined in [7]. This presentation should be sufficient to explain the subsequent motivation of the new calculus from the viewpoint of a certain problem encountered in diagnosis tasks. In Section 2 we bring merge paths into trees and define an ordering on merge paths. It is employed in Section 3 in the new calculus. In Section 4 we show how merge paths can be simulated by atomic cuts and, based on that, prove soundness and completeness. Section 5 discusses certain aspects of the calculus (memory requirements, atomic cuts vs. merge paths).

Clause trees. Merge paths are introduced and studied in [7] in the context of clause trees. Clause trees are a data structure that represent equivalence classes of resolution derivations. Merge paths are a unified inference rule and generalize the folding up/folding down technique of [9].

Clause trees consist of *clause* nodes and *atom* nodes. Clause nodes are indicated by a ∘. Every clause node N corresponds to some input clause $\lambda(N) = L_1 \vee \ldots \vee L_n$ as can be seen from the n emerging edges; these edges are labeled by the signs of the L_i's, and the atom parts of the L_i's can be found in the adjacent atom nodes. Clause trees are built in such a way that from every atom node exactly two edges with opposite sign emerge. This corresponds to a binary resolution inference. Here is an example:

Clause tree: 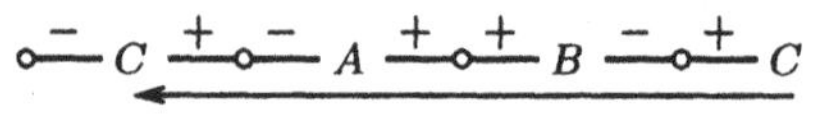

Clause set: $\leftarrow C$ $\quad C \leftarrow A$ $\quad A, B \leftarrow$ $\quad C \leftarrow B$

Now, in addition, *merge paths* can be drawn between equally labeled atom nodes, provided that the first and final edges are also equally labelled. In the preceeding figure, there is a merge path from the right C-node (called the *tail* of the merge path), to the left C-node (called the *head* of the merge path). The idea is "in order to find a proof at the tail of a merge path, look it up (copy it) from the head of the merge path". Thus, tail nodes are considered as proven and need no further extension. Thus a proof is a clause tree where every leaf is proven in this way or is a clause node.

Head nodes can be part of another merge path, and then there is a dependency of the nodes on the path on the head node. In this case the "lookup" of proofs is done recursively. In order to terminate this, cyclic dependencies must be excluded. The absence of cycles in a set of merge paths is referred to by the term "legal". Many of the results in [7] concerning legality and relation notions are derived as general properties of paths in trees. They thus can be readily applied to our case of hyper tableaux as well.

Motivation: A diagnosis application. We consider consistency-based diagnosis according to Reiter [16]. In this scenario, a model of a device under consideration is constructed and is used to predict its normal behavior. By comparing this prediction with the actual behavior it is possible to derive a diagnosis. More precisely, a *diagnosis* Δ is a (minimal) subset of the components of the device, such that the observed behavior is consistent with the assumption that exactly the components in Δ are behaving abnormally. Computing diagnosis can also be formalized as a circumscription problem.

The figure below depicts a hypothetical diagnosis scenario of an electrical circuit where merge paths are useful. The notation [0] in the left picture means that at this point the circuit is logical zero. The [0]'s at the bottom refer to input values of the actually observed behavior. The "Huge" box is meant to stand for a large circuit. The lightning at the output indicates that the predicted output is different from the actual output. We assume that two possible diagnoses are $\Delta_1 = \{inv1\}$ and $\Delta_2 = \{inv2\}$. Then it is consistent to have [0] at the output of the *and*-gate, and we assume that this renders the whole description consistent.

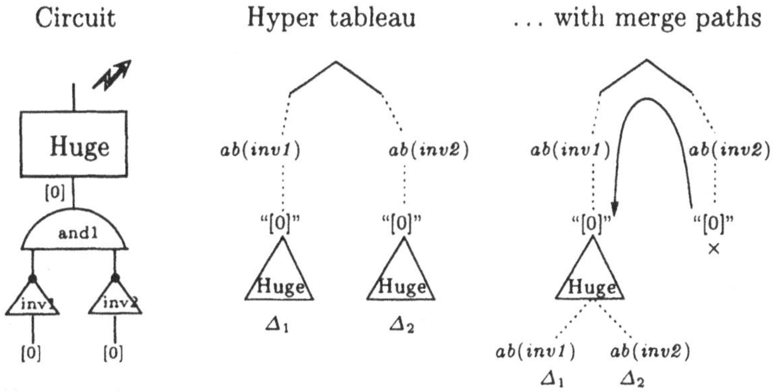

Now, the crucial observation is that the computation of Δ_1 and Δ_2 show considerable redundancies. The hyper tableau based diagnosis approach of [2] would result in the tableau depicted in the middle of the figure. Diagnoses are read off from open branches by collecting the *ab*-literals found there. The triangles stand for sub-tableaux containing diagnoses of the "Huge" part. There are two open branches containing Δ_1 and Δ_2 respectively.

Notice that the "Huge" part has to be diagnosed twice *although for its diagnosis exactly the same situation applies, namely* [0] *at its input*. This is reflected by the nodes "[0]". Clearly, for the diagnosis of "Huge" it is irrelevant what caused the "[0]"-situation. The generalized underlying problem is well-known in the diagnosis community and is referred to as "reconvergent fanouts".

So, the symmetry hidden in this problem was not exploited. In fact, the merge path technique just realizes this. It is indicated in the right part of the figure above: after the diagnosis Δ_1 is computed in the left branch, and the computation reaches the "[0]" node in the right subtree, a merge path is drawn as indicated, and the branch with the right "[0]" node is closed. The price to be paid is that Δ_1 as computed so far is invalid now. Technically, the $ab(inv1)$ literal can be thought of as being removed from the branch (it becomes "invisible" in our terminology). Hence, the computation starts again as indicated below the triangle. Eventually, both Δ_1 and Δ_2 can be found there.

Why is it attractive to use such a "non-monotonic" strategy? The answer is that it is little effort to recompute the initial segment of the diagnosis and better to save recomputing the "huge" part. We do not suggest to use the merge paths in all possible situations. In order to be flexible and allow guidance by heuristics, merge paths are thus always *optional* in the calculus defined below.

Preliminaries. We assume that the reader is familiar with the basic concepts of first-order logic. Throughout this paper, we are concerned with finite ground clause sets. A *clause* is an expression of the form $\mathcal{A} \leftarrow \mathcal{B}$, where $\mathcal{A} = (A_1, \ldots, A_m)$ and $\mathcal{B} = (B_1, \ldots, B_n)$ are finite sequences of atoms ($m, n \geq 0$); $\mathcal{A}$ is called the *head*, and $\mathcal{B}$ is called the *body* of the clause. Whenever convenient, a clause is also identified with the disjunction $A_1 \vee \cdots \vee A_m \vee \neg B_1 \vee \cdots \vee \neg B_n$ of literals.

Quite often, the ordering of atoms does not play a role, and we identify $\mathcal{A}$ and $\mathcal{B}$ with the sets $\{A_1, \ldots, A_m\}$ and $\{B_1, \ldots, B_n\}$, respectively. Thus, set-theoretic operations (such as "$\subset$", "$\cap$" etc.) can be applied meaningfully.

By $\overline{L}$ we denote the complement of a literal L. Two literals L and K are *complementary* if $\overline{L} = K$. In the sequel, the letters K and L always denote literals, A and B always denote atoms, C and D always denote clauses, $\mathcal{S}$ always denotes a finite ground clause set, and Σ denotes its signature, i.e. $\Sigma = \bigcup\{\mathcal{A} \cup \mathcal{B} \mid \mathcal{A} \leftarrow \mathcal{B} \in \mathcal{S}\}$.

As usual, we represent a Σ-interpretation $\mathcal{I}$ by the set of *true* atoms, i.e. $\mathcal{I}(A) = \mathit{true}$ iff $A \in \mathcal{I}$. Define $\mathcal{I} \models \mathcal{A} \leftarrow \mathcal{B}$ iff $\mathcal{B} \subseteq \mathcal{I}$ implies $\mathcal{A} \cap \mathcal{I} \neq \emptyset$. Notice that this is consistent with other usual definitions when clauses are treated as disjunctions of literals. Usual model-theoretical notions of "satisfiability", "validity" etc. of clauses and clause sets are applied without defining them explicitly here.

Minimal models are of central importance in various fields, like (logic) programming language semantics, non-monotonic reasoning (e.g. GCWA, WGCWA) and knowledge representation. Of particular interest are Γ-minimal models, i.e. minimal models only wrt. the Γ-subset of Σ. From a circumscriptive point of view, Γ is thus the set of atoms to be minimized, and $\Sigma \setminus \Gamma$ varies. In the sequel, Γ always denotes some subset of the signature Σ.

Definition 1 (Γ-Minimal Models). *For any atom set M define the* restriction of M to Γ *as* $M|\Gamma = M \cap \Gamma$. *In order to relate atom sets M_1 and M_2 define $M_1 <_\Gamma M_2$ iff $M_1|\Gamma \subset M_2|\Gamma$, and $M_1 =_\Gamma M_2$ iff $M_1|\Gamma = M_2|\Gamma$. As usual, the relation $M_1 \leq_\Gamma M_2$ is defined as $M_1 <_\Gamma M_2$ or $M_1 =_\Gamma M_2$. We say that a model $\mathcal{I}$ for a clause set M is* Γ-minimal (for M) *iff there is no model $\mathcal{I}'$ for M such that $\mathcal{I}' <_\Gamma \mathcal{I}$*

It is easy to see that $\leq_\Gamma$ is a partial order and that $=_\Gamma$ is an equivalence relation. Notice that the "general" minimal models can simply be expressed by setting $\Gamma = \Sigma$. Henceforth, by a *minimal* model we mean a Σ-minimal one.

An obvious consequence of this definition is that every minimal model of $\mathcal{S}$ is also a Γ-Minimal model of $\mathcal{S}$ (but the converse does not hold in general).

2 Literal Trees and Merge Paths

We consider finite ordered trees T where the nodes, except the root node, are labeled with literals. The labeling function is denoted by λ. A *branch* of T is a sequence $b = (N_0, N_1, \dots, N_n)$ of nodes of T such that N_0 is the root, N_i is an immediate successor node of N_{i-1} (for $1 \leq i \leq n$) and N_n is a leaf node. The fact that b is a branch of T is also written as $b \in T$.

Any subsequence $b' = (N_i, \dots, N_j)$ with $0 \leq i \leq j \leq n$ is called a *partial branch of* b; if $i = 0$ then this subsequence is called *rooted*. Define $last(b') = N_j$. In the sequel the letter b always denotes a branch or a partial branch. The expression (b_1, b_2) denotes the concatenation of partial branches b_1 and b_2; similarly, the expression (b, N) denotes $(N_i, \dots, N_j, N)$, where b is the partial branch $(N_i, \dots, N_j)$. For convenience we write "the node L", where L is a literal, instead of the more lengthy "the node N labeled with L", where N is some node given by the context. In the same spirit, we write $(L_1, \dots, L_n)$ and mean the partial branch $(N_1, \dots, N_n)$, or even $(N_0, N_1, \dots, N_n)$ in case N_0 is the root and N_i is an immediate successor node of the root, where N_i is labelled with L_i (for $1 \leq i \leq n$). Further, (b, L) means (b, N), where N is some node labeled with L and b is a partial branch.

A branch b is labeled either as "open", "closed" or with some subset of Γ. In the latter case, b is called a MM-branch, and MM(b) denotes that set, which is called the *minimal model of* b. A tree or subtree is *closed* iff every of its branches is closed, otherwise it is *non-closed*. A tree or subtree is *open* if some of its branches are open.

Definition 2 (Ancestor Path, Merge Path). *Let T be a tree and suppose that T contains a rooted partial branch b of the form $b = (N_0, N_1, \dots, N_i, \dots, N_n)$ with N_0 being the root. Any sequence $ancp(b, N_i) := (N_n, N_{n-1}, \dots, N_i)$, where $n \geq i > 0$, is called an* ancestor path (of b)*. The node N_n is called the* tail *and the node N_i is called the* head *of this ancestor path. Now, if it additionally holds that $\lambda(N_i) = A$ and $\lambda(N_n) = \neg A$ (for some atom A) then $ancp(b, N_i)$ is called an* ancestor merge path (of b).
Let T contain rooted partial branches $b^T = (N_0, N_1, \dots, N_i, N_{i+1}, \dots N_n)$ and $b^H = (N_0, N_1, \dots, N_i, M_{i+1}, \dots M_m)$ with N_0 being the root and $m, n > i \geq 0$ and $M_{i+1} \neq N_{i+1}$ and such that $\lambda(N_n) = \lambda(M_m) = A$ for some atom A. Define $p^T = N_n, \dots, N_{i+1}$, $p^H = M_{i+1}, \dots, M_m$, and $p = (p^T, p^H)$. Here, p is understood as a concatenation of p^T and p^H. By this definition, nodes on paths are written in order from tail to head. We assume that p can always be decomposed into its constituents p^T and p^H; p is called a non-ancestor merge path of T from b^T to b^H with tail N_n and head M_m*. It is also denoted by $mergep(b^T, b^H)$. The node N_i is called the* turn point *of p. Note that the turn point is not on p.*

By a merge path *we mean a non-ancestor merge path or an ancestor merge path. The letters p and q are used in the sequel to denote ancestor paths or merge paths, and the letter $\mathcal{P}$ will be used to refer to sets of merge paths.*

A non-ancestor merge path with $m = n = i + 1$ is called *factoring*, the case $m = i + 1$ is called a *hook*, and the case $m > i + 1$ is called a *deep merge path.*

Definition 3 (Ordering on paths). *Suppose the paths $p = (N_1, \ldots, N_n)$ and $q = (M_1, \ldots, M_m)$ as given. Define q* precedes *p, as $q \prec p$ iff $M_m \in \{N_2, \ldots, N_{n-1}\}$. We say that a finite set of paths $\mathcal{P}$ is* legal *iff the $\prec$ relation on $\mathcal{P}$ can be extended to a partial order $\ll$ on $\mathcal{P}$.* Illegal *means not legal.*

Notice that the $\prec$ relation is irreflexive but in general not transitive. One could also define a set of paths to be illegal if it contains a cycle, i.e. if there are paths $p_1, \ldots, p_n \in \mathcal{P}$ such that $p_1 \prec p_2 \prec \cdots \prec p_n \prec p_1$, for some $n > 1$. Avoiding cycles is important to guarantee the soundness of the calculus.

Example 1 (Ordering). The figure below contains examples of trees equipped with merge paths. The underlying clause sets can be left implicit. Merge paths are indicated using arrow notation. For instance, in the right tree, the arrow from the leaf node $\neg A$ to A indicates an (the) ancestor merge path $p_1 = (\neg A, C, A)$ of the branch $(A, C, \neg A)$ with tail $\neg A$ and head A. In the same tree, the arrow from the rightmost node C to the other node C indicates a non-ancestor merge path $p_2 = mergep((B, C), (A, C)) = (C, B, A, C)$ with tail C (the right node) and head C (the other node C) and the root as turn point. In terms of Definition 2 we have $p_2^T = (C, B)$ and $p_2^H = (A, C)$. The path p_2 is an example of a *deep merge path*. The merge path set $\{p_1, p_2\}$ is not legal because both $p_1 \prec p_2$ and $p_2 \prec p_1$ and hence $\prec$ cannot be extended to a partial order. The left tree contains two non-ancestor merge paths and both are "hooks".

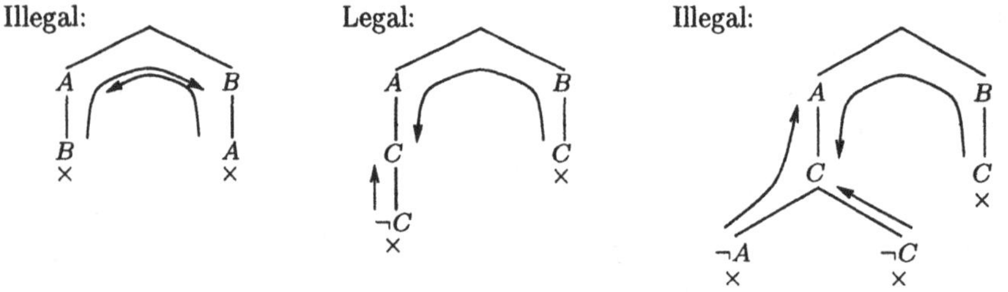

The left and right cases are the simplest cases for illegality, as in both cases only two merge paths are involved. These are illegal, because the heads of the merge paths are mutually contained as inner nodes. The left tableau would correspond to an unsound combination of the "folding up" and "folding down" inference rules, usually avoided in implementations by choosing not to combine them at all.

The new calculus to be presented below does not only construct a tableaux T as the derivation proceeds, but also a *legal* set of merge paths $\mathcal{P}$. This guarantees soundness.

In order to achieve minimal model computation, we have to define how interpretations are extracted from open branches.

Definition 4 (Visibility, Branch Semantics). *Let $b = (N_0, N_1 \ldots, N_n)$ be a rooted partial branch in a tree T (not necessarily a hyper tableau) with $n \geq 0$,* *and let* $\mathcal{P}$ *be a legal set of merge paths in* T. *The node* N_i *(where* $0 < i \leq n$*) that is not the tail of a merge path in* $\mathcal{P}$ *is said to be* visible from N_n wrt. $\mathcal{P}$ *iff* $\mathcal{P} \cup \{ancp(b, N_i)\}$ *is legal. Define*

$$[\![(N_0, N_1, \ldots, N_n)]\!]_{\mathcal{P}} = \{\lambda(N_i) \mid N_i \textit{ is visible from } N_n \textit{ wrt. } \mathcal{P}, \textit{ for } 0 < i \leq n\} \ .$$

The set $[\![b]\!]_{\mathcal{P}}$ *is called* inconsistent *iff* $\{A, \neg A\} \subseteq [\![b]\!]_{\mathcal{P}}$ *for some atom* A*;* consistent *means "not inconsistent". We omit "wrt.* $\mathcal{P}$*" when* $\mathcal{P}$ *is given by the context.*

The head of a merge path hides nodes that are on the path from nodes beyond the head, i.e. away from the direction that the head points. Those nodes that are not hidden from a node are visible to that node. In the definition of branch semantics an atom A is true in a consistent branch if and only if it is visible from the leaf. For instance, in the middle tableau in Example 1 we have $[\![(A, C, \neg C)]\!]_{\mathcal{P}} = \{\neg C, C\}$ and $[\![(B, C)]\!]_{\mathcal{P}} = \{B, C\}$, where $\mathcal{P}$ consists of the two merge paths drawn there. Notice that the case $n = 0$ is not excluded, and it holds that $[\![(N_0)]\!] = \emptyset$.

3 Hyper Tableaux with Merge Paths

Before defining the new calculus we take one more preliminary step: suppose that $B \in [\![b]\!]_{\mathcal{P}}$ for given open branch b and legal path set $\mathcal{P}$. In the trees constructed in Definition 5, there is a *unique* node N_B in b with $\lambda(N_B) = B$ such that N_B is visible from the leaf of b[1]. Consequently, the ancestor merge path $ancp((b, \neg B), N_B)$ is uniquely defined, and it is denoted by $ancp((b, \neg B))$ alone.

Definition 5 (Hyper tableaux with merge paths). *Let* T *be a tree,* b *be a branch in* T *and let* $L_1 \vee \cdots \vee L_n$ *be a disjunction of literals. We say that* T' *is an* extension of T at b with $L_1 \vee \cdots \vee L_n$ *iff* T' *is obtained from* T *by attaching to the leaf of* b n *new successor nodes* $N_1, \ldots, N_n$ *that are labeled with the literals* $L_1, \ldots, L_n$ *in this order.*

A selection function *is a total function* f *that maps an open tree to one of its open branches. If* $f(T) = b$ *we also say that* b is selected in T by f.

Hyper tableaux T for $\mathcal{S}$ with merge path set $\mathcal{P}$ *– or* $(T, \mathcal{P})$ *for short – are defined inductively as follows.*

Initialization step: $(\epsilon, \emptyset)$ *is a hyper tableau for* $\mathcal{S}$*, where* ϵ *is a tree consisting of a root node only. Its single branch is marked as "open".*

Hyper extension step with C***:*** *If (i)* $(T, \mathcal{P})$ *is an open hyper tableau for* $\mathcal{S}$ *with selected branch* b*, and (ii)* $C = A_1, \ldots, A_m \leftarrow B_1, \ldots, B_n$ *is a clause from* $\mathcal{S}$ *(for some* $A_1, \ldots, A_m$ *and* $B_1, \ldots, B_n$ *and* $m, n \geq 0$*), and (iii)* $\{B_1, \ldots, B_n\} \subseteq [\![b]\!]_{\mathcal{P}}$*, and (iv)* $\{A_1, \ldots, A_m\} \cap [\![b]\!]_{\mathcal{P}} = \emptyset$ *(regularity), then* $(T', \mathcal{P}')$ *is a hyper tableau for* $\mathcal{S}$*, where (i)* T' *is an extension of* T *at* b *with* $A_1 \vee \cdots \vee A_m \vee \neg B_1 \vee \cdots \vee \neg B_n$*,*

[1] Most proofs are omitted or only sketched for space reasons; the full version [4] contains all proofs.

and (ii) every branch $(b, \neg B_1) \ldots, (b, \neg B_n)$ *of* T' *is labeled as closed, and (iii) every branch* $(b, A_1) \ldots, (b, A_m)$ *of* T' *is labeled as open, and (iv)* $\mathcal{P}' = \mathcal{P} \cup \{ancp((b, \neg B_1)), \ldots, ancp((b, \neg B_n))\}$. *If conditions (i) – (iv) hold, we say that an "extension step with clause* $\mathcal{A} \leftarrow \mathcal{B}$ *is applicable to* b*".*

Merge path step with p*: If (i)* $(T, \mathcal{P})$ *is an open hyper tableau for* $\mathcal{S}$ *with selected branch* b*, and (ii)* $p = mergep(b, b^H)$ *is a non-ancestor merge path from* b*, for some rooted partial branch* b^H *of* T*, and (iii)* $last(b^H)$ *is not the tail of a merge path in* $\mathcal{P}$*, and (iv)* $\mathcal{P} \cup \{p\}$ *is legal, then* $(T', \mathcal{P}')$ *is a hyper tableau for* $\mathcal{S}$*, where (i)* T' *is the same as* T*, except that* b *is labeled as closed in* T'*, and every* MM*-branch* b' *of* T *with* $[\![b']\!]_{\mathcal{P}\cup\{p\}}|\Gamma \subset \mathrm{MM}(b')$ *is labeled as open in* T'*, and (ii)* $\mathcal{P}' = \mathcal{P} \cup \{p\}$. *If conditions (i) – (iv) hold, we say that a "merge path step with merge path* p *is applicable to* b*".*

Minimal Model Test: *If (i)* $(T, \mathcal{P})$ *is an open hyper tableau for* $\mathcal{S}$ *with selected branch* b*, and (ii)* $[\![b]\!]_{\mathcal{P}}$ *is a* Γ*-minimal model of* $\mathcal{S}$*, then* $(T', \mathcal{P})$ *is a hyper tableau for* $\mathcal{S}$*, where* T' *is the same as* T *except that* b *is labeled in* T' *with* $[\![b]\!]_{\mathcal{P}}|\Gamma$*. If applicability conditions (i) and (ii) hold, we say that the minimal model test inference rule is* applicable *(to* b*).*

A (possibly infinite) sequence $((\epsilon, \emptyset) = (T_0, \mathcal{P}_0)), (T_1, \mathcal{P}_1), \ldots, (T_n, \mathcal{P}_n), \ldots$ *of hyper tableaux for* $\mathcal{S}$ *is called a* derivation*, where* $(T_0, \mathcal{P}_0)$ *is obtained by an initialization step, and for* $i > 0$ *the tableau* $(T_i, \mathcal{P}_i)$ *is obtained from* $(T_{i-1}, \mathcal{P}_{i-1})$ *by a single application of one of the other inference rules. A* derivation of $(T_n, \mathcal{P}_n)$ *is a finite derivation that ends in* $(T_n, \mathcal{P}_n)$*. A* refutation of $\mathcal{S}$ *is a derivation of a closed tableau.*

This definition is an extension of previous ground versions of hyper tableaux (mentioned in the introduction) by bringing in an inference rule for merge paths and explicitly handling Γ-minimal models. The introduction of non-ancestor merge paths requires to explicitly keep track of the ancestor merge paths as well.

The purpose of the hyper extension step rule is to satisfy a clause that is not satisfied in the selected branch b. An implicit legality check for the ancestor paths added in an extension step is carried out by excluding those atoms from the branch semantics that would cause illegality when drawing an ancestor path to them.

An obvious invariant of the inference rules is that every open or MM-branch b is labeled with positive literals only and hence $[\![b]\!]_{\mathcal{P}}$ is consistent. Thus $[\![b]\!]_{\mathcal{P}}$ conforms to our convention of representing interpretations as the set of atoms being true in it.

The purpose of the minimal model test rule is to remember that a Γ-minimal model is computed and to attach it to the selected branch b. Since usually one is interested only in the Γ-subset of models, we keep only the Γ-atoms. These are thought to be the output of the computation. Notice that for MM-branches, a hyper extension step is not applicable, because MM-branches are not open and only open branches can be selected. For the same reason merge path steps are also not applicable to MM-branches.

The purpose of the merge path step inference rule is to close branches because a "proof" or a model is to be found in the branch where the drawn merge path is pointing to. But in the course of a derivation, a previously computed Γ-minimal model MM(b) of a branch b might no longer be the same as $[\![b]\!]_{\mathcal{P}}|\Gamma$, because of a deep merge path step with head node (for instance) in b. Therefore, the label MM(b) has to be rejected and the branch has to be opened again for further extension. This is expressed in item (i) in the conclusion of the merge path step inference rule (Def. 5). Notice, however, that this happens only if some atom $A \in \Gamma$ in $[\![b]\!]_{\mathcal{P}}$ becomes invisible, not if some other literal from $\Sigma \setminus \Gamma$ becomes invisible. Thus, some deep merge paths can still be drawn without causing recomputation.

3.1 Examples

(1) Consider the figure in Example 1 again. Closed branches are marked with the symbol "×" as closed. Only the tableau in the middle is constructible by the calculus, because the calculus rules forbid the derivation of a tableau with an illegal set of merge paths. In this middle tableau the left branch gets closed by a hyper extension step with the clause $\leftarrow C$, and the right branch is closed by a non-ancestor merge path step as indicated. This application of a non-ancestor merge path step corresponds to a folding-up step in model elimination [9].

The right tableau shows that both ancestor and non-ancestor merge paths have to be taken into account for legality.

(2) The figure below serves as an example to demonstrate the change of branch semantics as the derivation proceeds and the computation of models. We forget about the minimal model test rule for a moment.

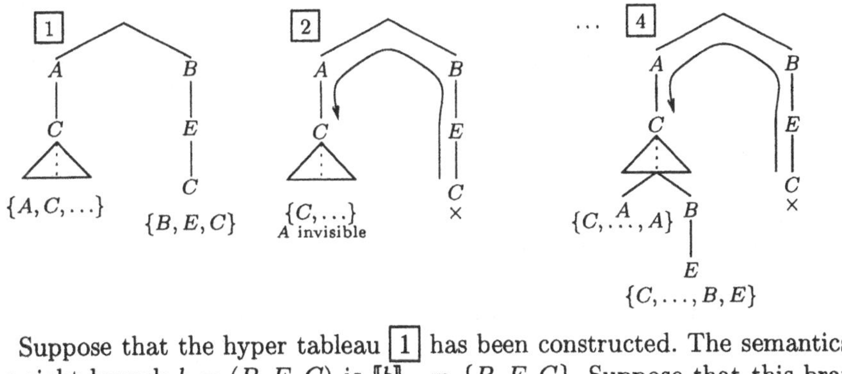

Suppose that the hyper tableau [1] has been constructed. The semantics of the right branch $b = (B, E, C)$ is $[\![b]\!]_{\mathcal{P}} = \{B, E, C\}$. Suppose that this branch can be extended further. Suppose that the left subtree contains an open branch $b_{\ldots}$ that makes A and C true. This is indicated by the set $[\![b_{\ldots}]\!]_{\mathcal{P}} = \{A, C, \ldots\}$. Further suppose that this is a minimal model.

Next, let a merge path step be applied with non-ancestor merge path p to the tableau [1], yielding the tableau [2]. By this step, b is closed and hence its interpretation is rejected for the time being. A second effect of this step is that the node labeled with A becomes invisible from the leaf of $b_{\dots}$. Thus $[\![b_{\dots}]\!]_{\mathcal{P}\cup\{p\}} = \{C, \dots\}$. Now, this new interpretation has to be "repaired" by bringing in A again. This is done in the next step by extending with $A \vee B$ yielding a tableau $\boxed{3}$ (which is not depicted). Notice that the minimal model $[\![b_{\dots}]\!]_{\mathcal{P}}$ is indeed reconstructed, only in a different order. In order to reconstruct the rejected interpretation $\{B, E, C\}$ from above that was rejected by the merge path step, a hyper extension step below the new B node with E is carried out. This leads to the tableaux $\boxed{4}$. Notice that the new branch with semantics $\{C, \dots, B, E\}$ possibly contains more elements than the corresponding one with semantics $\{B, E, C\}$.

It is worth emphasizing that the re-computation of models happens only in the case of non-ancestor merge paths with their head in *open* branches. Merge paths into *closed* branches are "cheap" in that no re-computation is necessary. Thus, in a sense, refutational theorem proving, which would stop with failure after the first open finished branch (cf. Def. 6 below) is found, is "simpler" than computing models.

In order to demonstrate the effect of the minimal model test inference rule let now $\Gamma = \{C, E\}$. We start with tableau $\boxed{1}$ again. For the branch $b_{\dots}$ the minimal model $[\![b_{\dots}]\!]_{\mathcal{P}} = \{A, C, \dots\}$ was supposed. Suppose that E is not contained in that set. Then $[\![b_{\dots}]\!]_{\mathcal{P}}|\Gamma = \{C\}$ is a Γ-minimal model, because $[\![b_{\dots}]\!]_{\mathcal{P}}$ is a minimal model. According to the minimal model test inference rule, the branch $b_{\dots}$ can be labeled with $\{C\}$ then.

Now, consider tableau $\boxed{2}$. The merge path p there eliminates the Γ-minimal model candidate in the right branch by closing it. Concerning the left branch $b_{\dots}$, although A has been removed from its previous interpretation $[\![b_{\dots}]\!]_{\mathcal{P}} = \{A, C, \dots\}$, its Γ-minimal model $\{C\}$ has not been changed, i.e. $[\![b_{\dots}]\!]_{\mathcal{P}}|\Gamma = [\![b_{\dots}]\!]_{\mathcal{P}\cup\{p\}}|\Gamma = \{C\}$. Consequently the branch label $\{C\}$ has not to be removed and $b_{\dots}$ has not to be opened again. This is reflected by the result description (i) in the definition of merge path step. If Γ were Σ, the branch $b_{\dots}$ would have to be opened again and the computation could continue as above leading to $\boxed{4}$.

3.2 Finite Derivations

Unfortunately, our calculus does not terminate in general, i.e. there are infinite derivations (for finite clause sets), although we employ the "regularity" test (cf. Def. 5). This is due to deep merge paths – without them, termination is straightforward to prove. For instance, the satisfiable clause set $\{(A, B \leftarrow), (B, C \leftarrow), (A, D \leftarrow), (C \leftarrow A)\}$ admits an infinite derivation (cf. [4]) even under very reasonable assumptions, namely that only hooks are mandatory, and that deep merge paths are carried out only to close branches holding non-minimal models. As a consequence we propose the following technique:

Theorem 1 (Termination Criterion). *A derivation $(T_0, \mathcal{P}_0), \dots, (T_n, \mathcal{P}_n), \dots$ is finite, provided that for every $(T_i, \mathcal{P}_i)$, where $i \geq 0$, an applicable merge path step with merge path p is not carried out if for some open branch b in T_i more* *than an a priori fixed number max of occurrences of some label A is invisible from last(b) wrt. $\mathcal{P}_i \cup \{p\}$.*

This criterion avoids infinite derivations by bounding repetitions of the same literal along branches. A trivial instance is $max = 0$. Then no deep merge paths but only hooks are possible. The idea underlying the criterion is that one should not without bound repeat the derivation of an atom that becomes repeatedly invisible on a branch. Due to this criterion we consider from now on only finite derivations.

Definition 6 (Redundancy, Fairness). *Suppose as given some hyper tableau $(T, \mathcal{P})$ for $\mathcal{S}$. A clause $\mathcal{A} \leftarrow \mathcal{B}$ is called* redundant *in an open branch b of T wrt. $\mathcal{P}$ iff $[\![b]\!]_\mathcal{P} \models \mathcal{A} \leftarrow \mathcal{B}$ (iff $\mathcal{B} \subseteq [\![b]\!]_\mathcal{P}$ implies $\mathcal{A} \cap [\![b]\!]_\mathcal{P} \neq \emptyset$).*

A branch b of T is called finished (wrt. $\mathcal{P}$) *iff (i) b is closed, or (ii) b is an* MM*-branch, or else (iii) the minimal model test inference rule is not applicable to b and every clause $\mathcal{A} \leftarrow \mathcal{B} \in \mathcal{S}$ is redundant in b wrt. $\mathcal{P}$. The term* unfinished *means "not finished".*

Now suppose as given a finite derivation $D = (T_0, \mathcal{P}_0), \ldots, (T_n, \mathcal{P}_n)$ from $\mathcal{S}$ with selection function f. D is called fair *iff (i) D is a refutation, i.e. T_n is closed, or else (ii) $f(T_n)$ is finished wrt. $\mathcal{P}_n$.*

The selection function f is called a model computation selection function *iff f maps a given open hyper tableau $(T, \mathcal{P})$ to an unfinished branch wrt. $\mathcal{P}$, provided one exists, else f maps T to some other open (finished) branch.*

According to this definition, the only possibility to be unfair is to terminate a derivation with a selected open branch that could be either labeled with a Γ-minimal model or extended further.

The *existence* of fair derivations is straightforward because we insist on *finite* derivations. Notice that any input clause not redundant so far in a branch b can be made redundant by simply carrying out an extension step with that clause.

The idea behind a *model-computation selection function* is that no derivation should stop with an unfinished branch. Since finished open branches constitute Γ-models, with such a selection function every Γ-minimal model is computed.

4 Soundness and Completeness

Lemma 1 (Soundness lemma). *Let $(T, \mathcal{P})$ be a hyper tableau for satisfiable clause set $\mathcal{S}$. Then for every minimal model $\mathcal{I}$ of $\mathcal{S}$ there is an open branch b of T such that $[\![b]\!]_\mathcal{P} \subseteq \mathcal{I}$.*

The proof of Lemma 1 is done by simulating non-ancestor merge paths by atomic cuts, i.e. by β-steps applied to disjunctions of the form $A \vee \neg A$, for some atom A. The branch semantics in presence of atomic cuts is given by forgetting about the negative literals, i.e. $[\![b]\!]^+_\mathcal{P} = \{A \in [\![b]\!]_\mathcal{P} \mid A \text{ is a positive literal}\}$ for any consistent branch b in a hyper tableau with atomic cuts.

The transformation t defined below takes a hyper tableau with cut $(T, \mathcal{P})$ where $\mathcal{P}$ is legal and contains at least one non-ancestor merge path, and returns a hyper tableau with cut $(T', \mathcal{P}') = t(T, \mathcal{P})$ that contains one less non-ancestor merge path in $\mathcal{P}'$ (which is legal as well). The transformation t preserves the following ***invariant***: for every consistent and open branch b' of T' there is a consistent and open branch b of T such that $[\![b]\!]^+_{\mathcal{P}} \subseteq [\![b']\!]^+_{\mathcal{P}'}$. Repeated application of t as long as possible results in a tableau $(T_{\text{cut}}, \mathcal{P}_{\text{cut}})$ with cuts but without non-ancestor merge paths. All literals along all branches are visible there, and hence we have a "standard tableau" with cuts then. The lemma then is proven for this tableau, and using the ***invariant*** above it can be translated back for the originally given tableau $(T, \mathcal{P})$.

The transformation t itself is depicted in the figure below. The left side displays the most general situation. Dashed lines mean partial branches. For instance, the top leftmost dashed line leading to B means the partial branch p_B from the root to the node (inclusive) labeled with B. Triangles are certain forests. The most appropriate intuition is to think of trees as branch sets. Then the triangle T^B is simply the set of the branches obtained from T by deleting all branches that contain p_B.

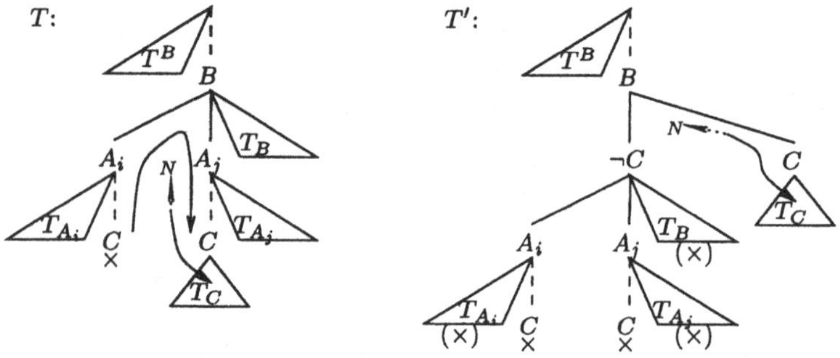

Since $\mathcal{P}$ is legal it is extendible to a partial order $\ll$. Let p be a minimal element in this order. This is the one to be transformed away. It is important to use a minimal element in order to prove the invariant.

The solid lines, just like the ones below B indicate a hyper extension step; here, it is supposed that a hyper extension step with clause $C = A_1, \ldots, A_n \leftarrow B$ has been carried out to p_B, and all the literals short of A_i and A_j (for some $i, j \in \{1, \ldots, n\}$ and $i \neq j$) are attached to nodes in the subtree T_B. The assumed non-ancestor merge path p is indicated with tail node C (left) and head node C (right) and turn point B. There might be other non-ancestor merge paths in $\mathcal{P}$, in particular some where the head of p is an inner node. This possibility is indicated in the figure as well, by the arrow pointing into T_C. The tail of this non-ancestor merge path, say p_C is a leaf node N somewhere in T.

Inconsistent or closed branches are marked by "×". The effect of the transformation t is shown on the right. Notice the cut with $C \vee \neg C$ at the turn point B. The transformation is understood to move merge paths as well. For example, the non-ancestor merge path p_C still has the same head and tail node, but they are possibly located in different places in T' now, and also a different turn point might result. After transformation some branches might get closed due to the presence of $\neg C$. This is indicated by "(×)". Notice that the transformation only introduces new *negative* literals into branches, $\neg C$, so that the branch semantics wrt. positive literals does not change, as required in the *invariant*.

The central properties that have to be argued for are (i) that the tableau resulting from the transformation is a hyper tableau (i.e. that all negative leaf nodes can still be closed by legal ancestor paths), and (ii) that the *invariant* holds. This is done by expressing the *invariant* in terms of visibility from leaf nodes and then arguing with the orderings underlying $\mathcal{P}$ and $\mathcal{P}'$.

This lemma is applied in the proof of the next theorem, which is our main result.

Theorem 2 (Soundness and Completeness). *Let f be a model computation selection function and D be a finite, fair derivation from clause set $\mathcal{S}$ of the hyper tableau $(T, \mathcal{P})$. Then $\{\mathrm{MM}(b) \mid b$ is a MM-branch of $T\} = \{\mathcal{I}|\Gamma \mid \mathcal{I}$ is a Γ-minimal model of $\mathcal{S}\}$ Furthermore, if $\mathcal{S}$ is unsatisfiable then T is closed (refutational completeness).*

Proof. Minimal model soundness – the first theorem statement in the "$\subseteq$"-direction – is an immediate consequence of the applicability condition (ii) in the minimal model test inference rule and the result description (i) in the merge path step inference rule. Regarding minimal model completeness – the first theorem statement in the "$\supseteq$"-direction –, suppose to the contrary that for some Γ-minimal model $\mathcal{I}$ of $\mathcal{S}$ there is no MM-branch of T such that $[\![b]\!]_{\mathcal{P}} =_{\Gamma} \mathcal{I}$.

Clearly $\mathcal{I}|\Gamma \subseteq \mathcal{I}$ for some minimal model $\mathcal{I}$ of $\mathcal{S}$. Now, label all MM-branches of T as open and let T' be the resulting tableau. By the soundness lemma (Lemma 1) we know that T' contains an open branch b with $[\![b]\!]_{\mathcal{P}} \subseteq \mathcal{I}$. Suppose that b is a MM-branch of T. The case $[\![b]\!]_{\mathcal{P}} =_{\Gamma} \mathcal{I}$ is impossible by the assumption to the contrary. Hence from $[\![b]\!]_{\mathcal{P}} \neq_{\Gamma} \mathcal{I}$ and $[\![b]\!]_{\mathcal{P}} \subseteq \mathcal{I}$ it follows $[\![b]\!]_{\mathcal{P}} <_{\Gamma} \mathcal{I}$. This, however, is impossible by soundness, as it contradicts the given fact that $\mathcal{I}$ is a Γ-minimal model. Therefore b is not an MM-branch in T. Since it is open in T' it must be open in T as well. We are given that D is fair. Since f is a model computation selection function, this implies that b is finished.

For this particular b we show next that $[\![b]\!]_{\mathcal{P}} =_{\Gamma} \mathcal{I}$ holds. For, suppose to the contrary, that $[\![b]\!]_{\mathcal{P}} \neq_{\Gamma} \mathcal{I}$ holds. Again, with $[\![b]\!]_{\mathcal{P}} \subseteq \mathcal{I}$ it follows $[\![b]\!]_{\mathcal{P}} <_{\Gamma} \mathcal{I}$. Since b (of T) is open – i.e. neither closed nor a MM-branch – and finished the minimal model test rule is not applicable and every clause from $\mathcal{S}$ is redundant in b wrt. $\mathcal{P}$. In other words, $[\![b]\!]_{\mathcal{P}} \models \mathcal{S}$. With $[\![b]\!]_{\mathcal{P}} <_{\Gamma} \mathcal{I}$ this is a contradiction to the given Γ-minimality of $\mathcal{I}$. Hence, $[\![b]\!]_{\mathcal{P}} =_{\Gamma} \mathcal{I}$. But then the minimal model test inference rule is applicable to b, because $\mathcal{I}$ is given as a Γ-minimal model, and so $[\![b]\!]_{\mathcal{P}}$ is a Γ-minimal model as well. Hence b is not finished, contradicting the given fairness of D. So the outermost assumption to the contrary must have been wrong, and the theorem follows.

Refutational completeness is proven as follows: suppose that $\mathcal{S}$ is unsatisfiable but T is not closed. By the minimal model soundness result then T must contain an open branch b (because MM-branches are impossible). Since $[\![b]\!]_{\mathcal{P}}$ is an interpretation and $\mathcal{S}$ is unsatisfiable, $[\![b]\!]_{\mathcal{P}}$ falsifies some input clause from $\mathcal{S}$. But then a hyper extension step is applicable to b with this clause. This contradicts the given fact that D is fair. □

5 Further Considerations and Conclusions

Calculi like ours and related calculi need some extra test or device to ensure Γ-minimal model soundness as well. This is due to the inherent complexity of the problem [6]. Fortunately, every Γ-minimal model candidate can be tested in a branch-local way for actual Γ-minimality. More specifically, the approach suggested as the *groundedness test* in [12, 13] is adapted in the full paper. This approach is attractive due to its low (polynomial) memory consumption. Since our approach, when forgetting about merge path steps, is an instance of the method of in [13], low memory assumption can be achieved in our case as well. This does not hold for related methods like MILO-resolution [15], or the minimal-model computation extension of MGTP proposed in [8], or the tableau method of [14], whose worst-case space complexity is exponential.

In the proof of Lemma 1 we indicated how atomic cuts can be used to simulate non-ancestor merge paths. So, the question might arise why not directly use these cuts. The answer is manifold. First, by the mere fact that the simulation exists we get insights how merge paths relate to atomic cuts. Second, the graphical notation might be a helpful metaphor to study the topic. Third, merge paths correspond only to *certain* cuts, much like folding-down [9] or related techniques like complement splitting [10] also correspond only to certain cuts. Fourth, with merge paths, the effect is that they are surgically inserted into the path, and thus in this sense we procrastinate insertion of cuts until useful.

Our approach can be viewed as a Davis-Putnam (DP) procedure. In DP, splitting in a certain order is advantageous for deterministic computation (unit-resulting steps). Our procedure can use the entire set of visible literals to achieve the same determinism, without pre-selecting this splitting order.

It is generally accepted that analytic or even atomic cuts should be applied with care in order not to drown in the search space. This is our viewpoint as well. We emphasize one particular property of the transformation t (cf. the figure in the proof of Lemma 1): in the cut simulation, the subtree T_C is moved to a different place in the tree. By the bare fact that the considered non-ancestor merge path p is legal in the merge path set containing it, we can be *sure* that the destination of T_C (the C node) contains enough ancestor literals so that T_C *remains* a hyper tableau – that all branches with negative leaves remain inconsistent. Clearly, opening branches again would be undesirable as it is unclear if any progress is achieved then. The alternative, forgetting about T_C would cause a lot of recomputation.

Of course, this and other effects and how to avoid them could be formulated as conditions on cuts as well. Non-termination would result if the same atomic cut occurs without bound on a branch.

Conclusions. In this paper we extended previous versions of the hyper tableau calculus by inference rules for merge paths, a device that was originally conceived to speed up refutational theorem proving in the context of clause trees [7]. Our primary goal was to investigate the consequences for model computation purposes. Our main result is therefore a minimal model sound and complete calculus to compute circumscription in the presence of minimized and varying predicates. The motivation was given by the potential to solve a certain problem in diagnosis applications.

We argued that the new calculus generalizes other approaches developed in comparable calculi (folding-up/down, complement splitting). How to apply the new technique *practically*, in particular in the envisaged diagnosis domain, is subject to further investigations. Fortunately, the legality test is $O(|\mathcal{P}|)$ and only negligible overhead is introduced. An algorithm is described in [7].

Acknowledgements. We thank the reviewers for their valuable comments.

References

1. C. Aravindan and P. Baumgartner. A Rational and Efficient Algorithm for View Deletion in Databases. In *Proc. ILPS*, New York, 1997. The MIT Press.
2. P. Baumgartner, P. Fröhlich, U. Furbach, and W. Nejdl. Semantically Guided Theorem Proving for Diagnosis Applications. In *Proc. IJCAI 97*, pages 460–465, Nagoya, 1997.
3. P. Baumgartner, U. Furbach, and I. Niemelä. Hyper Tableaux. In *Proc. JELIA 96*, LNAI 1126. Springer, 1996.
4. P. Baumgartner, J.D. Horton, and B. Spencer. Merge Path Improvements for Minimal Model Hyper Tableaux. Fachberichte Informatik 1–99, Universität Koblenz-Landau, 1999. URL: `http://www.uni-koblenz.de/fb4/publikationen/gelbereihe/RR-1-99.ps.gz`
5. F. Bry and A. Yahya. Minimal Model Generation with Positive Unit Hyper-Resolution Tableaux. In Miglioli et al. [11], pages 143–159.
6. T. Eiter and G. Gottlob. Propositional circumscription and extended closed world reasoning are π_2^p-complete. *Theoretical Computer Science*, 114:231–245, 1993.
7. J. D. Horton and B. Spencer. Clause trees: a tool for understanding and implementing resolution in automated reasoning. *Artificial Intelligence*, 92:25–89, 1997.
8. K. Inoue, M. Koshimura, and R. Hasegawa. Embedding Negation as Failure into a Model Generation Theorem Prover. In D. Kapur, editor, In *Proc. CADE 11*, LNAI 607, pp. 400–415. Springer, 1992.
9. R. Letz, K. Mayr, and C. Goller. Controlled Integrations of the Cut Rule into Connection Tableau Calculi. *Journal of Automated Reasoning*, 13, 1994.
10. R. Manthey and F. Bry. SATCHMO: a theorem prover implemented in Prolog. In E. Lusk and R. Overbeek, editors, *Proc. CADE 9*, LNCS 310, pp. 415–434. Springer, 1988.
11. P. Miglioli, U. Moscato, D. Mundici, and M. Ornaghi, editors. *Theorem Proving with Analytic Tableaux and Related Methods*, LNAI 1071. Springer, 1996.
12. I. Niemelä. A Tableau Calculus for Minimal Model Reasoning. In Miglioli et al. [11].
13. I. Niemelä. Implementing circumscription using a tableau method. In *Proc. ECAI*, pages 80–84, Budapest, 1996. John Wiley.
14. N. Olivetti. A tableaux and sequent calculus for minimal entailment. *Journal of Automated Reasoning*, 9:99–139, 1992.
15. T. Przymusinski. An Algorithm to Compute Circumscription. *Artificial Intelligence*, 38:49–73, 1989.
16. R. Reiter. A Theory of Diagnosis from First Principles. *Artificial Intelligence*, 32(1):57–95, Apr. 1987.

CLDS for Propositional Intuitionistic Logic

Krysia Broda[1] and Dov Gabbay[2]

[1] Dept. of Computing, Imperial College kb@doc.ic.ac.uk
[2] Dept. of Computer Science, King's College, London, dg@dcs.kcl.ac.uk

Abstract. The *compilation approach* for Labelled Deductive Systems (CLDS) is used to obtain a decidable theorem prover for propositional intuitionistic logic. Previous applications of the CLDS method were based around a natural deduction system, together with the notion of a theory as a structure of points, called a *configuration*, and a semantic approach using a translation technique based on first-order logic. In this paper the same semantic method is used, but the proof system is instead a first order theorem prover using techniques drawn from the Davis Putnam and Hyper-resolution procedures. This is shown to be sound and complete with respect to the semantics. The resulting system is a generalisation of intuitionistic logic in a sense that is explained and it is briefly compared with other first order translation techniques.

1 Introduction

A general methodology based on Gabbay's Labelled Deductive Systems (LDS) [7], called the Compiled Labelled Deductive Systems approach (CLDS), is described in [11][4]. The method allows various logics to be formalised within a single framework. In this paper the method is specifically applied to intuitionistic logic (IL). The motivation for using LDS derives from the observation that many logics only differ from each other in small ways. In the family of modal logics, for example, the differences can be captured semantically through the properties of the accessibility relation, or syntactically within various side-conditions on the proof steps. In substructural logics, the differences can be captured in the syntax by means of the structural proof rules. In a CLDS, capturing differences between logics is achieved through the use of a combined language, incorporating a language for wffs and a language for terms (known as labels), called a labelling language. Elements of the two languages are combined to produce *declarative units* of the form $\alpha:\lambda$, where α is a wff and λ is a label. The interpretation of a declarative unit depends on the particular family of logics being formalised, and in substructural, or resource, logics it names a combination of resources. A theory built from declarative units is called a *configuration* and consists both of declarative units and literals stating the relationships between labels of the configuration (called R-literals). In this LDS approach, in which IL is considered a resource logic, the declarative unit $\alpha : \lambda$ represents the statement that the "resource" λ verifies the wff α. This was first exploited in [7]. Resources can be combined using the operator $\circ$ and their power of verification compared using the relation $\preceq$. Thus $\lambda \preceq \lambda'$ is interpreted to mean that λ' can verify everything that λ can and is thus the more powerful of the two. Depending on the properties given to $\circ$ the power of combined resources is controlled. In IL, resources can be copied, that is $\lambda \circ \lambda \preceq \lambda$, or λ is just as powerful as multiple copies of itself. Resources can also be extended, so that $\lambda \preceq \lambda \circ \lambda'$. These properties, contraction and monotonicity, respectively, correspond to the structural rules of contraction and weakening of the standard IL sequent calculus. In fact, in LDS, all substructural logics can be treated in a uniform way, simply by including different axioms in the labelling algebra [1].

The semantics of a CLDS is given by translating a configuration into first order logic in a particular way, the notion of semantic entailment being defined with respect to such translated configurations. A set of axioms to capture the meanings of the logical operators, and a theory, called the *labelling algebra*, are given and are used for manipulating labels and the relations between them. The language, axiom theory and labelling algebra considered in this paper for IL are referred to as I_{CLDS}. An example of a semantic axiom, in this case that captures the meaning of the $\rightarrow$ operator, using monadic predicates of the form $[\alpha]^*$, one for each different wff α, is $\forall x([\alpha \rightarrow \beta]^*(x) \leftrightarrow \forall y([\alpha]^*(y) \rightarrow [\beta]^*(x \circ y)))$. For a given problem, the set of semantic axioms is implicitly instantiated for every wff that occurs in the problem; this set of instances together with a translation of the initial configuration, in which $\alpha : \lambda$ is translated as $[\alpha]^*(\lambda)$ can also be taken as a compiled form of the problem and any standard first order theorem prover could be used to find refutations. In previous work using CLDS [11], [4] a natural deduction system to manipulate configurations was defined and shown to be sound and complete with respect to the translated semantics. Instead, in this paper a decidable refutation theorem prover AlgDP based on the methods of Davis Putnam [5] and Hyper-resolution [10] is taken as the proof system.

Although the CLDS approach may appear similar to the translation methods in [9], as used here it is part of a systematic general framework that can be applied to any logic, either old or new. It is also similar in spirit, for IL, to the standard way of translating intutionistic theorems into first order logic using a modal S4 theory [6]. A comparison is made with these approaches at the end of Sect. 3. The theorem prover developed here could easily be adapted for other substructural logics, although the properties of the labelling algebra for IL give a particularly simple system, not completely shared with the other logics. In case a CLDS corresponds to a known logic, the correspondence with a standard presentation of that logic must also be provided. First, it is shown that every derivation in a standard presentation of that logic can be simulated by the rules of the CLDS, in this case the refutation theorem prover. Second, it is shown how to build an interpretation such that, if a formula α is not a theorem of the logic in question, then there is an appropriate model in which a suitable declarative unit derived from α is false.

In the rest of the paper, Sect. 2 details the language and axioms used for I_{CLDS}, Sect. 3 describes the theorem prover and Sect. 4 states and proves the results concerning soundness, completeness and correspondence. The general approach will be referred to as the CLDS system whereas the refined version for IL is referred to as the $\mathrm{I_{CLDS}}$ system. The paper concludes with a brief discussion.

2 The Refutation CLDS Approach for $\mathrm{I_{CLDS}}$

The CLDS approach for $\mathrm{I_{CLDS}}$ is now described more formally. Definitions of the language, syntax and semantics are given, and *configurations* are introduced.

2.1 Languages and Syntax

A basic CLDS propositional language is defined as an ordered pair $\langle \mathcal{L}_P, \mathcal{L}_L \rangle$, where $\mathcal{L}_L$ is a *labelling language* and $\mathcal{L}_P$ is a *propositional language.* For $\mathrm{I_{CLDS}}$ the language $\mathcal{L}_P$ is composed of a countable set of proposition symbols, $\{p, q, r, \ldots\}$, a unary connective $\neg$, and the binary connectives $\wedge, \vee, \rightarrow$. Two special proposition symbols are $\top$ and $\bot$, where $\neg A$ is defined also as $A \rightarrow \bot$ and $\top$ is defined also as $\neg\bot$. The labelling language $\mathcal{L}_L$ used in $\mathrm{I_{CLDS}}$ is a fragment of a first-order language composed of a binary operator $\circ$, a countable set of variables $\{x, y, z, \ldots\}$, a binary predicate $\preceq$, the set of logical connectives $\{\neg, \wedge, \vee, \rightarrow, \leftrightarrow\}$, and the quantifiers $\forall$ and $\exists$. Literals using $\preceq$ are called *constraints.* Let the set of all wffs in $\mathcal{L}_P$ be $\{\alpha_1, \alpha_2, \ldots\}$, then the semi-extended labelling language $Func(\mathcal{L}_P, \mathcal{L}_L)$ comprises $\mathcal{L}_L$ extended with a set of *skolem* constant symbols $\{c_{\alpha_1}, c_{\alpha_2}, \ldots\}$, also referred to as *characteristic labels* or *parameters.* Terms of $Func(\mathcal{L}_P, \mathcal{L}_L)$ are defined inductively, as consisting of parameters and variables, together with expressions of the form $\lambda \circ \lambda'$, for terms λ and λ', and are also called labels. Note that all parameters will have a special role in the semantics, especially $c_\bot$, and that the parameter c_α represents the smallest label verifying α. For the wff $\top$ there is the parameter 1 (shorthand for $c_\top$) that represents the empty resource, since $\top$ is always provable.

To capture different classes of logics within the CLDS framework an appropriate first-order theory written in the language $\mathcal{L}_L$, called the *labelling algebra,* needs to be defined. In the case of $\mathrm{I_{CLDS}}$, the labelling algebra, $\mathcal{A}_\mathcal{I}$, is a binary first-order theory which axiomatises (i) the binary predicate $\preceq$ as a pre-ordering relation, (ii) the properties *identity* and *order preserving* of the commutative and associative function symbol $\circ$, and (iii) the structural properties *contraction* and *monotonicity.*

Definition 1. *The labelling algebra $\mathcal{A}_\mathcal{I}$ is the first order theory given by the following axioms, where x, y and z all belong to* $\mathrm{Func}(\mathcal{L}_P, \mathcal{L}_L)$.

1. **(identity)** $\forall x[1 \circ x \preceq x \wedge x \preceq 1 \circ x]$
2. **(order-preserving)** $\forall x, y, z[x \preceq y \rightarrow x \circ z \preceq y \circ z \wedge z \circ x \preceq z \circ y]$
3. **(pre-ordering)** $\forall x[x \preceq x]$ *and* $\forall x, y, z[x \preceq y \wedge y \preceq z \rightarrow x \preceq z]$
4. **(commutativity)** $\forall x, y[x \circ y \preceq y \circ x]$
5. **(associativity)** $\forall x, y, z[(x \circ y) \circ z \preceq x \circ (y \circ z)]$
6. **(contraction)** $\forall x[x \circ x \preceq x]$
7. **(monotonicity)** $\forall x, y[x \preceq x \circ y]$ ◇

Syntax. The CLDS language facilitates the formalisation of two types of information, (i) what holds at particular points, given by the declarative units, and (ii) which points are in relation with each other and which are not, given by R-literals. A declarative unit is defined as a pair *"formula:label"* expressing that a formula "holds" at a point. The label component is a ground term of the language $Func(\mathcal{L}_P, \mathcal{L}_L)$ and the formula is a wff of the language $\mathcal{L}_P$. An R-literal is any ground literal (constraint) in the semi-extended labelling language of the form $\lambda_1 \preceq \lambda_2$, $\lambda_1 \not\preceq \lambda_2$, where λ_1 and λ_2 are labels, expressing that λ_2 is, or is not, related to λ_1. In the $\mathrm{I_{CLDS}}$ system "related to" is interpreted as "subset of" and no explicit use is made of negative R-literals. This combined aspect of the CLDS syntax yields a definition of a CLDS theory, called a *configuration*, which is composed of a set of R-literals and a set of declarative units. An example of a $\mathrm{I_{CLDS}}$ configuration is the set of declarative units $\{\neg(p \rightarrow (q \rightarrow p)) : 1, p : a, \neg(q \rightarrow p) : a, q : b, \neg p : a \circ b\}$ and R-literals $\{1 \preceq a, 1 \preceq b\}$.

Definition 2. *Given a CLDS language, a configuration is a tuple $\langle \mathcal{D}, \mathcal{F} \rangle$, where $\mathcal{D}$ is a finite set of R-literals (referred to as a* diagram*) and $\mathcal{F}$ is a function from the set of ground terms of* Func*($\mathcal{L}_P$, $\mathcal{L}_L$) to the set $PW(wff(\mathcal{L}_P))$ of sets of wffs of $\mathcal{L}_P$. Statements of the form $A \in \mathcal{F}(\lambda)$ will be written as $A{:}\lambda \in \mathcal{C}$.*

2.2 Semantics

The model-theoretic semantics of CLDS is defined in terms of a first-order semantics using a translation method. This enables the development of a model-theoretic approach which is equally applicable to any logic whose operators have a semantics which can be expressed in a first-order theory. As mentioned before, a declarative unit $\alpha : \lambda$ represents that the formula is verified (or holds) at the point λ, whose interpretation is strictly related to the type of underlying logic. These notions are expressed in terms of first-order statements of the form $[\alpha]^*(\lambda)$, where $[\alpha]^*$ is a predicate symbol. The relationships between these predicate symbols are constrained by a set of first-order axiom schemas which capture the satisfiability conditions of each type of formula α. The language $Func(\mathcal{L}_P, \mathcal{L}_L)$ is extended given by adding a monadic predicate symbol $[\alpha]^*$ for each wff α of $\mathcal{L}_P$.

Definition 3. *Let $Func(\mathcal{L}_P, \mathcal{L}_L)$ be a semi-extended labelling language. Let the ordered set of wffs of $\mathcal{L}_P$ be $\alpha_1, \ldots, \alpha_n, \ldots,$, then the* extended labelling language, *called $Mon(\mathcal{L}_P, \mathcal{L}_L)$, is defined as the language $Func(\mathcal{L}_P, \mathcal{L}_L)$ extended with the set of unary predicate symbols: $\{[\alpha_1]^*, \ldots, [\alpha_n]^*, \ldots\}$.*

The *extended algebra* $\mathcal{A}_{\mathrm{I}}^+$ for $\mathrm{I_{CLDS}}$ is a first-order theory written in $Mon(\mathcal{L}_P, \mathcal{L}_L)$ which extends the labelling algebra $\mathcal{A}_{\mathcal{I}}$ with the axiom schemas given in Table 1. A $\mathrm{I_{CLDS}}$ system S can now be defined as $S = \langle \langle \mathcal{L}_P, \mathcal{L}_L \rangle, \mathcal{A}_{\mathrm{I}}^+, \mathrm{AlgDP} \rangle$.

In Table 1 there are the *basic axioms*, (Ax1) - (Ax7), and clausal axioms ((Ax3a), (Ax3b), etc.) derived from them by taking each half of the $\leftrightarrow$ in turn. The first axiom (Ax1) characterises the property that increasing labels λ and

λ', such that $\lambda \preceq \lambda'$, imply the sets of wffs verified by those labels are also increasing. The second axiom (Ax2) characterises a special property that states that, if a wff α is verified by some label, then it is verified by a smallest label, called the α-characteristic label. Both these axioms relate declarative units to constraints. The others, (Ax3) - (Ax6), characterise the operators $\rightarrow$, $\neg$, $\wedge$ and $\vee$ respectively, whilst (Ax7) corresponds to the rule in Intuitionistic logic that falsum implies any formula.

Table 1. Basic and clausal semantic axioms for $\mathrm{I_{CLDS}}$

Ax1: $\forall x \forall y(x \preceq y \wedge [\alpha]^*(x) \rightarrow [\alpha]^*(y))$	
Ax2: $\forall x([\alpha]^*(x)) \rightarrow \exists y([\alpha]^*(y) \wedge \forall z([\alpha]^*(z) \rightarrow y \preceq z)))$	
Ax3: $\forall x([\alpha \rightarrow \beta]^*(x) \leftrightarrow \forall y([\alpha]^*(y) \rightarrow [\beta]^*(x \circ y)))$	
Ax4: $\forall x([\neg\alpha]^*(x) \leftrightarrow \forall y([\alpha]^*(y) \rightarrow \bot : x \circ y))$	
Ax5: $\forall w([\alpha \wedge \beta]^*(w) \leftrightarrow [\alpha]^*(w) \wedge [\beta]^*(w))$	
Ax 6: $\forall x, y \left(\begin{array}{l} [\alpha \vee \beta]^*(x) \leftrightarrow \\ (([\alpha]^*(c_\alpha) \rightarrow [\gamma]^*(c_\alpha \circ y)) \wedge ([\beta]^*(c_\beta) \rightarrow [\gamma]^*(c_\beta \circ y)) \rightarrow [\gamma]^*(x \circ y) \end{array} \right)$	
Ax7: $\forall x([\bot]^*(x) \rightarrow [\alpha]^*(x))$	
Ax2a: $\forall x([\alpha]^*(x) \rightarrow [\alpha]^*(c_\alpha)$	Ax2b: $\forall x([\alpha]^*(x) \rightarrow c_\alpha \preceq x)$
Ax3a: $\forall x \forall y([\alpha \rightarrow \beta]^*(x) \wedge [\alpha]^*(y) \rightarrow [\beta]^*(x \circ y)))$	
Ax3b: $\forall x([\alpha \rightarrow \beta]^*(x) \leftarrow [\beta]^*(x \circ c_\alpha))$	Ax3c: $\forall x([\alpha \rightarrow \beta]^*(x) \vee [\alpha]^*(c_\alpha))$
Ax4a: $\forall x \forall y([\neg\alpha]^*(x) \wedge [\alpha]^*(y) \rightarrow [\bot]^*(x \circ y))$	
Ax4b: $\forall x([\neg\alpha]^*(x) \leftarrow [\bot]^*(x \circ c_\alpha)$	Ax4c: $\forall x([\neg\alpha]^*(x) \vee [\alpha]^*(c_\alpha))$
Ax5a: $\forall x([\alpha \wedge \beta]^*(x) \rightarrow [\alpha]^*(x)$	Ax5b: $\forall x([\alpha \wedge \beta]^*(x) \rightarrow [\beta]^*(x)$
Ax5c: $\forall x([\alpha]^*(x) \wedge [\beta]^*(x) \rightarrow [\alpha \wedge \beta]^*(x))$	
Ax6a: $\forall x([\alpha]^*(x) \rightarrow [\alpha \vee \beta]^*(x))$	Ax6b: $\forall x([\beta]^*(x) \rightarrow [\alpha \vee \beta]^*(x))$
Ax6c: $\forall x \left(\begin{array}{l} [\alpha \vee \beta]^*(x) \rightarrow \\ \forall y\, ([\alpha]^*(c_\alpha) \rightarrow [\gamma]^*(c_\alpha \circ y)) \wedge ([\beta]^*(c_\beta) \rightarrow [\gamma]^*(c_\beta \circ y)) \rightarrow [\gamma]^*(x \circ y) \end{array} \right)$	

Several of the axioms have been simplified by the use of parameters and (Ax1) and (Ax2) (effectively applying Skolemisation). In the special case of IL the properties of (monotonicity) and (contraction) allow also for the 'only if' direction of (Ax6) to be simplified to $\forall x([\alpha \vee \beta]^*(x) \rightarrow [\alpha]^*(x) \vee [\beta]^*(x))$, called (Ax6d). This is proved in the longer report, [2]. A further simplification, due to the (monotonicity) property, is possible in $\mathrm{I_{CLDS}}$. Since $1 \preceq 1 \circ x$ for all x, it follows that $1 \preceq x$, by (identity) and (transitivity). By means of this property it suffices for (Ax3c) to be replaced by $[\alpha \rightarrow \beta]^*(1) \vee [\alpha]^*(a)$ (called (Ax3d)), since the original is then implied using (Ax1). The clausal axioms in Table 1 (using (Ax3d) and (Ax6d) in place of (Ax3c) and (Ax6c) respectively), together with the properties of the Labelling Algebra are also called the Extended Labelling Algebra, $\mathcal{A}_{\mathrm{I}}^{+}$. It is for finite sets of instances of these axioms that a refutation theorem prover is given in Sect. 3.

The notions of satisfiability and semantic entailment are common to any CLDS and based on a translation method which associates configurations with first-order theories in the language $Mon(\mathcal{L}_P, \mathcal{L}_L)$. Each declarative unit $\alpha:\lambda$ is translated into the sentence $[\alpha]^*(\lambda)$, and R-literals are translated as themselves.

Definition 4. *Let $\mathcal{C} = \langle \mathcal{D}, \mathcal{F} \rangle$ be a configuration. The* first-order translation *of $\mathcal{C}$, $FOT(\mathcal{C})$, is a theory in $Mon(\mathcal{L}_P, \mathcal{L}_L)$ and is defined by the expression: $FOT(\mathcal{C}) = \mathcal{D} \cup \mathcal{DU}$, where $\mathcal{DU} = \{[\alpha]^*(\lambda) \mid \alpha \in \mathcal{F}(\lambda)$, λ is a ground term of $Func(\mathcal{L}_P, \mathcal{L}_L)\}$.*

The notion of semantic entailment for $\mathrm{I_{CLDS}}$ as a relation between configurations is given in terms of classical semantics using the above definition.

Definition 5. *Let $S = \langle\langle \mathcal{L}_P, \mathcal{L}_L, \rangle, \mathcal{A}_I^+, AlgDP\rangle$ be a I_{CLDS}, $\mathcal{C} = \langle \mathcal{D}, \mathcal{F} \rangle$ and $\mathcal{C}' = \langle \mathcal{D}', \mathcal{F}' \rangle$ be two configurations of S, and $FOT(\mathcal{C}) = \mathcal{D} \cup \mathcal{DU}$ and $FOT(\mathcal{C}') = \mathcal{D}' \cup \mathcal{DU}'$ be their respective first-order translations. The configuration $\mathcal{C}$ semantically entails $\mathcal{C}'$, written $\mathcal{C} \models_I \mathcal{C}'$, iff for each $\Delta \in \mathcal{D}'$, $\mathcal{A}_I^+ \cup FOT(\mathcal{C}) \models_{FOL} \Delta$, and for each $[\alpha]^*(\lambda) \in \mathcal{DU}'$, $\mathcal{A}_I^+ \cup FOT(\mathcal{C}) \models_{FOL} [\alpha]^*(\lambda)$.*

Declarative units of the form $\alpha:1$, such that $\mathcal{T}_\emptyset \models_I \alpha:1$, where $\mathcal{T}_\emptyset$ is an empty configuration, are called *theorems*. In order to show a theorem $\alpha : 1$ holds in $\mathrm{I_{CLDS}}$, appropriate instances of the axioms in $\mathcal{A}_I^+$ are first formed for each subformula of α, and then $\neg[\alpha]^*(1)$ is added. This set of clauses is refuted by AlgDP. More generally, to show that α follows from the wffs $\beta_1, \ldots, \beta_n$, the appropriate instances include those for each subformula of $\alpha, \beta_1, \ldots, \beta_n$, together with $\neg[\alpha]^*(i)$, where $i = c_{\beta_1} \circ \ldots \circ c_{\beta_n}$, and the set $\{[\beta_i]^*(c_{\beta_i})\}$.

3 A Theorem Prover for the $\mathrm{I_{CLDS}}$ System

As remarked earlier, the Extended Labelling Algebra $\mathcal{A}_I^+$ enjoys a very simple clausal form. The theorem prover described, built in Prolog, uses an adaptation of the Davis Putnam method with Hyper-resolution, called AlgDP. The axioms of the Labelling Algebra, (monotonicity), (contraction) and so on, together with Axioms (Ax1) and (Ax2a) are incorporated into the unification algorithm, called AlgU. Axioms (Ax1), (Ax2a) and (Ax2b) were otherwise accounted for in the derivation of the remaining axioms and are not explicitly needed any further. First, some definitions are given for this particular first order theory, $\mathcal{A}_I^+$.

Note 1. In this section, a clause will either be denoted by C, or by $L \vee D$, where L is a literal and D is a disjunction of none or more literals. All variables are implicitly universally quantified. Literals are generally denoted by L, but may also be of the form: $L(x)$, when the argument is exactly the variable x, or $L(u), L(v), L(w)$, when the argument contains no variables.

For a given set of clauses S, the set $\mathcal{D} = \{c_\alpha | c_\alpha$ is a parameter occuring in $S\}$ is called the *Herbrand Domain* of S and the *Herbrand Universe* of S is the set of terms formed using the operator $\circ$ applied to elements from the Herbrand Domain. A *ground instance* of a clause C or literal L (written $C\theta$ or $L\theta$) is the result of replacing each variable x_i in C or L by a ground term t_i from the Herbrand Universe, where the substitution $\theta = \{x_i := t_i\}$. $L(u)$ *unifies* with $L(v)$

(with respect to AlgU) iff $u \preceq v$. Notice that unification is not symmetric. $L(u)$ unifies with L' iff there is a ground instance $L(v)$ of L', $L(v) = L'\theta$, such that $L(u)$ unifies with $L(v)$ and θ is the minimal substitution. That is, $L(v) \preceq L(w)$ for any other ground instance $L(w)$ of L', such that $L(u)$ unifies with $L(w)$. The unifier is the substitution θ. Subsumption is applied between literals in AlgDP in only two cases: $L(u)$ ***subsumes*** $L(v)$ iff $u \preceq v$, and $\neg[\bot]^*(x)$ subsumes any negative literal with predicate $[\bot]^*$. Literal L subsumes clause C iff L subsumes a literal in C. Positive unit clause $L(u)$ resolves with $D \vee \neg L'$ to give $D\theta$ iff $L(u)$ unifies with L' with unifier θ. A *Hyper-resolvent* is a clause with no negative literals formed by resolving a clause with one or more positive unit clauses.

Overview of AlgDP. AlgDP operates on sets of clauses, which may be any of the following types: unit clauses, Horn clauses, or non-Horn clauses with one of the forms: $[\alpha]^*(c_\alpha) \vee [\alpha \to \beta]^*(1)$, $[\alpha]^*(u) \vee [\beta]^*(u)$ or $\forall x([\alpha \vee \beta]^*(x) \to [\alpha]^*(x) \vee [\beta]^*(x))$, where u is a ground term. There is just one kind of negative unit clause, $\neg[\alpha]^*(i)$, derived from the initial goal, where α is the wff to be proved and $i = i_1 \circ \ldots \circ i_n$ is the label consisting of the parameters $i_1, \ldots, i_n$ that verify the formulas from which α is to be proved. Furthermore, since, as argued below, it is only necessary to maintain compound terms as sets, label combinations such as $x \circ y \circ z$ will be written as xyz. Consequently, as the Herbrand Domain $\mathcal{D}$ is finite, for any particular problem the size of the label terms has a known upper bound, equal to the size of $\mathcal{D}$. This fact is used to prove termination.

AlgDP incorporates a special unification algorithm AlgU, which is used to unify two literals $[\alpha]^*(u)$ and $[\alpha]^*(z)$, where z may contain a variable, implicitly taking into account the properties of $\mathcal{A}_{\mathrm{I}}^+$. These properties allow two labels λ and λ' to satisfy $\lambda \preceq \lambda'$ iff $\lambda \subseteq \lambda'$ (λ, λ' treated as sets), for the following reason. The order of parameters in a label does not matter because of the properties (associativity) and (commutativity). Duplicate parameters in λ can be ignored by (contraction) and in λ' they can be ignored by (monotonicity). The parameter 1 satisfies additionally $1 \preceq \lambda$ by (monotonicity). By (identity), the parameter 1 is only necessary in the label 1 itself, which is treated as the empty set. Furthermore, in any ground clause, because of contraction, each literal can be simplified by removing from any label any duplicate parameters. Thus $[\alpha]^*(aba) \vee [\beta]^*(acd)$ can be simplified to $[\alpha]^*(ab) \vee [\beta]^*(acd)$. In fact, the two clauses are equivalent in the first order theory $\mathcal{A}_{\mathrm{I}}^+$: The first clause implies the second because of (contraction) and the second implies the first because of (monotonicity). As for unification, there are only a restricted number of kinds, which will be considered after the steps of AlgDP have been described. (The rule embodied in (Ax7) is included in the following way. Instead of explicitly deriving $[\alpha]^*(x)$ from $[\bot]^*(x)$, for every "useful" α, the matching algorithm AlgU allows $[\bot]^*(x)$ to be unified with $[\alpha]^*(y)$ if x unifies with y.)

The initial set of clauses for refuting a formula α are derived from instances of the semantic axioms appropriate for the predicates occurring in the first order translation of α (called the "appropriate set of clauses for showing α"). There are seven different rules in AlgDP, which can be applied to a finite list of clauses.

Five of these are defined below. The other two are a purity rule and a simplify rule and are only necessary for efficiency sake; they are omitted here for space considerations but can be found in the full version [2]. Ground unit clauses in a list, derived by the (Hyper) or (Split) rule, are maintained as a partial model of the initial clauses. An outline Prolog version of AlgDP is given, which is shown to be correct in Sect. 4. The actual implementation is rather less non-deterministic to avoid making redundant checks. For example, subsumption is checked after any new unit clause is generated. The following rules are available:

End A list containing an atom and its complement is marked as successfully finished. The only negative unit clause is the ground clause stating the initial goal.

Subsumption Any clause subsumed by a unit clause L is removed.

Fail A list in which no more steps are possible is marked as failed and can be used to give a model of the initial clauseset.

Hyper A hyper-resolvent (with respect to AlgU) is formed from a non-unit clause in the list and (positive) unit clauses in the list. Only hyper-resolvents that cannot immediately be subsumed are generated.

Split Given a list of clauses L containing ground clause $L' \vee L''$, two new lists $[L'|L^-]$ and $[L''|L^-]$ are formed, where L^- results from removing $L' \vee L''$ from L. The algorithm is then applied to each list.

The outline Prolog program for AlgDP is given next. Given a list of clauses S derived from a particular I_{CLDS}, to show S are unsatisfiable or to find a model of S, call $dp(S, F, R)$, where

> $dp(S, F, R)$ holds iff $R = false$ and F can be extended to a model of clauses in S, or $R = true$ and S has no model.

There can be no tautologies in S because of the way the clauses are set up and assume there are no initially subsumed clauses. In $dp1$ the first argument is the current set of positive unit clauses and F and R are initially variables.

```
0(start). dp(S,F,R) :- dp1 ([ ],S,F,R).
1(fail). dp1(M,S,M,false) :- noRulesApplicable(M,S). (The Fail rule)
2(end). dp1(M,S,[],true) :- endIsApplicable(S,M).
3(subsume). dp1(M,S,F,R) :- subsumed(C,M,S), remove(C,S,NewS),
                dp1( M,NewS,F.R).
4(hyper). dp1(M,S,F,R) :- hyper(M,S,New), add(New,S,M,NewS,NewM),
                dp1(NewM,NewS,F,R).
5(split). dp1(M,S,F,R) :- split(M,S,NewS,S1,S2),
                dp1([S1|M],NewS,F1,R1),dp1([S2|M],NewS,F2,R2),
                join(F1,F2,F), and(R1,R2,R).
```

The predicates used in the Prolog version of AlgDP can be interpreted as follows: `add(New,S,M,NewS,NewM)` holds iff the units in New derived from the (Hyper) rule are added to M to form $NewM$ and disjunctions in New are added to S to form $NewS$. `and(X,Y,Z)` holds iff $Z = X \wedge Y$. `endIsApplicable(S,M)` holds iff (End) can be applied to $(S,\ M)$. `hyper(M,S,New)` holds iff New is the set of hyper-resolvents using unit clauses in M and a clause in S, that do not already occur in M. `join(F1,F2,F)` holds iff F is the union of $F1$ and $F2$. `noRulesApplicable(M,S)` holds iff there are no applicable rules to (M, S). `remove(P,S,NewS)` holds iff clause P is removed from S to give $NewS$. `split(M,S,NewS, S1,S2)` holds iff $S1 \vee S2$ is removed from S to leave $NewS$. `subsumed(C,M,S)` holds if Clause C in S is subsumed by clauses from S or M.

Overview of AlgU. An analysis of the unifications that need to be made in the system reveals them to be of the following kinds. (In the following, z is always a variable and g, g_1 and g_2 are ground labels, w is an arbitrary label.) (1) Unification of g in a positive literal with z in a negative literal in the (Hyper) step. The unifier is $\{z := g\}$. (2) Unification of g_1 in a positive literal with g_2 in a negative literal in the (End) step. It succeeds either if $g_1 \preceq g_2$, that is if $g_1 \subseteq g_2$. (3) Unification of $g = g_1a$ in a positive literal with a label za, which succeeds with unifier $\{z := g_1\}$. In the case that g does not contain a, then the unifier is $\{z := g\}$. (4) Special case of the (Hyper) step applied to axiom (Ax5a); consider, as an illustration, the clause $[\alpha]^*(z) \wedge [\beta]^*(z) \rightarrow [\alpha \wedge \beta]^*(z)$ and the literals $[\alpha]^*(a)$ and $[\beta]^*(b)$. By monotonicity, $a \preceq ab$ and $b \preceq ab$, so $[\alpha \wedge \beta]^*(ab)$ can be derived. However, when using the (Hyper) rule, if a simple-minded unification is made between a and z, binding z to a, the second unification will fail as it would require $b \subseteq a$. In such a case, the first binding to z should be $\{z := az_1\}$ and then the second yields $\{z_1 := b\}$, with the final unifier $\{z := ab\}$. In all four unification cases, the resolvent is either a ground positive unit clause or a ground disjunction of two positive literals. According to the definition of unification, a variable z is always bound to the smallest ground term g_1 that is possible. This is correct because for any larger term $g_2 = g_1x$, $g_1 \preceq g_2$ by (monotonicity) and is catered for by AlgU. Moreover, any duplicate atomic labels in the label arguments, which can only arise in the (Hyper) rule using a clause with two negative literals, are removed.

Examples. An example of a refutation is given in Figure 1, in which the theorem $(\alpha \rightarrow \beta) \rightarrow (\neg\beta \rightarrow \neg\alpha)$ is proved. For simplicity, the parameters used are called $a, b, c, \ldots$ instead of having the form $c_{\alpha\rightarrow\beta}$, etc. and the predicates A and B are used in place of $[\alpha]^*$ and $[\beta]^*$. The calls to *dpl* can be arranged into a tree, bifurcation occurring when the (Split) rule is used. In the derivation in Fig. 1 each line, after the initial clauses, records a derived clause. Derived unit clauses would be added to an accumulating partial model M, which is returned in case of a branch ending in failure. In Fig. 1. for example, there are three branches in the tree of calls to *dpl*, which all terminate with the use of the (End) rule. They all contain lines (1) - (8) implicitly, and then the first branch contains lines (9) - (15), the second branch contains lines (9), (10), (16), (17), and the third contains lines (9), (10), (18) - (20). On the other hand, Fig. 2 gives an example of a failed derivation for a non-theorem of Intuitionistic logic, namely $\neg\neg\alpha \rightarrow \alpha$.

There are three branches followed in the tree of calls to *dpl*, the last of them ending at line (21). Note that in line (16) (Ax7) is used implicitly to derive $A(a)$ before using (3). The resulting model is $M = \{P_0(c), P_1(1), A(c)\}$ (the atom

Initial clauses:

(1) $P_0(d)$
(2) $\neg P_3(d)$
(3) $P_0(x) \wedge A(y) \rightarrow B(xy)$
(4) $P_2(c) \vee P_3(1)$
(5) $P_1(xc) \rightarrow P_3(x)$
(6) $P_2(x) \wedge B(y) \rightarrow [\bot]^*(xy)$
(7) $A(a) \vee P_1(1)$
(8) $[\bot]^*(ax) \rightarrow P_1(x)$

Initial translation:

$P_0(x)$ $[\alpha \rightarrow \beta]^*(x)$
$P_1(x)$ $[\neg\alpha]^*(x)$
$P_2(x)$ $[\neg\beta]^*(x)$
$P_3(x)$ $[\neg\beta \rightarrow \neg\alpha]^*(x)$

Derivation:

(9) (Split (7)) $A(a)$
(10) (Hyper (3)) $B(da)$
(11) (Split (4)) $P_2(c)$
(12) (Hyper (6)) $[\bot]^*(cda)$
(13) (Hyper (8)) $P_1(cd)$
(14) (Hyper (5)) $P_3(d)$
(15) (End)
(16) (Split(4)) $P_3(1)$
(17) (End)
(18) (Split (7) $P_1(1)$
(19) (Hyper (5)) $P_3(1)$
(20) (End)

Fig. 1. Refutation of $(\alpha \rightarrow \beta) \rightarrow (\neg\beta \rightarrow \neg\alpha)$ in $\mathrm{I_{CLDS}}$ using AlgDP

Initial clauses:

(1) $\neg P_0(1)$
(2) $P_1(a) \vee P_0(1)$
(3) $A(ax) \rightarrow P_0(x)$
(4) $P_0(x) \wedge P_1(y) \rightarrow A(xy)$
(5) $P_2(b)) \vee P_1(1)$
(6) $[\bot]^*(bx) \rightarrow P_1(x)$
(7) $P_1(x) \wedge P_2(y) \rightarrow [\bot]^*(xy)$
(8) $A(c) \vee P_2(1)$
(9) $[\bot]^*(cx) \rightarrow P_2(x)$
(10) $P_2(x) \wedge A(y) \rightarrow [\bot]^*(xy)$

Initial translation:

$P_0(x)$ $[\neg\neg\alpha \rightarrow \alpha]^*(x)$
$P_1(x)$ $[\neg\neg\alpha]^*(x)$
$P_2(x)$ $[\neg\alpha]^*(x)$

Derivation:

(11) (Split (2)) $P_0(1)$
(12) (End)
(13) (Split (2)) $P_1(a)$
(14) (Split (8)) $P_2(1)$
(15) (Hyper (7)) $[\bot]^*(a)$
(16) (Hyper (3)) $P_0(1)$
(17) (End)
(18) (Split (8)) $A(c)$
(19) (Hyper (3)) $P_0(c)$
(20) (Split (5)) $P_1(1)$
(21) (Fail)

Fig. 2. Attempted refutation of $\neg\neg\alpha \rightarrow \alpha$ in $\mathrm{I_{CLDS}}$ using AlgDP

$P_1(a)$ is subsumed by $P_1(1)$). A model of the initial clauses, *EndM*, is extracted, by assigning true to all literals in the Herbrand Base that are subsumed by a literal in M and assigning false to all other literals in the Herbrand Base. The reader can check that this gives a model of the clauses (1) - (10) in Fig. 2. This model can also be seen to correspond to a standard Kripke countermodel for this formula. Notice, that in Fig. 1, only some of the appropriate axioms have been included. For example, there might have been expected clauses such as $P_1(x) \wedge A(y) \rightarrow [\bot]^*(xy)$, that is clauses derived from both halves of the appropriate equivalence schemas. However, it is only necessary to include a restricted number of clauses, based on the polarity of the sub-formula occurrences (see [2]). It is, however, easier to show the correspondence with intuitionistic logic when both halves of the schema equivalences are included, and this is the assumption made in this paper.

Comparison. The example in Fig. 2 is used to make a comparison with other approaches to embedding IL in classical logic. In the standard translation approach for the example, based on a possible worlds semantics, the sentences of FOL that are obtained for refutation are the following: (i) $\forall x[R(x,y) \wedge \alpha(x) \rightarrow \alpha(y)]$, which expresses that a true formula remains true in all accessible worlds, together with the reflexivity and transitivity of the accessibility relation R, and

(ii) $\forall x \forall y[\forall z[R(y,z) \rightarrow \exists w[R(z,w) \wedge \alpha(w)]] \wedge R(x,y) \rightarrow \alpha(y)]$, which is the translation of the formula $\neg\neg\alpha \rightarrow \alpha$, which is to be proved. Sentence (ii) is then negated ready for refutation, yielding $R(a,b)$, $\neg\alpha(b)$ and $\forall z[R(b,z) \rightarrow \exists w[R(z,w) \wedge \alpha(w)]]$, in which a and b are Skolem constants. Without some careful strategies, standard resolution will not, in general, terminate for such translated formulas. On the other hand, the CLDS approach allows for IL to be treated as a resource logic and additional properties in the labelling algebra such as (monotonicity) enable simple decidable strategies to be used. There is also similarity with the functional translation method [9], which for this example gives the translation $\forall\gamma[\forall\delta\exists\delta'[\alpha(0.\gamma.\delta.\delta')] \rightarrow \alpha(0.\gamma)]$. An argument such as $0.\gamma.\delta$ represents a path obtained by applying functors δ and γ to world 0 that leads from 0 to an R accessible world. In this case, a refutation is not possible, as after negating the two clauses $\alpha(0.a.x.b(x))$ and $\neg\alpha(0.a)$ are obtained, which do not unify (using the special unification algorithm of that approach). In general, careful unification strategies are again needed for termination, see [12], in which it is also shown that the Skolem function $b(x)$ of this example can be eliminated in favour of a constant. In the CLDS approach the difficulties with termination are compiled into the use of the structural rules in the labelling algebra. Moreover, although in this example a model can be extracted from the failure, it is not as obvious as in the more explicit CLDS approach.

Properties of AlgDP. There are several properties that can be stated about the relationship between the Semantics given by the Axioms in the Extended Labelling Algebra $\mathcal{A}_{\mathrm{I}}^{+}$ and the procedure AlgDP. They are all stated in Theorem 1 and are proved in Sect. 4.

Theorem 1. *Let $\mathcal{S}$ be a I_{CLDS}, α be a propositional IL formula and $\mathcal{A}_I^+(\alpha)$ be the particular clauses and instances of the Semantic Axioms for showing α, and $\mathcal{G}_\alpha = \mathcal{A}_I^+(\alpha) \cup \{\neg[\alpha]^*(1)\}$. Let AlgDP be initiated by the call $dp(\mathcal{G}_\alpha, F, R)$ for variables F and R, then the following properties hold:*

1. *If AlgDP returns $R = true$ then $\mathcal{G}_\alpha \models_{FOL}$.*
2. *If AlgDP returns $R = false$ then F is a partial model of $\mathcal{G}_\alpha$ and $\mathcal{G}_\alpha \not\models_{FOL}$.*
3. *AlgDP terminates.*
4. *If α is also a Hilbert theorem of propositional intuitionistic logic (i.e. α can be derived from the Hilbert Axioms for IL and Modus Ponens), then $\mathcal{G}_\alpha \models_{FOL}$.*
5. *If $\mathcal{G}_\alpha \models_{FOL}$ then α is a theorem of IL.*

Properties (1) and (2) are soundness and completeness results for AlgDP, in the sense that they show the algorithm is correct with respect to finding refutations. These properties, together with Property (3), are proved in Sect. 4.1 and show that AlgDP is decidable. Properties (4) and (5) show that AlgDP corresponds with IL, (4) showing it gives a refutation for any theorem of IL, and (5) showing it only succeeds for theorems. These properties are shown in Sect. 4.2.

4 Proving the Properties of AlgDP

In this section properties (1)-(3) of Theorem 1 are proved. The proof of Property (3) is given by Lemma 1, whilst Lemma 2 shows Properties (1) and (2).

4.1 Soundness and Completeness of AlgDP

Definition 6. *The* DPSize *of a call* $dp1(M, S, F, R)$ *is a pair* $(clausect, unitct)$, *where clausect counts the number of clauses in* S *and unitct counts the size of* M. *Given DPSizes* (x, y) *and* (u, v), *then* $(x, y) \leq_{DP} (u, v)$ *iff* $x < u$ *or* $x = u \wedge y < v$.

Lemma 1. *Given an initial call* $dp1(M, S, F, R)$, *AlgDP will always terminate.*

Proof. Note first that in all cases of AlgDP except (Hyper), the DPSize of the recursive call is smaller than the DPSize of the conclusion. Since the relation $\leq_{DP}$ is well-founded, after a finite number of steps either there must be a (Hyper) step or there is termination. For (Hyper) steps, notice that once a unit H has been generated by (Hyper) there is always a unit in M that subsumes H (which may be H itself), and so H is never again generated. Since there are only a finite number of possible units, limited by the finiteness of parameters, there is a maximum number of (Hyper) steps that can be made. Thereafter the only possible steps are those that reduce the DPSize.

□

Lemma 2. *Each clause of* $dp1$ *satisfies the following invariant, called (INV).*

> *Either,* $R = false$, $M \subseteq F$ *and* F *can be extended to a model of* S, *or,*
> $R = true$, $F = [\,]$ *and* $M \cup S$ *have no models.*

Proof. For each of the five clauses of $dp1$ it is shown that if the $dp1$ conditions of the clause satisfy invariant (INV) and the other conditions are also true, then the $dp1$ conclusion of the clause satisfies (INV) also.

Fail R is false; all rules have been applied and $F = M$. Certainly, $M \subseteq F$, and also F can be extended to a model M_0 of S (which may now be empty) as follows. Any literal subsumed by a literal in M is true in M_0. All other literals are false in M_0. The clauses left in S can only generate subsumed clauses or they are negative units. Suppose there is a non-negative clause C in S that is false in M_0. That is, for some instance C', of C, its condition literals are true in M_0 and its conclusion is false in M_0. If the conclusion is a single literal then, as (Hyper) has been applied, the conclusion is either true in M, and hence in M_0, or it is subsumed by a clause in M, and again is true in M_0, a contradiction. If the conclusion is a disjunction, then (Split) must have eventually been applied and the conclusion will again be true in M, or the disjunction is subsumed by a literal in M, contradicting the assumption. In case C is a negative clause in S, then if it is false, some instance $C' = \neg L$ is false, or L is true in M_0. But in that case (End) would have been applied, leading to a contradiction.

End R is true; since (End) is applicable, $M \cup S$ have no models; also $F = [\,]$.

Subsume Suppose (INV) is satisfied by $dp1(M, NewS, F, R)$ and R = false. Then $M \subseteq F$ and some model F_0 of F is a model of $NewS$. Let C be the subsumed clause removed from S. Then in case C is subsumed by a positive ground unit in M, by the axiom (Ax1) F_0 makes C true. No clause can be subsumed by the negated goal clause since it is ground and no other negative literals in S are ground. Thus F_0 is also a model of S. In case R = true, then $NewS \cup M$ has no models so $S \cup M$ have no models either; also $F = [\,]$.

Hyper Suppose (INV) is satisfied by $dp1(NewM, NewS, F, R)$ and R = false, $NewM \subseteq F$ and some model F_0 of F satisfies $NewS$. Then $M \subseteq F$ and F_0 is also a model of M that makes S true. In case R = true, $F = [\,]$, then every model of $NewM$ falsifies $NewS$. Suppose there is a model M_0 of M that is also a model of S. Therefore, there is an instance C' of clause C in S to which (Hyper) is applied, but such that the conclusion of C', which is either in $NewS$ or $NewM$, is false in M_0. Since (Hyper) is applicable to C', the conditions must occur in M and hence be true in M_0. But then the conclusion must also be true in M_0, a contradiction. Hence all models of M do falsify S as well and $M \cup S$ have no models.

Split Suppose that $dp1([S1|M], NewS, F1, R1)$ and $dp1([S2|M], NewS, F2, R2)$ both satisfy (INV) and that both $R1 = R2$ = true. Then $F = [\,]$, since $F1 = [\,]$ and $F2 = [\,]$. Also every model of $[S1|M]$ and of $[S2|M]$ falsifies $NewS$. Therefore, any model of M must make either $S1$ true and hence $NewS$ and S false, or $S2$ true and $NewS$ and S false, or both $S1$ and $S2$ false, and again S false as $S1 \vee S2 \in S$. On the other hand, suppose one of $R1$ or $R2$ is false, say $R1$, $[S1|M] \subseteq F1$ and some model F_0 of $F1$ satisfies $NewS$. In this case F_0 also satisfies $S1 \vee S2$. Similarly, if $R2$ is false, there is a model of $F2 \supseteq [S2|M]$ that satisfies $S1 \vee S2$. Finally, $M \subseteq F$ as $M \subseteq F1$ or $M \subseteq F2$.

Suppose that on termination, after the initial call $dp1([], S, F, R)$, the final values of S, M, R and F are given by S', M', F' and R'. If the value of R' is true, then the invariant (INV) implies that $F' = [\,]$ and $M' \cup S'$ have no models. Therefore, the initial call of $dp1([\,], S, R', F')$ also satisfies the invariant (INV) and S has no models. (R' and F' are used since their values are only assigned at termination of $dp1$.) On the other hand, if the value of R' is false, then F' yields a model for S'. Therefore, by the invariant (INV), the initial call $dp1([\,], S, R', F')$ also yields a model of S. Properties (1), (2) and (3) of Theorem 1 are therefore true. □

4.2 Correspondence of I_{CLDS} with Intuitionistic Logic

In order to show that the refutation system I_{CLDS} presented here for Intuitionistic Logic does indeed correspond to a standard Hilbert axiom presentation it is necessary to show that theorems in the two systems correspond (Properties 4 and 5 of Theorem 1). The complete set of axioms is shown in Table 2. Axioms (I2), (I3), (I4) and (I5) correspond, respectively, to monotonicity, contraction, distributivity and permutation. A useful axiom, (I14), is derivable also and is included for convenience. Axioms (I6) to (I8) capture negation and (I9) to (I13) capture conjunction and disjunction. Respectively, Theorems 2 and 3 state that theorems in IL obtained from a standard Hilbert presentation of IL, together with the rule of Modus Ponens (MP), are also theorems of AlgDP and that theorems of I_{CLDS} are also theorems in the Hilbert System of Intuitionistic Logic.

Table 2. The Hilbert axioms for I_{CLDS}

$\alpha \rightarrow \alpha$	(I1)	$\bot \rightarrow \alpha$	(I8)
$\alpha \rightarrow (\beta \rightarrow \alpha)$	(I2)	$\alpha \rightarrow (\beta \rightarrow (\alpha \wedge \beta))$	(I9)
$(\alpha \rightarrow (\alpha \rightarrow \beta)) \rightarrow (\alpha \rightarrow \beta)$	(I3)	$(\alpha \rightarrow (\beta \rightarrow \gamma)) \rightarrow ((\alpha \wedge \beta) \rightarrow \gamma)$	(I10)
$(\alpha \rightarrow \beta) \rightarrow ((\gamma \rightarrow \alpha) \rightarrow (\gamma \rightarrow \beta))$	(I4)	$\alpha \rightarrow \alpha \vee \beta$	(I11)
$(\alpha \rightarrow (\beta \rightarrow \gamma)) \rightarrow (\beta \rightarrow (\alpha \rightarrow \gamma))$	(I5)	$\beta \rightarrow \alpha \vee \beta$	(I12)
$\neg\alpha \rightarrow (\alpha \rightarrow \bot)$	(I6)	$(\alpha \rightarrow \gamma) \rightarrow ((\beta \rightarrow \gamma) \rightarrow (\alpha \vee \beta) \rightarrow \gamma)$	(I13)
$(\alpha \rightarrow \bot) \rightarrow \neg\alpha$	(I7)	$(\alpha \rightarrow \beta) \rightarrow ((\beta \rightarrow \gamma) \rightarrow (\alpha \rightarrow \gamma))$	(I14)

It is fairly easy to show that a refutation of a translated theorem $\mathcal{T}$ of IL exists using the appropriate equivalence schemas from the semantic axioms. But a stronger result, namely, that a refutation exists when only the restricted set of axioms for $\mathcal{T}$ is used, can also be shown. This allows a failed refutation (for non-theorems) to be found more quickly as fewer axioms are included, but it is more complex to prove.

Theorem 2. *Let P be a Hilbert theorem of IL then $\{\neg[P]^*(1)\}$ and the appropriate set of instances of the semantic axioms (equivalences) for $\neg[P]^*(1)$, P_S, has no models.*

Proof. (*Outline only.*) Let P_S be the set of defining equivalences for P and its subformulas, $\forall x[[P]^*(x) \leftrightarrow R(x)]$ be the defining equivalence for $[P]^*$ and $\forall x[[P]^*(x) \leftrightarrow T_P(x)]$ be the resulting equivalence after replacing every occurrence in $R(x)$ of an atom that has a defining equivalence in P_S by the right-hand side of that equivalence. Then $T_P(1)$ is always true. Therefore, there are no models of P_S and $\neg[P]^*(1)$. This property of $T_P(1)$ is shown by induction on the number of (MP) steps in the Hilbert proof of P. In case P is an axiom and uses no applications of (MP) in its proof then the property can be seen to hold by construction. Let the property hold for all theorems that have Hilbert proofs using $< n$ applications of (MP), and consider a theorem P such that its proof uses n (MP)steps, with the last step being a derivation from P' and $P' \rightarrow P$. By hypothesis, $T_{P'}(1)$ is true and $T_{P' \rightarrow P}(1)$ is true. Hence, since $\forall x[T_{P' \rightarrow P}(x) \leftrightarrow \forall u[T_{P'}(u) \rightarrow T_P(ux)]]$, then $T_P(1)$ is also true.

□

Theorem 3. *Let $\mathcal{G}_\alpha$ be the set of instances of $\mathcal{A}_I^+$ for showing α (not including $\neg[\alpha]^*(1)$), then if there exists an AlgDP refutation in I_{CLDS} of $\mathcal{G}_\alpha \cup \neg[\alpha]^*(1)$ then there is a Hilbert proof in IL of α, which is therefore a theorem of IL. That is, if $\mathcal{G}_\alpha, \neg[\alpha]^*(1) \models_{FOL}$ then $\vdash_{HI} \alpha$.*

Proof. Suppose $\mathcal{G}_\alpha, \neg[\alpha]^*(1) \models_{\mathrm{FOL}}$, hence any model of $\mathcal{G}_\alpha$ is also a model of $[\alpha]^*(1)$; it is required to show $\vdash_{\mathrm{HI}} \alpha$. Lemma 3 below states there is a model M of $\mathcal{A}_{\mathrm{I}}^+$, and hence of $\mathcal{G}_\alpha$, with the property that $[\alpha]^*(1) = true$ iff $\vdash_{\mathrm{HI}} \alpha$. Therefore, since M is a model of $\mathcal{A}_{\mathrm{I}}^+$ it is a model of $[\alpha]^*(1)$ and hence $\vdash_{\mathrm{HI}} \alpha$ is true, as required. The desired model is based on the canonical interpretation introduced in [1].

□

Definition 7. *The* canonical interpretation *for I_{CLDS} is an interpretation from* Func*$(\mathcal{L}_P, \mathcal{L}_L)$ onto $PW(\mathcal{L}_P)$ defined as follows:*

- $||c_\alpha|| = \{z \mid \vdash_{HI} \alpha \rightarrow z\}$, *for each characteristic label c_α;*
- $||\lambda \circ \lambda'|| = \{z \mid \vdash_{HI} \alpha \wedge \beta \rightarrow z\}$, *where $\alpha \in ||\lambda||$ and $\beta \in ||\lambda'||$;*
- $||1|| = \{z \mid \vdash_{HI} z\}$ *and* $||c_\perp|| = \{z \mid \vdash_{HI} \perp \rightarrow z\} = \mathcal{L}_P$;
- $|| \preceq || = \{(||x||, ||y||) \mid ||x|| \subseteq ||y||\}$.
- $||[\alpha]^*|| = \{||x|| \mid \alpha \in ||x||\}$.

The canonical interpretation is used to give a Herbrand model for $\mathcal{A}_{\mathrm{I}}^+$, by setting $[\alpha]^*(x) = true$ iff $\alpha \in ||x||$. This means, in particular, that if $[\alpha]^*(1) = true$ then $\alpha \in ||1||$ and hence $\vdash_{\mathrm{HI}} \alpha$. The following Lemma, proved in the full version [2], states that the canonical interpretation of Def. 7 is a model of $\mathcal{A}_{\mathrm{I}}^+$.

Lemma 3. *The properties of the labelling algebra $\mathcal{A}_{\mathcal{I}}$ given in Def. 1 and the semantic axioms of $\mathcal{A}_I^+$ are satisfied by the canonical interpretation for I_{CLDS}.*

5 Conclusions

In this paper a new method, that of Compiled Labelled Deductive Systems, based on the principles in [7], is applied to Intuitionistic Logic. The method of CLDS provides logics with a uniform presentation of their derivability relations and semantic entailments and its semantics is given in terms of a translation approach into first-order logic. The method is used to give a presentation of $\mathrm{I}_{\mathrm{CLDS}}$, which is seen to be a generalisation of Intuitionistic Logic through the correspondence results stated in Section 4. In fact, the CLDS approach yields a generalisation of IL, although this hasn't been exploited here.

The translation results in a compiled theory of a configuration. A refutation system based on an extension of the Davis Putnam procedure is defined for this theory, that is well suited to the case of $\mathrm{I}_{\mathrm{CLDS}}$. The prover also uses Hyper-resolution with splitting and a particular unification algorithm, which together result in only ground clauses ever being derived. It yields a decidability test for formulas of propositional Intuitionistic Logic. Other standard approaches to providing a first order representation of IL do so by translating IL sentences into the modal logic S4 [6], and the CLDS method and such approaches were compared through examples. However, it is emphasised once more that the method of CLDS is a uniform approach that can be applied to give new logics, as well as old ones. Only the case of Intuitionistic Logic has been considered here, but Linear Logic is considered in [4]. Labelling algebrae for Linear Logic use the properties

(1) - (5) of Def. 1 and for Relevance logic the (contraction) property is added too. (See [1] and [4] for a full discussion of this issue.) In the presence of monotonicity the algorithm AlgDP can be restricted to deriving ground clauses and it would also be suitable for other logics that include the monotonicity property, such as Lukasiewicz fuzzy logic. On the other hand, the monotonicity property does not hold for Linear Logic, and, for example, instances of (Ax3b) would take the form $\forall x([\alpha]^*(a) \vee [\alpha \rightarrow \beta]^*(x))$ and one branch of a (Split) rule application would include $[\alpha \rightarrow \beta]^*(x)$ for all values of x. Together with an instance of (Ax3a) this could lead to atoms of the form $[\beta]^*(x \circ \lambda)$, for some ground or variable label λ. Furthermore, in Linear Logic, for instance, labels must be treated as multisets of the composing parameters, so, for example, $[\alpha]^*(a)$ does not subsume $[\alpha]^*(aa)$ any more. Decidability becomes a more difficult issue. For a classical system, the requirement $c_\alpha = c_{\neg\neg\alpha}$ can be added to the labelling algebra, which allows the double negation rule to be derived. In Fig. 2, this allows for a and c to be identified, so allowing the proof to terminate successfully.

Acknowledgement. The authors acknowledge their debt to foundation work in [1] and thank the anonymous referee who indicated a potential error.

References

1. M. D'Agostino and D. Gabbay. A generalisation of analytic deduction via labelled deductive systems. Part I: Basic substructural Logics. Journal of Automated Reasoning, 13:243-281, 1994
2. K. Broda, A compiled labelled deductive system for propositional intuitionistic logic (full version) available from K. Broda, 1998.
3. K. Broda, M. Finger and A. Russo. Labelled Natural Deduction for Substructural Logics. Accepted, Journal of the International Group for Pure and Applied Logics.
4. K. Broda and A. Russo. A Unified Compilation Style Labelled Deductive System for Modal and Substructural Logic using Natural Deduction. Technical Report 10/97. Department of Computing, Imperial College 1997.
5. C. L. Chang and R. Lee. Symbolic Logic and Mechanical Theorem Proving. Academic Press 1973.
6. M. Fitting. Proof Methods for Modal and Intuitionistic Logic. D. Reidel, 1983.
7. D. Gabbay. Labelled Deductive Systems, Volume I - Foundations. OUP, 1996
8. J. H. Gallier. Logic for Computer Science. Harper and Row, 1986.
9. H.J. Ohlbach. Semantics-based translation methods for modal logics. Journal of Logic and Computation, 1 (5):691-746 1991.
10. J.A. Robinson. Logic, Form and Function. Edinburgh Press 1979.
11. A. Russo. Modal Logics as Labelled Deductive Systems. PhD. Thesis, Department of Computing, Imperial College, 1996.
12. R. A. Schmidt. Resolution is a decision procedure for many propositional modal logics. Advances in Modal Logic, Vol.1: 189-208, CSLI 1998.

Intuitionisitic Tableau Extracted

James Caldwell

Department of Computer Science
University of Wyoming
Laramie, WY
caldwell@denali.cs.uwyo.edu

Abstract. This paper presents a formalization of a sequent presentation of intuitionisitic propositional logic and proof of decidability. The proof is implemented in the Nuprl system and the resulting proof object yields a "correct-by-construction" program for deciding intuitionisitc propositional sequents. The extracted program turns out to be an implementation of the tableau algorithm. If the argument to the resulting decision procedure is a valid sequent, a formal proof of that fact is returned, otherwise a counter-example in the form of a Kripke Countermodel is returned. The formalization roughly follows Aitken, Constable and Underwood's presentation in [1] but a number of adjustments and corrections have been made to ensure the extracted program is clean (no non-computational junk) and efficient.

1 Introduction

Confronted with the notion of automated verification the astute skeptic correctly asks, "Who verifies the verifier?" This paper, presenting a formally developed decision procedure for a sequent presentation of intuitionistic propositional logic, addresses the skeptics question, even if only peripherally. We describe the formalization and mechanical checking, in Nuprl, of a proof that intuitionistic propositional logic is decidable. The program extracted from the formal proof is a tableau decision procedure: invoked with a sequent as its argument, it returns either a multi-succedent sequent proof or a Kripke counter-example depending on whether the formula to be decided is valid or not. With the proof of decidability as our focus, we describe the formal development of a sequent proof theory, the tableau construction, and a formal theory of Kripke counter-examples which are used here as evidence of unprovability. A principle goal of the work reported here is the extraction of a reasonably readable and efficient program from the formal proof via the "proof-as-programs" interpretation implemented in Nuprl.

1.1 Related Work

In a series of papers [19, 18, 20, 1], Underwood and her colleagues presented constructive completeness proofs for intuitionistic propositional logic having tableau decision procedures as their computational content. The work reported on here extends those efforts. Underwood worked out a type theoretic presentation of the problem and presented informal proofs, including a new termination argument for the tableau construction. The formalization and proof presented here follows the proof presented in the paper by Aitken, Constable and Underwood [1] (hereafter referred to as ACU.) A fuller account of the formalization and proof can be found in [6]. In this paper we describe the formal implementation in Nuprl and adjustments made to the formalization that result in a readable and "efficient"[1] extracted program.

The idea of verifying decision procedures is not new but actual verifications are not common. One example that has published at least five times and in a number of systems is Boyer and Moore's (classical) propositional tautology checker which takes the form of an `IF-THEN-ELSE` normalization procedure. Of those efforts, Paulin-Mohring and Werner's extraction of an ML program [14] is closest in spirit to the presentation here. Both Shankar [16] and Hayashi [12] have verified deciders for implicational fragments of classical propositional logic presented in sequent forms. Caldwell [4, 6] extracted a tableau decision procedure from a proof of the decidability of a sequent presentation of classical propositional logic.

Weich [21] formalized a proof of decidability for the implicational fragment of propositional intuitionistic logic in MINLOG. His work is also closely related to the proof presented here; indeed, his effort was also inspired by Underwood's formulation of constructive decidability. Weich's proof differs from the one reported on here in that it is based on a contraction-free calculus. He reports [22] that the extracted program is huge (about 60KB) and efforts are underway to minimize its size.

1.2 Results

The program extracted from the proof of intuitionistic decidability presented here is the first to include a full propositional logic, *i.e.* the logic formalized here includes propositional variables, a constant denoting false, and operators for conjunction, disjunction, and implication. The extracted program is readable and efficient in the sense that it does not perform extraneous computation related to the logical part of the specification, nor does it contain unreadable artifacts of the proof in its text. These qualities will be most evident to those familiar with the state of the art in program extraction.

In the course of the development presented here, a number of minor errors in the ACU presentation were discovered, additionally a more serious error was uncovered. Indeed, discovering errors like these is one point of formal machine checked proofs. The presentation here differs from that of ACU in two significant ways. First, we have made modifications to the type theoretic formalization to guarantee the program extracted from the proof is free of the

[1] Of course intuitionistic propositional logic is known to be PSPACE complete, what we mean here by "efficient" is that the extracted program doesn't do unnecessary computation and that the program does not contain non-computational artifacts of the proof.

non-computational junk that often clutters programs extracted from constructive proofs. The methodology of using set types in place of existential quantifiers to generate efficient extracts has been described elsewhere [5,6]. The second difference between the formalization presented here and that of ACU is in the proof type used as evidence of validity. We formalize a multi-succedent sequent calculus while ACU attepted to push the argument through for a single succedent calculus. Although the overall structure most of the details of the ACU proof survive in the version presented here, the ACU proof is incorrect. We simply remark that ACU failed to fully consider the case of reconstructing a proof object after the application of the tableau rule for a negatively occurring disjunction.

2 Nuprl

The Nuprl type theory is a sequent presentation of a constructive type theory via type assignment rules. The underlying programming language is untyped and the objective of a proof is to either prove a type is inhabited, *i.e.* to show that some term (program) is a member of the type, or to show that a term inhabits a particular type. A complete presentation of the type theory can be found in the Nuprl book [7].

The Nuprl system supports construction of proofs by top-down refinement. The prover is implemented as a tactic based prover in the style of LCF. The tactic language is ML. Nuprl differs from other LCF-style provers in that tactic invocations define the structure of an explicitly represented proof tree which is directly manipulated in the editor, stored in the Nuprl library, and retrieved for later editing. The Nuprl system also supports a unique and powerful display mechanism. Nuprl terms are edited using a structure editor; term structure is independent of display which is user specified. All Nuprl terms occurring in this paper are set in `typewriter font` and appear on the page as they do in the Nuprl editor and library.

Complete documentation is included in the Nuprl V4.2 distribution. [2]

2.1 Clean and Efficient Extracts

Methods of generating efficient and readable extracts by the use of the set type (as opposed to the existential type) and by efficient general recursion combinators have been presented by the author in [5,4,6]. We reiterate the main points here.

Inhabitants of the existential type `∃x:T.P[x]` are pairs `<a,b>` where `a∈T` and `b∈P[a]`. The term `b` inhabiting `P[a]` specifies, as far as the proofs-as-programs interpretation goes, how to prove `P[a]`. When an existential type occurs as a hypothesis it can be decomposed into two hypotheses, one of the form `a:T` and another asserting `b:P[a]`. If `v` is the name of the variable denoting the existential hypothesis, occurrences of `a` in the final extract appear as `v.1`, and occurrences of `b` appear as `v.2` (the first and second projections).

[2] The Nuprl system is freely available on the Nuprl group web pages at Cornell, `http://www.cs.cornell.edu/Info/Projects/NuPrl/nuprl.html`.

Alternatively, consider the Nuprl set type {y∈T|P[y]}. Its inhabitants are elements of type T, say a, such that P[a] holds. Thus, a set type does not carry the computational content associated with the logical part P[a]. Since the proof that P[a] holds is not witnessed by inhabitants of the set type, the fact that P[a] holds is not freely available in parts of a proof where it might find its way into an extract. When a set type occurring as a hypothesis is decomposed it results in two new hypotheses: one of the form a:T; and the other, a "hidden" hypothesis, of the form b:P[a]. The Nuprl system prevents the variable of a hidden hypothesis from appearing free in the extract of a proof by restrictions on its use. Hidden hypotheses are unhidden by the system in parts of the proof where no computational content is constructed.

Although these issues may appear to be Nuprl specific technicalities, they arise in all constructive systems implementing the proofs-as-programs interpretation.

2.2 Efficient Induction Schemes

We are interested in extracting efficient programs from proofs; to do so we carefully construct proofs of the induction principles to ensure their extracts are efficient recursion combinators.

The Nuprl standard library includes the following type characterizing well-founded binary relations:

$$\texttt{WellFnd(A;x,y.R[x;y])} \stackrel{\text{def}}{=}$$
$$\forall \texttt{P:A} \rightarrow \texttt{Prop.}(\forall \texttt{j:A.}\ (\forall \texttt{k:A.}\ \texttt{R[k; j]} \Rightarrow \texttt{P[k]}) \Rightarrow \texttt{P[j]}) \Rightarrow \forall \texttt{n:A.}\ \texttt{P[n]}$$

Well-founded induction on the natural numbers over the ordinary less-than ordering is specified by a lemma of the form WellFnd(ℕ;x,y. x < y).

The following recursion scheme inhabits this type.

$$\lambda\texttt{P,g.}\ \texttt{(letrec f(n) = g(n)(}\lambda\texttt{k,p. f(k)))}$$

Here P is a proposition (over type A), and g corresponds to the computational content of the induction hypothesis. In this scheme, g takes two arguments, the first being the principal argument on which the recursion is formed, while its second argument is a function inhabiting the proposition ∀k:A. R[k;j]⇒ P[k], *i.e.* a function which accepts some element k of type A along with evidence for R[k;j] and which produces evidence for P[j]. In the scheme, the evidence that R[k;j] holds takes the form of the argument p to the innermost λ-binding. The variable p occurs nowhere else in the term and does not contribute to the actual computation of P[j]; instead it is a vestige of the typing. In the context of any complete proof, this argument will be a term justifying R[k;j]. In any program extracted from a proof using this scheme, the useless argument p must be supplied. This term is non-computational junk.

As an alternative, we give the following definition of well-founded binary relations that hides the ordering in a set type; this type, simply called WF is defined as follows:

$$\texttt{WF(A;x,y.R[x; y])} \stackrel{\text{def}}{=}$$
$$\forall \texttt{P:A} \rightarrow \texttt{Prop.}(\forall \texttt{j:A.}\ (\forall \texttt{k:\{k:A|}\ \texttt{R[k; j]\}}\ .\ \texttt{P[k]}) \Rightarrow \texttt{P[j]}) \Rightarrow \forall \texttt{n:A.}\ \texttt{P[n]}$$

Since the ordering relation is now hidden in the right side of a set type, it does not contribute to the computational content of the extracted programs. The recursion scheme extracted from a proof of this type is nearly identical to the previous one, but the extra (useless) lambda-abstraction is gone.

```
λP,g. (letrec f(n) = g(n)(λk. f(k)))
```

For an arbitrary type T and a measure function ρ:T→N, following lemma defines an efficient measure induction principle.

```
∀T:Type. ∀ρ:T → N.  WF(T;x,y.ρ(x) < ρ(y))
Extraction:
  λT,ρ,P,g.(letrec f(n) = g(n)(λk.f (k)))
```

Note that the measure function ρ does not occur in the body of the extract, logically it belongs to the termination argument which is not part of the computational content.

The proof of intuitionistic decidability presented below is by induction on the lexicographic ordering of a pair of inverse images (measures functions mapping systems onto the natural numbers.) This induction principle is established by the following lemma.

```
∀T:Type. ∀ρ,ρ':T → N.
  WF(T;k,j.ρ(k) < ρ(j) ∨ (ρ(k) = ρ(j) ∧ ρ'(k) < ρ'(j)))
Extraction:
  λT,ρ,ρ',P,g.(letrec f(n) = g(n)(λj.f j))
```

Note that the recursion combinator does not mention the measure functions.

3 The Tableau Algorithm

Our goal is to extract a tableau decision procedure from the formal proof. Tableau methods for proof search in intuitionistic logic go back to Beth [3] and are analyzed in detail by Fitting [11]. Roughly, tableau methods are search procedures that work by systematically exploring all consequences of an assumption in the search for a counter-example. For example, if a formula of the form $P \wedge Q$ is assumed to be false, then one of P or Q must also be false; the step of tableau development for this formula will split into two paths, one with the added assumption that P is false and the other with the added assumption that Q is false. The *tableau* is the tree-like structure that records the development of the search, keeping track in each node of those formulas assumed to true and those formulas assumed to be false.

If, in the process of developing a path of the tableau, it occurs that a formula is assumed to be both true and false, then that path is contradictory and we say it is *closed*. If a path is developed to the point where further application of the tableau rules can only result in redundant nodes being added to the path, then we stop development and say the path is *open*. If all the paths developed in this process are closed then the initial assumption must be false and the formula is provable; *i.e.* if the initial assumption that the formula is false always leads to a contradiction, then the formula must be true. Using the tableau so constructed we construct a proof of the formula. If on the other hand some path in the tableau is open, that path is interpreted as a Kripke counter-example to the initial formula.

It is easy to check whether a path is closed. The complexity of the decidability argument arises in determining whether further development of an open path is redundant. Underwood [18] provided a new termination argument based on a lexicographic ordering of tableau systems based on two measures:

i1: bounding the number of nodes that can be added to a tableau system, and
i2: bounding the number of formulas that can be added to any node.

Ultimately, these measures depend on the fact that tableau construction has the *subformula property*, *i.e.* in the tableau development, only subformulas of formulas already occurring in the tableau are ever added.

Measures i1 and i2 are calculated by computing conservative upper bounds on the sizes of the respective structures they measure and then by taking the difference between these bounds and the actual sizes of the objects in the tableau being constructed. Since nodes and systems grow during each step of tableau development, the difference decreases. Thus, at each step of the tableau construction process, one or the other measure decreases, which is enough to show termination. The bounds are never achievable in an actual tableau development and so we terminate the process when all nodes are completely developed and when the system is completely developed.

4 Intuitionistic Proof Systems, Kripke Counter-Examples and Tableau Systems

The final output of the algorithm we are interested in will either be a proof that the initial system is valid or a Kripke model serving as a counter-example, we formalize these structures now.

4.1 Formulas and Sequents

Propositional formulas are formalized by the following Nuprl recursive type:

$$\texttt{Formula} \stackrel{\text{def}}{=} \texttt{rec(F.Var | Unit | F} \times \texttt{F | F} \times \texttt{F | F} \times \texttt{F)}$$

Reading left to right, a formula is either: a variable (which is displayed as $\ulcorner\texttt{x}\urcorner$); the constant inhabiting the type Unit which is interpreted as *false* and displayed $\ulcorner\texttt{false}\urcorner$; a pair of formulas representing a conjunction displayed as $\texttt{p}\ulcorner\wedge\urcorner\texttt{q}$; a pair of formulas, representing a disjunction displayed $\texttt{p}\ulcorner\vee\urcorner\texttt{q}$); or a pair of formulas, representing an implication and displayed $(\texttt{p}\ulcorner\Rightarrow\urcorner\texttt{q})$. Negation $(\neg\texttt{P})$ is defined as $(\texttt{P}\ulcorner\Rightarrow\urcorner\ulcorner\texttt{false}\urcorner)$ and we do not include it explicitly in our formula type; neither do we include an operator for equivalence. Formula is a discrete type, *i.e.* it is decidable whether two formulas are equal.

We model the type of variables using the Nuprl Atom type; however, any discrete type may be substituted. other than this constraint, Var may be considered an uninterpreted type.

The sequent type (Sequent) consists of pairs of formula lists. If S is a sequent, Hyps(S) denotes the list of formulas that are in the antecedent of S (the hypotheses) and `Concl(S)` denotes the list of formulas in the succedent of `S` (the conclusions.) `Sequent` is a discrete type since `Formula` is.

A sequent is deemed true whenever the conjunction of the antecedents implies the disjunction of the succedents (by convention, an empty disjunction is true and an empty conjunction is false.)

4.2 Multi-Succedent Proofs

Our proof type is based on the sequent calculus *MJ* presented in Figure 1. *MJ* is essentially the propositional fragment of Dragalin's [8, pg.11] multi-succedent calculus. The form of our rules differs from Dragalin's in logically insignificant ways that support the use of lists instead of sets.

$$\frac{}{M, \mathtt{false}, N \vdash C}\ (\mathtt{false}\,l) \qquad \frac{}{M, q, N \vdash M', q, N'}\ (Ax)$$

$$\frac{q, M, q\vee r, N \vdash C \qquad r, M, q\vee r, N \vdash C}{M, q\vee r, N \vdash C}\ (\vee l) \qquad \frac{H \vdash q, M, q\vee r, N}{H \vdash M, q\vee r, N}\ (\vee r1) \qquad \frac{H \vdash r, M, q\vee r, N}{H \vdash M, q\vee r, N}\ (\vee r2)$$

$$\frac{q, M, q\wedge r, N \vdash C}{M, q\wedge r, N \vdash C}\ (\wedge l1) \qquad \frac{r, M, q\wedge r, N \vdash C}{M, q\wedge r, N \vdash C}\ (\wedge l2) \qquad \frac{H \vdash q, M, q\wedge r, N \qquad H \vdash r, M, q\wedge r, N}{H \vdash M, q\wedge r, N}\ (\wedge r)$$

$$\frac{M, q\Rightarrow r, N \vdash q, C \qquad r, M, q\Rightarrow r, N \vdash C}{M, q\Rightarrow r, N \vdash C}\ (\Rightarrow l) \qquad \frac{q, H \vdash r}{H \vdash M, q\Rightarrow r, N}\ (\Rightarrow r)$$

Fig. 1. System *MJ*

To read these rule schemas, M, N, C and H denote (possibly empty) formula lists and q and r denote individual formulas. Consider the figure for the rule labelled $(\Rightarrow r)$, this rule characterizes the multi-conclusion intuitionistic sequent calculus. To derive the sequent $H \vdash M, q \Rightarrow r, N$ it is enough to show the sequent $q, H \vdash r$. Note that, in distinction to the other rules, the formulas in the succedent of the conclusion of $(\Rightarrow r)$ (formulas in the list $M, q \Rightarrow r, N$) have been replaced by the single formula r.

MJ proofs are formally modeled in the Nuprl implementation in two stages. In the first, a recursive type of pre-proofs is defined to represent the shape (tree structure) of a proof. In the second stage, the type of pre-proofs is narrowed to include only those trees representing actual proofs.

```
pre_proof  ≝  rec(P. Sequent
                   | Sequent × Sequent × P
                   | Sequent × Sequent × P × Sequent × P)
```

We display the three classes of **pre_proofs** as C\, C\<H,p>, and C\<H,p>,<H',p'> respectively where C, H, and H' are sequents and p and p' are pre-proofs.

For a pre-proof P let Concl(P) be the sequent that is the root of the pre-proof.

Excluding axioms, the rules of system *MJ* have either one or two hypotheses. These rule classes are characterized by two definitions, one for rules having a single hypothesis (**proof_rule1**: $\vee r1$, $\vee r2$, $\Rightarrow r$, $\wedge l1$, and $\wedge l2$) and another for rules having two hypotheses (**proof_rule2**: $\vee l$, $\wedge r$, and $\Rightarrow r$). We give the definition of **proof_rule1** here.

```
c\h is a rule instance  ≝
  ∃a,b:Formula.
     ((a⌜∨⌝b) ∈ Concl(c)  ∧ h = <Hyps(c),a::Concl(c)>)
     ∨ ((a⌜∨⌝b) ∈ Concl(c)  ∧ h = <Hyps(c),b::Concl(c)>)
     ∨ ((a⌜⇒⌝b) ∈ Concl(c)  ∧ h = <a::Hyps(c), b::[]>)
     ∨ ((a⌜∧⌝b) ∈ Hyps(c)  ∧ h = <a::Hyps(c), Concl(c)>)
     ∨ ((a⌜∧⌝b) ∈ Hyps(c)  ∧ h = <b::Hyps(c), Concl(c)>)
```

The equality used here is the type equality for sequents (defined as pairs of formula lists) and so order counts; this is not the semantic (permutation) equality on sequents. The reader can verify by inspection that these clauses match the appropriate rules of system *MJ*.

In the second stage of modeling *MJ* proofs. A well-formedness predicate is defined to narrow the class of pre-proofs to those structures that actually model proofs of system *MJ*. For a pre-proof P we write P is a Proof if:

i.) its leaves are all instances of the false*l* rule or the *Ax* rule, and
ii.) every non-leaf node matches a conclusion of some rule instance and its children match the premises of that rule.

This characterization is formalized by a recursive function we omit for lack of space. Thus proofs are characterized by the subtype of pre-proofs that are well formed.

```
Proof  ≝  {p:pre_proof | p is a Proof}
```

A proof P proves a sequent S if Concl(P) = S.

4.3 Kripke Counter-examples as Evidence of Unprovability

It is a well known negative result that no finite valuation captures intuitionistic propositional logic. Thus, models for intuitionistic logic are necessarily more complex than models for classical logics. Following the account given by Underwood in [18], we use Kripke models to witness the unprovability of a formula. This interpretation is not without some subtlety as Kripke models provide for classical analyses of intuitionistic logic but are not faithful to intuitionistic semantics. Smorynski [17] and Dummett [9] discuss this in some detail. Never-the-less, following Underwood [18, pg.11–15], Kripke models are used here as evidence of unprovability. Failed tableau searches yield Kripke counter-examples. This use of Kripke models as counter-examples to intuitionistic provability has received attention elsewhere [15, 13].

The type of Kripke models is a dependent triple consisting of a type (of states), a reflexive and transitive relation on the states, and an atomic forcing function.

```
Kripke ≝ T:Type
      ×R:{R:(T × T) → Prop | Reflexive(R) ∧ Transitive(R)}
      ×{af:T → Var → Prop |
          ∀a:T. ∀v:Var. af(a)(v) ⇒ (∀b:T. R(<a, b>) ⇒ af(b)(v))}
```

The selectors for the three components of a Kripke model `K` are displayed as `Σ(K)`, `≤{K}`, and `K.af` respectively. For states `s` and `s'` we display `s≤{K}s'` for `≤{K}(<s,s'>)`.

Truth in a Kripke model is defined by the forcing relation. The statement of the main theorem requires definitions of both *forces*, and its complement *not forces*. The reader may realize that we cannot simply define the complementary notion by taking the constructive negation of the definition of forcing. To avoid this problem, following a suggestion of Underwood, we define the forces and not-forces relations simultaneously by mutual recursion. Definition by mutual recursion is not directly supported by Nuprl tactics (although there is no technical reason it cannot be) and we use the pairing trick to implement it.

```
<forces,not_forces>{K} ≝
    (letrec f_nf(s)(f) =
      case f:
        ⌜x⌝ → <K.af(s)(x), ¬(K.af(s)(x))>;
        ⌜false⌝ → <False, True>;
        a⌜∧⌝b → <(f_nf(s)(a)).1 ∧ (f_nf(s)(b)).1,
                 (f_nf(s)(a)).2 ∨ (f_nf(s)(b)).2>;
        a⌜∨⌝b → <(f_nf(s)(a)).1 ∨ (f_nf(s)(b)).1,
                 (f_nf(s)(a)).2 ∧ (f_nf(s)(b)).2>;
        a⌜⇒⌝b → <∀s':Σ(K). s ≤{K} s' ⇒
                    (f_nf(s')(a)).2 ∨ (f_nf(s')(b)).1,
                 ∃s':Σ(K). s ≤{K} s' ∧
                    (f_nf(s')(a)).1 ∧ (f_nf(s')(b)).2>;
    )
```

Using this definition we further define `forces(K,S,f)` and `not_forces(K,S,f)` to be the first and second projections of the term `<forces,not_forces>{K}(S)(f)`.

4.4 Tableau Systems

The tree structure representing an actual tableau is never explicitly constructed by the program extracted from the proof presented here. Rather, the paths in the tableau are represented by lists of tableau nodes, these lists are called *Systems* and the overall structure of the tableau is implicit in the unfolding of the recursion.

Like sequents, tableau nodes (type `Node`) are represented by pairs of formula lists. The elements in the first component of a node are those formulas assumed to be true, the elements in the second component are those elements assumed to be false. We refer to these components by writing `T(N)` for the true part and

`F(N)` for the false part. Of course, `Node` is a discrete type. `asSequent(N)` casts the node `N` to the type `Sequent`.

A `System` is a non-empty list of nodes.

There is a close correspondence between the steps of tableau construction and the proof rules of system *MJ*. For each proof rule there is a corresponding step of tableau development. For proof rules having a single premise there is a corresponding tableau development step in which an existing node is extended or, in the case of $\Rightarrow r$, the tableau system itself is extended by the addition of a new node. For proof rules having two premises, the corresponding tableau step extends an existing node in the tableau in two different ways, invoking the induction hypothesis (unfolding a step of recursion) on these extended systems. This bifurcation of systems corresponds to a branching in the tableau structure. We call the tableau steps corresponding to rules other than the $\Rightarrow r$ rule *local* rules, as they only extend existing nodes.

When a node has been developed as far as possible under the local rules we say it is *node complete* (we write `nComplete(N)`.) The type of *eligible systems* (`ESystem`) are those systems restricted to contain at most one member that is not node complete. Tableau systems containing all possible node extensions induced by occurrences of $\Rightarrow r$ are called *system complete*; for a system `S` we write `sComplete(S)` to indicate `S` is system complete.

In the case of a failed tableau search, culminating in a system `S`, the corresponding Kripke structure `K(S)` will serve as the counter-example. Eventually, we are interested in viewing tableau systems as Kripke structures. The following function serves to map systems into a triple which is a Kripke model.

$$\texttt{K(S)} \stackrel{\text{def}}{=} \texttt{<}\{\texttt{N:Node} \mid \texttt{N}\in\texttt{S}\}\texttt{, }\lambda\texttt{<n,m>.T(n)}\subseteq\texttt{T(m), }\lambda\texttt{N,x.}\ulcorner\texttt{x}\urcorner\in\texttt{T(N)>}$$

Thus, under the interpretation, states of the corresponding Kripke model consist of the type whose members are those nodes in the system. The ordering on pairs of nodes is defined by sublist inclusion on the formulas assumed to be true in the nodes. The atomic forcing function for a state `N` and a variable `x` is defined by membership of the atomic formula $\ulcorner$`x`$\urcorner$ among formulas assumed true at `N`. That systems do indeed map to Kripke models under `K` is established by a well-formedness theorem for `K`.

5 Intuitionistic Decidability

A proof of a constructive disjunction $(P \vee Q)$ must indicate which of P or Q was proved and also must give evidence for its truth. Thus, if intuitionistic decidability is stated as follows:

$$\forall\texttt{S:Sequent. }(\exists\texttt{p:Proof. p proves S}) \vee (\exists\texttt{c:counter\_example. c refutes S})$$

the resulting computational content is a function that takes a sequent as input and which either returns evidence for its validity or returns a counter-example.

We do not prove this theorem directly, but instead prove a more general theorem having the structure to support an inductive proof. The more general theorem does not apply directly to formulas, but applies to systems (lists of tableau nodes) satisfying the eligibility condition of being members of the type

ESystem. Evidence for the provability of an ESystem takes the form of a formal proof in the sequent calculus *MJ*. Evidence for its absurdity takes the form of a Kripke counter-example. Formally stated, the theorem we eventually prove here is the following:

```
∀S:ESystem
    (∃N:{N:Node| N∈S} . {p:Proof| p proves asSequent(N)} )
    ∨ {K:Kripke| ∃f:Node → Σ(K)
        ∀N:{N:Node| N∈S}
          ∀F:Formula. (F∈(T(N)) ⇒ forces(K,f N,F))
                    ∧ (F∈(F(N)) ⇒ not_forces(K,f N,F))}
```

To decide a formula ϕ, we will apply the computational content of this more general theorem to an eligible system containing a single node in which ϕ is assumed to be false. Should ϕ turn out to be provable, the result is a pair consisting of a tableau node and a proof of that node regarded as a sequent. Since the computational content of the theorem is intended to be applied to systems consisting of single nodes which contain a single formula, this evidently corresponds to a proof of the sequent <[],[ϕ]>. Should ϕ turn out not to be provable, the result is a Kripke counter-example. Kripke counter-examples here take the form of Kripke models defined over tableau nodes N∈S such that every formula in the true portion of the node (T(N)) is forced and every element in the false portion of the node (F(N)) is not forced. Since we will be applying the extracted program to initial systems consisting of a single nodes containing a single formula assumed to be false, the formula is not forced in the resulting Kripke model and so it serves as a counter-example.

5.1 The Proof

The proof of the theorem stated above is by induction on eligible systems, *i.e.* on systems having at most one node that is not node complete. The induction principle is the lexicographic measure induction presented above in Section 2.2. We apply it here using the measure functions i1 and i2 defined above in Section 3. Recall that the first measure decreases with every node added to the system while the second decreases as formulas are added to the eligible node.

After inducting on the eligible system S we are left with the following Nuprl state.

```
1. S: ESystem
2. ∀k:{k:ESystem| k < S}
     (∃N:{N:Node| N∈k} . {p:Proof| p proves asSequent(N)})
     ∨ {K:Kripke| ∃g:Node → Σ(K)
         ∀N:{N:Node| N∈k}
           ∀f:Formula. (f∈(T(N)) ⇒ forces(K,g(N),f))
                     ∧ (f∈(F(N)) ⇒ not_forces(K,g(N),f))}
⊢ (∃N:{N:Node| N∈S} . {p:Proof| p proves asSequent(N)})
  ∨ {K:Kripke| ∃g:Node → Σ(K)
      ∀N:{N:Node| N∈S}
        ∀f:Formula. (f∈(T(N)) ⇒ forces(K,g(N),f))
                  ∧ (f∈(F(N)) ⇒ not_forces(K,g(N),f))}
```

Thus, we may assume (by hypothesis 2) that there is either a proof or a Kripke counter example for eligible systems lexicographically below S. The recursive structure (the outermost `letrec`) of the extracted program (see Fig. 2) arises from this step of induction.

Consider the eligible system S decalred in hypothesis 1 above; either all nodes in S are node complete or not. This property is decidable and appears in the extracted program as the first if-then-else clause.

Consider the else case first, *i.e.* there exists some node N in S that is not node complete (`¬nComplete(N)`). Since eligible nodes are expanded in place by adding subformulas of formulas already occurring in S, the tableau expansion steps for these rules reduce the measure i2. The proof rules $\vee r1$, $\vee r2$, $\wedge l1$, and $\wedge l2$ correspond to local tableau steps and all have one premise. In these cases, the induction hypothesis is instantiated with the system constructed from S by extending the eligible node with subformulas as specified by the corresponding proof rule. The proof rules $\vee l$, $\wedge r$, and $\Rightarrow l$ all have two premises and so we instantiate two copies of the induction hypothesis; one with the system constructed by expanding the eligible node with the subformulas specified in the left premise of the corresponding proof rule; and the other with a system created by expanding the eligible node by adding subformulas as specified by the right premise of the corresponding rule. In each case, the result of instantiating the induction hypothesis is a new hypothesis asserting the existence of a node-proof pair system or a Kripke counter-example for the extended (and therefore lexicographically smaller) system. Whenever a Kripke counter-example exists, it serves to refute the S as well. In the case a node-proof pair results from the instantiated induction hypotheses, they are used to identify a node in S and to construct a proof for it. Instantiations of the induction hyptothesis in the proof generates a recursive call to the tableau procedure in the extract (Fig. 2). The computations corresponding to the seven local rules can be identified in the extract.

Suppose instead that there is no eligible node in S (this is the then-clause of the outermost if-then-else in the extracted program.) Either the system is system complete (`sComplete(S)`) or not. If it is not system complete then there is some node containing an occurrence of $\Rightarrow r$ (say of the form P⌜⇒⌝Q) which has not been accounted for in S, call this node N. In this case, decompose the induction hypothesis with the system constructed by extending S with a new node constructed from N which accounts for the application of the $\Rightarrow r$ rule. This new node is constructed by replacing `F(N)` with the single formula Q and by adding the formula P to the formulas in T(N) . This extended system is lower in the lexicographic ordering of systems since the measure i1 is reduced whenever a node is added to S. As above, the instantiation of the induction hypothesis results in a recursive call to the tableau procedure in the extracted program, which returns either a node-proof pair or a Kripke counter-example for the expanded system.

Finally, if all nodes are complete and the system is complete, then we are in the base case where one of a node-proof pair or a Kripke counter example is constructed directly without reference to the induction hypothesis. This is accounted for in the extract by a call to the extract of the lemma (decidability_base):

```
∀S:ESystem
    sComplete(S)
    ⇒ ∀N∈S.nComplete(N)
    ⇒ (∃N:{N:Node| N∈S} . {p:Proof| p proves asSequent(N)})
       ∨ {K:Kripke| ∃g:Node → Σ(K)
           ∀N:{N:Node| N∈S}
             ∀f:Formula. (f∈(T(N)) ⇒ forces(K,g(N),f))
                       ∧ (f∈(F(N)) ⇒ not_forces(K,g(N),f))}
```

If the system contains a node that, viewed as a sequent, is an instance of an axiom, then that node is returned paired with the instance of the axiom rule. If not, then a Kripke counter-model is constructed by applying the function K to the system (defined above in Section 4.4.)

This completes the proof of decidability in the intuitionistic case.

5.2 Remarks on the Extract

Figure 2 exhibits the extracted decision procedure. The program shown there has been symbolically transformed within Nuprl using the direct computation system to eliminate some unnecessary steps of computation. This mostly entails β-reducing occurrences of applications of the identity function. These transformations are entirely formal and since, by the semantics of Nuprl, direct computation is allowed anywhere within a term, they do not change the meaning of the program. The program has further been hand edited to format it and to rename unreadable system generated variable names. This is only for display.

6 Future Work

Study of the extracted program reveals that there is room for the introduction of abstractions which would both make the extracted program clearer and would result in a shorter proof. This process of tuning a proof by examination of the extract and of tuning the extract by studying the proof is an interesting part of the methodology of using a constructive system like Nuprl.

Integrating of the extracted decider for intuitionistic propositions into Nuprl is an immediate goal. However, if we are to preserve Nuprl's program extraction capabilities, this poses some problems. Nuprl's proof system is a single succedent sequent calculus. To repair the error in the ACU proof we have resorted to a multi-succedent calculus. Egly and Schmidtt [10] give cut-free translations of multi-succedent proofs into single succedent proofs which preserve reasonable extracts.

The program extracted here can easily be translated into ML and used as part of a tactic to decide propositional fragments of Nuprl's type theory. The resulting tactic would fail, returning the Kripke model as evidence against the validity of a formula should it turn out not to be valid; alternatively, it would use the formal proof returned by the decision procedure, in concert with the Egly

```
letrec tableau(S) =
  if ∀N∈S.nComplete(N) then
    if sComplete(S) then
      ext{decidability_base}(S)(·)(·)
    else let <N,a,b,mp,_> = (ext{not_system_complete}(S)(·)) in
            case tableau(<a::T(N), b::[]>::S)
            of inl(<N1,p1>) =>
              inl(if (N1 = <a::T(N), b::[]>)
                  then <N, let <p',_> =
                              (ext{imp_right_proof}
                                (N)(a)(b)(mp)(p1)(Ax)) in p'>
                  else <N1, p1>)
            | inr(K) => inr(K)
  else
    let <N,t> = (∃N:{N:Node | N∈S}. ¬nComplete(N))
      let <a,b,op_type> = (ext{not_node_complete}(N)(t)) in
        case op_type of inl(<_,V14>) => case V14
           of inl(_) =>
             case tableau(<a::T(N), F(N)>::remove(N;S))
             of inl(<N1,p1>) =>
               inl(if (N1 = <a::T(N), F(N)>)
                   then <N, mk_proof(N,<N1,p1>)>
                   else <N1, p1>)
             | inr(K) => inr(K)
           | inr(_) =>
               case tableau(<b::T(N), F(N)>::remove(N;S))
               of inl(<N1,p1>) =>
                 inl(if (N1 = <b::T(N), F(N)>)
                     then <N, mk_proof(N,<N1,p1>)>
                     else <N1, p1>)
               | inr(K) => inr K
        | inr(V13) => case V13
           of inl(_) =>
             case tableau(<a::T(N), F(N)>::remove(N;S))
             of inl(<N1,p1>) =>
                 if (N1 = <a::T(N), F(N)>) then
                   case tableau(<b::T(N), F(N)>::remove(N;S))
                   of inl(<N2,p2>) =>
                     inl(if (N2 = <b::T(N), F(N)>)
                          then <N, mk_proof(N,<N1,p1>,<N2,p2>)>
                          else <N2, p2>)
                   | inr(K) => inr(K)
                 else  inl(<N1, p1>)
             | inr(K) => inr(K)
| inr(V15) => case V15
    of inl(_) =>
      case tableau(<b::T(N),F(N)>::remove(N;S))
      of inl(<N1,p1>) =>
        if (N1 = <b::T(N), F(N)>) then
          case tableau(<T(N), a::F(N)>::remove(N;S))
          of inl(<N2,p2>) =>
            inl(if (N2 = <T(N), a::F(N)>)
                then <N, mk_proof(N,<N1,p1>,<N2,p2>)>
                else <N2, p2>)
          | inr(K) => inr(K)
        else  inl(<N1, N2>)
      | inr(K) => inr(K)
    | inr(V17) => case V17
        of inl(_) =>
          case tableau(<T(N), b::F(N)>::remove(N;S))
          of inl(<N1,p1>) =>
            if (N1 = <T(N), b::F(N)>) then
              case tableau(<T(N), a::F(N)>::remove(N;S))
              of inl(<N2,p2>) =>
                inl(if (N2 = <T(N), a::F(N)>)
                  then <N, mk_proof(N,<N2,p2>,<N1,p1>)>
                  else <N2, p2>)
              | inr(K) => inr(K)
            else inl(<N1, p1>)
          | inr(K) => inr(K)
        | inr(V19) => let <_,V21> = V19 in
              case V21
              of inl(_) =>
                case
                 tableau(<T(N), a::F(N)>::remove(N;S))
                of inl(<N1,p1>) =>
                  inl(if (N1 = <T(N), a::F(N)>)
                  then  <N, mk_proof(N,<N1,p1>)>
                  else <N1, p1>)
            | inr(K) => inr(K)
          | inr(_) =>
              case tableau(<T(N), b::F(N)>::remove(N;S))
              of inl(<N1,p1>) =>
                inl(if (N1 = <T(N), b::F(N)>)
                    then <N, mk_proof(N,<N1,p1>)>
                    else <N1, p1>)
              | inr(K) => inr(K)
```

Fig. 2. The extract of the decidiability proof

and Schmidtt procedure, to construct a Nuprl tactic, which it could then apply to discharge the goal.

Another line of development that needs to be explored is the reflection of this decision procedure into Nuprl. Reflection [2, 1] was the motivation for the proof outlined in [1].

References

1. William Aitken, Robert Constable, and Judith Underwood. Metalogical frameworks II: Using reflected decision procedures. *Unpublished Manuscript.*
2. Stuart F. Allen, Robert L. Constable, Douglas J. Howe, and William Aitken. The semantics of reflected proof. In *Proceedings of the Fifth Symposium on Logic in Computer Science*, pages 95–197. IEEE, June 1990.
3. E. W. Beth. *The Foundations of Mathematics.* North-Holland, 1959.
4. J. L. Caldwell. Classical propositional decidability via Nuprl proof extraction. In Jim Grundy and Malcolm Newey, editors, *Theorem Proving In Higer Order Logics*, volume 1479 of *Lecture Notes in Computer Science*, 1998.
5. James Caldwell. Moving proofs-as-programs into practice. In *Proceedings, 12th IEEE International Conference Automated Software Engineering*, pages 10–17. IEEE Computer Society, 1997.

6. James Caldwell. *Decidability Extracted: Synthesizing "Correct-by-Construction" Decision Procedures from Constructive Proofs.* PhD thesis, Cornell University, Ithaca, NY, August 1998.
7. Robert L. Constable, et al. *Implementing Mathematics with the Nuprl Proof Development System.* Prentice-Hall, Englewood Cliffs, New Jersey, 1986.
8. A. G. Dragalin. *Mathematical Intuitionism: Introduction to Proof Theory*, volume 67 of *Translations of Mathematical Monographs.* American Mathematical Society, 1987.
9. Michael Dummett. *Elements of Intuitionism.* Oxford Logic Series. Clarendon Press, 1977.
10. U. Egly and S. Schmitt. Intuitionistic proof transformations and their application to constructive program synthesis. In J. Calmet and J. Plaza, editors, *Proceedings of the 4th International Conference on Artificial Intelligence and Symbolic Computation (AISC'98)*, number 1476 in Lecture Notes in Artificial Intelligence, pages 132–144. Springer Verlag, Berlin, Heidelberg, New-York, 1998.
11. Melvin Fitting. *Proof Methods for Modal and Intuitionistic Logics*, volume 169 of *Synthese Library.* D. Reidel, 1983.
12. Susumu Hayashi and Hiroshi Nakano. *PX: A Computational Logic.* Foundations of Computing. MIT Press, Cambridge, MA, 1988.
13. J. Hudelmaier. A note on Kripkean countermodels for intuitionistically unprovable sequents. In W. Bibel, U. Furbach, R. Hasegawa, and M. Stickel, editors, *Seminar on Deduction*, February 1997. Dagstuhl report 9709.
14. C. Paulin-Mohring and B. Werner. Synthesis of ML programs in the system Coq. *Journal of Symbolic Computation*, 15(5-6):607–640, 1993.
15. L. Pinto and R. Dyckhoff. Loop-free construction of counter-models for intuitionistic propositional logic. In *Symposia Gaussiana*, pages 225–232, Berlin, New York, 1995. Walter de Gruyter and Co.
16. N Shankar. Towards mechanical metamathematics. *J. Automated Reasoning*, 1(4):407–434, 1985.
17. C. A. Smorynski. Applications of Kripke models. In A. Troelstra, editor, *Metamathematical Investigation of Intuitionistic Mathematics*, volume 344 of *Lecture Notes in Mathematics*, pages 324–391. Springer-Verlag, 1973.
18. J. Underwood. *Aspects of the Computational Content of Proofs.* PhD thesis, Cornell University, 1994.
19. Judith Underwood. The tableau algorithm for intuitionistic propositional calculus as a constructive completeness proof. In *Proceedings of the Workshop on Theorem Proving with Analytic Tableaux, Marseille, France*, pages 245–248, 1993.
20. Judith Underwood. Tableau for intuitionistic predicate logic as metatheory. In Peter Baumgartner, Reiner Hähnle, and Joachim Posegga, editors, *Theorem Proving with Analytic Tableaux and Related Methods*, volume 918 of *Lecture Notes in Artificial Intelligence.* Springer, 1995.
21. K. Weich. Decision procedures for intuitionistic propositional logic by program extraction.
22. K. Weich. Private communication. February 1998.

A Tableau-Based Decision Procedure for a Fragment of Set Theory Involving a Restricted Form of Quantification*

Domenico Cantone[1] and Calogero G. Zarba[2]

[1] Università di Catania, Dipartimento di Matematica,
Viale A. Doria 6, I-95125 Catania, Italy,
e-mail: `cantone@cs.unict.it`

[2] Stanford University, Computer Science Department,
Gates Building, Stanford CA 94305, USA,
e-mail: `zarba@theory.stanford.edu`

Abstract. We extend the unquantified set-theoretic fragment discussed in [1] with a restricted form of quantification, we prove decidability of the resulting fragment by means of a tableau calculus and we address the efficiency problem of the underlying decision procedure, by showing that the model-checking steps used in [1] are not necessary.

1 Introduction

In *Computable Set Theory*, a "core" decidable fragment is *Multi-Level Syllogistic* (in short **MLS**), namely the unquantified set-theory involving the constant $\emptyset$ (empty set), the operators $\cup$ (union), $\cap$ (intersection) and $\setminus$ (set difference), and the predicates $\in$ (membership), $=$ (equality) and $\subseteq$ (set inclusion). Its satisfiability decision problem was first solved in [7], the paper which started the research field of computable set theory.

Several extensions of **MLS** were proved decidable, among them *Multi-Level Syllogistic with Singleton* (in short **MLSS**), which extends **MLS** with the singleton operator $\{\bullet\}$. A decision procedure for **MLSS** was first stated as a tableau calculus in [4]. However, it was not until 1997 that the problem of *efficiently* deciding fragments of set-theory was seriously tackled, when a fast saturation strategy based on interleaving model-checking steps with saturation ones was introduced in [3] for a tableau calculus for **MLSS**.

In [1] another tableau calculus for **MLSS**, still based on the model-checking approach, was presented where formulae do not need to be expressed in a normalized form, in contrast to [3], where formulae need a preprocessing normalization phase. The same paper presented also a complete tableau calculus for the

* This work has been partially supported by the C.N.R. of Italy, coordinated project SETA, by M.U.R.S.T. Project "Tecniche speciali per la specifica, l'analisi, la verifica, la sintesi e la trasformazione di programmi", and by project "Deduction in Set Theory: A Tool for Software Verification" under the 1999 Vigoni Program.

fragment **MLSSF**, resulting from the extension of **MLSS** with uninterpreted function symbols. However, the tableau calculus for **MLSSF** presented in [1] is not a decision procedure, though a promising optimization based on the concept of rigid E-unification was given.

Recently, in [5] we have proposed a more efficient strategy which does not require the model-checking steps, though limited to the fragment **MLSS**. In this paper we apply and further improve the same idea of [5] to the larger fragment $\mathbf{MLSSF}^{\forall}$, which is obtained by extending **MLSSF** with a restricted form of quantification. In contrast with [1], we not only provide a sound and complete tableau calculus for $\mathbf{MLSSF}^{\forall}$, but even a practical saturation strategy which is guaranteed to terminate.

$\mathbf{MLSSF}^{\forall}$ is related to the theory presented in [2]. However, the decision procedure described there, which is not stated as a tableau calculus, is highly non-deterministic and not suitable for automation.

The paper is organized as follows. In Section 2 we introduce the syntax and semantics of $\mathbf{MLSSF}^{\forall}$ and we give also some examples to illustrate its expressive power. In Section 3 we present a tableau calculus for $\mathbf{MLSSF}^{\forall}$ and introduce some restrictions to the applicability of some of its rules to enforce termination. Soundness and completeness of the $\mathbf{MLSSF}^{\forall}$-tableau calculus is proved in Section 4. In Section 5 we discuss some optimizations of the $\mathbf{MLSSF}^{\forall}$-tableau calculus and make comparisons with those presented in [1] and [3]. Finally, in Section 6 we hint at some directions for future research.

2 Syntax and Semantics

The basic elements of the language of $\mathbf{MLSSF}^{\forall}$ are:

- denumerable many variables, denumerable many uninterpreted constants, and denumerable many uninterpreted unary function symbols;
- the interpreted constant $\emptyset$ (empty set), and the interpreted function symbols $\sqcup$ (union), $\sqcap$ (intersection), $-$ (set difference) and $[\bullet]$ (singleton);
- the interpreted predicate symbols $\sqsubset$ (membership) and $\approx$ (equality);
- the logical connectives $\neg$ and $\wedge$;[1]
- the universal quantifier symbol $\forall$.

To simplify notation, we use the abbreviations $s \not\sqsubset t$ and $s \not\approx t$ to denote $\neg(s \sqsubset t)$ and $\neg(s \approx t)$, respectively.

Next we define the fragment $\mathbf{MLSSF}^{\forall}$.

Definition 1. *An* $\mathbf{MLSSF}^{\forall}$*-formula* φ *is a logical formula in the language* $\mathbf{MLSSF}^{\forall}$ *such that each subformula of* φ *of type* $\forall x \sqsubset t : \psi$ *has a positive polarity*[2] *and moreover satisfies the following technical conditions:*

(A) t *is ground, and*

[1] In our treatment, $\neg\neg p$ is considered to be a syntactic variation of p.

[2] We recall that a subformula S of a formula F has a positive (resp. negative) polarity if it occurs within an even (resp. odd) number of negation symbols $\neg$.

(B) the variable x cannot be a proper subterm of a term t' in ψ such that
- *t' involves some interpreted symbols, or*
- *t' occurs on the left-hand side of a membership literal.*

Thus, for instance, if s and t are ground terms, then $\forall x \sqsubseteq t : f(x) \approx s$ and $s \approx t$ are **MLSSF**$^{\forall}$-formulae, whereas $\forall x \sqsubseteq t : [x] \approx s$, $\forall x \sqsubseteq t : f(x) \sqsubseteq s$, and $\forall x \sqsubseteq t : \forall y \sqsubseteq x : \varphi$ are not **MLSSF**$^{\forall}$-formulae. It is to be noticed that the decision problem for the fragment obtained from **MLSSF**$^{\forall}$ by dropping technical conditions (A) and (B) is still open.

Definition 2. *The* DEGREE *of an* **MLSSF**$^{\forall}$*-formula is the number of symbols occurring in it.*

Semantics of **MLSSF**$^{\forall}$ is based upon the von Neumann standard cumulative hierarchy $\mathcal{V}$ of sets defined by:

$$\begin{aligned} \mathcal{V}_0 &= \emptyset \\ \mathcal{V}_{\alpha+1} &= \mathcal{P}(\mathcal{V}_\alpha)\,, && \text{for each ordinal } \alpha \\ \mathcal{V}_\lambda &= \textstyle\bigcup_{\mu<\lambda} \mathcal{V}_\mu\,, && \text{for each limit ordinal } \lambda \\ \mathcal{V} &= \textstyle\bigcup_{\alpha\in\mathcal{O}} \mathcal{V}_\alpha\,, \end{aligned}$$

where $\mathcal{P}(S)$ is the power set of S and $\mathcal{O}$ denotes the class of all ordinals. It can easily be seen that there can be no membership cycle in $\mathcal{V}$, namely sets in $\mathcal{V}$ are well-founded with respect to the membership relation.

Definition 3. *A* SET MODEL *M interprets each constant c with a set c^M in $\mathcal{V}$, and each function symbol f with a function $f^M : \mathcal{V} \to \mathcal{V}$.*

An **MLSSF**$^{\forall}$*-formula φ is said to be* SATISFIABLE *if there exists a set model M such that, after interpreting the interpreted symbols occurring in an φ according to their standard meaning*[3] *and the uninterpreted ones according to M one obtains the truth-value* true. *We write $M \models \varphi$ to say that the set model M satisfies φ.*

2.1 Expressivity of MLSSF$^{\forall}$-formulae

A variety of interesting set-theoretic constructs can be expressed by means of **MLSSF**$^{\forall}$-formulae. Here we list some of them.

- $[x_1, \ldots, x_n] \equiv_{Def} [x_1] \sqcup \ldots \sqcup [x_n]$ (finite enumeration);
- the inclusion relation $s \sqsubseteq t$ can be expressed both by $s \sqcup t \approx t$ and by $\forall x \sqsubseteq s : x \sqsubseteq t$, but the latter is preferable for efficiency reasons, since it does not introduce new terms;

[3] Thus, for instance, $\sqcup$, $\sqcap$, $-$, $[\bullet]$, $\sqsubseteq$, and $\approx$ are interpreted as the set operators $\cup$, $\cap$, $\setminus$, $\{\bullet\}$, and as the set predicates $\in$ and $=$, respectively.

- the comprehension schema $c \approx [x \sqsubseteq t : P(x)]$ can be expressed by means of the $\mathbf{MLSSF}^{\forall}$-formula

$$(\forall x \sqsubseteq c : (x \sqsubseteq t \wedge P(x))) \wedge (\forall x \sqsubseteq t : (P(x) \rightarrow x \sqsubseteq c)),$$

  provided that t is ground and x is not used to form compound terms in $P(x)$, with the only exceptions allowed by Definition 1;
- some important function related constructs can be expressed:
  - $injective(f,t) \equiv_{Def} \forall x_1 \sqsubseteq t : \forall x_2 \sqsubseteq t : (f(x_1) \approx f(x_2) \rightarrow x_1 \approx x_2)$ (the restriction of f to t is injective);
  - $identity(f,t) \equiv_{Def} \forall x \sqsubseteq t : f(x) \approx x$ (the restrictions of f to t is the identity function over t);
  - $idempotent(f,t) \equiv_{Def} \forall x \sqsubseteq t : f(f(x)) \approx f(x)$ (the restriction of f to t is idempotent);
  - $equal(f,g,t) \equiv_{Def} \forall x \sqsubseteq t : f(x) \approx g(x)$ (the restrictions of f and g to t are equal);
  - $composition(f,g,h,t) \equiv_{Def} \forall x \sqsubseteq t : f(g(x)) \approx h(x)$ (h is equal to the function composition of f and g, when restricted to t);
  - $left\text{-}inverse(f,g,t) \equiv_{Def} \forall x \sqsubseteq t : g(f(x)) \approx x$ (g is a left-inverse of f, relative to t);
- by using Kuratowski's order pair $(a,b) \equiv_{Def} [[a],[a,b]]$, one can also express functions with multiple arguments; for instance, $f(a,b)$ could be considered as a shorthand for $f([[a],[a,b]])$.

It is to be noted, though, that the theory $\mathbf{MLSSF}^{\forall}$ is not expressive enough to force infinite models. This will follow as a by-product of the completeness proof.

Finally, we conclude by pointing out that in contrast to the language studied in [2], though the $\mathbf{MLSSF}^{\forall}$-language does not deal currently with the interpreted constants $\mathbb{N}$ and $\mathcal{O}$ (respectively the set of natural numbers and the class of all ordinals), on the other hand it allows, as shown above, to express predicates related to functions (such as *idempotent*, *composition*, and *left-inverse*) which are not expressible in [2].

3 The Tableau Calculus

The rules of the tableau calculus for $\mathbf{MLSSF}^{\forall}$ are listed in Table 3.

Next we define how to construct $\mathbf{MLSSF}^{\forall}$-tableaux.

Definition 4. *Let φ be an $\mathbf{MLSSF}^{\forall}$-formula. An* INITIAL TABLEAU *for φ is a tree with only one node labeled with φ.*

*An $\mathbf{MLSSF}^{\forall}$-*TABLEAU *for φ is a tableau labeled with $\mathbf{MLSSF}^{\forall}$-formulae, which can be constructed from an initial tableau for φ by a finite number of applications of rules (1)–(18) in Table 3.*

Closure conditions must take into account also the semantics of set theory, as the following definition indicates.

$$\frac{s \in t_1 \sqcup t_2}{s \in t_1 \mid s \in t_2}\ (1) \qquad \frac{s \in t_1}{s \in t_1 \sqcup t_2}\ (2) \qquad \frac{s \in t_2}{s \in t_1 \sqcup t_2}\ (3)$$

$$\frac{s \in t_1 \sqcap t_2}{\begin{array}{c} s \in t_1 \\ s \in t_2 \end{array}}\ (4) \qquad \frac{\begin{array}{c} s \in t_1 \\ s \in t_2 \end{array}}{s \in t_1 \sqcap t_2}\ (5) \qquad \frac{s \in t_1 - t_2}{\begin{array}{c} s \in t_1 \\ s \notin t_2 \end{array}}\ (6)$$

$$\frac{\begin{array}{c} s \in t_1 \\ s \notin t_2 \end{array}}{s \in t_1 - t_2}\ (7) \qquad \frac{s \in [t]}{s \approx t}\ (8) \qquad \frac{}{t \in [t]}\ (9)$$

$$\frac{\begin{array}{c} s \approx t \\ \ell \end{array}}{\begin{array}{c} \ell^s_t \\ \ell^t_s \end{array}}\ (10)^a \qquad \frac{\begin{array}{c} s_1 \in t \\ s_2 \notin t \end{array}}{s_1 \not\approx s_2}\ (11) \qquad \frac{t_1 \approx t_2}{f(t_1) \approx f(t_2)}\ (12)$$

$$\frac{t_1 \not\approx t_2}{\begin{array}{c|c} c \in t_1 & c \notin t_1 \\ c \notin t_2 & c \in t_2 \end{array}}\ (13)^b \qquad \frac{}{s \in t \mid s \notin t}\ (14) \qquad \frac{}{s \approx t \mid s \not\approx t}\ (15)$$

$$\frac{\varphi \wedge \psi}{\begin{array}{c} \varphi \\ \psi \end{array}}\ (16) \qquad \frac{\neg(\varphi \wedge \psi)}{\neg\varphi \mid \neg\psi}\ (17) \qquad \frac{\begin{array}{c} s \in t \\ \forall x \in t : \psi \end{array}}{\psi^x_s}\ (18)$$

[a] ℓ^s_t denotes the literal obtained from ℓ by substituting each occurrence of s in ℓ with t.
[b] c is a new uninterpreted constant not occurring in the branch to which the rule is applied

Table 1. Tableau calculus for $\mathbf{MLSSF}^{\forall}$

Definition 5. *A branch of an* $\mathbf{MLSSF}^{\forall}$*-tableau is closed if it contains two complementary formulae* φ, $\neg\varphi$, *or a membership cycle of the form* $t_0 \in t_1 \in \ldots \in t_0$, *or a literal of the form* $t \not\approx t$, *or a literal of the form* $s \in \emptyset$.

A tableau is CLOSED *if all its branches are closed.*

Notice that tableau rules (10) and (12), in combination with the fact that a branch containing the term $t \not\approx t$ is closed, are used to compute the congruence closure of the equality relation between the terms occurring in the branch.

3.1 Ensuring Termination

In order to force termination, some restrictions need to be imposed on the applicability of the rules in Table 3 during the construction of an $\mathbf{MLSSF}^{\forall}$-tableau.

Given an $\mathbf{MLSSF}^{\forall}$-tableau $\mathcal{T}$ for a formula φ, we make use of the following notation:

- $\mathcal{T}_\varphi$ denotes the collection of ground terms occurring in φ;
- $\mathcal{T}^{\theta}_{(13)}$ (resp. $\mathcal{T}^{\theta}_{(18)}$) denotes the collection of ground terms introduced on the branch θ of $\mathcal{T}$ by applications of rule (13) (resp. (18)).

We require that an $\mathbf{MLSSF}^{\forall}$-tableau is constructed according to the following restrictions.

R1. No new term can be created by applications of any rule other than (13) or (18). Thus, for instance, rule (2) can be applied to a branch θ of a tableau only if the term $t_1 \sqcup t_2$ occurs already in θ (not necessarily as a top-level term). Notice also that, by definition of $\mathbf{MLSSF}^{\forall}$-formulae, only terms of the form $f_1(\ldots f_n(c)\ldots)$, with c an uninterpreted constant, can be created by rule (18).
R2. In rule (10), ℓ stands for a literal, and the substituted term is restricted to be a *top-level* term occurring in ℓ.
R3. Rule (13) can be applied only if the terms t_1, t_2 are in $\mathcal{T}_\varphi$, and at most once for each such pair of terms.
R4. The cut rule (14) can be applied to the pair of terms s and t only if for some term t' the literal $s \sqsubseteq t'$ and one of the two terms $t' \sqcap t$ and $t' - t$ occur in the branch to which the rule is applied.
R5. The cut rule (15) can be applied only to pairs of terms s and t such that both $f(s)$ and $f(t)$ occur in the branch to which the rule is applied, for some function symbol f.
R6. Rule (18) can be applied to pairs of formulae $s \sqsubseteq t$ and $\forall x \sqsubseteq t : \psi$ occurring in a branch θ, provided that the term s is in $\mathcal{T}_\varphi \cup \mathcal{T}^{\theta}_{(13)}$.

Definition 6. *A branch of an* $\mathbf{MLSSF}^{\forall}$*-tableau is said to be* SATURATED *if no application of any rule subject to restrictions R1–R6 can add new formulae to it.*

3.2 Examples

Example 1. Figure 1 shows a proof of the unsatisfiability of the following $\mathbf{MLSSF}^{\forall}$-formula $(\forall x \sqsubseteq d - (a \sqcup b) : f(c \sqcup \emptyset) \sqsubseteq f(x)) \wedge (c \sqsubseteq (d-a) \sqcap (d-b))$ in the form of a closed tableau. Notice that x is the only variable in φ, whereas a, b, c and d are constants.

We denote with φ_i the formula labeling node i, and provide justifications for the construction of the tableau in Figure 1.

- φ_1 and φ_2 are obtained from φ_0 by means of rule (16);
- φ_3 and φ_4 are obtained from φ_2 by means of rule (4);
- φ_5, φ_6 and φ_7 are obtained from φ_3 and φ_4 by applying twice rule (6);
- φ_8 and φ_{11} are obtained by an application of the cut rule (14), according to restriction R4;

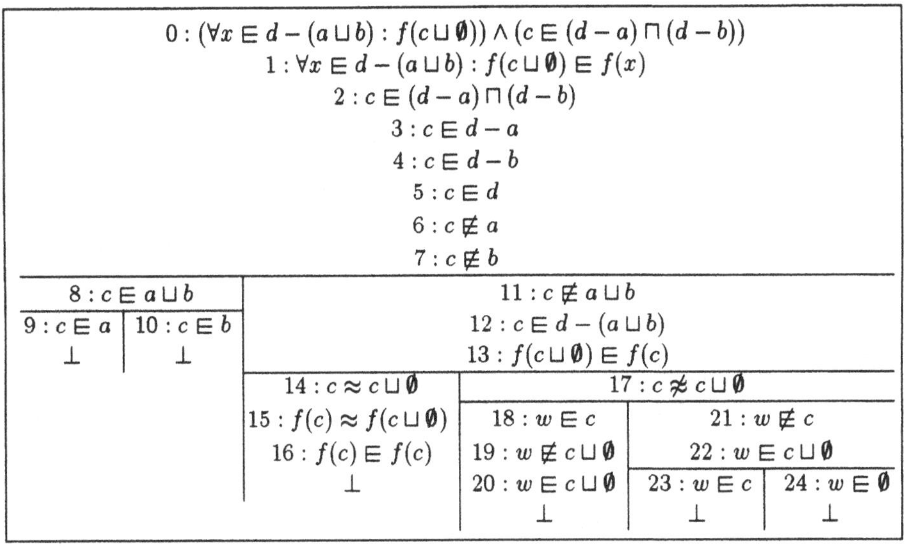

Fig. 1. A tableau proof

- φ_9 and φ_{10} are obtained from φ_8 by means of rule (1); the resulting branches are closed because they contain complementary literals;
- φ_{12} is obtained from φ_5 and φ_{11} by means of rule (7);
- φ_{13} is obtained from φ_1 and φ_{12} by means of rule (18);
- φ_{14} and φ_{17} are obtained by an application of the cut rule (15), according to restriction R5;
- φ_{15} is obtained from φ_{14} by means of rule (12);
- φ_{16} is obtained from φ_{15} by means of rule (10); the branch is closed for a membership cycle;
- $\varphi_{18}, \varphi_{19}, \varphi_{21}$ and φ_{22} are obtained from φ_{17} by means of rule (13);
- φ_{20} is obtained from φ_{18} by means of rule (2); the branch is closed because it contains two complementary literals;
- φ_{23} and φ_{24} are obtained from φ_{22} by means of rule (1); the left branch is closed because it contains two complementary literals, while the right one contains the contradiction $d \sqsubseteq \emptyset$.

Example 2. Figure 2 shows a tableau for the satisfiable formula $(\forall x \sqsubseteq a : x \sqsubseteq a \sqcup f(a)) \wedge (a \not\approx a \sqcup f(a))$.

The deductions can be justified as follows:

- φ_1 and φ_2 are obtained from φ_0 by means of rule (16);
- $\varphi_3, \varphi_4, \varphi_6$ and φ_7 are obtained from φ_2 by means of rule (13);
- φ_5 is obtained from φ_1 and φ_3 by means of rule (18). The branch is closed because it contains two complementary literals;
- φ_8 and φ_9 are obtained from φ_7 by means of rule (1). The left branch is closed because it contains two complementary literals.

<table>
<tr><td colspan="3" align="center">$0 : (\forall x \sqsubseteq a : x \sqsubseteq a \sqcup f(a)) \wedge (a \not\approx a \sqcup f(a))$
$1 : (\forall x \sqsubseteq a : x \sqsubseteq a \sqcup f(a))$
$2 : (a \not\approx a \sqcup f(a))$</td></tr>
<tr><td rowspan="2" align="center">$3 : w \sqsubseteq a$
$4 : w \not\sqsubseteq a \sqcup f(a)$
$5 : w \sqsubseteq a \sqcup f(a)$
$\bot$</td><td colspan="2" align="center">$6 : w \not\sqsubseteq a$
$7 : w \sqsubseteq a \sqcup f(a)$</td></tr>
<tr><td align="center">$8 : w \sqsubseteq a$
$\bot$</td><td align="center">$9 : w \sqsubseteq f(a)$</td></tr>
</table>

Fig. 2. A non-closed saturated tableau

We do not yet have all the tools needed to extract a model for φ from the non-closed and saturated rightmost branch in Figure 2, and therefore we postpone this task to the next section.

4 Proof of Correctness

Our main claim in the present section is that the tableau rules presented in Table 3, together with a strict saturation strategy restricted only by rules R1–R6 of Section 3.1, constitute a decision procedure for the theory $\mathbf{MLSSF}^{\forall}$. In order to do so, we need to show termination of any saturation strategy subject to restrictions R1–R6 and prove that the tableau calculus for the theory $\mathbf{MLSSF}^{\forall}$ is sound and complete (even in presence of restrictions R1–R6).

4.1 Termination

Termination is based on the following elementary lemma, whose proof is omitted for brevity.

Lemma 1. *Let T be a finite collection of ground terms and $n \in \mathbb{N}$. Then the number of $\mathbf{MLSSF}^{\forall}$-formulae of degree less than or equal to n which can be constructed using only terms in T is finite (up to renaming of bound variables).*

Now, let φ be an $\mathbf{MLSSF}^{\forall}$-formula having degree n. Also, let $\mathcal{T}$ be the tableau limit for φ constructed by means of rules (1)-(18) of Table 3, subject to restrictions R1–R6. If $\mathcal{T}$ were infinite, then, by König's lemma, it would have an infinite branch θ. In view of the preceding lemma, in order to reach a contradiction it is then enough to show that the number of terms occurring in θ is finite, since all formulae occurring in θ must have degree less than or equal to n. Indeed, terms occurring in θ can be partitioned into the classes $\mathcal{T}_{\varphi}$, $\mathcal{T}^{\theta}_{(13)}$ and $\mathcal{T}^{\theta}_{(18)}$, which have been defined in Section 3.1. Clearly $\mathcal{T}_{\varphi}$ is finite. Also, $|\mathcal{T}^{\theta}_{(13)}|$ is bounded by $|\mathcal{T}_{\varphi}|^2$, in view of restriction R3. Finally, restriction R6 implies that only terms in $\mathcal{T}_{\varphi} \cup \mathcal{T}^{\theta}_{(13)}$ can be "used" in applications of rule (18), implying that even $\mathcal{T}^{\theta}_{(18)}$ must be finite.

Thus, we have proved

Lemma 2. *For any* **MLSSF**$^{\forall}$*-formula* φ, *it is possible to construct in a finite number of steps a saturated tableau for* φ.

4.2 Soundness

Soundness of the **MLSSF**$^{\forall}$-calculus follows immediately by inspection of the rules in Table 3 and by observing that all closure conditions listed in Definition 5 are indeed unsatisfiable. Hence we have the following result

Lemma 3. *If an* **MLSSF**$^{\forall}$*-formula has a closed tableau then it is unsatisfiable.*

4.3 Completeness

As a technical tool we need to define the concept of realization, which will be used later to construct models satisfying open and saturated branches.

Definition 7. *The* REALIZATION *of a directed acyclic graph* $G = (N, \widehat{\in})$ *relative to a family of sets* $\{u_p : p \in P\}$ *and to a bipartition* (P, T) *of* N *is the function* $R : N \rightarrow \mathcal{V}$ *recursively defined by:*

$$\begin{aligned} Rp &= \{Rs : s \,\widehat{\in}\, p\} \cup \{u_p\} && \textit{for } p \textit{ in } P \\ Rt &= \{Rs : s \,\widehat{\in}\, t\} && \textit{for } t \textit{ in } T \end{aligned}$$

Remark 1. Notice that if the u_p's, for $p \in P$, are pairwise distinct elements chosen in such a way that $u_p \neq Rt$, for all p in P and t in $P \cup T$, then one has readily that $Rp \neq Rt$, for all p in P and t in $P \cup T$.

Next we define the function $h : N \rightarrow \mathbb{N}$ (called the HEIGHT), by putting:

$$h(t) = \begin{cases} 0 & \text{if } s \,\widehat{\notin}\, t, \text{ for all } s \in N \\ \max\{h(s) : s \,\widehat{\in}\, t\} + 1 & \text{otherwise.} \end{cases}$$

The following lemma states the main properties of realizations.

Lemma 4. *Let* $G = (P \cup T, \widehat{\in})$ *be a directed acyclic graph, with* $P \cap T = \emptyset$. *Also, let* $\{u_p : p \in P\}$ *and* R *be respectively a family of sets and the realization of* G *relative to* $\{u_p : p \in P\}$ *and* (P, T). *Assume also that* $u_p \neq Rt$, *for all* p *in* P *and* t *in* $P \cup T$. *Then the following properties hold:*

(i) if $s \,\widehat{\in}\, t$ *then* $h(s) < h(t)$, *for all* s, t *in* $P \cup T$;
(ii) if $Rt_1 = Rt_2$ *then* $h(t_1) = h(t_2)$, *for all* t_1, t_2 *in* $P \cup T$;
(iii) if $Rs \in Rt$ *then* $h(s) < h(t)$, *for all* s, t *in* $P \cup T$.

In our proof of completeness, we also rely on the following notation and terminology.

Definition 8. *To any open branch θ of a tableau $\mathcal{T}$ for an* **MLSSF$^{\forall}$**-*formula φ, we associate the following objects:*[4]

$\mathcal{T}_\varphi$: *the collection of all ground terms occurring in φ;*

$\mathcal{T}^\theta_{(13)}$: *the collection of all ground terms introduced on the branch θ of $\mathcal{T}$ by applications of rule (13);*

$\mathcal{T}^\theta_{(18)}$: *the collection of all ground terms introduced on the branch θ of $\mathcal{T}$ by applications of rule (18);*

P_θ: *the collection $\mathcal{T}^\theta_{(13)} \cup \mathcal{T}^\theta_{(18)}$;*

P'_θ: *the collection $\{t \in P_\theta :$ there is no t' in $\mathcal{T}_\varphi$ such that $t \approx t'$ occurs in $\theta\}$;*

$\mathcal{T}'_\theta$: *the set $\mathcal{T}_\varphi \cup (P_\theta \setminus P'_\theta)$;*

G_θ: *the oriented graph $(P'_\theta \cup \mathcal{T}'_\theta, \hat{\in})$, where $s \,\hat{\in}\, t$ if and only if the literal $s \in t$ occurs in θ;*

R_θ: *a realization of G_θ relative to the bipartition $(P'_\theta, \mathcal{T}'_\theta)$ and to sets u_t, for $t \in P'_\theta$, each satisfying the requirements that $u_t \neq R'_t$, for all t in P'_θ and t' in $P'_\theta \cup \mathcal{T}'_\theta$, and that $u_{t_1} = u_{t_2}$ if and only if the literal $t_1 \approx t_2$ occurs in θ;*[5]

M_θ: *the set model defined by $M_\theta c = R_\theta c$, for each uninterpreted constant c, and $f^M(a) = \{R_\theta s : s \in f(t)$ is in θ, for some term t such that $R_\theta t = a\} \cup \{u_{f(t)} : R_\theta t = a$ and $f(t) \in P'_\theta\}$, for each uninterpreted function symbol f and for each a in $\mathcal{V}$.*

Definition 9. *Given a branch θ of a tableau for φ, the realization R_θ is said to be* COHERENT *if $R_\theta t = M_\theta t$, for all t in $P_\theta \cup \mathcal{T}_\varphi$.*

Before entering into the details of the completeness proof, let us return to Example 2.

Example 2 (contd.). Let θ be the rightmost branch of the tableau shown in Figure 2. Since θ is open and saturated, it is possible to construct all the objects of Definition 8. In particular, we have $P'_\theta = \{w\}$ and $\mathcal{T}'_\theta = \{a, f(a), a \sqcup f(a)\}$. Then, chosen an opportune set u_w, we can construct R_θ and M_θ:

$$\begin{aligned} R_\theta w &= \{u_w\} \\ R_\theta a &= \emptyset \\ R_\theta(f(a)) &= \{R_\theta w\} = \{\{u_w\}\} \\ R_\theta(a \sqcup f(a)) &= \{R_\theta w\} = \{\{u_w\}\} \end{aligned} \qquad \begin{aligned} M_\theta w &= R_\theta w = \{\{u_w\}\} \\ M_\theta a &= R_\theta w = \emptyset \\ f^{M_\theta}(x) &= \begin{cases} \{\{u_w\}\} & \text{if } x = \emptyset \\ \emptyset & \text{otherwise} \end{cases} \end{aligned}$$

It can easily be checked that R_θ is coherent and that $M_\theta \models \theta$. This fact is not incidental: indeed we are going to prove that if ϑ is any open and saturated branch of an **MLSSF$^{\forall}$**-tableau, then the set model R_ϑ is coherent and M_ϑ satisfies ϑ.

[4] For completeness, we repeat here also the definitions of $\mathcal{T}_\varphi$, $\mathcal{T}^\theta_{(13)}$, and $\mathcal{T}^\theta_{(18)}$ which were given at the beginning of Section 3.1.

[5] It can easily be shown that it is always possible to choose such u_t's.

Returning to the completeness proof, let φ be an **MLSSF**$^{\forall}$-formula, and let $\mathcal{T}$ be a saturated tableau for it. If $\mathcal{T}$ is closed, we have already observed in Section 4.2 that φ must be unsatisfiable. So let us assume that $\mathcal{T}$ is not closed. Hence it must contain an open and saturated branch θ. To prove completeness, it is enough to show that φ must be satisfiable. In fact, we will show that the assignment M_θ must satisfy the open branch θ.

The following lemma can be proved by induction on the number of applications of rules (1)-(18) in Table 3.

Lemma 5. *If a literal $s \sqsubseteq t$ occurs in a branch θ and s is a term in $\mathcal{T}^{\theta}_{(18)}$, then there exists a term s' in $\mathcal{T}_\varphi \cup \mathcal{T}^{\theta}_{(13)}$ such that the literal $s \approx s'$ is in θ.*

We first show in the following lemma that the realization R_θ models correctly all literals in an open and saturated branch θ, provided that terms are just considered as "complex names" for constants (namely operators are not interpreted).

Lemma 6. *Let θ be an open and saturated branch in a tableau for φ. Then:*

(i) if $s \sqsubseteq t$ occurs in θ, then $R_\theta s \in R_\theta t$;
(ii) if $t_1 \approx t_2$ occurs in θ, then $R_\theta t_1 = R_\theta t_2$;
(iii) if $t_1 \not\approx t_2$ occurs in θ, then $R_\theta t_1 \neq R_\theta t_2$;
(iv) if $s \not\sqsubseteq t$ occurs in θ, then $R_\theta s \notin R_\theta t$.

Proof. (i) Immediate.

(ii) Let $t_1 \approx t_2$ but $R_\theta t_1 \neq R_\theta t_2$ and without loss of generality suppose that there is some a such that $a \in R_\theta t_1$ and $a \notin R_\theta t_2$. If $t_1 \in P'_\theta$ it might be the case that $a = u_{t_1}$, and, by construction of R_θ, t_2 would be in P'_θ and $u_{t_1} = u_{t_2}$ in $R_\theta t_2$. If instead that is not the case, or if t_1 is in $\mathcal{T}'_\theta$, then there exists an s such that $R_\theta s = a$ and $s \sqsubseteq t_1$ occurs in θ. Since θ is saturated, $s \sqsubseteq t_2$ must also occur in θ, and by (i) $a = R_\theta s \in R_\theta t_2$, a contradiction.

(iii) Let $t_1 \not\approx t_2$ be in θ but $R_\theta t_1 = R_\theta t_2$. Without loss of generality we can assume that $t_1, t_2 \in \mathcal{T}_\varphi$, because otherwise θ would contain a literal $t'_1 \not\approx t'_2$ with t'_1, t'_2 in $\mathcal{T}_\varphi$ and such that $t_1 \approx t'_1$ and $t_2 \approx t'_2$ are in θ; then $t'_1 \not\approx t'_2$ could play the role of $t_1 \not\approx t_2$ in the following discussion (notice that if t_1 (resp. t_2) were in P'_θ then t_1 (resp. t_2) would contain among its elements a distinctive set u_{t_1} (resp. u_{t_2}) which would force $Rt_1 \neq Rt_2$). By Lemma 4 we have $h(t_1) = h(t_2)$. We proceed by induction on $h(t_1)$. In the base case ($h(t_1) = 0$) we reach a contradiction, since by saturation there is some s such that either $s \sqsubseteq t_1$ and $s \not\sqsubseteq t_2$ occur in θ, or $s \not\sqsubseteq t_1$ and $s \sqsubseteq t_2$ occur in θ, and we would have $h(t_1) > 0$ in either cases. For the inductive step, without loss of generality let $s \sqsubseteq t_1$ and $s \not\sqsubseteq t_2$ be in θ (their occurrence is due to saturation with respect to rule (13)), for some s. Then $R_\theta s \in R_\theta t_1$, which implies $R_\theta s \in R_\theta t_2$, so that by construction of R_θ there exists an s' such that $R_\theta s = R_\theta s'$ and $s' \sqsubseteq t_2$ occurs in θ. Notice that $s' \neq s$ (otherwise θ would be closed). Since by Lemma 4 we have $h(s) = h(s') < h(t_1)$, we can apply the induction hypothesis and obtain the contradiction $R_\theta s \neq R_\theta s'$.

(iv) Let $s \not\sqsubseteq t$ be in θ but $R_\theta s \in R_\theta t$. As $R_\theta s \neq u_p$, for $p \in P_\theta$, then there exists an s' different from s such that $R_\theta s = R_\theta s'$ and $s' \sqsubseteq t$ occurs in θ. By saturation $s \not\approx s'$ is in θ, and by (iii) $R_\theta s \neq R_\theta s'$, a contradiction.

Next we show that even operators are correctly modeled by R_θ (and therefore by M_θ), for an open and saturated branch θ.

Lemma 7. *Let θ be an open and saturated branch in a tableau for φ. Then the realization R_θ is coherent.*

Proof. Let θ be an open and saturated branch. We prove that $R_\theta t = M_\theta t$, for each t in $P_\theta \cup \mathcal{T}_\varphi$, by structural induction on t. The base case is trivial for uninterpreted constants. Concerning $\mathbf{\emptyset}$, notice that trivially $M_\theta \mathbf{\emptyset} = \emptyset$ and that $R_\theta \mathbf{\emptyset} = \emptyset$, since θ is open. For the inductive step we only prove that (a) $R_\theta(t_1 \sqcap t_2) = M_\theta(t_1 \sqcap t_2)$ and (b) $R_\theta(f(t)) = M_\theta(f(t))$ (other cases are similar).

Concerning (a), suppose that $a \in R_\theta(t_1 \sqcap t_2)$. Then there exists a term s such that $R_\theta s = a$ and $s \sqsubseteq t_1 \sqcap t_2$ occurs in θ. Since θ is saturated both $s \sqsubseteq t_1$ and $s \sqsubseteq t_2$ occur in θ. By Lemma 6, $R_\theta s \in R_\theta t_1$ and $R_\theta s \in R_\theta t_2$, and by induction hypothesis $a \in M_\theta t_1 \cap M_\theta t_2 = M_\theta(t_1 \sqcap t_2)$. Conversely, if $a \in M_\theta(t_1 \sqcap t_2)$ then $a \in M_\theta t_1 \cap M_\theta t_2$, and by induction hypothesis $a \in R_\theta t_1 \cap R_\theta t_2$. After noticing that, because of the restrictions imposed to the application of the rules, it must be the case that $t_1, t_2 \in \mathcal{T}'_\theta$, it follows that there exist s', s'' such that $R_\theta s' = R_\theta s'' = a$ and both $s' \sqsubseteq t_1$ and $s'' \sqsubseteq t_2$ occur in θ. By saturation, either $s' \sqsubseteq t_2$ or $s' \not\sqsubseteq t_2$ occurs in θ. In the former case $s' \sqsubseteq t_1 \sqcap t_2$ occurs in θ, and therefore $a \in R_\theta(t_1 \sqcap t_2)$. In the latter case $s' \not\approx s''$ occurs in θ, and therefore $R_\theta s' \neq R_\theta s''$, a contradiction.

Concerning (b), suppose that $a \in R_\theta(f(t))$. If $a = u_{f(t)}$ (which may happen only if $f(t) \in P'_\theta$) then, by construction of f^{M_θ}, $a \in f^{M_\theta}(R_\theta t)$, and by induction hypothesis $a \in f^{M_\theta}(M_\theta t) = M_\theta(f(t))$. Otherwise, there exists a term s such that $R_\theta s = a$ and $s \sqsubseteq f(t)$ occurs in θ. By definition of f^{M_θ}, $a \in f^{M_\theta}(R_\theta t)$ and, again by induction hypothesis, $a \in f^{M_\theta}(M_\theta t) = M_\theta(f(t))$. Conversely, if $a \in M_\theta(f(t))$ then $a \in f^{M_\theta}(M_\theta t)$, and by induction hypothesis $a \in f^{M_\theta}(R_\theta t)$. Now there are two cases to consider: (b_1) there exists a term t' such that $R_\theta t = R_\theta t'$ and $a = u_{f(t')}$, and (b_2) there exist terms s, t' such that $R_\theta s = a, R_\theta t = R_\theta t'$ and the literal $s \sqsubseteq f(t')$ is in θ. In case (b_1), by saturation, either $t \approx t'$ occurs in θ (and the claim would hold since $u_{f(t)} = u_{f(t')}$ and $u_{f(t)} \in R_\theta f(t)$), or $t \not\approx t'$ occurs in θ (which would lead to a contradiction). In case (b_2), by saturation either $t \approx t'$ or $t \not\approx t'$ occurs in θ. In the former case $f(t) \approx f(t')$ is in θ, as well as $s \sqsubseteq f(t)$, and therefore $a \in R_\theta(f(t))$. In the latter case $R_\theta t \neq R_\theta t'$, a contradiction.

The following lemma concludes the proof of completeness.

Lemma 8. *If θ is an open and saturated branch in a tableau for φ, then it is satisfiable, and indeed it is satisfied by M_θ.*

Proof. First notice that, by combining together Lemmas 6 and 7, it follows that $M \models \ell$, for each literal ℓ occurring in θ. Proceeding by induction on the degree of formulae in θ, it is easy to see that even formulae of the form $p \wedge q$ and $\neg(p \wedge q)$ are satisfied by M_θ. Therefore, it remains to show that each formula of the form $\forall x \sqsubseteq t : \varphi$ is satisfied by M_θ (notice that formulae of the form $\neg(\forall x \sqsubseteq t : \varphi)$ cannot occur in θ).

Thus, suppose by contradiction that a formula $\forall x \sqsubseteq t : \psi$ is in θ, but $M_\theta \not\models \forall x \sqsubseteq t : \psi$. Then there exists a set $a \in M_\theta t$ such that $M_\theta^{\{x \mapsto a\}} \not\models \psi$.[6] Since, by Lemma 7, R_θ is coherent, we have $a \in R_\theta t$ and therefore there exists a term s such that $R_\theta s = a$ and the literal $s \sqsubseteq t$ occurs in θ. Without loss of generality we can suppose that $s \in \mathcal{T}_\varphi \cup \mathcal{T}_{(13)}$ (otherwise, by Lemma 5 there would be a term s in $\mathcal{T}_\varphi \cup \mathcal{T}_{(13)}$ such that the literal $s \approx s'$ would be in θ, and s' would play the role of s in the following discussion). By saturation φ^x_s is in θ and by induction hypothesis $M_\theta \models \varphi^x_s$. But this is a contradiction since basic model properties and the fact that $M_\theta s = a$ yield that $M_\theta^{\{x \mapsto a\}} \not\models \varphi$ and $M_\theta \models \varphi^x_s$ cannot both hold simultaneously.

Summing up, we have proved

Theorem 1. *The tableau calculus for* **MLSSF**$^\forall$ *is complete, even if subject to restrictions R1–R6.*

5 Efficiency Issues

We first discuss some possible optimizations to the tableau calculus presented in the previous sections. Then, we compare our approach with those used in [1] and [3].

5.1 Minimizing the Branching Factor

It is possible to considerably lower the branching factor of a tableau constructed by means of the rules (1)-(18) of Table 3 by adopting the **KE** calculus, a tableau calculus with analytic cut introduced in [6]. As noticed in [6], Smullyan's tableaux suffer some anomalies. These can be solved by adopting an approach based on the calculus **KE**, which forces branches to be mutually exclusive andSmullyan's tableaux. Let us now show how the splitting rules (1), (13), and (17) in Table 3 can be redesigned, in order to make branches mutually exclusive (notice that cut rules (14) and (15) do not need to be changed). It is not difficult to fix rule (1), by substituting it with the rules

$$\frac{s \sqsubseteq t_1 \sqcup t_2 \qquad s \not\sqsubseteq t_1}{s \sqsubseteq t_2} \qquad\qquad \frac{s \sqsubseteq t_1 \sqcup t_2 \qquad s \not\sqsubseteq t_2}{s \sqsubseteq t_1}$$

[6] $M^{\{x \mapsto a\}}$ denotes the set model identical to M with the possible exception of x, which is modeled by a.

and by requiring the application of the cut rule (15) when a formula of the form $s \sqsubseteq t_1 \sqcup t_2$ is in a branch θ, but neither $s \sqsubseteq t_1$ nor $s \sqsubseteq t_2$ is in θ. While rule (17) can be handled in a similar way, rule (13) is more challenging. In the subfragment **MLSSF** there is no clear way of how to solve the problem in a simple and elegant manner. In fact, one could think to substitute rule (13) with, for instance,

$$\frac{t_1 \not\approx t_2}{\begin{array}{l|l} c \sqsubseteq t_1 & c \not\sqsubseteq t_1 \\ c \not\sqsubseteq t_2 & c \sqsubseteq t_2 \\ & t_1 \sqcup t_2 \approx t_2 \end{array}}$$

But doing so a new term $t_1 \sqcup t_2$ is introduced, and termination would be in jeopardy (or, at least, more difficult to prove). Instead, using the expressiveness of $\mathbf{MLSSF}^{\forall}$, one can substitute rule (13) with

$$\frac{t_1 \not\approx t_2}{\begin{array}{l|l} c \sqsubseteq t_1 & c \not\sqsubseteq t_1 \\ c \not\sqsubseteq t_2 & c \sqsubseteq t_2 \\ & \forall x \sqsubseteq t_1 : x \sqsubseteq t_2 \end{array}}$$

without generating new terms, therefore ensuring termination, and fully achieving our purposes to solve the anomalies of Smullyan's tableaux in the spirit of the **KE** calculus.

5.2 Model Checking or Exhaustive Saturation?

A legitimate question about the comparison between the interleaving model-checking approach used in [1, 3] and the exhaustive approach used in this paper and in [5] is *"does the new approach really do less work than the previous one?"* We claim that the new approach does not require more applications of split rules than the previous one. Moreover, useful cuts can be decided more efficiently. In fact, notice that

- the applications of rule (1), (or the corresponding cut rules required if one wishes to use the **KE** approach) correspond to rule (R7) in [1], and to rule (3) in [3];
- the applications of rule (17) correspond to the β-propositional schema given in [1]. There is no corresponding rule in [3], since there only *conjunctions of normalized literals* were considered;
- the applications of rule (13) hinted by restriction R3 (cf. Section 3.1) correspond to rule (R12) in [1] and to rule (12) in [3];
- literals of the form $s \not\sqsubseteq t_1 \sqcap t_2$ and $s \not\sqsubseteq t_1 - t_2$ do not trigger any split rule, in contrast to rules (R8) and (R9) in [1].

Roughly speaking, the cuts that in the previous approach were triggered by the model-checking steps correspond to the applications of the cut rule (14) hinted by restriction R4. (The part relative to the set difference operator – closely reminds rule (11) in [3]). Therefore, we can expect that the size of the tableau built with the new approach is not greater than the size of the tableau built with the old approach. Now, which is the new cost for deciding cuts? In the previous approach, deciding a cut is very costly, since one has to build a model and verify that the model satisfies the branch. Instead, in the new approach it is possible to decide more efficiently which cut to apply, provided that suitable information is collected in the linear saturation phase.[7] For instance, it could be enough to maintain a list L of *pending cuts* of the form

- $t_1 \not\approx t_2$, for rule (13),
- $s \sqsubseteq ?\, t$, for rule (14),
- $t_1 \approx ?\, t_2$, for rule (15),

and then the following high-level code

if $s \sqsubseteq t_1$ is in θ **or** $s \sqsubseteq t_2$ is in θ **then**
  skip
else if $s \not\sqsubseteq t_1$ is in θ **then**
  $\theta := \theta \cup (s \sqsubseteq t_2)$
else if $s \not\sqsubseteq t_2$ is in θ **then**
  $\theta := \theta \cup (s \sqsubseteq t_1)$
else
  $L := L \cup (s \sqsubseteq ?\, t_1)$
end if

could be called during the linear saturation phase when a literal $s \sqsubseteq t_1 \sqcup t_2$ occurs in a branch θ (other types of literals could be handled similarly). When θ is linearly saturated, and possibly after a closure check, it is enough to choose arbitrarily an element from L and apply the relative cut rule.

6 Conclusion and Future Developments

We have presented a sound and complete tableau calculus for the fragment $\mathbf{MLSSF}^{\forall}$, which extends **MLSSF** with a restricted form of quantification. We have also provided a saturation strategy which is guaranteed to terminate. The basic idea is the same as in [5], but applied to a more general case.

We plan to extend our approach to admit also the constants $\mathbb{N}$ and $\mathcal{O}$, which allow one to state interesting facts about natural numbers and ordinals (cf. [2]). We also plan to extend our approach to other fragments of set theory (cf. [4]).

[7] The linear saturation phase consists in the exhaustive application of all the rules in Table 3 except the splitting ones.

Acknowledgments

The authors wish to thank Tomás E. Uribe for helpful comments and Nikolaj S. Bjørner for insightful discussions. The second author wishes to thank Prof. Zohar Manna for having given him the opportunity to visit his REACT group.

References

1. B. Beckert and U. Hartmer. A tableau calculus for quantifier-free set theoretic formulae. In Harrie de Swart, editor, *Proceedings of the International Conference on Automated Reasoning with Analytic Tableaux and Related Methods, Oisterwijk, The Netherlands*, volume 1397 of *LNAI*, pages 93–107. Springer-Verlag, 1998.
2. M. Breban, A. Ferro, E. G. Omodeo, and J. T. Schwartz. Decision procedures for elementary sublanguages of set theory. I. Formulas involving restricted quantifiers, together with ordinals, integer, map and domain notions. *Comm. Pure Appl. Math.*, 34:177–195, 1981.
3. D. Cantone. A fast saturation strategy for set-theoretic tableaux. In Didier Galmiche, editor, *Proceedings of the International Conference on Automated Reasoning with Analytic Tableaux and Related Methods*, volume 1227 of *LNAI*, pages 122–137. Springer-Verlag, May 1997.
4. D. Cantone and A. Ferro. Techniques of computable set theory with applications to proof verification. *Comm. Pure Appl. Math.*, XLVIII:1–45, 1995.
5. D. Cantone and C. G. Zarba. A new fast decision procedure for an unquantified fragment of set theory. In *International Workshop in First-Order Theorem Proving FTP '98*, 1998.
6. M. D'Agostino and M. Mondadori. The taming of the cut. Classical refutations with analytic cut. *Journal of Logic and Computation*, 4(3):285–319, June 1994.
7. A. Ferro, E. G. Omodeo, and J. T. Schwartz. Decision procedures for elementary sublanguages of set theory. II. Multilevel syllogistic and some extensions. *Comm. Pure Appl. Math.*, 33:599–608, 1980.

Bounded Contraction in Systems with Linearity

Agata Ciabattoni

Dipartimento di Informatica: University of Milano. Via Comelico, 39, Milano, Italy
ciabatto@dsi.unimi.it

Abstract. The aim of this work is to perform a proof-theoretical investigation of some propositional logics underlying either finite-valued Gödel logic or finite-valued Łukasiewicz logic. We define cut-free hypersequent calculi for logics obtained by adding either the n-contraction law or the n-weak law of excluded middle to affine intuitionistic linear logic with the linearity axiom $(A \rightarrow B) \vee (B \rightarrow A)$. We also develop cut-free calculi for the classical counterparts of these logics. Moreover we define a hypersequent calculus for $Ł_3 \cap Ł_4$ in which the cut-elimination theorem holds. This calculus allows to define an alternative axiomatization of $Ł_4$ making no use of the Łukasiewicz axiom.

1 Introduction

In this paper we develop cut-free calculi for some propositional logics underlying either finite-valued Gödel logic or finite-valued Łukasiewicz logic.

In most of the logics considered here, the contraction law does not hold. This entails the splitting of the connectives "and" and "or" of classical logic CL into lattice (or additive[1]) connectives $\wedge$ and $\vee$, and monoidal (or multiplicative) connectives $\odot$ and $\oplus$. Moreover the truth values of all these logics are always linearly ordered.

All the logics we consider are extensions of the affine intuitionistic linear logic (without exponential connectives) a-MAILL[2], also known as H_{BCK} [15] or monoidal logic [12], with the linearity axiom $(A \rightarrow B) \vee (B \rightarrow A)$. Let A^n be an abbreviation of $A \odot \ldots \odot A$ (n times). By extending the aforementioned system by either the n-contraction law $A^n \rightarrow A^{n-1}$ or the n-weak law of excluded middle $A \vee \neg A^{n-1}$, with $n \geq 2$, one gets two families of systems, respectively denoted IC_n and IW_n. IC_2 coincides with Gödel logic while IW_2 is CL. We also consider the classical counterparts of IC_n and IW_n. We respectively denote by CC_n and CW_n the logics obtained by adding to IC_n and IW_n the law of double negation $\neg\neg A \rightarrow A$. CC_2 and CW_2 coincide with CL while CW_3 turns out to be 3-valued Łukasiewicz logic. CW_n is the system W_n, investigated in [7], with the linearity axiom. For $n > 3$ both CC_n and CW_n, are proper subsystems of n-valued Łukasiewicz logic $Ł_n$.

[1] The terminology is due to [9].

[2] a-MAILL stands for the Multiplicative Additive fragment of Intuitionistic Linear Logic [9] enriched with weakening rules.

In [17] Prijatelj considered related systems, namely, a-MAILL and a-MALL[3] with the n-contraction law. In [13] MAILL with $A^n \to A^k$, for $k > 0$, and $k \neq n$, is investigated. In both papers, the authors provided a Gentzen style formulation for these systems, lacking, however, the analiticity property.

In this paper we develop calculi for IC_n, IW_n, CC_n, and CW_n in which the cut-elimination theorem holds. These calculi are in the form of hypersequent calculi.

Both a-MAILL and a-MALL have natural formulations in terms of Gentzen calculi, see e.g. [15,18,9]. On the other hand, the linearity axiom can be enforced on a given sequent calculus by transferring it to a hypersequent calculus see [6] in analogy to Avron's work on Gödel logic [3]. Here we define some suitable hypersequent rules allowing to prove the n-contraction law and the n-weak law of excluded middle in both the intuitionistic and classical contraction-free contexts, thus obtaining cut-free calculi for IC_n, IW_n, CC_n and CW_n.

Finally, by adding a new rule to the hypersequent calculus for a-MALL extended by the 4-weak law of excluded middle [7] we define a cut-free calculus for $Ł_3 \cap Ł_4$. This calculus can be seen as a step forward to find a cut-free hypersequent calculus for $Ł_4$. Moreover it allows to define an alternative axiomatization for $Ł_4$ making no use of the Lukasiewicz axiom $((A \to B) \to B) \to ((B \to A) \to A)$.

2 Hypersequent Calculi

Hypersequent calculi are a simple and natural generalization of ordinary Gentzen calculi, see e.g. [1,2,4,3,5].

Definition 1. A *hypersequent* is an expression of the form $\Gamma_1 \vdash \Delta_1 | \cdots | \Gamma_n \vdash \Delta_n$, where for all $i = 1, \ldots n$, $\Gamma_i \vdash \Delta_i$ is an ordinary sequent. $\Gamma_i \vdash \Delta_i$ is called a *component* of the hypersequent. We say that a hypersequent is *single-conclusion* if for any $i = 1, \ldots, n$, Δ_i consists of at most one formula, otherwise the hypersequent is said to be *multiple-conclusion.*

The intended meaning of the symbol | is disjunctive. For the purposes of this paper it is convenient to treat sequents and hypersequents as multisets of formulas and multisets of sequents, respectively.

Like in ordinary sequent calculi, in a hypersequent calculus there are initial hypersequents and rules, which are divided into *logical* and *structural rules.* The logical ones are essentially the same as in sequent calculi, the only difference being the presence of dummy contexts, called *side hypersequents.* We will use the symbol G to denote a side hypersequent.

The structural rules are divided into *internal* and *external rules.* The former deal with formulas within components. If they are present, they are the same as in ordinary sequent calculi. The external rules manipulate whole components

[3] a-MALL stands for the Multiplicative Additive fragment of Linear Logic extended by weakening rules.

within a hypersequent. These are external weakening (EW) and contraction (EC). For instance, the hypersequent calculus for a-MALL is the following:

$$(id)\quad A \vdash A \qquad\qquad (cut)\quad \frac{G|\Gamma \vdash \Delta, A \qquad G'|A, \Gamma' \vdash \Delta'}{G|G'|\Gamma, \Gamma' \vdash \Delta, \Delta'}$$

Internal Structural Rules

$$(w,l)\quad \frac{G|\Gamma \vdash \Delta}{G|\Gamma, B \vdash \Delta} \qquad\qquad (w,r)\quad \frac{G|\Gamma \vdash \Delta}{G|\Gamma \vdash \Delta, B}$$

External Structural Rules

$$(EW)\quad \frac{G|\Gamma \vdash \Delta}{G|\Gamma \vdash \Delta|\Gamma' \vdash \Delta'} \qquad\qquad (EC)\quad \frac{G|\Gamma \vdash \Delta|\Gamma \vdash \Delta}{G|\Gamma \vdash \Delta}$$

Multiplicative fragment

$$(\oplus,l)\quad \frac{G|\Gamma, A \vdash \Delta \qquad G'|\Gamma', B \vdash \Delta'}{G|G'|\Gamma, \Gamma', A \oplus B \vdash \Delta, \Delta'} \qquad\qquad (\oplus,r)\quad \frac{G|\Gamma \vdash \Delta, A, B}{G|\Gamma \vdash \Delta, A \oplus B}$$

$$(\odot,l)\quad \frac{G|\Gamma, A, B \vdash \Delta}{G|\Gamma, A \odot B \vdash \Delta} \qquad\qquad (\odot,r)\quad \frac{G|\Gamma \vdash \Delta, A \qquad G'|\Gamma' \vdash \Delta', B}{G|G'|\Gamma, \Gamma' \vdash \Delta, \Delta', A \odot B}$$

$$(\rightarrow,l)\quad \frac{G|\Gamma \vdash \Delta, A \qquad G'|\Gamma', B \vdash \Delta'}{G|G'|\Gamma, \Gamma', A \rightarrow B \vdash \Delta, \Delta'} \qquad\qquad (\rightarrow,r)\quad \frac{G|\Gamma, A \vdash \Delta, B}{G|\Gamma \vdash \Delta, A \rightarrow B}$$

Additive fragment

$$(\vee,l)\quad \frac{G|\Gamma, A \vdash \Delta \qquad G'|\Gamma, B \vdash \Delta}{G|G'|\Gamma, A \vee B \vdash \Delta} \qquad\qquad (\vee,r_i)\quad \frac{G|\Gamma \vdash \Delta, A_i}{G|\Gamma \vdash \Delta, A_1 \vee A_2}\ \text{for } i = 1,2$$

$$(\wedge,l_i)\quad \frac{G|\Gamma, A_i \vdash \Delta}{G|\Gamma, A_1 \wedge A_2 \vdash \Delta} \qquad\qquad (\wedge,r)\quad \frac{G|\Gamma \vdash \Delta, A \qquad G'|\Gamma \vdash \Delta, B}{G|G'|\Gamma \vdash \Delta, A \wedge B}$$

$$(\neg,l)\quad \frac{G|\Gamma \vdash A, \Delta}{G|\Gamma, \neg A \vdash \Delta} \qquad\qquad (\neg,r)\quad \frac{G|\Gamma, A \vdash \Delta}{G|\Gamma \vdash \Delta, \neg A}$$

The above calculus is redundant, in the sense that if a hypersequent $\Gamma_1 \vdash \Delta_1|\ldots|\Gamma_k \vdash \Delta_k$ is derivable, then, for some $i \in \{1,\ldots,k\}$, $\Gamma_i \vdash \Delta_i$ is derivable too.

A hypersequent calculus for a-MAILL is obtainable by the single-conclusion version of the above calculus for a-MALL.

In hypersequent calculi it is possible to define new structural rules which simultaneously act on several components of one or more hypersequents. It is this type of rule which increases the expressive power of hypersequent calculi with respect to ordinary sequent calculi.

Effective use of this kind of rules is given by the following examples:

- The Hilbert-style axiomatization of the LQ logic is obtained by extending the axioms of IL with $\neg A \vee \neg\neg A$. A cut-free calculus for this logic is defined by adding the following rule to the hypersequent calculus for IL.

$$(lq)\quad \frac{G|\Gamma, \Gamma' \vdash}{G|\Gamma \vdash |\Gamma' \vdash}\quad [7]$$

- By extending the hypersequent calculus for a-MALL with either

$$(M)\quad \frac{G|\Gamma_1, \Gamma_2, \Gamma_3 \vdash \Delta_1, \Delta_2, \Delta_3 \qquad G'|\Gamma_1', \Gamma_2', \Gamma_3' \vdash \Delta_1', \Delta_2', \Delta_3'}{G|G'|\Gamma_1, \Gamma_1' \vdash \Delta_1, \Delta_1'|\Gamma_2, \Gamma_2' \vdash \Delta_2, \Delta_2'|\Gamma_3, \Gamma_3' \vdash \Delta_3, \Delta_3'}\quad [2] \quad \text{or}$$

$$(3\text{–weak})\quad \frac{G|\Sigma, \Gamma_1 \vdash \Delta_1, \Pi \qquad G'|\Sigma, \Gamma_2 \vdash \Delta_2, \Pi}{G|G'|\Gamma_1, \Gamma_2 \vdash \Delta_1, \Delta_2|\Sigma \vdash \Pi}\quad [7]$$

one gets a cut-free calculus for 3-valued Łukasiewicz logic.

– By adding the following rule

$$(com)\quad \frac{G|\Gamma,\Gamma' \vdash A \quad G'|\Gamma_1,\Gamma_1' \vdash A'}{G|G'|\Gamma,\Gamma_1 \vdash A|\Gamma',\Gamma_1' \vdash A'} \quad [3]$$

to the hypersequent calculus for IL one obtains a cut-free calculus for Gödel logic.

As shown in [6], cut-elimination in a single-conclusion sequent calculus entails cut-elimination in the corresponding hypersequent calculus extended with the (com) rule. As an immediate consequence, the cut rule is eliminable in the hypersequent calculus for a-MAILL with the (com) rule.

Let us consider the following generalization of the (com) rule to a multiple-conclusion hypersequent calculus:

$$(lin)\quad \frac{G|\Gamma,\Gamma' \vdash \Delta,\Delta' \quad G'|\Gamma_1,\Gamma_1' \vdash \Delta_1,\Delta_1'}{G|G'|\Gamma,\Gamma_1 \vdash \Delta,\Delta_1|\Gamma',\Gamma_1' \vdash \Delta',\Delta_1'}$$

It is not hard to see that the hypersequent calculus for a-MALL with the (lin) rule admits cut-elimination.

3 Bounded Contraction in Intuitionistic Systems with linearity

In this section we define cut-free hypersequent calculi for the systems IC_n and IW_n, with $n \geq 2$, respectively obtained by adding either the n-contraction law $A^{n-1} \to A^n$ or the n-weak law of excluded middle $A \vee \neg A^{n-1}$, to the Hilbert-style axiomatization of a-MAILL (see e.g. [18]) with $(A \to B) \vee (B \to A)$. The only rule of inference is modus ponens.

Definition 2. $\mathcal{M} = (M, \cdot, \Rightarrow, \wedge, \vee, \neg, 1, 0, \bot, \top)$ is an *intuitionistic linear algebra* (IL-algebra for short), see [18], if:

1. $(M, \cdot, 1)$ is a commutative monoid with unit element 1;
2. $(M, \wedge, \vee, \bot, \top)$ is a lattice with bottom $\bot$ and top $\top$;
3. $\cdot$ and $\Rightarrow$ are monotone with respect to the lattice order $\leq$, that is, for every $a, b, c \in M$ if $a \leq b$ then $a \cdot c \leq b \cdot c$ and $b \Rightarrow c \leq a \Rightarrow c$;
4. for every $a, b, c \in M, a \cdot b \leq c$ iff $a \leq b \Rightarrow c$;
5. $\neg a$ coincides with $a \Rightarrow 0$.

IL-algebras are a semantical counterpart of MAILL.

In an IL-algebra we have $a \Rightarrow b \geq 1$ if and only if $a \leq b$.

Definition 3. $\mathcal{M} = (M, \cdot, \Rightarrow, \wedge, \vee, \neg, 1, 0, \bot, T)$ is an *ILa-algebra* if it is an IL-algebra with the additional property:

$$\text{(w)}\quad \bot = 0 \quad \text{and} \quad \top = 1.$$

As is well known, from a deductive point of view, condition (w) corresponds to the presence of weakening rules in the associated sequent calculus.

Lemma 4. *In all ILa-algebras, for every $a, b \in M$, the following conditions hold:* (1) $a \cdot b \leq a \wedge b$ *and* (2) $a \cdot b \leq a$.

ILa-algebras are also known as *integral commutative residuated l-monoids* [12].

Lemma 5. *The class of all ILa-algebras forms a variety.*

Definition 6. An ILa_{lin}*-algebra* is an ILa-algebra satisfying

$$\text{(linearity)} \quad (a \Rightarrow b) \vee (b \Rightarrow a) = 1.$$

Let a^n be an abbreviation of $a \cdot \ldots \cdot a$ (n times). An $ILa_{lin}^{c_n}$*-algebra* is an ILa_{lin}-algebra such that

$$(n\text{-contraction}) \quad a^{n-1} \leq a^n.$$

An $ILa_{lin}^{w_n}$*-algebra* is an ILa_{lin}-algebra satisfying the additional condition

$$(n\text{-weak}) \quad a \vee \neg a^{n-1} = 1.$$

Remark 7. An $ILa_{lin}^{c_n}$-algebra is an IPL_n^a*-algebra* [17] satisfying the (linearity) condition. A *BL-algebra* [11] is an ILa$_{lin}$-algebra such that $a \wedge b = a \cdot (a \Rightarrow b)$.

Proposition 8. *IC_n and IW_n are respectively characterized by the class of all totally ordered $ILa_{lin}^{c_n}$ and $ILa_{lin}^{w_n}$-algebras.*

Proof. By Birkhoff's Theorem, one can show that IC_n (respectively, IW_n) is characterized by the class of all subdirectly irreducible ILa-algebras satisfying the (linearity) and the (n-contraction) (respectively, the (n-weak)) condition. Since in any subdirectly irreducible ILa-algebra $x \vee y = 1$ implies $x = 1$ or $y = 1$, see [14], the claim follows.

Definition 9. Given an $ILa_{lin}^{c_n}$-algebra $\mathcal{M}$. An *evaluation* v is a mapping $v : Var \to M$, where Var is the set of variables of the logic, which can be extended to formulas as follows:

$$\begin{array}{rr} v(\neg A) = \neg v(A) & v(0) = 0 \quad v(1) = 1 \\ v(A \to B) = v(A) \Rightarrow v(B) & v(A \odot B) = v(A) \cdot v(B) \\ v(A \vee B) = v(A) \vee v(B) & v(A \wedge B) = v(A) \wedge v(B). \end{array}$$

We say that a formula P is true in $\mathcal{M}$ if for all evaluations v on $\mathcal{M}$, $v(P) = 1$. A formula is $ILa_{lin}^{c_n}$*-valid* if it is true in every $ILa_{lin}^{c_n}$-algebra.

A sequent $\Gamma \vdash B$, where $\Gamma = A_1, \ldots, A_k$ is true in an $ILa_{lin}^{c_n}$-algebra $\mathcal{M}$ if the formula $A_1 \odot \ldots \odot A_k \to B$ is true in $\mathcal{M}$. Moreover we stipulate that $\Gamma \vdash$ and $\vdash B$ are true in $\mathcal{M}$ if so are $\Gamma \Rightarrow 0$ and $1 \Rightarrow B$, respectively.

A hypersequent $G_1 | \ldots | G_m$ is true in an $ILa_{lin}^{c_n}$-algebra $\mathcal{M}$ iff $v(G_1) \vee \ldots \vee v(G_m)$ is true in $\mathcal{M}$.

The same applies to $ILa_{lin}^{w_n}$-algebra.

Definition 10. For $n \geq 2$, the hIC_n calculus is obtained by adding the following rule

$$(ic_n)\ \frac{G_1|\Gamma, \overbrace{A_1, \ldots, A_1}^{n \text{ times}} \vdash B \quad \ldots \quad G_{n-1}|\Gamma, \overbrace{A_{n-1}, \ldots, A_{n-1}}^{n \text{ times}} \vdash B}{G_1|\ldots|G_{n-1}|\Gamma, A_1, \ldots, A_{n-1} \vdash B}$$

and the (com) rule to the hypersequent calculus for a-MAILL.

Note that (ic_2) is the internal contraction rule. Thus hIC_2 coincides with the calculus for Gödel logic introduced in [3].

We show that hIC_n is sound and complete with respect to validity in $ILa_{lin}^{c_n}$-algebras.

Theorem 11 (Soundness). *If a hypersequent H is derivable in hIC_n, then it is valid in all $ILa_{lin}^{c_n}$-algebras.*

Proof. By induction on the length of a derivation of H. By Proposition 8 it suffices to show that the rules of hIC_n are true in all totally ordered $ILa_{lin}^{c_n}$-algebras. It is an easy exercise for the reader to check that so are the (com) rule and the rules of the hypersequent calculus for a-MAILL. We will only show the soundness of the (ic_n) rule. To simplify the notation we can safely assume that there are no side hypersequents.

Let $\mathcal{M}$ be a totally ordered $ILa_{lin}^{c_n}$-algebra and v any interpretation. By hypothesis, $v(\Gamma) \cdot v(A_i)^n \leq v(B)$, for every $i = 1, \ldots, n-1$. We have to show that $v(\Gamma) \cdot v(A_1) \cdot \ldots \cdot v(A_{n-1}) \Rightarrow v(B) = 1$. If $v(A_m) = \max\{v(A_j) \mid j = 1, \ldots, n-1\}$, then $v(\Gamma) \cdot v(A_1) \cdot \ldots \cdot v(A_{n-1}) \leq v(\Gamma) \cdot v(A_m)^{n-1} = v(\Gamma) \cdot v(A_m)^n \leq v(B)$. Thus $v(\Gamma) \cdot v(A_1) \cdot \ldots \cdot v(A_{n-1}) \Rightarrow v(B) = 1$.

Theorem 12 (Completeness). *If a formula P is $ILa_{lin}^{c_n}$-valid, then $\vdash P$ is derivable in hIC_n.*

Proof. As usual we show that the Lindenbaum algebra M_n, determined by hIC_n, is an $ILa_{lin}^{c_n}$-algebra. The M_n algebra is constructed in the standard way: For any two formulas A and B of the language $\mathcal{L}$, we set $A \approx_n B$ iff $A \vdash B$ and $B \vdash A$ are both derivable in hIC_n. Then $\approx_n$ is a congruence relation. For each n, $M_n = (S_n, \cdot, \Rightarrow, \wedge, \vee, \neg, 0, 1)$, where S_n is $\mathcal{L}_{/\approx_n}$, and the operations are defined in the natural way:

$$\neg[A]_{\approx_n} := [\neg A]_{\approx_n}$$
$$[A]_{\approx_n} \Rightarrow [B]_{\approx_n} := [A \rightarrow B]_{\approx_n} \quad [A]_{\approx_n} \cdot [B]_{\approx_n} := [A \odot B]_{\approx_n}$$
$$[A]_{\approx_n} \wedge [B]_{\approx_n} := [A \wedge B]_{\approx_n} \quad [A]_{\approx_n} \vee [B]_{\approx_n} := [A \vee B]_{\approx_n}$$

$$1 := \{A \mid \vdash A \text{ is derivable in } hIC_n\} \quad 0 := \{A \mid A \vdash \text{ is derivable in } hIC_n\}.$$

It is not hard to prove that M_n is an $ILa_{lin}^{c_n}$-algebra. We only show the identity $[A^{n-1}]_{\approx_n} \Rightarrow [A^n]_{\approx_n}$. By definition, this identity holds if and only if the formula

$A^{n-1} \to A^n$ is derivable in hIC_n. The following derivation yields the desired result:

$$\dfrac{\dfrac{\dfrac{\dfrac{A \vdash A \quad \dots \quad A \vdash A}{\overbrace{A, \dots, A}^{n \text{ times}} \vdash A^n} \quad \dots\dots \quad \dfrac{A \vdash A \quad \dots \quad A \vdash A}{\overbrace{A, \dots, A}^{n \text{ times}} \vdash A^n}}{A, \dots, A \vdash A^n}\,(ic_n)}{A^{n-1} \vdash A^n}}{\vdash A^{n-1} \to A^n}$$

In [3] (or [6]) it is shown how to derive the linearity axiom.

If a formula P is $ILa^{c_n}_{lin}$-valid, then in particular P is true in M_n and $v(P) = 1$, under the canonical evaluation v, defined as $v(P) = [P]_{\approx_n}$. This implies that $P \in 1$, so that $\vdash P$ is derivable in hIC_n.

We show that the cut rule is eliminable in hIC_n:

Theorem 13. *If $G|\Gamma \vdash A$ and $G'|\Gamma', A \vdash B$ are provable in hIC_n, then so is $G|G'|\Gamma, \Gamma' \vdash B$.*

Proof. Cut elimination for hypersequent calculi works essentially in the same way as for the corresponding sequent calculi.

In order to deal with the (ic_n) rule we prove something stronger: that is if $G|\Gamma \vdash A$ and $G'|\Gamma', A^k \vdash B$ are provable, then so is $G|G'|\Gamma^k, \Gamma' \vdash B$, where A^k stands for $A, \dots, A$ (k times).

One way to make the inductive argument work in presence of the (EC) rule, is to consider the number of the applications of this rule in a given derivation as an independent parameter. The proof will proceed by induction on lexicographically-ordered triples of integers (r, c, h), where r is the number of applications of the (EC) rule in the proofs of the premises of the cut rule, c is the complexity of the cut formula, and h is the sum of the length of the proofs of the premises of the cut rule. It suffices to consider the following cases according to which inference rule is being applied just before the application of the cut rule:

1. either $G|\Gamma \vdash A$ or $G'|\Gamma', A^k \vdash B$ is an initial hypersequent, that is of the form $A \vdash A$
2. either $G|\Gamma \vdash A$ or $G'|\Gamma', A^k \vdash B$ is derived from a structural rule
3. both $G|\Gamma \vdash A$ and $G'|\Gamma', A^k \vdash B$ are lower sequents of some logical rules such that the cut formula is the principal formula of both rules.

We will give here a proof for some relevant cases, omitting the side hypersequents that are not involved in the derivation.

Suppose that the last inference in the proof of one premise of the cut is the (EC) rule, i.e.,

$$\dfrac{\dfrac{\Gamma \vdash A | \Gamma \vdash A}{\Gamma \vdash A}\,(EC) \qquad A, \Gamma' \vdash B}{\Gamma', \Gamma \vdash B}\,(cut)$$

Let r be the number of applications of the (EC) rule in the above proof. This proof can be replaced by

$$\dfrac{\dfrac{\dfrac{\Gamma \vdash A | \Gamma \vdash A \quad A, \Gamma' \vdash B}{\Gamma, \Gamma' \vdash B | \Gamma \vdash A}(cut) \qquad A, \Gamma' \vdash B}{\Gamma', \Gamma \vdash B | \Gamma', \Gamma \vdash B}(cut)}{\Gamma', \Gamma \vdash B}(EC)$$

which contains two cuts with $r-1$ applications of the (EC) rule. Then these cuts can be eliminated by induction hypothesis.

Suppose that the last inference in the proof of one premise of the cut is the (ic_n) rule and the proof ends as follows:

$$\dfrac{\dfrac{\Gamma, \overbrace{A_1, \ldots, A_1}^{n \text{ times}} \vdash B \quad \ldots \quad \Gamma, \overbrace{A_{n-1}, \ldots, A_{n-1}}^{n \text{ times}} \vdash B}{\Gamma, A_1, \ldots, A_{n-1} \vdash B}(ic_n) \qquad \Gamma' \vdash A_1}{\Gamma, \Gamma', A_2, \ldots, A_{n-1} \vdash B}(cut)$$

This proof can be replaced by:

$$\dfrac{\dfrac{\Gamma, \overbrace{A_1, \ldots, A_1}^{n \text{ times}} \vdash B \quad \Gamma' \vdash A_1}{\Gamma, \overbrace{\Gamma', \ldots, \Gamma'}^{n \text{ times}} \vdash B}(cut) \quad \ldots \quad \Gamma, \overbrace{A_{n-1}, \ldots, A_{n-1}}^{n \text{ times}} \vdash B}{\Gamma, \Gamma', A_2, \ldots, A_{n-1} \vdash B}(ic_n)$$

where the cut has been shifted upward, whence it can be eliminated by induction hypothesis.

In [3] it is shown how to eliminate cuts involving the (com) rule. The remaining cases can be treated as in the corresponding sequent calculi.

Remark 14. One can show that, for every $n \geq 2$, the *n-contraction rule*

$$(LC_n) \quad \dfrac{\Gamma, \overbrace{A, \ldots, A}^{n \text{ times}} \vdash B}{\Gamma, \underbrace{A, \ldots, A}_{n-1 \text{ times}} \vdash B} \quad [17]$$

is derivable in hIC_n. However, in contrast to our systems hIC_n, by adding the (LC_n) rules to the sequent calculus for a-MAILL, one obtains a family of calculi in which the cut rule is not eliminable. Indeed, in [16] it was shown that in these calculi, for any $n > 2$, the sequent $A, (B \to A)^{n-1}, (B \to A) \to ((B \to A) \to \ldots \to (B \to A) \to C) \ldots) \vdash C$, where $(B \to A)$ occurs n times in the indicated subformula of the antecedent, provides a counterexample for cut-elimination.

Remark 15. In [13] the extensions of MAILL with the so called ***knotted structural rules*** are discussed. For every $n \neq k$ and $k > 0$, each knotted structural rule has the following form:

$$(n,k)\quad \frac{\Gamma, \overbrace{A, \ldots, A}^{n \text{ times}} \vdash B}{\Gamma, \underbrace{A, \ldots, A}_{k \text{ times}} \vdash B}\quad [13]$$

The (LC_n) rule is a particular case of the (n, k) rule. The latter is a restricted form of the weakening rule when $n < k$, and of the contraction rule when $n > k$. In [13] it was proved that in the sequent calculus for MAILL extended by the (n, k) rule, the cut-elimination theorem holds if and only if $k = 1$.

For every $n \neq k$ and $k > 0$, let us consider the following rule, obtained by slightly modifiying the (ic_n) rule of Definition 10:

$$(ic_k^n)\quad \frac{\Gamma, \overbrace{A_1, \ldots, A_1}^{n \text{ times}} \vdash B \quad \ldots \quad \Gamma, \overbrace{A_k, \ldots, A_k}^{n \text{ times}} \vdash B}{\Gamma, A_1, \ldots, A_k \vdash B}$$

If we add to the sequent calculus for MAILL the (ic_k^n) rule we can derive (n, k). It easy to see that in this calculus the cut-elimination theorem holds for every $n, k \geq 1$.

Definition 16. For $n \geq 2$, the hIW_n calculus is obtained by adding the following rule to the hypersequent calculus for a-MAILL with the (com) rule

$$(iw_n)\quad \frac{G_1|\Gamma, A_1 \vdash B \quad \ldots \quad G_{n-1}|\Gamma, A_{n-1} \vdash B}{G_1|\ldots|G_{n-1}|A_1, \ldots, A_{n-1} \vdash |\Gamma \vdash B}$$

(iw_2) turns out to coincide with the (cl) rule introduced in [7] (see also [5]). Then hIW_2 is a (single-conclusion) hypersequent calculus for CL.

We show that hIW_n is sound and complete with respect to validity in $ILa_{lin}^{w_n}$-algebras.

Theorem 17 (Soundness). *If a hypersequent H is derivable in hIW_n, then it is $ILa_{lin}^{w_n}$-valid.*

Proof. We argue as in Theorem 11. As an example, we show the soundness of the (iw_n) rule with respect to all totally ordered $ILa_{lin}^{c_n}$-algebras. By hypothesis, $v(A_i) \cdot v(\Gamma) \leq v(B)$, for every $i = 1, \ldots, n-1$. We have to show that either $v(A_1) \cdot \ldots \cdot v(A_{n-1}) \leq 0$ or $v(\Gamma) \leq v(B)$. Let $v(A_m) = \max\{v(A_j) \mid j = 1, \ldots n-1\}$. Then $(*)$ $v(A_1) \cdot \ldots \cdot v(A_{n-1}) \leq v(A_m)^{n-1}$. By the $(n-\text{weak})$ condition there are two cases: $v(A_m) = 1$ or $v(A_m)^{n-1} = 0$. In the first case, from $v(A_m)\dot{v}(\Gamma) \leq v(B)$ it follows $v(\Gamma) \leq v(B)$. In the second case, from $(*)$ we have $v(A_1) \cdot \ldots \cdot v(A_{n-1}) \leq 0$.

Theorem 18 (Completeness). *If a formula P is $ILa^{w_n}_{lin}$-valid, then $\vdash P$ is derivable in hIW_n.*

Proof. The proof proceeds as in Theorem 12. We show how to derive the formula $A \vee \neg A^{n-1}$:

$$\dfrac{\dfrac{\dfrac{\dfrac{\dfrac{A \vdash A \quad \ldots \quad A \vdash A}{\vdash A|A, \ldots, A \vdash}\,(iw_n)}{\vdash A|A^{n-1} \vdash}}{\vdash A| \vdash \neg A^{n-1}}}{\vdash A \vee \neg A^{n-1}| \vdash A \vee \neg A^{n-1}}}{\vdash A \vee \neg A^{n-1}}$$

The following result shows that the cut is eliminable in hIW_n.

Theorem 19. *If $G|\Gamma \vdash A$ and $G'|\Gamma', A \vdash B$ are provable in hIW_n, so is $G|G'|\Gamma, \Gamma' \vdash B$.*

Proof. The proof is similar to the one for hIC_n. We only show how to eliminate a cut involving the (iw_n) rule

$$\dfrac{\dfrac{\Gamma, A_1, A \vdash B \quad \ldots \quad \Gamma, A_{n-1}, A \vdash B}{A_1, \ldots, A_{n-1} \vdash |\Gamma, A \vdash B} \qquad \Gamma' \vdash A}{A_1, \ldots, A_{n-1} \vdash |\Gamma, \Gamma' \vdash B}$$

This proof can be replaced by a proof having $n-1$ cuts in which the sum of the length of the proofs in the premises is smaller than in the above cut:

$$\dfrac{\dfrac{\Gamma, A_1, A \vdash B \quad \Gamma' \vdash A}{\Gamma, \Gamma', A_1 \vdash B} \quad \ldots \quad \dfrac{\Gamma, A_{n-1}, A \vdash B \quad \Gamma' \vdash A}{\Gamma, \Gamma', A_{n-1} \vdash B}}{A_1, \ldots, A_{n-1} \vdash |\Gamma, \Gamma' \vdash B}$$

Then these cuts can be eliminated by induction hypothesis.

Remark 20. It is easy to see that, for every $n \geq 2$, hIC_n is a proper subsystem of hIW_n.

4 Bounded Contraction in Classical Systems with linearity

This section is devoted to investigate the classical counterparts of IC_n and IW_n. We define cut-free hypersequent calculi for systems CC_n and CW_n, with $n \geq 2$, respectively obtained by adding either the n-contraction law $A^{n-1} \rightarrow A^n$ or the n-weak law of excluded middle $A \vee \neg A^{n-1}$, to a-MALL with the axiom $(A \rightarrow B) \vee (B \rightarrow A)$. CW_n is the system W_n considered in [7] plus the linearity axiom. By comparing their calculi, it is easy to see that, for every $n \geq 3$, CC_n is a proper subsystem of CW_n.

As we mentioned in the introduction, both CC_n and CW_n are subsystems of n-valued Lukasiewicz logic $Ł_n$. In the particular case $n = 3$, W_3 (and then CW_3) coincides with 3-valued Lukasiewicz logic, see [7].

By extending the calculus for W_4 with a new rule, we shall define a cut free hypersequent calculus for $Ł_3 \cap Ł_4$. This calculus allows to define an alternative Hilbert-style axiomatization of $Ł_4$ making no use of the Lukasiewicz axiom.

Definition 21. An IL-algebra is a *classical linear algebra* (CL-algebra for short) if for every $a \in M, \neg\neg a = a$.

CL-algebras are a semantical counterpart of MALL, see [18].

Definition 22. A *CLa-algebra* is a CL-algebra satisfying condition (w) in Definition 3. CLa_{lin}, $CLa_{lin}^{c_n}$ and $CLa_{lin}^{w_n}$*-algebras* are obtained, respectively, by adding to the ILa_{lin}, $ILa_{lin}^{c_n}$ and $ILa_{lin}^{w_n}$-algebras of Definition 6, $\neg\neg a = a$.

In CL-algebras one defines $a + b = \neg(\neg a \cdot \neg b)$. Thus the ($n-$contraction) and ($n-$weak) conditions can be respectively expressed, dually, as $na \leq (n-1)a$ and $\neg a \vee (n-1)a = 1$ where $na = a + \ldots + a$ (n times).

Remark 23. The W_n-algebras [7] are CLa-algebras satisfying the ($n-$weak) condition. MV-algebras, that are the algebraic models of infinite-valued Lukasiewicz logic (see, e.g., [8]) are CLa-algebras satisfying in addition $a \wedge b = a \cdot (a \Rightarrow b)$.

Proposition 24. *CC_n and CW_n are respectively characterized by the class of all totally ordered $CLa_{lin}^{c_n}$ and $CLa_{lin}^{w_n}$-algebras.*

The semantic notions are the same as in Definition 9. They are extended to multiple-conclusion hypersequent calculi as follows:

A sequent $\Gamma \vdash \Delta$, where $\Gamma = A_1, \ldots, A_k$ and $\Delta = B_1, \ldots, B_m$ is true in a $CLa_{lin}^{c_n}$-algebra (respectively, in a $CLa_{lin}^{w_n}$-algebra) $\mathcal{M}$ if the formula $A_1 \odot \ldots \odot A_k \to B_1 \oplus \ldots \oplus B_m$ is true in $\mathcal{M}$, where $v(A \oplus B) = v(A) + v(B)$.

Definition 25. For $n \geq 2$, the hCC_n calculus is obtained by adding the (cc_n) rule below to the hypersequent calculus for a-MALL with the (lin) rule:

$$\frac{G_1|\Gamma, \overbrace{A_1, \ldots, A_1}^{n \text{ times}} \vdash \overbrace{B_1, \ldots, B_1}^{n \text{ times}}, \Delta \quad \ldots \quad G_{n-1}|\Gamma, \overbrace{A_{n-1}, \ldots, A_{n-1}}^{n \text{ times}} \vdash \overbrace{B_{n-1}, \ldots, B_{n-1}}^{n \text{ times}}, \Delta}{G_1|\ldots|G_{n-1}|\Gamma, A_1, \ldots, A_{n-1} \vdash B_1, \ldots, B_{n-1}, \Delta}$$

We show that hCC_n is sound and complete with respect to validity in $CLa_{lin}^{c_n}$-algebras.

Theorem 26 (Soundness). *If a hypersequent H is derivable in hCC_n, then it is $CLa_{lin}^{c_n}$-valid.*

Proof. We argue as in the proof of Theorem 11. We only show the soundness of the (cc_n) rule with respect to all totally ordered $CLa_{lin}^{c_n}$-algebras. By hypothesis for every $i = 1, \ldots n-1$, $v(\Gamma) \cdot v(A_i)^n \leq nv(B_i) + v(\Delta)$, that is $\neg v(\Gamma) + n\neg v(A_i) + nv(B_i) + v(\Delta) = 1$. Let $\neg v(A_m) + v(B_m) = \min\{\neg v(A_j) + v(B_j) \mid j = 1, \ldots, n-1\}$, thus $1 \leq \neg v(\Gamma) + n\neg v(A_m) + nv(B_m) + v(\Delta) \leq \neg v(\Gamma) + (n-1)\neg v(A_m) + (n-1)v(B_m) + v(\Delta) \leq \neg v(\Gamma) + \neg v(A_1) + \ldots + \neg v(A_{n-1}) + v(B_1) + \ldots + v(B_{n-1}) + v(\Delta)$.

Theorem 27 (Completeness). *If a formula P is $CLa_{lin}^{c_n}$-valid, then $\vdash P$ is derivable in hCC_n.*

Proof. The proof is similar to the one of Theorem 12.

The cut rule is eliminable in hCC_n.

Theorem 28. *If both $G|\Gamma \vdash A, \Delta$ and $G'|\Gamma', A \vdash \Delta'$ are provable in hCC_n, then so is $G|G'|\Gamma, \Gamma' \vdash \Delta, \Delta'$.*

Proof. By a straightforward adaptation of the proof for hIC_n, keeping into account the fact that we have now to deal with multiple-conclusion hypersequents.

In [7] it was proved that the hW_n calculus, with $n \geq 2$, obtained by adding to the hypersequent calculus for a-MALL the following rule:

$$(n\text{-}weak) \quad \frac{G_1|\Gamma, A_1 \vdash B_1, \Delta \quad \ldots \quad G_{n-1}|\Gamma, A_{n-1} \vdash B_{n-1}, \Delta}{G_1|\ldots|G_{n-1}|A_1, \ldots, A_{n-1} \vdash B_1, \ldots, B_{n-1}|\Gamma \vdash \Delta} \quad [7]$$

is sound and complete with respect to validity in W_n-algebras.

Definition 29. The hCW_n calculus coincides with the hW_n calculus with the (lin) rule.

Theorem 30. *A formula P is $CLa_{lin}^{w_n}$-valid if and only if $\vdash P$ is derivable in hCW_n.*

Proof. Since the (lin) rule is valid in all totally ordered CLa-algebras and allows one to derive the linearity axiom, the proof follows from the soundness and completeness of the hW_n-calculus with respect to W_n-algebras [7].

Theorem 31. *If $G|\Gamma \vdash A, \Delta$ and $G'|\Gamma', A \vdash \Delta'$ are provable in hCW_n, then so is $G|G'|\Gamma, \Gamma' \vdash \Delta, \Delta'$.*

Proof. The proof is similar to that of hIW_n. In [7] it was shown how to eliminate cuts involving the (n-weak) rule.

Lemma 32. *For all $n \geq 3$, hCC_n and hW_n are proper subsystem of hCW_n.*

As was pointed out in [7], hW_3 (and hence, also hCW_3) is a calculus for 3-valued Łukasiewicz logic Ł$_3$.
This is no longer true for hCW_n, when $n > 3$. Indeed the Hilbert-style axiomatization of Ł$_n$ is given by adding to the axioms for a-MALL the following [10]:

$$((A \to B) \to B) \to ((B \to A) \to A) \quad \text{(Łukasiewicz axiom)}$$

$$(n-1)A \leftrightarrow nA \quad (n\text{–contraction})$$

$$(pA^{p-1})^n \leftrightarrow nA^p \quad \text{(Grigolia axioms)}$$

for every integer $p = 2, \ldots, n-2$ that does not divide $n-1$. Here $A \leftrightarrow B$ stands for $(A \to B) \odot (B \to A)$, nA for $A \oplus \ldots \oplus A$ (n times) and A^n for $A \odot \ldots \odot A$ (n times).

For $n > 3$, hCW_n is strictly included in Ł$_n$. Indeed, all the rules of hCW_n are valid in the algebraic models of Ł$_n$, namely MV$_n$-algebras (see e.g. [8]). On the other hand there is no way to prove in hCW_n the Łukasiewicz axiom or the Grigolia axioms.

In the particular case $n = 4$ we shall define a new rule, that is valid in Ł$_4$ and allows us to prove the Łukasiewicz axiom.

Definition 33. The h4Łuk calculus is obtained by adding to the hW_4 hypersequent calculus the following rule:

$$(4\text{Ł}uk) \quad \frac{G|\Gamma_1, \Gamma_1, \Gamma_1', \Gamma_1' \vdash \Delta_1, \Delta_1, \Delta_1', \Delta_1' \qquad G'|\Gamma_2, \Gamma_2' \vdash \Delta_2, \Delta_2'}{G|G'|\Gamma_1, \Gamma_2 \vdash \Delta_1, \Delta_2|\Gamma_1', \Gamma_2' \vdash \Delta_1', \Delta_2'}$$

Remark 34. Notice that the (4Łuk) rule is a mix between the (lin) rule and internal contraction rules.

Theorem 35 (Soundness). *If a hypersequent is derivable in h4Łuk then it is valid in 4-valued Łukasiewicz logic.*

Proof. The proof proceeds as in Theorem 30. We only show validity of the (4Łuk) rule with respect to algebraic models of Ł$_4$, namely MV$_4$-algebras. By the completeness theorem of MV$_4$-algebras (see, e.g. [8]), it suffices to check validity of the (4Łuk) rule in the MV$_4$-algebra M_4 on the set of truth values $\{0, \frac{1}{3}, \frac{2}{3}, 1\}$, where the connectives $+$ and $\neg$ are interpreted in the following way: $A + B = min\{1, A + B\}$ and $\neg A = 1 - A$, where $+$ and $-$ respectively denote the ordinary sum and subtraction. By hypothesis, (a) $1 - v(\Gamma_1) + 1 - v(\Gamma_1) + 1 - v(\Gamma_1') + 1 - v(\Gamma_1') + v(\Delta_1) + v(\Delta_1) + v(\Delta_1') + v(\Delta_1') = 1$ and (b) $1 - v(\Gamma_2) + 1 - v(\Gamma_2') + v(\Delta_2) + v(\Delta_2') = 1$. We have to prove that either (c) $1 - v(\Gamma_1) + 1 - v(\Gamma_2) + v(\Delta_1) + v(\Delta_2) = 1$ or (d) $1 - v(\Gamma_1') + 1 - v(\Gamma_2') + v(\Delta_1') + v(\Delta_2') = 1$.

Suppose that (c) does not hold. We show that (d) must be true. Being ($*$) $1 - v(\Gamma_1) + 1 - v(\Gamma_2) + v(\Delta_1) + v(\Delta_2) < 1$, there are three cases: $1 - v(\Gamma_2) + v(\Delta_2)$ can be equal to 0, $\frac{1}{3}$ or $\frac{2}{3}$. In the first case, from (b) it follows that (d) holds. In the second case, from (b) we have ($\star$) $1 - v(\Gamma_2') + v(\Delta_2') \geq \frac{2}{3}$. Since $1 - v(\Gamma_2) + v(\Delta_2) =$

$\frac{1}{3}$ and $(*)$ holds, $1 - v(\Gamma_1) + v(\Delta_1)$ must be $\leq \frac{1}{3}$, thus (d) follows from (a) and $(\star)$. In the third case, $1 - v(\Gamma_1) + v(\Delta_1)$ must be equal to 0, so, from (a) we have $1 - v(\Gamma_1') + v(\Delta_1') \geq \frac{2}{3}$. On the other hand, from (b) it follows $1 - v(\Gamma_2') + v(\Delta_2') \geq \frac{1}{3}$. Thus (d) holds.

The $(4\text{Ł}uk)$ rule is not valid in Ł_n for $n > 4$. A simple counterexample, e.g. in Ł_5, can be obtained by taking $v(\Gamma_1) = \frac{1}{2}$, $v(\Gamma_2) = \frac{1}{4}$, $v(\Gamma_2') = \frac{3}{4}$ and $v(\Gamma_i') = v(\Delta_i) = v(\Delta_i') = 0$, for $i = 1, 2$.

Remark 36. In $h4\text{Ł}uk$ we can derive the Łukasiewicz axiom. An equivalent formulation of this axiom is $A \odot (A \to B) \to B \odot (B \to A)$, see e.g. [11]. Here we show how to prove it in $h4\text{Ł}uk$:

$$\dfrac{\dfrac{\dfrac{\dfrac{A \vdash A \quad \dfrac{B \vdash B \quad \dfrac{B \vdash B \quad \dfrac{A \vdash A \quad A \vdash A \quad \dfrac{B \vdash B \quad A \vdash A}{B, B, A \vdash B \odot (B \to A)}}{B, B \vdash A, A \mid A \vdash B \odot (B \to A)}\,(4\text{-weak})}{B, B \vdash A, B \odot (B \to A) \mid A \vdash B \odot (B \to A)}}{B, B \vdash B \odot (B \to A), B \odot (B \to A) \mid A \vdash B \odot (B \to A)}}{A \vdash B \odot (B \to A) \mid B \vdash A \mid A \vdash B \odot (B \to A)}\,(4\text{Ł}uk)}{A, A \to B \vdash B \odot (B \to A) \mid A, A \to B \vdash B \odot (B \to A) \mid A, A \to B \vdash B \odot (B \to A)}}{\dfrac{A, A \to B \vdash B \odot (B \to A)}{\dfrac{A \odot (A \to B) \vdash B \odot (B \to A)}{\vdash A \odot (A \to B) \to B \odot (B \to A)}}}$$

It is not hard to see that in $h4\text{Ł}uk$ the cut-elimination theorem holds.

$h4\text{Ł}uk$ is not a calculus for 4-valued Łukasiewicz logic. Indeed, in $h4\text{Ł}uk$ one cannot prove the Grigolia axiom

$$(\dagger)\ [(A \odot A) \oplus (A \odot A) \oplus (A \odot A)] \leftrightarrow [(A \oplus A) \odot (A \oplus A) \odot (A \oplus A)].$$

Let $\text{Ł}_4 \cap \text{Ł}_3$ the logic whose Hilbert-style axiomatization is given by adding to the axioms of a-MALL the Łukasiewicz axiom and the 4-weak law of excluded middle. Modus ponens is the only rule of inference. The tautologies of this logic are those formulas that simultaneously are verified in the 3-elements MV-algebra $MV_3 = \{0, \frac{1}{2}, 1\}$ and in the 4-elements MV-algebra $MV_4 = \{0, \frac{1}{3}, \frac{2}{3}, 1\}$ where connectives $\neg, \oplus, \odot, \to, \wedge, \vee$ are interpreted in the following way: $\neg A = 1 - A$, $A \oplus B = \min\{1, A + B\}$, $A \odot B = \max\{0, A + B - 1\}$, $A \to B = \min\{1, 1 - A + B\}$, $A \wedge B = \min\{A, B\}$ and $A \vee B = \max\{A, B\}$.

Proposition 37. *$h4\text{Ł}uk$ is a calculus for $\text{Ł}_4 \cap \text{Ł}_3$.*

Proof. (*Soundness*) Trivial, since every rule of the $h4\text{Ł}uk$ calculus is valid both in Ł_4 and in Ł_3. (*Completeness*) Every axiom of $\text{Ł}_4 \cap \text{Ł}_3$ is derivable in $h4\text{Ł}uk$ while modus ponens corresponds to the derivability of $A, A \to B \vdash B$ and the cut rule.

As an easy corollary we can define an alternative Hilbert-style axiomatization of 4-valued Łukasiewicz logic making no use of the Łukasiewicz axiom.

As a final remark we stress that in order to formulate a cut-free hypersequent calculus for 4-valued Łukasiewicz logic, it remains to find some rules that forbid (†) $\frac{1}{2}$ *to be a truth value of the logic.*

References

1. *A. Avron.* A constructive analysis of RM. *J. of Symbolic Logic*, vol. **52**. pp. 939-951. 1987.
2. *A. Avron.* Natural 3-valued Logics. Characterization and Proof Theory. *J. of Symbolic Logic*, vol. **56**. pp. 276-294. 1991.
3. *A. Avron.* Hypersequents, Logical Consequence and Intermediate Logics for Concurrency. *Annals of Mathematics and Artificial Intelligence*, vol. **4**. pp. 225-248. 1991.
4. *A. Avron.* The Method of Hypersequents in the Proof Theory of Propositional Nonclassical Logics. In: **Logic: from Foundations to Applications.** W. Hodges, M. Hyland, C. Steinhorn and J. Truss Eds., European Logic Colloquium. Oxford Science Publications. Clarendon Press. Oxford. pp. 1-32. 1996.
5. *A. Avron.* Two Types of Multiple-Conclusion Systems. *Logic Journal of the IGPL*, vol. **6**(5). pp. 695-717. 1998.
6. *M. Baaz, A. Ciabattoni, C.G. Fermüller, H. Veith.* Proof Theory of Fuzzy Logics: Urquhart's C and Related Logics. Prooceedings of MFCS'98. Lectures Notes in Computer Science. vol.**1450**. pp.203-212. 1998.
7. *A. Ciabattoni, D.M. Gabbay, N. Olivetti.* Cut-free Proof Systems for Logics of Weak Excluded Middle. *Soft Computing*. vol. **2**(4). To appear. 1998.
8. *R. Cignoli, D. Mundici, I.M.L. D'Ottaviano.* **Algebraic foundations of many-valued reasoning**. In preparation.
9. *J.Y. Girard.* Linear Logic. *Theoretical Comp. Science*, vol. **50**. pp. 1-102. 1987.
10. *R. Grigolia.* Algebraic analysis of Łukasiewicz-Tarski n-valued logical systems. In **Selected Papers on Łukasiewicz Sentential Calculi**. R. Wòjciki and G. Malinowski Ed., Polish Acad. of Sciences, Ossolineum, Wrocław. pp. 81-91. 1977.
11. *P. Hájek.* **Metamathematics of fuzzy logic**. Kluwer. 1998.
12. *U. Höhle.* Commutative, residuated l-monoids. In: **Nonclassical logics and their applications to fuzzy subsets**. U. Höhle and P. Klement Eds., Kluwer. Dordrecht. pp. 53-106. 1995.
13. *R. Hori, H. Ono, H. Schellinx.* Extending Intuitionistic Linear Logic with Knotted Structural Rules. *Notre Dame Journal of Formal Logic*. vol. **35**(2). pp. 219-242. 1994.
14. *H. Ono.* Logics without contraction rule and residuated lattices. Draft. 1997.
15. *H. Ono, Y. Komori.* Logics without the contraction rule. *J. of Symbolic Logic*, vol. **50**. pp.169-201. 1985.
16. *A. Prijatelj.* Bounded Contraction and Gentzen style Formulation of Łukasiewicz Logics. *Studia Logica*, vol. **57**. pp. 437-456. 1996.
17. *A. Prijatelj.* Connectification for n-contraction. *Studia Logica*, vol. **54**(2). pp. 149-171. 1995.
18. *A.S. Troelstra.* **Lectures on Linear Logic**. CSLI Lectures Notes n.29. 1991.

The Non-associative Lambek Calculus with Product in Polynomial Time

Philippe de Groote

LORIA UMR n° 7503 - INRIA
Campus Scientifique, B.P. 239
54506 Vandœuvre lès Nancy Cedex – France
e-mail: degroote@loria.fr

Abstract. We prove, by introducing a new kind of sequent calculus, that the decision problem for the non-associative Lambek calculus with product belongs to PTIME. This solves an open prolem.

1 Introduction

Modern categorial grammars [6] are based on a logical calculus introduced by Lambek more than thirty years ago [4,5]. Two variants of this calculus exist. The first, **L**, which is perhaps the most well-known, corresponds exactly to the non-commutative fragment of **IMLL**, i.e., intuitionistic multiplicative linear logic [2]. The second, **NL**, which was introduced three years later, is obtained from the first by dropping the hidden structural rule of associativity. Therefore intuitionistic multiplicative linear logic may be seen as the commutative extension of **L** which, in turn, may be seen as the associative extension of **NL**:

$$\mathbf{NL} \subset \mathbf{L} \subset \mathbf{IMLL}$$

If, in addition, we distinguish between the purely implicational fragments and the fragments with product, the picture becomes the following:

$$\begin{array}{ccccc} \mathbf{NL}^{\backslash/\bullet} & \subset & \mathbf{L}^{\backslash/\bullet} & \subset & \mathbf{IMLL}^{\multimap\otimes} \\ \cup & & \cup & & \cup \\ \mathbf{NL}^{\backslash/} & \subset & \mathbf{L}^{\backslash/} & \subset & \mathbf{IMLL}^{\multimap} \end{array}$$

where the superscripts make explicit the connectives of the systems.

The decidability of these six fragments follows immediately from easy cut elimination theorems. As for the complexity of the associated decision problems, the state of the art is as follows. Kanovich has shown both $\mathbf{IMLL}^{\multimap\otimes}$ and $\mathbf{IMLL}^{\multimap}$ to be NP-complete [3].[1] In the case of $\mathbf{L}^{\backslash/\bullet}$ and $\mathbf{L}^{\backslash/}$, the question is still open. Moreover, there is no proof that the two problems are equivalent. Aerts and Trautwein have shown that $\mathbf{NL}^{\backslash/}$ belongs to PTIME [1]. Our own contribution is to show that this is also the case for $\mathbf{NL}^{\backslash/\bullet}$.

[1] In fact, in this case, the two problems are easily seen to be equivalent by using a Goedel-like negative translation. This is not true for **L** and **NL** because Goedel-like translations do not work in a non-commutative setting.

2 The non-associative Lambek calculus

The formulas of the non-associative Lambek calculus with product ,$\mathbf{NL}^{\backslash/\bullet}$, are built from a set of atomic formulas $\mathcal{A}$ and the connectives $\backslash$, $/$, and $\bullet$ according to the following grammar:

$$\mathcal{F} \ ::= \ \mathcal{A} \mid (\mathcal{F} \backslash \mathcal{F}) \mid (\mathcal{F}/\mathcal{F}) \mid (\mathcal{F} \bullet \mathcal{F})$$

The consequence relation of $\mathbf{NL}^{\backslash/\bullet}$ may be specified by a Gentzen-like sequent calculus. The sequents have the form $\Gamma \vdash A$ where Γ is a non-empty binary tree of formulas, i.e., a fully bracketed structure. We take for granted the notion of context, i.e., a binary tree with a hole. If $\Gamma[\,]$ is such a context, $\Gamma[A]$ denotes the binary tree obtained by filling the hole in $\Gamma[\,]$ with the formula A.

$$A \vdash A \quad (\text{Id})$$

$$\frac{\Gamma \vdash A \quad \Delta[B] \vdash C}{\Delta[\,(\Gamma, (A \backslash B))\,] \vdash C}\ (\backslash\text{-L}) \qquad \frac{(A, \Gamma) \vdash B}{\Gamma \vdash (A \backslash B)}\ (\backslash\text{-R})$$

$$\frac{\Gamma \vdash A \quad \Delta[B] \vdash C}{\Delta[\,((B/A), \Gamma)\,] \vdash C}\ (/\text{-L}) \qquad \frac{(\Gamma, A) \vdash B}{\Gamma \vdash (B/A)}\ (/\text{-R})$$

$$\frac{\Gamma[\,(A, B)\,] \vdash C}{\Gamma[\,(A \bullet B)\,] \vdash C}\ (\bullet\text{-L}) \qquad \frac{\Gamma \vdash A \quad \Delta \vdash B}{(\Gamma, \Delta) \vdash (A \bullet B)}\ (\bullet\text{-R})$$

The binary-tree structure of the antecedents induces the non-associativity of the calculus. As an illustration, consider the following derivation:

$$\cfrac{a \vdash a \qquad \cfrac{b \vdash b \quad c \vdash c}{(b, b \backslash c) \vdash c}}{((a, a \backslash b), b \backslash c) \vdash c}$$

In the associative case, this derivation might be continued by applying the right introduction rule of $\backslash$, which would yield $(a \backslash b, b \backslash c) \vdash a \backslash c$. In the present case, the bracketing of the antecedent prevents Rule ($\backslash$-R) from being applied.

In order to show that one may decide in polynomial time whether a sequent of $\mathbf{NL}^{\backslash/\bullet}$ is derivable, we will focus on sequents made of two formulas. By doing so, we will not lose any generality, as explained below.

Proposition 1. *Rule $\bullet$-L is invertible.*

Proof. This follows from the fact that this rule is permutable with all the rules. □

From this, we immediately have:

Corollary 2. *For each sequent $\Gamma \vdash B$ there exist a formula A such that $\Gamma \vdash B$ is provable if and only if $A \vdash B$ is provable. Moreover, $\Gamma \vdash B$ and $A \vdash B$ have the same length.* □

Because of Corollary 2, we may reduce the decision problem of $\mathbf{NL}^{\backslash/\bullet}$ to the particular case of sequents made of two formulas. Let us call any such provable sequent a tautology of $\mathbf{NL}^{\backslash/\bullet}$. We end this section by giving a characterisation of these tautologies.

Proposition 3. *The set of tautologies of $\mathbf{NL}^{\backslash/\bullet}$ is the least set of sequents closed under the following clauses:*

(a) $A \vdash A$;
(b) $(B \backslash C) \vdash (A \backslash D)$ *if* $A \vdash B$ *and* $C \vdash D$;
(c) $(C/B) \vdash (D/A)$ *if* $A \vdash B$ *and* $C \vdash D$;
(d) $(A \bullet C) \vdash (B \bullet D)$ *if* $A \vdash B$ *and* $C \vdash D$;
(e) $B \vdash (A \backslash C)$ *if and only if* $(A \bullet B) \vdash C$;
(f) $A \vdash (C/B)$ *if and only if* $(A \bullet B) \vdash C$.

Proof. Let S be the least set closed under the above conditions, and let T be the set of tautologies of $\mathbf{NL}^{\backslash/\bullet}$. We first note that Clauses a, b, c, d, e, and f correspond to admissible rules of $\mathbf{NL}^{\backslash/\bullet}$. Therefore, $S \subset T$.

Then, to prove that $T \subset S$ consists in a routine induction on the length of the sequent proofs of $\mathbf{NL}^{\backslash/\bullet}$. □

3 The product-free case

Proof search in the non-associative Lambek calculus takes advantage of the structure of the sequents. However, the reconstruction of a proof from a sequent is not as simple as it might seem at first sight. Indeed the backward application of the inference rules is not completely deterministic, as shown by the following derivations, which correspond to two different proofs of the same sequent.

$$\dfrac{\dfrac{\dfrac{\dfrac{\dfrac{b \vdash b \quad a \vdash a}{b, b \backslash a \vdash a}}{b \backslash a \vdash b \backslash a} \quad a \vdash a}{a/(b \backslash a), b \backslash a \vdash a \quad a \vdash a}}{a/(b \backslash a) \vdash a/(b \backslash a) \quad a \vdash a}}{a/(b \backslash a), (a/(b \backslash a)) \backslash a \vdash a}$$

$$\dfrac{\dfrac{\dfrac{\dfrac{\dfrac{b \vdash b \quad a \vdash a}{b, b \backslash a \vdash a}}{b \vdash a/(b \backslash a)} \quad a \vdash a}{b, (a/(b \backslash a)) \backslash a \vdash a}}{(a/(b \backslash a)) \backslash a \vdash b \backslash a} \quad a \vdash a}{a/(b \backslash a), (a/(b \backslash a)) \backslash a \vdash a}$$

Now it is easy to construct, from the above example, sequents with an exponential number of possible proofs. Consequently a brute force search based on the sequent calculus of Section 2 cannot be polynomial in time.

In the product free case, the polynomiality of the decision problem may be obtained as a consequence of the following key property: *any derivation of a two-formula sequent may be transformed, by permuting the rules, into a derivation where each two-premise inference rule is immediately followed by a one-premise inference rule.* Consequently, any derivation of a two-formula sequent may be transformed into a derivation whose sequents contain at most three formulas. This key property fails when the product is present. This is shown, for instance, by the following counterexample.

$$\dfrac{\dfrac{\dfrac{\dfrac{a \vdash a \quad b \vdash b}{(a, b) \vdash a \bullet b} \quad c \vdash c}{((a, b), (a \bullet b) \backslash c) \vdash c}}{(a, b) \vdash c/((a \bullet b) \backslash c)}}{a \vdash (c/((a \bullet b) \backslash c))/b}$$

In order to better understand the meaning of the key property, consider the two-premise rules of the sequent calculus of Section 2. Each of these rules introduces two connectives: an actual conjunctive connective, which is the active connective of the rule (i.e., a negative implication, or a positive product), and a possible disjunctive connective, which is introduced by the rule as a meta-connective (i.e., a comma). When deriving a two formula sequent, this meta-connective will be eventually turned into a positive implication or a negative product.

In the product-free case, the key property says that each comma may be turned into an actual connective as soon as it is introduced. Consequently, by merging the left and the right introduction rules, one obtains a complete system whose rules introduce two dual connectives at the same time:

$$A \vdash A$$

$$\dfrac{A \vdash B \quad C \vdash D}{(B \backslash C) \vdash (A \backslash D)} \qquad\qquad \dfrac{A \vdash B \quad C \vdash D}{A \vdash (D/(B \backslash C))}$$

$$\frac{A \vdash B \quad C \vdash D}{(C/B) \vdash (D/A)} \qquad \frac{A \vdash B \quad C \vdash D}{A \vdash ((C/B) \setminus D)}$$

In the case of $\mathbf{NL}^{\setminus/\bullet}$, it is still possible to design such a system, where each rule introduces a pair of dual connectives. However, because of the failure of the key property, this system manipulates a notion of context. This is explained in the next section.

4 A calculus with contexts

In this section, we define a context to be a formula with a hole (remark that this notion of context is different from the one of Section 2):

$$\mathcal{C}[\,] ::= [\,] \mid (\mathcal{C}[\,]\backslash\mathcal{F}) \mid (\mathcal{F}\backslash\mathcal{C}[\,]) \mid (\mathcal{C}[\,]/\mathcal{F}) \mid (\mathcal{F}/\mathcal{C}[\,]) \mid (\mathcal{C}[\,]\bullet\mathcal{F}) \mid (\mathcal{F}\bullet\mathcal{C}[\,])$$

We let $\Gamma[\,], \Delta[\,], \ldots$ range over contexts, and we write $\Gamma[A]$ to denote the formula obtained by filling the hole in $\Gamma[\,]$ with the formula A. We also say that a context $\Gamma[\,]$ is a correct positive (respectively, negative) context if and only if $A \vdash \Gamma[B]$ (respectively, $\Gamma[A] \vdash B$) is a tautology whenever $A \vdash B$ is. This notion of correctness is the keystone of the following calculus, which includes inference rules that allow correct contexts to be derived.

Sequent rules

$$A \vdash A \quad \text{(Id)}$$

$$\frac{A \vdash B \quad C \vdash D}{(B \setminus C) \vdash (A \setminus D)} \ (\backslash) \qquad \frac{A \vdash B \quad C \vdash D}{(C/B) \vdash (D/A)} \ (/)$$

$$\frac{A \vdash B \quad C \vdash D}{(A \bullet C) \vdash (B \bullet D)} \ (\bullet)$$

$$\frac{A \vdash B \quad \vdash_N \Gamma[\,]}{\Gamma[A] \vdash B} \ (\mathrm{Cont}_N) \qquad \frac{A \vdash B \quad \vdash_P \Gamma[\,]}{A \vdash \Gamma[B]} \ (\mathrm{Cont}_P)$$

Negative context rules

$$\vdash_N [\,] \quad ([\,]\text{-N})$$

$$\frac{A \vdash B \quad \vdash_N \Gamma[\,] \quad \vdash_N \Delta[\,]}{\vdash_N (A \bullet \Gamma[(B \setminus \Delta[\,])])} \ (\bullet\backslash\text{-N}) \qquad \frac{A \vdash B \quad \vdash_N \Gamma[\,] \quad \vdash_N \Delta[\,]}{\vdash_N (\Gamma[(\Delta[\,]/B)] \bullet A)} \ (\bullet/\text{-N})$$

Positive context rules

$$\vdash_P [] \quad ([]\text{-P})$$

$$\frac{A \vdash B \quad \vdash_P \Gamma[] \quad \vdash_P \Delta[]}{\vdash_P (A \backslash \Gamma[(B \bullet \Delta[])])} (\backslash\bullet\text{-P}) \qquad \frac{A \vdash B \quad \vdash_P \Gamma[] \quad \vdash_P \Delta[]}{\vdash_P (\Gamma[(\Delta[] \bullet B)]/A)} (/\bullet\text{-P})$$

$$\frac{B \vdash A \quad \vdash_N \Gamma[] \quad \vdash_P \Delta[]}{\vdash_P (A/\Gamma[(\Delta[] \backslash B)])} (/\backslash\text{-P}) \qquad \frac{B \vdash A \quad \vdash_N \Gamma[] \quad \vdash_P \Delta[]}{\vdash_P (\Gamma[(B/\Delta[])] \backslash A)} (\backslash/\text{-P})$$

We now prove that the above system, which we call SC, is a sound and complete axiomatisation of $\mathbf{NL}^{\backslash/\bullet}$.

Proposition 4. *(Soundness) Let $A \vdash B$ be a sequent derivable according to system SC. Then $A \vdash B$ is a tautology of* $\mathbf{NL}^{\backslash/\bullet}$.

Proof. The proof is carried out by induction on the SC-derivation of $A \vdash B$. The cases of Axiom Id, Rules \, /, and • are straightforward because they correspond, respectively, to Conditions a, b c and d of Proposition 3. Rules Cont_N and Cont_P correspond to the definition of correctness for the contexts. Consequently, it remains to prove that the negative and positive context rules allow only correct contexts to be derived. We handle the case of the negative contexts and leave the other case, which is similar, to the reader.

Let $C \vdash D$ be a tautology of $\mathbf{NL}^{\backslash/\bullet}$ and let $\Theta[]$ be a context such that $\vdash_N \Theta[]$ is derivable. We must prove that $\Theta[C] \vdash D$ is a tautology.

The case where Θ is obtained by axiom []-N is obvious.

If Θ is obtained by Rule •\-N then $\Theta = (A \bullet \Gamma[(B \backslash \Delta[])])$ where, by induction hypothesis, $A \vdash B$ is a tautology and $\Gamma[], \Delta[]$ are correct negative contexts. Then $\Delta[C] \vdash D$ is a tautology, and so is $(B \backslash \Delta[C]) \vdash (A \backslash D)$. Hence $\Gamma[(B \backslash \Delta[C])] \vdash (A \backslash D)$ is also a tautology and, by Condition e of Proposition 3, so is $(A \bullet \Gamma[(B \backslash \Delta[C])]) \vdash D$.

The case where Θ is obtained by Rule •/-N is similar. □

In order to prove the completeness, we first establish two lemmas.

Lemma 5. *If $\vdash_N \Gamma[]$ and $\vdash_N \Delta[]$ are both derivable, so is $\vdash_N \Gamma[\Delta[]]$.*

Proof. A straightforward induction on the derivation of $\vdash_N \Gamma[]$. □

Lemma 6. *If $\vdash_P \Gamma[]$ and $\vdash_P \Delta[]$ are both derivable, so is $\vdash_P \Gamma[\Delta[]]$.*

Proof. A straightforward induction on the derivation of $\vdash_P \Gamma[]$. □

We say that an SC-derivation is normal if the three following conditions hold:

(a) it is not the case that the right premise of any occurrence of Rule Cont_N (respectively, Rule Cont_P) is obtained by the Axiom []-N (respectively, Axiom []-P);
(b) it is not the case that the left premise of any occurrence of Rule Cont_N (respectively, Rule Cont_P) is obtained as the conclusion of another occurrence of Rule Cont_N (respectively, Rule Cont_P);
(c) Axiom Id is restricted to atomic formulas.

Lemma 7. *Any SC-derivation may be turned into a normal derivation.*

Proof. The occurrences of Rule Cont_N or Cont_P that do not satisfy Condition a are clearly useless. On the other hand, the occurrences of Rule Cont_N and Cont_P that do not satisfy Condition b may be eliminated by Lemmas 5 and 6. Finally, Rules \, /, and • allow any tautology of the form $A \vdash A$ to be derived from axioms on atomic formulas. □

Proposition 8. *(Completeness) Let* $A \vdash B$ *be a tautology of* $\mathbf{NL}^{\backslash/\bullet}$. *Then* $A \vdash B$ *is derivable according to system SC.*

Proof. We prove that the set of SC-derivable sequents is closed under the conditions of Proposition 3. This is clearly the case for Conditions a, b, c, d since they respectively correspond to Axiom Id and Rules \, /, and •. Therefore, it remains to prove that the set of SC-derivable sequents is closed under Conditions e and f. This amounts to proving that the following rules are admissible:

$$\frac{(A \bullet B) \vdash C}{B \vdash (A \backslash C)}\,(\mathrm{e1}) \qquad \frac{B \vdash (A \backslash C)}{(A \bullet B) \vdash C}\,(\mathrm{e2}) \qquad \frac{(A \bullet B) \vdash C}{A \vdash (C / B)}\,(\mathrm{f1}) \qquad \frac{A \vdash (C / B)}{(A \bullet B) \vdash C}\,(\mathrm{f2})$$

We show that each of these rules is admissible by performing a case analysis of the normal SC-derivations.

A. Admissibility of Rule e1.

A.1. The last rule of the SC-derivation is Rule •:

$$\frac{\dfrac{A \vdash B \quad C \vdash D}{(A \bullet C) \vdash (B \bullet D)}\,(\bullet)}{C \vdash (A \backslash (B \bullet D))}\,(\mathrm{e1})$$

The derivation may be transformed as follows:

$$\frac{C \vdash D \qquad \dfrac{A \vdash B \quad \vdash_P [\,] \quad \vdash_P [\,]}{\vdash_P (A \backslash (B \bullet [\,]))}\,(\backslash\bullet\text{-P})}{C \vdash (A \backslash (B \bullet D))}\,(\mathrm{Cont}_P)$$

A.2. The last rule of the SC-derivation is Rule Cont_N. We distinguish between two subcases.

A.2.1. The right premise of Rule $Cont_N$ *is obtained by application of Rule* $\bullet\backslash$*-N:*

$$\dfrac{\dfrac{C \vdash D \qquad \dfrac{A \vdash B \quad \vdash_N \Gamma[\,] \quad \vdash_N \Delta[\,]}{\vdash_N (A \bullet \Gamma[(B \backslash \Delta[\,])])}(\bullet\backslash\text{-N})}{(A \bullet \Gamma[(B \backslash \Delta[C])]) \vdash D}(\text{Cont}_N)}{\Gamma[(B \backslash \Delta[C])] \vdash (A \backslash D)}(\text{e1})$$

The derivation may be transformed as follows:

$$\dfrac{\dfrac{A \vdash B \qquad \dfrac{C \vdash D \quad \vdash_N \Delta[\,]}{\Delta[C] \vdash D}(\text{Cont}_N)}{(B \backslash \Delta[C]) \vdash (A \backslash D)}(\backslash) \qquad \vdash_N \Gamma[\,]}{\Gamma[(B \backslash \Delta[C])] \vdash (A \backslash D)}(\text{Cont}_N)$$

A.2.2. The right premise of Rule $Cont_N$ *is obtained by application of Rule* $\bullet/$*-N:*

$$\dfrac{\dfrac{C \vdash D \qquad \dfrac{A \vdash B \quad \vdash_N \Gamma[\,] \quad \vdash_N \Delta[\,]}{\vdash_N (\Gamma[(\Delta[\,]/B)] \bullet A)}(\bullet/\text{-N})}{(\Gamma[(\Delta[C]/B)] \bullet A) \vdash D}(\text{Cont}_N)}{A \vdash (\Gamma[(\Delta[C]/B)] \backslash D)}\text{e1}$$

The derivation may be transformed as follows:

$$\dfrac{A \vdash B \qquad \dfrac{\dfrac{C \vdash D \quad \vdash_N \Delta[\,]}{\Delta[C] \vdash D}\text{Cont}_N \quad \vdash_N \Gamma[\,] \quad \vdash_P [\,]}{\vdash_P (\Gamma[(\Delta[C]/[\,])] \backslash D)}(\backslash/\text{-P})}{A \vdash (\Gamma[(\Delta[C]/B)] \backslash D)}(\text{Cont}_P)$$

A.3. The last rule of the SC-derivation is Rule $Cont_P$. Again, we distinguish between two subcases.

A.3.1. The left premise of Rule $Cont_P$ *is obtained by applying Rule* $\bullet$*:*

$$\dfrac{\dfrac{\dfrac{A \vdash B \quad C \vdash D}{(A \bullet C) \vdash (B \bullet D)}(\bullet) \qquad \vdash_P \Gamma[\,]}{(A \bullet C) \vdash \Gamma[(B \bullet D)]}(\text{Cont}_P)}{C \vdash (A \backslash \Gamma[(B \bullet D)])}(\text{e1})$$

The derivation may be transformed as follows:

$$\dfrac{C \vdash D \qquad \dfrac{A \vdash B \quad \vdash_P \Gamma[\,] \quad \vdash_P [\,]}{\vdash_P (A \backslash \Gamma[(B \bullet [\,])])}(\backslash\bullet\text{-P})}{C \vdash (A \backslash \Gamma[(B \bullet D)])}(\text{Cont}_P)$$

A.3.2. The left premise of Rule $Cont_P$ is obtained by applying Rule $Cont_N$:

$$\dfrac{\dfrac{A \vdash B \quad \vdash_N \Gamma[\,]}{\Gamma[A] \vdash B}\,(\mathrm{Cont}_N) \qquad \vdash_P \Delta[\,]}{\Gamma[A] \vdash \Delta[B]}\,(\mathrm{Cont}_P)$$

This case may be reduced to case A.2 by permuting the two rules as follows:

$$\dfrac{\dfrac{A \vdash B \quad \vdash_P \Delta[\,]}{A \vdash \Delta[B]}\,(\mathrm{Cont}_P) \qquad \vdash_N \Gamma[\,]}{\Gamma[A] \vdash \Delta[B]}\,(\mathrm{Cont}_N)$$

B. Admissibility of Rule e2.

B.1. The last rule of the SC-derivation is Rule \\:

$$\dfrac{\dfrac{A \vdash B \quad C \vdash D}{(B \backslash C) \vdash (A \backslash D)}\,(\backslash)}{(A \bullet (B \backslash C)) \vdash D}\,(\mathrm{e2})$$

The derivation may be transformed as follows:

$$\dfrac{C \vdash D \qquad \dfrac{A \vdash B \quad \vdash_N [\,] \quad \vdash_N [\,]}{\vdash_N (A \bullet (B \backslash [\,]))}\,(\bullet\backslash\text{-N})}{(A \bullet (B \backslash C)) \vdash D}\,(\mathrm{Cont}_N)$$

B.2. The last rule of the SC-derivation is Rule $Cont_N$. We distinguish between two subcases.

B.2.1. The left premise of Rule $Cont_N$ is obtained by applying Rule \\:

$$\dfrac{\dfrac{\dfrac{A \vdash B \quad C \vdash D}{(B \backslash C) \vdash (A \backslash D)}\,(\backslash) \qquad \vdash_N \Gamma[\,]}{\Gamma[\,(B \backslash C)\,] \vdash (A \backslash D)}\,(\mathrm{Cont}_N)}{(A \bullet \Gamma[\,(B \backslash C)\,]) \vdash D}\,(\mathrm{e2})$$

The derivation may be transformed as follows:

$$\dfrac{C \vdash D \qquad \dfrac{A \vdash B \quad \vdash_N \Gamma[\,] \quad \vdash_N [\,]}{\vdash_N (A \bullet \Gamma[\,(B \backslash [\,])\,])}\,(\bullet\backslash\text{-N})}{(A \bullet \Gamma[\,(B \backslash C)\,]) \vdash D}\,(\mathrm{Cont}_N)$$

B.2.2. The left premise of Rule $Cont_N$ is obtained by applying Rule $Cont_P$:

$$\dfrac{\dfrac{A \vdash B \quad \vdash_P \Gamma[\,]}{A \vdash \Gamma[B]}\,(\mathrm{Cont}_P) \qquad \vdash_N \Delta[\,]}{\Delta[A] \vdash \Gamma[B]}\,(\mathrm{Cont}_N)$$

This case is reduced to case B.3 by permuting the two rules:

$$\dfrac{\dfrac{A \vdash B \quad \vdash_N \Delta[\,]}{\Delta[A] \vdash B}(\mathrm{Cont}_N) \qquad \vdash_P \Gamma[\,]}{\Delta[A] \vdash \Gamma[B]}(\mathrm{Cont}_P)$$

B.3. The last rule of the SC-derivation is Rule Cont$_P$. There are two subcases.

B.3.1. The right premise of Rule Cont$_P$ is obtained by application of Rule \\•-P:

$$\dfrac{\dfrac{C \vdash D \qquad \dfrac{A \vdash B \quad \vdash_P \Gamma[\,] \quad \vdash_P \Delta[\,]}{\vdash_P (A \backslash \Gamma[(B \bullet \Delta[\,])])}(\backslash\bullet\text{-P})}{C \vdash (A\backslash \Gamma[(B\bullet\Delta[D])])}\mathrm{Cont}_P}{(A\bullet C) \vdash \Gamma[(B\bullet\Delta[D])]}(\mathrm{e2})$$

The derivation may be transformed as follows:

$$\dfrac{\dfrac{A\vdash B \qquad \dfrac{C\vdash D \quad \vdash_P \Delta[\,]}{C\vdash \Delta[D]}(\mathrm{Cont}_P)}{(A\bullet C)\vdash (B\bullet\Delta[D])}(\bullet) \qquad \vdash_P \Gamma[\,]}{(A\bullet C)\vdash \Gamma[(B\bullet\Delta[D])]}(\mathrm{Cont}_P)$$

B.3.1. The right premise of Rule Cont$_P$ is obtained by application of Rule \\/-P:

$$\dfrac{\dfrac{C\vdash D \qquad \dfrac{A\vdash B \quad \vdash_N \Gamma[\,] \quad \vdash_P \Delta[\,]}{\vdash_P (\Gamma[(A/\Delta[\,])]\backslash B)}(\backslash/\text{-P})}{C\vdash (\Gamma[(A/\Delta[D])]\backslash B)}(\mathrm{Cont}_P)}{(\Gamma[(A/\Delta[D])]\bullet C)\vdash B}(\mathrm{e2})$$

The derivation may be transformed as follows:

$$\dfrac{A\vdash B \qquad \dfrac{\dfrac{C\vdash D \quad \vdash_P\Delta[\,]}{C\vdash\Delta[D]}(\mathrm{Cont}_P) \qquad \vdash_N \Gamma[\,] \quad \vdash_N [\,]}{\vdash_N (\Gamma[([\,]/\Delta[D])]\bullet C)}(\bullet/\text{-N})}{(\Gamma[(A/\Delta[D])]\bullet C)\vdash B}(\mathrm{Cont}_N)$$

C. Admissibility of Rule f1. This part of the proof is symmetric to Part A.

D. Admissibility of Rule f2. This part of the proof is symmetric to Part B. □

5 Polynomiality

Let A be a formula and $\Gamma[\,]$ be a context. We say that $\Gamma[\,]$ is a subcontext of A if and only if there exists a context $\Delta[\,]$ and a formula B such that $A = \Delta[\Gamma[B]]$.

Remark that if A is a formula of length n then the number of subformulas of A is bounded by n, and the number of subcontexts of A is bounded by n^2.

We immediately obtain the following property.

Lemma 9. *The SC-derivations satisfy the subformula/subcontext property, i.e., all the formulas and contexts occurring in an SC-derivation are subformulas and subcontexts of the conclusion of this SC-derivation.*

Proof. A straightforward induction on SC-derivations. □

From this lemma, we easily derive our main result.

Theorem 10. *The non-associative Lambek calculus is decidable in polynomial time.*

Proof. Let $A \vdash B$ be a two formula sequent of $\mathbf{NL}^{\backslash/\bullet}$. By Propositions 4 and 8, $A \vdash B$ is a tautology of $\mathbf{NL}^{\backslash/\bullet}$ if and only if there exist an SC-derivation of it. Now, by Lemma 9, any possible SC-derivation of $A \vdash B$ will be made up of two kinds of expressions:

- subcontexts of either A or B,
- sequents of the form $C \vdash D$, where C and D are subformulas of A or B.

The number of such expressions is bounded by $2n^2$, where n is the sum of the lengths of A and B. Consequently, a brute force search algorithm for constructing a possible SC-derivation of $A \vdash B$ will terminate in polynomial time if its search space is organised as a DAG rather than as a tree. □

Remark 11. Organizing the proof-search space in such a way that different possible proofs share the sub-proofs they have in common is needed in order to get a polynomial algorithm. Nevertheless, the bottum-up strategy suggested by the proof of Theorem 10 is not the only possible way. In practice, one could prefer top-down strategies, such as the so-called inverse method, that take advantage of dynamic programming techniques.

Acknowledgements I wish to thank Glyn Morrill, François Lamarche, Jean-Yves Marion and Adam Cichon for helpful discussions and comments.

References

1. E. Aarts and K. Trautwein. Non-associative lambek categorial grammar in polynomial time. *Mathematical Logic Quaterly*, 41:476–484, 1995.
2. J.-Y. Girard. Linear logic. *Theoretical Computer Science*, 50:1–102, 1987.
3. M. Kanovich. Horn programming in linear logic is np-complete. In *7-th annual IEEE Symposium on Logic in Computer Science*, pages 200–210. IEEE Computer Society Press, 1992.
4. J. Lambek. The mathematics of sentence structure. *Amer. Math. Monthly*, 65:154–170, 1958.

5. J. Lambek. On the calculus of syntactic types. In *Studies of Language and its Mathematical Aspects*, pages 166–178, Providence, 1961. Proc. of the 12th Symp. Appl. Math..
6. M. Moortgat. Categorial type logic. In J. van Benthem and A. ter Meulen, editors, *Handbook of Logic and Language*, chapter 2. Elsevier, 1997.

Sequent Calculi for Nominal Tense Logics: A Step Towards Mechanization?

Stéphane Demri

Laboratoire LEIBNIZ- U.M.R. 5522
46 Avenue Felix Viallet, 38031 Grenoble, France
Email: demri@imag.fr

Abstract. We define sequent-style calculi for nominal tense logics characterized by classes of modal frames that are first-order definable by certain Π_1^0-formulae and Π_2^0-formulae. The calculi are based on d'Agostino and Mondadori's calculus KE and therefore they admit a restricted cut-rule that is not eliminable. A nice computational property of the restriction is, for instance, that at any stage of the proof, only a finite number of potential cut-formulae needs to be taken under consideration. Although restrictions on the proof search (preserving completeness) are given in the paper and most of them are theoretically appealing, the use of those calculi for mechanization is however doubtful. Indeed, we present sequent calculi for fragments of classical logic that are syntactic variants of the sequent calculi for the nominal tense logics.

1 Introduction

Background. The nominal tense logics are extensions of Prior tense logics (see e.g. [Pri57, RU71]) by adding *nominals* (also called *names*) to the language (see e.g. [Bla93]). *Nominals* are understood as atomic propositions that hold true in a unique world of the Kripke-style models. The nominal tense logics are quite expressive since not only do they extend the standard (mono)modal logics by adding a past operator (giving the tense flavour) but they also admit nominals in the language. In spite of the analogy between nominals (in the object language of the logic) and *prefixes*, also called *labels*, used in various proof systems for modal logics (see e.g. [Fit83, Wal90]), no proof systems for nominal tense logics using this conceptual similarity exist. This is all the more surprising because during the last years, prefixed calculi have regained some interest (see e.g. [Ogn94, Mas94, Gov95, Rus96, Gab96, BMV97, BG97]).

Although designing general frameworks defining proof systems for modal logics is a fundamental task, other works deal with the difficult problem of improving significantly the mechanization of logics by finding refined properties, mostly proof-theoretical, that provide better complexity bounds or that allow the design of efficient decision procedures (see e.g. [Hud96, GHM98, Heu98]). We claim that the latter approach is the most promising for mechanization. As witness, the present paper illustrates that for many nominal tense logics, it is not so difficult to find a general framework for mechanization as long as only qualitative properties (soundness, completeness, ...) are investigated.

Our contribution. For any nominal tense logic $\mathcal{L}$ from the class $\mathcal{C}_{\Pi_2^0}$ defined in this paper, we define a sequent-style calculus, say $G\mathcal{L}$, that is based on the sequent-style counterpart of the calculus KE defined in [dM94]. Our calculi admit a cut rule satisfying the following nice computational properties. When reading the proof upwards, at any stage of the construction of the proof,

(CR1) the number of potential cut-formulae is linear in the size of the part of the proof constructed so far;
(CR2) any potential cut-formula can be computed in linear-time in the size of the part of the proof constructed so far.
(CR3) the size of any potential cut-formula is linear in the size of the part of the proof constructed so far (consequence of (CR2));

(CR1) means for instance that when growing the proofs upwards, if one decides to apply the cut rule at some stage, only a limited amount of candidate cut formulae could be useful to end the construction of the proof. The non-determinism of the cut rule is therefore weakened. Analycity is however not guaranteed because new nominals shall be introduced during the construction of the proofs. It is known (see e.g. [Boo84, dM94]) that cut-elimination is not always a guarantee for (efficient) mechanization. The search for some *analytic* cut rule is often desirable and the calculi defined in this paper follow that line of research. Furthermore, we take advantage of the presence of nominals in the modal language to use "implicit prefixes" in the proof systems. As far as we know, the idea of using such implicit prefixes when nominals are involved is due to Konikowska [Kon97]. In [Kon97], Rasiowa-Sikorski-style calculi for relative similarity logics are defined. Herein, we generalize the use of implicit prefixes to a class of nominal tense logics and we introduce various restrictions on the applications of the rules while preserving completeness. Although, for some particular logics, decision procedures can be obtained using the restrictions, in the general case, the design of decision procedures (when possible) is not straightforward from our calculi. It is also fair to state that the paper [Kon97] has been a source of inspiration in order to develop some of the ideas present in this paper.

In the last part of the paper, we define sequent-style calculi (based on KEQ [d'A90]), say $GFOL_{\mathcal{L}}$, for fragments of the classical logic such that the calculi $G\mathcal{L}$ and $GFOL_{\mathcal{L}}$ can be clearly viewed as syntactic variants. This allows to observe that $G\mathcal{L}$ is first-order in nature and to explain why it is so. Moreover, it clearly raises the questions about the relevancy of defining calculi within a general proof-theoretical framework when mechanization is wanted. Apart from the technical results of the paper, we wish to formally illustrate why numerous calculi for modal logics can be viewed as an encoding into classical logic. Although this fact is widely recognized for particular systems, we want here to propose a more general picture since the class $\mathcal{C}_{\Pi^0_2}$ is quite large.

Related work. Most of the proof systems designed for nominals tense logics are Hilbert-style ones [Bla93]. Calculi for (non nominal) tense logics can be for instance found in [RU71, Kra96, Heu98, BG98] but these calculi do not treat the nominal case and they do not consider so large a class of logics as $\mathcal{C}_{\Pi^0_2}$. In [DG99], display calculi for nominal tense logics have been defined and cut is not only eliminable but also a strong normalization theorem is established. For all the calculi designed in the present paper, cut (or equivalently the principle of bivalence) is not eliminable. Furthermore, the sequent calculi defined in the present paper are based on a completely different approach: we rather use the nominals as "implicit prefixes". In that sense, our calculi are *explicit systems* following [Gor99] but without introducing any extra proof-theoretical device that does not belong to the object modal language. Furthermore, the calculi defined in this paper does not differ very much in spirit with those defined in [Rus96, BMV98]. Indeed, we associate syntactically rules to formulas defining relational theories. However, we are able to capture all the conditions on frames for the properly displayable modal logics defined in [Kra96]. We wish also to thank one of the referees for pointing us to [Bla98, Tza99] where tableau-style calculi having technical similarities with ours have been defined.

2 Nominal tense logics

Given a countably infinite set[1] $\mathtt{For}_0 = \{\mathtt{p}_0, \mathtt{p}_1, \mathtt{p}_2, \ldots\}$ of *atomic propositions* and a countably infinite set $\mathtt{For}_0^N = \{\mathtt{i}_0, \mathtt{i}_1, \ldots\}$ of *names*, the formulas $\phi \in \mathtt{NTL}(G, H)$ are inductively defined as follows: $\phi ::= \mathtt{p}_k \mid \mathtt{i}_k \mid \phi_1 \wedge \phi_2 \mid \phi_1 \Rightarrow \phi_2 \mid \neg\phi \mid G\phi \mid H\phi$ for $\mathtt{p}_k \in \mathtt{For}_0$ and $\mathtt{i}_k \in \mathtt{For}_0^N$. Standard abbreviations include $\Leftrightarrow$, F, P. We write $|\phi|$ to denote the *length* of the formula ϕ for some (unspecified) succinct encoding. An occurrence of the formula ψ is said to be a subformula of the formula ϕ of *secondary disjunctive force* $\overset{\text{def}}{\Leftrightarrow}$ ψ is a subformula of ϕ and ψ is the immediate subformula either of a conjunction in ϕ of *negative polarity* or of an implication in ϕ of *positive polarity*. We use here the usual notion of polarity. For instance, $\mathtt{p}_0$ occurs negatively in $(\mathtt{p}_1 \wedge \mathtt{p}_0) \Rightarrow \mathtt{p}_1$. A *modal frame* $\mathcal{F} = \langle W, R \rangle$ is a pair such that W is a non-empty set and R is a binary relation on W. We use $R(w) \overset{\text{def}}{=} \{v \in W : (w, v) \in R\}$. A *model* $\mathcal{M}$ is a structure $\mathcal{M} = \langle W, R, m \rangle$ such that $\langle W, R \rangle$ is a frame and m is a mapping $m : \mathtt{For}_0 \cup \mathtt{For}_0^N \rightarrow \mathcal{P}(W)$ where for any $\mathtt{i} \in \mathtt{For}_0^N$, $m(\mathtt{i})$ is a singleton. Let $\mathcal{M} = \langle W, R, m \rangle$ be a model and $w \in W$. The formula ϕ is *satisfied by the world* $w \in W$ *in* $\mathcal{M}$ $\overset{\text{def}}{\Leftrightarrow}$ $\mathcal{M}, w \models \phi$ where the satisfaction relation $\models$ is inductively defined as follows: $\mathcal{M}, w \models \mathtt{p} \overset{\text{def}}{\Leftrightarrow} w \in m(\mathtt{p})$, for every $\mathtt{p} \in \mathtt{For}_0 \cup \mathtt{For}_0^N$; $\mathcal{M}, w \models G\phi \overset{\text{def}}{\Leftrightarrow}$ for every $w' \in R(w)$, $\mathcal{M}, w' \models \phi$; $\mathcal{M}, w \models H\phi \overset{\text{def}}{\Leftrightarrow}$ for every $w' \in R^{-1}(w)$, $\mathcal{M}, w' \models \phi$ (R^{-1} is the converse of R). We omit the standard conditions for the propositional connectives. A formula ϕ is *true* in a model $\mathcal{M}$ (written $\mathcal{M} \models \phi$) $\overset{\text{def}}{\Leftrightarrow}$ for every $w \in W$, $\mathcal{M}, w \models \phi$. A formula ϕ is *true* in a frame $\mathcal{F}$ (written $\mathcal{F} \models \phi$) $\overset{\text{def}}{\Leftrightarrow}$ ϕ is true in every model based on $\mathcal{F}$. In what follows, by a *logic* $\mathcal{L}$ we understand a pair $\langle \mathtt{NTL}(H, G), \mathcal{C} \rangle$ where $\mathcal{C}$ is a non-empty class of modal frames. A formula ϕ is said to be $\mathcal{L}$*-valid* $\overset{\text{def}}{\Leftrightarrow}$ ϕ is true in all the models based on the frames of $\mathcal{C}$. A formula ϕ is said to be $\mathcal{L}$*-satisfiable* $\overset{\text{def}}{\Leftrightarrow}$ $\neg\phi$ is not $\mathcal{L}$-valid. Now, we define the class $\mathcal{C}_{\Pi_2^0}$ of nominal tense logics announced in the introduction. First, we need to present preliminary definitions. Here, we consider the fragment of FOL built using the following vocabulary: $\top$ is the *verum* logical constant; $\{\mathtt{P}_k : k \in \omega\}$ is a countable set of unary predicate symbols; $\mathtt{R}$ and $=$ (identity) are the unique binary predicate symbols; $\{\mathtt{a}_k : k \in \omega\}$ is a countable set[2] of individual constants;

[1] The metavariables for atomic propositions [resp. for nominals] are $\mathtt{p}, \mathtt{q}, \ldots$ [resp. $\mathtt{i}, \mathtt{j}, \ldots$]. When $\mathtt{p}$ [resp. $\mathtt{i}$] is subscripted by some natural number, we mean exactly the members from $\mathtt{For}_0$ [resp. from $\mathtt{For}_0^N$].

[2] The metavariables for individual constants [resp. for individual variables] are $\mathtt{a}, \mathtt{b}, \ldots$ [resp. $\mathtt{x}, \mathtt{y}, \ldots$]. When $\mathtt{a}$ [resp. $\mathtt{x}$ and $\mathtt{y}$] are subscripted by some natural numbers we mean exactly the members from $\{\mathtt{a}_k : k \in \omega\}$ [resp. from $\{\mathtt{x}_k : k \in \omega\} \cup \{\mathtt{y}_k : k \in \omega\}$].

$\{\mathbf{x}_k : k \in \omega\} \cup \{\mathbf{y}_k : k \in \omega\}$ is a countable set of individual variables. A Π_1^0-formula is a FOL-formula of the form $\forall \mathbf{x}_1 \ldots \forall \mathbf{x}_n\ \phi$ where ϕ is quantifier-free and $n \geq 1$. A Π_2^0-formula is a FOL-formula of the form $\forall \mathbf{x}_1 \ldots \forall \mathbf{x}_n\ \exists \mathbf{y}_1 \ldots \exists \mathbf{y}_m\ \phi$ where ϕ is quantifier-free and $n, m \geq 1$. A *restricted Π_2^0-formula* ψ is defined here as a FOL-formula of the form $\forall \mathbf{x}_1 \ldots \forall \mathbf{x}_n\ \exists \mathbf{y}_1 \ldots \exists \mathbf{y}_m\ (\phi_1 \Rightarrow \phi_2)$ where

1. ψ is in *prenex normal form* (PNF) and $\phi_1 \Rightarrow \phi_2$ is precisely its *matrix*;
2. ϕ_1 and ϕ_2 are formulas built upon the binary predicate symbols R, =, the truth logical constant $\top$ and from $\{\mathbf{x}_1, \ldots, \mathbf{x}_n, \mathbf{y}_1, \ldots, \mathbf{y}_m\}$ (no individual constant occurs in $\phi_1 \Rightarrow \phi_2$); $n \geq 1$; $m \geq 0$;
3. ϕ_1 is either the logical constant $\top$ or a finite conjunction of literals (atomic formulae or negated atomic formulae) where no $\mathbf{y}_i$ occurs in ϕ_1;
4. ϕ_2 is a disjunction of conjunctions of literals.

A nominal tense logic $\mathcal{L} = \langle \mathtt{NTL}(G, H), \mathcal{C} \rangle$ is an element of the class $\mathcal{C}_{\Pi_2^0} \overset{\text{def}}{\Leftrightarrow}$ there is a set[3] Φ of restricted Π_2^0-formulae such that $\mathcal{C}$ is exactly the set of frames satisfying each formula from Φ (in the first-order sense). The class $\mathcal{C}$ of modal frames is also said to be $\mathcal{C}_{\Pi_2^0}$*-definable.* The class $\mathcal{C}_{\Pi_2^0}$ is quite large. By manipulation at the first-order level one can show:

1. For any closed (unrestricted) Π_2^0-formula $\psi \overset{\text{def}}{=} \forall \mathbf{x}_1 \ldots \forall \mathbf{x}_n\ \exists \mathbf{y}_1 \ldots \exists \mathbf{y}_m\ (\phi_1 \Rightarrow \phi_2)$ in PNF such that the only variables in ϕ_1 belong to $\{\mathbf{x}_1, \ldots, \mathbf{x}_n\}$, there exists a *finite* conjunction of *restricted Π_2^0-formulae* equivalent to ψ.
2. Every *primitive* first-order formula in the sense of [Kra96] is logically equivalent to a restricted Π_2^0-formula.
3. There exist $\mathcal{C}_{\Pi_2^0}$-definable classes of frames that contain only *infinite* frames (see e.g. [Bla93]).

Expressivity of the restricted Π_2^0-formulae is also well-illustrated by the fact that not only are there $\mathcal{C}_{\Pi_2^0}$-definable classes of frames that are not modally definable but also all the first-order classes of frames defined by a conjunction of conditions from Figure 2 and Figure 3 in [Gor99] are $\mathcal{C}_{\Pi_2^0}$-definable. All the first-order definable classes of frames considered in [Rus96, CFdCGH97] are $\mathcal{C}_{\Pi_2^0}$-definable and $\mathcal{C}_{\Pi_2^0}$ contains all the modal logics (in their nominal tense version) defined with Horn clauses from [BMV98]. Furthermore, for any nominal tense logic $\mathcal{L} = \langle \mathtt{NTL}(G, H), \mathcal{C} \rangle$ such that $\mathcal{C}$ is first-order definable by a finite set Φ of restricted Π_2^0-formulae, it is known that the $\mathcal{L}$-validity problem can be translated into FOL-validity (using [Ben83, GG93]). However, there is no guarantee that $\mathcal{L}$ admits a proof system (based on KE for instance) such that the cut rule satisfies the conditions (CR1), (CR2) and (CR3) -see Section 1. In the present paper, the delimitations of the class $\mathcal{C}_{\Pi_2^0}$ has been designed in such a way that the sequent calculi (based on KE) admit a cut-rule satisfying the computationnally nice conditions (CR1), (CR2) and (CR3) -other restrictions on the applications of various rules shall be introduced. Those criteria distinguish our work from the standard translation into FOL but other criteria are of course possible as done in [BMV97, Section 4] where enlighting analyses about the behaviour of the falsum $\perp$ can be found. To conclude this section, we warn the reader that although $\mathcal{C}_{\Pi_2^0}$ is undoubtly a very large class, we ignore whether it contains any logic *useful in practice.*

[3] Φ should be understood as a (possibly infinite) conjunction.

3 Sequent-style calculi for nominal tense logics

In this section, $\mathcal{L}$ denotes a nominal tense logic $\langle \mathtt{NTL}(G,H), \mathcal{C} \rangle$ in $\mathcal{C}_{\Pi^0_2}$ characterized by the set Φ of restricted Π^0_2-formulae.

3.1 Preliminaries

Most of the prefixed tableaux calculi for modal logics use prefixes as a compact way to *represent* sets of positive literals in first-order logic. It partly explains why numerous calculi can be viewed as a "clever translation"[4] into classical logic (see e.g. [Gen92]). For instance, in [Fit83], a prefix is defined as a (non-empty) sequence of natural numbers. A sequence $i_1 \ldots i_n \in \omega^*$ $(n \geq 1)$ can be understood (for example for the modal logic S4) as the set[5] $\{\mathtt{R}(\mathtt{a}_{i_1 \ldots i_m}, \mathtt{a}_{i_1 \ldots i_{m'}}) : 1 \leq m \leq m' \leq n\}$ of positive literals (the $\mathtt{a}_\sigma$'s are individual constants). It is therefore inaccurate to believe that since prefixes can be interpreted at the metalevel by worlds, then prefixes and nominals have the same expressive power. Actually, the prefixes are more expressive since the nominals do not contain any information about the accessibility relation. However, formulas involving nominals can encode first-order literals, positive and *negative* ones as shown below. For any model $\mathcal{M} = \langle W, R, m \rangle$, it is easy to show that $\mathtt{i}_1 \Rightarrow G\neg \mathtt{i}_2$ is true in $\mathcal{M}$ iff $(m(\mathtt{i}_1), m(\mathtt{i}_2)) \notin R$. So, $\mathtt{i}_1 \Rightarrow G\neg\mathtt{i}_2$ can be used as a negative literal. What seems to be lost here, is a conciseness of the representation: each literal is represented by one nominal tense formula of the same length (modulo some constant) and it is the approach chosen in the calculi defined in Section 3.2. However, since we are dealing with logics whose satisfiability is **NP**-hard, the following argument shows that conciseness is a secondary issue for mechanization. Indeed, let $i_1 \ldots i_n$ be a (non-empty) sequence of natural numbers representing a set X of first-order positive literals subset of $\{\mathtt{R}(\mathtt{a}_{i_1 \ldots i_m}, \mathtt{a}_{i_1 \ldots i_{m'}}) : m, m' \in \{1, \ldots, n\}\}$ (it depends on the modal logic we consider but let us treat the general case). The length of $i_1 \ldots i_n$, say $|i_1 \ldots i_n|$, is naturally defined as the sum of the length (in binary writing) of each natural number occurring in $i_1 \ldots i_n$. For instance, $|i_1 \ldots i_n| \geq n$ and $card(X) \leq n^2$. Let ϕ_X be the following nominal tense formula $\bigwedge_{\mathtt{R}(\mathtt{a}_{i_1 \ldots i_m}, \mathtt{a}_{i_1 \ldots i_{m'}}) \in X} \mathtt{i}_{i_1 \ldots i_m} \Rightarrow \neg G \neg \mathtt{i}_{i_1 \ldots i_{m'}}$ that encodes the prefix $i_1 \ldots i_n$ (or equivalently that encodes X). The generalized conjunction $\bigwedge$ should be here understood as an abbreviation for a certain amount of binary conjunctions. $|\phi_X|$ is in $\mathcal{O}(|i_1 \ldots i_n|^3)$ and therefore, if a formula ϕ has a proof Π with the "concise representation" of the positive literals, then ϕ has a proof Π' with the representation of literals "in extension" where $|\Pi'|$ is in $\mathcal{O}(|\Pi|^3)$. The *length* of the proof Π, denoted $|\Pi|$, is defined as the number of nodes in the tree. In a more general setting, it would be necessary to use a more refined definition of proof complexity which takes into account the length of proof steps. Since the calculi involved in the paper use a very restricted cut-rule (the size of the cut-formula is linear in the size of the conclusion), our definition is sufficient for our needs. As no subexponential algorithm for any **NP**-hard problem is known, such a cubic overhead

[4] [BG97] is one of the rare papers where such a relationship is explicitly recognized.

[5] Since ω^* and ω have the same cardinality, without any loss of generality, we can assume that the individual constants and the nominals are respectively of the form $\mathtt{a}_\sigma$ and $\mathtt{i}_\sigma$ where $\sigma \in \omega^*$.

($|\phi_X| \in \mathcal{O}(|i_1 \ldots i_n|^3)$) is not so significant (even in the worst-case) when dealing with **NP**-hard problems (and *a fortiori* with **PSPACE**-hard problems). Of course, this is highly significant to establish tight complexity upper bounds as done in [Hud96]. In [Kri63, CFdCGH97] and [Heu98, Chapter 4], some of the graphical representations of the sets of (positive) first-order literals enjoy some conciseness property comparable to the one for prefixes.

3.2 Definition

The basic syntactic objects in the calculus are *sequents*. A *sequent* is an expression of the form $\Gamma \vdash \Delta$ where Γ and Δ are finite multisets of nominal tense formulae, i.e. unordered collections of formulae that may contain several occurrences of the same formula. We write ϕ for $\{\phi\}$ and let "," denote the multiset union. The length of the sequent $\Gamma \vdash \Delta$, denoted $|\Gamma \vdash \Delta|$, is the sum of the length of each element from Γ, Δ. The sequent calculus, say $G\mathcal{L}$, for the logic $\mathcal{L}$ contains the rules in Figures 1-3. Other rules depending on Φ are presented when needed. In Figure 2, the rules $(refl)$, (sym) and $(trans)$ encode properties of identity (reflexivity, symmetry and transitivity). Similarly, the rules $(sub \vdash)$ and $(\vdash sub)$ ("sub" stands for substitution) encode that identical terms can be substituted. The $(start)$-rule has a special status since in any proof, this rule is applied exactly once, at the root (with the forthcoming restriction (R_{start})). This initiates the introduction of nominals that behave as prefixes. Observe that $\mathtt{i} \Rightarrow \phi$ is $\mathcal{L}$-valid iff ϕ is $\mathcal{L}$-valid when $\mathtt{i}$ does not occur in ϕ.

$$\Gamma, \mathtt{i} \Rightarrow \psi \vdash \Delta, \mathtt{i} \Rightarrow \psi \text{ (initial sequents)} \qquad \frac{\vdash \mathtt{i} \Rightarrow \phi}{\vdash \phi}\ (start)$$

For the $(start)$-rule, $\mathtt{i}$ does not occur in ϕ.

Fig. 1. Initial sequents and the rule $(start)$

We continue here the definition of $G\mathcal{L}$. Let σ be a finite sequence of formulas of the form $\mathtt{i} \Rightarrow \mathtt{j}$, $\mathtt{i} \Rightarrow \neg G \neg \mathtt{j}$, $\mathtt{i} \Rightarrow \neg \mathtt{j}$, $\mathtt{i} \Rightarrow G \neg \mathtt{j}$. Those formulae precisely "encodes" positive and negative first-order literals whose (binary) predicate symbol is either = or R. We define the sequent $(\Gamma \vdash \Delta) \otimes \sigma$ inductively on the length of σ as follows (λ denotes the empty string and $\otimes$ is simply an operator that inserts formulae in sequents):

- $(\Gamma \vdash \Delta) \otimes \lambda \stackrel{\text{def}}{=} \Gamma \vdash \Delta$;
- $(\Gamma \vdash \Delta) \otimes (\mathtt{i} \Rightarrow \mathtt{j}).\sigma' \stackrel{\text{def}}{=} (\Gamma, \mathtt{i} \Rightarrow \mathtt{j} \vdash \Delta) \otimes \sigma'$;
- $(\Gamma \vdash \Delta) \otimes (\mathtt{i} \Rightarrow G \neg \mathtt{j}).\sigma' \stackrel{\text{def}}{=} (\Gamma, \mathtt{i} \Rightarrow G \neg \mathtt{j} \vdash \Delta) \otimes \sigma'$;
- $(\Gamma \vdash \Delta) \otimes (\mathtt{i} \Rightarrow \neg \mathtt{j}).\sigma' \stackrel{\text{def}}{=} (\Gamma \vdash \Delta, \mathtt{i} \Rightarrow \mathtt{j}) \otimes \sigma'$;
- $(\Gamma \vdash \Delta) \otimes (\mathtt{i} \Rightarrow \neg G \neg \mathtt{j}).\sigma' \stackrel{\text{def}}{=} (\Gamma \vdash \Delta, \mathtt{i} \Rightarrow G \neg \mathtt{j}) \otimes \sigma'$.

Let ψ be a restricted Π^0_2-formula of the form

$$\frac{\Gamma, \mathrm{i} \Rightarrow \phi \vdash \Delta}{\Gamma \vdash \Delta, \mathrm{i} \Rightarrow \neg\phi} (\vdash \neg) \quad \frac{\Gamma \vdash \Delta, \mathrm{i} \Rightarrow \phi}{\Gamma, \mathrm{i} \Rightarrow \neg\phi \vdash \Delta} (\neg \vdash) \quad \frac{\Gamma, \mathrm{i} \Rightarrow \phi_1 \vdash \Delta, \mathrm{i} \Rightarrow \phi_2}{\Gamma \vdash \Delta, \mathrm{i} \Rightarrow (\phi_1 \Rightarrow \phi_2)} (\vdash\Rightarrow)$$

$$\frac{\Gamma, \mathrm{i} \Rightarrow \phi_1, \mathrm{i} \Rightarrow \phi_2 \vdash \Delta}{\Gamma, \mathrm{i} \Rightarrow \phi_1, \mathrm{i} \Rightarrow (\phi_1 \Rightarrow \phi_2) \vdash \Delta} (\Rightarrow\vdash)_1 \quad \frac{\Gamma \vdash \Delta, \mathrm{i} \Rightarrow \phi_1, \mathrm{i} \Rightarrow \phi_2}{\Gamma, \mathrm{i} \Rightarrow (\phi_1 \Rightarrow \phi_2) \vdash \Delta, \mathrm{i} \Rightarrow \phi_2} (\Rightarrow\vdash)_2$$

$$\frac{\Gamma, \mathrm{i} \Rightarrow \phi \vdash \Delta, \mathrm{i} \Rightarrow \psi}{\Gamma, \mathrm{i} \Rightarrow \phi \vdash \Delta, \mathrm{i} \Rightarrow (\phi \wedge \psi)} (\vdash \wedge)_1 \quad \frac{\Gamma, \mathrm{i} \Rightarrow \psi \vdash \Delta, \mathrm{i} \Rightarrow \phi}{\Gamma, \mathrm{i} \Rightarrow \psi \vdash \Delta, \mathrm{i} \Rightarrow (\phi \wedge \psi)} (\vdash \wedge)_2$$

$$\frac{\Gamma, \mathrm{i} \Rightarrow \phi, \mathrm{i} \Rightarrow \psi \vdash \Delta}{\Gamma, \mathrm{i} \Rightarrow (\phi \wedge \psi) \vdash \Delta} (\wedge \vdash)$$

$$\frac{\Gamma, \mathrm{i} \Rightarrow G\psi, \mathrm{j} \Rightarrow \psi \vdash \Delta, \mathrm{i} \Rightarrow G\neg\mathrm{j}}{\Gamma, \mathrm{i} \Rightarrow G\psi \vdash \Delta, \mathrm{i} \Rightarrow G\neg\mathrm{j}} (G \vdash) \quad \frac{\Gamma \vdash \Delta, \mathrm{j} \Rightarrow \psi, \mathrm{i} \Rightarrow G\neg\mathrm{j}}{\Gamma \vdash \Delta, \mathrm{i} \Rightarrow G\psi} (\vdash G)$$

$$\frac{\Gamma, \mathrm{j} \Rightarrow H\psi, \mathrm{i} \Rightarrow \psi \vdash \Delta, \mathrm{i} \Rightarrow G\neg\mathrm{j},}{\Gamma, \mathrm{j} \Rightarrow H\psi \vdash \Delta, \mathrm{i} \Rightarrow G\neg\mathrm{j}} (H \vdash) \quad \frac{\Gamma \vdash \Delta, \mathrm{j} \Rightarrow \psi, \mathrm{j} \Rightarrow G\neg\mathrm{i}}{\Gamma \vdash \Delta, \mathrm{i} \Rightarrow H\psi} (\vdash H)$$

in $(\vdash H)$ and $(\vdash G)$, j does not occur in the conclusion

$$\frac{\Gamma, \mathrm{i} \Rightarrow \mathrm{j}, \mathrm{i}' \Rightarrow \mathrm{j}, \mathrm{i} \Rightarrow \mathrm{i}' \vdash \Delta}{\Gamma, \mathrm{i} \Rightarrow \mathrm{j}, \mathrm{i}' \Rightarrow \mathrm{j} \vdash \Delta} (NOM_= \vdash)$$

$$\frac{\Gamma, \mathrm{i} \Rightarrow \psi \vdash \Delta, \mathrm{i}' \Rightarrow \psi, \mathrm{i} \Rightarrow \mathrm{i}'}{\Gamma, \mathrm{i} \Rightarrow \psi \vdash \Delta, \mathrm{i}' \Rightarrow \psi} (\vdash NOM_=)$$

$$\frac{\Gamma, \mathrm{i} \Rightarrow G\psi, \mathrm{i} \Rightarrow G\neg\mathrm{i}' \vdash \Delta, \mathrm{i}' \Rightarrow \psi}{\Gamma, \mathrm{i} \Rightarrow G\psi \vdash \Delta, \mathrm{i}' \Rightarrow \psi} (NOM_G \vdash)$$

$$\frac{\Gamma, \mathrm{i} \Rightarrow \mathrm{j} \vdash \Delta, \mathrm{i}' \Rightarrow G\neg\mathrm{j}, \mathrm{i}' \Rightarrow G\neg\mathrm{i}}{\Gamma, \mathrm{i} \Rightarrow \mathrm{j} \vdash \Delta, \mathrm{i}' \Rightarrow G\neg\mathrm{j}} (\vdash NOM_G)$$

$$\frac{\Gamma, \mathrm{i} \Rightarrow H\psi, \mathrm{i}' \Rightarrow G\neg\mathrm{i} \vdash \Delta, \mathrm{i}' \Rightarrow \psi}{\Gamma, \mathrm{i} \Rightarrow H\psi \vdash \Delta, \mathrm{i}' \Rightarrow \psi} (NOM_H \vdash)$$

$$\frac{\Gamma, \mathrm{i} \Rightarrow \mathrm{j} \vdash \Delta, \mathrm{i}' \Rightarrow H\neg\mathrm{j}, \mathrm{i} \Rightarrow G\neg\mathrm{i}'}{\Gamma, \mathrm{i} \Rightarrow \mathrm{j} \vdash \Delta, \mathrm{i}' \Rightarrow H\neg\mathrm{j}} (\vdash NOM_H)$$

$$\frac{\Gamma, \mathrm{i} \Rightarrow \mathrm{i} \vdash \Delta}{\Gamma \vdash \Delta} (refl) \quad \frac{\Gamma, \mathrm{j} \Rightarrow \mathrm{i}, \mathrm{i} \Rightarrow \mathrm{j} \vdash \Delta}{\Gamma, \mathrm{i} \Rightarrow \mathrm{j} \vdash \Delta} (sym) \quad \frac{\Gamma, \mathrm{i} \Rightarrow \mathrm{k}, \mathrm{i} \Rightarrow \mathrm{j}, \mathrm{j} \Rightarrow \mathrm{k} \vdash \Delta}{\Gamma, \mathrm{i} \Rightarrow \mathrm{j}, \mathrm{j} \Rightarrow \mathrm{k} \vdash \Delta} (trans)$$

$$\frac{\Gamma, \mathrm{i} \Rightarrow \phi, \mathrm{i} \Rightarrow \mathrm{j}, \mathrm{j} \Rightarrow \phi \vdash \Delta}{\Gamma, \mathrm{i} \Rightarrow \mathrm{j}, \mathrm{j} \Rightarrow \phi \vdash \Delta} (sub \vdash) \quad \frac{\Gamma, \mathrm{i} \Rightarrow \mathrm{j} \vdash \Delta, \mathrm{i} \Rightarrow \phi, \mathrm{j} \Rightarrow \phi}{\Gamma, \mathrm{i} \Rightarrow \mathrm{j} \vdash \Delta, \mathrm{j} \Rightarrow \phi} (\vdash sub)$$

$$\frac{\Gamma, \mathrm{j} \Rightarrow \mathrm{j}', \mathrm{i} \Rightarrow G\neg\mathrm{j}, \mathrm{i} \Rightarrow G\neg\mathrm{j}' \vdash \Delta}{\Gamma, \mathrm{j} \Rightarrow \mathrm{j}', \mathrm{i} \Rightarrow G\neg\mathrm{j} \vdash \Delta} (sub' \vdash)$$

$$\frac{\Gamma, \mathrm{j} \Rightarrow \mathrm{j}' \vdash \Delta, \mathrm{i} \Rightarrow G\neg\mathrm{j}, \mathrm{i} \Rightarrow G\neg\mathrm{j}'}{\Gamma, \mathrm{j} \Rightarrow \mathrm{j}' \vdash \Delta, \mathrm{i} \Rightarrow G\neg\mathrm{j}} (\vdash sub')$$

Fig. 2. Common core of (introduction) rules in $G\mathcal{L}$

$$\frac{\Gamma \vdash \Delta, \mathtt{i} \Rightarrow \psi \quad \Gamma, \mathtt{i} \Rightarrow \psi \vdash \Delta}{\Gamma \vdash \Delta} \; (PB)$$

Fig. 3. Principle of bivalence

$$\forall \mathbf{x}_1, \ldots, \mathbf{x}_n \; \exists \mathbf{y}_1, \ldots, \mathbf{y}_m s_0^1 P_0^1(z_{1,0}^1, z_{2,0}^1) \wedge \ldots \wedge s_0^{l(0)} P_0^{l(0)}(z_{1,0}^{l(0)}, z_{2,0}^{l(0)}) \Rightarrow \bigvee_{i=1}^{k} s_i^1 P_i^1(z_{1,i}^1, z_{2,i}^1) \wedge \ldots \wedge s_0^{l(i)} P_0^{l(i)}(z_{1,i}^{l(i)}, z_{2,i}^{l(i)})$$

where

1. each P_i^j belongs to $\{=, \mathtt{R}\}$; each s_i^j belongs to $\{\lambda, \neg\}$;
2. each $z_{\alpha,0}^{\beta}$ $(1 \leq \alpha \leq 2,\, 1 \leq \beta \leq l(0))$ belongs to $\{\mathbf{x}_1, \ldots, \mathbf{x}_n\}$;
3. each $z_{\alpha,i}^{\beta}$ $(1 \leq \alpha \leq 2, 1 \leq i \leq k, 1 \leq \beta \leq l(i))$ belongs to $\{\mathbf{x}_1, \ldots, \mathbf{x}_n, \mathbf{y}_1, \ldots, \mathbf{y}_m\}$.

We shall now define the (ψ)-rule that mimicks the syntactic structure of ψ. For any $\mathtt{i}, \mathtt{j} \in \mathbf{For}_0^N$, for any $s, s' \in \{\lambda, \neg\}$ such that $s \neq s'$ and for any $P \in \{=, \mathtt{R}\}$, let us define the formula $\Sigma(sP, \mathtt{i}, \mathtt{j})$ as follows:

$$\Sigma(sP, \mathtt{i}, \mathtt{j}) \stackrel{\text{def}}{=} \begin{cases} \mathtt{i} \Rightarrow s'G\neg\mathtt{j} \text{ if } P = \mathtt{R}; \\ \mathtt{i} \Rightarrow s\mathtt{j} \text{ otherwise.} \end{cases}$$

Roughly speaking, a literal $sP(\mathbf{x}_k, \mathbf{x}_{k'})$ in ψ shall be encoded by $\Sigma(sP, \mathtt{i}_k, \mathtt{i}_{k'})$. For any formula ψ in Φ, we add the (ψ)-rule in Figure 4 to $G\mathcal{L}$. The conditions 1.

$$\frac{(\Gamma \vdash \Delta) \otimes \sigma_1 \quad \ldots \quad (\Gamma \vdash \Delta) \otimes \sigma_k}{(\Gamma \vdash \Delta) \otimes \sigma_0} \; (\psi)$$

1. $\sigma_0 = \Sigma(s_0^1 P_0^1, \mathtt{i}_{1,0}^1, \mathtt{i}_{2,0}^1), \ldots, \Sigma(s_0^{l(0)} P_0^{l(0)}, \mathtt{i}_{1,0}^{l(0)}, \mathtt{i}_{2,0}^{l(0)})$;
2. for $1 \leq u \leq k$, $\sigma_u = \sigma_0.\Sigma(s_u^1 P_u^1, \mathtt{i}_{1,u}^1, \mathtt{i}_{2,u}^1). \ldots .\Sigma(s_u^{l(u)} P_u^{l(u)}, \mathtt{i}_{1,u}^{l(u)}, \mathtt{i}_{2,u}^{l(u)})$;
3. for any $\alpha, \alpha' \in \{1, 2\}$, $q, q' \in \{1, \ldots, k\}$, $r \in \{1, \ldots .l(q)\}$ and $r' \in \{1, \ldots .l(q')\}$,
   (a) $z_{\alpha,q}^{r} = z_{\alpha',q'}^{r'}$ iff $\mathtt{i}_{\alpha,q}^{r} = \mathtt{i}_{\alpha',q'}^{r'}$;
   (b) if $z_{\alpha,q}^{r}$ is equal to some $\mathbf{y}_i$, then $\mathtt{i}_{\alpha,q}^{r}$ does not occur in the conclusion.

Fig. 4. (ψ)-rule for $\psi \in \Phi$

and 2. in Figure 4 relate the (ψ)-rule with the structure of ψ (without taking care of the variables). Condition 3.(a) roughly states that each variable occurring in ψ corresponds to a unique nominal in the application of the (ψ)-rule. Condition 3.(b) states that the nominals corresponding to the $\mathbf{y}_i$'s are new on the branch. The (ψ)-rule can be viewed as a generalization of the "ρ-rule" in [Bal98] and of the "Horn relational rule" in [BMV97, BMV98]. More generally, the (ψ)-rules merely encodes the logical consequence relation of the first-order relational theory of $\mathcal{L}$ (as also done in [Gen92]). Furthermore, since the definition of the (ψ)-rules is purely syntactic, it is *not* guaranteed that for logics $\mathcal{L}$, $\mathcal{L}'$ in $\mathcal{C}_{\Pi^0_2}$ characterized by Φ and Φ' respectively, if Φ and Φ' define the same class of frames, then $G\mathcal{L}$ and $G\mathcal{L}'$ have exactly the same rules.

Example 1. Let $\mathcal{L}_{\neq} \stackrel{\text{def}}{=} \langle \mathtt{NTL}(G,H), \mathcal{C}_{\neq}\rangle$ be the nominal tense logic such that $\Phi \stackrel{\text{def}}{=} \{\forall \mathtt{x},\mathtt{y}\ \mathtt{R}(\mathtt{x},\mathtt{y}) \Rightarrow \neg(\mathtt{x}{=}\mathtt{y}), \forall \mathtt{x},\mathtt{y}\ \neg(\mathtt{x}{=}\mathtt{y}) \Rightarrow \mathtt{R}(\mathtt{x},\mathtt{y})\}$. The tense operators G and H are actually equivalent and G is merely the difference modal operator $[\neq]$. The rules of $G\mathcal{L}_{\neq}$ are those in Figures 1-3 plus the rules defined from Φ:

$$\frac{\Gamma \vdash \Delta, \mathtt{i} \Rightarrow \mathtt{j}, \mathtt{i} \Rightarrow G\neg\mathtt{j}}{\Gamma \vdash \Delta, \mathtt{i} \Rightarrow G\neg\mathtt{j}} \qquad \frac{\Gamma \vdash \Delta, \mathtt{i} \Rightarrow G\neg\mathtt{j}, \mathtt{i} \Rightarrow \mathtt{j}}{\Gamma \vdash \Delta, \mathtt{i} \Rightarrow \mathtt{j}}$$

A proof Π in $G\mathcal{L}$ is a tree whose nodes are labelled by sequents satisfying the following conditions: the topmost sequents of Π are initial sequents and every sequent of Π, except the lowest one is an upper sequent of an inference whose lower sequent is also in Π. A formula ϕ is *provable in* $G\mathcal{L}$ $\stackrel{\text{def}}{\Leftrightarrow}$ there is a proof Π in $G\mathcal{L}$ such that $\vdash \phi$ is the lowest sequent of Π.

3.3 Soundness, restrictions and completeness

Lemma 1. *Let $\Gamma \vdash \Delta$ be a sequent provable in $G\mathcal{L}$. Then, for any $\mathcal{L}$-model $\mathcal{M}$, for all $\psi \in \Gamma$, ψ is true in $\mathcal{M}$ implies that ϕ' is true in $\mathcal{M}$ for some $\phi' \in \Delta$.*

The proof is by induction on the length of the derivation. It is more standard to prove soundness by using the notion of *satisfiability* in a model rather than the notion of *truth* in a model as done here.

Theorem 2. *If $\phi \in \mathtt{NTL}(G,H)$ is provable in $G\mathcal{L}$, then ϕ is $\mathcal{L}$-valid.*

The system $G\mathcal{L}$ is not minimal since for instance, the $(\vdash NOM_=)$-rule, the $(NOM_H \vdash)$-rule and the $(NOM_G \vdash)$-rule are derivable from the rest of $G\mathcal{L}$. These rules are included for the sake of symmetry. The system $G\mathcal{L}$ is considerably improved for the mechanization by imposing the restrictions (R_{init}), (R_{start}), $(R_=)$, $(R_{no-renaming})$, (R_{PB}), (R_{NOM}), $(R_{witness})$, $(R_{sub'})$ and (R_ψ) for $\psi \in \Phi$ defined below. *In the rest of the paper, by $G\mathcal{L}$, we mean the calculus with such restrictions.* First, any nominal $\mathtt{j}$ that occurs on a branch of a (possibly partial) proof whose root is labeled by ϕ is a *p-name* (standing for "implicit prefix") $\stackrel{\text{def}}{\Leftrightarrow}$ $\mathtt{j}$ has been placed on the branch by application of a rule that introduces new nominals. The notion of p-names is similar to that of Skolem constants.

- (R_{init}) for the initial sequent is: any ϕ' occurring in $\Gamma, \mathtt{i} \Rightarrow \psi \vdash \Delta, \mathtt{i} \Rightarrow \psi$ is of the form $\mathtt{j} \Rightarrow \psi''$ where $\mathtt{j}$ is a p-name, ψ'' is either a subformula of ϕ (syntactically) equal to an atomic proposition in the case when $\mathtt{j} \Rightarrow \psi'' = \mathtt{i} \Rightarrow \psi$ or a p-name, or a nominal occurring in the root sequent $\vdash \phi$ or a formula of the form $G\neg\mathtt{j}'$ with $\mathtt{j}'$ a p-name.
- (R_{start}) for the $(start)$-rule is: ϕ is not of the form $\mathtt{j} \Rightarrow \phi'$ where $\mathtt{j}$ is a p-name.
- $(R_=)$ concerns the rules $(refl)$, (sym), $(trans)$, $(\vdash sub)$ and $(sub \vdash)$: all the names $\mathtt{i}, \mathtt{j}, \mathtt{k}$ are p-names.

- $(R_{no-renaming})$ is: in $(\vdash G)$ and in $(\vdash H)$ ψ is not a negated p-name.
- (R_{PB}) is: $\mathtt{i}$ is a p-name and ψ is either a subformula in ϕ of secondary disjunctive force or $G\neg\mathtt{j}$ with $\mathtt{j}$ a p-name or a p-name $\mathtt{j}$.
- (R_{NOM}) concerns the rules $(\vdash NOM_=)$, $(NOM_= \vdash)$, $(\vdash NOM_G)$, $(NOM_G \vdash)$, $(\vdash NOM_H)$, $(NOM_H \vdash)$: $\mathtt{i}$ and $\mathtt{i}'$ are p-names whereas $\mathtt{j}$ is not a p-name.
- $(R_{witness})$ concerns the rules $(G\vdash)$ and $(H\vdash)$: $\mathtt{i}$ and $\mathtt{j}$ are p-names.
- $(R_{sub'})$ is: in the $(sub'\vdash)$-rule and the $(\vdash sub')$-rule, $\mathtt{i}, \mathtt{j}$ and $\mathtt{j}'$ are p-names.
- The restriction (R_ψ) for the (ψ)-rule for $\psi \in \Phi$ is: all the nominals occurring in σ_0 are p-names.

The sequent calculus $G\mathcal{L}$ (in its restricted form) has the following separation property: any p-name $\mathtt{i}$ occurring in a branch does not occur in a formula $\mathtt{j} \Rightarrow \psi$ occurring on the same branch, except when either $\mathtt{j} = \mathtt{i}$ or $\psi = G\neg\mathtt{i}$ or $\psi = \mathtt{i}$. This separation property illustrates the control on the use of nominals imposed by the above restrictions.

Theorem 3. *If $\phi \in$ NTL(G, H) is $\mathcal{L}$-valid, then ϕ is provable in $G\mathcal{L}$.*

The proof of Theorem 3 (using Schütte's method) is based on a similar proof for *classical logic*. In Section 4, we formally state in which sense $G\mathcal{L}$ is equivalent to a calculus for a fragment of classical logic.

4 Sequent calculi for fragments of classical logic with relational theories

In this section, we define a first-order Gentzen-style calculus $GFOL_\mathcal{L}$ (based on the calculus KEQ [d'A90, Section 3.5]) such that $G\mathcal{L}$ and $GFOL_\mathcal{L}$ can be viewed as syntactic variants. This is the opportunity to formally present (once and for all) how a tableaux calculus can be viewed as a translation into classical logic. Let us briefly recall the translation ST ("Standard Translation") defined in [Ben83, GG93] of nominal tense formulae into the first-order language (here $\mathtt{t}$ is either a variable or a constant): $ST(\mathtt{p}_j, \mathtt{t}) \stackrel{\text{def}}{=} \mathtt{P}_j(\mathtt{t})$; $ST(\mathtt{i}_j, \mathtt{t}) \stackrel{\text{def}}{=} \mathtt{t}{=}\mathtt{a}_j$; $ST(\neg\psi, \mathtt{t}) \stackrel{\text{def}}{=} \neg ST(\psi, \mathtt{t})$; $ST(\psi \oplus \phi', \mathtt{t}) \stackrel{\text{def}}{=} ST(\psi, \mathtt{t}) \oplus ST(\phi', \mathtt{t})$ for $\oplus \in \{\wedge, \Rightarrow\}$; $ST(G\psi, \mathtt{t}) \stackrel{\text{def}}{=} \forall\, \mathtt{x}'\ (\mathtt{R}(\mathtt{t}, \mathtt{x}') \Rightarrow ST(\psi, \mathtt{x}'))$ where $\mathtt{x}'$ is a *new* variable; $ST(H\psi, \mathtt{t}) \stackrel{\text{def}}{=} \forall\, \mathtt{x}'\ (\mathtt{R}(\mathtt{x}', \mathtt{t}) \Rightarrow ST(\psi, \mathtt{x}'))$ where $\mathtt{x}'$ is a *new* variable. It is known that ϕ is $\mathcal{L}$-valid iff $\Phi \Rightarrow \forall \mathtt{x}_0\ ST(\phi, \mathtt{x}_0)$ is FOL-valid. The previous statement assumes that Φ is a *finite* conjunction. By contrast, the developments in this section *does not* assume that Φ is finite. The rules of the calculus $GFOL_\mathcal{L}$ are those presented in Figure 5 - Figure 6 (other rules are added later on). Like the notion of p-name in $G\mathcal{L}$, an individual constant $\mathtt{a}$ occurring on a branch is said to be a *p-constant* (or Skolem constant) $\stackrel{\text{def}}{\Leftrightarrow}$ $\mathtt{a}$ does not occur in the root sequent of the proof (possibly in construction) and it has been introduced on the branch by a rule putting new constants on the branches. We write $\psi(\mathtt{a}_k)$ [resp. $\psi(\mathtt{x})$] to denote the formula whose $\mathtt{a}_k$ is a p-constant occurring in it [resp. whose $\mathtt{x}$ is a *free* individual variable occurring in it.].

For instance, the rules $(\forall\vdash)_1$ and $(\forall\vdash)_2$ can be seen as derived rules in the calculus KEQ [d'A90] using the rules from KEQ recalled below

$$\Gamma, \psi \vdash \Delta, \psi \text{ (initial sequents)}$$

under the proviso: any formula ϕ' in Γ, ψ, Δ is (1) either a subformula $\psi''(\mathtt{a})$ of $\forall \mathtt{x}_0\ ST(\phi, \mathtt{x}_0)$ where a is the unique p-constant in $\psi''(\mathtt{a})$ and in the case when $\psi = \psi''$, ψ is atomic (2) or a formula a=b where a is a p-constant and b is either a p-constant or a constant occurring in $\forall \mathtt{x}_0\ ST(\phi, \mathtt{x}_0)$ (3) or a formula $\mathtt{R}(\mathtt{a}, \mathtt{b})$ where a and b are p-names.

$$\frac{\Gamma \vdash \Delta, \psi \quad \Gamma, \psi \vdash \Delta}{\Gamma \vdash \Delta} \ (PB)$$

where either ψ is a formula of secondary disjunctive force occurring below in the proof containing a unique p-constant or ψ is of the form $\mathtt{a}_k=\mathtt{a}_{k'}$ or $\mathtt{R}(\mathtt{a}_k, \mathtt{a}_{k'})$ where $\mathtt{a}_k$ and $\mathtt{a}_{k'}$ are p-constants.

$$\frac{\vdash ST(\phi, \mathtt{a}_k)}{\vdash \forall \mathtt{x}_0\ ST(\phi, \mathtt{x}_0)} \ (start)$$

the application of $(start)$ is under the proviso that $\mathtt{a}_k$ does not occur in $ST(\phi, \mathtt{x})$ (or equivalently, $\mathtt{i}_k$ does not occur in ϕ) and $\forall \mathtt{x}_0\ ST(\phi, \mathtt{x}_0)$ does not contain p-constants.

Fig. 5. First bunch of rules for $GFOL_{\mathcal{L}}$

$$\frac{\Gamma, \forall \mathtt{x}\ \phi(\mathtt{x}), \phi(\mathtt{a}) \vdash \Delta}{\Gamma, \forall \mathtt{x}\ \phi(\mathtt{x}) \vdash \Delta} \qquad \frac{\Gamma, \phi_1, \phi_2, \vdash \Delta}{\Gamma, \phi_1, \phi_1 \Rightarrow \phi_2, \vdash \Delta}$$

This explains why the universal quantification in modal logic can be naturally encoded in KEQ .

Let σ be a finite sequence of formulas of the form $\mathtt{R}(\mathtt{a}, \mathtt{a}')$, $\neg\mathtt{R}(\mathtt{a}, \mathtt{a}')$, $\mathtt{a}=\mathtt{a}'$, $\neg(\mathtt{a}=\mathtt{a}')$. We define the sequent $(\Gamma \vdash \Delta) \otimes' \sigma$ inductively as follows:

- $(\Gamma \vdash \Delta) \otimes' \lambda \stackrel{\text{def}}{=} \Gamma \vdash \Delta$; $(\Gamma \vdash \Delta) \otimes' \mathtt{a}=\mathtt{a}'.\sigma' \stackrel{\text{def}}{=} (\Gamma, \mathtt{a}=\mathtt{a}' \vdash \Delta) \otimes' \sigma'$;
- $(\Gamma \vdash \Delta) \otimes' \neg\mathtt{R}(\mathtt{a}, \mathtt{a}').\sigma' \stackrel{\text{def}}{=} (\Gamma \vdash \Delta, \mathtt{R}(\mathtt{a}, \mathtt{a}')) \otimes' \sigma'$;
- $(\Gamma \vdash \Delta) \otimes' \neg(\mathtt{a}=\mathtt{a}').\sigma' \stackrel{\text{def}}{=} (\Gamma \vdash \Delta, \mathtt{a}=\mathtt{a}') \otimes' \sigma'$;
- $(\Gamma \vdash \Delta) \otimes' \mathtt{R}(\mathtt{a}, \mathtt{a}').\sigma' \stackrel{\text{def}}{=} (\Gamma, \mathtt{R}(\mathtt{a}, \mathtt{a}') \vdash \Delta) \otimes' \sigma'$.

Let ψ be a restricted Π^0_2-formula in Φ (we use the notations from Section 3). The rule associated to ψ is presented in Figure 7.

By construction, the calculi $G\mathcal{L}$ and $GFOL_{\mathcal{L}}$ have (almost) the same amount of rules and there is a natural correspondence between the rules of $G\mathcal{L}$ and $GFOL_{\mathcal{L}}$. For instance, the $(\forall \vdash)_1$-rule in $GFOL_{\mathcal{L}}$ correspond to the $(G \vdash)$-rule in $G\mathcal{L}$ and the $(sub \vdash)$-rule and $(sub' \vdash)$-rule in $G\mathcal{L}$ correspond to the (sub_{fol})-rule in $GFOL_{\mathcal{L}}$.

Let $\phi \in \mathtt{For}$ and Π be a proof of $\forall \mathtt{x}_0\ ST(\phi, \mathtt{x}_0)$ in $GFOL_{\mathcal{L}}$. By induction on the length of Π one can show that any formula ψ occurring in Π has at most two p-constants occurring in it. Moreover, if ψ is not an atomic formula whose predicate symbol is binary, then exactly one p-constant occurs in ψ unless ψ is the root formula $\forall \mathtt{x}_0 ST(\phi, \mathtt{x}_0)$ itself. This is reminiscent of the facts that

$$\frac{\Gamma, \phi \vdash \Delta}{\Gamma \vdash \Delta, \neg\phi}\ (\vdash \neg) \qquad \frac{\Gamma \vdash \Delta, \phi}{\Gamma, \neg\phi \vdash \Delta}\ (\neg \vdash) \qquad \frac{\Gamma, \phi_1 \vdash \Delta, \phi_2}{\Gamma \vdash \Delta, \phi_1 \Rightarrow \phi_2}\ (\vdash \Rightarrow)$$

$$\frac{\Gamma, \phi_1, \phi_2 \vdash \Delta}{\Gamma, \phi_1, \phi_1 \Rightarrow \phi_2 \vdash \Delta}\ (\Rightarrow \vdash)_1 \qquad \frac{\Gamma \vdash \Delta, \phi_1, \phi_2}{\Gamma, \phi_1 \Rightarrow \phi_2 \vdash \Delta, \phi_2}\ (\Rightarrow \vdash)_2$$

$$\frac{\Gamma, \phi \vdash \Delta, \psi}{\Gamma, \phi \vdash \Delta, \phi \wedge \psi}\ (\vdash \wedge)_1 \qquad \frac{\Gamma, \psi \vdash \Delta, \phi}{\Gamma, \psi \vdash \Delta, \phi \wedge \psi}\ (\vdash \wedge)_2 \qquad \frac{\Gamma, \phi, \psi \vdash \Delta}{\Gamma, \phi \wedge \psi \vdash \Delta}\ (\wedge \vdash)$$

$$\frac{\Gamma, \mathrm{R}(\mathrm{a}, \mathrm{b}), \forall \mathrm{x}\ (\mathrm{R}(\mathrm{a}, \mathrm{x}) \Rightarrow \phi(\mathrm{x})), \phi(\mathrm{b}) \vdash \Delta}{\Gamma, \mathrm{R}(\mathrm{a}, \mathrm{b}), \forall \mathrm{x}\ (\mathrm{R}(\mathrm{a}, \mathrm{x}) \Rightarrow \phi(\mathrm{x})) \vdash \Delta}\ (\forall \vdash)_1 \qquad \frac{\Gamma, \mathrm{R}(\mathrm{b}, \mathrm{a}), \forall \mathrm{x}\ (\mathrm{R}(\mathrm{x}, \mathrm{a}) \Rightarrow \phi(\mathrm{x})), \phi(\mathrm{b}) \vdash \Delta}{\Gamma, \mathrm{R}(\mathrm{b}, \mathrm{a}), \forall \mathrm{x}\ (\mathrm{R}(\mathrm{x}, \mathrm{a}) \Rightarrow \phi(\mathrm{x})) \vdash \Delta}\ (\forall \vdash)_2$$

$$\frac{\Gamma, \mathrm{R}(\mathrm{a}, \mathrm{b}), \vdash \Delta, \phi(\mathrm{b})}{\Gamma \vdash \Delta, \forall \mathrm{x}\ (\mathrm{R}(\mathrm{a}, \mathrm{x}) \Rightarrow \phi(\mathrm{x}))}\ (\vdash \forall)_1 \qquad \frac{\Gamma, \mathrm{R}(\mathrm{b}, \mathrm{a}), \vdash \Delta, \phi(\mathrm{b})}{\Gamma \vdash \Delta, \forall \mathrm{x}\ (\mathrm{R}(\mathrm{x}, \mathrm{a}) \Rightarrow \phi(\mathrm{x}))}\ (\vdash \forall)_2$$

under the proviso that b does not occur in the lower sequent.

$$\frac{\Gamma, \mathrm{a}_{k_1}{=}\mathrm{a}_k, \mathrm{a}_{k_2}{=}\mathrm{a}_k, \mathrm{a}_{k_1}{=}\mathrm{a}_{k_2} \vdash \Delta}{\Gamma, \mathrm{a}_{k_1}{=}\mathrm{a}_k, \mathrm{a}_{k_2}{=}\mathrm{a}_k \vdash \Delta}\ (NOM'_= \vdash)$$

$$\frac{\Gamma, \psi(\mathrm{a}_{k_1}) \vdash \Delta, \psi(\mathrm{a}_{k_2}), \mathrm{a}_{k_1}{=}\mathrm{a}_{k_2}}{\Gamma, \psi(\mathrm{a}_{k_1}) \vdash \Delta, \psi(\mathrm{a}_{k_2})}\ (\vdash NOM'_=)$$

$$\frac{\Gamma, \forall \mathrm{x}(\mathrm{R}(\mathrm{a}_{k_1}, \mathrm{x}) \Rightarrow \psi(\mathrm{x})) \vdash \Delta, \psi(\mathrm{a}_{k_2}), \mathrm{R}(\mathrm{a}_{k_1}, \mathrm{a}_{k_2})}{\Gamma, \forall \mathrm{x}(\mathrm{R}(\mathrm{a}_{k_1}, \mathrm{x}) \Rightarrow \psi(\mathrm{x})) \vdash \Delta, \psi(\mathrm{a}_{k_2})}\ (NOM'_G \vdash)$$

$$\frac{\Gamma, \mathrm{a}_{k_1}{=}\mathrm{a}_k, \mathrm{R}(\mathrm{a}_{k_2}, \mathrm{a}_{k_1}) \vdash \Delta, \forall \mathrm{x}(\mathrm{R}(\mathrm{a}_{k_2}, \mathrm{x}) \Rightarrow \neg(\mathrm{x}{=}\mathrm{a}_k))}{\Gamma, \mathrm{a}_{k_1}{=}\mathrm{a}_k \vdash \Delta, \forall \mathrm{x}(\mathrm{R}(\mathrm{a}_{k_2}, \mathrm{x}) \Rightarrow \neg(\mathrm{x}{=}\mathrm{a}_k))}\ (\vdash NOM'_G)$$

$$\frac{\Gamma, \forall \mathrm{x}(\mathrm{R}(\mathrm{a}_{k_1}, \mathrm{x}) \Rightarrow \psi(\mathrm{x})) \vdash \Delta, \psi(\mathrm{a}_{k_2}), \mathrm{R}(\mathrm{a}_{k_2}, \mathrm{a}_{k_1})}{\Gamma, \forall \mathrm{x}(\mathrm{R}(\mathrm{x}, \mathrm{a}_{k_1}) \Rightarrow \psi(\mathrm{x})) \vdash \Delta, \psi(\mathrm{a}_{k_2})}\ (NOM'_H \vdash)$$

$$\frac{\Gamma, \mathrm{a}_{k_1}{=}\mathrm{a}_k, \mathrm{R}(\mathrm{a}_{k_1}, \mathrm{a}_{k_2}) \vdash \Delta, \forall \mathrm{x}(\mathrm{R}(\mathrm{a}_{k_2}, \mathrm{x}) \Rightarrow \neg(\mathrm{x}{=}\mathrm{a}_k))}{\Gamma, \mathrm{a}_{k_1}{=}\mathrm{a}_k \vdash \Delta, \forall \mathrm{x}(\mathrm{R}(\mathrm{x}, \mathrm{a}_{k_2}) \Rightarrow \neg(\mathrm{x}{=}\mathrm{a}_k))}\ (\vdash NOM'_H)$$

in the above rules, a_{k_1} and a_{k_2} are p-constants and a_k is not a p-constant.

$$\frac{\Gamma, \mathrm{a}{=}\mathrm{a} \vdash \Delta}{\Gamma \vdash \Delta}\ \mathrm{a}\ occurs\ in\ \Gamma, \Delta \qquad \frac{\Gamma, \mathrm{a}{=}\mathrm{b}, \mathrm{b}{=}\mathrm{a}, \vdash \Delta}{\Gamma, \mathrm{a}{=}\mathrm{b} \vdash \Delta} \qquad \frac{\Gamma, \mathrm{a}{=}\mathrm{b}, \mathrm{b}{=}\mathrm{b}', \mathrm{a}{=}\mathrm{b}', \vdash \Delta}{\Gamma, \mathrm{a}{=}\mathrm{b}, \mathrm{b}{=}\mathrm{b}' \vdash \Delta}$$

$$\frac{\Gamma, \mathrm{a}{=}\mathrm{b} \vdash \Delta, \phi(\mathrm{a}), \psi(\mathrm{b})}{\Gamma, \mathrm{a}{=}\mathrm{b} \vdash \Delta, \psi(\mathrm{a})}\ (\vdash sub_{fol}) \qquad \frac{\Gamma, \mathrm{a}{=}\mathrm{b}, \psi(\mathrm{a}), \psi(\mathrm{b}) \vdash \Delta}{\Gamma, \mathrm{a}{=}\mathrm{b}, \psi(\mathrm{a}) \vdash \Delta}\ (sub_{fol} \vdash)$$

In the above rules, a, b and b′ are p-constants

Fig. 6. Common core of (introduction rules) for $GFOL_{\mathcal{L}}$

$$\frac{(\Gamma \vdash \Delta) \otimes' \sigma_1 \quad \ldots \quad (\Gamma \vdash \Delta) \otimes' \sigma_k}{(\Gamma \vdash \Delta) \otimes' \sigma_0} \ (\psi)$$

1. $\sigma_0 = s_0^1 P_0^1(\mathrm{a}_{1,0}^1, \mathrm{a}_{2,0}^1), \ldots, s_0^{l(0)} P_0^{l(0)}(\mathrm{a}_{1,0}^{l(0)}, \mathrm{a}_{2,0}^{l(0)})$ and all the constants in σ_0 are p-constants;
2. for $1 \leq u \leq k$, $\sigma_u = \sigma_0.s_u^1 P_u^1(\mathrm{a}_{1,u}^1, \mathrm{a}_{2,u}^1), \ldots, s_0^{l(u)} P_0^{l(u)}(\mathrm{a}_{1,u}^{l(u)}, \mathrm{a}_{2,u}^{l(u)})$;
3. for any $\alpha, \alpha' \in \{1, 2\}$, $q, q' \in \{1, \ldots, k\}$, $r \in \{1, \ldots .l(q)\}$ and $r' \in \{1, \ldots .l(q')\}$,
   (a) $z_{\alpha,q}^r = z_{\alpha',q'}^{r'}$ iff $\mathrm{a}_{\alpha,q}^r = \mathrm{a}_{\alpha',q'}^{r'}$;
   (b) if $z_{\alpha,q}^r$ is equal to some $\mathbf{y}_i$, then $\mathrm{a}_{\alpha,q}^r$ does not occur in the conclusion.

Fig. 7. (ψ)-rule for $\psi \in \Phi$

in standard modal logic, one can deal with only one world at a time and two individual variables are sufficient for encoding the quantification $\Box$ in first-order logic. Theorem 4 below helps understanding the relationships between $G\mathcal{L}$ and $GFOL_{\mathcal{L}}$.

Theorem 4. *(I) Let Π be a proof of ϕ in $G\mathcal{L}$. Then, there is a proof Π' of $\forall \boldsymbol{x}_0\ ST(\phi, \boldsymbol{x}_0)$ in $GFOL_{\mathcal{L}}$ such that $|\Pi'|$ is in $\mathcal{O}(|\Pi|)$.*
(II) Let Π be a proof of $\forall \boldsymbol{x}_0\ ST(\phi, \boldsymbol{x}_0)$ in $GFOL_{\mathcal{L}}$ for some nominal tense formula ϕ. Then, there is a proof Π' of ϕ in $G\mathcal{L}$ such that $|\Pi'|$ is in $\mathcal{O}(|\Pi|)$.

5 Concluding remarks

The results of the previous sections can be extended to the polymodal case. Indeed, it is easy to consider for some countable set I of "modal terms", the family $\{G_i : i \in I\} \cup \{H_i : i \in I\}$ of tense operators by appropriately considering polymodal Kripke models. The class $\mathcal{C}^I_{\Pi^2_0}$ is defined as the class of polymodal logics such that the class of frames is determined by a (possibly infinite) set of restricted Π^0_2-formulae over the vocabulary containing $\{\mathtt{R}_i : i \in I\}$. This extension does not generate any new technical problems and it is quite powerful as shown below. Let $I_0 = \{\mathtt{c}_0, \ldots, \mathtt{c}_i, \ldots\}$ be a set of *modal constants* and I be the set of modal terms $\mathtt{t}$ inductively defined as follows: $\mathtt{t} ::= \mathtt{id} \mid \mathtt{c}_i \mid -\mathtt{t} \mid \mathtt{t}^{-1} \mid \mathtt{t}_1 \cup \mathtt{t}_2 \mid \mathtt{t}_1 \cap \mathtt{t}_2 \mid \mathtt{t}_1 \circ \mathtt{t}_2$ for $\mathtt{c}_i \in I_0$. We wish to interpret the operators $-$, $^{-1}$, $\cup$, $\cap$ and $\circ$ and the identity constant $\mathtt{id}$ as in the Relation Calculus. Although it is known that the Relation Calculus can be translated in classical logic, surprisingly, we can also capture such a semantics in our framework using *only restricted Π^0_2-formulae*. So, by using our framework we can deal with nominal (poly)tense logics admitting the operators $-, ^{-1}, \cap, \cup, \circ$ and this is done uniformly[6] (this list of operators is not exhaustive). By contrast, in [Bal98, Chapter VI], only the operators $\cup$ and $\circ$ and the constant $\mathtt{id}$ are treated.

In this paper, we defined sequent calculi for nominal tense logics. The idea of using "implicit prefixes" in the calculi, due to [Kon97], allows a great flexibility and we have been able to consider most of the classes of modal frames first-order definable that can be found in the literature. Using standard correspondences, it

[6] Numerous description logics can be also treated within our framework

is easy to define tableaux calculi for nominal tense logics from our sequent-style calculi. Extensions of the calculi to cope with the logical consequence relations are also possible. Moreover, by appropriately modifying the (*start*)-rule, one can deal with *finite configuration* in the sense of [Rus96, Chapters 2 and 3]. Similarly, prefixed calculi (either sequent-based or tableaux-based) could be easily defined for the corresponding (non nominal) tense logics. Because of lack of space, such developments are omitted here but they are not difficult to derive from the present paper. Similarly, the design of decision procedures from our calculi was out of the scope of this paper but it is a question worth being investigated in the future.

The adequateness of our framework for mechanization cannot be stated without further investigations although it seems theoretically appealing (see for instance in Section 3.3 how the application of rules can be restricted). There is no reason to be overly optimistic since we have shown that the non prefixed sequent calculi are syntactic variants of restricted calculi for classical logic (augmented with relational theories). This property is shared by numerous calculi from the literature. As a conclusion, it is an open question whether any general framework defining sequent-style proof systems for modal (or nominal tense, ...) logics characterized by first-order definable classes of modal frames (take for instance $\mathcal{C}_{\Pi^0_2}$) is bound to define syntactic variants of calculi for fragments of classical logic augmented with relational theories.

Acknowledgments The author thanks Rajeev Goré for suggestions about a preliminary version of this work and for many discussions about prefixed tableaux and related matters while being an International ARC Fellow at the A.R.P. Thanks are also due to the referees for many useful suggestions and remarks and to Nicolas Peltier for reading a preliminary version.

References

[Bal98] M. Baldoni. *Normal Multimodal Logics: Automated Deduction and Logic Programming*. PhD thesis, Università degli Studi di Torino, 1998.

[Ben83] J. van Benthem. *Modal logic and classical logic*. Bibliopolis, 1983.

[BG97] B. Beckert and R. Goré. Free variable tableaux for propositional modal logics. In *TABLEAUX'97*, pages 91–106. LNAI 1227, Springer, 1997.

[BG98] N. Bonnette and R. Goré. A labelled sequent systems for tense logic K_t. In *Australian Joint Conference of Articifial Intelligence*, pages 71–82. LNAI 1502, Springer, 1998.

[Bla93] P. Blackburn. Nominal tense logic. *Notre Dame Journal of Formal Logic*, 34(1):56–83, 1993.

[Bla98] P. Blackburn. Internalizing labeled deduction. Technical Report 102, Computerlinguistik, Universität des Saarlandes, 1998.

[BMV97] D. Basin, S. Matthews, and L. Viganò. Labelled propositional modal logics: Theory and practice. *J. of Logic and Computation*, 7(6):685–717, 1997.

[BMV98] D. Basin, S. Matthews, and L. Viganò. Natural deduction for non-classical logics. *Studia Logica*, 60(1):119–160, 1998.

[Boo84] G. Boolos. Don't eliminate cut. *J. of Philosophical Logic*, 13:373–378, 1984.

[CFdCGH97] M. Castilho, L. Fariñas del Cerro, O. Gasquet, and A. Herzig. Modal tableaux with propagation rules and structural rules. *Fundamenta Informaticae*, 32(3/4):281-297 1997.

[d'A90] M. d'Agostino. *Investigations into the complexity of some propositional calculi.* PhD thesis, Oxford University Computing Laboratory, 1990.

[DG99] S. Demri and R. Goré. Cut-free display calculi for nominal tense logics. In this volume, 1999.

[dM94] M. d'Agostino and M. Mondadori. The taming of the cut. Classical refutations with analytic cut. *J. of Logic and Computation*, 4(3):285–319, 1994.

[Fit83] M. Fitting. *Proof methods for modal and intuitionistic logics.* D. Reidel Publishing Co., 1983.

[Gab96] D. Gabbay. *Labelled Deductive Systems.* Oxford University Press, 1996.

[Gen92] I. Gent. *Analytic proof systems for classical and modal logics of restricted quantification.* PhD thesis, University of Warwick, 1992.

[GG93] G. Gargov and V. Goranko. Modal logic with names. *J. of Philosophical Logic*, 22(6):607–636, 1993.

[GHM98] H. Ganzinger, U. Hustadt, and R. Meyer and C. Schmidt. A resolution-based decision procedure for extensions of K4. In *2nd Workshop on Advances in Modal Logic*, 1998. to appear.

[Gor99] R Goré. Tableaux methods for modal and temporal logics. In *Handbook of Tableaux Methods.* Kluwer, Dordrecht, 1999. to appear.

[Gov95] G. Governatori. Labelled tableaux for multi-modal logics. In *TABLEAUX-4*, pages 79–94. LNAI 918, Springer, 1995.

[Heu98] A. Heuerding. *Sequent Calculi for Proof Search in Some Modal Logics.* PhD thesis, University of Bern, 1998.

[Hud96] J. Hudelmaier. Improved decision procedures for the modal logics K, KT and S4. In *CSL'95*, pages 320–334. LNCS 1092, Springer, 1996.

[Kon97] B. Konikowska. A logic for reasoning about relative similarity. *Studia Logica*, 58(1):185–226, 1997.

[Kra96] M. Kracht. Power and weakness of the modal display calculus. In H. Wansing, editor, *Proof theory of modal logic*, pages 93–121. Kluwer Academic Publishers, 1996.

[Kri63] S. Kripke. Semantical analysis of modal logic I: normal modal propositional calculi. *Zeitschrift für Mathematik Logik und Grundlagen der Mathematik*, 9:67–96, 1963.

[Mas94] F. Massacci. Strongly analytic tableaux for normal modal logics. In *CADE-12*, pages 723–737. Springer, LNAI 814, 1994.

[Ogn94] Z. Ognjanović. A tableau-like proof procedure for normal modal logics. *TCS*, 129:167–186, 1994.

[Pri57] A. Prior. *Time and Modality.* Clarendon Press, Oxford, 1957.

[RU71] N. Rescher and A. Urquhart. *Temporal Logic.* Springer-Verlag, 1971.

[Rus96] A. Russo. *Modal logics as labelled deductive systems.* PhD thesis, Imperial College, London, 1996.

[Tza99] M. Tzakova. Tableau calculi for hybrid logics. In this volume, 1999.

[Wal90] L. Wallen. Automated Deduction in Nonclassical Logics. MIT Press, 1990.

Cut-Free Display Calculi for Nominal Tense Logics

Stéphane Demri[1*] and Rajeev Goré[2†]

[1] Laboratoire LEIBNIZ - C.N.R.S.
46 av. Félix Viallet, 38000 Grenoble, France
demri@imag.fr
[2] Automated Reasoning Project and Dept. of Computer Science
Australian National University
ACT 0200 Canberra, Australia
rpg@arp.anu.edu.au

Abstract. We define cut-free display calculi for nominal tense logics extending the minimal nominal tense logic (MNTL) by addition of primitive axioms. To do so, we use a translation of MNTL into the minimal tense logic of inequality ($\mathtt{MTL}_{\neq}$) which is known to be properly displayable by application of Kracht's results. The rules of the display calculus δMNTL for MNTL mimic those of the display calculus $\delta\mathtt{MTL}_{\neq}$ for $\mathtt{MTL}_{\neq}$. Since δMNTL does not satisfy Belnap's condition (C8), we extend Wansing's strong normalisation theorem to get a similar theorem for any extension of δMNTL by addition of structural rules satisfying Belnap's conditions (C2)-(C7). Finally, we show a weak Sahlqvist-style theorem for extensions of MNTL, and by Kracht's techniques, deduce that these Sahlqvist extensions of δMNTL also admit cut-free display calculi.

1 Introduction

Background: The addition of *names* (also called *nominals*) to modal logics has been investigated recently with different motivations; see e.g. [Orło84, PT85, Bla90]. A *name* is usually understood as an atomic proposition that holds true in a unique world of a Kripke model. Most of the time, the addition of names is intended to increase the expressive power of the initial logics. For instance, there is a tense formula with names that characterises the class of irreflexive frames [Bla93] although there is no such formula without names. Another remarkable breakthrough due to the inclusion of names is the ability to define the intersection operator (see e.g. [PT91]) although it is known that intersection is not modally definable in the standard modal language [GT75]. Adding the difference operator $[\neq]$, which allows access to worlds different from the current world, is another way to obtain names (see e.g. [Koy92, Rij92, Ven93]). As far as expressive power is concerned, adding $[\neq]$ is more powerful than adding only names: in [GG93], the relationships between names and $[\neq]$ are fully established with respect to definability. So most of the literature for modal logics with names concerns their

* Visit to ARP supported by an Australian Research Council International Fellowship.
† Supported by an Australian Research Council Queen Elizabeth II Fellowship.

expressive power, decidability, complexity (see e.g. [Bla90, Rij93, GG93, PT91]) and Hilbert-style systems [Bla90, PT91, Ven93, Rij93].

Display Logic: Display Logic (abbreviated by **DL**) is a proof-theoretical framework due to Belnap [Bel82] that generalises the structural language of Gentzen's sequents by using multiple structural connectives instead of Gentzen's comma. Display calculi enjoy various nice properties. The first is that any display calculus that obeys eight simple conditions C1-C8 (see the appendix) also enjoys a cut-elimination theorem [Bel82]. The second is that, in the rules introducing logical connectives, the principal formula is alone as an antecedent or succedent, thereby giving a clear *definition* of the introduced connective. Consequently, interactions between logical connectives are reduced to a minimum. All of this is possible because any occurrence of a structure in a sequent can be displayed either as the entire antecedent or as the entire succedent of some sequent *structurally equivalent* to the initial sequent.

Our contribution: We define cut-free display calculi for two classes of extensions of the minimal nominal tense logic (MNTL) [Bla90], by addition of two types of primitive axioms in the sense of [Kra96]. These display calculi break (C8). We extend various results for displayed tense logics (including strong normalisation) from [Wan94, Kra96, Wan98] to nominals. Our main contribution is to show that Belnap's condition C8 can be weakened while preserving cut-elimination.

We first define the basic display calculus δMNTL by using a natural translation from MNTL into $\mathtt{MTL}_{\neq}$, the minimal tense logic augmented with the difference operator. Indeed, $\mathtt{MTL}_{\neq}$ is properly displayable in the sense of [Kra96] thanks to the Hilbert-style axiomatisation given in [Rij92] (see also [Seg81, Koy92]). The rules for δMNTL mimic those of $\delta\mathtt{MTL}_{\neq}$, the display calculus for $\mathtt{MTL}_{\neq}$. We prove soundness of δMNTL by showing that the rules preserve MNTL-validity. We prove completeness of δMNTL by showing that δMNTL can simulate the rules of the Hilbert-style calculus $\vdash_{\mathtt{MNTL}}$ for MNTL given in [Bla90]. Cut-elimination cannot be proved via that proof because cut is needed to simulate the *modus ponens* rule.

An interesting (and at first glance very unpleasant) feature of δMNTL is that it does not satisfy the condition (C8) [Bel82] which is crucial for the cut-elimination proofs from [Bel82, Wan98]. We show that the failure of (C8) is caused by the introduction rules for nominals and then show a limited cut-elimination theorem by observing that one of these rules is not really necessary. By appropriately modifying a proof from [Wan98], we then prove a strong normalisation theorem for any extension of δMNTL obtained by the addition of structural rules satisfying the conditions (C2)-(C7) from [Bel82] (condition (C8) only makes sense for logical rules). From a technical viewpoint, we have modified the definitions of *parametric* and *principal* moves to view a sequent in a proof as its equivalence class with respect to structural equivalence. Consequently, a display postulate inference in a proof does not add to the size of the proof. This can be generalised for any invertible structural rule with a single premiss.

We then have to make a connection between axiomatic extensions of $\vdash_{\mathtt{MNTL}}$ and corresponding extensions of δMNTL obtained by adding structural rules à la Kracht [Kra96]. Since δMNTL is based upon $\delta\mathtt{MTL}_{\neq}$, we proceed via axiomatic extensions of $\vdash_{\neq}$, the Hilbert-style calculus for $\mathtt{MTL}_{\neq}$. Many such extensions of $\mathtt{MTL}_{\neq}$ require the powerful (and sometimes redundant) irreflexivity rule (see e.g. [Gab81]) and, unfortunately, the corresponding rule in **DL** lacks various nice properties of standard display calculi. Although it is not always known when the irreflexivity rule is really needed, it is not needed in the axiomatisation $\vdash_{\neq}$ of $\mathtt{MTL}_{\neq}$. We therefore prove cut-elimination and completeness of δMNTL with respect to primitive axiomatic extensions of $\vdash_{\mathtt{MTL}_{\neq}}$ which do not require the irreflexivity rule, by backward translation (Theorem 14). These primitive axioms possibly *contain the difference operator*, which is foreign to MNTL.

Finally, although many extensions of MNTL are not canonical [Bla90], we show a weak Sahlqvist-style theorem for nominal tense logics. This allows us to define cut-free display calculi for any extension of $\vdash_{\mathtt{MNTL}}$ by addition of another class of primitive axioms *using only the language of* MNTL, *and hence without the difference operator*. Furthermore, we can characterise the semantical extensions of MNTL which correspond to these calculi.

Related work: Existing proof systems for nominal tense logics [Bla90, Bla93] or for modal logics with the difference operator [Seg81, Koy92, Rij92, Ven93] are mostly Hilbert-style. And although the prefixed tableaux defined in [BD97] for several modal logics with the difference operator give decision procedures, a cut rule present in these calculi is not eliminable in many cases (for reasons similar to those that apply to calculi from [dM94]). Gentzen-style calculi for similarity logics with names have been defined in [Kon97] where the nominals play the rôle of prefixes in an elegant manner. These calculi contain no prefixed formulae as such since the language of the logic already contains names.

Our treatment of nominals in δMNTL is different since we instead use the double nature of a nominal: as atomic proposition i and as necessity formula $[\neq]\neg\mathtt{i}$. In that sense, it is similar to the treatment of atomic propositions in display calculi for intuitionistic logic in [Gor95]. In [Bla98, Dem99], sequent calculi for nominal tense logics are given in which the nominals roughly play the role of labels. Cut-free display calculi have also been defined for substructural logics (see e.g. [Gor98]) and for modal and polymodal logics [Wan94, Kra96]. In [Ven93], a Sahlqvist theorem for tense logics with the difference operator has been established for calculi with the irreflexivity rule (see also [Rij93]).

Plan of the paper: In Section 2, we recall the definitions of the logics under study [Bla90, Rij92, Ven93]. In Section 3, we define the cut-free display calculus δMNTL for MNTL, show its completeness and prove a (weak) cut-elimination theorem. In Section 4, we prove a strong normalisation theorem for any *reasonable* extension of δMNTL although δMNTL does not satisfy Belnap's condition (C8). In Section 5 we establish a weak Sahlqvist-style theorem and, by using [Kra96], define cut-free display calculi for extensions of MNTL. Space limits preclude detailed proofs, but these can be found in the full version [DG98a]. Belnap's eight conditions, and our weaker version of (C8), can be found in the appendix.

2 Nominal Tense Logics

Given a set $\mathtt{PRP} = \{\mathtt{p}_0, \mathtt{p}_1, \mathtt{p}_2, \ldots\}$ of *atomic propositions* and a set $\mathtt{NOM} = \{\mathtt{i}_0, \mathtt{i}_1, \ldots\}$ of *names*, the formulas $\phi \in \mathtt{NTL}(G, H, [\neq])$ are inductively defined as follows for $\mathtt{p}_j \in \mathtt{PRP}$, $\mathtt{i}_k \in \mathtt{NOM}$:

$$\phi ::= \top \mid \bot \mid \mathtt{p}_j \mid \mathtt{i}_k \mid \phi_1 \wedge \phi_2 \mid \phi_1 \vee \phi_2 \mid \phi_1 \Rightarrow \phi_2 \mid \neg\phi \mid H\phi \mid G\phi \mid [\neq]\phi$$

Standard abbreviations include $\Leftrightarrow$, $\langle\neq\rangle$, F, P. For instance $F\phi \stackrel{\text{def}}{=} \neg G \neg \phi$.

For any sequence $\overline{\mathtt{OP}}$ from $\{H, G, [\neq]\}$, we write $\mathtt{NTL}(\overline{\mathtt{OP}})$ to denote the fragment of $\mathtt{NTL}(G, H, [\neq])$ with the unary modal operators from $\overline{\mathtt{OP}}$. Similarly, $\mathtt{TL}(\overline{\mathtt{OP}})$ denotes the fragment of $\mathtt{NTL}(\overline{\mathtt{OP}})$ with no names. In the rest of the paper, we study logics whose languages are strict fragments of $\mathtt{NTL}(G, H, [\neq])$ (the whole language contains all that we need in the paper). For any $\phi \in \mathtt{NTL}(G, H, [\neq])$, we write $dg(\phi)$ to denote the *degree* of ϕ: that is the number of occurrences of members of $\mathtt{PRP} \cup \mathtt{NOM} \cup \{\top, \bot\} \cup \{\neg, \wedge, \vee, \Rightarrow, G, H, [\neq]\}$. For instance $dg(\bot \Rightarrow (\mathtt{i}_0 \vee \neg \mathtt{p}_1)) = 6$.

A *modal frame* (W, R) is a pair where W is a non-empty set and R is a binary relation over W, with R^{-1} the converse of R. We write Fr for the set of all modal frames and use $R(w) \stackrel{\text{def}}{=} \{v \in W : (w, v) \in R\}$. A *model* is a triple (W, R, m) such that (W, R) is a frame, $\mathcal{P}(W)$ is the set of all subsets of W, and m is a mapping $m : \mathtt{PRP} \cup \mathtt{NOM} \to \mathcal{P}(W)$ where for $\mathtt{i} \in \mathtt{NOM}$, $m(\mathtt{i})$ is a singleton.

Let $\mathcal{M} = (W, R, m)$ be a model and $w \in W$. As usual, the formula ϕ is *satisfied by the world* $w \in W$ *in* $\mathcal{M}$ $\stackrel{\text{def}}{\Leftrightarrow}$ $\mathcal{M}, w \models \phi$ where the satisfaction relation $\models$ is inductively defined as follows:

$\mathcal{M}, w \models \mathtt{p} \stackrel{\text{def}}{\Leftrightarrow} w \in m(\mathtt{p})$, for every $\mathtt{p} \in \mathtt{PRP} \cup \mathtt{NOM}$;
$\mathcal{M}, w \models G\phi \stackrel{\text{def}}{\Leftrightarrow}$ for every $v \in R(w)$, $\mathcal{M}, v \models \phi$;
$\mathcal{M}, w \models H\phi \stackrel{\text{def}}{\Leftrightarrow}$ for every $v \in R^{-1}(w)$, $\mathcal{M}, v \models \phi$;
$\mathcal{M}, w \models [\neq]\phi \stackrel{\text{def}}{\Leftrightarrow}$ for every $v \neq w$, $\mathcal{M}, v \models \phi$.

We omit the standard conditions for the propositional connectives and the logical constants. A formula ϕ is *true* in a model $\mathcal{M}$ (written $\mathcal{M} \models \phi$) $\stackrel{\text{def}}{\Leftrightarrow}$ for every $w \in W$, $\mathcal{M}, w \models \phi$. A formula ϕ is *true* in a frame $\mathcal{F}$ (written $\mathcal{F} \models \phi$) $\stackrel{\text{def}}{\Leftrightarrow}$ ϕ is true in every model based on $\mathcal{F}$. By a *logic* $\mathcal{L}$ we understand a pair $\langle \mathtt{L}, \mathcal{C} \rangle$ consisting of a language $\mathtt{L} \subseteq \mathtt{NTL}(H, G, [\neq])$ and a nonempty set of frames $\mathcal{C} \subseteq Fr$. A formula $\phi \in \mathtt{L}$ is $\mathcal{L}$-*valid* $\stackrel{\text{def}}{\Leftrightarrow}$ ϕ is true in all the models based on the frames in $\mathcal{C}$. A formula $\phi \in \mathtt{L}$ is $\mathcal{L}$-*satisfiable* $\stackrel{\text{def}}{\Leftrightarrow}$ $\neg\phi$ is not $\mathcal{L}$-valid.

The *minimal nominal tense logic* is $\mathtt{MNTL} \stackrel{\text{def}}{=} \langle \mathtt{NTL}(H, G), Fr \rangle$. The *minimal tense logic of inequality* is $\mathtt{MTL}_{\neq} \stackrel{\text{def}}{=} \langle \mathtt{TL}(G, H, [\neq]), Fr \rangle$. Moreover, for any formula ϕ of some language $\mathtt{L} \subseteq \mathtt{NTL}(H, G, [\neq])$ with names [resp. without names], we write $\mathtt{NTL}_{\phi}$ [resp. $\mathtt{TL}_{\phi}$] to denote the logic $\langle \mathtt{L}, \{\mathcal{F} \in Fr : \mathcal{F} \models \phi\} \rangle$.

By a *universal modality* [resp. *existential modality*] σ, we mean a (possibly empty) finite sequence of elements from $\{G, H\}$ [resp. $\{F, P\}$]. We write $\vdash_{\neq}$ to denote the axiomatic system defined in [Rij93, pp. 36-37] for $\mathtt{MTL}_{\neq}$. We write $\vdash_{\mathtt{MNTL}}$ for the smallest subset of $\mathtt{NTL}(G, H)$ closed under *modus ponens*, closed under *necessitation* for G and H, and containing every formula of the form

- the tautologies of the propositional calculus;
- $(G(\phi \Rightarrow \psi) \wedge G\phi) \Rightarrow G\psi$; $(H(\phi \Rightarrow \psi) \wedge H\phi) \Rightarrow H\psi$; $\phi \Rightarrow HF\phi$; $\phi \Rightarrow GP\phi$;
- $\mathtt{i} \wedge \phi \Rightarrow \sigma(\mathtt{i} \Rightarrow \phi)$ where $\mathtt{i} \in \mathtt{NOM}$ and σ is any universal modality.

We write $\vdash \psi$ to mean that ψ is derivable in the Hilbert-style calculus $\vdash$. We write $\vdash + \phi$ to denote the minimal extension of the axiomatic system $\vdash$ by adding all formulae of the form ϕ (thus ϕ is just an axiom schema).

Theorem 1. *[Bla90] Any $\phi \in \mathtt{NTL}(H, G)$ is* MNTL*-valid iff $\vdash_{\mathtt{MNTL}} \phi$.*

3 A Display Calculus for MNTL

As stated previously there are numerous existing display calculi. We use Wansing's [Wan94] formulation since it is tailored to modal logics. On the structural side, we have the structural connectives $*$ (unary), $\circ$ (binary), I (nullary), $\bullet$ (unary) and $\bullet_{\neq}$ (unary). A *structure* $\mathtt{X} \in \mathtt{struc}(\delta\mathtt{MNTL})$ is inductively defined as

$$\mathtt{X} ::= \phi \mid *\mathtt{X} \mid \mathtt{X}_1 \circ \mathtt{X}_2 \mid I \mid \bullet\mathtt{X} \mid \bullet_{\neq}\mathtt{X}$$

for $\phi \in \mathtt{NTL}(G, H)$. A logical interpretation of the structural connectives can be found in the proof of the forthcoming Theorem 3. A *sequent* is defined as an expression of the form $\mathtt{X} \vdash \mathtt{Y}$ with $\mathtt{X}$ the *antecedent* and $\mathtt{Y}$ the *succedent*. For any finite set S of structures, we write $\mathtt{NOM}(S)$ for the set of names from $\mathtt{NOM}$ that occur in S. We write φ_S to denote the formula (in $\mathtt{TL}(G, H, [\neq])$) below:

$$\bigwedge_{\mathtt{i}_k \in \mathtt{NOM}(S)} (\mathtt{p}_{2\times k+1} \wedge [\neq]\neg \mathtt{p}_{2\times k+1}) \vee \langle\neq\rangle(\mathtt{p}_{2\times k+1} \wedge [\neq]\neg \mathtt{p}_{2\times k+1})$$

The rules of δMNTL are those in Figures 1-5.

The *display postulates* (reversible rules) in Figure 2 deal with the manipulation of structural connectives. In what follows, we write

$$\frac{s}{s'}\ (dp)$$

to denote that the sequent s' is obtained from the sequent s by an unspecified finite number (possibly zero) of applications of display postulates.

$$(\mathrm{Id})\ \mathtt{p} \vdash \mathtt{p} \qquad (\mathrm{Id}')\ \mathtt{i} \vdash \mathtt{i} \qquad \frac{\mathtt{X} \vdash \phi \quad \phi \vdash \mathtt{Y}}{\mathtt{X} \vdash \mathtt{Y}}\ (\mathrm{cut})$$

Fig. 1. Fundamental logical axioms and cut rule

$$\frac{X \circ Y \vdash Z}{X \vdash Z \circ *Y} \quad \frac{X \circ Y \vdash Z}{Y \vdash *X \circ Z} \quad \frac{X \vdash Y \circ Z}{X \circ *Z \vdash Y} \quad \frac{X \vdash Y \circ Z}{*Y \circ X \vdash Z}$$

$$\frac{*X \vdash Y}{*Y \vdash X} \quad \frac{X \vdash *Y}{Y \vdash *X} \quad \frac{**X \vdash Y}{X \vdash Y} \quad \frac{X \vdash **Y}{X \vdash Y} \quad \frac{X \vdash \bullet_{\neq} Y}{\bullet_{\neq} X \vdash Y} \quad \frac{X \vdash \bullet Y}{\bullet X \vdash Y}$$

Fig. 2. Display postulates

In any structure Z, the structure X occurs *negatively* [resp. *positively*] $\overset{\text{def}}{\Leftrightarrow}$ X occurs in the scope of an odd number [resp. an even number] of occurrences of $*$ [Bel82]. In a sequent $V \vdash W$, an occurrence of X is an *antecedent part* [resp. *succedent part*] $\overset{\text{def}}{\Leftrightarrow}$ it occurs positively in V [resp. negatively in W] or it occurs negatively in W [resp. positively in V] [Bel82]. Two sequents $X \vdash Y$ and $X' \vdash Y'$ are said to be *structurally equivalent* $\overset{\text{def}}{\Leftrightarrow}$ there is a derivation of the first sequent from the second (and vice-versa) using only the display postulates.

Theorem 2. *[Bel82] For every sequent $V \vdash W$ and every antecedent [resp. succedent] part X of $V \vdash W$, there is a structurally equivalent sequent $X \vdash Y$ [resp. $Y \vdash X$] that has X (alone) as its antecedent [resp. succedent]. X is said to be* displayed *in $X \vdash Y$ [resp. $Y \vdash X$].*

A *structural rule* contains only structural connectives and structure variables like X, Y, Z. Following [Kra96], a formula is said to be *primitive* $\overset{\text{def}}{\Leftrightarrow}$ it is of the form $\phi \Rightarrow \psi$ where both ϕ and ψ are built only from $\mathtt{PRP} \cup \{\top\}$ with the help of $\wedge$, $\vee$, F, P and $\langle\neq\rangle$, and such that ϕ contains each atomic proposition at most once. The rules in Figure 5 are translations of primitive axioms from the axiomatisation $\vdash_{\neq}$ of $\mathtt{MTL}_{\neq}$ [Rij93] into structural rules following [Kra96]. Thus $\bullet_{\neq}$ is *implicitly* associated with the pair $\langle[\neq], \langle\neq\rangle\rangle$ of *dual* modal operators (since $\neq$ is symmetric), and $\bullet$ is associated with the pair of *residuated* operators $\langle G, P\rangle$.

An easy way to understand the way the rules $(\mathtt{i} \vdash)$ and $(\vdash \mathtt{i})$ in Figure 3 work is to observe that the formula $\mathtt{i} \Leftrightarrow [\neq]\neg\mathtt{i}$ from the language $\mathtt{NTL}([\neq])$ is valid in any Kripke model. Thus, the rules $(\mathtt{i} \vdash)$ and $(\vdash \mathtt{i})$ use the intensional nature of a name whereas the fundamental axiom $\mathtt{i} \vdash \mathtt{i}$ uses its atomic nature.

Theorem 3. *(soundness) If $I \vdash \phi$ is derivable in $\delta\mathtt{MNTL}$, then ϕ is $\mathtt{MNTL}$-valid.*

Proof. Consider maps a and s from $\mathtt{struc}(\delta\mathtt{MNTL})$ to $\mathtt{TL}(H, G, [\neq])$ as below:

a and s are homomorphic for $\neg$, $\wedge$, $\vee$, $\Rightarrow$, H and G
for every $\mathtt{p}_j \in \mathtt{PRP}$, $a(\mathtt{p}_j) \overset{\text{def}}{=} s(\mathtt{p}_j) \overset{\text{def}}{=} \mathtt{p}_{2\times j}$
for every $\mathtt{i}_k \in \mathtt{NOM}$, $a(\mathtt{i}_k) \overset{\text{def}}{=} s(\mathtt{i}_k) \overset{\text{def}}{=} \mathtt{p}_{2\times k+1} \wedge [\neq]\neg\mathtt{p}_{2\times k+1}$
$a(\top) \overset{\text{def}}{=} s(\top) \overset{\text{def}}{=} \top$ $\qquad a(\bot) \overset{\text{def}}{=} s(\bot) \overset{\text{def}}{=} \bot$

$$\frac{}{I \vdash \top}\ (\vdash \top) \quad \frac{I \vdash X}{\top \vdash X}\ (\top \vdash) \quad \frac{X \vdash I}{X \vdash \bot}\ (\vdash \bot) \quad \frac{}{\bot \vdash I}\ (\bot \vdash) \quad \frac{X \vdash *\phi}{X \vdash \neg\phi}\ (\vdash \neg) \quad \frac{*\phi \vdash X}{\neg\phi \vdash X}\ (\neg \vdash)$$

$$\frac{X \circ \phi \vdash \psi}{X \vdash \phi \Rightarrow \psi}\ (\vdash\Rightarrow) \quad \frac{X \vdash \phi \quad \psi \vdash Y}{\phi \Rightarrow \psi \vdash *X \circ Y}\ (\Rightarrow\vdash) \quad \frac{X \vdash \phi \quad Y \vdash \psi}{X \circ Y \vdash \phi \wedge \psi}\ (\vdash \wedge) \quad \frac{\phi \circ \psi \vdash X}{\phi \wedge \psi \vdash X}\ (\wedge \vdash)$$

$$\frac{X \vdash \phi \circ \psi}{X \vdash \phi \vee \psi}\ (\vdash \vee) \quad \frac{\phi \vdash X \quad \psi \vdash Y}{\phi \vee \psi \vdash X \circ Y}\ (\vee \vdash) \quad \frac{\phi \vdash X}{G\phi \vdash \bullet X}\ (G \vdash) \quad \frac{X \vdash \bullet\phi}{X \vdash G\phi}\ (\vdash G)$$

$$\frac{\phi \vdash X}{H\phi \vdash * \bullet * X}\ (H \vdash) \quad \frac{X \vdash * \bullet * \phi}{X \vdash H\phi}\ (\vdash H) \quad \frac{i \vdash \bullet_{\neq} * X}{X \vdash i}\ (\vdash i) \quad \frac{X \vdash i}{i \vdash \bullet_{\neq} * X}\ (i \vdash)$$

Fig. 3. Operational rules

$$\begin{array}{c} X \vdash Z \\ \hline\hline I \circ X \vdash Z \end{array}\ (I_l) \quad \begin{array}{c} X \vdash Z \\ \hline\hline X \vdash I \circ Z \end{array}\ (I_r) \quad \begin{array}{c} I \vdash Y \\ \hline\hline *I \vdash Y \end{array}\ (Q_l) \quad \begin{array}{c} X \vdash I \\ \hline\hline X \vdash *I \end{array}\ (Q_r)$$

$$\frac{X \vdash Z}{Y \circ X \vdash Z}\ (weak_l) \quad \frac{X \vdash Z}{X \circ Y \vdash Z}\ (weak_r) \quad \begin{array}{c} X_1 \circ (X_2 \circ X_3) \vdash Z \\ \hline\hline (X_1 \circ X_2) \circ X_3 \vdash Z \end{array}\ (assoc_l)$$

$$\begin{array}{c} Z \vdash X_1 \circ (X_2 \circ X_3) \\ \hline\hline Z \vdash (X_1 \circ X_2) \circ X_3 \end{array}\ (assoc_r)$$

$$\frac{Y \circ X \vdash Z}{X \circ Y \vdash Z}\ (com_l) \quad \frac{Z \vdash Y \circ X}{Z \vdash X \circ Y}\ (com_r) \quad \frac{X \circ X \vdash Y}{X \vdash Y}\ (contr_l) \quad \frac{Y \vdash X \circ X}{Y \vdash X}\ (contr_r)$$

$$\frac{I \vdash X}{\bullet I \vdash X}\ (nec^l_G) \quad \frac{X \vdash I}{X \vdash \bullet I}\ (nec^r_G) \quad \frac{I \vdash X}{\bullet_{\neq} I \vdash X}\ (nec^l) \quad \frac{X \vdash I}{X \vdash \bullet_{\neq} I}\ (nec^r)$$

Fig. 4. Other basic structural rules

$$\frac{X \vdash Y \quad * \bullet_{\neq} * X \vdash Y}{* \bullet_{\neq} \bullet_{\neq} * X \vdash Y}\ (alio) \quad \frac{* \bullet_{\neq} *(Z \circ * \bullet_{\neq} * X) \vdash Y}{X \circ * \bullet_{\neq} * Z \vdash Y}\ (sym)$$

$$\frac{X \vdash Y \quad * \bullet_{\neq} * X \vdash Y}{* \bullet * X \vdash Y}\ (uni1) \quad \frac{X \vdash Y \quad * \bullet_{\neq} * X \vdash Y}{\bullet X \vdash Y}\ (uni2)$$

Fig. 5. Other structural rules

$$
\begin{array}{lclclcl}
a(I) & \stackrel{\text{def}}{=} & \top & \quad & s(I) & \stackrel{\text{def}}{=} & \bot \\
a(*\mathtt{X}) & \stackrel{\text{def}}{=} & \neg s(\mathtt{X}) & & s(*\mathtt{X}) & \stackrel{\text{def}}{=} & \neg a(\mathtt{X}) \\
a(\mathtt{X}\circ\mathtt{Y}) & \stackrel{\text{def}}{=} & a(\mathtt{X})\wedge a(\mathtt{Y}) & & s(\mathtt{X}\circ\mathtt{Y}) & \stackrel{\text{def}}{=} & s(\mathtt{X})\vee s(\mathtt{Y}) \\
a(\bullet\mathtt{X}) & \stackrel{\text{def}}{=} & P\, a(\mathtt{X}) & & s(\bullet\mathtt{X}) & \stackrel{\text{def}}{=} & G\, s(\mathtt{X}) \\
a(\bullet_{\neq}\mathtt{X}) & \stackrel{\text{def}}{=} & \langle\neq\rangle a(\mathtt{X}) & & s(\bullet_{\neq}\mathtt{X}) & \stackrel{\text{def}}{=} & [\neq]s(\mathtt{X})
\end{array}
$$

By induction on the length of the given derivation of $\mathtt{X} \vdash \mathtt{Y}$, we can show that if $\mathtt{X} \vdash \mathtt{Y}$ is derivable in δ**MNTL**, then $\varphi_{\{\mathtt{X},\mathtt{Y}\}} \Rightarrow (a(\mathtt{X}) \Rightarrow s(\mathtt{Y}))$ is $\mathbf{MTL}_{\neq}$-valid. Furthermore, for any $\phi \in \mathtt{NTL(H,G)}$, ϕ is **MNTL**-valid iff $a(\phi)$ is $\mathbf{MTL}_{\neq}$-valid iff $s(\phi)$ is $\mathbf{MTL}_{\neq}$-valid iff $\varphi_{\{\phi\}} \Rightarrow a(\phi)$ is $\mathbf{MTL}_{\neq}$-valid iff $\varphi_{\{\phi\}} \Rightarrow s(\phi)$ is $\mathbf{MTL}_{\neq}$-valid. In particular, if $I \vdash \phi$ is derivable in δ**MNTL**, then $\varphi_{\{\phi\}} \Rightarrow (a(I) \Rightarrow s(\phi))$ (i.e. $\top \Rightarrow s(\phi)$) is $\mathbf{MTL}_{\neq}$-valid and hence ϕ is **MNTL**-valid.

Next, we give a completeness proof of δ**MNTL** using the system $\vdash_{\mathtt{MNTL}}$.

Lemma 4. *Let* $\mathtt{X} \vdash \mathtt{Y}$ *and* $\mathtt{X}' \vdash \mathtt{Y}'$ *be sequents such that* $\mathtt{X}' \vdash \mathtt{Y}'$ *can be obtained from* $\mathtt{X} \vdash \mathtt{Y}$ *by replacing some occurrences of* $* \bullet_{\neq} *\mathtt{Z}$ *by* $\bullet_{\neq}\mathtt{Z}$ *and by replacing some occurrences of* $\bullet_{\neq}\mathtt{W}$ *by* $* \bullet_{\neq} *\mathtt{W}$*. Then, any display calculus* δ *containing the display postulates from Figure 2, (sym),* $(contr_r)$*,* $(weak_r)$ *and* $(weak_l)$ *satisfies:* $\mathtt{X} \vdash \mathtt{Y}$ *is derivable [resp. has a cut-free proof] in* δ *iff* $\mathtt{X}' \vdash \mathtt{Y}'$ *is derivable [resp. has a cut-free proof] in* δ*.*

Lemma 4 is unsurprising since (sym) corresponds to the axiom schema $F\,\phi \Leftrightarrow P\,\phi$ characterising symmetry. However, Lemma 4 is purely syntactic.

Theorem 5. *(completeness) If* $\vdash_{\mathtt{MNTL}} \phi$*, then* $I \vdash \phi$ *is derivable in* δ**MNTL**.

The proof of Theorem 5 relies only on the completeness of δKt [Kra96] and on the derivability of the axiom schema $\mathtt{i}\wedge\phi \Rightarrow \sigma(\mathtt{i} \Rightarrow \phi)$. Moreover, it highlights how the rules (*uni*1), (*uni*2), (*sym*) and (*alio*) are needed to get completeness. In what follows, we write

$$\begin{array}{c}\vdots\;\Pi\\ s\end{array}$$

to denote that the sequent s has a proof Π in δ**MNTL**.

Proof. (sketch) The proof is by induction on the length of the derivation of ϕ in $\vdash_{\mathtt{MNTL}}$. Actually, most of the cases have been already proved in [Wan94, Kra96, Wan98]. It remains to show that $I \vdash \mathtt{i} \wedge \phi \Rightarrow \sigma(\mathtt{i} \Rightarrow \phi)$ is derivable in δ**MNTL** where $\mathtt{i} \in \mathtt{NOM}$, $\phi \in \mathtt{NTL}(H,G)$ and σ is a (possibly empty) finite sequence of elements from $\{H, G\}$. To do so, we prove by induction on the length of σ that $\mathtt{i}\circ\phi \vdash \sigma(\mathtt{i} \Rightarrow \phi)$ and $\bullet_{\neq}(\mathtt{i}\circ\phi) \vdash \sigma(\mathtt{i} \Rightarrow \phi)$ are derivable in δ**MNTL** (see [DG98a]).

Unfortunately, as shown shortly in Example 1, the rules ($\vdash \mathtt{i}$) and ($\mathtt{i} \vdash$) from δ**MNTL** do not satisfy (C8), so we cannot prove cut-elimination using [Bel82, Wan98]. However, δ**MNTL** minus the rule ($\vdash \mathtt{i}$), say δ^-**MNTL**, obeys (C1)-(C8) since, in δ^-**MNTL**, $\mathtt{i}$ can be a succedent principal formula only in the fundamental axiom $\mathtt{i} \vdash \mathtt{i}$. Belnap's cut-elimination proof applies and therefore $\mathtt{X} \vdash \mathtt{Y}$ has a proof in δ^-**MNTL** iff $X \vdash Y$ has a cut-free proof in δ^-**MNTL**. A similar "trick" is used in [Gor95]. Surprisingly, the proof of Theorem 5 also shows that if $\vdash_{\mathtt{MNTL}} \phi$, then $I \vdash \phi$ is derivable in δ^-**MNTL** since the ($\vdash$ i)-rule is simply not used. Consequently,

Theorem 6. *(weak cut-elimination) If* $\vdash_{\mathtt{MNTL}} \phi$*, then* $I \vdash \phi$ *has a cut-free proof in* δ^-**MNTL**.

Whether δ**MNTL** enjoys cut-elimination is still open at this stage of the paper since all the provable sequents $X \vdash Y$ are not necessarily of the form $I \vdash \phi$. Moreover, Theorem 6 does not guarantee that any *reasonable* extension of δ**MNTL** enjoys cut-elimination. In the next section we extend Wansing's strong normalisation theorem to δ**MNTL** in such a way that any extension of δ**MNTL** by addition of structural rules satisfying (C2)-(C7) also satisfies the strong normalisation theorem (condition (C8) is relevant only for logical rules).

4 A Strong Normalisation Theorem

A very important feature of the proof-theoretical framework **DL** is the existence of a very general cut-elimination theorem [Bel82]. Indeed, any display calculus satisfying the conditions (C2)-(C8) [Bel82] admits cut-elimination. In [Wan98], such a result is strengthened by proving that any classical modal display calculus defined from [Kra96] for a properly displayable classical modal logic [Kra96] admits a strong normalisation theorem: that is, the process of cut-elimination terminates for any sequence of the reduction steps to be defined shortly. Similar theorems exist for numerous formal systems such as for example those for typed λ-terms (see e.g. [TS96]).

Unfortunately δ**MNTL** does not satisfy (C8) recalled below (see e.g. [Wan98]):

(C8) If there are inferences $\mathcal{I}_1$ and $\mathcal{I}_2$ with respective conclusions $X \vdash \phi$ and $\phi \vdash Y$ with ϕ *principal* in both inferences, and if cut is applied to obtain $X \vdash Y$, then either $X \vdash Y$ is identical to one of $X \vdash \phi$ and $\phi \vdash Y$; or there is a derivation of $X \vdash Y$ from the premisses of $\mathcal{I}_1$ and $\mathcal{I}_2$ in which every cut-formula of any application of cut is a proper subformula of ϕ.

Example 1. Consider the proof,

$$\dfrac{\dfrac{\overset{\vdots\ \Pi_1}{\mathtt{i} \vdash \bullet_{\neq} * X}}{X \vdash \mathtt{i}}\ (\vdash \mathtt{i}) \qquad \dfrac{\overset{\vdots\ \Pi_2}{Y \vdash \mathtt{i}}}{\mathtt{i} \vdash \bullet_{\neq} * Y}\ (\mathtt{i} \vdash)}{X \vdash \bullet_{\neq} * Y}\ (cut)$$

Since i does not have proper subformulae, δ**MNTL** does not satisfy (C8) which is absolutely crucial in the proofs of cut-elimination in [Bel82, Wan98]. However, δ**MNTL** enjoys a (weak) cut-elimination theorem (see Theorem 6).

At first sight, C4 also seems to be violated since an inference of ($\mathtt{i}\vdash$) [resp. ($\vdash\mathtt{i}$)] changes the displayed antecedent [resp. succedent] part occurrence of $\mathtt{i}$ in the conclusion into a succedent [resp. antecedent] part occurrence in the premiss. However, all is well, for the occurrences of a name in some ($\mathtt{i}\vdash$)-rule [resp. ($\vdash\mathtt{i}$)-rule] inference are not *parameters* since they are not substructures of some structure obtained by instantiating some *structure* variable.

We now show that any *reasonable* extension of δ**MNTL** admits a strong normalisation theorem by adapting arguments from [Wan98]. By a *reasonable* extension, we mean a calculus δ obtained from δ**MNTL** by addition of structural rules that satisfy the conditions (C2)-(C7) (see e.g. [Bel82, Kra96, Wan98]).

As usual, our strong normalisation theorem is relative to a given reduction concept. Indeed, we shall define legitimate moves that define the authorised reductions. Basically, each reduction removes a cut at the cost of cuts of lesser rank, or permutes a cut with a rule application in one of its premisses or replaces a cut by a cut of the same rank but decreases the number of *significant* inferences. In the rest of the section, δ is assumed to be *reasonable*.

The reduction process consists of *SE-principal moves* and *parametric moves*. First, let us recall that in **DL**, every structure occurrence in an inference $\mathcal{I}$ is called a *constituent* of $\mathcal{I}$. Constituents of an inference $\mathcal{I}$ are *congruent* $\overset{\text{def}}{\Leftrightarrow}$ they occupy similar positions in occurrences of structures assigned to the same structure variable.

Definition 7. In the proof Π_1 from Definition 8 below left, the *congruence class* of ϕ is the smallest set Q_ϕ of occurrences of ϕ in Π_1 such that

- the displayed occurrence of ϕ in $\mathtt{X}\vdash\phi$ is in Q_ϕ;
- for every inference $\mathcal{I}$ in Π_1, each constituent of a premiss of $\mathcal{I}$ which is *congruent* (w.r.t. $\mathcal{I}$) to a constituent of the conclusion of $\mathcal{I}$ already in Q_ϕ, is in Q_ϕ.

Q_ϕ can be viewed as a finite tree of occurrences of ϕ. A *path* in the tree defined by Q_ϕ is a maximal finite sequence $\phi_{occ_1},\ldots,\phi_{occ_l}$ ($l\geq 1$) of elements of Q_ϕ such that for $k\in\{1,\ldots,l-1\}$, ϕ_{occ_k} is congruent to $\phi_{occ_{k+1}}$ for some inference.

Definition 8. In the proof Π below left, ϕ is said to be *SE-principal* ('principal modulo structural equivalence') in $\mathtt{X}\vdash\phi$ $\overset{\text{def}}{\Leftrightarrow}$ the subproof Π_1 is of the form Π_1' shown below right, ϕ is principal in the instance of rule (ru) and the two occurrences of ϕ in $\mathtt{X}'\vdash\phi$ and $\mathtt{X}\vdash\phi$ in Π_1' belong to the same *congruence class*:

$$\dfrac{\begin{array}{c}\vdots\,\Pi_1\\ \mathtt{X}\vdash\phi\end{array}\qquad\begin{array}{c}\vdots\,\Pi_2\\ \phi\vdash\mathtt{Y}\end{array}}{\mathtt{X}\vdash\mathtt{Y}}\,(cut)\qquad\qquad\dfrac{\dfrac{\vdots\,\Pi_1'}{\mathtt{X}'\vdash\phi}\,(ru)}{\mathtt{X}\vdash\phi}\,(dp)$$

We use an analogous definition for ϕ, SE-principal in $\phi\vdash\mathtt{Y}$.

Consider an application of (cut) as shown in proof Π from Definition 8. If the cut-formula ϕ is *SE-principal* in $\mathtt{X}\vdash\phi$ and $\phi\vdash\mathtt{Y}$, then an *SE-principal move* is done otherwise a *parametric move* is done.

SE-principal moves There are three cases:
Case 1: $X \vdash Y$ is $X \vdash \phi$ [resp. $\phi \vdash Y$]. Then, Π is transformed into Π_1 [resp. Π_2].
Case 2: ϕ is not a name. The treatment of the similar case in [Wan98] (see also [Bel82]) applies except that one has to take into account the display postulate inferences. For instance, when $\phi = \neg\psi$ the proof fragment below left is transformed into the proof fragment below right:

$$\dfrac{\dfrac{\dfrac{X' \vdash *\psi}{X' \vdash \neg\psi}\,(\vdash \neg)}{X \vdash \neg\psi}\,(dp1) \qquad \dfrac{\dfrac{*\psi \vdash Y'}{\neg\psi \vdash Y'}\,(\neg \vdash)}{\neg\psi \vdash Y}\,(dp2)}{X \vdash Y}\,(cut) \qquad\qquad \dfrac{\dfrac{\dfrac{\dfrac{\dfrac{X' \vdash *\psi}{\psi \vdash *X'}\,(dp) \qquad \dfrac{*\psi \vdash Y'}{*Y' \vdash \psi}\,(dp)}{*Y' \vdash *X'}\,(cut)}{X' \vdash Y'}\,(dp)}{X \vdash Y'}\,(dp1)}{X \vdash Y}\,(dp2)$$

Observe that, in the transformed proof, the cut-formula ψ has $dg(\psi) < dg(\phi)$.
Case 3: ϕ is the name $\mathtt{i}$. Then Π is as shown below left and is transformed into the proof Π' shown below right:

$$\dfrac{\dfrac{\dfrac{\mathtt{i} \vdash \bullet_{\neq} * X'}{X' \vdash \mathtt{i}}\,(\vdash \mathtt{i})}{X \vdash \mathtt{i}}\,(dp1) \qquad \dfrac{\dfrac{Y' \vdash \mathtt{i}}{\mathtt{i} \vdash \bullet_{\neq} * Y'}\,(\mathtt{i} \vdash)}{\mathtt{i} \vdash Y}\,(dp2)}{X \vdash Y}\,(cut) \qquad\qquad \dfrac{\dfrac{\dfrac{\dfrac{\mathtt{i} \vdash \bullet_{\neq} * X' \quad Y' \vdash \mathtt{i}}{Y' \vdash * \bullet_{\neq} X'}\,(cut)}{X' \vdash \bullet_{\neq} * Y'}\,(dp)}{X \vdash \bullet_{\neq} * Y'}\,(dp1)}{X \vdash Y}\,(dp2)$$

It is obvious that (dp) moves do not alter a sequent in any significant way. So let us consider only significant (i.e. non (dp)) inferences. In Case 3, the degree of the cut-formula in Π' equals the degree of the cut-formula ϕ but the number of significant inferences in Π' is less than in Π. In the proof of the strong normalisation theorem (see [DG98a]), the measure on the size of proofs counts only the number of *significant* inferences (and this measure decreases when required). Indeed, we *implicitly* consider as identical the sequents that are structurally equivalent (i.e. interderivable by using only the display postulates from Figure 2).

Parametric moves The parametric moves can be viewed simply as non SE-principal moves. Suppose ϕ is not SE-principal in the inference ending in $X \vdash \phi$ from Definition 8 in proof Π (the other case is analogous). Viewing the congruence class Q_ϕ of this occurrence of ϕ as a tree, if the tree Q_ϕ contains an application of cut, then no reduction is performed and we instead consider one of the applications of cut above $X \vdash \phi$ for reduction. Thus the shown application of cut from Π is not subject to reduction at this stage. If the tree contains no application of cut, then for each path in Q_ϕ consider ϕ_u the uppermost member of Q_ϕ on the path and let $\mathcal{I}_u$ be the inference ending in the sequent s which contains ϕ_u.
Case (i): ϕ_u is principal in $\mathcal{I}_u$. So ϕ_u is the entire succedent of s. We cut with Π_2 and replace every occurrence of ϕ below ϕ_u in the path by Y.
Case (ii): ϕ_u is not principal in $\mathcal{I}_u$. Then, w.r.t. $\mathcal{I}$, ϕ_u is congruent only to itself so we just replace every occurrence of ϕ below ϕ_u in the path by Y. Π_2 is deleted.

Primitive Reduction. The result of simultaneously carrying out these operations for every path of occurrences of ϕ in Π_1 and removing the initial occurrence of $X \vdash Y$ is by definition a *primitive reduction.*

The treatment of the last two cases is exactly what is done in [Wan98] (see also [Bel82]). Fortunately, by close examination of Case (i) and Case (ii), it also works when ϕ is a name. Indeed, as mentioned previously, the two occurrences of $\mathtt{i}$ in both rules $(\mathtt{i} \vdash)$ and $(\vdash \mathtt{i})$ *are not congruent* by definition, and therefore, there is no need to treat the case $\phi = \mathtt{i}$ separately.

The reduction process does not systematically remove the uppermost cut (this is just a particular case) and not all the cuts in a proof are necessarily subject to primitive reduction. For any non cut-free proof Π, we write $\Pi' < \Pi$ to denote that Π' is obtained from Π by application of a primitive reduction.

Theorem 9. *(strong normalization) The relation $<$ on proofs of δ is* well-founded *(no infinite decreasing chains) and the terminal proofs (those that cannot be reduced) are cut-free.*

These proofs are impervious to additional *structural* rules obeying (C1)-(C7). The full proof of Theorem 9 can be found in [DG98a].

5 Properly Displayable Nominal Tense Logics

The aim of this section is to identify classes of properly displayable nominal tense logics by adapting developments from [Bla90, Kra96]. In what follows, we write $\delta + \mathcal{R}$ to denote the display calculus δ augmented with the set $\mathcal{R}$ of rules.

Definition 10. Logic $\mathcal{L} = \langle \mathtt{NTL}(H,G), \mathcal{C} \rangle$ is *properly displayable* $\stackrel{\text{def}}{\Leftrightarrow}$ there is a display calculus $\delta \stackrel{\text{def}}{=} \delta\mathtt{MNTL} + \mathcal{R}$ such that $\mathcal{R}$ is a set of structural rules satisfying (C2)-(C7) and for any $\phi \in \mathtt{NTL}(H,G)$, ϕ is $\mathcal{L}$-valid iff $I \vdash \phi$ is derivable in δ.

Theorem 11. *Every properly displayable logic has a cut-free display calculus.*

Indeed, by Theorem 9, $\delta\mathtt{MNTL} + \mathcal{R}$ admits a (strongly normalising) cut-elimination theorem since all the rules in $\mathcal{R}$ satisfy the conditions (C2)-(C7).

Sahlqvist tense formulae are useful to study the nominal tense logics characterized by classes of frames modally definable by such formulae. A formula is *positive* [resp. *negative*] $\stackrel{\text{def}}{\Leftrightarrow}$ every propositional variable occurs under an even [resp. odd] number of negation symbols (when $\phi_1 \Rightarrow \phi_2$ is treated as $\neg\phi_1 \vee \phi_2$). A *simple Sahlqvist tense formula* in $\mathtt{TL}(H,G)$ is an implication $\phi \Rightarrow \psi$ such that ψ is *positive* and ϕ is built up from *negative* formulae, formulae without occurrences of atomic propositions and formulae of the form $\sigma\mathrm{p}$ with σ a universal modality and $\mathrm{p} \in \mathtt{PRP}$ using only $\wedge, \vee$ and the existential modalities; see e.g. [Rij93]. A *Sahlqvist tense formula* is a conjunction of formulae of the form $\sigma(\phi \Rightarrow \psi)$ where σ is a universal modality and $\phi \Rightarrow \psi$ is a simple Sahlqvist tense formula.

Theorem 12. *Let ϕ be a Sahlqvist tense formula and let $\vdash \stackrel{\text{def}}{=} \vdash_{\mathtt{MNTL}} + \phi$. Then, any $\psi \in \mathtt{NTL}(H,G)$ is $\mathtt{NTL}_{\phi}$-valid iff $\vdash \psi$.*

Theorem 12 does *not* follow from Sahlqvist's Theorem [Sah75] since $\mathtt{NTL}_\phi$ is known to be non canonical for any Sahlqvist tense formula ϕ where $\{\mathcal{F} \in Fr : \mathcal{F} \models \phi\}$ contains a frame with a reflexive world and a frame with an irreflexive world [Bla90, Proof of Theorem 4.3.1]. For instance take ϕ to be $\mathtt{p} \Rightarrow \mathtt{p}$. That is, there is no (single canonical) $\mathtt{NTL}_\phi$-model $\mathcal{M} = (W, R, m)$ such that for every $\vdash$-*consistent set* X there is $w \in W$ such that for all $\psi \in X$, $\mathcal{M}, w \models \psi$.

Theorem 13. *Any logic* $\mathcal{L} = \langle \mathtt{NTL}(H, G), \mathcal{C}\rangle$ *where* $\mathcal{C} = \{\mathcal{F} \in Fr : \mathcal{F} \models \phi\}$ *for some conjunction* ϕ *of primitive formulae in* $\mathtt{TL}(G, H)$ *is properly displayable.*

The primitive formulae in Theorem 13 do not contain the difference operator. Another class of properly displayable nominal tense logics can be identified.

Theorem 14. *Let* $\mathcal{L}_{\neq} = \langle \mathtt{TL}(H, G, [\neq]), \mathcal{C}\rangle$ *and let* γ *be a conjunction of primitive formulae over the language* $\mathtt{TL}(H, G, [\neq])$ *such that* $\vdash_{\neq} + \gamma$ *axiomatizes* $\mathcal{L}_{\neq}$ *and* $\mathcal{C}$ *is closed under disjoint unions and isomorphic copies. Then the logic* $\mathcal{L} = \langle \mathtt{NTL}(H, G), \mathcal{C}\rangle$, *is properly displayable.*

The irreflexivity rule is *not* present in $\vdash_{\neq} + \gamma$. However, unlike Theorem 13, the primitive axioms in Theorem 14 may contain the difference operator.

Proof. (sketch) Since $\mathtt{struc}(\delta\mathtt{MNTL})$ contains $\bullet_{\neq}$, we first transform γ into a collection $\mathcal{R}_\gamma$ of structural rules over $\mathtt{struc}(\delta\mathtt{MNTL})$ using Kracht's method [Kra96]. This gives a display calculus $\delta\mathcal{L}_{\neq} \stackrel{\text{def}}{=} \delta\mathtt{MTL}_{\neq} + \mathcal{R}_\gamma$ where $\delta\mathtt{MTL}_{\neq}$ is the display calculus for $\mathtt{MTL}_{\neq}$. Actually, $\delta\mathtt{MTL}_{\neq}$ can be defined from $\delta\mathtt{MNTL}$ by: considering the same set of structural connectives but building up the structures from $\mathtt{TL}(H, G, [\neq])$ instead of $\mathtt{TL}(H, G)$; deleting the fundamental axioms of the form $\mathtt{i} \vdash \mathtt{i}$ and the rules $(\mathtt{i} \vdash)$ and $(\vdash \mathtt{i})$; and adding the rules below:

$$\frac{\phi \vdash \mathtt{X}}{[\neq]\phi \vdash \bullet_{\neq}\mathtt{X}}\ ([\neq]\vdash) \qquad \frac{\mathtt{X} \vdash \bullet_{\neq}\phi}{\mathtt{X} \vdash [\neq]\phi}\ (\vdash [\neq])$$

Since $\delta\mathcal{L}_{\neq}$ obeys (C1)-(C8), it enjoys cut-elimination. To show that $\delta\mathcal{L} \stackrel{\text{def}}{=} \delta\mathtt{MNTL}+\mathcal{R}_\gamma$ properly displays $\mathcal{L}$, let $\mathtt{struc}(\delta\mathcal{L}_{\neq})$ be the set of structures involved in $\delta\mathcal{L}_{\neq}$ and define a *partial function* $g : \mathtt{struc}(\delta\mathcal{L}_{\neq}) \to \mathtt{struc}(\delta\mathtt{MNTL})$ as follows:

- $g(\mathtt{X})$ is undefined if $\mathtt{X}$ contains some occurrences of $[\neq]\psi$ where ψ is not of the form $\neg\mathtt{p}_{2\times k+1}$ for $k \in \omega$; otherwise
- g is homomorphic for the Boolean connectives, for H and for G;
- for any $k \in \omega$, $g(\mathtt{p}_{2\times k+1}) \stackrel{\text{def}}{=} g([\neq]\neg\mathtt{p}_{2\times k+1}) \stackrel{\text{def}}{=} \mathtt{i}_k$ and $g(\mathtt{p}_{2\times k}) \stackrel{\text{def}}{=} \mathtt{p}_k$;
- $g(\bot) \stackrel{\text{def}}{=} \bot$; $g(\top) \stackrel{\text{def}}{=} \top$;
- g is homomorphic for the structural connectives and $g(I) \stackrel{\text{def}}{=} I$.

Let ϕ be a formula of $\mathtt{NTL}(G, H)$.

- (soundness) If $I \vdash \phi$ has a cut-free proof in $\delta\mathcal{L}$, then $s(\phi)$ is $\mathcal{L}_{\neq}$-valid (where s is from the proof of Theorem 3 and we use the closure properties of $\mathcal{C}$). We also have that ϕ is $\mathcal{L}$-valid iff $s(\phi)$ is $\mathcal{L}_{\neq}$-valid. Hence, ϕ is $\mathcal{L}$-valid. Note that in general $\phi \neq s(\phi)$!

- (completeness) We must show that if ϕ is $\mathcal{L}$-valid, then $I \vdash \phi$ has a cut-free proof in $\delta\mathcal{L}$. The proof contains five parts: (1) if ϕ is $\mathcal{L}$-valid, then $a(\phi)$ is $\mathcal{L}_{\neq}$-valid (here we use the closure properties of $\mathcal{C}$); (2) if $a(\phi)$ is $\mathcal{L}_{\neq}$-valid, then $I \vdash a(\phi)$ has a cut-free proof in $\delta\mathcal{L}_{\neq}$; (3) if $I \vdash a(\phi)$ has a cut-free proof in $\delta\mathcal{L}_{\neq}$, then $I \vdash g(a(\phi))$ has a cut-free proof in $\delta\mathcal{L}$; (4) $I \vdash g(a(\phi))$ has a cut-free proof in $\delta\mathcal{L}$ iff $I \vdash \phi$ has a cut-free proof in $\delta\mathcal{L}$; (5) hence, if ϕ is $\mathcal{L}$-valid, then $I \vdash \phi$ has a cut-free proof in $\delta\mathcal{L}$ (see the details in [DG98a]).

The proof of Theorem 14 is very informative since for instance, it also shows that any formula $\phi \in \mathtt{NTL}(H, G)$ is $\mathtt{MNTL}$-valid iff $I \vdash \phi$ has a cut-free proof in $\delta\mathtt{MNTL}$. Unlike the proof of Theorem 5, the ($\vdash$ i)-rule is used. The rules (i $\vdash$) and ($\vdash$ i) are obviously equivalent to the reversible rule below:

$$\frac{\mathtt{X} \vdash \mathtt{i}}{\mathtt{i} \vdash \bullet_{\neq} * \mathtt{X}}$$

Hence, as in the case with the display postulates, or indeed any reversible rule, backward proof search may enter loops. However, all is not lost, for the proof of Theorem 14 also yields

Corollary 15. *In a backward proof attempt, if we apply* (i $\vdash$) *[resp.* ($\vdash$ i)*], giving rise to some name* i *in the premiss, then we do not need to apply* ($\vdash$ i) *[resp.* (i $\vdash$)*] to this name in the rest of the backward proof search.*

6 Concluding Remarks

To define cut-free display calculi for nominal tense logics, we have extended Wansing's strong normalization theorem [Wan98] to any *reasonable* extension of $\delta\mathtt{MNTL}$. Although $\delta\mathtt{MNTL}$ does not satisfy (C8), the proof in Section 4 provides a new condition (C′8) (see the appendix).

Are the classes of properly displayable nominal tense logics characterised by Theorem 13 and Theorem 14 really different? One solution is to characterize the class of Sahlqvist tense formulae ϕ such that $\vdash_{\neq} + \phi$ axiomatizes $\langle \mathtt{TL}(H, G, [\neq]), \{\mathcal{F} : \mathcal{F} \models \phi\}\rangle$. This is roughly equivalent to knowing when the irreflexivity rule is superfluous (see e.g. [Ven93]). How to define structural rules in **DL** from axioms containing names?

Kracht and Wolter [KW97] show how to eliminate the difference operator by means of a pair of tense operators. Unfortunately, one operator must satisfy the Gödel-Lob axiom G, which is not Sahlqvist. Using our recent work on cut-free display calculi for such "second-order" modal logics [DG99], we may be able to design yet another display calculus for nominal tense logics.

References

[BD97] Ph. Balbiani and S. Demri. Prefixed tableaux systems for modal logics with enriched languages. In *IJCAI-15*, pages 190–195. Morgan Kaufmann, 1997.

[Bel82] N. Belnap. Display logic. *Journal of Philosophical Logic*, 11:375–417, 1982.

[Bla90] P. Blackburn. *Nominal Tense Logic and Other Sorted Intensional Frameworks*. PhD thesis, University of Edinburgh, Edinburgh, 1990.

[Bla93] P. Blackburn. Nominal tense logic. *NDJFL*, 34(1):56–83, 1993.

[Bla98] P. Blackburn. Internalizing labeled deduction. Technical Report 102, Computerlinguistik, Universität des Saarlandes, 1998.

[Dem99] S. Demri. *Sequent Calculi for Nominal Tense Logics: a step toward mechanization?*. In this volume.

[DG98a] S. Demri and R. Goré. Cut-free display calculi for nominal tense logics. TR-ARP-07-98, A.R.P., A.N.U., 1998. `http://arp.anu.edu.au/`.

[DG99] S. Demri and R. Goré. Theoremhood Preserving Maps as a Characterisation of Cut Elimination for Provability Logics. TR-ARP-??-99, forthcoming 1999.

[dM94] M. d'Agostino and M. Mondadori. The taming of the cut. Classical refutations with analytic cut. *J. of Logic and Computation*, 4(3):285–319, 1994.

[Gab81] D. Gabbay. An irreflexivity lemma with applications to axiomatization of conditions on tense frames. In U. Mönnich, editor, *Aspects of Philosophical Logic*, pages 67–89. Reidel, 1981.

[GG93] G. Gargov and V. Goranko. Modal logic with names. *J. of Philosophical Logic*, 22(6):607–636, 1993.

[Gor95] R. Goré. Intuitionistic logic redisplayed. TR-ARP-1-95, ARP, ANU, 1995.

[Gor98] R. Goré. Substructural logics on display. *LJIGPL*, 6(3):451–504, 1998.

[GT75] R. Goldblatt and S. Thomason. Axiomatic classes in propositional modal logic. In *Algebra and Logic*, LNM 450:163–173, 1975, Springer-Verlag.

[Kon97] B. Konikowska. A logic for reasoning about relative similarity. *Studia Logica*, 58(1):185–226, 1997.

[Koy92] R. Koymans. *Specifying message passing and time-critical systems with temporal logic*. LNCS 651, Springer-Verlag, 1992.

[Kra96] M. Kracht. Power and weakness of the modal display calculus. In H. Wansing, editor, *Proof theory of modal logic*, pages 93–121. Kluwer, 1996.

[KW97] M. Kracht and F. Wolter. Simulation and transfer results in modal logic - A survey. *Studia Logica*, 59:149–1997, 1997.

[Orło84] E. Orłowska. Logic of indiscernibility relations. In *5th Symposium on Computation Theory*, pages 177–186. LNCS 208, Springer-Verlag, 1984.

[PT85] S. Passy and T. Tinchev. PDL with data constants. *IPL*, 20:35–41, 1985.

[PT91] S. Passy and T. Tinchev. An essay in combinatory dynamic logic. *Information and Computation*, 93:263–332, 1991.

[Rij92] M. de Rijke. The modal logic of inequality. *JSL*, 57(2):566–584, 1992.

[Rij93] M. de Rijke. *Extending modal logic*. PhD thesis, ILLC, Amsterdam, 1993.

[Sah75] H. Sahlqvist. Completeness and correspondence in the first and second order semantics for modal logics. In S. Kanger, editor, *3rd Scandinavian Logic Symposium*, pages 110–143. North Holland, 1975.

[Seg81] K. Segerberg. A note on the logic of elsewhere. *Theoria*, 47:183–187, 1981.

[TS96] A. Troelstra and H. Schwichtenberg. *Basic Proof Theory*. Cambridge Tracts in Theoretical Computer Science 43. Cambridge University Press, 1996.

[Ven93] Y. Venema. Derivation rules as anti-axioms in modal logic. *JSL*, 58(3):1003–1034, 1993.

[Wan94] H. Wansing. Sequent calculi for normal modal propositional logics. *J. of Logic and Computation*, 4(2):125–142, 1994.

[Wan98] H. Wansing. *Displaying Modal Logic*, volume 3 of *Trends in Logic*. Kluwer Academic Publishers, Dordrecht, 1998.

Appendix: Belnap's Conditions.

For every sequent rule Belnap [Bel82, page 388] first defines the following notions: in an application *Inf* of a sequent rule (ρ), "constituents occurring as part of occurrences of structures assigned to structure-variables are defined to be **parameters** of *Inf* ; all other constituents are defined as **nonparametric**, including those assigned to formula-variables. Constituents occupying similar positions in occurrences of structures assigned to the same structure-variable are defined as **congruent** in *Inf*". The eight (actually seven) conditions shown below are from [Kra96]:

(C1) Each formula which is a constituent of some premiss of a rule ρ is a subformula of some formula in the conclusion of ρ.

(C2) Congruent parameters are occurrences of the same structure.

(C3) Each parameter is congruent to at most one constituent in the conclusion. Equivalently, no two constituents of the conclusion are congruent to each other.

(C4) Congruent parameters are either all antecedent parts or all succedent parts of their respective sequent.

(C5) If a formula is non-parametric in the conclusion of a rule ρ, it is either the entire antecedent, or the entire succedent. Such a formula is called a **principal** formula.

(C6/7) Each rule is closed under simultaneous substitution of arbitrary structures for congruent parameters.

(C8) If there are inference rules ρ_1 and ρ_2 with respective conclusions $\mathtt{X} \vdash \phi$ and $\phi \vdash \mathtt{Y}$ with ϕ principal in both inferences (in the sense of C5), and if (cut) is applied to yield $\mathtt{X} \vdash \mathtt{Y}$ then, either $\mathtt{X} \vdash \mathtt{Y}$ is identical to $\mathtt{X} \vdash \phi$ or to $\phi \vdash \mathtt{Y}$; or it is possible to pass from the premisses of ρ_1 and ρ_2 to $\mathtt{X} \vdash \mathtt{Y}$ by means of inferences falling under (cut) where the cut-formula is always a proper subformula of ϕ. If ϕ satisfies the "if" part of this condition it is known as a "matching principal constituent".

Our new condition (C8′)

(C8′) There exist a non-empty set S with $<$ a well-founded ordering on S and a map $dg : \mathtt{For} \to S$ such that if there are inferences $\mathcal{I}_1$ and $\mathcal{I}_2$ with respective conclusions $\mathtt{X} \vdash \phi$ and $\phi \vdash \mathtt{Y}$ with ϕ *SE-principal* in both inferences, and if cut is applied to obtain $\mathtt{X} \vdash \mathtt{Y}$, then

- either $\mathtt{X} \vdash \mathtt{Y}$ is identical to one of $\mathtt{X} \vdash \phi$ and $\phi \vdash \mathtt{Y}$;
- or there is a derivation of $\mathtt{X} \vdash \mathtt{Y}$ from the premisses of $\mathcal{I}_1$ and $\mathcal{I}_2$ in which every cut-formula ψ of any application of cut satisfies $dg(\psi) < dg(\phi)$;
- or there is a derivation of $\mathtt{X} \vdash \mathtt{Y}$ from the premisses of $\mathcal{I}_1$ and $\mathcal{I}_2$ in which every cut-formula ψ of any application of cut satisfies $dg(\psi) = dg(\phi)$ and in that derivation every inference, except possibly one, falls under an invertible structural rule with a single premiss.

Hilbert's ϵ-Terms in Automated Theorem Proving

Martin Giese and Wolfgang Ahrendt

Institut für Logik, Komplexität und Deduktionssysteme,
Universtät Karlsruhe, Germany
{giese|ahrendt}@ira.uka.de

Abstract. ϵ-terms, introduced by David Hilbert [8], have the form $\epsilon x.\phi$, where x is a variable and ϕ is a formula. Their syntactical structure is thus similar to that of a quantified formulae, but they are terms, denoting 'an element for which ϕ holds, if there is any'.

The topic of this paper is an investigation into the possibilities and limits of using ϵ-terms for automated theorem proving. We discuss the relationship between ϵ-terms and Skolem terms (which both can be used alternatively for the purpose of $\exists$-quantifier elimination), in particular with respect to efficiency and intuition. We also discuss the consequences of allowing ϵ-terms in theorems (and cuts). This leads to a distinction between (essentially two) semantics and corresponding calculi, one enabling efficient automated proof search, and the other one requiring human guidance but enabling a very intuitive (i.e. semantic) treatment of ϵ-terms. We give a theoretical foundation of the usage of both variants in a single framework. Finally, we argue that these two approaches to ϵ are just the extremes of a range of ϵ-treatments, corresponding to a range of different possible Skolemization variants.

1 Introduction

Calculi for full first-order predicate logic have to cope with the elimination of existential quantifiers. Quantified variables are usually replaced by terms, which have to obey certain restrictions. Many approaches in proof theory and almost all approaches in automated deduction use the concept of Skolem functions (resp. constants) for this purpose. An alternative concept for terms replacing existentially quantified variables is that of ϵ-terms. An ϵ-term has the form $\epsilon x.\phi$, where x is a variable and ϕ is a formula. The intended meaning is 'an element for which ϕ holds, if there is any, and an arbitrary element otherwise'. If ϕ holds for more than one element, or for none, ϵ acts as a choice operator.

A Skolem term introduced during elimination of the quantifier in $\exists x.\phi(x)$ also denotes an element e for which $\phi(e)$ holds. But in contrast to the Skolem term, the ϵ-term refers explicitly (on an object language level) to the property ϕ it satisfies.

1.1 Short History of ϵ-Terms

The ϵ-symbol was introduced by Hilbert in the context of the formalist effort to prove the consistency of arithmetic and analysis by finitary means. In particular, ϵ-terms are used to give a finitary justification of the use of (non-finitary) quantifier reasoning in predicate logic. The arguments in this context are typically based on proof transformations. Model-theoretic reasoning would have been inappropriate, as reasoning about models is usually non-finitary. The principal work in this area is by Hilbert and Bernays [8]. Leisenring [9] gives a more condensed and up-to-date survey of the field.

In the context of *automated deduction,* reasoning with models is not regarded as problematic. Indeed, soundness or completeness statements are almost always relative to a given model semantics. Possible model semantics for ϵ-terms are investigated by Meyer Viol [10] and also to a certain degree by Leisenring.

To our knowledge, in the context of automated deduction, calculi do not use ϵ-terms as a syntactical construct. On the other hand, the development of improved δ-rule versions (see below) can be seen as a progressing approximation of ϵ-like behaviour.

1.2 Short History of δ-Rules

Elimination of existential quantifiers takes place either in a preprocessing step or, in particular in analytic non-normal form calculi (i.e. tableaux and sequent calculi), in a special expansion rule, called δ-rule. The evolution of different δ-rules that we sketch now took place in the framework of tableaux. We use the tableau notation in the rest of this paper.[1]

In a Smullyan style *ground* tableau calculus [11], there is a δ-rule of the form

$$\frac{\exists x.\phi(x)}{\phi(c)} ,$$

where c is a constant symbol, which must be new relative to the tableau or branch to which the rule is applied. The intuition behind this requirement is to make sure that all we know about c is $\phi(c)$. (Sometimes, we *do* know more about c, however, which is where some liberalized δ-rules come in.)

In a *free variable* tableau calculus, where free variables stand for instances not yet known, the δ-rule

$$\frac{\exists x.\phi(x)}{\phi(f(x_1,\ldots,x_n))}$$

introduces a term $t = f(x_1,\ldots,x_n)$, where the choice of both the function symbol and the variables has to meet certain requirements, which vary from one δ-rule to the other. Early versions of this rule, e.g. [5], required that the function symbol f is new and that all free variables present on the current branch are

[1] Note, however, that it is trivial to translate the discussion to a sequent calculus notation.

parameters of t. These parameters guarantee that t stays new w.r.t. the branch even after applying arbitrary substitutions.

Later versions of the δ-rule for free variable tableaux modified the restrictions for t, always shortening the minimal proof length. At first, the δ^+-rule, introduced by Hähnle and Schmitt [7], reduced the parameters of t to the free variables of the expanded formula only. Now, t is actually a *Skolem term* in the sense, that the soundness argument for this rule uses the semantic properties of Skolemization. Note that, with this rule, it is possible to unify t with a free variable occurring above in the branch. Consequently, after applying such a unifier to the tableau, the term replacing the existentially bound variable occurs in the proof prior to the rule that introduced it. It is not trivial to formulate a sound δ-rule for a *ground* tableau, which corresponds one to one to δ^+, see [2, Sect. 3.6].

A further modification of restrictions for t is formulated in the δ^{++}-rule by Beckert et. al.[3]. Now, the function symbol of the Skolem term need not be new in general. Instead, the same functor can be used when the δ^{++}-rule is applied to formulae that are identical up to renaming of (free and bound) variables. In theory, classes of such formulae *are* the functors. This way of Skolemization is closely related to the idea of ϵ-terms, because the chosen element is identified by a class of formulae it satisfies. However, Skolemization of two formulae, where one is an instance of the other, leads to non-unifiable results. Consequently, δ^{++}-rule application and substitution of free variables are not exchangeable, which is unsatisfying from an intuitive point of view.

There are already δ-rules going beyond δ^{++}, e.g. δ^* [1] and δ^{**} [4], which we shall come back to in the course of this paper.

1.3 This Paper

This paper is concerned with the embedding of ϵ-terms in a calculus well suited for automated theorem proving. Moreover, our issue is the border between ϵ-handling that fits purely automated proof search, and ϵ-handling requiring human guidance. The context of our work is research on concepts for integrating automated and interactive theorem proving in a *homogeneous* way. By 'homogeneous' we mean an integration of the two paradigms in *one* prover, based on *one* calculus. In this setting, a calculus must be intuitive, as well as efficient, which shall be an issue in Sect. 3 and 4.

In this paper, we present a spectrum of treatments of ϵ-terms, discussing their suitability for automated proof search. ϵ essentially is a choice operator. Therefore, fixing its semantics means fixing the features of the choice. Given $\exists x.\phi(x)$, the choice of an element e, for which $\phi(e)$ holds, may for example depend only on the semantics (i.e. the extension) of ϕ. Another possibility is to let the choice depend only on the syntax of a formula (compare δ^{++} above). But then, the choice function should have some basic properties, which we discuss below.

We start, in Sect. 2, with the introduction of a δ^ϵ-rule and, because of the similarity to the δ^{++}-rule, compare both with respect to minimal proof length.

Then, we turn to the semantics of ϵ-terms in Sect. 3, defining a hierarchy of ϵ-structures. The distinction between different structures is justified in Sect. 4, where two calculi that are complete for different semantics are presented and discussed with respect to automated theorem proving.

2 Using ϵ-Terms Instead of Skolem Functions

2.1 Introducing ϵ-Terms

We begin by defining a number of basic syntactic notions.

Definition 1 (Syntax, free/bound variables, substitutions). *Let* $\mathbf{V}$ *be a fixed (infinite) set of* **variables**. *The sets* $\mathbf{Tm}$, *resp.* $\mathbf{Fm}$, *of well formed first order* **terms**, *resp.* **formulae**, *are defined as usual, with the additional requirement, that for all* $x \in \mathbf{V}$ *and* $\phi \in \mathbf{Fm}$, *there is a term* $\epsilon x.\phi \in \mathbf{Tm}$.[2]

For a term or formula α, *define* $\mathrm{bv}(\alpha) \subseteq \mathbf{V}$, *resp.* $\mathrm{fv}(\alpha) \subseteq \mathbf{V}$, *the sets of* **bound**, *resp.* **free variables** *of* α. *A term, resp. formula is called* **closed** *if it has no free variables. The sets of all closed terms, resp. closed formulae are denoted by* $\mathbf{Tm}^0$, *resp.* $\mathbf{Fm}^0$.

A **substitution** *is a mapping* $\sigma : \mathbf{V} \to \mathbf{Tm}$, *where* $\mathrm{dom}(\sigma) := \{x \in \mathbf{V} \mid \sigma(x) \neq x\}$ *(called the* **domain** *of* σ*) is finite. The notation* $\sigma = [x_1/t_1, \ldots, x_n/t_n]$ *is used for the substitution with* $\sigma(x_i) = t_i$, $\mathrm{dom}(\sigma) = \{x_1, \ldots, x_n\}$.

The most important point here is that terms may contain bound variables, which is not the case in ordinary first order logic: $\epsilon x.\phi$ is a term in which the variable x is bound. This means that a little more care needs to be taken, when arguing about substitutions.

Instead of giving a formal semantics for ϵ-terms right away, we first show what we want to use them for, and defer the rigorous discussion to Sect. 3. The given intuition behind ϵ-terms captures the essence of $\exists$-quantifier elimination: given $\exists x.\phi$, $\epsilon x.\phi$ denotes a value of which we know nothing, except that it makes ϕ true. Accordingly, we use the δ-rule

$$\frac{\exists x.\phi(x)}{\phi(\epsilon x.\phi(x))}\ \delta^\epsilon \ .$$

To give the reader a general idea of how this works, here is a proof of the inconsistency of the set of formulae

$$\{\forall u.p(u,a,b), (\forall y.\exists x.\neg p(x,y,b)) \vee (\forall z.\exists x.\neg p(x,a,z))\}$$

[2] This means, that *unlike* the usual practice, terms and formulae are defined by *mutual* recursion.

in an unsigned tableau-calculus with free variables:

$$1:\ \forall u.p(u,a,b)$$
$$2:\ (\forall y.\exists x.\neg p(x,y,b)) \vee (\forall z.\exists x.\neg p(x,a,z))$$
$$3,\gamma(1):\ p(U,a,b)$$

$$4,\beta(2):\ \forall y.\exists x.\neg p(x,y,b) \qquad 5,\beta(2):\ \forall z.\exists x.\neg p(x,a,z)$$
$$6,\gamma(4):\ \exists x.\neg p(x,Y,b) \qquad 7,\gamma(5):\ \exists x.\neg p(x,a,Z)$$
$$8,\delta^{\epsilon}(6):\ \neg p(\epsilon x.\neg p(x,Y,b),Y,b) \qquad 9,\delta^{\epsilon}(7):\ \neg p(\epsilon x.\neg p(x,a,Z),a,Z)$$

The tableau is closed after applying the following substitution:

$$[U/\epsilon x.\neg p(x,a,b), Y/a, Z/b]$$

With the δ, δ^{+}, δ^{++} or δ^{*} rules, different skolem functions would be chosen for the skolemization of formulae 6 and 7, so the tableau could not be closed without a second instance of the γ-formula 1.

It should be mentioned at this point, that ϵ-terms (a) may be nested, (b) may contain free variables, and (c) may lead to rather large formulae, as they repeat most of the δ-formula. The problem of large formulae can be addressed in an implementation using structure sharing.

The main benefit of using ϵ-terms to handle δ-formulae is that identical formulae lead to introduction of the same term. The same idea is realized in the δ^{++}-rule. Therefore, in the next section we compare that rule to δ^{ϵ}.

2.2 Exponentially Shorter Proofs with ϵ-terms than with δ^{++}

We shall now show that the δ^{ϵ}-rule can cut down minimal proof-length exponentially with respect to a certain modification of the δ^{++}-rule: while the original δ^{++}-rule allows to assign the same Skolem-function symbol to any two formulae which are equal up to renaming of *bound and free* variables, we require the formulae to be equal up to renaming of *free variables only.* We refer to this modification as the δ^{+^-}-rule.

Theorem 1 (Proof length with δ^{ϵ} vs. δ^{+^-}). *There is a family $\phi_n, n \in \mathbb{N}$ of valid first order formulae, such that the minimal number b^{ϵ}, resp. b^{+^-} of branches in a closed tableau for ϕ_n with the δ^{ϵ}-rule, resp. δ^{+^-}-rule satisfy $b^{\epsilon}(n) \in \Theta(n)$, and $b^{+^-}(n) \in \Theta(2^n)$.*

Proof. The proof is based on the same ideas as the one in [3], where it is shown, that the δ^{++}-rule permits exponentially shorter proofs than the δ^{+}-rule. Define

$$\phi_0 := \mathit{true}$$
$$\phi_{n+1} := \exists x.\Big(\phi_n \wedge \big(p_n(x,a,b) \rightarrow (\exists y.\forall x.p_n(x,y,b) \wedge \exists z.\forall x.p_n(x,a,z))\big)\Big) \qquad \text{for } n \in \mathbb{N}.$$

The proof proceeds analogous to that of [3]. As in the introductory example of section 2.1, the inclusion of the skolemized formula in the ϵ-terms provides the necessary information to permit the simultaneous closure of two branches in the δ^ϵ case, where another γ-rule application is needed with δ^{+^-}. □

Clearly, any δ^{+^-}-proof can be simulated using δ^ϵ, so the δ^ϵ-rule is strictly stronger than δ^{+^-}.

Remark 1. It is not hard to modify the δ^ϵ-rule to obtain exponentially shorter minimal proofs than with the origninal δ^{++}-rule of [3]: one only needs to define closure by means of unification *modulo* renaming of bound variables. Alternatively, normalize the names of bound variables when applying the δ^ϵ-rule. We will omit this technical detail here, however.

Remark 2. Baaz and Fermüller [1] show a stronger speed-up result, namely that the δ^{++} rule gives *non-elementary* speedup w.r.t. to the δ^+ rule. We are currently investigating whether their proof technique can be applied to show that δ^ϵ yields non-elementary speed-up w.r.t. δ^{++}.

Remark 3. It is also possible to strengthen the δ^ϵ-calculus in a way that makes it *strictly stronger* than the δ^*-rule of Baaz and Fermüller [1], which in turn gives non-elementary speed-up w.r.t. the δ^{++}-rule. For lack of space, we are not going to develop this any further in this paper.

3 Semantics of ϵ-Terms

In the last section, we have introduced ϵ-terms as syntactical entities, but we have not given them a formal model-semantics, which is the topic of this section.

3.1 Valuation in Pre-Structures

We want our logic with ϵ-terms to be a conservative extension of classical predicate logic, i.e. the validity of terms and formulae that do not contain ϵ-terms should remain the same. Accordingly, the valuation functions correspond closely to the classical case. On the other hand, we will discuss several possible semantics for ϵ-terms, so we give some minimal semantic definitions first and refine them later.

Definition 2 (Variable assignments, pre-structures). *A* **variable assignment** *of* **V** *to a set $\mathcal{D}$ is a function $\beta : \mathbf{V} \to \mathcal{D}$. We denote by $\beta\{x \leftarrow d\}$ the modified assignment with*

$$\beta\{x \leftarrow d\}(y) := \begin{cases} d & \text{if } y = x, \\ \beta(y) & \text{otherwise.} \end{cases}$$

A **pre-structure** *is a triple $\mathcal{S} = (\mathcal{D}, \mathcal{I}, \mathcal{A})$ with the following properties:*

- *$(\mathcal{D}, \mathcal{I})$ is a classical first order structure with* **carrier** *$\mathcal{D}$ and* **interpretation** *$\mathcal{I}$.*

- *The* **ε-valuation** $\mathcal{A}$ *is a function that maps any ε-term* $\epsilon x.\phi$ *and any variable assignment* β *on* $\mathcal{D}$ *to a value* $\mathcal{A}(\epsilon x.\phi, \beta) \in \mathcal{D}$.

This definition contains no restriction whatsoever on the valuation of ε-terms. We will add restrictions that reflect the intended behaviour of these terms later. Here, we proceed by defining the valuation of terms and formulae on pre-structures.

Definition 3 (Term and formula valuation). *The* **valuation** $\mathrm{val}(\mathcal{S}, \beta, t) \in \mathcal{D}$ *of a term* $t \in \mathbf{Tm}$ *in a pre-structure* $\mathcal{S} = (\mathcal{D}, \mathcal{I}, \mathcal{A})$ *under a variable assignment* β *is defined as for classical first order logic, except for the valuation of ε-terms, where we set*

$$\mathrm{val}(\mathcal{S}, \beta, \epsilon x.\phi) := \mathcal{A}(\epsilon x.\phi, \beta) \ .$$

The validity relation for formulae, $\mathcal{S}, \beta \models \phi$ *is defined exactly as for classical first order logic.*

Note, that – in contrast to the syntax – *no* mutual recursion between terms and formulae is needed in these semantic definitions: the whole valuation of ε-terms is delegated to the function $\mathcal{A}$, so the semantic definitions do not take the formula in an ε-term into account so far.

3.2 A Hierarchy of Structures

In this section, we give several concrete restrictions leading to more useful semantics for ε-terms. In particular, we define the *substitutive* and *extensional* semantics, for which we give complete calculi in Sect. 4.

Two minimal requirements are needed to ensure a sensible semantics for ε-terms: first, the valuation of an ε-term should depend only on the valuation of variables occurring free in that term. Second, an ε-term $\epsilon x.\phi$ should actually denote a value that satisfies ϕ, if any such value exists. These requirements are captured in the following definition:

Definition 4 (Intensional structure). *A pre-structure* $\mathcal{S} = (\mathcal{D}, \mathcal{I}, \mathcal{A})$ *is called* **intensional structure** *or* **I-structure**, *if*

- *any ε-term* $\epsilon x.\phi$ *and two assignments* β_1, β_2 *with* $\beta_1|_{\mathrm{fv}(\epsilon x.\phi)} = \beta_2|_{\mathrm{fv}(\epsilon x.\phi)}$ *satisfy* $\mathcal{A}(\epsilon x.\phi, \beta_1) = \mathcal{A}(\epsilon x.\phi, \beta_2)$.
- *for any* β, $x \in \mathbf{V}$, $\phi \in \mathbf{Fm}$, *if* $\mathcal{S}, \beta \models \exists x.\phi$, *then* $\mathcal{S}, \beta\{x \leftarrow \mathcal{A}(\epsilon x.\phi, \beta)\} \models \phi$.

A formula which is valid in all I-structures under all variable assignments is called **I-valid**. *If it is valid in at least one I-structure under at least one variable assignment, it is called* **I-satisfiable**.

This intensional semantics lacks an important property: it is not *substitutive.* E.g., from $\forall x.q(\epsilon y.p(x, y))$ it is not possible to infer $q(\epsilon y.p(a, y))$. Similarly, from the equality $a = b$, we can not infer $\epsilon x.p(x, a) = \epsilon x.p(x, b)$. However, these inferences become possible, if we further constrain the set of permissible structures.

Definition 5 (Substitutive structure). *An I-structure* $\mathcal{S} = (\mathcal{D}, \mathcal{I}, \mathcal{A})$ *is called* **substitutive** *or* **S-structure,** *if for all* $x, y \in \mathbf{V}$, $\phi \in \mathbf{Fm}$, $\beta : \mathbf{V} \to \mathcal{D}$ *and* $t \in \mathbf{Tm}$ *with* $\mathrm{fv}(t) \cap \mathrm{bv}(\epsilon x.\phi) = \emptyset$,

$$\mathcal{A}([y/t](\epsilon x.\phi), \beta) = \mathcal{A}(\epsilon x.\phi, \beta\{y \leftarrow \mathrm{val}(\mathcal{S}, \beta, t)\}) \ .$$

S-validity *and* **S-satisfiability** *are defined analogous to Definition 4.*

Substitutivity, namely the fact that

$$\mathrm{val}(\mathcal{S}, \beta, [y/t]\alpha) = \mathrm{val}(\mathcal{S}, \beta\{y \leftarrow \mathrm{val}(\mathcal{S}, \beta, t)\}, \alpha)$$

for any term or formula α with $\mathrm{fv}(\alpha) \cap \mathrm{bv}(\epsilon x.\phi) = \emptyset$, follows directly from this definition for S-structures. Substitutivity is a central property for the construction of a calculus, as it captures the semantic effects of the syntactic operation of substituting parts of a term or formula.

Classical first order logic has the property that replacing an arbitrary subformula ψ of a formula ϕ by a logically equivalent formula ψ' maintains the validity of ϕ. This is not necessarily the case with S-validity. In fact, from $\forall x.p(x) \leftrightarrow q(x)$ it does not follow that $\epsilon x.p(x) = \epsilon x.q(x)$. As long as we use ϵ-terms for $\exists$-quantifier elimination only, this would not be a problem. But, as we argue in the next section, it is reasonalbe to permit the use of ϵ-terms in the formulation of problems, which might well be done by a human. In that case, it is vital to make the behaviour of ϵ-terms as intuitive as possible. The main intuition behind logical equivalence is that replacing part of a formula by something equivalent should not change the meaning of the whole. We therefore define a semantics that has this property, by making the interpretation of an ϵ-term $\epsilon x.\phi$ depend on the *semantics* of the formula ϕ.

Definition 6 (Extensional structure). *For an* ϵ*-term* $\epsilon x.\phi$, *an I-structure* $\mathcal{S} = (\mathcal{D}, \mathcal{I}, \mathcal{A})$ *and a variable assignment* $\beta : \mathbf{V} \to \mathcal{D}$, *define the* **extension**

$$\mathrm{Ext}(\mathcal{S}, \beta, \epsilon x.\phi) := \{d \in \mathcal{D} \mid \mathcal{S}, \beta\{x \leftarrow d\} \models \phi\}$$

An I-structure is called **extensional** *or* **E-structure,** *if for all* $x, y \in \mathbf{V}$, $\phi, \psi \in \mathbf{Fm}$, $\beta : \mathbf{V} \to \mathcal{D}$,

$$\textit{if} \ \ \mathrm{Ext}(\mathcal{S}, \beta, \epsilon x.\phi) = \mathrm{Ext}(\mathcal{S}, \beta, \epsilon y.\psi), \ \ \textit{then} \ \ \mathcal{A}(\epsilon x.\phi, \beta) = \mathcal{A}(\epsilon y.\psi, \beta) \ .$$

E-validity *and* **E-satisfiability** *are defined analogous to Definition 4.*

The three variations of ϵ-term semantics constitute a hierarchy, as stated in the following theorem.

Theorem 2 (Hierarchy Theorem). *Let* $\phi \in \mathbf{Fm}$. *If* ϕ *is E-satisfiable, then it is S-satisfiable. If* ϕ *is S-satisfiable, then it is I-satisfiable.*

Proof. The only non-trivial part of the proof is to show that extensional structures are always substitutive, which is done by showing substitutivity for all formulae and terms, using structural induction. For the complete proof, see [6] or [9]. □

It was mentioned at the beginning of this section, that the logic with ϵ-terms should be a conservative extension of classical first order logic, whatever the exact semantics chosen for the ϵ-terms. This is ensured by the following theorem.[3]

Theorem 3 (Embedding Theorem). *Let* $\phi \in \mathbf{Fm}$ *be a formula* without ϵ-terms. *The following statements are equivalent:*

1. *ϕ is satisfiable in classical first order logic.*[4]
2. *ϕ is I-satisfiable.*
3. *ϕ is S-satisfiable.*
4. *ϕ is E-satisfiable.*

Proof. **1.⇒4.**: Let $\mathcal{S}_0 = (\mathcal{D}, \mathcal{I})$ be a classical first order structure, and $\beta : \mathbf{V} \to \mathcal{D}$ a variable assignment such that $\mathcal{S}_0, \beta \models \phi$. We show the existence of an E-structure $\mathcal{S} = (\mathcal{D}, \mathcal{I}, \mathcal{A})$ with $\mathcal{S}, \beta \models \phi$. As ϕ does not contain ϵ-terms, the validity of ϕ does not depend on $\mathcal{A}$. Thus, it suffices to construct *any* E-structure with carrier $\mathcal{D}$ and interpretation $\mathcal{I}$.

Using the axiom of choice, we may assume the existence of a function $\alpha : \mathcal{P}(\mathcal{D}) \to \mathcal{D}$ satisfying $\alpha(M) \in M$ for all non-empty sets $M \subseteq \mathcal{D}$. The ϵ-valuation $\mathcal{A}$ is defined by successive approximation. We define the family of sets $F_i \subset \mathbf{Fm}$ for $i \in \mathbb{N}$ by:

$$\begin{aligned} F_0 &:= \{\phi \in \mathbf{Fm} \mid \phi \text{ contains no } \epsilon\text{-terms}\} \\ F_{i+1} &:= F_i \cup \{\phi \in \mathbf{Fm} \mid \phi \text{ contains only } \epsilon\text{-terms } \epsilon x.\phi' \text{ with } \phi' \in F_i\} \end{aligned}$$

Obviously, we have $\mathbf{Fm} = \bigcup_{i=0}^{\infty} F_i$. Let $\iota(\phi) := \min\{i \mid \phi \in F_i\}$ be the first of these sets containing a given formula ϕ. We now define a family of ϵ-valuations $\mathcal{A}_i$ for $i \in \mathbb{N}$ as follows:

$$\begin{aligned} \mathcal{A}_0(\epsilon x.\phi, \beta) &:= d_\perp \\ \mathcal{A}_{i+1}(\epsilon x.\phi, \beta) &:= \begin{cases} \alpha(\mathrm{Ext}_{\iota(\phi)}(\epsilon x.\phi)) & \text{for } \phi \in F_i, \\ d_\perp & \text{otherwise,} \end{cases} \end{aligned}$$

where $\mathrm{Ext}_i(\epsilon x.\phi) := \{d \in \mathcal{D} \mid (\mathcal{D}, \mathcal{I}, \mathcal{A}_i), \beta\{x \leftarrow d\} \models \phi\}$, and $d_\perp \in \mathcal{D}$ is an arbitrary carrier element. Defining

$$\mathcal{A}(\epsilon x.\phi, \beta) := \mathcal{A}_{\iota(\phi)+1}(\epsilon x.\phi, \beta)$$

makes $\mathcal{S} := (\mathcal{D}, \mathcal{I}, \mathcal{A})$ an E-structure. The proof that this is the case is not very hard, though somewhat technical, and can be found in [6].

4.⇒3. and **3.⇒2.** follow immediately from Theorem 2.

2.⇒1.: The validity of ϕ is independent of the ϵ-valuation, as ϕ contains no ϵ-terms. Therefore, $(\mathcal{D}, \mathcal{I}, \mathcal{A}), \beta \models \phi$ implies $(\mathcal{D}, \mathcal{I}), \beta \models \phi$ in classical first order logic. □

---

[3] This is the semantic equivalent of Hilbert's Second ϵ-Theorem. It is of course much easier to show, because we argue with model-semantics instead of proof theory.

[4] The definition of satisfiability differs slightly between authors. We call a formula satisfiable if there are a structure and a variable assignment which satisfy the formula.

It should be remarked, that there are many more variants of ϵ-semantics than the three proposed in this paper. The intensional semantics is minimal, in the sense, that it captures only the most basic properties of ϵ-terms. The extensional semantics, on the other hand, assures an intuitive structural property. Finally, as the next section shows, the substitutive semantics has pleasant properties when it comes to constructing a calculus. But there are of course many other possible restrictions on the evaluation of ϵ-terms, that give rise to as many different semantics. E.g., it is possible to require the value of ϵ-terms to remain the same under renaming of bound variables, a property that is guaranteed in E-structures, but not in S-structures. That would permit a full simulation of the δ^{++}-rule. It is also possible to construct an even stronger semantics than the extensional one: for instance, one might require the existence of a well-ordering on the carrier set $\mathcal{D}$, such that the value of an ϵ-term is always the *minimal* element of its extension. In view of the results of the next section, however, stronger semantics are probably not of much interest to automated theorem proving.

4 Proving theorems with ϵ-Terms

If we restricted the use of ϵ-terms to $\exists$-quantifier elimination, the completeness of the resulting calculus for first order problems – without ϵ-terms – would be an easy consequence of the completeness of less liberal δ-rules, like δ^{+} or δ^{++}. The main thing to show would be the soundness of the new rule.

However, the work presented in this paper was done with the aim of integrating automated and interactive proof systems using a common calculus. In that setting, it seemed unnatural to forbid the use of ϵ-terms in the formulation of the proof obligations themselves. The user might want to formulate lemmata or cut-formulae that use ϵ-terms. So the question was, whether we could find a calculus that was complete for the whole logic with ϵ-terms, or more precisely, for which semantics such a calculus could be found.

We now present variants of the free-variable tableau calculus for the substitutive and extensional semantics; the intensional semantics, lacking substitutivity, is to weak to allow a reasonable free-variable calculus. The calculus for the extensional semantics will use a logic with equality, but we shall not discuss equality *handling* here, as the problems arising are largely orthogonal. For a more detailed discussion, including equality handling with constraints, see [6].

4.1 A Complete Calculus for the Substitutive Semantics

We consider a standard unsigned free-variable tableau calculus with the usual α, β and γ expansion rules, as well as a closure rule based on syntactic unification, that applies a substitution to all formulae in the tableau. We use the following δ^{ϵ} expansion rules:

$$\frac{\exists x.\phi}{[x/\epsilon x.\phi]\phi} \quad \text{and} \quad \frac{\neg\forall x.\phi}{[x/\epsilon x.\neg\phi]\neg\phi} .$$

Additionally we introduce an ϵ expansion rule,

$$\frac{}{\forall x.\neg\phi \quad | \quad [x/\epsilon x.\phi]\phi.}$$

In the left branch, one has to show, that there exists at least one element satisfying ϕ. In the right branch, we can use the fact that $\epsilon x.\phi$ denotes one such element.

By taking $x \notin \text{fv}(\phi)$, this rule can easily be seen to be equivalent to the *cut*-rule! So, to permit the application of the ϵ-rule in an automated theorem prover without exploding the search space, we have to make sure that it is only applied in a very limited way. We show that the calculus remains complete, if we allow the application of the ϵ-rule only if

1. the branch contains an atomic formula $(\neg)p(t_1, \ldots, t_n)$, such that
   (a) $\epsilon x.\phi$ is a subterm of one of the terms t_i,
   (b) no free variable of $\epsilon x.\phi$ is bound by a containing ϵ-term in t_i,
2. $\epsilon x.\phi$ was not introduced by a δ-rule, and
3. the ϵ-rule has not previously been applied for $\epsilon x.\phi$ on this branch.

For instance, given an atom

$$p(f(\epsilon x.q(x,y)), \epsilon x.r(g(\epsilon y.s(x,y)))) \quad ,$$

the ϵ-rule is applied for $\epsilon x.q(x,y)$ and $\epsilon x.r(g(\epsilon y.s(x,y)))$, but not for $\epsilon y.s(x,y)$, as the variable x is bound in the containing ϵ-term. Note, that these restrictions ensure, that the ϵ-rule is not applied at all, if there are no ϵ-terms in the original problem. Of course, the ϵ-rule is also sound without these restrictions.

Theorem 4 (Soundness of Calculus with δ^ϵ- and ϵ-Rules). *Let $\phi \in \mathbf{Fm}^0$ be a closed formula. If there is a closed tableau for $\neg\phi$ using the δ^ϵ and ϵ expansion rules, then ϕ is S-valid.*

Proof. The proof follows the proof for the classical free-variable tableau calculus with the δ^+-rule, see [7]. An S-structure $\mathcal{S} = (\mathcal{D}, \mathcal{I}, \mathcal{A})$ is said to ***satisfy*** a tableau T, if for all variable assignments $\beta : \mathbf{V} \to \mathcal{D}$ there is a branch on which $\mathcal{S}, \beta \models \phi$ for all formulae ϕ on the branch. We must show, that if $\mathcal{S}$ satisfies T, then $\mathcal{S}$ also satisfies any tableau T' constructed by the application of an expansion rule. Here, only the δ^ϵ- and ϵ-rules are interesting.

If T' is constructed by applying the δ^ϵ-rule for a formula $\exists x.\phi$ on a branch B of T, and $\mathcal{S} = (\mathcal{D}, \mathcal{I}, \mathcal{A})$ satisfies T, let $\beta : \mathbf{V} \to \mathcal{D}$ be a variable assignment, and B_0 a branch, such that all formulae on B_0 are valid under $\mathcal{S}, \beta$. If B_0 and B are not the same, the branch B_0 has not changed, and we are finished. Otherwise, we show that the new formula on B is also valid under $\mathcal{S}, \beta$. We know $\mathcal{S}, \beta \models \exists x.\phi$. From Def. 4 we get $\mathcal{S}, \beta\{x \leftarrow \mathcal{A}(\epsilon x.\phi, \beta)\} \models \phi$, and with $\text{val}(\mathcal{S}, \beta, \epsilon x.\phi) = \mathcal{A}(\epsilon x.\phi, \beta)$ and substitutivity, we have $\mathcal{S}, \beta \models [x/\epsilon x.\phi]\phi$, what we needed to show. Note that there can be no problems with collisions between free variables in $\epsilon x.\phi$ and bound variables in ϕ, as any free variables in ϕ must have been introduced by a γ-rule, and are thus new with respect to any quantified variable. The case for $\neg\forall x.\phi$ is, of course, analogous.

If B is extended using the ϵ-rule, yielding two extended branches, and $\mathcal{S},\beta$ satisfy every formula on B, there are two cases:

1. $\mathcal{S},\beta \models \exists x.\phi$. Then, due to Def. 4, we have $\mathcal{S},\beta\{x \leftarrow \mathcal{A}(\epsilon x.\phi,\beta)\} \models \phi$, and as in the δ^ϵ-case, it follows that $\mathcal{S},\beta \models [x/\epsilon x.\phi]\phi$. So $\mathcal{S},\beta$ satisfy all formulae on the right branch.
2. $\mathcal{S},\beta \not\models \exists x.\phi$. Then we obviously get $\mathcal{S},\beta \models \forall x.\neg\phi$, and $\mathcal{S},\beta$ satisfy all formulae on the left branch.

The rest of the proof is identical to the one without ϵ-terms. □

If the formula ϕ to be proved does not contain ϵ-terms, the ϵ-rule can never be applied, so this theorem also proves the soundness of the δ^ϵ-rule, if ϵ-terms are used for $\exists$-quantifier elimination only. Also note that the restrictions of the ϵ-rule were not used in this proof.

Theorem 5 (Completeness of Calculus with δ^ϵ- and ϵ-Rules). *Let $\phi \in$ $\mathbf{Fm}^0$ be a closed S-valid formula. Then there is a closed tableau for $\neg\phi$ using the δ^ϵ and ϵ expansion rules.*

We do not give the proof of this theorem here, as it is rather lengthy and technical. A full proof is given in [6]. Here, we only point out the two main difficulties:

- While the Hintikka-set construction proceeds as usual, the definition of an S-structure satisfying all formulae of the Hintikka-set poses some problems: if we chose the set of all closed terms as carrier set, we would have to apply the ϵ-rule to *all possible* closed ϵ-terms to ensure completeness, contrary to the restrictions of the ϵ-rule. So we need to limit ourselves to all closed terms occurring in atomic formulae of the Hintikka-set. But then, it becomes difficult define the structure in a way that ensures substitutivity for all ϵ-terms and not only for the ones constituting the carrier.
- The restrictions of the ϵ-rule make lifting a trifle more complicated: in the ground version, we restrict the application of the ϵ-rule to closed ϵ-terms occurring in atomic formulae on the current branch. When we lift a ground tableau, these closed ϵ-terms may disappear into a free variable that has not yet been instantiated when the ϵ-rule is applied. In this case, we must show, that there must be a corresponding ϵ-term – possibly containing not-yet-instantiated free variables – somewhere else on the branch. This is the case because the free variable in question will at some time be instantiated by unification, so the instance is necessarily 'somewhere' on the branch from the beginning. Of course, the formal proof is a little involved.

4.2 A Complete Calculus for the Extensional Semantics

We have argued, that the extensional semantics is more intuitive than the substitutive one. Thus, it would be good to have a complete calculus for the extensional semantics too. We now present such a calculus, but it will turn out that it is *not* suited for use in an automated theorem prover.

We obtain a complete calculus for the extensional semantics, if we add another tableau expansion rule to the calculus described in Sec. 4.1, namely

$$\frac{}{\neg\forall z.([x/z]\phi \leftrightarrow [y/z]\phi') \quad | \quad \epsilon x.\phi = \epsilon y.\phi'} ,$$

referred to as the *ext* expansion rule.[5] Intuitively the rule says that, whenever we can show that the equivalence of two formulae is a consequence of the current branch, we can identify the values of the corresponding ϵ-terms. Together with any complete set of rules for equality handling, this yields a sound and complete calculus for the extensional semantics, as is shown in [6]. (The completeness proof is much easier as that of Theorem 5, as we do not impose any restrictions on the application of the *ext* or ϵ-rule.)

There is a number of problems with the *ext*-rule:

- We currently do not know – though it seems plausible – whether the rule remains complete if we restrict its application to ϵ-terms already occurring on the branch.
- Even if this were the case, it would have to be applied to any *pair* of occurring ϵ-terms, which would give rise to a quadratic number of rule applications.
- The formula introduced on the left branch is a δ-formula, leading to the introduction of another ϵ-term, which would in turn have to be taken into account for the *ext*-rule. Maybe, it is not necessary for completeness to apply the *ext*-rule to these new ϵ-terms, but that is not yet known.
- Most possible applications of the ϵ-rule would be completely useless for a proof, as two formulae are normally *not* equivalent. Each such unnecessary split would at least double the size of the proof.

Clearly, the *ext*-rule is as dangerous for a machine to apply as a non-atomic cut! Unfortunately, there does not seem to be any other way to cope with extensional semantics.

In the setting of an integrated automated and interactive proof system, we decided to adopt the following view: human users may consider ϵ-terms to have extensional semantics. They are given a complete calculus including the *ext*-rule for interactive work. The automated part of the system uses the calculus described in Sect. 4.1, which is not complete for the extensional semantics. But thanks to the Hierarchy Theorem 2, it is sound: any S-valid formula is also E-valid. And we also provide a precise *semantic* characterization of the incompleteness, namely the automated system can find proofs only for theorems that are not only E-valid, but also S-valid.

[5] This rule was designed for a logic with equality. In a logic without equality, extensionality could be handled with a rule like

$$\frac{\psi(\epsilon x.\phi)}{\neg\forall z.([x/z]\phi \leftrightarrow [y/z]\phi') \quad | \quad \psi(\epsilon y.\phi')} .$$

5 Conclusion

The idea of eliminating existential quantifiers by means of ϵ-terms is known for decades. So far, however, this concept is not used (on an object language level) in frameworks for automated deduction. Traditionally, most approaches there deal with Skolem terms instead, e.g. in the context of δ-rules. Compared to simple (i.e. earlier) versions of Skolemization, the ϵ-terms seem to be more complicated. During the last years, on the other hand, the investigation into more efficient δ-rules lead to more sophisticated Skolemization techniques. We interpret this evolution as a movement towards ϵ-like behaviour. Therefore, in this paper we proposed to use ϵ-terms themselves in the context of automated theorem proving, as they have several desirable properties. Compared to Skolem terms, the representation of some information about the 'chosen' element is shifted to the level of the object language. Therefore, the origin and usage of that information is made transparent. For the same reason, object language operations like substitution can be applied to this information. (This exactly is the reason for the exponential speedup discussed in Sect. 2.2.)

Moreover, the usage of ϵ-terms enables us to add a property like extensionality, if desired, by just adding a rule to the calculus. This is the consequence of the semantic hierarchy presented in Sect. 3 and the corresponding rules of Sect. 4. We discussed the suitability of these different variants of an ϵ-calculus for automated proof search. Here, we want to add that substitutivity on the one hand and extensionality on the other hand can be seen as the extremes of a range of ϵ-treatments. Between both, there are other possibilities to exploit special cases of (easily checkable) equivalences. An example for this is the usage of the concept of relevant formulae, used in the δ^{**}-rule of Cantone and Nicolosi [4]. We believe that ϵ-terms provide a framework in which many possible approaches to existential quantifier handling may be expressed.

Acknowledgments

We would like to thank Bernhard Beckert for many fruitful discussions about ϵ-terms and Reiner Hähnle, as well as the referees for their helpful comments on drafts of this paper.

References

1. M. Baaz and C.G. Fermüller. Non-elementary speedups between different versions of tableaux. In 4th *International Workshop, TABLEAUX'95*, LNCS 918, 1995.
2. Bernhard Beckert. *Integrating and Unifying Methods of Tableau-based Theorem Proving.* PhD thesis, Universität Karlsruhe, Fakultät für Informatik, 1998.
3. Bernhard Beckert, Reiner Hähnle, and Peter H. Schmitt. The even more liberalized δ-rule in free variable semantic tableaux. In G. Gottlob, A. Leitsch, and D. Mundici, editors, *Proceedings, 3rd Kurt Gödel Colloquium (KGC), Brno, Czech Republic*, LNCS 713, pages 108–119. Springer, 1993.

4. Domenico Cantone and Marianna Nicolosi Asmundo. A further and effective liberalization of the δ-rule in free variable semantic tableaux. In Ricardo Caferra and Gernot Salzer, editors, *Int. Workshop on First-Order Theorem Proving (FTP'98)*, Technical Report E1852-GS-981, pages 86–96. Technische Universität Wien, Austria, 1998. Electronically available from `http://www.logic.at/ftp98`.
5. Melvin C. Fitting. *First-Order Logic and Automated Theorem Proving*. Springer, 1990.
6. Martin Giese. Integriertes automatisches und interaktives Beweisen: Die Kalkülebene. Diploma Thesis, Fakultät für Informatik, Universität Karlsruhe, June 1998.
7. Reiner Hähnle and Peter H. Schmitt. The liberalized δ-rule in free variable semantic tableaux. *Journal of Automated Reasoning*, 13(2):211–222, 1994.
8. D. Hilbert and P. Bernays. *Grundlagen der Mathematik*, volume 2. Springer Verlag, 1968.
9. A.C. Leisenring. *Mathematical Logic and Hilbert's ϵ-Symbol*. MacDonald, London, 1969.
10. W.P.M. Meyer Viol. *Instantial Logic. An Investigation into Reasoning with Instances*. Number DS–1995–11 in ILLC Dissertation Series. Universiteit van Amsterdam, 1995.
11. Raymond M. Smullyan. *First-Order Logic*, volume 43 of *Ergebnisse der Mathematik und ihrer Grenzgebiete*. Springer-Verlag, New York, 1968.

Partial Functions in an Impredicative Simple Theory of Types

Paul C. Gilmore

Department of Computer Science, University of British Columbia,
2366 Main Mall, Vancouver, B.C., Canada, V6T 1Z4
gilmore@cs.ubc.ca

Abstract. A functional notation is not a necessity for a predicate logic since a function of n arguments can be represented as a predicate of $n + 1$ arguments. But a functional notation in a predicate logic with identity can greatly simplify some assertions , and for this reason a functional notation is frequently assumed for predicate logics, both first order and higher. But a functional notation that is admitted as primitive in a predicate logic must of necessity be interpreted as a notation for total functions, not partial functions, over the domain of the functions. The traditional way of introducing a notation for partial functions into a predicate logic with an assumed or defined identity is using the notation $(\iota x)F$ of Russell's definite descriptions that is read "the x such that F". But the traditional manner of introduction requires the treatment of what Quine has called "the waste cases"; that is when there is no x or more than one x such that F. The purpose of this paper is to demonstrate that the tableaux method of formalizing logics permits the introduction of definite descriptions without the need to provide a denotation for waste case definite descriptions. As a result the distortions of meaning that result from Quine's treatment of the waste cases is avoided. The technique is illustrated by introducing a notation for partial functions into an impredicative version ITT of the simple theory of types. The resulting logic ITTf is shown to be a conservative extension of ITT. The tableaux proof theory of ITT is of independent interest both for its motivation and for the strength of its proof theory. The logic has a nominalist motivation appropriate for a logic intended for applications in computer science. Its extension of the membership of the type of the individuals of the simple theory of types avoids the abuses of use and mention that can result when higher order predication is given a nominalist interpretation. The proof theory does not require an axiom of infinity. As a result, the definition of both well-founded and non-well-founded recursive predicates is much simpler than in the simple theory of types with an axiom of infinity.

1 Introduction

A functional notation is not a necessity for a predicate logic since a function of n arguments can be represented as a predicate of $n + 1$ arguments. But as remarked by Farmer in [6], where he introduces a partial function notation into a version PF of the simple theory of types of [1], "Reasoning about functions strictly using relations is neither natural nor efficient, since function application must be represented in a verbose, indirect fashion. Nevertheless, this approach is perfectly adequate if pragmatic concerns are not important. This approach shows that the problem of reasoning about partial functions is not a matter of making classical logic more expressive. The problem is, rather, to find a notationally efficient way of reasoning about partial functions that is reasonably faithful to mathematical practice and that upsets the framework of classical logic as little as possible."

The classical approach to partial functions has been through Russell's definite description $(\iota x)F$ that is read "the x such that F". Farmer dismisses this approach as well as seven others for various reasons that he describes. He dismisses the classical approach because he believes it requires attention to what a nondenoting description actually denotes; that is, to considerations of what Quine has called the "waste cases" when there does not exist an x such that F, or there exists more than one. [15]

The purpose of this paper is to demonstrate that the tableaux method of formalizing logics permits the introduction of definite descriptions without the need to provide a denotation for a nondenoting definite description; consequently the distortions of meaning that result from Quine's treatment of the waste cases are avoided. In a tableaux proof theory for a logic, each of the rules of deduction is an elimination rule for a logical constant that need only be applied when in some sense the constant appears in a principal position. Such a logic can be extended to admit Russell's definite description notation by adding one rule of deduction for eliminating the notation when it appears in a principal position. As a consequence it is unnecessary to consider interpreting a nondenoting definite description.

The technique is illustrated by introducing a notation for partial functions into an impredicative version ITT of the simple theory of types that has evolved from [7]. The resulting logic ITTf is shown to be a conservative extension of ITT. A step in the proof of this result is the definition in §6.3 of a mapping of some of the terms of ITTf into terms of ITT. The treatment of partial functions in this mapping turns out to be somewhat similar in effect to that of Farmer's logic PF which takes approach (h) of [6]:

> (h) Partial evaluation for [function] terms but total valuation for formulas.

This adds the following two rules to the standard rules of valuation:

1. A [function] term denotes a value only if all its subterms denote values.
2. An atomic formula is false if any [function] term occurring in it is nondenoting.

However, ITTf provides a more flexible treatment of partial functions than does PF, since there is no sharp distinction between the treatment of partial and of total or many-valued functions.

The tableaux proof theory of ITT is of independent interest both for its motivation and for the strength of its proof theory. The logic has a nominalist motivation appropriate for a logic intended for applications in computer science. Its extension of the types of the simple theory of types avoids the abuses of use and mention that can result when higher order predication is given a nominalist interpretation. The proof theory does not require an axiom of infinity. As a result, the definition of both well-founded and non-well-founded recursive predicates is much simpler than in the simple theory of types with an axiom of infinity. [8], [11]

The motivation for ITT, described in §2, has been adapted from [9] and [11] where a semantic proof of the redundancy of cut is provided. The syntax of the logic is described in §3 and its proof theory in §4. The reader is referred to [8] or [9] for a description of its semantics. In §5 some elementary and novel derivations of ITT are presented in preparation for the introduction in §6 for the syntax and proof theory for the extension ITT*f* of ITT with a partial function notation. A proof that ITT*f* is a conservative extension of ITT is given in §6.4.

The financial support of the Natural Science and Engineering Research Council of Canada is gratefully acknowledged.

2 MOTIVATION FOR ITT

Consider a form TT of the simple theory of types in which predicates of any number of arguments are admitted, but no functions. The types of such a predicate logic can be inductively defined as follows:

1. 1 is the type of individuals;
2. $[\tau_1, \ldots, \tau_n]$ is the type of the predicates with arguments of the types $\tau_1, \ldots, \tau_n$, $n \geq 0$.

The type $[]$, introduced in (2) when $n = 0$, is the type of the truth values. Apart from notation and the exclusion of functions, these are the types of Schütte's type theory [16].

Although the types of TT are traditionally thought of as necessary for the consistency of the logic, the types can just as well be seen to arise naturally from the predicate and subject distinction of natural languages, for these become the distinction between a function and its argument(s) when predicates are regarded as functions with range the truth values.

Scepticism has often been expressed that a violation of the type restrictions is the ultimate source of the paradoxes. For example, in the concluding paragraph of [4] Church comments on a remark of Frege's "... Frege's criticism seems to me still to retain much of its force, and to deserve serious consideration by those who hold that the simple theory of types is the final answer to the riddle of the paradoxes". Here an alternative explanation of the paradoxes is offered, namely that they result from a confusion of use and mention, and is used to motivate an impredicative simple theory of types ITT. The confusion can arise when higher order predication is given a nominalist interpretation. This was first suggested as a source of the paradoxes in [17] and [18].

2.1 Intensional and Extensional Identity

Traditionally the basis for an interpetation of TT is the assignment of a set $D(\tau)$ to each type τ as follows: $D(1)$ is a given fixed non-empty set of individuals, $D([])$ is the set of the two truth values, and $D([\tau_1, \ldots, \tau_n]), n > 0$, is the set of all subsets of the Cartesian product $D(\tau_1) \times \ldots \times D(\tau_n)$. A predicate of type $[\tau_1, \ldots, \tau_n]$ may have as its i'th argument any member of the domain $D(\tau_i)$.

Intensional and extensional identity are defined in TT:

$$= \langle df \rangle \ (\lambda u, v.\forall X.[X(u) \rightarrow X(v)])$$
$$=_e \langle df \rangle \ (\lambda u, v.\forall x_1, \ldots, x_n.[u(x_1, \ldots, x_n) \leftrightarrow v(x_1, \ldots, x_n)])$$

The type restrictions necessary for the definitions can be expressed as $v : \mathrm{T}[u]$ and $X : [\mathrm{T}[u]]$ for the first, and as $u, v : [\mathrm{T}[x_1], \ldots, \mathrm{T}[x_n]]$ for the second. Here $\mathrm{T}[cv]$ denotes the type of a constant or variable cv that is assigned to it by the primitive syntax; and ':' denotes the relationship between a term and its type.

Using the usual infix notation for the identities, a theorem of TT is:

IEId $\quad\quad \vdash \forall X, Y.[X = Y \rightarrow X =_e Y]$

where necessarily $\mathrm{T}[X] \neq 1$. The comparable result in the set theory ZF [19] is

IEIdZF $\quad\quad \vdash \forall x, y.[x = y \rightarrow x =_e y]$

where here = is the primitive identity of a first order logic with identity; (IEIdZF) is actually a theorem of that logic.

The converse of (IEIdZF), the axiom of extensionality, is the first axiom in the first formulation of ZF. [20] It is traditional to accept the converse of (IEId) as an axiom of TT:

Ext $\quad\quad \vdash \forall X, Y.[X =_e Y \rightarrow X = Y]$

This may be acceptable for a pure logic, but it is not for an applied logic trying to meet the needs of computer science. For in some such applications, the intension of a predicate is known only informally and its extension is provided by data entry. For example, the extension of an Employee predicate in a company database is maintained in this manner along with usually a Sex predicate among others. From these two predicates the intension of a predicate MaleEmployee can be defined, and its extension retrieved and printed. [10] By an accident of hiring, however, the two predicates Employee and MaleEmployee may have the same extension; but clearly their intensions must be distinguished. For this reason the axiom (Ext) concluding the intensional identity of predicates from their extensional identity is not accepted in ITT. It will be seen that intensional identity can be expressed in ITT by lambda convertability.

2.2 Nominalism and Higher Order Predication

In a logic of extensions such as TT, a higher order predicate with predicates as arguments is understood to have the extensions of the predicates as arguments. But in a logic in which the intension of a predicate is distinguished from its extension, higher order predication must be reexamined.

A nominalist understands a predicate of a universal to be a predicate of a name of the universal. For example, a nominalist understands 'Yellow is a colour' to mean 'Yellow is a colour-word'; the sentence is understood as a description of the use of the word 'Yellow' in English. Since computers are consumate nominalists, nominalist interpretations of languages intended for computer applications are needed. But this does require a careful distinction between the use and mention of predicate names, especially when treating abstraction and quantification. For example, in 'Yellow is a colour-word' the predicate name 'Yellow' is being mentioned while the predicate name 'colour-word' is being used. An excellant discussion of use and mention appears in §4 of chapter one of [15].

The distinction between the use and mention of predicate names is maintained in the logic ITT as follows: The types of ITT are the same as the types of TT, but the membership of the type 1 of individuals in ITT is an extension of the membership of the same type in TT. The extension consists in adding to the membership of the type 1 any higher order term in which at most variables of type 1 have a free occurrence. For example, a constant P that is a predicate name is necessarily of some type $\tau \neq 1$ and always has that type in contexts where it is used. But since no variable has a free occurrence in it P, P is also of type 1 and it has that type in contexts in which it is being mentioned.

Mentioning the name of a predicate means that the name is implicitly quoted. This is the reason why higher order terms that are also of type 1 must be restricted to those in which only variables of type 1 have free occurrences. For only such terms can be given a Herbrand interpretation when quoted. For example, let P be a constant of type [1] and x a variable of type 1. Then $P(x)$ is of type [], and also of type 1. As a type 1 term, $P(x)$ is to be interpreted as the function with domain and range the type 1 terms in which no variable has a free occurrence: The value of the function $P(x)$ for a term t in its domain is the term $P(t)$ in its range. Such an interpretation can't be given for higher order terms not satisfying the restriction. For example, if X is a variable of type [1] and c a constant of type 1, then $X(c)$ is of type [] but not also of type 1, since $X(c)$ cannot be given a Herbrand interpretation.

2.3 Set Theory and the Lambda Calculus

For (IEId) to be derivable in TT it is necessary that $\mathrm{T}[X] \neq 1$. Although (IEId) is not derivable in ITT when $\mathrm{T}[X] = 1$, each instance of the following sequent scheme is derivable when R and S are terms of type $\tau, \tau \neq 1$, that are also of type 1 by virtue of their free variables being of type 1:

IEIds $\qquad R = S \vdash R =_e S$

This scheme is similar to the scheme that would result from all possible instantiations of (IEIdZF) of ZF. As a consequence, the logic ITT combines features from set theory and from a lambda calculus based logic; for this reason it may satisfy the requirements for such a logic described in [13].

Consider for example the following definitions of zero and successor

$$0 < \mathit{df} > (\lambda u.\neg u = u)$$
$$S < \mathit{df} > (\lambda u, v.u = v)$$

where $=: [1,1]$. They are definitions in the style of set theory, but all of Peano's axioms are derivable in ITT including the following pair:

S.1. $\vdash \forall x, y.[S(x) = S(y) \rightarrow x = y]$
S.2. $\vdash \forall x.\neg S(x) = 0$

Dual typing is critical for their derivations: 0:[1] and S:[1,1], but also 0:1 and S(x):1 when x:1. But also the lambda calculus definition of ordered pair from [5] is available

$$\langle\rangle < \mathit{df} > (\lambda u, v, w.w(u, v))$$

and the following sequents can be derived

OP.1. $\vdash \forall x1, y1, x2, y2.[\langle x1, y1\rangle = \langle x2, y2\rangle \rightarrow x1 = x2 \wedge y1 = y2]$
OP.2. $\vdash \forall x, y.\neg\langle x, y\rangle = 0$

Just as the sequents (S.1) and (S.2) justify the use of S as a "constuctor" in Horn clause definitions of recursive predicates, so do (OP.1) and (OP.2) justify the use of ordered pair. Further definitions, derivations and details are provided in [8] and [11]. Also provided there is a foundation for recursions. Both well-founded and non-well-founded recursive predicates are defined there using a decidable set of terms called *recursion generators*; the technique is demonstrated using higher order Horn sequent definitions with computations being defined as iterations of recursion generators. This overcomes the complications that arise from the need for an axiom of infinity in the applied versions TPS, HOL, and PVS of the simple theory of types. [2], [12], [14].

3 THE SYNTAX

The logic ITT is assumed to have denumerably many constants and variables of each type. The type of a constant or variable is not displayed but must be either declared or inferred from context. For a constant or variable cx,$\mathrm{T}[cx]$ denotes its type; this is expressed in the usual fashion as $cx : \mathrm{T}[cx]$.

In the style of [5], special constants introduce the logical connectives and the quantifiers. The binary logical connective of joint denial, denoted by $\downarrow$, is a special constant of type $[[], []]$; that is, it is a predicate of two arguments of type $[]$; it is the only primitive logical connective needed since the more usual logical connectives can be defined in terms of it. Similarly a special constant $\forall$ of type $[[\tau]]$ is introduced for each type τ; it is the universal quantifier for a type τ variable. The type of each $\forall$ is not displayed but must be inferred from context. The existential quantifier $\exists$ is defined in terms of $\forall$ in the usual way.

Definition of Type Membership

1. cv :$\mathrm{T}[cx]$, for each constant or variable cx; $\downarrow$: $[[],[]]$; and $\forall : [[\tau]]$ for each type τ.
2. $M : [\tau, \tau_1, \ldots, \tau_n] \& N : \tau \Rightarrow (MN) : [\tau_1, \ldots, \tau_n], n \geq 0$.
3. $M : [\tau_1, \ldots, \tau_n] \Rightarrow (\lambda x.M) : [\,\mathrm{T}[x], \tau_1, \ldots, \tau_n], n \geq 0$.
4. $M : [\tau_1, \ldots, \tau_n] \Rightarrow M : 1, n \geq 0$, provided each variable with a free occurrence in M is of type 1.

The unusual clause (4) results from the nominalist interpretation discussed in §2. The type 1 assigned to M in (4) is called the dual type of M. Note that no term of type 1 and no variable has a dual type. However a constant c for which $\mathrm{T}[c] \neq 1$ has 1 as a dual type; neverthess, $\mathrm{T}[c]$ is always to be understood to be the type assigned by the primitive syntax, and never the dual type 1 assigned by clause (4).

By a term is meant a member of a type. Note that a term of type 1 is a constant, a variable, or a term of dual type 1 since clauses (1) and (4) are the only ones that yield terms of type 1.

Let N :$\mathrm{T}[x]$. The substitution notation $[N/x]M$ denotes the result of replacing each free occurrence of x in a term M by N. The notation can result in changes of bound variables within M; a change is necessary if a free occurrence of x in M is within the scope of an abstractor λy for which y has a free occurrence in N.

A formula of ITT is a term of type $[]$. Formulas are the basis for the proof theory for ITT. But first the sparse notation of the lambda calculus is extended by definitions that introduce notations more common to predicate logics. The application notation is "sugared" by the definitions

$$M(N) < df > MN$$
$$M(N1, \ldots, N_m, N) < df > M(N_1, \ldots, N_m)(N), m \geq 1.$$

The prefix notation for $\downarrow$ is replaced by an infix notation. All of the usual logical connectives can be defined from $\neg$ and $\vee$ which are defined

$$\neg M < df > [M \downarrow M]$$
$$[M \vee N] < df > [[M \downarrow N] \downarrow [M \downarrow N]]$$

A conventional notation for the universal quantifier is defined:

$$\forall x.M(x) < df > \forall(M),$$
where $M : [\mathrm{T}[x]]$ and x has no free occurrence in M.

Here is a definition of formula in the style of [16]:

1. $cv(S_1, \ldots, S_n)$ is a *prime* formula and a formula if $cv : [\tau_1, \ldots, \tau_n]$ and $S_i : \tau_i, 0 \leq i \leq n$.
2. $[F \downarrow G]$ is a formula if F and G are formulas.
3. $\forall x.F$ is a formula if F is.
4. $(\lambda x.T)(S, S_1, \ldots, S_n)$ is a formula if $([S/x]T)(S_1, \ldots, S_n)$ is a formula and $S :\mathrm{T}[x]$.

That an expression defined in this way is a term of type [] follows from the definition of type membership. That a term of type [] can be defined as a formula in Schütte's style follows from the fact that all terms of a typed lambda calculus have a normal form.[3]

The relation of immediate lambda reduction between terms is denoted here by >, and allows $\alpha-$, $\beta-$, and $\eta-$ reductions [3]. It is recursively defined as follows:

1. $(\lambda x.M) > (\lambda.[y/x]M)$, provided y has no free occurrence in M.
   $(\lambda x.M)N > [N/x]M$.
   $(\lambda x.(Mx)) > M$, provided x has no free occurrence in M.
2. Let $M > N$. Then
   .1. $MP > NP$ and $PM > PN$.
   .2. $(\lambda x.M) > (\lambda x.N)$.

4 PROOF THEORY

The proof theory is presented as a logic of sequents using analytic tableaux derivations. The rules for the logical connectives $\neg$ and $\wedge$ and for the quantifier $\forall$ are the usual; rules for the other logical connectives and the quantifier $\exists$ are left to the reader to derive. Rules are added for λ removal. The proof theory can be seen to be equivalent to the theory presented in [8], [9] and [11].

$\neg$ $$\frac{\neg\neg F}{F}$$

$\wedge$ $$\frac{[F \wedge G]}{F} \qquad \frac{[F \wedge G]}{G}$$

$\neg\wedge$ $$\frac{\neg[F \wedge G]}{\neg F \qquad \neg G}$$

$\forall$ $$\frac{\forall x.F}{[T/x]F}$$
$T :\mathrm{T}[x]$ *[the eigenterm]*

$\neg\forall$ $$\frac{\neg\forall x.F}{\neg[y/x]F}$$
$y :\mathrm{T}[x]$ and is new

$$\lambda \quad \frac{F}{G} \qquad\qquad \neg\lambda \quad \frac{\neg F}{\neg G}$$

where for each rule, $F > G$.

An analytic tableaux *based* on a sequent $F_1, \ldots, F_m \vdash G_1, \ldots, G_n$ has initial nodes consisting of a selection from the formulas $F_1, \ldots, F_m, \neg G_1, \ldots, \neg G_n$. A branch of an analytic tableaux is *closed* if there is a *closing pair* of nodes F and $\neg F$ on the branch. An analytic tableaux is *closed* if each of its branches is closed. A *derivation* of a sequent is a closed analytic tableaux based on the sequent.

By a subsequent of a sequent is meant one with possibly some formulas removed. It is not difficult to establish that if a sequent has a derivation then a derivation exists for a subsequent in which each branch of the derivation has a single pair of closing nodes and every node of the derivation has a descendant that is a member of a closing pair. For the remainder of the paper by a derivation is meant a derivation with these two properties.

5 EXAMPLE DERIVATIONS

The following notational conventions will be followed. Strings of lower and upper case Latin letters and numerals beginning with the letters u, v, w, x, y, and z are variables. When a term is known to be a formula, the types of constants and variables occurring it it can often be inferred and in these cases will not be declared. Strings which are not variables may be used, along with special symbols such as $=$ and $<$, as names of predicates introduced by definition. Such a string may often be assumed to be polymorhic since the type of a predicate and the relationship between the types of its arguments can often be determined from its definition.

The following type and type declaration notation will be used here and in the remainder of the paper. The notation $\bar{\tau}$ denotes a sequence of n types $\tau_1, \ldots, \tau_n$, for some $n \geq 0$; thus $[\bar{\tau}, \tau]$ is the type $[\tau_1, \ldots, \tau_n, \tau]$. A type declaration $\bar{z} : \bar{\tau}$ is to be understood as declaring that $\bar{z}$ is a sequence $z_1, \ldots, z_n$ of distinct variables of types $\tau_1, \ldots, \tau_n$ respectively, and a declaration $\bar{s} : \bar{\tau}$ that $\bar{s}$ is a sequence $s_1, \ldots, s_n$ of terms of types $\tau_1, \ldots, \tau_n$ respectively for some $n \geq 0$.

A Derivation of (IEIds) of §2.3

Here is a full annotated derivation.

R=S	initial node
$\neg R =_e S$	initial node
$(\lambda u, v.\forall Z.[Z(u) \to Z(v)])(R, S)$	df =
$(\lambda u.\forall Z.[Z(R) \to Z(v)])(S)$	λ
$\forall Z.[Z(R) \to Z(S)]$	λ
$T(R) \to T(S)]$	$\forall$ with $T <$ *df* $> \lambda w.R =_e w$

L	R	
$\neg T(R)$		$\rightarrow$
$\neg(\lambda w.R =_e w)(R)$		df T
$\neg R =_e R$		$\neg\lambda$
$\neg\forall\bar{z}.[R(\bar{z}) \leftrightarrow R(\bar{z})]$		df $=_e$
$\neg[R(\bar{z}) \leftrightarrow R(\bar{z})]$		$\neg\forall$
$\neg[[R(\bar{z} \rightarrow R(\bar{z})] \wedge [R(\bar{z} \rightarrow R(\bar{z}]]$		df $\leftrightarrow$

LL	LR	
$\neg[R(\bar{z}) \rightarrow R(\bar{z})]$		$\neg\wedge$
$R(\bar{z})$		$\neg \rightarrow$
$\neg R(\bar{z})$		$\neg \rightarrow$

=======

LR

repeat LL

=======

R	
$T(S)$	$\rightarrow$
$(\lambda w.R =_e w)(S)$	df T
$R =_e S$	λ

=======

A Derivation of (S.1) of §2.3

An abbreviated derivation follows:

$\neg\forall x, y.[S(x) = S(y) \rightarrow x = y]$

$\neg[S(x) = S(y) \rightarrow x = y$

$S(x) = S(y)$

$\neg x = y$

$S(x) =_e S(y)$	$\neg S(x) =_e S(y)$	Cut
$\forall z.[S(x)(z) \leftrightarrow S(y)(z)]$	$S(x) =_e S(y)$	IEIds
$[S(x)(y) \leftrightarrow S(y)(y)]$	========	
$[S(y)(y) \rightarrow S(x)(y)]$		

$\neg S(y)(y)$	$S(x)(y)$
$\neg y = y$	$x = y$
=====	=====

A Derivation of (S.2) of §2.3

$\neg\forall x.\neg S(x) = 0$

$\neg\neg S(x) = 0$

$S(x) = 0$

$S(x) =_e 0$	$\neg S(x) =_e 0$	Cut
$\forall z.[S(x)(z) \leftrightarrow 0(z)]$	$S(x) =_e 0$	IEIds
$[S(x)(x) \leftrightarrow 0(x)]$	======	
$[S(x)(x) \rightarrow 0(x)]$		

$\neg S(x)(x)$	$0(x)$	Cut
$\neg x = x$	$\neg x = x$	
====	====	

6 FUNCTIONAL NOTATIONS

An implicit notation for functions is available in ITT in the form of higher order terms that are also first order terms. The term S defined in §2.3, for example, was used in this way in the derivations of (S.1) and (S.2) in §5: For a first order term t, S(t) is a first order term. ITT is extended here to a logic ITTf with an explicit partial function notation for functions with arguments of any type and values of type 1. A simplified version of Russell's notation for definite descriptions is used to introduce the functional notation. It makes use of the following definition in which $=: [1, 1]$.

$$\exists ! y.F < df > \exists y.[F \wedge \forall x.[[x/y]F \rightarrow y = x]]$$

6.1 Syntax and Proof Theory of ITTf

The notation introduced in the second paragraph of §5 is used in the following definition of the terms of ITTf:

1. A term of ITT is a term of ITTf of the same type.
2. Let $T : [\bar{\sigma}, 1]$ and $\bar{s} : \bar{\sigma}$ be terms of ITTf. Then $fT(\bar{s})$ is a term of ITTf of type 1.
3. $M : [\tau, \tau_1, \ldots, \tau_n] \& N : \tau \Rightarrow (MN) : [\tau_1, \ldots, \tau_n], n \geq 0$.
4. $M : [\tau_1, \ldots, \tau_n] \Rightarrow (\lambda x.M) : [\mathrm{T}[x], \tau_1, \ldots, \tau_n], n \geq 0$.

The terms $fT(\bar{s})$ are called f-terms. Note that (3) and (4) are (2) and (3) of the definition of type membership in §3, while (4) from §3 does not apply to terms in which f-terms occur. Using Russell's notation, the f-term $fT(\bar{s})$ would be expressed as $(\iota x)T(\bar{s}, x)$, where $x : 1$ has no free occurrence in $T(\bar{s})$. Thus the f notation takes advantage of λ abstraction and assumes that the $n + 1$'st argument of the predicate T is used for the value of the function to be represented.

6.2 The Proof Theory of ITTf

The definition in §3 of the lambda reduction relation $>$ on the formulas of ITT is extended to the formulas of ITTf by defining: If $R > G$, then $fR > fG$. The *domain* δT of the partial function fT obtained from a term $T : [\bar{\sigma}, 1]$ is defined

$$\delta T < df > \lambda \bar{u}.\exists ! x.T(\bar{u}, x)$$

The rules of ITT given in §5 are also rules of ITTf. One additional rule permits the removal of f-terms:

$$f \quad \frac{[fT(\bar{s})/x]F}{\exists x.[T(\bar{s}, x) \wedge F] \qquad \neg \partial T(\bar{s})}$$

where x is a variable without a free occurrence in $T(\bar{s})$, and no f-term has a free occurrence in $T(\bar{s})$.

The term $fT(\bar{s})$ is called the removed term of an application of the rule. The closure condition on a branch of a tree of ITTf is exactly the same as that for ITT; that is, a branch is closed if there is a closing pair of nodes F and $\neg F$ on the branch, where F is a formula of ITT. Thus for a branch to be closed, it is necessary to have a closing pair of nodes in which f-terms do not occur.

Examples As noted before, S can be understood to be a total function; that is the following sequent is derivable:

1) $\vdash \forall x.\exists ! y.S(x) = y$

The inverse of S is a partial function, the "destructor" for the "constructor" S. It is fIS where IS is defined to be $\lambda u, v.u = S(v)$. That is, the following sequent is derivable:

2) $\vdash \forall x.f\text{IS}(S(x)) = x$

An abbreviated derivation follows:

$\neg \forall x.fIS(S(x)) = x$
$\neg fIS(S(x)) = x$

$\exists y.[IS(S(x), y) \wedge \neg y = x]$	$\neg \delta IS(S(x))$
$[IS(S(x), y) \wedge \neg y = x]$	$\neg(\lambda u.\exists ! x.IS(u, x))(S(x))$
$IS(S(x), y)$	$\neg \exists ! y.IS(S(x), y))$
$\neg y = x$	$\neg \exists y.[IS(S(x), y)) \wedge \forall z.[IS(S(x), z) \rightarrow z = y]]$
$S(x) = S(y)$	$\neg [IS(S(x), x)) \wedge \forall z.[IS(S(x), z) \rightarrow z = x]]$
$x = y$ (S.1)	
===	

$\neg IS(S(x), x))$	$\neg \forall z.[IS(s(x), z) \rightarrow z = x]$
$\neg S(x) = S(x)$	$IS(S(x), z)$
========	$\neg z = x$
	$S(x) = S(z)$
	$x = z$ (S.1)
	===

The following sequent, on the other hand, is not derivable because of (S.2):

3) $\vdash \exists y.f\mathrm{IS}(0) = y$

6.3 Translating a Derivation in ITTf to a Derivation in ITT

A term of ITTf that is not a term of ITT is called an f-extended term. Thus one or more f-terms occur free or bound in an f-extended term. An f-term fS in which no f-term has a free occurrence is said to be f-prime. A prime component of an f-extended term T is an f-prime f-term fR for which for some variable x and term T' in which x occurs free, T is $[fR/x]T'$. Since all the f-prime f-terms can be linearly ordered, it is possible to define the first prime component of an f-extended term that is not f-prime.

A mapping * of some terms of ITTf into terms of ITT is defined:

1. If R is a term of ITT, then $*R$ is R.
2. Consider the formulas of ITTf that are not formulas of ITT.
   (a) If $cv(S_1, \ldots, S_n)$ is f-prime then $*cv(S_1, \ldots, S_n)$ is $cv(*S_1, \ldots, *S_n)$. Otherwise let fR be the first prime component of $cv(S_1, \ldots, S_n)$. Then $*cv(S_1, \ldots, S_n)$ is $*\delta R \wedge \exists x.[*R(x) \wedge *cv(S'_1, \ldots, S'_n)]$, where S_i is $[fR/x]S'_i$, and fR has no free occurrence in any S'_i.
   (b) $*\neg F$ is $\neg * F$, $*[F \wedge G]$ is $[*F \wedge *G]$, and $*\forall x.F$ is $\forall x. * F$.
   (c) $*(\lambda x.T)(S, S_1, \ldots, S_n)$ is $*[S/x]T(S_1, \ldots, S_n)$
3. Consider the f-prime terms of ITTf of type $[\bar{\tau}]$, where is $\bar{\tau}$ not empty, that are not terms of ITT.
   (a) $*(MN)$ is $(*M * N)$
   (b) $*(\lambda x.T)$ is $(\lambda x. * T)$

The case of an f-prime term of type 1, that is not a term of ITT, is not considered since such terms cannot exist. For an f-term can only be bound by λ-abstraction, and λ-abstraction cannot be applied to a term of type 1. Thus $*F$ is a formula of ITT for each formula F of ITTf.

6.4 ITTf is a Conservative Extension of ITT

This section is devoted to a proof that ITTf is a conservative extension of ITT; that is, to a proof of the following theorem:

Theorem

A sequent of ITT that is derivable in ITTf is derivable in ITT.

Proof

Let Derv$f$ be a derivation in ITTf of a sequent of ITT. Each node H of Derv$f$ is replaced by $*H$ to produce a tree *Derv$f$ of formulas of ITT that may not be a derivation in ITT.

Lemma
Let F be the premiss and G the conclusion of a single conclusion rule other than $\forall$, or let G and H be the two conclusions of $\neg\wedge$, or of f with a removed term that is f-prime. Then $*F \vdash *G$ and $*F \vdash *G, *H$ are derivable sequents of ITT.

The lemma follows immediately from the definition of * for all the rules other than f. The sequent for the f-rule, namely $*[fR/x]F \vdash \exists x.[*R(x) \wedge *F], \neg * \delta R$ where R is f-prime, can be shown to be derivable for any F by induction on the definition of F, thus also when F is replaced by $\neg F$.

The $\forall$-rule has been excluded from the lemma because its premiss $\forall x.F$ may be a formula of ITT while its conclusion $[T/x]F$ may not. But note that if T is f-prime, then $*[T/x]F$ is $[*T/x]F$ which is a formula of ITT if F is. Thus in order to construct a derivation of ITT from the tree *Derv$f$, it is sufficient to show that each application of $\forall$ in Derv$f$ with an eigenterm that is not f-prime can be justified in *Derv$f$. The proof proceeds by induction on the number of prime components that can be extracted from T with the case of zero prime components being immediate.

Consider a first application of $\forall$ in Derv$f$ for which the premiss $\forall x.F$ is a formula of ITT and the conclusion $[T/x]F$ is not. Let fR be the first prime component of T so that T is $[fR/u]T'$, for some term T' in which fR has no free occurrence. There are two cases to consider:

a) There is no application of f with premiss a descendant of $[[fR/u]T'/x]F$ in which fR is the removed term. In this case consider each free occurrence of fR in $[[fR/u]T'/x]F$, and in each descendant $[fR/u]G$. All these free occurrences may be replaced by a first order constant. The result is a derivation in which T' has one fewer prime components than T does.

b) There is an application of f with premiss a descendant $[fR/u]G$ of $[[fR/u]T'/x]F$ with fR the removed term.

By induction on the number of applications of rules used to obtain $[fR/u]G$ as a descendant of $[[fR/u]T'/x]F$ it can be proved that the application of f with premiss $[fR/u]G$ can be replaced by an application with premiss $[[fR/u]T'/x]F$. Thus the chosen application of $\forall$ can be assumed to appear as follows in Derv$f$:

$\forall x.F$

...

$[[fR/u]T'/x]F \quad \forall$

...

$\exists u.[R(u) \wedge [T'/x]F]$ $\qquad\qquad$ $\neg\delta R$

Tree 1 $\qquad\qquad$ *Tree 2*

Before translation by *, this portion of Derv$f$ is first transformed to

$\forall x.F$
$\bullet\bullet\bullet$
$[[c/u]T'/x]F \qquad \forall$ where $c:1$

<table>
<tr><td>$[[fR/u]T'/x]F$
$\bullet\bullet\bullet$</td><td></td><td>$\neg[[fR/u]T'/x]F$
$\bullet\bullet\bullet\dagger$</td><td>Cut</td></tr>
<tr><td>$\exists u.[R(u) \wedge [T'/x]F]$
Tree 1</td><td>$\neg\delta R$
Tree 2</td><td>$\exists u.[R(u) \wedge \neg[T'/x]F]$
$[R(w) \wedge \neg[[w/u]T'/x]F]$
$\neg[[w/u]T'/x]F$
$[[w/u]T'/x]F \qquad \forall$
$=======\dagger$</td><td>$\neg\delta R$
Tree 2 $\dagger$</td></tr>
</table>

The nodes of $\bullet\bullet\bullet\dagger$ and of the tree *Tree 2* $\dagger$ are obtained respectively from the corresponding nodes $\bullet\bullet\bullet$ in Derv$f$ and *Tree 2* as follows. Consider the free occurrences of fR in nodes of $\bullet\bullet\bullet$ and *Tree 2* that are descendants of $[[fR/u]T'/x]F$ and that correspond to free occurrences in $[[fR/u]T'/x]F$. The nodes of $\bullet\bullet\bullet\ \dagger$ and of the *Tree 2* $\dagger$ are obtained from $\bullet\bullet\bullet$ and *Tree 2* by replacing each such free occurrence of fR by c.

Each of the terms $[c/u]T'$ and $[w/u]T'$ in the conclusions of the applications of $\forall$ in the transformed Derv$f$, has one fewer prime components than T. Since the "closure" indicated by $===\ \dagger$ is a proper closure in *Derv$f$, this completes a proof of the theorem.

End of proof

References

1. Peter B. Andrews. *An Introduction to Mathematical Logic and Type Theory: to Truth Through Proof*, Academic Press, 1986.
2. Peter B. Andrews, Sunil Issar, Daniel Nesmith, & Frank Pfenning. The TPS Theorem Proving System,*9'th International Conference on Automated Deduction (CADE)*, volume 310, Lecture Notes in Computer Science, E. Lusk & R. Overbeek (Eds), 760-761, Springer-Verlag 1988.
3. H.P. Barendregt. *The Lambda Calculus, Its Syntax and Semantics*, Revised Edition. North-Holland. 1985.
4. Alonzo Church. Schröder's Anticipation of the Simple Theory of Types. *The Journal of Unified Science (Erkenntnis)* Vol IX, 149-152, 1939.
5. Alonzo Church. A Formulation of the Simple Theory of Types,*J. Sym. Logic*, 5, 56-68, 1940.
6. William M. Farmer, A Partial Functions Version of Church's Simple Theory of Types, *J. Sym. Logic*, 55, 1269-1290, 1990.
7. Paul C. Gilmore. Natural Deduction Based Set Theories: A New Resolution of the Old Paradoxes, *J.Sym. Logic*, 51, 393-411, 1986.
8. Paul C. Gilmore. An Impredicative Simple Theory of Types, presented at the Fourteenth Workshop on Mathematical Foundations for Programming Systems, Queen Mary College, London, May 1998. The paper is available at: http://www.cs.ubc.ca/spider/gilmore

9. Paul C. Gilmore. Cut-Elimination for an Impredicative Simple Theory of Types, July 1998. The paper is to appear in the Journal of Symbolic Logic and is available at: http://www.cs.ubc.ca/spider/gilmore
10. Paul C. Gilmore. A Foundation for the Entity Relationship Approach: How and Why, *Proceedings of the 6th Entity Relationship Conference*, S.T. March (Ed.), North-Holland 95-113, 1988.
11. *An Impredicative Higher Order Logic and Some Applications*, a monograph on ITT in preparation.
12. Michael J.C. Gordon. A Proof Generating System for Higher-order Logic, *VLSI Specification, Verification and Synthesis*, G. Birtwistle, P. Subrahmanyam, Eds., Academic Publishers, Boston, pp. 73-128, 1987. Also, University of Cambridge Computer Laboratory Technical Report No. 103
13. Mike Gordon. Set Theory, Higher Order Logic or Both? The 1996 International Conference on Theorem Proving in Higher order Logics, Lecture Notes in Computer Science No. 1125, pp191-202, Springer-Verlag, 1996.
14. S. Owre, N. Shankar, and J. M. Rushby. The PVS Specification Language (Beta Release), Computer Science Laboratory, SRI International, Menlo Park CA 940 25, June 14, 1993.
15. Willard Van Orman Quine, *Mathematical Logic*, Revised Edition, Harvard University Press, 1951.
16. K. Schütte. Syntactical and Semantical Properties of Simple Type Theory, *J. Sym. Logic*, 25, 305-326, 1960.
17. Wilfred Sellars. Abstract Entities, *Rev. of Metaphysics*, vol. 16, 625-671, 1963.
18. Wilfred Sellars. Classes as Abstract Entities and the Russell Paradox, *Rev. of Metaphysics*, vol. 17, 67-90, 1963.
19. Joseph R. Shoenfield, *Mathematical Logic*, Addison-Wesley, 1967.
20. Ernst Zermelo, Investigations in the Foundations of Set Theory, *From Frege to Gödel*, Ed. Jean van Heijenoort, Harvard University Press, 199-215, 1967.

A Simple Sequent System for First-Order Logic with Free Constructors

Jean Goubault-Larrecq

G.I.E. Dyade & Projet Coq, Inria, France (Jean.Goubault@dyade.fr)

1 Introduction

First-order logic with equality is one of the most pervasive logics in use, whether in mathematics, logic or computer science. For real applications, however, automated provers need to be complemented with axioms of interest, e.g. for arithmetic, or for associative-commutative operations. It is then interesting to build these axioms inside the prover itself, for performance reasons. This has been done for a variety of theories, whether equational [13] or not [14].

One form of theory that has not yet been investigated is that of *datatype constructors*. Consider for instance the specification of the type `nat` of unary integers and `natlist` of lists of unary integers in Standard ML [9]:

```
datatype nat = 0 | S of nat;
datatype natlist = nil | cons of nat * natlist;
```

This specifies a many-sorted signature $\mathtt{0} : \mathtt{nat}$, $\mathtt{S} : \mathtt{nat} \to \mathtt{nat}$, $\mathtt{nil} : \mathtt{natlist}$ and $\mathtt{cons} : \mathtt{nat} \times \mathtt{natlist} \to \mathtt{natlist}$. This also states that the only ground terms of sort `nat` are those built up using `0` and `S`, and that the only ground terms of sort `natlist` are those built up using `nil` and `cons` atop ground terms of sort `nat`. This can be expressed by structural induction schemes:

$$\forall P_{\mathtt{nat}\to o} \cdot P(\mathtt{0}) \wedge (\forall n_{\mathtt{nat}} \cdot P(n) \supset P(\mathtt{S}(n))) \supset \forall n_{\mathtt{nat}} \cdot P(n)$$
$$\forall P_{\mathtt{natlist}\to o} \cdot P(\mathtt{nil}) \wedge (\forall n_{\mathtt{nat}}, \ell_{\mathtt{natlist}} \cdot P(\ell) \supset P(\mathtt{cons}(n, \ell))) \supset \forall \ell_{\mathtt{natlist}} \cdot P(\ell)$$

The ML declarations above also imply that distinct ground terms always denote distinct values. This can be described by *non-confusion axioms* ($\approx$ is equality):

$$\forall n_{\mathtt{nat}} \cdot \neg \mathtt{S}(n) \approx \mathtt{0} \qquad \forall m_{\mathtt{nat}}, n_{\mathtt{nat}} \cdot \mathtt{S}(m) \approx \mathtt{S}(n) \supset m \approx n$$
$$\forall \ell_{\mathtt{natlist}}, m_{\mathtt{nat}} \cdot \neg \mathtt{cons}(m, \ell) \approx \mathtt{nil}$$
$$\forall \ell_{\mathtt{natlist}}, \ell'_{\mathtt{natlist}}, m_{\mathtt{nat}}, n_{\mathtt{nat}} \cdot \mathtt{cons}(m, \ell) \approx \mathtt{cons}(n, \ell') \supset \ell \approx \ell' \wedge m \approx n$$

and also e.g. $\forall n_{\mathtt{nat}} \cdot \neg n \approx \mathtt{S}(n)$, which forbid cycles and are inductive consequences of the above. Symbols like `0`, `S`, `nil`, `cons` that obey non-confusion are usually referred to as *free constructors* of the datatypes `nat` and `natlist`.

These theories are very natural, and have been considered elegant foundations for inductive datatypes both in programming language design and in proof assistants, like Coq [1]. Recently, frameworks for analyzing and proving properties of cryptographic protocols [3, 12] also used similar inductive definitions: messages are typically described as the following datatype `msg`:

```
datatype base = K of key | ...;
datatype msg = B of base | P of msg * msg | C of msg * key;
```

where key is some type of encryption keys, and the informal ellipsis ... indicates that there may be other base messages than keys: there is no induction principle on base. Encrypting a message m with a key k is done by applying the constructor C, *viz.* $\mathtt{C}(m, k)$; that C is a free constructor automatically implies the desired features that an encrypted message cannot be confused with a pair or a base message ($\neg\mathtt{C}(m, k) \approx \mathtt{P}(m_1, m_2)$, $\neg\mathtt{C}(m, k) \approx \mathtt{B}(b)$), that there are no semantical overlaps between encrypted messages ($\mathtt{C}(m_1, k_1) \approx \mathtt{C}(m_2, k_2) \supset m_1 \approx m_2 \wedge k_1 \approx k_2$), and that there are no cycles, in particular we cannot decipher a message by encrypting it repetitively ($\neg\mathtt{C}(\mathtt{C}(\ldots\mathtt{C}(m, k_1)\ldots, k_{n-1}), k_n) \approx m$).

Working with non-confusion axioms atop a generic first-order prover is awkward, and it is fruitful to build them in. This is all the more desirable, as the semantics of free constructors is extremely simple: take any (many-sorted) Herbrand model, and insist that equality denote exactly identity on ground terms. We introduce a new sequent system, $\mathrm{LKc}_{\approx}$, for theories with free constructors and equality, and where non-confusion axioms are built in; our motto here is simplicity, and we believe that $\mathrm{LKc}_{\approx}$ is as simple as the semantics allows.

The paper is organized as follows: we introduce all preliminary notions in Section 2, and vindicate the rules of our sequent system $\mathrm{LKc}_{\approx}$ in Section 3. $\mathrm{LKc}_{\approx}$ is a sound, complete proof system for first-order logic with equality and free constructors. We show this in Section 4, and also that cuts can be eliminated. The latter is indispensable if we are to derive a practical tableau calculus from $\mathrm{LKc}_{\approx}$, a task which we defer for lack of space. We give a short tour of related ideas in Section 5, and conclude in Section 6. For space reasons, we won't consider structural induction, and most proofs are abridged; see [7] for details.

2 Preliminaries

Let $\mathcal{S}$ be a fixed set of sorts τ, τ', τ_1, ..., and $\mathcal{C}$ be a fixed set of function symbols c, d, ..., which we call *constructors*. Each constructor c is given a unique *arity* $\alpha(c)$, which is an expression of the form $\tau_1 \times \ldots \times \tau_n \to \tau$. Let $\mathcal{V}$ be a set of so-called *variables* x_τ, y_τ, z_τ, ...; we assume that for each sort τ, there are infinitely many variables with τ as subscript. The *pre-terms* t are defined inductively as either variables x_τ or applications $c(t_1, \ldots, t_n)$, where t_1, ..., t_n are pre-terms. We define a *typing judgment* $\triangleright t : \tau$ by the following rules: $\triangleright x_\tau : \tau$, and $\triangleright c(t_1, \ldots, t_n) : \tau$ whenever $\alpha(c) = \tau_1 \times \ldots \times \tau_n \to \tau$, $\triangleright t_1 : \tau_1, \ldots, \triangleright t_n : \tau_n$. The *terms* are the pre-terms t such that $\triangleright t : \tau$ for some τ. In this case, τ is unique; we call it the *type* of the term t. When the type τ of x_τ is understood, we also drop the sort subscript and write x. The set $\mathrm{fv}(t)$ of *free variables* of t is defined in the usual way. A term t such that $\mathrm{fv}(t) = \emptyset$ is called *closed* or *ground*.

A *substitution* σ is a map from variables x_τ to terms of type τ such that $\sigma(x) = x$ for all but finitely many variables x. The *domain* $\mathrm{dom}\,\sigma$ of σ is $\{x \in \mathcal{V} \mid \sigma(x) \neq x\}$. The notation $[x_1 := t_1, \ldots, x_m := t_m]$ denotes the substitution mapping each x_i to t_i, $1 \leq i \leq m$, and mapping every other variable y to y; in particular, $[]$ is the *identity substitution*. Let Σ be the set of all substitutions.

Substitution application $t \mapsto t\sigma$ is defined by $x\sigma =_{\mathrm{df}} \sigma(x)$, $c(t_1, \ldots, t_n)\sigma =_{\mathrm{df}} c(t_1\sigma, \ldots, t_n\sigma)$. The *composition* $\sigma\sigma'$ of σ and σ' is the unique substitution such that $t(\sigma\sigma') = (t\sigma)\sigma'$ for all t; this defines a monoid law, with $[]$ as unit. The relation $\succeq$ defined by $\sigma \succeq \sigma\sigma'$ is then a preorder: we say that σ is *more general than* $\sigma\sigma'$. We write $\sigma \equiv \sigma'$ iff $\sigma \succeq \sigma'$ and $\sigma' \succeq \sigma$.

A *system of equations* E is any finite set of *equations* $s \approx t$, where s and t are terms of the same type. E, E' denotes the union of E and E'. A substitution σ *unifies* E, or is a *unifier* of E, iff $s\sigma = t\sigma$ for every $s \approx t$ in E. σ is *idempotent* iff $\mathrm{fv}(\sigma(x)) \cap \mathrm{dom}\,\sigma = \emptyset$ for every $x \in \mathrm{dom}\,\sigma$; this implies that $\sigma\sigma = \sigma$. It is well-known [15] that every unifiable system of equations E has an idempotent *most general unifier*, or *mgu* σ_0. Conversely, any substitution $\sigma =_{\mathrm{df}} [x_1 := t_1, \ldots, x_m := t_m]$ with $\mathrm{dom}\,\sigma = \{x_1, \ldots, x_m\}$ defines a unique system of equations $\overline{\sigma} =_{\mathrm{df}} \{x_1 \approx t_1, \ldots, x_m \approx t_m\}$. Let *mgu* be any function mapping each unifiable system E of equations to an idempotent unifier of E.

Let $\bot$ be an element outside Σ, designed to represent non-unifiable systems. Extend $\succeq$ so that $\sigma \succeq \bot$ for every $\sigma \in \Sigma$. We may then extend the *mgu* function so that $mgu(E) = \bot$ for every non-unifiable system E. Let also $\overline{\bot} =_{\mathrm{df}} \bot$, and extend again the *mgu* function so that $mgu(\bot, E) =_{\mathrm{df}} \bot$, $mgu(E, \bot) =_{\mathrm{df}} \bot$. This makes $\Sigma_\bot =_{\mathrm{df}} \Sigma \cup \{\bot\}$ equipped with the pre-order $\succeq$ a meet-semi-lattice with bottom element $\bot$, meet $\sqcap$ defined by $\sigma \sqcap \sigma' =_{\mathrm{df}} mgu(\overline{\sigma}, \overline{\sigma'})$ for every $\sigma, \sigma' \in \Sigma_\bot$. For readability, we shall again write $mgu(\sigma, \sigma')$ for $\sigma \sqcap \sigma'$.

We build atomic formulae using predicate symbols P, Q, ..., taken from a fixed set $\mathcal{P}$; each predicate symbol is equipped with an *arity* $\alpha(P) = \tau_1 \times \ldots \times \tau_n \to o$, where o is the type of propositions, assumed not to be a sort. The *atoms* are either *non-equality atoms* A, B, ..., which are expressions of the form $P(t_1, \ldots, t_n)$ where P is as above, and $\triangleright t_1 : \tau_1$, ..., $\triangleright t_n : \tau_n$; or *equalities* $s \approx t$, where s and t have the same type, whatever it is. We assume that $\approx$ is not in $\mathcal{P}$.

Formulae F, G, ..., are built upon atoms using $\mathbf{0}$ (false), $\supset$ (implication), and $\forall x \cdot$ (universal quantification) in the usual way; $\neg F$ abbreviates $F \supset \mathbf{0}$, and $\supset$ associates to the right. For conciseness, we see $\wedge$, $\vee$, $\exists x \cdot$ as defined connectives.

Our algebra of sorts is designed to keep type-checking and unification problems simple. Undoubtedly, we can enrich the type system, but this comes at a price, and it is not our purpose to pay for it here.

To sum up (the role of ϕ will be explained later):

Definition 1. *A* language *is a tuple* $(\mathcal{C}, \mathcal{P}, \alpha, \phi)$, *where* $\mathcal{C} \cap \mathcal{P} = \emptyset$, $(\approx) \notin \mathcal{P}$; *the* arity function α *maps each element* $c \in \mathcal{C}$ *to an expression of the form* $\tau_1 \times \ldots \times \tau_n \to \tau$, *and each element* $P \in \mathcal{P}$ *to an expression of the form* $\tau_1 \times \ldots \times \tau_n \to o$; *and* ϕ *maps each* $P \in \mathcal{P}$ *such that* $\alpha(P) = \tau_1 \times \ldots \times \tau_n \to o$ *to a set of subsets of* $\{1, \ldots, n\}$; *these subsets are called the* functionalities *of* P. *We assume that for every sort* τ, *there is at least one ground term of type* τ.

The Tarskian semantics of this language is as usual. An *interpretation* I is a family $I(\tau)$ of pairwise disjoint non-empty sets indexed by sorts τ, a function $I(c)$ from $I(\tau_1) \times \ldots \times I(\tau_n)$ to $I(\tau)$ for each constructor c, of arity $\tau_1 \times \ldots \times \tau_n \to$

τ, a subset $I(P)$ of $I(\tau_1) \times \ldots \times I(\tau_n)$ for each predicate symbol P, of arity $\tau_1 \times \ldots \times \tau_n \to o$, and a subset $I(\approx)$ of $\bigcup_\tau I(\tau) \times I(\tau)$. *Valuations* ρ map variables x_τ to elements of $I(\tau)$. The semantics $I[\![t]\!]\rho$ of terms t is: $I[\![x]\!]\rho =_{\mathrm{df}} \rho(x)$, $I[\![c(t_1, \ldots, t_n)]\!]\rho =_{\mathrm{df}} I(c)(I[\![t_1]\!]\rho, \ldots, I[\![t_n]\!]\rho)$. The semantics of formulae is given by: $I, \rho \models P(t_1, \ldots, t_n)$ iff $(I[\![t_1]\!]\rho, \ldots, I[\![t_n]\!]\rho) \in I(P)$, and $I, \rho \models s \approx t$ iff $(I[\![s]\!]\rho, I[\![t]\!]\rho) \in I(\approx)$, and logical connectives are defined as usual. We write $I \models F$ iff $I, \rho \models F$ for every valuation ρ.

An *equational* interpretation I is such that $I, \rho \models s \approx t$ iff $I[\![s]\!]\rho = I[\![t]\!]\rho$, i.e. such that $I(\approx) = \{(v, v) \mid v \in \bigcup_\tau I(\tau)\}$. We shall also be interested in interpretations that are *free*, in that they obey non-confusion [4]:

Definition 2. *An interpretation I is* free *iff:*
whenever $I[\![c(s_1, \ldots, s_m)]\!]\rho = I[\![d(t_1, \ldots, t_n)]\!]\rho$, then $c = d$, $m = n$, and $I[\![s_i]\!]\rho = I[\![t_i]\!]\rho$ for every i, $1 \leq i \leq m$;
and whenever $I[\![x]\!]\rho = I[\![t]\!]\rho$, then either $x = t$ or x is not free in t.

3 Design of $\mathrm{LKc}_\approx$

Because our domains are free, an equation $c(s_1, \ldots, s_m) \approx d(t_1, \ldots, t_n)$ can only hold when $c = d$, and the equations $s_1 \approx t_1, \ldots, s_m \approx t_m$ hold; also, $x \approx t$ can only hold when $x = t$ or when x is not free in t. The astute reader will have recognized the basic rules for Martelli-Montanari-style first-order unification [10]. So, to prove $s_1 \approx t_1 \supset s_2 \approx t_2$, replace $s_1 \approx t_1$ by its most general unifier σ; if $s_2\sigma = t_2\sigma$, the implication is proved. For example, $\mathtt{S}(x) \approx \mathtt{S}(y) \supset x \approx y$ holds because $mgu(\mathtt{S}(x) \approx \mathtt{S}(y)) \equiv [x := y]$, and $x[x := y] = y[x := y]$. We therefore consider sequents of the following form:

Definition 3. *An* $\mathrm{LKc}_\approx$ *sequent is a triple $\sigma; \Gamma \vdash \Delta$, where $\sigma = \bot$ or σ is an idempotent substitution in Σ, and Γ and Δ are multisets of formulae.*

The substitution part σ collects a preprocessed form of some equalities on the left of $\vdash$: the above sequent has the same semantics as the usual sequent $\overline{\sigma}, \Gamma \vdash \Delta$. If σ is the identity substitution [], we also write $; \Gamma \vdash \Delta$ instead of $[]; \Gamma \vdash \Delta$. We write S, S' for the multiset union of S and S'.

The example above also justifies a *reflexivity rule* $(\approx R)$, where $\sigma; \Gamma \vdash s \approx t, \Delta$ is inferred, whenever $\sigma \neq \bot$ and $s\sigma = t\sigma$. When $\sigma = \bot$, the equalities that σ represents are non-unifiable, i.e. they are contradictory. For example, consider the equation $\mathtt{0} \approx \mathtt{S}(x)$: if it occurs on the left of $\vdash$, then the sequent is proved. Hence we add an *absurdity rule* $(\bot L)$, allowing us to infer $\bot; \Gamma \vdash \Delta$, whatever Γ and Δ may be. We must not forget to process the equalities in the Γ part, and have them mix with the σ part—this is done by the $(\approx L)$ rule, see Figure 1—and we must also allow the system to conclude when the same formula occurs in the Γ and in the Δ parts, up to equalities represented by σ: this is the $(\approx)$ rule of Figure 1. (Recall that, by convention, A and B are non-equality atoms.) Finally, note that our use of unification has nothing to do with proof search.

Adding rules for the logical connectives is all we need to get a sound and complete sequent system for first-order logic with equality—i.e., the special case where there are no constructors—, as we shall see in Section 4. On the downside, we do not have any function symbols, apart from constructors: functions must be coded as predicates, as in Prolog (say, the binary + function as a ternary $\oplus(x, y, z)$ meaning $z \approx x+y$), obeying new axioms, *functionality axioms* expressing the uniqueness of the result (e.g., $\forall x, y, z, z' \cdot \oplus(x, y, z) \supset \oplus(x, y, z') \supset z \approx z'$), and *totality axioms* stating its existence (e.g., $\forall x, y \cdot \exists z \cdot \oplus(x, y, z)$).

There does not seem to be any clever way of building in totality axioms. However, it is possible to build in functionality axioms (this will therefore make $\mathrm{LKc}_{\approx}$ a theory of *partial functions*). To do this, we equip each predicate symbol P with a set $\phi(P)$ of *functionalities* f: f is a set of argument positions for P such that, given some values at these positions, the values at the positions outside f are uniquely determined. For instance, the predicate $\oplus$ above has functionality $\{1, 2\}$, since whenever its first two arguments are given, its third is determined uniquely. It also has the functionalities $\{1, 3\}$ and $\{2, 3\}$; that is, $\phi(\oplus) = \{\{1, 2\}, \{1, 3\}, \{2, 3\}\}$. Formally, if $\alpha(P) = \tau_1 \times \ldots \times \tau_n \rightarrow o$, $\phi(P)$ is a set of subsets of $\{1, \ldots, n\}$, as announced in Definition 1.

$$\frac{}{\bot; \Gamma \vdash \Delta}\,(\bot L) \qquad \frac{\sigma \neq \bot, \quad A\sigma = B\sigma}{\sigma; \Gamma, A \vdash B, \Delta}\,(\approx) \qquad \frac{\sigma \neq \bot, \quad s\sigma = t\sigma}{\sigma; \Gamma \vdash s \approx t, \Delta}\,(\approx R)$$

$$\frac{\begin{array}{c}\sigma \neq \bot,\\ mgu(s \approx t, \overline{\sigma}); \Gamma \vdash \Delta\end{array}}{\sigma; \Gamma, s \approx t \vdash \Delta}\,(\approx L) \qquad \frac{\begin{array}{c}f \in \phi(P), \quad \sigma \neq \bot, \quad \vec{s}_f\sigma = \vec{t}_f\sigma\\ \sigma; \Gamma, P(s_1, \ldots, s_n), P(t_1, \ldots, t_n), \vec{s}_{\overline{f}^n} \approx \vec{t}_{\overline{f}^n} \vdash \Delta\end{array}}{\sigma; \Gamma, P(s_1, \ldots, s_n), P(t_1, \ldots, t_n) \vdash \Delta}\,(\approx\uparrow)$$

$$\frac{\sigma; \Gamma, G \vdash \Delta \quad \sigma; \Gamma \vdash F, \Delta}{\sigma; \Gamma, F \supset G \vdash \Delta}\,(\supset L) \qquad \frac{\sigma; \Gamma, F \vdash G, \Delta}{\sigma; \Gamma \vdash F \supset G, \Delta}\,(\supset R)$$

$$\frac{\sigma; \Gamma, \forall x \cdot F, F[x := t] \vdash \Delta}{\sigma; \Gamma, \forall x \cdot F \vdash \Delta}\,(\forall L) \qquad \frac{\sigma; \Gamma \vdash F[x := y_\tau], \Delta}{\sigma; \Gamma \vdash \forall x_\tau \cdot F, \Delta}\,(\forall R)$$
$$(y \text{ not free in } \overline{\sigma}, \Gamma, \forall x_\tau \cdot F, \Delta)$$

$$\frac{}{\sigma; \Gamma, \mathbf{0} \vdash \Delta}\,(\mathbf{0}L) \qquad \frac{\sigma; \Gamma \vdash F, \Delta \quad \sigma; \Gamma, F \vdash \Delta}{\sigma; \Gamma \vdash \Delta}\,(Cut)$$

Fig. 1. System $\mathrm{LKc}_{\approx}$

Semantically, interpretations will have to respect functionalities:

Definition 4. *An interpretation* I respects functionalities *iff, for every* $P \in \mathcal{P}$, *where* $\alpha(P) = \tau_1 \times \ldots \times \tau_n \rightarrow \tau$, *for every* $f \in \phi(P)$, *for every* $v_1, v_1' \in I(\tau_1)$, $\ldots$, $v_n, v_n' \in I(\tau_n)$, *if* $(v_1, \ldots, v_n) \in I(P)$ *and* $(v_1', \ldots, v_n') \in I(P)$, *and* $v_i = v_i'$ *for every* $i \in f$, *then* $v_i = v_i'$ *for every* $i \in \{1, \ldots, n\}$.

To express this in the proof system, we add one rule. Given $f \in \phi(P)$, let $\overline{f}^n$ denote $\{1, \ldots, n\} \setminus f$; given a finite set $f =_{\mathrm{df}} \{i_1, \ldots, i_k\}$ of integers, and families of terms $(s_i)_{i \geq 0}$, $(t_i)_{i \geq 0}$, write $\vec{s}_f \approx \vec{t}_f$ for $s_{i_1} \approx t_{i_1}, \ldots, s_{i_k} \approx t_{i_k}$. The desired rule should express that $P(s_1, \ldots, s_n) \supset P(t_1, \ldots, t_n) \supset \vec{s}_f \approx \vec{t}_f \supset \vec{s}_{\overline{f}^n} \approx \vec{t}_{\overline{f}^n}$. This is best expressed as a left rule (where $f = \{i_1, \ldots, i_k\} \in \phi(P)$):

$$\frac{\sigma; \Gamma', \vec{s}_{\overline{f}^n} \approx \vec{t}_{\overline{f}^n} \vdash \Delta \quad \sigma; \Gamma' \vdash s_{i_1} \approx t_{i_1}, \Delta \quad \ldots \quad \sigma; \Gamma' \vdash s_{i_k} \approx t_{i_k}, \Delta}{\sigma; \underbrace{\Gamma, P(s_1, \ldots, s_n), P(t_1, \ldots, t_n)}_{\Gamma'} \vdash \Delta}$$

But the only (non-trivial) way we can prove an equality $s_{i_j} \approx t_{i_j}$ is by reflexivity, so we simplify this to the ($\approx\uparrow$) rule of Figure 1, where $\vec{s}_f\sigma = \vec{t}_f\sigma$ abbreviates the list $s_{i_1}\sigma = t_{i_1}\sigma, \ldots, s_{i_k}\sigma = t_{i_k}\sigma$. This terminates the description of $\mathrm{LKc}_{\approx}$.

4 Soundness, Completeness

We shall use the following algorithm U as a guide for proving certain properties of most general unifiers:

(Delete) $E, s \approx s \to E$
(Check1) $E, x \approx t \to \bot$ $\quad (x \neq t, x \in \mathrm{fv}(t))$
(Check2) $E, t \approx x \to \bot$ $\quad (x \neq t, x \in \mathrm{fv}(t))$
(Bind1) $E, x \approx t \to E[x := t], x \approx t$ $\quad (x \notin \mathrm{fv}(t), x$ not solved in $E, x \approx t)$
(Bind2) $E, t \approx x \to E[x := t], x \approx t$ $\quad (x \notin \mathrm{fv}(t), x$ not solved in $E, x \approx t)$
(Clash) $E, c(s_1, \ldots, s_m) \approx d(t_1, \ldots, t_n) \to \bot$ $\quad (c \neq d)$
(Decomp) $E, c(s_1, \ldots, s_m) \approx c(t_1, \ldots, t_m) \to E, s_1 \approx t_1, \ldots, s_m \approx t_m$

This is a variant of Martelli and Montanari's algorithm [10]. A variable x is *solved in* E iff E is of the form $E', x \approx s$, where x is free neither in s nor in E'. E is *solved* if all the variables occurring on either side of any equation in E are solved in E. Let $\#E$ be the number of free unsolved variables in E. Let also $|E|$ be the *size* of E, defined as the sum of $|s \approx t|$, $(s \approx t) \in E$, where $|s \approx t| =_{\mathrm{df}} |s| + |t|$, and the size of terms is defined by: $|x| =_{\mathrm{df}} 1$, $|c(t_1, \ldots, t_n)| =_{\mathrm{df}} 1 + |t_1| + \ldots + |t_n|$. Here, $\bot$ is a token denoting the absence of unifiers.

Any sequence of steps $E_0 \to E_1 \to \ldots \to E_n \to \ldots$ by the rules of U terminates, since each rule makes $(\#E, |E|)$ decrease in the lexicographic ordering. Each rule also preserves the sets of all unifiers, and for any maximal sequence $E_0 \to E_1 \to \ldots \to E_n$ of rule applications, E_n must be $\bot$ or a solved system $x_1 \approx t_1, \ldots, x_k \approx t_k$; in the first case, E_0 is not unifiable, in the second case $[x_1 := t_1, \ldots, x_k := t_k]$ is an mgu of E_0. We might define $mgu(E_0)$ as the output of this algorithm, but we wish to prove results independently of a particular algorithm. To this end, we use the following facts, stated without proof.

Proposition 1. *Consider the following rule on systems of equations:*

$$\textbf{(Swap)}\ E, x \approx y \to E[y := x], y \approx x$$

The **(Swap)** *rule transforms solved systems E_1 into solved systems E_2 that have the same set of unifiers, and such that* $\mathrm{dom}\, E_2 = (\mathrm{dom}\, E_1 \setminus \{x\}) \cup \{y\}$.

Proposition 2. *Let E a solved system, and σ be an idempotent most general unifier of E. There is a finite sequence of* **(Swap)** *steps leading from E to $\overline{\sigma}$.*

4.1 Soundness

We extend the $\models$ notation: $I, \rho \models \sigma$, where $\sigma \in \Sigma_\perp$, iff $\sigma \neq \perp$ and $I[\![x]\!]\rho = I[\![\sigma(x)]\!]\rho$ for every x. $I, \rho \models (\sigma; \Gamma \vdash \Delta)$ is defined as: if $I, \rho \models \sigma$, and for every F in Γ, $I, \rho \models F$, then there is a formula G in Δ such that $I, \rho \models G$. Again, $I \models (\sigma; \Gamma \vdash \Delta)$ iff $I, \rho \models (\sigma; \Gamma \vdash \Delta)$ for every valuation ρ.

Theorem 1 (Soundness). *If $\sigma; \Gamma \vdash \Delta$ is provable in* $\mathrm{LKc}_{\approx}$*, then for every free equational interpretation I that respects functionalities, for every valuation ρ, it holds : $I, \rho \models (\sigma; \Gamma \vdash \Delta)$.*

Proof. By structural induction on the proof, looking at the last rule used. We only deal with the most important cases:

– Rule ($\approx$): assume $\sigma \neq \perp$, $A\sigma = B\sigma$. To show that $I, \rho \models (\sigma; \Gamma, A \vdash B, \Delta)$ for every ρ, we need to state a few auxiliary lemmas:

Proposition 3. *For every s, t, if $s\sigma = t\sigma$ and $I, \rho \models \sigma$, then $I[\![s]\!]\rho = I[\![t]\!]\rho$.*

Proposition 4. *For every non-equality atoms A, B, whenever $A\sigma = B\sigma$ and $I, \rho \models \sigma$, then $I, \rho \models A$ iff $I, \rho \models B$.*

Now if $I, \rho \models \sigma$ and $I, \rho \models F$ for every F in Γ, A, then in particular $I, \rho \models A$, and by Proposition 4 $I, \rho \models B$; therefore $I, \rho \models (\sigma; \Gamma, A \vdash B, \Delta)$.

– Rule ($\approx R$): similarly, using Proposition 3.

– Rule ($\approx L$): again, we first make a few auxiliary claims. Write $I, \rho \models E$ to say that $I, \rho \models s \approx t$ for every equation $s \approx t$ in E.

Lemma 1. *For every system of equations E, for every ρ, if $I, \rho \models E$, then E is unifiable and $I, \rho \models \sigma$, for all idempotent mgus σ of E.*

Proof. First, show that E is unifiable by some idempotent mgu σ_0 with $I, \rho \models \sigma_0$: σ_0 is the mgu that algorithm U computes, under some fixed strategy. The claim is proved by an easy induction on $(\#E, |E|)$ ordered lexicographically, considering whether E is solved or not, and in case E is not solved, by considering each of the rules of U in turn. Note that the claim is trivial when E is solved. We then show that $I, \rho \models \sigma$, for all idempotent mgus σ of E. Now, σ is obtained from E by a finite sequence of rules in U, followed by finitely many instances of **(Swap)**, by Proposition 2. We show that $I, \rho \models \sigma$ by another easy induction on the number of instances of rules that we used, noticing that all rules, including **(Swap)** (by Proposition 1), preserve the set of unifiers. □

We now show that ($\approx L$) is sound. Assume that $mgu(s \approx t, \overline{\sigma}); \Gamma \vdash \Delta$ is derived. By induction hypothesis: (a) $I, \rho \models (mgu(s \approx t, \overline{\sigma}); \Gamma \vdash \Delta)$. Now assume that: (b) $I, \rho \models \sigma$ and $I, \rho \models F$ for every formula F in $\Gamma, s \approx t$. In particular, $I, \rho \models s \approx t$. Moreover, (b) implies $I, \rho \models \overline{\sigma}$, so $I, \rho \models s \approx t, \overline{\sigma}$. By Lemma 1, $I, \rho \models mgu(s \approx t, \overline{\sigma})$, whatever the definition of the function mgu. Since by (b) $I, \rho \models F$ for every F in Γ, by (a) $I, \rho \models G$ for some G in Δ. □

4.2 Completeness

Lemma 2. *For every formulae F, G, $\sigma; \Gamma, F \vdash G, \Delta$ is provable in* LKc$_\approx$ *as soon as $\sigma = \bot$ or $\sigma \neq \bot$ and $F\sigma = G\sigma$.*

Proof. Easy structural induction on F. (Observe that $(\approx)$ cannot be used directly, since the closing formulae A and B are non-equality atoms.)

Lemma 3 (Weakening). *If $\sigma; \Gamma \vdash \Delta$ is provable in* LKc$_\approx$*, then $mgu(\overline{\sigma}, E)$; $\Gamma', \Gamma \vdash \Delta, \Delta'$ is provable in* LKc$_\approx$*, for every system of equations E, for every multisets of formulas Γ' and Δ'.*

Proof. By structural induction on the given proof π of $\sigma; \Gamma \vdash \Delta$. Use $(\bot L)$ when $\sigma' = \bot$. Otherwise, this is straightforward, using the fact that mgu is associative in the case of $(\approx L)$. □

Theorem 2 (Completeness). *If $I \models (\sigma; \Gamma \vdash \Delta)$ for every free equational interpretation I that respects functionalities, then $\sigma; \Gamma \vdash \Delta$ is provable in* LKc$_\approx$.

Proof. Let T be the following infinite set of formulae:

1. (Reflexivity) $\forall x_\tau \cdot x \approx x$;
2. (Symmetry) $\forall x_\tau \cdot \forall y_\tau \cdot x \approx y \supset y \approx x$;
3. (Transitivity) $\forall x_\tau \cdot \forall y_\tau \cdot \forall z_\tau \cdot x \approx y \wedge y \approx z \supset x \approx z$;
4. (FCongruence) $\forall x_{1\,\tau_1} \cdot \forall y_{1\,\tau_1} \cdot \ldots \cdot \forall x_{n\,\tau_n} \cdot \forall y_{n\,\tau_n} \cdot x_1 \approx y_1 \supset \ldots \supset x_n \approx y_n \supset c(x_1, \ldots, x_n) \approx c(y_1, \ldots, y_n)$ for every constructor c of arity $\tau_1 \times \ldots \times \tau_n \to \tau$;
5. (PCongruence) $\forall x_{1\,\tau_1} \cdot \forall y_{1\,\tau_1} \cdot \ldots \cdot \forall x_{n\,\tau_n} \cdot \forall y_{n\,\tau_n} \cdot x_1 \approx y_1 \supset \ldots \supset x_n \approx y_n \supset P(x_1, \ldots, x_n) \supset P(y_1, \ldots, y_n)$ for every predicate P of arity $\tau_1 \times \ldots \times \tau_n \to o$;
6. (Clash) $\forall x_{1\,\tau_1} \cdot \ldots \cdot \forall x_{n\,\tau_n} \cdot \forall y_{1\,\tau'_1} \cdot \ldots \cdot \forall y_{m\,\tau'_m} \cdot \neg c(x_1, \ldots, x_n) \approx d(y_1, \ldots, y_m)$ for every distinct constructors of c and d, of respective arities $\tau_1 \times \ldots \times \tau_n \to \tau$ and $\tau'_1 \times \ldots \times \tau'_m \to \tau'$;
7. (Decomp) $\forall x_{1\,\tau_1} \cdot \forall y_{1\,\tau_1} \cdot \ldots \cdot \forall x_{n\,\tau_n} \cdot \forall y_{n\,\tau_n} \cdot c(x_1, \ldots, x_n) \approx c(y_1, \ldots, y_n) \supset x_i \approx y_i$ for every c of arity $\tau_1 \times \ldots \times \tau_n \to \tau$, $n \geq 1$, and every i, $1 \leq i \leq n$;
8. (Check) $\forall y_1 \cdot \ldots \cdot \forall y_n \cdot \neg x \approx t$ for every term t such that $x \neq t$ and x is free in t, where $\{y_1, \ldots, y_n\} = \mathrm{fv}(t)$;
9. (Function) $\forall x_1 \cdot \forall y_1 \cdot \ldots \cdot \forall x_n \cdot \forall y_n \cdot \bigwedge \vec{x}_f \approx \vec{y}_f \supset P(x_1, \ldots, x_n) \supset P(y_1, \ldots, y_n) \supset x_i \approx y_i$ for every predicate P of arity $\tau_1 \times \ldots \times \tau_n \to o$, every $f \in \phi(P)$ and every $i \in \{1, \ldots, n\}$; by $\bigwedge \vec{x}_f \approx \vec{y}_f \supset F$, we denote the formula $x_{i_1} \approx y_{i_1} \supset \ldots \supset x_{i_k} \approx y_{i_k} \supset F$, where $f = \{i_1, \ldots, i_k\}$, $1 \leq i_1 < \ldots < i_k \leq n$.

Say that $I \models T$ iff $I \models F$ for every F in T.

Proposition 5. *For every interpretation I such that $I \models T$, there is an interpretation, the* quotient interpretation $I/\!\approx$, *which is free, equational and respects functionalities, and such that $I \models F$ iff $I/\!\approx\, \models F$, for every F.*

Proof. Take for $I/\!\approx$ the quotient of I by the equivalence relation $I(\approx)$. □

Now assume that: (a) $I_0 \models (\sigma; \Gamma \vdash \Delta)$ for every free equational interpretation I_0 that respects functionalities. If $\sigma = \perp$, then $\sigma; \Gamma \vdash \Delta$ is proved by ($\perp L$).

So assume that $\sigma \neq \perp$, and let I be an arbitrary interpretation. If $I \models T$, by Proposition 5 we may take $I_0 =_{\text{df}} I/\approx$ in (a), so $I/\approx\ \models (\sigma; \Gamma \vdash \Delta)$. By Proposition 5 again, $I \models (\sigma; \Gamma \vdash \Delta)$. So $I \models T$ implies $I \models (\sigma; \Gamma \vdash \Delta)$, hence: (b) $I \models (T, \overline{\sigma}, \Gamma \vdash \Delta)$, where the latter notation means that for every valuation ρ, if $I, \rho \models F$ for every $F \in T, \overline{\sigma}, \Gamma$, then $I, \rho \models G$ for some $G \in \Delta$.

Since first-order logic is compact [8], there is a finite subset T_{fin} of T such that $T_{fin}, \overline{\sigma}, \Gamma, \neg\Delta$ is unsatisfiable, where $\neg\Delta =_{\text{df}} \{\neg G \mid G \in \Delta\}$. Consider the following system ND:

$$\frac{}{\Lambda, F \vdash F}(Ax) \qquad \frac{\Lambda, F \vdash G}{\Lambda \vdash F \supset G}(\supset I) \qquad \frac{\Lambda \vdash F \supset G \quad \Lambda \vdash F}{\Lambda \vdash G}(\supset E)$$

$$\frac{\Lambda \vdash \mathbf{0}}{\Lambda \vdash F}(\mathbf{0}E) \quad \frac{\Lambda, \neg F \vdash \mathbf{0}}{\Lambda \vdash F}(\neg\neg E) \quad \frac{\Lambda \vdash F[x := y_\tau]}{\Lambda \vdash \forall x_\tau \cdot F}(\forall I) \quad \frac{\Lambda \vdash \forall x_\tau \cdot F \quad \rhd t : \tau}{\Lambda \vdash F[x := t]}(\forall E)$$

$$(y \text{ not free in } \Lambda)$$

which is complete in the following sense: for every multiset of formulae Λ, for every formula F, if $I \models (\Lambda \vdash F)$ for every I, then $\Lambda \vdash F$ is provable. It follows that: (c) $T_{fin}, \overline{\sigma}, \Gamma, \neg\Delta \vdash \mathbf{0}$ is provable in ND. We now translate this ND proof into an $\text{LKc}_\approx$ proof.

Lemma 4. *Whenever σ is an idempotent substitution, other than $\perp$, and T_{fin}, $\overline{\sigma}, \Lambda \vdash F$ is provable in* ND, *then $\sigma; \Lambda \vdash F$ is provable in* $\text{LKc}_\approx$.

Proof. By structural induction on the given ND proof of $T_{fin}, \overline{\sigma}, \Lambda \vdash F$. The most important case is when the last rule is (Ax), then F is in T_{fin}, $\overline{\sigma}$ or Λ. If F is in Λ, then the result follows from Lemma 2, since $\sigma \neq \perp$. If F is in $\overline{\sigma}$, then F is of the form $x \approx t$, and we derive $\sigma; \Lambda \vdash x \approx t$ by ($\approx R$). Indeed, $x\sigma = t$ (since $x \approx t$ is in $\overline{\sigma}$) $= t\sigma$ (since σ is idempotent). If $F \in T_{fin}$, we consider the cases of the 9 kinds of formulae in T. We only deal with a few cases (in each case, complete by Lemma 3 to get the desired proof):

3. (Transitivity)
$$\cfrac{\cfrac{\cfrac{\cfrac{}{mgu(x \approx z, y \approx z); \vdash x \approx z}(\approx R)}{; x \approx y, y \approx z \vdash x \approx z}2 \times (\approx L)}{; \vdash x \approx y \wedge y \approx z \supset x \approx z}(\wedge L), (\supset R)}{; \vdash \forall x_\tau \cdot \forall y_\tau \cdot \forall z_\tau \cdot x \approx y \wedge y \approx z \supset x \approx z}3 \times (\forall R)$$

4. (FCongruence) We go a bit faster now:

$$\cfrac{\cfrac{\cfrac{}{mgu(x_1 \approx y_1, \ldots, x_n \approx y_n); \vdash c(x_1, \ldots, x_n) \approx c(y_1, \ldots, y_n)}(\approx R)}{; x_1 \approx y_1, \ldots, x_n \approx y_n \vdash c(x_1, \ldots, x_n) \approx c(y_1, \ldots, y_n)}n \times (\approx L)}{\forall x_1, y_1, \ldots, x_n, y_n \cdot x_1 \approx y_1 \supset \ldots \supset x_n \approx y_n \supset c(x_1, \ldots, x_n) \approx c(y_1, \ldots, y_n)}$$

where the last line is by ($\supset R$) n times, then ($\forall R$) $2n$ times.

6. (Clash) Recall that $\neg F$ abbreviates $F \supset \mathbf{0}$. If c and d are distinct constructors, then $mgu(c(x_1,\dots,x_n) \approx d(y_1,\dots,y_m)) = \bot$, therefore:

$$\dfrac{\dfrac{\dfrac{\dfrac{}{\bot; \vdash \mathbf{0}}\,(\bot L)}{; c(x_1,\dots,x_n) \approx d(y_1,\dots,y_m) \vdash \mathbf{0}}\,(\approx L)}{; \vdash \neg c(x_1,\dots,x_n) \approx d(y_1,\dots,y_m)}\,(\supset R)}{; \vdash \forall x_1 \cdot \ldots \cdot \forall x_n \cdot \forall y_1 \cdot \ldots \cdot \forall y_m \cdot \neg c(x_1,\dots,x_n) \approx d(y_1,\dots,y_m)}\,(n+m) \times (\forall R)$$

9. (Function) Let k be the cardinality of f:

$$\dfrac{\dfrac{\dfrac{\dfrac{}{mgu(\vec{x}_{\{1,\dots,n\}} \approx \vec{y}_{\{1,\dots,n\}}); P(x_1,\dots,x_n), P(y_1,\dots,y_n) \vdash x_i \approx y_i}\,(\approx R)}{; \vec{x}_f \approx \vec{y}_f, P(x_1,\dots,x_n), P(y_1,\dots,y_n), \vec{x}_{\overline{f}^n} \approx \vec{y}_{\overline{f}^n} \vdash x_i \approx y_i}\,n \times (\approx L)}{; \vec{x}_f \approx \vec{y}_f, P(x_1,\dots,x_n), P(y_1,\dots,y_n) \vdash x_i \approx y_i}\,(\approx\uparrow)}{; \vdash \forall x_1, y_1, \dots, x_n, y_n \cdot \bigwedge \vec{x}_f \approx \vec{y}_f \supset P(x_1,\dots,x_n) \supset P(y_1,\dots,y_n) \supset x_i \approx y_i}$$

where the last line uses $(\supset R)$ $k+2$ times, and $(\forall R)$ $2n$ times.

When the last rule in the ND proof of $T_{fin}, \overline{\sigma}, \Lambda \vdash F$ is not (Ax), then we use standard arguments [8] to build an LKc$_\approx$ proof of $\sigma; \Lambda \vdash F$, using Lemma 3 and Lemma 2. This uses (Cut) in the cases of $(\supset E)$, $(\forall E)$, $(\mathbf{0}E)$, $(\neg\neg E)$. □

By Lemma 4 and (c), $\sigma; \Gamma, \neg\Delta \vdash \mathbf{0}$ is therefore provable in LKc$_\approx$. We then deduce $\sigma; \Gamma \vdash \Delta$ easily, using (Cut) several times. □

4.3 Cut Elimination

Theorem 2 heavily relies on the (Cut) rule. The purpose of this section is to show that all instances of (Cut) can be eliminated. We roughly follow [6], Chapter 13.

Referring to the notations of Figure 1, call a formula occurrence *principal* in a rule if it is explicitly shown in the conclusion of this rule (i.e., if it is not an occurrence inside the Γ or Δ components), and *active* in some premise if it is explicitly shown in this premise (again, this means not in Γ or Δ).

Define the *degree* $\partial(F)$ of a formula F by: $\partial(A) =_{\mathrm{df}} \partial(s \approx t) =_{\mathrm{df}} \partial(\mathbf{0}) =_{\mathrm{df}} 1$, $\partial(F \supset G) =_{\mathrm{df}} \max(\partial(F), \partial(G)) + 1$, $\partial(\forall x_\tau \cdot F) =_{\mathrm{df}} \partial(F) + 1$. In an instance of (Cut), the occurrences of the active formula F are called the *cut formulae*. Their common degree is called the *degree* of the cut rule. The *degree* $\partial(\pi)$ of a proof π is the sup of the degrees of its cut rules, or 0 if π is cut-free. Let $h(\pi)$ denote the *height* of a proof, defined as 1 if it ends in a rule with no premise, otherwise as $\max_i(h(\pi_i)) + 1$, where π_i ranges over all immediate subproofs of π.

Proposition 6. *Let σ be an idempotent substitution, such that $s\sigma = s'\sigma$ and $t\sigma = t'\sigma$; then $mgu(s \approx t, \overline{\sigma}) \equiv mgu(s' \approx t', \overline{\sigma})$.*

Proposition 7 (Substitution Replacement). *Assume $\sigma \equiv \sigma'$. If $\sigma; \Gamma \vdash \Delta$ has a proof of degree d and height h in* LKc$_\approx$*, then so does $\sigma'; \Gamma \vdash \Delta$.*

Lemma 5 (Rewriting). *If $\sigma; \Gamma \vdash \Delta$ has an* LKc$_\approx$ *proof of degree d and height n, $\sigma \neq \bot$, and $\Gamma\sigma = \Gamma'\sigma$, $\Delta\sigma = \Delta'\sigma$, then $\sigma; \Gamma' \vdash \Delta'$ has an* LKc$_\approx$ *proof of degree at most d and height at most n.*

Proof. By structural induction on the given LKc$_\approx$ proof π of $\sigma; \Gamma \vdash \Delta$, using Proposition 6 in case the last rule is $(\approx L)$. □

Lemma 6 (Weakening). *If $\sigma; \Gamma \vdash \Delta$ has a proof of degree d and height n in* LKc$_\approx$*, then $mgu(\overline{\sigma}, E); \Gamma', \Gamma \vdash \Delta, \Delta'$ has a proof of degree at most d and height at most n in* LKc$_\approx$*, for every system of equations E, for every multisets of formulas Γ' and Δ'.*

Proof. As for Lemma 3, taking care of degrees and heights. □

The main difficulty in showing cut-elimination occurs in the case of quantifier rules: we need to show that we can replace variables by terms in proofs without increasing the degree or the height of the proof. This will be Lemma 8 below.

Given two systems of equations E_1 and E_2, write $E_1 \Vdash E_2$ iff E_1 is not unifiable, or $mgu(E_1)$ unifies E_2. For short, we agree that $\bot \Vdash E$ for every system of equations E, that $\bot \Vdash \bot$, and that $E \Vdash \bot$ iff E is not unifiable. A *reflexivity equation* is an equation of the form $t \approx t$.

Lemma 7. *The following hold:*

(*i*) *If $E_1 \Vdash E_2$, then $E_1\sigma \Vdash E_2\sigma$ for every substitution σ.*
(*ii*) *If $E_1, E_2 \Vdash E_3$, and E_2 is a collection of reflexivity equations, then $E_1 \Vdash E_3$.*
(*iii*) *If $E_1\sigma, \overline{\sigma} \Vdash E_2$, then $E_1, \overline{\sigma} \Vdash E_2$.*
(*iv*) *If $E_1, \overline{\sigma} \Vdash E_2\sigma$, then also $E_1, \overline{\sigma} \Vdash E_2$.*
(*v*) *If $E_1 \Vdash E_3$, then $E_1, E_2 \Vdash E_3$.*
(*vi*) *If θ is an idempotent substitution, then $E_1\theta \Vdash E_2\theta$ iff $E_1, \overline{\theta} \Vdash E_2$.*

Proof. (*i*): let $\sigma_1 =_{\mathrm{df}} mgu(E_1)$ and $\sigma_1' =_{\mathrm{df}} mgu(E_1\sigma)$; if $\sigma_1' = \bot$, (*i*) is clear. Otherwise, σ_1' unifies $E_1\sigma$, so $\sigma\sigma_1'$ unifies E_1. Hence $\sigma_1 = mgu(E_1) \succeq \sigma\sigma_1'$. Since $E_1 \Vdash E_2$, σ_1 unifies E_2, so its instance $\sigma\sigma_1'$ also unifies E_2; so σ_1' unifies $E_2\sigma$.

(*ii*): let σ be $mgu(E_1)$: $\sigma \equiv mgu(E_1, E_2)$ as well, so σ unifies E_3.

(*iii*): let σ' be $mgu(E_1, \overline{\sigma})$. Then σ' unifies every equation $s \approx t$ in E_1, and also s with $s\sigma$ and t with $t\sigma$ (since σ' unifies $\overline{\sigma}$); so it unifies $s\sigma$ with $t\sigma$, and this for every equation $s \approx t$ in E_1. So σ' unifies $E_1\sigma$. Moreover, by definition σ' unifies $\overline{\sigma}$, so σ' unifies $E_1\sigma, \overline{\sigma}$. Since $E_1\sigma, \overline{\sigma} \Vdash E_2$, σ' unifies E_2.

(*iv*): let σ' be $mgu(E_1, \overline{\sigma})$. By assumption, σ' unifies $E_2\sigma$, so σ' unifies every equation $s\sigma \approx t\sigma$, for every $s \approx t$ in E_2. Since σ' unifies $\overline{\sigma}$, σ' unifies s with $s\sigma$ and t with $t\sigma$, so σ' unifies $s \approx t$, for every $s \approx t$ in E_2. Therefore, σ' unifies E_2.

(*v*): let σ be $mgu(E_1, E_2)$. Then σ unifies E_1, so it is an instance of $mgu(E_1)$. Since $E_1 \Vdash E_3$, σ also unifies E_3.

(*vi*), if direction: since $E_1, \overline{\theta} \Vdash E_2$, we have $E_1\theta, \overline{\theta}\theta \Vdash E_2\theta$ by (*i*). But $\overline{\theta}\theta = \{x\theta \approx x\theta\theta \mid x \in \operatorname{dom}\theta\}$. Since θ is idempotent, $x\theta\theta = x\theta$, so by (*ii*), $E_1\theta \Vdash E_2\theta$.

(*vi*), only if direction: since $E_1\theta \Vdash E_2\theta$, by (*v*) $E_1\theta, \overline{\theta} \Vdash E_2\theta$, so by (*iii*) and (*iv*), $E_1, \overline{\theta} \Vdash E_2$. □

Lemma 8. *For every idempotent substitution θ, if $\sigma; \Gamma \vdash \Delta$ has a proof of degree d and height n in* $\mathrm{LKc}_{\approx}$*, then $mgu(\overline{\sigma}\theta); \Gamma\theta \vdash \Delta\theta$ has a proof of degree at most d and height at most n.*

Proof. That is, we can apply substitutions θ to whole proofs. We prove the result by structural induction on the given proof of $\sigma; \Gamma \vdash \Delta$. We examine the last rule: if this is $(\perp L)$, the result is trivial. Otherwise, if $mgu(\overline{\sigma}\theta) = \perp$, then $mgu(\overline{\sigma}\theta); \Gamma\theta \vdash \Delta\theta$ has a proof by $(\perp L)$, with degree 0 and height 1, so the result is clear. So assume that $\sigma \neq \perp$, $mgu(\overline{\sigma}\theta) \neq \perp$, and examine each rule in turn:

– $(\approx R)$: we have derived $\sigma; \Gamma \vdash s \approx t, \Delta$, using $s\sigma = t\sigma$. The latter means $\overline{\sigma} \Vdash s \approx t$. By Lemma 7 (v), $\overline{\sigma}, \overline{\theta} \Vdash s \approx t$. By Lemma 7 (i), $\overline{\sigma}\theta, \overline{\theta}\theta \Vdash s\theta \approx t\theta$. Since θ is idempotent, $\overline{\theta}\theta$ is a collection of reflexivity equations, so by Lemma 7 (ii), $\overline{\sigma}\theta \Vdash s\theta \approx t\theta$. So $mgu(\overline{\sigma}\theta); \Gamma\theta \vdash \Delta\theta, s\theta \approx t\theta$ is provable by $(\approx R)$ again. The case of $(\approx)$ is similar.

– $(\approx L)$: we have derived $\sigma; \Gamma, s \approx t \vdash \Delta$ from a proof of $mgu(s \approx t, \overline{\sigma}); \Gamma \vdash \Delta$ of depth d and height $n-1$. By induction hypothesis: $(*)$ there is a proof of $mgu(mgu(s \approx t, \overline{\sigma})\theta); \Gamma\theta \vdash \Delta\theta$ of depth d at most and height $n-1$ at most.

We claim that: $(*)$ $mgu(\overline{\sigma}\theta, s\theta \approx t\theta)$ is an instance of $mgu(mgu(s \approx t, \overline{\sigma})\theta)$. Indeed, $\overline{\sigma}, s \approx t, \overline{\theta} \Vdash mgu(s \approx t, \overline{\sigma})$ since the mgu of the left-hand side is clearly an instance of the mgu of the right-hand side. By Lemma 7 (vi), since θ is idempotent, $\overline{\sigma}\theta, s\theta \approx t\theta \Vdash mgu(s \approx t, \overline{\sigma})\theta$. This means that $mgu(\overline{\sigma}\theta, s\theta \approx t\theta)$ unifies $mgu(s \approx t, \overline{\sigma})\theta$. This shows $(*)$.

In particular, $mgu(\overline{\sigma}\theta, s\theta \approx t\theta)$ is equivalent w.r.t. the $\equiv$ relation to the mgu of $mgu(mgu(s \approx t, \overline{\sigma})\theta)$ and some system of equations E: just take $E =_{\mathrm{df}} mgu(\overline{\sigma}\theta, s\theta \approx t\theta)$ itself. It follows from $(*)$, Lemma 6 and Proposition 7 that we can build a proof of $mgu(\overline{\sigma}\theta, s\theta \approx t\theta); \Gamma\theta \vdash \Delta\theta$ of depth d at most and height $n-1$ at most. By rule $(\approx L)$, we infer a proof of $mgu(\overline{\sigma}\theta); \Gamma\theta, s\theta \approx t\theta \vdash \Delta\theta$ of depth d at most and height n at most, as desired.

– The cases of all other rules are straightforward. □

Lemma 9. *Given any* $\mathrm{LKc}_{\approx}$ *proof of the form:*

$$\dfrac{\dfrac{\vdots\ \pi_1}{\sigma; \Gamma \vdash F_0, \Delta} \quad \dfrac{\vdots\ \pi_2}{\sigma; \Gamma, F_0 \vdash \Delta}}{\sigma; \Gamma \vdash \Delta}\ (Cut)$$

where $\partial(F_0) = d$, $\partial(\pi_1) < d$ and $\partial(\pi_2) < d$, then we can build effectively an $\mathrm{LKc}_{\approx}$ *proof π of $\sigma; \Gamma \vdash \Delta$ with $\partial(\pi) < d$.*

Proof. By induction on $h(\pi_1) + h(\pi_2)$. If F_0 is not principal either in the last rule R_1 of π_1 or in the last rule R_2 of π_2, then this is by induction. So deal with the cases where F_0 is principal in R_1 and in R_2. We have the following cases:

– $R_1 = (\approx)$, then F_0 is a non-equality atom, hence R_2 must be one of:
  • $R_2 = (\approx)$:

$$\dfrac{\dfrac{\sigma \neq \perp,\ A\sigma = F_0\sigma}{\sigma; \Gamma, A \vdash F_0, B, \Delta} \quad \dfrac{\sigma \neq \perp,\ F_0\sigma = B\sigma}{\sigma; \Gamma, A, F_0 \vdash B, \Delta}}{\sigma; \Gamma, A \vdash B, \Delta}\ (Cut) \longrightarrow \dfrac{}{\sigma; \Gamma, A \vdash B, \Delta}\ (\approx)$$

• $R_2 = (\approx\uparrow)$, then F_0 is of the form $P(s_1,\dots,s_n)$; letting $f \in \phi(P)$, with $\sigma \neq \bot$, $\vec{s}_f\sigma = \vec{t}_f\sigma$; we transform:

$$\dfrac{\dfrac{A\sigma = P(s_1,\dots,s_n)\sigma}{\sigma;\Gamma,P(t_1,\dots,t_n),A \vdash P(s_1,\dots,s_n),\Delta}(\approx) \qquad \dfrac{\begin{array}{c}\vdots\,\pi_2'\\ \sigma;\Gamma,A,P(s_1,\dots,s_n),P(t_1,\dots,t_n),\vec{s}_{\overline{f}^n} \approx \vec{t}_{\overline{f}^n} \vdash \Delta\end{array}}{\sigma;\Gamma,A,P(s_1,\dots,s_n), P(t_1,\dots,t_n) \vdash \Delta}(\approx\uparrow)}{\sigma;\Gamma,A,P(t_1,\dots,t_n) \vdash \Delta}(Cut)$$

as follows. First, $A\sigma = P(s_1,\dots,s_n)\sigma$, so A is of the form $P(u_1,\dots,u_n)$, with $u_i\sigma = s_i\sigma$ for every i, so $u_i\sigma = t_i\sigma$ for every $i \in f$ and we produce:

$$\dfrac{\dfrac{\dfrac{}{\sigma;\Gamma,A,P(t_1,\dots,t_n),\vec{u}_{\overline{f}^n} \approx \vec{t}_{\overline{f}^n} \vdash A,\Delta}(\approx) \qquad \begin{array}{c}\vdots\,\pi_2''\\ \sigma;\Gamma,A,A,P(t_1,\dots,t_n),\\ \vec{u}_{\overline{f}^n} \approx \vec{t}_{\overline{f}^n} \vdash \Delta\end{array}}{\sigma;\Gamma,A,P(t_1,\dots,t_n),\vec{u}_{\overline{f}^n} \approx \vec{t}_{\overline{f}^n} \vdash \Delta}(*)}{\sigma;\Gamma,A,P(t_1,\dots,t_n) \vdash \Delta}(\approx\uparrow)$$

where π_2'' is obtained from π_2' by Lemma 5, and $(*)$ is by induction.

– $R_1 = (\approx R)$, and F_0 is an equality $s \approx t$, then since F_0 is principal in R_2 as well, R_2 must be $(\approx L)$, and we transform:

$$\dfrac{\dfrac{\sigma \neq \bot,\ s\sigma = t\sigma}{\sigma;\Gamma \vdash s \approx t,\Delta}(\approx R) \qquad \dfrac{\begin{array}{c}\vdots\,\pi_2'\\ mgu(s \approx t,\overline{\sigma});\Gamma \vdash \Delta\end{array}}{\sigma;\Gamma,s \approx t \vdash \Delta}(\approx L)}{\sigma;\Gamma \vdash \Delta}(Cut)$$

into the proof of $\sigma;\Gamma \vdash \Delta$ obtained from π_2' by Proposition 7, noticing that, since $s\sigma = t\sigma$, $mgu(s \approx t,\overline{\sigma}) \equiv mgu(\overline{\sigma}) \equiv \sigma$.

– The case $R_1 = (\supset R)$, $R_2 = (\supset L)$ is standard [6].

– $R_1 = (\forall R)$, $R_2 = (\forall L)$; let t of type τ, and y_τ not free in $\overline{\sigma},\Gamma,\Delta$. We transform:

$$\dfrac{\dfrac{\begin{array}{c}\vdots\,\pi_1'\\ \sigma;\Gamma \vdash F[x := y_\tau]\end{array}}{\sigma;\Gamma \vdash \forall x_\tau \cdot F,\Delta}(\forall R) \qquad \dfrac{\begin{array}{c}\vdots\,\pi_2'\\ \sigma;\Gamma,\forall x_\tau \cdot F, F[x := t] \vdash \Delta\end{array}}{\sigma;\Gamma,\forall x_\tau \cdot F \vdash \Delta}(\forall L)}{\sigma;\Gamma \vdash \Delta}(Cut)$$

into:

$$\dfrac{\begin{array}{c}\vdots\,\pi_1'[y := t]\\ \sigma;\Gamma \vdash F[x := t],\Delta\end{array} \qquad \dfrac{\begin{array}{c}\vdots\,(\forall R)\\ \sigma;\Gamma \vdash \forall x_\tau \cdot F,\Delta\end{array} \quad \begin{array}{c}\vdots\,\pi_2'\\ \sigma;\Gamma,\forall x_\tau \cdot F, F[x := t] \vdash \Delta\end{array}}{\sigma;\Gamma,F[x := t] \vdash \Delta}(*)}{\sigma;\Gamma \vdash \Delta}(Cut)$$

which we now explain and justify. We may assume without loss of generality that $[y := t]$ is an idempotent substitution. By Lemma 8 there is a proof of $mgu(\overline{\sigma}); \Gamma \vdash F[x := t], \Delta$, hence also of $\sigma; \Gamma \vdash F[x := t], \Delta$ by Proposition 7: this is the proof named $\pi_1'[x := t]$ above. This proof has degree $< d$ and height at most $n - 1$. On the other hand, step $(*)$ is obtained by induction hypothesis. Note that the remaining instance of (Cut) has degree $\partial(F[x := t]) = \partial(F) < d$.

Finally, it is clear that the processes described above are all effective. □

By easy inductions on degrees, then on the structure of proofs, it follows:

Theorem 3 (Cut Elimination). *Every proof of $\sigma; \Gamma \vdash \Delta$ in* $\mathrm{LKc}_{\approx}$ *can be effectively transformed into one of the same sequent that does not use* (Cut).

5 Related Works

It appears that reducing equality to syntactic equality as we did is not a new idea. Girard ([5], Section 3.1) mentioned a similar trick in the framework of linear logic and proposed the following rules:

$$\frac{}{\vdash t \approx t} \qquad \frac{mgu(t \approx u) = \bot}{\vdash \Gamma, \neg(t \approx u)} \qquad \frac{\vdash \Gamma\sigma \quad (\sigma = mgu(t \approx u))}{\vdash \Gamma, \neg(t \approx u)}$$

This is very close to our rules $(Refl)$, $(\approx L)/(\bot L)$ and $(\approx L)$, with some immediate instantiation going on. Again, this forces an encoding of non-constructor functions as predicates, as we did. Our import is then, apart from a rigorous account of the idea above, the notion of functionalities of predicates, and the associated $(\approx\uparrow)$ rule.

Encoding functions as predicates is a very old idea, and the Principia [16] is already based on a formalization of logic without function symbols. Parikh [11] warns against it, arguing that this may increase proof length greatly: reflexivity proofs (of $s \approx s$, where s contains non-constructor function symbols) may take $O(|s|)$ proof steps to derive. However, Girard [5] argues in favor of it on esthetic grounds, while Baumgartner [2] shows that a similar technique, based on translating clauses with equality to Horn clauses without equality, gives good results in practice, while implementations remain simple enough.

6 Conclusion

We have presented a sound and complete sequent system for a natural first-order logic with free constructors and equality. This system can then be seen as an prelude to the definition of a tableau calculus, designed to automate the search for proofs involving equality, free constructors (and even structural induction, although we have not shown it here): $\mathrm{LKc}_{\approx}$ is not only sound and complete, but cuts can be eliminated, allowing for practical proof search, at least in principle. We shall deal with the problem of proof search in $\mathrm{LKc}_{\approx}$ in another paper.

References

1. B. Barras, S. Boutin, C. Cornes, J. Courant, J.-C. Filliâtre, E. Giménez, H. Herbelin, G. Huet, C. Muñoz, C. Murthy, C. Parent, C. Paulin, A. Saïbi, and B. Werner. The Coq proof assistant reference manual - version V6.1. Technical Report 0203, INRIA, 1997.
2. P. Baumgartner. A predicative encoding of equality. Slides available at `http://www.uni-koblenz.de/~peter/DFG-Impl-Equality.ps.gz`.
3. D. Bolignano. Formal verification of cryptographic protocols. In *3rd ACM Conf. on Computer and Communication Security*, 1996.
4. H. Comon. Disunification: a survey. In *Computational Logic: Essays in Honor of Alan Robinson*. MIT Press, 1991.
5. J.-Y. Girard. A fixpoint theorem in linear logic. Note on the linear logic mailing list, `http://www.csl.sri.com/linear/mailing-list-traffic/www/07/mail_3.html`, 1992.
6. J.-Y. Girard, Y. Lafont, and P. Taylor. *Proofs and Types*. Cambridge University Press, 1989.
7. J. Goubault-Larrecq. A simple deduction system for first-order logic with equality, free constructors and induction. Research report, INRIA, March 1999.
8. J. Goubault-Larrecq and I. Mackie. *Proof Theory and Automated Deduction*, volume 6 of *Applied Logic Series*. Kluwer, 1997.
9. R. Harper, R. Milner, and M. Tofte. *The Definition of Standard ML*. MIT Press, 1990.
10. A. Martelli and U. Montanari. An efficient unification algorithm. *ACM Trans. Prog. Lang. Sys.*, 4(2):258–282, 1982.
11. R. Parikh. Some results on the lengths of proofs. *Trans. AMS*, 177:29–36, 1973.
12. L. Paulson. Proving properties of security protocols by induction. In *IEEE Computer Security Foundations Workshop X*, pages 70–83, 1997.
13. G. Plotkin. Building in equational theories. *Machine Intelligence*, 7:73–90, 1972.
14. M. E. Stickel. Automated deduction by theory resolution. In *9th IJCAI*, pages 1181–1186, 1985.
15. C. Walther. Many-sorted unification. *J. ACM*, 35(1):1–17, 1988.
16. A. N. Whitehead and B. Russell. *Principia Mathematica*. Cambridge University Press, 1910, 1927.

linTAP : A Tableau Prover for Linear Logic

Heiko Mantel[1] Jens Otten[2]

[1] *German Research Center for Artificial Intelligence (DFKI)*
Stuhlsatzenhausweg 3, 66123 Saarbrücken, Germany
mantel@dfki.de

[2] *Fachgebiet Intellektik, Fachbereich Informatik, Darmstadt University of Technology*
Alexanderstr. 10, 64283 Darmstadt, Germany
jeotten@informatik.tu-darmstadt.de

Abstract. linTAP is a tableau prover for the multiplicative and exponential fragment $\mathcal{M}?\mathcal{LL}$ of Girards linear logic. It proves the validity of a given formula by constructing an analytic tableau and ensures the linear validity using prefix unification. We present the tableau calculus used by linTAP, an algorithm for prefix unification in linear logic, the linTAP implementation, and some experimental results obtained with linTAP.

1 Introduction

Linear logic [12] can be regarded as a refinement of classical as well as of intuitionistic logic. It subsumes these logics because both of them can be embedded into linear logic. Mainly, linear logic has become known as a very expressive logic of action and change. It has found applications in logic programming [14,20], planing [19], modeling concurrent computation [11], and other areas. Its expressiveness, however results in a high complexity. Validity is undecidable for propositional linear logic. The multiplicative fragment is already $\mathcal{NP}$-complete [16]. The complexity of the multiplicative exponential fragment ($\mathcal{MELL}$) is still unknown. Consequently, proof search in linear logic is difficult to automate.

Various calculi have been developed for linear logic. Beginning with the sequent calculus and proof nets by Girard [12], several optimizations have been proposed. More recently, the connection method has been extended to fragments of linear logic [8,9,15,17]. In this article, we propose a tableau calculus for $\mathcal{MELL}$ and for $\mathcal{M}?\mathcal{LL}$ which is the theoretical basis for our theorem prover linTAP.

linTAP is implemented in a very compact way but uses sophisticated techniques to reduce the search space and thus follows the idea of *lean theorem proving*. It was inspired by the classical tableau prover lean*TAP* [2,3] and by the intuitionistic tableau prover ileanTAP [21]. Like in ileanTAP, string unification is used to deal with the non-permutabilities specific to linear logic. This approach has been invented by Wallen in the context of matrix characterizations for non-classical logics [25]. The prefixes used by linTAP are motivated by a matrix characterization for $\mathcal{MELL}$ [17]. In our implementation of linTAP we use a lean*TAP* like technique for path checking and then try to unify the so-called prefixes of atoms which are closing the branches of the tableau proof like in ileanTAP. Some additional checks are required because of the resource sensitivity of linear logic. Some of these checks are tested already during proof construction.

After some preliminaries we propose a tableau calculus for $\mathcal{MELL}$ in Section 3. The application of a calculus rule to a formula de-constructs the formula and constructs a prefix for the resulting sub-formulas. An algorithm for the unification of such prefixes is presented in Section 4. A tableau calculus for $\mathcal{M?LL}$, where ? and ! can only occur, respectively, positvely and negatively, some details about our theorem prover linTAP, and some experimantal results are discussed in Section 5. We conclude with some remarks on related and on future work.

2 Preliminaries

Linear logic [12] treats formulas like resources that disappear after their use unless they are explicitly marked as reusable. It can be seen as the outcome of removing the rules for contraction and weakening from the classical sequent calculus and re-introducing them in a controlled manner. Linear negation $^\perp$ is involutive like classical negation. The two traditions for writing the sequent rule for conjunction result in two different conjunctions $\otimes$ and & and two different disjunctions $⅋$ and $\oplus$. The constant `true` splits up into $\mathbf{1}$ and $\top$ and `false` into $\perp$ and $\mathbf{0}$. The unary connectives ? and ! mark formulas for a controlled application of weakening and contraction. Quantifiers $\forall$ and $\exists$ are added as usual.

Linear logic can be divided into the multiplicative, additive, and exponential fragment. While in the multiplicative fragment resources are used exactly once, resource sharing is enforced in the additive fragment. Exponentials mark formulas as reusable. All fragments exist on their own right and can be combined freely. The full power of linear logic comes from combining all of them.

In this article we focus on multiplicative exponential linear logic ($\mathcal{MELL}$ and $\mathcal{M?LL}$), the combination of the multiplicative and exponential fragments, leaving the additive fragment and the quantifiers out of consideration. $^\perp$, $\otimes$, $⅋$, $\multimap$, $\mathbf{1}$, $\perp$, !, and ? are the connectives of $\mathcal{MELL}$. In $\mathcal{M?LL}$, ? and ! only occur, respectively, with positive and negative polarity. Linear negation $^\perp$ expresses the difference between resources that are to be used up and resources to be produced. In order to use up $F^\perp$ a resource F must be produced. Having a resource $F_1 \otimes F_2$ means having F_1 as well as F_2. $F_1 \multimap F_2$ allows the construction of F_2 from F_1. $F_1 ⅋ F_2$ is equivalent to $F_1{}^\perp \multimap F_2$ and to $F_2{}^\perp \multimap F_1$. Having a resource $\mathbf{1}$ has no impact while nothing can be constructed when $\perp$ is used up. A resource $!F$ acts like a machine which produces any number of copies of F. During the construction of $!F$ only such machines can be used. ? is the dual to !.

We adopt Smullyan's uniform notation to $\mathcal{MELL}$. A *signed formula* $\varphi = F^k$ denotes an occurrence of F in Δ or Γ. Depending on the *label* F and its *polarity* $k \in \{+, -\}$, a signed formula will receive a *type* α, β, ν, π, o, τ, ω, or a according to the tables below. The functions $succ_1$ and $succ_2$ return the major signed subformulas of a signed formula. Note that during the decomposition of a formula the polarity switches only for $^\perp$ and $\multimap$. We use type symbols as meta-variables for signed formulas of the respective type, e.g. α stands for a signed formula of type α and a stands for atomic formulas, i.e. signed predicates.

The validity of a linear logic formula can be proven syntactically by using a sequent calculus. For multi-sets Γ and Δ of formulas $\Gamma \longrightarrow \Delta$ is called a *sequent*.

a	A^-	A^+
τ	$\bot^-$	$\mathbf{1}^+$
ω	$\mathbf{1}^-$	$\bot^+$

α	$(F_1 \otimes F_2)^-$	$(F_1 \parr F_2)^+$	$(F_1 \multimap F_2)^+$
$succ_1(\alpha)$	F_1^-	F_1^+	F_1^-
$succ_2(\alpha)$	F_2^-	F_2^+	F_2^+

β	$(F_1 \otimes F_2)^+$	$(F_1 \parr F_2)^-$	$(F_1 \multimap F_2)^-$
$succ_1(\beta)$	F_1^+	F_1^-	F_1^+
$succ_2(\beta)$	F_2^+	F_2^-	F_2^-

o	$(F^\bot)^-$	$(F^\bot)^+$
$succ_1(o)$	F^+	F^-

ν	$(!F)^-$	$?F^+$
$succ_1(\nu)$	F^-	F^+

π	$(?F)^-$	$!F^+$
$succ_1(\pi)$	F^-	F^+

Table 1. Uniform notation for signed $\mathcal{MELL}$ formulas

It can be understood as the specification of a transformation which constructs Δ from Γ. The formulas in Γ are connected implicitly by $\otimes$ while the formulas in Δ are connected implicitly by $\parr$.

A sequent calculus Σ_1' for $\mathcal{MELL}$ based on our uniform notation is depicted in Table 2. Omitting the π-rule yields a calculus for $\mathcal{M?LL}$. In a rule, the sequents above the line are the *premises* and the one below is the *conclusion*. A *principal formula* is a formula that occurs in the conclusion but not in any premise. Formulas that occur in a premise but not in the conclusion are called *active*. All other formulas compose the *context*. Σ_1' is correct and complete wrt. Girard's original sequent calculus [12].

$$\frac{}{\longrightarrow A^+, A^-}\ axiom \qquad \frac{}{\longrightarrow \tau}\ \tau \qquad \frac{\longrightarrow \Upsilon}{\longrightarrow \Upsilon, \omega}\ \omega \qquad \frac{\longrightarrow \Upsilon, succ_1(o)}{\longrightarrow \Upsilon, o}\ o$$

$$\frac{\longrightarrow \Upsilon, succ_1(\alpha), succ_2(\alpha)}{\longrightarrow \Upsilon, \alpha}\ \alpha \qquad \frac{\longrightarrow \Upsilon_1, succ_1(\beta) \quad \longrightarrow \Upsilon_2, succ_2(\beta)}{\longrightarrow \Upsilon_1, \Upsilon_2, \beta}\ \beta$$

$$\frac{\longrightarrow \Upsilon, succ_1(\nu)}{\longrightarrow \Upsilon, \nu}\ \nu \qquad \frac{\longrightarrow \nu, succ_1(\pi)}{\longrightarrow \nu, \pi}\ \pi \qquad \frac{\longrightarrow \Upsilon}{\longrightarrow \Upsilon, \nu}\ w \qquad \frac{\longrightarrow \Upsilon, \nu, \nu}{\longrightarrow \Upsilon, \nu}\ c$$

Table 2. Sequent calculus Σ_1' for $\mathcal{MELL}$ in uniform notation

In *analytic proof search*, one starts with the sequent to be proven and reduces it by application of rules until the *axiom*-rule or the τ-rule can be applied. There are several choice points within this process. As in classical logic, first, a principal formula must be chosen. Unless the principal formula has type ν, this choice determines which rule must be applied. Formulas of type ν are *generic*. They can be duplicated using the *contraction* rule c and are removed by the *weakening* rule w. When the β-rule is applied the context of the sequent must be split, i.e. Υ_1 and Υ_2 must be a partition of the context. Several solutions have been proposed in order to optimize these choices [1,10,23,6,13]. Additional difficulties arise from the rules *axiom*, τ, and π. The rules *axiom* and τ require an empty context which expresses that all formulas must be used up in a proof. The π rule requires that all formulas in the context are of type ν. The careful handling of the context reflects the resource sensitivity of linear logic.

Example 1. Figure 1 presents a Σ_1'-proof of $\varphi = (((A \parr \bot) \otimes !A) \parr ?(A^\bot))^+$. We abbreviate occurrences of subformulas of φ by position markers as shown in the table on the right. Note that any proof of φ requires that the contraction rule c is applied before the β-rule.

$$\frac{\quad}{\to a_{1111}, a_{1211}}\ axiom$$
$$\frac{}{\to a_{1111}, o_{121}}\ o$$
$$\frac{}{\to a_{1111}, \nu_{12}}\ \nu$$
$$\frac{}{\to a_{1111}, \omega_{1112}, \nu_{12}}\ \omega$$
$$\frac{}{\to \alpha_{111}, \nu_{12}}\ \alpha$$

$$\frac{\quad}{\to a_{1121}, a'_{1211}}\ axiom$$
$$\frac{}{\to a_{1121}, o'_{121}}\ o$$
$$\frac{}{\to a_{1121}, \nu'_{12}}\ \nu$$
$$\frac{}{\to \pi_{112}, \nu'_{12}}\ \pi$$
$$\beta$$

$$\frac{}{\to \beta_{11}, \nu_{12}, \nu'_{12}}$$
$$\frac{}{\to \beta_{11}, \nu_{12}}\ c$$
$$\frac{}{\to \alpha_1}\ \alpha$$

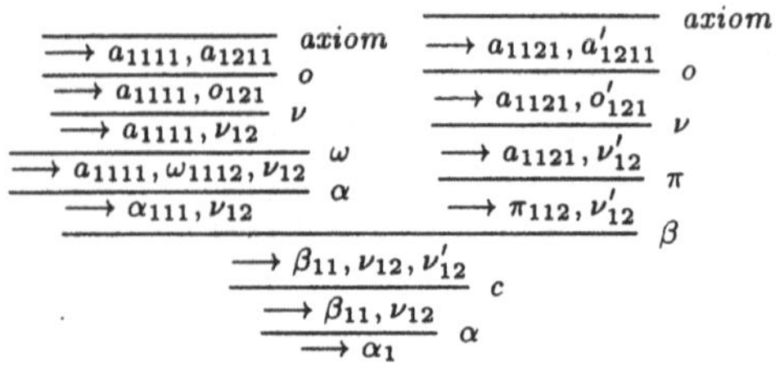

$lab(\varphi')$	φ'
$((A \,⅋\, \bot) \otimes !A) \,⅋\, ?(A^\bot)$	α_1
$(A \,⅋\, \bot) \otimes !A$	β_{11}
$A \,⅋\, \bot$	α_{111}
A	a_{1111}
$\bot$	ω_{1112}
$!A$	π_{112}
A	a_{1121}
$?(A^\bot)$	ν_{12}, ν'_{12}
$A^\bot$	o_{121}, o'_{121}
A	a_{1211}, a'_{1211}

Fig. 1. An example Σ'_1-proof.

3 A Tableau Calculus

The tableau calculus presented in this section is motivated by a matrix characterization for $\mathcal{MELL}$ [17].

Basic Definitions. We assume disjoint sets Φ^M, Ψ^M, Φ^E, and Ψ^E of characters. ϕ^M, ψ^M, ϕ^E, and ψ^E are used as meta-variables for characters from the respective set. Elements of Φ^M and Ψ^M are called *multiplicative* and elements of Φ^E, and Ψ^E are called *exponential*. Characters in Φ^M and Φ^E are called *variable* and characters in Ψ^M and Ψ^E are called *constant*. The intuition is that variable characters can be substituted while constant characters cannot. A *prefix* s is a string over these sets, i.e. $s \in (\Phi^M \cup \Psi^M \cup \Phi^E \cup \Psi^E)^*$. A *multiplicative string substitution* is a mapping $\sigma_M : \Phi^M \to (\Phi^M \cup \Psi^M)^*$. An *exponential string substitution* is a mapping $\sigma_E : \Phi^E \to (\Phi^M \cup \Psi^M \cup \Phi^E \cup \Psi^E)^*$. A *string substitution* is a mapping $\sigma : (\Phi^M \cup \Phi^E) \to (\Phi^M \cup \Psi^M \cup \Phi^E \cup \Psi^E)^*$ such that the restriction of σ to Φ^M is a multiplicative string substitution and the restriction to Φ^E is an exponential string substitution. We extend σ homomorphically to strings from $(\Phi^M \cup \Psi^M \cup \Phi^E \cup \Psi^E)^*$ where σ is the identity on constant characters.[1]

A *position* p is a string from $\mathcal{P} = \{l, r\}^* \cup \{0\}$. p is a *sub-position* of a position p' if p' is a proper prefix of p, e.g. lrl is a sub-position of lr. A *multiplicity* μ is a function which assigns natural numbers to positions, i.e. $\mu : \mathcal{P} \to \mathbb{N}$. Using multiplicities, we determine the number of duplicates of generic formulas in a tableau. We mark each occurrence of a formula in a tableau proof with a position. In a tableau for φ, φ is marked with position 0. If φ is marked with p then the left and right subformula of φ are marked with $p \circ l$ and $p \circ r$, respectively. For a generic formula φ the jth instance of the subformula is marked with $p \circ l^j$.

Definition 2. Let φ be a signed formula, s be a prefix, and p be a position. Then $\varphi : s\ (p)$ is called a *prefixed formula*. If φ is of type a, τ, ω, or ν then $[\varphi] : s\ (p)$ is *prefixed formula* as well. We refer to the later kind as *marked prefixed formulas*.

The type of a prefixed formula $\varphi : s\ (p)$ is the type of φ. We use the same meta-variables for prefixed formulas as for signed formulas. If necessary, we will point out what kind of formula is denoted by a specific meta-variable.

Definition 3. A *connection* is a one-element set containing a marked prefixed formula of type τ or a two-element set containing two marked atomic prefixed formulas with the same label and opposite signs. A *weakening map* is a set of marked prefixed formulas of type ω and of type ν with multiplicity 0.

---

[1] For $\mathcal{M?LL}$ the set Ψ^E is not needed. Thus, Φ^M and Φ^E need not be distinguished.

For example, $\{[\mathbf{1}]^+ : s'\ (p')\}$ and $\{[A]^+ : s''\ (p''), [A]^- : s'''\ (p''')\}$ are connections; $\emptyset$, $\{[\bot]^+ : t'\ (q')\}$, and $\{[?F]^+ : t''\ (q''), [\mathbf{1}]^- : t'''\ (q''')\}$ are weakening maps.

Note, that Definition 3 imposes the same restrictions on the elements of a connection as the Σ_1'-rules τ and *axiom* do for the principal formulas in order to close a branch. It requires the same properties for the elements of a weakening map as the Σ_1'-rules ω and w do for the principal formulas in order to remove a formula. This resembles the relation between a proof according to the connection method and the set of sequent proofs represented by it [17]. It should be helpful to keep this in mind in order to grasp the intuition behind the following definitions.

Complementarity Conditions and Closed Tableaux. We now define some *complementarity conditions* which are crucial for our definition of closed tableaux in $\mathcal{MELL}$. Each condition is motivated by a property of the sequent calculus Σ_1' in Table 2 and, if possible, an intuitive explanation based on the resource sensitivity of linear logic is given. In the following we always assume $\mathcal{C}$ to be a set of connections, $\mathcal{W}$ to be a weakening map, and σ to be a string substitution.

- Resources can be used at most once and disappear after their use. In Σ_1' this is reflected by the lack of a general rule for contraction and by the context split in the β-rule. *$\mathcal{C}$ is linear* if each prefixed formula occurs in at most one connection. *$\mathcal{C}$ and $\mathcal{W}$ are linear* if $\mathcal{C}$ is linear and p is not a sub-position of p' for any $\varphi : s\ (p)$ which occurs in a connection from $\mathcal{C}$ and any $\varphi' : s'\ (p') \in \mathcal{W}$. Intuitively, this linearity condition says that a formula cannot contribute to an axiom in a corresponding sequent proof if it has been weakened and that it cannot contribute to more than one axiom.
- Resources cannot disappear without a reason. They must be consumed. In Σ_1' this is reflected by the lack of a general rule for weakening and by the requirement of an empty context in the rules *axiom* and τ. *$\mathcal{C}$ and $\mathcal{W}$ are relevant for a set of prefixed formulas Υ* if each $\varphi : s\ (p) \in \Upsilon$ occurs at least in one connection or a $\varphi' : s'\ (p') \in \Upsilon$ occurs in $\mathcal{W}$ where p is a sub-position of p'. Intuitively, relevance demands for a corresponding sequent proof that a formula must contribute to an axiom unless it has been weakened.
- In Σ_1', the context only is divided by the application of a β-rule. Let $\boldsymbol{\beta}$ be a set of prefixed formulas of type β and let $\boldsymbol{\beta}_{\mathcal{W}} = \{(\beta : s\ (p)) \in \boldsymbol{\beta} \mid$ *there is no* $(\varphi : s'\ (p')) \in \mathcal{W}$ *such that p is a sub-position of p'*$\}$. *$\mathcal{C}$ and $\mathcal{W}$ have the right cardinality for $\boldsymbol{\beta}$* if $|\mathcal{C}| = |\boldsymbol{\beta}_{\mathcal{W}}| + 1$.
- In Σ_1', certain rule applications can be permuted while others cannot. The non-permutability of rules for linear logic has been investigated e.g. in [10]. The existence of a suitable order of non-permutable rule applications is expressed by the unifiability of prefixes. *$\mathcal{C}$ and $\mathcal{W}$ are unified by σ* if
  - for each $c \in \mathcal{C}$ the prefixes of all elements of c are identical under σ and
  - for each $\varphi \in \mathcal{W}$ there is a $c \in \mathcal{C}$ such that the prefix of φ is an initial substring of the prefix of the elements of c under σ.

Definition 4. Let φ be a prefixed formula.

1. The one-branch tree φ is a *tableau* for φ.
2. If T is a tableau for φ and T^* results from T by the application of a tableau expansion rule from Table 3 then T^* is a tableau for φ.

α-rules

$$\frac{(F_1 \parr F_2)^+ :\ s \quad (p)}{\begin{array}{ll} F_1^+ & : s \circ s' \ (p \circ l) \\ F_2^+ & : s \circ s' \ (p \circ r) \end{array}} \qquad \frac{(F_1 \otimes F_2)^- :\ s \quad (p)}{\begin{array}{ll} F_1^- & : s \circ s' \ (p \circ l) \\ F_2^- & : s \circ s' \ (p \circ r) \end{array}} \qquad \frac{(F_1 \multimap F_2)^+ :\ s \quad p}{\begin{array}{ll} F_1^- & : s \circ s' \ (p \circ l) \\ F_2^+ & : s \circ s' \ (p \circ r) \end{array}}$$

ν-rules (for $\mu(F_1) > 0$)

$$\frac{(!F_1)^- \ :\ s \quad (p)}{\begin{array}{lll} (F_1^1)^- & : s \circ s' \circ \phi^E_{pol} & (p \circ l) \\ \vdots & \vdots & \vdots \\ (F_1^{\mu(F_1)})^- & : s \circ s' \circ \phi^E_{pol^{\mu(F_1)}} & (p \circ l^{\mu(F_1)}) \end{array}} \qquad \frac{(?F_1)^+ \ :\ s \quad (p)}{\begin{array}{lll} (F_1^1)^+ & : s \circ s' \circ \phi^E_{pol} & (p \circ l) \\ \vdots & \vdots & \vdots \\ (F_1^{\mu(F_1)})^+ & : s \circ s' \circ \phi^E_{pol^{\mu(F_1)}} & (p \circ l^{\mu(F_1)}) \end{array}}$$

w-rules (for $\mu(F_1) = 0$)

$$\frac{(!F_1)^- \ :\ s \ (p)}{[!F_1]^- : s \circ s' \ (p \circ l)} \qquad \frac{(?F_1)^+ \ :\ s \ (p)}{[?F_1]^+ : s \circ s' \ (p \circ l)}$$

ω-rules

$$\frac{\mathbf{1}^- \ :\ s \ (p)}{[\mathbf{1}]^- : s \circ s' \ (p \circ l)} \qquad \frac{\bot^+ \ :\ s \ (p)}{[\bot]^+ : s \circ s' \ (p \circ l)}$$

a-rules

$$\frac{A^- \ :\ s \ (p)}{[A]^- : s \circ s' \circ \phi^M_p (p \circ l)} \qquad \frac{A^+ \ :\ s \ (p)}{[A]^+ : s \circ s' \circ \phi^M_p (p \circ l)}$$

τ-rules

$$\frac{\bot^- \ :\ s \ (p)}{[\bot]^- : s \circ s' \circ \phi^M_p (p \circ l)} \qquad \frac{\mathbf{1}^+ \ :\ s \ (p)}{[\mathbf{1}]^+ : s \circ s' \circ \phi^M_p (p \circ l)}$$

$s' = \psi^M_p$ if $s = \tilde{s} \circ \phi$ with $\phi \in \Phi^E \cup \Phi^M$
$s' = \varepsilon$ if $s = \tilde{s} \circ \psi$ with $\psi \in \Psi^E \cup \Psi^M$

β-rules

$$\frac{(F_1 \parr F_2)^- \ :\ s \ (p)}{F_1^- : s \circ s'' \ (p \circ l) \ \mid \ F_2^- : s \circ s'' \ (p \circ r)} \qquad \frac{(F_1 \otimes F_2)^+ \ :\ s \ (p)}{F_1^+ : s \circ s'' \ (p \circ l) \ \mid \ F_2^+ : s \circ s'' \ (p \circ r)}$$

$$\frac{(F_1 \multimap F_2)^- \ :\ s \ (p)}{F_1^+ : s \circ s'' \ (p \circ l) \ \mid \ F_2^- : s \circ s'' \ (p \circ r)}$$

π-rules

$$\frac{(!F_1)^+ \ :\ s \quad (p)}{F_1^+ \ :\ s \circ s'' \circ \psi^E_{pol} \ (p \circ l)} \qquad \frac{(?F_1)^- \ :\ s \quad (p)}{F_1^- \ :\ s \circ s'' \circ \psi^E_{pol} \ (p \circ l)}$$

$s'' = \phi^M_p$ if $s = \tilde{s} \circ \psi$ with $\psi \in \Psi^E \cup \Psi^M$
$s'' = \varepsilon$ if $s = \tilde{s} \circ \phi$ with $\phi \in \Phi^E \cup \Phi^M$

o-rules

$$\frac{(F_1{}^{\bot})^+ \ :\ s \ (p)}{F_1^- \ :\ s \ (p \circ l)} \qquad \frac{(F_1{}^{\bot})^- \ :\ s \ (p)}{F_1^+ \ :\ s \ (p \circ l)}$$

Table 3. A prefixed-based tableau calculus for $\mathcal{MELL}$

Expansion rules are applied as usual [7]. The application of a rule de-constructs a formula, possibly enlarges the prefix, and constructs a position. A tableau is *strict* if each occurrence of a formula is reduced at most once on a branch. In a strict tableau, prefixed formulas can be uniquely identified by their positions. In the sequel, we will consider only strict tableaux and will extensively use the isomorphism between formulas in a given tableaux and their positions.

Definition 5. A *branch of a tableau is closed* by a connection c if all elements of c occur on that branch.

Let T be a tableau for φ, Υ_T be the set of prefixed formulas of type a, τ, ω, and ν (with multiplicity 0) which occur in T, and β_T be the set of prefixed formulas of type β in T. Further, let $\mathcal{C}$ be a set of connections where the elements of connections are from Υ_T. Let $\mathcal{W}$ be a weakening map with elements from Υ_T. Let σ be a string substitution. Then $\mathcal{C}$ and $\mathcal{W}$ *fulfill linearity in* T if $\mathcal{C}$ and $\mathcal{W}$ are linear. $\mathcal{C}$ and $\mathcal{W}$ *fulfill relevance in* T if $\mathcal{C}$ and $\mathcal{W}$ are relevant for Υ_T. $\mathcal{C}$ and $\mathcal{W}$ *fulfill cardinality in* T if $\mathcal{C}$ and $\mathcal{W}$ have the right cardinality for β_T. $\mathcal{C}$, $\mathcal{W}$, and σ *fulfill unifiability for* T if $\mathcal{C}$ and $\mathcal{W}$ are unified by σ.

Definition 6. Let T be a tableau for a prefixed formula φ. Further, let $\mathcal{C}$ be a set of connections, $\mathcal{W}$ be a weakening map, and σ be a string substitution. T is *closed by* $\mathcal{C}$*,* $\mathcal{W}$*, and* σ *iff* the following conditions hold:

- Each branch of T is closed by a connection from $\mathcal{C}$.
- $\mathcal{C}$, $\mathcal{W}$, and σ fulfill linearity, relevance, cardinality, and unifiability for T.

Example 7. A tableau T for $((A \parr \bot) \otimes !A) \parr ?(A^{\bot})$ is depicted in Figure 2. The set of connections $\mathcal{C}=\{\{0llll, 0rlll\}, \{0lrll, 0rllll\}\}$ closes the branches of the tableau. Let $\mathcal{W} = \{0llrl\}$ be a weakening map and σ be a substitution with $\sigma(\phi^E_{0rl}) = \phi^M_{0l}\psi^M_{0ll}\phi^M_{aux1}$, $\sigma(\phi^M_{0lll}) = \phi^M_{aux1}\psi^M_{0rll}\phi^M_{0rll}$, $\sigma(\phi^E_{0rll}) = \phi^M_{0l}\psi^E_{0lrl}\phi^M_{aux2}$, and $\sigma(\phi^M_{0lrl}) = \phi^M_{aux2}\psi^M_{0rlll}\phi^M_{0rlll}$. Then T is closed by $\mathcal{C}$, $\mathcal{W}$, and σ.

The following theorems state that the tableau calculus in Table 3 is correct and complete. In order to follow the proof sketches prior knowledge of [17] is required.

Theorem 8 (Correctness). *If there is a closed tableau for a prefixed formula* $\varphi = F^+ : \psi^M_0\ (0)$ *for some multiplicity* μ *then* F *is valid.*

Proof Sketch: Let T be a tableau for φ with multiplicity μ which is closed by $\mathcal{C}$, $\mathcal{W}$, and σ. We construct a matrix proof for the matrix M of φ. The correctness of the matrix characterization in [17] then implies that φ is valid.

For every prefixed formula φ' in T there is a corresponding node n in M with the same label, polarity, type, and ancestors which are equivalent under this relation. Let m be an injective mapping which assigns to a formula in T a corresponding node in M. All non-special nodes in M are in the image of m. We define the application of m to sets as the application of m to the elements. For any path of leaves P through M there is branch B in T with marked formulas Υ_B such that $m(\Upsilon_B) \subseteq P$ holds. Let $\mathcal{C}_M = m(\mathcal{C})$ and $\mathcal{W}_M = m(\mathcal{W})$. Since all branches of T are closed by $\mathcal{C}$, $\mathcal{C}_M$ is spanning for M. $\mathcal{C}_M$ and $\mathcal{W}_M$ are linear,

$$1: ((A \,\mathord{\invamp}\, \bot) \otimes !A) \,\mathord{\invamp}\, ?(A^\bot)^+ \; : \; \psi_0^M \;\; (0)$$

α on (1)

$$2: (A \,\mathord{\invamp}\, \bot) \otimes !A^+ \; : \; \psi_0^M \;\; (0l)$$
$$3: \; ?(A^\bot)^+ \qquad\quad : \; \psi_0^M \;\; (0r)$$

ν on (3)

$$4: (A^\bot)^+ \; : \; \psi_0^M \phi_{0rl}^E \;\; (0rl)$$
$$5: (A^\bot)^+ \; : \; \psi_0^M \phi_{0rll}^E \;\; (0rll)$$

β on (2) β on (2)

$$6: (A \,\mathord{\invamp}\, \bot)^+ \; : \; \psi_0^M \phi_{0l}^M \;\; (0ll) \qquad\qquad 7: (!A)^+ \; : \; \psi_0^M \phi_{0l}^M \;\; (0lr)$$

α on (6) π on (7)

$$8: A^+ \; : \; \psi_0^M \phi_{0l}^M \psi_{0ll}^M \;\; (0lll)$$
$$9: \bot^+ \; : \; \psi_0^M \phi_{0l}^M \psi_{0ll}^M \;\; (0llr) \qquad\qquad 14: A^+ \; : \; \psi_0^M \phi_{0l}^M \psi_{0lrl}^E \;\; (0lrl)$$

o on (4) o on (5)

$$10: A^- \; : \; \psi_0^M \phi_{0rl}^E \;\; (0rll) \qquad\qquad 15: A^- \; : \; \psi_0^M \phi_{0rll}^E \;\; (0rlll)$$

ω on (9) $\quad$ a on (8), (10) a on (14), (15)

$$11: [\bot]^+ \; : \; \psi_0^M \phi_{0l}^M \psi_{0ll}^M \qquad\qquad (0llrl) \qquad 16: [A]^+ \; : \; \psi_0^M \phi_{0l}^M \psi_{0lrl}^E \phi_{0lrl}^M \qquad (0lrll)$$
$$12: [A]^+ \; : \; \psi_0^M \phi_{0l}^M \psi_{0ll}^M \phi_{0lll}^M \qquad (0llll) \qquad 17: [A]^- \; : \; \psi_0^M \phi_{0rll}^E \psi_{0rlll}^M \phi_{0rlll}^M \quad (0rllll)$$
$$13: [A]^- \; : \; \psi_0^M \phi_{0rl}^E \psi_{0rll}^M \phi_{0rll}^M \;\; (0rlll)$$

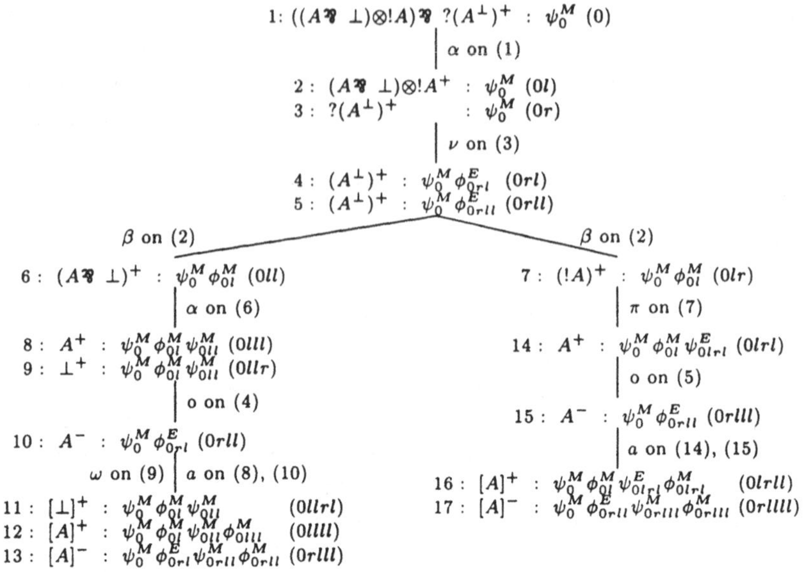

Fig. 2. An example tableau

relevant, and have the cardinality property for M. Marked formulas of type a, τ, ω, and ν have the same prefix (under renaming) as the correspondent nodes in M. Therefore, σ is a unifier for $\mathcal{C}_M$ and $\mathcal{W}_M$ in M. Thus, M is complementary for $\mathcal{C}_M$, $\mathcal{W}_M$, and σ.

Theorem 9 (Completeness). *If a formula F is valid then there exists a closed tableau for the prefixed formula $\varphi = F^+ : \psi_0^M (0)$.*

Proof Sketch: From any matrix proof of the matrix M of φ a closed tableau for φ can be constructed. The completeness of the matrix characterization then implies that a tableau for any valid formula exists.

The crucial step is that if there is a complementary matrix M' for φ with multiplicity μ' then there is a multiplicity μ, a set of connections $\mathcal{C}$, a weakening map $\mathcal{W}$ without elements of type ϕ^E, and a string substitution σ such that the matrix M for φ with multiplicity μ is complementary for $\mathcal{C}$, $\mathcal{W}$, and σ. Using $\mathcal{C}$, $\mathcal{W}$, and σ, a closed tableau for φ can be constructed.

4 Prefix Unification

The computation of a string substitution σ is one of the key components necessary to perform proof search in the prefix-based tableau calculus introduced in the previous section. A single string substitution σ has to unify the prefixes of each connection in the set $\mathcal{C}$. Furthermore the weakening map $\mathcal{W}$ has to fulfill the unifiability condition under this substitution σ. This condition can be reduced to unification since a prefix s is an initial substring of a prefix t iff $s \circ V$ and t can be unified where V is a new variable.

String unification in general is rather complicated but fortunately unifying prefixes is much easier since there are two *restrictions on prefixes*: prefixes are strings without duplicates and in any two prefixes (corresponding to atoms of the same formula) equal characters can only occur within a common substring at the beginning of the prefixes. In [22] we introduced a prefix unification algorithm, so-called *T-String Unification*, to unify prefixes in matrix based proof methods for non-classical logics, i.e. intuitionistic logic and the modal logics D, K, D4, K4, S5, and T. Only minor modifications are necessary to adapt this algorithm to deal with the prefixes arising in our tableau calculus for $\mathcal{MELL}$: we have to distinguish between characters (i.e. positions) of type ϕ^M/ψ^M and type ϕ^E/ψ^E.

Similar to the ideas of Martelli and Montanari [18] we consider the process of unification as a sequence of transformation steps. We start with the given set of (prefix-) equations $\Gamma = \{p_1{=}t_1, \ldots, p_n{=}t_n\}$ and an empty substitution $\sigma{=}\emptyset$. Each transformation step replaces the tuple (Γ,σ) by a modified tuple (Γ',σ') where Γ' is the result of replacing one equation $\{p_i{=}t_i\}$ in Γ by $\{p_i'{=}t_i'\}$ and applying the substitution σ' to the resulting equation set. The algorithm is described by transformation rules " $\{s_i{=}t_i\},\sigma \rightarrow \{s_i'{=}t_i'\},\sigma'$ " which can be applied nondeterministically to the selected equation $\{s_i{=}t_i\} \in \Gamma$. The set Γ is solvable, iff there are some transformation steps transforming the tuple $(\Gamma,\emptyset)$ into the tuple $(\emptyset,\tilde{\sigma})$. In this case the substitution $\tilde{\sigma}$ represents an idempotent most general unifier for Γ. The set of all resulting most general unifiers is *minimal*. For technical reasons we divide the right part t_i of each equation into two parts $t_i^1|t_i^2$ where the left part contains the substring which is not yet assigned to a variable. Therefore we start with the set of prefixes $\Gamma = \{s_1{=}\varepsilon|t_1, \ldots, s_n{=}\varepsilon|t_n\}$.

Definition 10. Let $\mathcal{V}{=}\Phi^M{\cup}\Phi^E$ be a set of variables, $\mathcal{C}{=}\Psi^M{\cup}\Psi^E$ be a set of constants, $\tilde{\mathcal{V}}^M$ and $\tilde{\mathcal{V}}^E$ be disjoint sets of *auxiliary variables*, $\mathcal{V}'{=}\tilde{\mathcal{V}}^M{\cup}\tilde{\mathcal{V}}^E$ (with $\mathcal{V}{\cap}\mathcal{V}'{=}\emptyset$), $\mathcal{V}^M{=}\Phi^M{\cup}\tilde{\mathcal{V}}^M$, and $\mathcal{V}^E{=}\Phi^E{\cup}\tilde{\mathcal{V}}^E$. The set of *transformation rules for* $\mathcal{MELL}$ is defined in Table 4.

R1.	$\{\varepsilon = \varepsilon\|\varepsilon\},\ \sigma$	$\rightarrow$	$\{\},\ \sigma$	
R2.	$\{\varepsilon = \varepsilon\|t^+\},\ \sigma$	$\rightarrow$	$\{t^+ = \varepsilon\|\varepsilon\},\ \sigma$	
R3.	$\{Xs = \varepsilon\|Xt\},\ \sigma$	$\rightarrow$	$\{s = \varepsilon\|t\},\ \sigma$	
R4.	$\{Cs = \varepsilon\|Vt\},\ \sigma$	$\rightarrow$	$\{Vt = \varepsilon\|Cs\},\ \sigma$	
R5.	$\{Vs = z\|\varepsilon\},\ \sigma$	$\rightarrow$	$\{s = \varepsilon\|\varepsilon\},\ \{V\backslash z\}\cup\sigma$	
R6.	$\{Vs = \varepsilon\|C_1t\},\ \sigma$	$\rightarrow$	$\{s = \varepsilon\|C_1t\},\ \{V\backslash\varepsilon\}\cup\sigma$	
R7.	$\{Vs = z\|C_1C_2t\},\ \sigma$	$\rightarrow$	$\{s = \varepsilon\|C_2t\},\ \{V\backslash zC_1\}\cup\sigma$	$(V \in \mathcal{V}^E$ or $C_1 \in \Psi^M)$
R8.	$\{Vs^+ = \varepsilon\|V_1t\},\ \sigma$	$\rightarrow$	$\{V_1t = V\|s^+\},\ \sigma$	$(V_1 \in \mathcal{V}^E$ or $V \in \mathcal{V}^M)$
R8′.	$\{Vs^+ = \varepsilon\|V_1t\},\ \sigma$	$\rightarrow$	$\{V_1t = V\|s^+\},\ \{V\backslash\tilde{V}^M\}\cup\sigma$	$(V_1 \in \mathcal{V}^M$ and $V \in \mathcal{V}^E)$
R9.	$\{Vs^+ = z^+\|V_1t\},\ \sigma$	$\rightarrow$	$\{V_1t = V'\|s^+\},\ \{V\backslash z^+V'\}\cup\sigma$	(if $V_1,V \in \mathcal{V}^E$ then $V' \in \tilde{\mathcal{V}}^E$ else $V' \in \tilde{\mathcal{V}}^M$)
R10.	$\{Vs = z\|Xt\},\ \sigma$	$\rightarrow$	$\{Vs = zX\|t\},\ \sigma$	$(V \in \mathcal{V}^E$ or $X \in (\mathcal{V}^M\cup\Psi^M))$
R10′.	$\{Vs = z\|Xt\},\ \sigma$	$\rightarrow$	$\{Vs = zX\|t\},\ \{X\backslash\tilde{V}^M\}\cup\sigma$	$(V \in \mathcal{V}^M$ and $X \in \mathcal{V}^E)$

$s,t,z \in (\mathcal{V}\cup\mathcal{C}\cup\mathcal{V}')^*$ denote (arbitrary) strings, $s^+,t^+,z^+ \in (\mathcal{V}\cup\mathcal{C}\cup\mathcal{V}')^+$ denote non-empty strings. X, V, V_1, C, C_1 and C_2 denote single characters with $X \in \mathcal{V}\cup\mathcal{C}\cup\mathcal{V}'$, $V, V_1 \in \mathcal{V}\cup\mathcal{V}'$ (with $V{\neq}V_1$), and $C, C_1, C_2 \in \mathcal{C}$. V' and $\tilde{V}^M \in \tilde{\mathcal{V}}^M$ are new variables which do not occur in the substitution σ computed so far. To apply rule R10 or R10′ the following must hold: $V{\neq}X$, and $s{=}\varepsilon$ or $t{\neq}\varepsilon$ or $X \in \mathcal{C}$.

Table 4. Transformation rules for $\mathcal{MELL}$

These rules are identical with the transformation rules presented in [22]. We only added rules R8′, R10′ (which are applied instead of rules R8 and R10 in certain cases) and some additional restrictions for the rules R7 and R9 (characters $X \in \mathcal{V}^E \cup \Psi^E$ cannot be assigned to variables $V \in \mathcal{V}^M$). We use the notion $\{x \backslash t \mid \sigma(x)=t \text{ and } x \neq t\}$ to specify a substitution σ and omit the string concatenation operator "$\circ$". See [22] for a graphical motivation of these rules, a more detailed description of the algorithm, and some complexity results.

Example 11. Consider the formula $((A \parr \bot) \otimes !A) \parr ?(A^\perp)$ from Example 7 and the unification of the two prefixes $\psi_0^M \phi_{0l}^M \psi_{0lrl}^E \phi_{0lrl}^M$ and $\psi_0^M \phi_{0rll}^E \psi_{0rlll}^M \phi_{0rlll}^M$. To keep the notation simple we substitute each character ϕ_p and ψ_p by $V_{|p|}$ and $C_{|p|}$, respectively, i.e. we start the unification process with the tuple $\{C_0^M V_2^M C_4^E V_4^M = \varepsilon | C_0^M V_4^E C_5^M V_5^M\}, \{\}$ and apply the transformation rules according to Table 4:

$$\{C_0^M V_2^M C_4^E V_4^M = \varepsilon|C_0^M V_4^E C_5^M V_5^M\}, \{\} \xrightarrow{R3} \{V_2^M C_4^E V_4^M = \varepsilon|V_4^E C_5^M V_5^M\}, \{\}$$
$$\xrightarrow{R8} \{V_4^E C_5^M V_5^M = V_2^M|C_4^E V_4^M\}, \{\} \xrightarrow{R10} \{V_4^E C_5^M V_5^M = V_2^M C_4^E|V_4^M\}, \{\}$$
$$\xrightarrow{R9} \{V_4^M = V'|C_5^M V_5^M\}, \{V_4^E \backslash V_2^M C_4^E V'\} \xrightarrow{R10} \{V_4^M = V' C_5^M|V_5^M\}, \{V_4^E \backslash V_2^M C_4^E V'\}$$
$$\xrightarrow{R10} \{V_4^M = V' C_5^M V_5^M|\varepsilon\}, \{V_4^E \backslash V_2^M C_4^E V'\}$$
$$\xrightarrow{R5} \{\varepsilon = \varepsilon|\varepsilon\}, \{V_4^E \backslash V_2^M C_4^E V', V_4^M \backslash V' C_5^M V_5^M\}$$
$$\xrightarrow{R1} \{\}, \{V_4^E \backslash V_2^M C_4^E V', V_4^M \backslash V' C_5^M V_5^M\}$$

The only successful transformation sequence, leading to a tuple $\{\}, \tilde{\sigma}$, yields the substitution $\tilde{\sigma} = \{V_4^E \backslash V_2^M C_4^E V', V_4^M \backslash V' C_5^M V_5^M\}$ Applying rule R10 instead of rule R8 doesn't lead to any successful transformation sequence. Thus the only (most gerneral) unifier is $\{\phi_{0rll}^E \backslash \phi_{0l}^M \psi_{0lrl}^E V', \phi_{0lrl}^M \backslash V' \psi_{0rlll}^M \phi_{0rlll}^M\}$ where V' is a new introduced variable.

For the fragment $\mathcal{M}?\mathcal{LL}$ of linear logic (on which we will focus in the following section of this paper) we do not need to deal with characters of type ϕ^E or ψ^E. Furthermore *all* prefixes to be unified have the form $C_1 V_1 C_2 V_2 ... C_n V_n$ (where $V_i \in \mathcal{V}$ and $C_i \in \mathcal{C}$), allowing us to drop rules R2, R4, R6, and R7 (see also [15]).

Definition 12. Let $\mathcal{V}=\Phi^M$ be a set of variables, $\mathcal{C}=\Psi^M$ be a set of constants, and $\mathcal{V}'$ be a set of *auxiliary variables* (with $\mathcal{V} \cap \mathcal{V}'=\emptyset$). The set of *transformation rules for $\mathcal{M}?\mathcal{LL}$* is defined in Table 5.

R1.	$\{\varepsilon = \varepsilon\|\varepsilon\}, \sigma$	$\rightarrow$	$\{\}, \sigma$	
R3.	$\{Xs = \varepsilon\|Xt\}, \sigma$	$\rightarrow$	$\{s = \varepsilon\|t\}, \sigma$	
R5.	$\{Vs = z\|\varepsilon\}, \sigma$	$\rightarrow$	$\{s = \varepsilon\|\varepsilon\}, \{V\backslash z\} \cup \sigma$	
R8.	$\{Vs^+ = \varepsilon\|V_1 t\}, \sigma$	$\rightarrow$	$\{V_1 t = V\|s^+\}, \sigma$	
R9.	$\{Vs^+ = z^+\|V_1 t\}, \sigma$	$\rightarrow$	$\{V_1 t = V'\|s^+\}, \{V\backslash z^+ V'\} \cup \sigma$	
R10.	$\{Vs = z\|Xt\}, \sigma$	$\rightarrow$	$\{Vs = zX\|t\}, \sigma$	($V \neq X$, and $s=\varepsilon$ or $t \neq \varepsilon$ or $X \in \mathcal{C}$)

$s,t,z \in (\mathcal{V} \cup \mathcal{C} \cup \mathcal{V}')^*$ denote (arbitrary) strings, $s^+, z^+ \in (\mathcal{V} \cup \mathcal{C} \cup \mathcal{V}')^+$ denote non-empty strings. X, V, and V_1 denote single characters with $X \in \mathcal{V} \cup \mathcal{C} \cup \mathcal{V}'$ and $V, V_1 \in \mathcal{V} \cup \mathcal{V}'$ (with $V \neq V_1$). $V' \in \mathcal{V}'$ is a new variable which does not occur in the substitution σ computed so far.

Table 5. Transformation rules for $\mathcal{M}?\mathcal{LL}$

5 A Tableau Prover

In this section we present an implementation of the tableau calculus for the fragment $\mathcal{M?LL}$. We first present the calculus and repeat some definitions.

A Tableau Calculus for $\mathcal{M?LL}$. The tableau calculus for $\mathcal{M?LL}$ is similar to the calculus for $\mathcal{MELL}$ presented in Table 3. Since ? and ! can only occur, respectively, with positive and negative polarity we do not need the π-rule anymore. Because of that there are no positions of type ϕ^E or ψ^E anymore. Furthermore the ν-rules use a stepwise contraction and the τ- and ω-rules are modified. Let $\mathcal{A}_F$ be the set of all predicate symbols in the formula F. A *tableaux* for a formula F is defined as usual (see Definition 4) but with the tableau expansion rules from Table 6 where $A_p \in \mathcal{A}'$ is a predicate symbol and $X_p \in \mathcal{X}$ is a predicate variable. Let T be a tableau, $\sigma{:}\Phi^M \to (\Phi^M \cup \Psi^M)$ be a string substitution, and $\sigma_{\mathcal{X}}{:}\mathcal{X} \to (\mathcal{A}_F \cup \mathcal{A}')$ be a predicate substitution.

Definition 13. A *branch of T is closed* iff it contains a *complementary* connection, i.e $\{[A]^- : s\ (p),\ [B]^+ : t\ (q)\}$ where $\sigma(s)=\sigma(t)$ and $\sigma_{\mathcal{X}}(A)=\sigma_{\mathcal{X}}(B)$.

Let T be a tableau, $\mathcal{C}$ be a set of connections, α_T and β_T be the set of all positions of formulas of type α and β, respectively, in T.

Definition 14. A *tableau T is closed* iff (1.) every branch of T is closed by a $c \in \mathcal{C}$ under σ and $\sigma_{\mathcal{X}}$, (2.) if $\{a,b\} \in \mathcal{C}$ and $\{a,c\} \in \mathcal{C}$ then $b{=}c$ *(linearity)*, (3.) $2|\mathcal{C}| = |\alpha_T| + |\beta_T| + 1$ *(relevance)*, and (4.) $2|\mathcal{C}| = 2|\beta_T| + 2$ *(cardinality)*.

Theorem 15 (Correctness & Completeness). *A formula F is valid in the fragment $\mathcal{M?LL}$ iff there is a closed tableau for the prefixed formula $F^+ : \psi_0\ (0)$.*

Proof (Sketch). We show that our calculi for $\mathcal{M?LL}$ and $\mathcal{MELL}$ (without using rule π) are equivalent for the fragment of $\mathcal{M?LL}$: both ν-rules are equivalent (consider an appropriate multiplicity μ); rules τ and ω are correct and complete, i.e $\mathbf{1}^+ \equiv \bot^- \equiv (A \multimap A)^+$ for a new predicate symbol A and $\bot^+ \equiv \mathbf{1}^- \equiv (X \multimap X)^-$ for an arbitrary predicate symbol X (so that one-element connections are omited and the weakening map is empty), since the rules for $\mathbf{1}^+/\bot^-$ and the axiom rule present leafs in the sequent proof and the rules for $\bot^+/\mathbf{1}^-$ can always applied at the leafs in the sequent proof; linearity and cardinality conditions are identical (with empty weakening map); if $\mathcal{C}$ is linear and $2|\mathcal{C}|{=}|\alpha_T|{+}|\beta_T|{+}1$ then every atomic formula occurs in $\mathcal{C}$ (relevance condition), since the number of leaves in the (binary) formula tree is equal to the number of inner nodes plus one.

The linTAP Implementation. The previous calculus has been implemented in Prolog (see Table 7). For the syntax of formulas we use the logical connectives "~" (negation $^\perp$), "*" (conjunction $\otimes$), "@" (disjunction $⅋$), "@>" (implication $\multimap$), the exponentials "?" and "!", the constants "1" (for $\mathbf{1}$) and "0" (for $\bot$), and Prolog atoms for atomic formulas. For example to express the formula $((A ⅋ \bot) \otimes !A) ⅋ ?(A^\perp)$ we use the Prolog term `((a@0)*!a)@ ? (~a)`.

We use 0 and 1 to present the polarities + and −, respectively. Positions are constructed from right to left. Like in ileanTAP we use two predicates for path checking: `fml` and `prove`.

α-rules

$$\frac{(F_1 \parr F_3)^+ \ :\ s \quad (p)}{\begin{array}{ll} F_1^+ & : s\circ s'\ (p\circ l)\\ F_3^+ & : s\circ s'\ (p\circ r)\end{array}} \qquad \frac{(F_1 \otimes F_3)^- \ :\ s \quad (p)}{\begin{array}{ll} F_1^- & : s\circ s'\ (p\circ l)\\ F_3^- & : s\circ s'\ (p\circ r)\end{array}}$$

$$\frac{(F_1 \multimap F_3)^+ \ :\ s \quad (p)}{\begin{array}{ll} F_1^- & : s\circ s'\ (p\circ l)\\ F_3^+ & : s\circ s'\ (p\circ r)\end{array}} \qquad s' = \begin{cases} \psi_p \ , & \text{if } s=\tilde{s}\circ\phi,\ \phi\in\Phi^M \\ \varepsilon \ , & \text{else} \end{cases}$$

β-rules

$$\frac{(F_1 \parr F_2)^- \ :\ s\ (p)}{F_1^- : s\circ s'\ (p\circ l) \ \mid\ F_2^- : s\circ s'\ (p\circ r)} \qquad \frac{(F_1 \otimes F_2)^+ \ :\ s\ (p)}{F_1^+ : s\circ s'\ (p\circ l) \ \mid\ F_2^+ : s\circ s'\ (p\circ r)}$$

$$\frac{(F_1 \multimap F_2)^- \ :\ s\ (p)}{F_1^+ : s\circ s'\ (p\circ l) \ \mid\ F_2^- : s\circ s'\ (p\circ r)} \qquad s' = \begin{cases} \phi_p \ , & \text{if } s=\tilde{s}\circ\psi,\ \psi\in\Psi^M \\ \varepsilon \ , & \text{else} \end{cases}$$

ν-rules

$$\frac{(!F_1)^- : \ s\ (p)}{\bot^- \ :\ s\ (p)} \qquad \frac{(!F_1)^- : \ s \quad (p)}{\begin{array}{ll} F_1^- & : s\circ s'\ (p\circ l)\\ (!F_1)^- & : s\circ s'\ (p\circ r)\end{array}} \qquad \frac{(?F_1)^+ : \ s\ (p)}{\bot^+ \ :\ s\ (p)} \qquad \frac{(?F_1)^+ : \ s \quad (p)}{\begin{array}{ll} F_1^+ & : s\circ s'\ (p\circ l)\\ (?F_1)^+ & : s\circ s'\ (p\circ r)\end{array}}$$

$$s' = \begin{cases} \psi_p \ , & \text{if } s=\tilde{s}\circ\phi,\ \phi\in\Phi^M \\ \varepsilon \ , & \text{else} \end{cases}$$

o-rules

$$\frac{(F_1{}^\bot)^+ \ :\ s\ (p)}{F_1^- \ :\ s\ (p\circ l)} \qquad \frac{(F_1{}^\bot)^- \ :\ s\ (p)}{F_1^+ \ :\ s\ (p\circ l)}$$

τ-rules

$$\frac{\bot^- \ :\ s\ (p)}{(A_p \multimap A_p)^+ \ :\ s\ (p\circ l)} \qquad \frac{\mathbf{1}^+ \ :\ s\ (p)}{(A_p \multimap A_p)^+ \ :\ s\ (p\circ l)}$$

ω-rules

$$\frac{\mathbf{1}^- \ :\ s\ (p)}{(X_p \multimap X_p)^- : s\ (p\circ l)} \qquad \frac{\bot^+ \ :\ s\ (p)}{(X_p \multimap X_p)^- : s\ (p\circ l)}$$

***a(tom)*-rules**

$$\frac{A^+ : \ s \quad (p)}{[A]^+ : \ s\circ s'\circ\phi_p\ (p)} \qquad \frac{A^- : \ s \quad (p)}{[A]^- : \ s\circ s'\circ\phi_p\ (p)} \qquad s' = \begin{cases} \psi_p \ , & \text{if } s=\tilde{s}\circ\phi,\ \phi\in\Phi^M \\ \varepsilon \ , & \text{else} \end{cases}$$

Table 6. A prefixed-based tableau calculus for $\mathcal{M}?\mathcal{LL}$

`fml(F,Pol,P,F1,F2,F3,PrN,Ctr)` is used to specify the rules of our prefix-based tableau calculus. It succeeds if there is a rule to expand the formula `F`. `Pol` is the polarity, `P`, `F1`, `F2`, `F3`, and `PrN` are the position p, formulas F_1, F_2, F_3, and the new prefix character s', respectively. `Ctr` is bound to `c` if a contraction (rule) is applied. According to our calculus we need 18 clauses to specify all rules.

```
%%% Specification of Tableau Rules

fml(A,    Pol, P,[A,Pol],[],        [],[P],0):-var(A).
fml((A@B), 0, P, (A,0), [],   (B,0),[P],0).          fml((A@B), 1, _, (A,1), (B,1),[],[_],0).
fml((A*B), 1, P, (A,1), [],   (B,1),[P],0).          fml((A*B), 0, _, (A,0), (B,0),[],[_],0).
fml((A@>B),0, P, (A,1), [],   (B,0),[P],0).          fml((A@>B),1, _, (A,0), (B,1),[],[_],0).
fml((!A),  1, P, (A,1), [],((!A),1),[P],c).          fml((!_),  1, _, (1,1), [],    [], [],0).
fml((?A),  0, P, (A,0), [],((?A),0),[P],c).          fml((?_),  0, _, (0,0), [],    [], [],0).
fml(0,     1, P, (P,0), [],   (P,1),[P],0).          fml(1,     1, _, (X,0), (X,1),[],[_],0).
fml(1,     0, P, (P,0), [],   (P,1),[P],0).          fml(0,     0, _, (X,0), (X,1),[],[_],0).
fml((~A),  0, _, (A,1), [],      [], [],0).          fml((~A),  1, _, (A,0), [],    [], [],0).
fml(A,    Pol, P,[A,Pol],[],        [],[P],0).

%%% Path Checking

prove([(F,Pol),Pre,P],UnExp,Lits,Exp,ExpLim,PU,At,Bt,C,C1) :-
   fml(F,Pol,P,F1,F2,F3,PrN,Ctr), append(_,[Lp],Pre),              % look up tableau rule
   ( Ctr=c -> Exp<ExpLim, Exp1 is (Exp+1) ; Exp1=Exp, ! ),           % control contraction
   ( (F2\=[],var(Lp);F2=[],\+var(Lp)) -> Pre1=Pre;append(Pre,PrN,Pre1) ),% Pre1 is new prefix
   ( F3=[] -> UnExp1=UnExp, At=At3;
              UnExp1=[[F3,Pre1,r(P)]|UnExp], At=[P|At3] ),            % update UnExp1
   prove([F1,Pre1,l(P)],UnExp1,Lits,Exp1,ExpLim,PU1,At1,Bt1,C,C2),     % continue with F1
   ( F2=[] -> PU=PU1, At3=At1, Bt=Bt1, C1=C2 ;
     prove([F2,Pre1,r(P)],UnExp1,Lits,Exp1,ExpLim,PU2,At2,Bt2,C2,C1),  % continue with F2
     append(PU1,PU2,PU), union(At1,At2,At3), union([P|Bt1],Bt2,Bt) ).

prove([[Lit,Pl],Pr,P],_,[[[L,Pl1],Pr1,P1]|Lits],_,_,PU,At,Bt,C,C1) :-  % close branch
   ( Lit=L, Pl is 1-Pl1, Lit=L,  At=[], Bt=[],                     % connection found ?
     (member([P,S],C)  -> (S=P1 -> C1=C, PU=[]) ;                  % relevance condition
     (member([P1,S],C) -> (S=P  -> C1=C, PU=[]) ;
      PU=[[Pr,_]=[Pr1,_]], C1=[[P,P1],[P1,P]|C])) ) ;              % add prefixes and connection
   prove([[Lit,Pl],Pr,P],[],Lits,_,_,PU,At,Bt,C,C1).               % otherwise check next literal
prove(Lit,[Next|UnExp],Lits,Exp,ExpLim,PU,At,Bt,C,C1) :-           % add Lit to current branch
   prove(Next,UnExp,[Lit|Lits],Exp,ExpLim,PU,At,Bt,C,C1).          % expand Next formula

%%% T-String Unification

t_string_unify([]).
t_string_unify([S=T|G]):- flatten(S,S1,[]), flatten(T,T1,[]),         % flatten prefix lists
                          tunify(S1,[],T1), t_string_unify(G).        % solve first equation
tunify([],[],[]).                                                     % transfor. rule R1
tunify([X1|S],[],[X2|T])       :- X1==X2, !, tunify(S,[],T).          %      -''-      R3
tunify([V|S],Z,[])             :- V=Z, tunify(S,[],[]).               %      -''-      R5
tunify([V,X|S],[],[V1|T])      :- var(V1), tunify([V1|T],[V],[X|S]).  %      -''-      R8
tunify([V,X|S],[Z1|Z],[V1|T]) :- var(V1), append([Z1|Z],[Vnew],V),   %      -''-      R9
                                 tunify([V1|T],[Vnew],[X|S]).
tunify([V|S],Z,[X|T])          :- (S=[]; T\=[]; \+var(X)) ->          %      -''-      R10
                                 append(Z,[X],Z1), tunify([V|S],Z1,T).

flatten(A,[A|B],B) :- (var(A); A\=[], A\=[_|_]), !.                   % flatten list
flatten([],A,A).
flatten([A|B],C,D) :- flatten(A,C,E), flatten(B,E,D).
```

Table 7. The source code of linTAP

`prove([(F,Pol),Pre,P],UnExp,Lits,Exp,ExpLim,PU,At,Bt,C,C1)` performs the actual proof search. `(F,Pol)` is the formula currently expanded, `Pre` its prefix s, `P` its position p. `UnExp` and `Lits` represent lists of formulas not yet expanded and the atomic formulas on the current branch of the tableau. `Exp` is the number of contractions on the current branch, `ExpLim` the maximum number of contractions allowed on a branch, `PU` a list of prefix equations, `At` and `Bt` represent the sets α_T and β_T, and `C` represents the current set of connections $\mathcal{C}$ (more precisely each connection is stored twice, i.e. `C`$=\bigcup_{\{p,q\}\in\mathcal{C}}[[p,q],[q,p]]$).

After a tableau has been found the prefix equations in PU have to be solved. This is done by `t_string_unify(PU)` and `tunify(S,[],T)` where PU is a system of string equations to be unified, S and T are two strings to be unified (see [22]).

The following goal succeeds if the formula F is valid in $\mathcal{M}?\mathcal{LL}$ using not more than ExpLim contractions on each branch:

```
prove([(F,0),[0],0],[],[],0,ExpLim,PU,At,Bt,[],C),
      length(Bt,Nbt), length(C,Nc), Nc=:=(2*Nbt)+2,          % cardinality
      length(At,Nat), Nc=:=Nat+Nbt+1,                        % linearity
      t_string_unify(PU).                          % unifiability of prefixes
```

Some experimental results. There are only a few provers and even fewer examples available for $\mathcal{M}?\mathcal{LL}$. Table 8 contains some problems for $\mathcal{M}?\mathcal{LL}$. The timings for these (valid) formulas are given in Table 9.[2] We compare linTAP[3] (with iterative deepening) with the sequent calculus provers llprover (implemented in Prolog; see [24]) and linseq, as well as the resolution prover linres (both last-mentioned provers are implemented in Scheme and compiled to C; see [23]).

F_1	$((A \parr \perp) \otimes A) \parr ?(A^\perp)$
F_2	$!(A \otimes C \multimap B) \otimes !(B \otimes D \otimes D \multimap C \otimes D) \otimes A \otimes C \otimes D \otimes D \multimap C \otimes D$
F_3	$(C_1^\perp \otimes (C_2^\perp \otimes (\ldots (C_{11}^\perp \otimes C_{12}^\perp)..))) \parr (C_{12} \parr (C_{11} \parr \ldots \parr (C_2 \parr C_1)..))$
F_4	$(C_1^\perp \otimes (C_2^\perp \otimes (\ldots (C_{11}^\perp \otimes C_{12}^\perp)..))) \parr ((C_{12} \otimes (D_{12} \parr D_{12}^\perp)) \parr$ $((C_{11} \otimes (D_{11} \parr D_{11}^\perp)) \parr \ldots \parr ((C_2 \otimes (D_2 \parr D_2^\perp)) \parr (C_1 \otimes (D_1 \parr D_1^\perp)))..))$
F_5	$D \otimes !(D \multimap C \otimes Q) \otimes !(D \otimes Q \otimes Q \multimap I) \multimap C \otimes ?Q$
F_6	$D \otimes D \otimes D \otimes !(D \multimap C \otimes Q) \otimes !(D \otimes Q \otimes Q \multimap I) \multimap C \otimes I \otimes C$
F_7	$D \otimes D \otimes D \otimes D \otimes Q \otimes Q \otimes !(D \multimap C \otimes Q) \otimes !(D \otimes Q \otimes Q \multimap I) \multimap C \otimes I \otimes C \otimes I$
F_8	$D \otimes D \otimes D \otimes Q \otimes Q \otimes Q \otimes !(D \multimap C \otimes Q) \otimes !(D \otimes Q \otimes Q \multimap I) \multimap C \otimes I \otimes X$

Table 8. Some problems for $\mathcal{M}?\mathcal{LL}$

F_i	llprover	linseq	linres	linTAP
F_1	0.08	0.02	0.02	< 0.01
F_2	61.05	0.17	0.05	0.03
F_3	–	0.33	0.08	0.05
F_4	–	–	–	0.28

F_i	llprover	linseq	linres	linTAP
F_5	0.95	0.03	0.03	< 0.01
F_6	–	0.15	0.05	0.13
F_7	–	4.63	0.07	13.67
F_8	n/a	n/a	n/a	11.75

Table 9. Timings for the problems from Table 8

[2] Measured on a Sun SPARC10 in seconds; "–" means that no proof was found within 100 seconds. F_2 is the most difficult example from [24] (linTAP solves all other problems from [24] in less than 30ms); F_3 is from [23]. The predicates in F_5 to F_8 can be interpreted as follows: D="dollar", Q="quarter", C="Coke", I="ice-cream". Formula F_6, e.g., then expresses the following situation: for one dollar I can buy a Coke and get a quarter back, and for one dollar and two quarters I can buy an ice-cream; so if I have three dollars I can buy two Cokes and one ice-cream (see [5] for a similar approach on deductive planning). It is possible to use (free) variables: formula F_8 contains a variable X which will be bound to an appropriate predicate symbol (i.e. I) to make the formula valid (only linTAP offers this feature).

[3] The linTAP implementation uses an additional technique to simplify formulas of type α of the form $F \odot \omega$ or $\omega \odot F$ replacing them by F (where $\odot \in \{\parr, \otimes, \multimap\}$).

6 Conclusion

We have presented prefix-based tableau calculi for $\mathcal{MELL}$ and $\mathcal{M?LL}$. We encoded the additional non-permutabilities arising in multiplicative linear logic by an additional string unification. These calculi are the basis for our tableau prover linTAP. linTAP is not only a very compact implementation but compares favourable with other (larger) implementations. Due to the compact code the program can easily be modified for special purposes or applications.

Future work include the extension to larger fragments of linear logic and the comparison of linTAP with a connection driven proof search procedure (see [15]).

Besides the original leanTAP implementation for classical first-order logic, lean tableau provers are also available for various non-classical logics, i.e. first-order intuitionistic logic (ileanTAP, [21]), and the propositional modal logics K, KD, KT, and S4 (ModLeanTAP, [4]). The linTAP implementation fills the gap for the multiplicative linear logic. The source code of linTAP can be obtained at `http://www.intellektik.informatik.tu-darmstadt.de/~jeotten/linTAP/`.

References

1. J.-M. Andreoli. Logic programming with focusing proofs in linear logic. *Journal of Logic and Computation*, 2(3):297–347, 1992.
2. B. Beckert, J. Posegga. leanTAP: Lean Tableau-Based Theorem Proving. *12th Conference on Automated Deduction*, LNAI 814, pp. 793–797. Springer, 1994.
3. B. Beckert, J. Posegga. leanTAP: Lean Tableau-Based Deduction. *Journal of Automated Reasoning*, 15 (3), pp. 339–358, 1995.
4. B. Beckert, R. Goré. Free Variable Tableaux for Propositional Modal Logics. *Proc. 6th TABLEAUX Conference*, LNAI 1227, pp. 91–106, Springer 1997.
5. W. Bibel. Let's plan it deductively!. In *IJCAI-97*, Morgan Kaufmann, 1997.
6. I. Cervesato, J.S. Hodas, F. Pfenning. Efficient resource management for linear logic proof search. In *Extensions of Logic Programming*, LNAI 1050, pages 67–81. Springer, 1996.
7. M. Fitting. *First-Order Logic and Automated Theorem Proving*. Springer, 1996.
8. B. Fronhöfer. *The action-as-implication paradigm*. CS Press, 1996.
9. D. Galmiche. Connection methods in linear logic fragments and proof nets. Technical report, CADE-13 workshop on proof search in type-theoretic languages, 1996.
10. D. Galmiche & G. Perrier. On proof normalization in linear logic. *TCS*, 135:67–110, 1994.
11. V. Gehlot and C. Gunter. Normal process representatives. *Sixth Annual Symposium on Logic in Computer Science*, pages 200–207, 1991.
12. J.-Y. Girard. Linear logic. *TCS*, 50:1–102, 1987.
13. J. Harland and D. Pym. Resource-Distribution via Boolean Constraints. *14th Conference on Automated Deduction*, LNCS 1249, pp. 222–236. Springer, 1997.
14. J.S. Hodas & D. Miller. Logic programming in a fragment of linear logic. *Journal of Information and Computation*, 110(2):327–365, 1994.
15. C. Kreitz, H. Mantel, J. Otten, S. Schmitt. Connection-Based Proof Construction in Linear Logic. *14th Conference on Automated Deduction*, LNCS 1249, pp. 207–221. Springer, 1997.
16. P. Lincoln and T. Winkler. Constant-only multiplicative linear logic is NP-complete. *TCS*, 135:155–169, 1994.
17. H. Mantel, C. Kreitz. A Matrix Characterization for MELL. *Logics in Artificial Intelligence*, JELIA '98, LNAI 1489, pp. 169–183, Springer, 1998.
18. A. Martelli and U. Montanari. An efficient unification algorithm. *ACM TOPLAS*, 4:258–282, 1982.
19. M. Masseron, C. Tollu, J. Vauzeilles. Generating plans in linear logic. In *Foundations of Software Technology and Theoretical Computer Science*, LNCS, Springer,1991.
20. D. Miller. FORUM: A Multiple-Conclusion Specification Logic. *TCS*, 165(1):201-232, 1996.
21. J. Otten. ileanTAP: An Intuitionistic Theorem Prover. *Proc. 6th TABLEAUX Conference*, LNAI 1227, pp. 307–312, Springer 1997.
22. J. Otten, C. Kreitz. T-String-Unification: Unifying Prefixes in Non-Classical Proof Methods. *Proc. 5th TABLEAUX Workshop*, LNAI 1071, pp. 244–260, 1996.
23. T. Tammet. Proof strategies in linear logic. *JAR*, 12:273–304, 1994.
24. N. Tamura. User's Guide of a Linear Logic Theorem Prover (llprover). Technical report. Faculty of Engineering, Kobe University, Japan, 1995.
25. L. Wallen. *Automated deduction in nonclassical logic*. MIT Press, 1990.

A Tableau Calculus for a Temporal Logic with Temporal Connectives

Wolfgang May

Institut für Informatik, Universität Freiburg, Germany,
may@informatik.uni-freiburg.de

Abstract. The paper presents a tableau calculus for a linear time temporal logic for reasoning about processes and events in concurrent systems. The logic is based on temporal connectives in the style of Transaction Logic [BK94] and explicit quantification over states. The language extends first-order logic with sequential and parallel conjunction, parallel disjunction, and temporal implication. Explicit quantification over states via state variables allows to express temporal properties which cannot be formulated in modal logics.
Using the tableau representation of temporal Kripke structures presented for CTL in [MS96] which represents states by prefix terms, explicit quantification over states is integrated into the tableau calculus by an adaptation of the δ-rule from first-order tableau calculi to the linear ordering of the universe of states.
Complementing the CTL calculus, the paper shows that this tableau representation is both suitable for *modal temporal logics* and for logics using *temporal connectives*.

1 Introduction

When extending first-order logic to temporal logic, most approaches are based on *modal operators*, such as LTL/CTL or Dynamic Logic. Here, formulas are modified via modalities – inducing an implicit quantification over states. Formulas are evaluated wrt. states or (infinite) paths, thus they do not support an intuitive notion of sequentiality or parallelism.

For reasoning about processes and events in concurrent systems, *temporal connectives* such as sequential, parallel, and alternative composition or iteration are well-known from process algebraic formalisms. First-order-logic based formalisms using temporal connectives (which implies evaluating formulas wrt. finite path segments) are rare, although they have obvious advantages when reasoning about temporal behavior of processes. For Transaction Logic [BK94], it has been shown how to write executable specifications in such a formalism.

There are some temporal constraints which cannot be expressed in temporal modal logics, e.g., that "if some state is reached such that a given predicate p has the same extension as now, then q holds in this state" (cf. [TN96,CT98]). In [CT98], it is shown that this can be expressed in 2-FOL which is a two-sorted first order language for dealing with a linear temporal state space by

$$\forall s_1, s_2 : (\forall x : p(x, s_1) \leftrightarrow p(x, s_2) \wedge s_1 < s_2) \rightarrow q(s_2) .$$

This example motivates that an explicit quantification and addressing of states via state variables would be useful in a temporal logic.

In [MS96], a tableau semantics for first-order Kripke structures has been presented, together with a tableau calculus for first-order CTL. There, states have been described by *prefix terms* which provide a natural way to adapt the γ and δ-rule to quantification by state variables.

In the present paper, it is shown how the same approach applies for this temporal logic based on *temporal connectives* and explicit quantification over states.

The paper is structured as follows: After introducing some basic notions in Section 2, a (linear-time) logic for formulating complex events and dynamic constraints is presented in Section 3. Section 4 contains the tableau semantics for linear Kripke structures, and the tableau calculus is given in Section 5. Section 6 closes with some concluding remarks.

Related Work. Most of the work in Temporal Logics focuses on modal logics, e.g., CTL, modal μ-calculus, or Dynamic Logic. An overview of tableau calculi for (modal) temporal logics have been summarized in [Wol85], a recent one is described in [MP95]. *Interval Logics* contain operators for sequential composition and iteration similar to those known from programming languages [Mos86]. A tableau method for interval logic has, e.g., been presented in [BT98]. Other formalisms for expressing temporal constraints in non-modal logics are dealt with in [Sin95], [BK94], [Pra90], [Jab94], and [TN96,CT98].

2 Basic Notions

Let Σ be a *signature* consisting of a set Σ_{func} of function symbols a set Σ_{pred} of predicate symbols with fixed arities $\mathsf{ord}(f)$ resp. $\mathsf{ord}(p)$, and $\mathsf{Var} := \{x_1, x_2, \dots\}$ an infinite set of variables. Let Term_Σ denote the set of terms over Σ and Var. The notions of bound and free variables are defined as usual, $\mathsf{free}(\mathcal{F})$ denoting the set of variables occurring free in a set $\mathcal{F}$ of formulas.

A *substitution* (over a signature Σ) is a mapping $\sigma : \mathsf{Var} \to \mathsf{Term}_\Sigma$ where $\sigma(x) \neq x$ for only finitely many $x \in \mathsf{Var}$, here denoted by $[\sigma(x)/x]$. Substitutions are extended to terms and formulas as usual.

A first-order structure $\boldsymbol{I} = (I, \boldsymbol{U})$ over a signature Σ consists of a universe $\boldsymbol{U}$ and a *first-order interpretation* I of Σ which maps every function symbol $f \in \Sigma$ to a function $I(f) : \boldsymbol{U}^{\mathsf{ord}(f)} \to \boldsymbol{U}$ and every predicate symbol $p \in \Sigma$ to a relation $I(p) \subseteq \boldsymbol{U}^{\mathsf{ord}(p)}$.

A *variable assignment* is a mapping $\chi : \mathsf{Var} \to \boldsymbol{U}$. For a variable assignment χ, a variable x, and $d \in \boldsymbol{U}$, the *modified* variable assignment χ_x^d is identical with χ except that it assigns d to x. Let Ξ denote the set of variable assignments.

Every interpretation induces an *evaluation* $\boldsymbol{I} : \mathsf{Term}_\Sigma \times \Xi \to \boldsymbol{U}$ s.t. $\boldsymbol{I}(x, \chi) := \chi(x)$ for $x \in \mathsf{Var}$, and $\boldsymbol{I}(f(t_1, ..., t_n), \chi) := (I(f))(\boldsymbol{I}(t_1, \chi), ..., \boldsymbol{I}(t_n, \chi))$ for $f \in \Sigma$, $\mathsf{ord}(f) = n$ and $t_1, ..., t_n \in \mathsf{Term}_\Sigma$. The truth of a formula F in a first-order structure $\boldsymbol{I}$ under a variable assignment χ, $(\boldsymbol{I}, \chi) \models F$ is defined as usual.

3 Temporal Connectives and Quantification

Temporal specifications consist of combining subformulas by *temporal connectives*. The logic presented here incorporates the following facilities:

- $\otimes$ denotes sequential conjunction via subsequent path segments and $\times$ denotes a parallel conjunction on the same path segment.
- E^* denotes finite iteration, mostly limited by a first-order condition on a state which is tested between each two iterations.
- Constraints are specified by constraint formulas in an if-then-style. In temporal context, there are three possible implication constructs (if ... then before/later/sometimes ...). With a suitable synchronization formalism, they can be formulated by a single causal implication $\text{E} \leadsto \text{F}$.
- Via temporal quantification, formulas introduce "private" synchronization points which represent agreements local to processes.

From the modeling point of view, synchronization points are *virtual* entities. This idea shows some similarities with first-order existential quantification of a variable x: there is a local agreement (binding), which entity is meant by x, without identifying it extensionally. This information is kept local to the scope of the quantifier. Following this idea, synchronization points are handled via a set SVar of *state variables* s_i which can be bound to states.

The logic is interpreted by linear first-order Kripke structures which are augmented by a *transition oracle* (cf. [BK94]) representing the actions which are executed in the state transitions. A *linear first-order Kripke structure* over a signature Σ is a pair $\boldsymbol{K} = (\boldsymbol{U}, \boldsymbol{M})$, where $\boldsymbol{U}$ is a universe and $\boldsymbol{M}$ is a mapping from the natural numbers to first-order interpretations $\boldsymbol{M}(n)$ over Σ. Since a constant universe is presumed, the notion of a *variable assignment* is defined as in the first-order case. For every transition from n to $n+1$, the *transition oracle* yields an interpretation $\boldsymbol{N}(n)$ of a set Σ_A of *action symbols* similar to predicates. Having $(u_1, \ldots u_n) \in (\boldsymbol{N}(n))(a)$ for $a \in \Sigma_A$ in the transition oracle means that $a(u_1, \ldots, u_n)$ is executed in the transition from n to $n+1$.

Definition 1 (Action Formulas). Action formulas *are first-order formulas over the signature $\Sigma_A \cup \Sigma_{func}$. Action formulas are evaluated wrt.* transitions $\boldsymbol{K}\langle i, i+1\rangle$ *as* $(\boldsymbol{K}\langle i, i+1\rangle, \chi) \models a(t_1, \ldots, t_n) \Leftrightarrow (\boldsymbol{M}(i)(t_1, \chi), \ldots, \boldsymbol{M}(i)(t_n, \chi)) \in \boldsymbol{N}(n)(a)$, *using the transition oracle.*

Definition 2 (ECL-Event Formulas). *The language of* ECL formulas *over a first-order signature Σ and an action signature Σ_A is defined inductively. With every ECL formula* E, *a* length $\mathsf{len}(\text{E}) \subseteq \mathbb{N} \cup \{\infty\}$, *is associated; the addition "+" on subsets of* $\mathbb{N} \cup \{\infty\}$ *is defined as* $N+M := \{k : \exists n \in N, m \in N \mid k = n+m\}$.

1. *Every first-order formula φ is an ECL formula of length* $\mathsf{len}(\varphi) = \{0\}$.
2. ∂ *and* $\perp$ *are ECL formulas with length* $\mathsf{len}(\partial) = \mathsf{len}(\perp) = \mathbb{N} \cup \{\infty\}$. ∂ *denotes idling for an arbitrary time,* $\perp$ *denotes an action which can never be executed successfully (often called* deadlock*).*

3. *Every action formula* E *is an ECL formula of length* $\mathsf{len}(\mathrm{E}) = \{1\}$.
4. *With* s *a state variable and* E *an ECL formula such that* s *is not free in* E,
   - $s \rhd \mathrm{E}$ *is an ECL formula with* $\mathsf{len}(s \rhd \mathrm{E}) = \mathsf{len}(\mathrm{E})$, *and*
   - *if* $\mathsf{len}(\mathrm{E}) \cap \mathbb{N} \neq \emptyset$, $\mathrm{E} \lhd s$ *is an ECL formula with* $\mathsf{len}(\mathrm{E} \lhd s) = \mathsf{len}(\mathrm{E}) \cap \mathbb{N}$.

   Then, s *is free in* $s \rhd \mathrm{E}$ *and* $\mathrm{E} \lhd s$ *(prefixing or postfixing with a synchronization point).*
5. *With* E *an ECL formula with* $\mathsf{len}(\mathrm{E}) \cap \mathbb{N} \neq \emptyset$ *and* F *an ECL formula,* $\mathrm{E} \otimes \mathrm{F}$ *is an ECL formula,* $\mathsf{len}(\mathrm{E} \otimes \mathrm{F}) = (\mathsf{len}(\mathrm{E}) \cap \mathbb{N}) + \mathsf{len}(\mathrm{F})$ *(sequential composition).*
6. *With* E *and* F *ECL formulas with* $\mathsf{len}(\mathrm{E}) \cap \mathsf{len}(\mathrm{F}) \neq \emptyset$, $\mathrm{E} \times \mathrm{F}$ *is an ECL formula with* $\mathsf{len}(\mathrm{E} \times \mathrm{F}) = \mathsf{len}(\mathrm{E}) \cap \mathsf{len}(\mathrm{F})$ *(parallel composition).*
7. *With* $\mathrm{E}_1, \ldots, \mathrm{E}_n$ *ECL formulas,* $\sum_{1 \leq i \leq n} \mathrm{E}_i$ *is an ECL formula with* $\mathsf{len}(\sum_{1 \leq i \leq n} \mathrm{E}_i) = \bigcup_{1 \leq i \leq n} \mathsf{len}(\mathrm{E}_i)$ *(alternative composition).*
8. *With* E *an ECL formula,* E^* *is an ECL formula with* $\mathsf{len}(\mathrm{E}^*) = \{n \mid \exists k \in \mathbb{N}, n_1, \ldots, n_k \in \mathsf{len}(\mathrm{E})$ *and* $n = n_1 + \ldots + n_k\}$ *(finite iteration).*
9. *With* E *an ECL formula and* x *a variable,* $\forall x : \mathrm{E}$ *and* $\exists x : \mathrm{E}$ *are ECL formulas,* $\mathsf{len}(\forall x : \mathrm{E}) = \mathsf{len}(\exists x : \mathrm{E}) = \mathsf{len}(\mathrm{E})$.
10. *With* s *a state variable and* E *an ECL formula,* $\blacklozenge s : \mathrm{E}$ *and – if* $\infty \in \mathsf{len}(\mathrm{E})$ – $\blacksquare s : \mathrm{E}$ *are ECL formulas,* $\mathsf{len}(\blacklozenge s : \mathrm{E}) = \mathsf{len}(\mathrm{E})$, $\mathsf{len}(\blacksquare s : \mathrm{E}) = \{\infty\}$ *(introducing a state variable).*

- *Each of the above ECL formulas is an ECL-*event *formula.*

ECL-event formulas hold on a segment of a Kripke structure. For a linear Kripke structure $\boldsymbol{K}$ and $i \leq j$ such that $i \in \mathbb{N}$, $j \in \mathbb{N} \cup \{\infty\}$, the expression $\boldsymbol{K}[i,j]$ denotes the whole structure, with the *focus* on the segment $[i,j]$.

Definition 3 (Assignment of State Variables). *For a linear Kripke structure, an* assignment ζ of state variables *is a function which maps every state variable to a state of* $\boldsymbol{K}$*, i.e., a natural number.*
The modification of an assignment ζ *of state variables at one element is defined in the same way as for first-order variable-assignments: For an assignment* ζ *of state variables, a state variable* x*, and* $n \in \mathbb{N}$*, the* modification ζ_s^n *is identical with* ζ *except that it assigns* n *to the state variable* s*:*

$$\zeta_s^n : \mathsf{SVar} \to \mathbb{N} : \begin{cases} t \mapsto \zeta(t) & \textit{if } t \neq s \quad , \\ s \mapsto n & \textit{otherwise} \; . \end{cases}$$

Definition 4 (Semantics of Event Formulas). *Let* $\boldsymbol{K}$ *be a linear Kripke structure with a universe* $\boldsymbol{U}$, χ *a variable assignment,* ζ *an assignment of state variables. Then,* $\models$ *is extended to ECL formulas as follows:*

1. *For* φ *a first-order formula:* $(\boldsymbol{K}[i,j], \chi) \models \varphi \;:\Leftrightarrow\; i = j$ *and* $(\boldsymbol{M}(i), \chi) \models \varphi$.
2. $(\boldsymbol{K}[i,j], \chi, \zeta) \models \partial$ *for all* $i \leq j$*, and* $(\boldsymbol{K}[i,j], \chi, \zeta) \models \bot$ *for no* i, j .
3. *For* φ *an action formula:* $(\boldsymbol{K}[i,j], \chi) \models \varphi \;:\Leftrightarrow\; j = i+1$ *and* $(\boldsymbol{K}\langle i,j \rangle, \chi) \models \varphi$.
4. $(\boldsymbol{K}[i,j], \chi, \zeta) \models s \rhd \mathrm{E} \;:\Leftrightarrow\; \zeta(s) = i$ *and* $(\boldsymbol{K}[i,j], \chi, \zeta) \models \mathrm{E}$ *, and*
   $(\boldsymbol{K}[i,j], \chi, \zeta) \models \mathrm{E} \lhd s \;:\Leftrightarrow\; \zeta(s) = j \in \mathbb{N}$ *and* $(\boldsymbol{K}[i,j], \chi, \zeta) \models \mathrm{E}$.
5. $(\boldsymbol{K}[i,j], \chi, \zeta) \models \mathrm{E} \otimes \mathrm{F} \;:\Leftrightarrow\;$ *there is a* $k \in \mathbb{N}$ *s.t.* $(\boldsymbol{K}[i,k], \chi, \zeta) \models \mathrm{E}$ *and* $(\boldsymbol{K}[k,j], \chi, \zeta) \models \mathrm{F}$.

6. $(K[i,j],\chi,\zeta) \models \mathrm{E} \times \mathrm{F} \;:\Leftrightarrow\; (K[i,j],\chi,\zeta) \models \mathrm{E}$ *and* $(K[i,j],\chi,\zeta) \models \mathrm{F}$.
7. $(K[i,j],\chi,\zeta) \models \sum_{1\ldots n} \mathrm{E}_i \;:\Leftrightarrow$ *there is a* $1 \leq k \leq n$ *s.t.* $(K[i,j],\chi,\zeta) \models \mathrm{E}_k$.
8. $(K[i,j],\chi,\zeta) \models \mathrm{E}^\star \;:\Leftrightarrow$ *there is a* $k \geq 0$ *s.t.* $(K[i,j],\chi,\zeta) \models \underbrace{\mathrm{E} \otimes \mathrm{E} \otimes \ldots \otimes \mathrm{E}}_{k\text{-times}}$.
   (note that for $k = 0$*, this means true)*
9. $(K[i,j],\chi,\zeta) \models \exists x : \mathrm{E} \;:\Leftrightarrow$ *there is a* $d \in U$ *s.t.* $(K[i,j],\chi^d_x,\zeta) \models \mathrm{E}$,
   $(K[i,j],\chi,\zeta) \models \forall x : \mathrm{E} \;:\Leftrightarrow$ *for all* $d \in U$, $(K[i,j],\chi^d_x,\zeta) \models \mathrm{E}$.
10. $(K[i,j],\chi,\zeta) \models \blacklozenge s : \mathrm{E} \;:\Leftrightarrow$ *there is a* $k : i \leq k \leq j$ *and* $(K[i,j],\chi,\zeta^k_s) \models \mathrm{E}$,
   $(K[i,j],\chi,\zeta) \models \blacksquare s : \mathrm{E} \;:\Leftrightarrow$ $j = \infty$ *and for all* $k \geq i$, $(K[i,j],\chi,\zeta^k_s) \models \mathrm{E}$.

As short notations, $\mathrm{E} \cdot \mathrm{F} := \mathrm{E} \otimes \partial \otimes \mathrm{F}$ *and* $\mathrm{E}_1 + \cdots + \mathrm{E}_n := \sum_{i\in\{1,\ldots,n\}} \mathrm{E}_i$ *are used.*

Remark 1 (Semantics of ECL). Note, that in this definition, if F is an ECL formula and E is a subformula of F, the segment of the Kripke structure which is looked at for E is always contained in the segment which is looked at for F. This will not be the case in Definition 6 where the semantics of temporal implication is defined.

ECL-event formulas without universal temporal quantification describe *finitely detectable* events:

Proposition 1 (Finite Satisfiability). *Let* E *be an ECL-event formula which does not contain* $\blacksquare s$. *Then, if a (possibly infinite computation) satisfies* E *(i.e., an event described by* E *occurs in the computation) then already a finite prefix of this computation satisfies* E. *Formally,* $(K[i,j],\chi,\zeta) \models \mathrm{E}$ *implies that there is a (unique least)* $i \leq k \leq j$ *such that* $k < \infty$ *and* $(K[i,k],\chi,\zeta) \models \mathrm{E}$.

For the proof, one must consider that an infinite sequence only satisfies formulas which contain either $\blacksquare$ or a final delay (this will change with the introduction of temporal implication in Sec. 5).
As a consequence, events of infinite length, i.e., $\mathsf{len}(\mathrm{E}) = \{\infty\}$ (note that these are exactly those events which contain $\blacksquare$ in all their alternatives), cannot be postfixed: there is no state where an action "raising" such an event can be terminated.

Example 1 (Event Formulas).

- Iteration: a state will be reached where F holds, an then, E is iterated until G is satisfied: $\partial \otimes F \otimes \mathrm{E}^\star \otimes G$.
- Conditional execution: If the set of elements for which some ECL formula $\mathrm{E}(x)$ should be satisfied should be restricted by some first-order formula $\varphi(x)$, this can be formulated as $\blacklozenge s : \forall x : ((\varphi(x) \otimes \mathrm{E}(x)) + (\neg\varphi(x) \otimes \partial)) \lhd s$.
- Consider a workflow, consisting of several jobs, each of them can be performed by several ways, consisting of a first and a second part. The additional condition is that all first parts are finished before some second part is started: This is done by a synchronization variable local to the process:

$$\mathrm{Workflow} = \blacklozenge s : (\mathrm{Job}_1 \times \mathrm{Job}_2 \times \ldots \times \mathrm{Job}_n) ,$$
$$\mathrm{Job}_i = \mathrm{Way}_{i,1} + \cdots + \mathrm{Way}_{i,k_i} ,$$
$$\mathrm{Way}_{i,j} = \partial \otimes \mathrm{First}_{i,j} \otimes \partial \lhd s \otimes \partial \otimes \mathrm{Second}_{i,j} \otimes \partial .$$

3.1 Constraints

Constraints can be used for describing processes from another point of view: in a declarative way, computations not satisfying a given set of constraints can be ruled out. Temporal constraints are specified by constraint formulas in an if-then-style. With the above synchronization formalism, the temporal implication constructs "*if ... then before/later/sometimes ...* " can be formulated by a single implication and state variables.

Definition 5 (Constraint Formulas). *For expressing temporal constraints, an additional connective is added to the syntax of ECL formulas:*

11. For ECL formulas E, F, E $\rightsquigarrow$ F *is an ECL (constraint) formula with* $\mathrm{len}(\text{E} \rightsquigarrow \text{F}) = 0$ *(temporal implication).*

Definition 6 (Semantics of Constraints). *Let K be a linear Kripke structure, χ a variable assignment, ζ an assignment of state variables. Then, $\models$ is extended to $\rightsquigarrow$ as follows:*

11. $(\boldsymbol{K}[i,j],\chi,\zeta) \models (\text{E} \rightsquigarrow \text{F}) \;:\Leftrightarrow\; i=j$ *and if* $(\boldsymbol{K}[i,k_1],\chi,\zeta) \models \text{E}$ *for some* k_1, *then* $(\boldsymbol{K}[0,k_2],\chi,\zeta) \models \text{F}$ *for some* k_2 .

Note that E $\rightsquigarrow \bot$ is ECL's negation, i.e., requires that an event E is *not* detected. In contrast to ECL-event formulas (cf. Remark 1), for a general ECL-constraint formula, the whole path has to be considered for evaluating the consequence. For negation via temporal implication, the focused segment has *not* to be extended. A constraint is evaluated wrt. one state and has length 0.

Proposition 2 (Connectives of [Jab94]). *The constraint connectives used in [Jab94] can be defined as derived symbols:*

- *"Deadline": eventually D will be satisfied, and before, C has to be satisfied:*
$$D < C \;:\Leftrightarrow\; (\partial \otimes D \otimes \partial) \times \blacksquare s : ((\partial \otimes s \rhd D) \rightsquigarrow (\partial \otimes C \otimes \partial \lhd s)) .$$
- *"Delay": C can only occur if D occured before:*
$$C > D \;:\Leftrightarrow\; \blacksquare s : (\partial \otimes s \rhd C) \rightsquigarrow ((\partial \otimes D \otimes \partial \lhd s)) .$$

Example 2 (Constraints). (assume E, F, and G to be action formulas)

- After F, E will never be satisfied: $(\partial \otimes \text{F} \cdot \text{E}) \rightsquigarrow \bot$,
- if E and later F are satisfied, then between them, G must eventually be satisfied: $\blacksquare s_1, s_2 : (\partial \otimes \text{E} \lhd s_1 \cdot s_2 \rhd \text{F}) \rightsquigarrow (\partial \otimes s_1 \rhd \partial \otimes \text{G} \otimes \partial \lhd s_2)$.
- between E and the next F, G is not satisfied:
$\blacksquare s_1, s_2 : ((\partial \otimes \text{E} \lhd s_1 \cdot s_2 \rhd \text{F}) \times ((\partial \otimes s_1 \rhd \partial \otimes \text{F} \otimes \partial \lhd s_2) \rightsquigarrow \bot)) \rightsquigarrow$
$((\partial \otimes s_1 \rhd \partial \otimes \text{G} \otimes \partial \lhd s_2) \rightsquigarrow \bot)$.
- if E is satisfied, in the state before, F holds: $\blacksquare s : (\partial \otimes s \rhd \text{E}) \rightsquigarrow (\partial \otimes F \lhd s)$.

Example 3 (2-FOL). The 2-FOL formula given in the introduction which is not expressible in LTL, CTL etc. can be expressed in ECL by

$$\blacksquare s_1, s_2 (\forall x((\partial \otimes (s_1 \rhd p(x)) \otimes \partial \otimes (s_2 \rhd p(x)) \otimes \partial) + (\partial \otimes (s_1 \rhd (\neg p(x))) \otimes \partial \otimes (s_2 \rhd (\neg p(x))) \otimes \partial))) \rightsquigarrow \partial \otimes (s_2 \rhd q) .$$

4 Tableau Semantics for Linear Kripke Structures

The tableau semantics and -calculus is a linear-time adaptation of the one presented for first-order CTL in [MS96] which uses branching time first-order Kripke structures as underlying semantics. For the first-order part, the well-known first-order tableau calculus is embedded into the tableau calculus which is constructed. It is necessary to describe many individual states as well as the relations between them in the tableau, including the ordering of states. Thus, three kinds of entities have to be described: Elements of the universe inside states, states, and the path with its transitions. In the chosen semantics, elements of the universe and states will be explicitly named when their existence is stated by a formula:

- Elements of the universe: a new constant resp. function symbol is introduced by the usual δ-rule when an existential quantifier is processed.
- States: states are named when their existence is required by a complex event.

In general, between two known states there can be many other still unknown states. These can be named when needed. Thus, a straightforward resolving of eventualities at any time is possible. A similar approach for PLTL where only the relevant states are generated has been used in [SGL97].

To allow the naming of states at any position of the model, the description of the path contains, apart from the (partial) ordering of known states, additional information about formulas which have to be true in still unknown states on the segments in-between. These are used when new states are explicitly named.

Representation. As a conceptional extension of first-order tableaux, every branch of the tableau corresponds to a linear Kripke structure with a transition oracle. Apart from the first-order portion, information about the frame and the transitions has to be coded in tableau nodes. For distinguishing and naming of states, a tableau calculus based on the free variable tableau calculus given in [Fit90] augmented with *prefixes* is employed: A formula F, assumed to be true in a certain state, occurs in the tableau as ***state prefixed formula*** $\gamma{:}F$. Additionally, path information formulas contain the information about the prefixes situated on the path.

Thus, the signature Σ_T used in the tableau is partitioned into Σ_L (first-order part), Σ_A (action symbols), and Σ_F (prefix symbols).

Σ_L is obtained by augmenting Σ with a countable infinite set of n-ary skolem function symbols for every $n \in \mathbb{N}$ and a countable infinite set of variables X_i.

Σ_F is a set of ***prefix symbols*** containing an infinite set of n-ary prefix symbols for every $n \in \mathbb{N}$. The construction of prefixes corresponds to the use of skolem functions in the first-order tableau calculus. Here the prefix symbols take the role of the skolem function symbols. Analogously to the skolem terms containing free variables resulting from invocations of the γ-rule, prefixes γ are terms consisting of a prefix symbol $\hat{\gamma}$ of an arity n and an n-tuple of terms as arguments. Additionally, there is a 0-ary symbol $\hat{\infty}$ which is no prefix symbol but is used in a similar way.

Definition 7. *Let Σ_F be the set of prefix symbols and Σ^c the subset of Σ which is interpreted state-independently. Then the following sets Σ_L and Γ are simultaneously recursively defined:*

$\Sigma_L := \Sigma \cup \{f \mid f \text{ an } n\text{-ary skolem function symbol}\} \cup \{f_\gamma \mid f \in \Sigma\backslash\Sigma^c, \gamma \in \Gamma\}$,

with $\mathsf{ord}(f_\gamma) = \mathsf{ord}(f)$ *and skolem functions and all* f_γ *interpreted state-independently, thus*

$\Sigma_L^c := \Sigma^c \cup \{f \mid f \text{ an } n\text{-ary skolem function symbol}\} \cup \{f_\gamma \mid f \in \Sigma\backslash\Sigma^c, \gamma \in \Gamma\}$.

The set of prefixes *is given as*
$\Gamma := \{\hat{\gamma}(t_1, \dots, t_n) \mid \hat{\gamma} \in \Sigma_F \text{ is an } n\text{-ary prefix symbol, } t_1, \dots, t_n \in \mathsf{Term}_{\Sigma_L^c}\}$.

For $\Gamma \subset \mathsf{Term}_{\Sigma_\mathcal{T}}$, it is precisely the leading function symbol which is a prefix symbol taken from Σ_F, and all argument terms are in $\mathsf{Term}_{\Sigma_L^c}$. For Σ_L^c, $\boldsymbol{K}$ induces a state-independent interpretation $(\boldsymbol{K}, \boldsymbol{U})$.

An interpretation of $\Sigma_\mathcal{T}$ – describing a Kripke structure $\boldsymbol{K} = (\boldsymbol{U}, \boldsymbol{M})$ – is accordingly partitioned: The interpretation of Σ_L is taken over by the set $\{\boldsymbol{M}(i) \mid i \in \mathbb{N}\}$ of first-order interpretations, and the symbols of Σ_A are interpreted by the transition oracle. Complementary to this, an "interpretation" of the prefix symbols in Σ_F is defined. The corresponding evaluation maps prefixes to natural numbers:

Definition 8. *A prefix interpretation of a set Σ_F of prefix symbols to a linear Kripke structure $\boldsymbol{K} = (\boldsymbol{U}, \boldsymbol{M})$ is a mapping $\pi : (\Sigma_F \cup \{\hat{\infty}\}) \to \boldsymbol{U}^m \to \mathbb{N} \cup \{\infty\}$ which maps every m-ary prefix symbol $\hat{\gamma} \in \Sigma_F$ to a function $\pi(\hat{\gamma}) : \boldsymbol{U}^m \to \mathbb{N} \cup \{\infty\}$ with $\pi(\gamma) = \infty \Leftrightarrow \gamma = \hat{\infty}$. Defining $\Pi_{\boldsymbol{K}} := (\pi \cup K, \mathbb{N} \cup \{\infty\})$, Π is organized similarly to a first-order interpretation $\boldsymbol{I} = (I, \boldsymbol{U})$ with a mapping π and the "universe" $\mathbb{N} \cup \{\infty\}$, inducing an* evaluation $\Pi_{\boldsymbol{K}} : (\Gamma \cup \{\hat{\infty}\}) \times \mathsf{Term}_{\Sigma_L^c} \to \mathbb{N} \cup \{\infty\}$ *of prefixes as follows:*
For $\gamma = \hat{\gamma}(t_1, \dots, t_n) \in \Gamma$ (thus $t_i \in \mathsf{Term}_{\Sigma_L^c}$ evaluated state-independently by $\boldsymbol{K}$),

$$\Pi_{\boldsymbol{K}}(\gamma, \chi) := (\pi(\hat{\gamma}))(\boldsymbol{K}(t_1, \chi), \dots, \boldsymbol{K}(t_n, \chi)) \ .$$

Finally, the interpretation of the derived function symbols f_γ is defined state-independently for all $i \in \mathbb{N}$ as

$$(\boldsymbol{M}(n))(f_\gamma(t_1, \dots, t_n), \chi) := (\boldsymbol{M}(\Pi_{\boldsymbol{K}}(\gamma, \chi)))(f(t_1, \dots, t_n), \chi) \quad .$$

Tableau formulas. Logical formulas occur in the tableau as prefixed formulas, additionally, the Kripke frame is encoded in ***path information formulas*** (*pif*s): An additional symbol ∇ can occur instead of prefixes and state variables as an auxiliary "generic prefix". ∇ is instantiated by a prefix when a state on the respective segment is explicitly named.

Definition 9 (Syntax of $\mathcal{TE}$ Tableau Formulas).

1. *For an ECL formula P with state variables $s_1, \dots, s_n$ and prefixes $\gamma_1, \dots, \gamma_n \in \Gamma \cup \{\nabla\}$, $P[\gamma_1/s_1, \dots, \gamma_n/s_n]$ is a $\mathcal{TE}$-path formula.*
2. *With $\blacklozenge s : P$ and $\blacksquare s : P$ a $\mathcal{TE}$-path formula and γ a prefix, $\blacklozenge s_{\geq\gamma} : P$ and $\blacksquare s_{\geq\gamma} : P$ are $\mathcal{TE}$-path formulas.*

3. *For a $\mathcal{TE}$-path formula P and $\gamma \in \Gamma \cup \{\nabla\}$, $\gamma{:}P$ is a $\mathcal{TE}$-prefixed formula.*
4. *Every $\mathcal{TE}$-prefixed formula which does not contain ∇ is also a $\mathcal{TE}$-node formula.*
5. *With $\gamma_0, \gamma_1, \ldots$ prefixes and L_i a conjunction of $\mathcal{TE}$-prefixed formulas, $[\gamma_0, L_0, \gamma_1, L_1, \ldots, \gamma_n, L_n, \hat{\infty}]$ is a $\mathcal{TE}$-path information formula.*
6. *Every $\mathcal{TE}$-path information formula is a $\mathcal{TE}$-node formula.*

Remark 2 (Properties of $\mathcal{TE}$ formulas). Note that, $\mathcal{TE}$-path formulas do *not* contain any free state variables, and the restricted quantifiers $\blacklozenge s_{\geq\gamma}$ and $\blacksquare s_{\geq\gamma}$ occur only in the outermost positions of $\mathcal{TE}$-path formulas.

Definition 10 (Semantics of $\mathcal{TE}$ Tableau Formulas). *The relation $\Vdash$ of a linear Kripke structure with a transition oracle $\boldsymbol{K} = (\boldsymbol{U}, \boldsymbol{M})$, a prefix interpretation Π, a variable assignment χ, and a $\mathcal{TE}$-node formula is defined as follows:*

- *For every $\mathcal{TE}$-path formula* E *neither containing ∇ nor beginning with $\blacklozenge s_{\geq\gamma}$ or $\blacksquare s_{\geq\gamma}$ and every prefix γ: let $\gamma_1, \ldots, \gamma_n$ be the prefixes occurring in* E*, $s_1, \ldots, s_n$ new state variables and $\zeta = \{s_j \mapsto \Pi(\gamma_j, \chi) \mid 1 \leq j \leq n\}$. Then,*

$$(\boldsymbol{K}, \Pi, \chi) \Vdash \gamma{:}\mathrm{E} \;:\Leftrightarrow\; \text{there is an } i \in \mathbb{N} \cup \{\infty\} \text{ s.t. } (\boldsymbol{K}[\Pi(\gamma, \chi), i], \chi, \zeta) \models \mathrm{E}[s_1/\gamma_1, \ldots, s_n/\gamma_n]\ .$$

  (In particular, for an action formula E*,*

$$(\boldsymbol{K}, \Pi, \chi) \Vdash \gamma : \mathrm{E} \quad :\Leftrightarrow \quad (\boldsymbol{K}\langle \Pi(\gamma, \chi), \Pi(\gamma, \chi){+}1\rangle, \chi) \models \mathrm{E}\ ,$$

  i.e., if the transition from $\Pi(\gamma, \chi)$ to $\Pi(\gamma, \chi){+}1$ satisfies E *under χ.)*
- *For every $\mathcal{TE}$-path formula beginning with $\blacklozenge s_{\geq\gamma}$ or $\blacksquare s_{\geq\gamma}$ and every prefix α,*

$$(\boldsymbol{K}, \Pi, \chi) \Vdash \alpha : \blacklozenge s_{\geq\gamma}{:}P \;:\Leftrightarrow\; (\boldsymbol{K}, \Pi \cup \{\hat{\delta} \mapsto i\}, \chi) \Vdash \alpha{:}P[\hat{\delta}/s] \text{ for some } i \geq \Pi(\gamma, \chi),$$
$$(\boldsymbol{K}, \Pi, \chi) \Vdash \alpha : \blacksquare s_{\geq\gamma}{:}P \;:\Leftrightarrow\; (\boldsymbol{K}, \Pi \cup \{\hat{\delta} \mapsto i\}, \chi) \Vdash \alpha{:}P[\hat{\delta}/s] \text{ for all } i \geq \Pi(\gamma, \chi)\ .$$

- *For every path information formula $I = [\gamma_0, L_0, \gamma_1, L_1, \ldots, \gamma_n, L_n, \hat{\infty}]$:*

$$(\boldsymbol{K}, \Pi, \chi) \Vdash [\gamma_0, L_0, \gamma_1, L_1, \ldots, \gamma_n, L_n, \hat{\infty}]$$

  iff $\Pi(\gamma_0, \chi) = 0$ and for all $0 \leq i \leq n$:

$$\Pi(\gamma_i, \chi) < \Pi(\gamma_{i+1}, \chi)\ , \text{ and for all } j \text{ with } \Pi(\gamma_i, \chi) < j < \Pi(\gamma_{i+1}, \chi):$$
$$(\boldsymbol{K}, \Pi \cup \{\hat{\delta} \mapsto j\}, \chi) \Vdash L_i[\hat{\delta}/\nabla] \text{ with } \hat{\delta} \text{ a new 0-ary prefix symbol.}$$

  This condition means that for all (finitely, but arbitrary many) states j situated between $\Pi(\gamma_i, \chi)$ and $\Pi(\gamma_{i+1}, \chi)$ in $\boldsymbol{K}$, the instantiation of L_i for a new prefix which is mapped to j holds in $\boldsymbol{K}$.
  Note that $L_i =$ false implies $\Pi(\gamma_{i+1}, \chi) = \Pi(\gamma_i, \chi){+}1$.

Note that the semantics for $\mathcal{TE}$-prefixed formulas containing ∇ is not defined. They occur only in the list components of path information formulas, and ∇ is instantiated by a prefix when the list is used.

A set $\mathcal{F}$ of path information formulas and prefixed formulas is *valid* in a linear Kripke structure $\boldsymbol{K} = (\boldsymbol{U}, \boldsymbol{M})$ under a variable assignment χ if there is a prefix-interpretation Π such that $(\boldsymbol{K},\Pi,\chi) \Vdash \mathcal{F}$. Since a branch of a tableau is a set of formulas like this, validity is a relation on Kripke structures with transition oracles and branches.

The construction of Kripke structures and consistent prefix-interpretations to a given set of formulas plays an important role in the proof of correctness.

5 The Tableau Calculus $\mathcal{TE}$

As usual, the tableau is initialized with a set of formulas which should be proven to be inconsistent, i.e., it is shown that there is no linear Kripke structure $\boldsymbol{K} = (\boldsymbol{U}, \boldsymbol{M})$ such that F does holds in $\boldsymbol{M}(0)$. Thus the initialization of the tableau is

$$\frac{}{\begin{array}{c}[\hat{0}, \mathsf{true}, \infty] \\ \hat{0} : F\end{array}}$$

The α-, β-, γ-, δ-rules for first-order formulas are as usual (extended with prefixes), boolean combinations of prefixed formulas are resolved analogously.

Atomic Closure Rule. For a substitution σ and a prefix γ, σ_γ is the γ-*localization*, i.e. $\sigma_\gamma(X)$ is obtained from $\sigma(X)$ by replacing every function symbol $f \in \Sigma \backslash \Sigma^c$ by its localized symbol f_γ. So the substitutes in σ_γ contain only function symbols which are interpreted state-independently. In the rule shown at the right, σ is a substitution and A, B are atomic formulas.

$$\frac{\begin{array}{c}\gamma : A \\ \gamma : B \\ \sigma(A) = \neg\sigma(B)\end{array}}{\begin{array}{c}\mathsf{close} \\ \text{apply } \sigma_\gamma \text{ to the whole tableau.}\end{array}}$$

For resolving modalities, the information about the frame of the Kripke structure, which is encoded in the *pif*s, is used. In a single step, a prefixed formula is resolved "along" a *pif*, inducing the following form of tableau rules:

$$\frac{\begin{array}{c}\text{prefixed formula} \\ \text{path information formula}\end{array}}{\begin{array}{c}\text{prefixed formulas} \\ \text{path information formulas}\end{array}}$$

where the premise takes the latest *pif* on the current branch. The connection between the prefixed formula being resolved and the *pif* is established by the prefix.

In the sequel, T denotes the current branch of the tableau, $\mathsf{free}(T)$ the free variables on T, $\hat{\gamma}$ is a new prefix symbol, and E is an ECL-formula.

Prefixed Event Formulas. For a prefixed event formula, the prefix must coincide with the respective prefix of the prefixed formula in the tableau (i.e., $\alpha : \beta \rhd \mathrm{E}$) requires $\alpha \equiv \beta$.[1](Here and in the following, $\beta \equiv \alpha$ evaluates to close if α and β are different prefixes, and to true otherwise.)

$$\frac{\alpha : (\beta \rhd \mathrm{E})}{\begin{array}{c}\beta \equiv \alpha \\ \alpha : \mathrm{E}\end{array}}$$

Postfixed Event Formulas. For a postfixed formula $\mathrm{E} \lhd \beta$, it has to be distinguished whether E is elementary, i.e., a delay, a deadlock, an action formula,

[1] here, the reader is asked to distinguish between a prefix $\gamma : \mathrm{E}$ and prefixing or postfixing a formula by $\gamma \rhd \mathrm{E}$ or $\mathrm{E} \lhd \gamma$.

or a first-order formula, or whether it is itself a complex event. The postfixing-operator $\lhd$ associates a synchronization point with the last elementary component of an event. Thus, postfixes can only be resolved if this final event is associated with a transition, otherwise, the formula has to be rewritten. The base cases also act as closure rules if the assignment of prefixes is inconsistent:

$$\frac{\alpha : \mathrm{E} \lhd \gamma \,,\ \mathsf{len}(\mathrm{E}) = \{1\} \,,\quad [\ldots, \alpha, L, \beta, \ldots]}{\begin{array}{c}[\ldots, \alpha, \mathsf{false}, \beta, \ldots] \\ \beta \equiv \gamma \\ \alpha : \mathrm{E}\end{array}} \qquad \frac{\alpha : F \lhd \beta \,,\ \mathsf{len}(F) = \{0\}}{\begin{array}{c}\beta \equiv \alpha \\ \alpha : F\end{array}} \qquad \frac{\alpha : \partial \lhd \beta \quad [\ldots, \beta, \ldots, \alpha, \ldots]}{\mathsf{close}}$$

Definition 11 (Normal Form wrt. Postfixes). *The* syntactic *operator Θ rewrites postfixed complex ECL formulas such that* $\mathsf{len}(\mathrm{E}) \cap \{2, 3, \ldots\} \neq \emptyset$ *by moving the postfix inside the outermost event connective:*

$$\Theta((\mathrm{E} \lhd t) \lhd s) := \begin{cases} (\mathrm{E} \lhd t) \lhd s & \textit{if } \mathsf{len}(\mathrm{E}) \in \{\{0\}, \{1\}\} \,, \\ \Theta(\Theta(\mathrm{E} \lhd t) \lhd s) & \textit{otherwise} \,, \end{cases}$$

$$\begin{array}{ll}
\Theta((t \rhd \mathrm{E}) \lhd s) := t \rhd (\mathrm{E} \lhd s) \,, & \Theta((\mathrm{E}^\star) \lhd s) := \mathsf{true} \lhd s + \mathrm{E}^\star \otimes (\mathrm{E} \lhd s) \,, \\
\Theta((\mathrm{E} \otimes \mathrm{F}) \lhd s) := \mathrm{E} \otimes (\mathrm{F} \lhd s) \,, & \Theta((\exists x : \mathrm{E}) \lhd s) := \exists x : (\mathrm{E} \lhd s) \,, \\
\Theta((\mathrm{E} \times \mathrm{F}) \lhd s) := (\mathrm{E} \lhd s) \times (\mathrm{F} \lhd s) \,, & \Theta((\forall x : \mathrm{E}) \lhd s) := \forall x : (\mathrm{E} \lhd s) \,, \\
\Theta((\mathrm{E} + \mathrm{F}) \lhd s) := (\mathrm{E} \lhd s) + (\mathrm{F} \lhd s) \,, & \Theta((\blacklozenge s' : \mathrm{E}) \lhd s) := \blacklozenge s' : (\mathrm{E} \lhd s) \,.
\end{array}$$

Note that formulas of length $\mathsf{len}(\mathrm{E}) = \{0\}$ are (possibly pre- or postfixed) first-order formulas or temporal implications, and formulas of $\mathsf{len}(\mathrm{E}) = \{1\}$ are (possibly pre- or postfixed) action formulas. Thus, Θ is the identity on temporal implications $\mathrm{E} \leadsto \mathrm{F}$ (since $\mathsf{len}(\mathrm{E} \leadsto \mathrm{F}) = \{0\}$). Postfixing of formulas of the form $\blacksquare s : \mathrm{E}$ is not defined. ∂ is not a complex event formula.
The above definition is *not* recursive, but denotes only a one-level rewriting of the parse-tree of the formula (which is typical for tableau calculi) – Θ does not occur on the right hand side. Only when Θ is iterated, a *normal form* is obtained:

Proposition 3 (Normal Form wrt. Prefixes and Postfixes). *For every linear Kripke structure $\boldsymbol{K}$, ECL formula E, variable assignment χ and assignment ζ of state variables, $(\boldsymbol{K}[i,j], \chi, \zeta) \models \mathrm{E} \Leftrightarrow (\boldsymbol{K}[i,j], \chi, \zeta) \models \Theta(\mathrm{E})$* and iterated *application of Θ yields an expression where only formulas E s.t. $\mathsf{len}(\mathrm{E}) \in \{\{0\}, \{1\}\}$ or delays are postfixed.*

In non-base cases, the operator Θ is applied for rewriting the formula:

$$\frac{\alpha : \mathrm{E} \lhd \beta, \quad \mathsf{len}(\mathrm{E}) \cap \{2, 3, \ldots\} \neq \emptyset}{\alpha : \Theta(\mathrm{E} \lhd \beta)}$$

Alternative and parallel compositions.
These connectives are disjunctive and conjunctive, respectively, and are resolved analogously to the α- and β-rules of first-order tableau calculi:

$$\frac{\alpha : \sum_{i=1\ldots n} \mathrm{E}_i}{\alpha : \mathrm{E}_1 \;\big|\; \ldots \;\big|\; \alpha : \mathrm{E}_n} \qquad \frac{\alpha : (\mathrm{E}_1 \times \ldots \times \mathrm{E}_n)}{\begin{array}{c}\alpha : \mathrm{E}_1 \\ \vdots \\ \alpha : \mathrm{E}_n\end{array}}$$

Sequential Composition: $E \otimes F$. Semantically, the brackets around composite events of the form $(\sum ... E_i)$ and $(E_1 \times ... \times E_n)$ can be regarded as synchronization points, i.e., (virtual) entities in the sense of the tableau representation: Detecting an event $E \otimes F$ in α is equivalent to the event $\blacklozenge s : (E \lhd s) \otimes (s \rhd F)$ where s must be bound to a state after the current state.
With the rules for $\blacklozenge_{\geq \gamma}$ (see below), the state variable in $\alpha : \blacklozenge s_{\geq \alpha} : (E \lhd s) \otimes (s \rhd F)$ is instantiated systematically with the prefixes. Then, the resulting formula $\alpha : (E \lhd \beta) \otimes (\beta \rhd F)$ can be split into two parts ("sequential conjunction").

$$\frac{\alpha : E \otimes F}{\alpha : \blacklozenge s_{\geq \alpha} : (E \lhd s) \otimes (s \rhd F)}$$

$$\frac{\alpha : (E \lhd \beta) \otimes (\beta \rhd F)}{\begin{array}{c} \alpha : E \lhd \beta \\ \beta : F \end{array}}$$

Shortcuts can be defined when one of the events is a base case, i.e., a delay, a first-order formula, or an action formula.

Iterative Composition. Iterative composition is reduced to sequential composition:

$$\frac{\alpha : E^{\star}}{\alpha : \mathsf{true} \;\Big|\; \alpha : E \otimes E^{\star}}$$

Temporal Quantification.
Due to the fact that there is a linear ordering between states, the γ- and δ-rules cannot be adapted to temporal quantification of synchronization points; instead, every synchronization point must be integrated into this ordering. For this, analogous to the resolving of eventuality formulas in the tableau calculus for CTL, synchronization points are shifted along path formulas. The rules correspond to a systematic application of the γ- or δ-rules, known from first-order tableau calculi for universal and existential quantification, along the state sequence.

$$\frac{\alpha : \blacksquare s : E}{\alpha : \blacksquare s_{\geq \alpha} : E} \qquad \frac{\alpha : \blacklozenge s : E}{\alpha : \blacklozenge s_{\geq \alpha} : E}$$

$$\frac{\begin{array}{c} \alpha : \blacksquare s_{\geq \beta} : E \\ [..., \beta, L, \gamma, ...] \end{array}}{\begin{array}{c} [..., \beta, L \wedge \alpha : E[\nabla/s], \gamma, ...] \\ \alpha : E[\beta/s] \\ \text{if } \gamma \neq \infty\text{:} \;\; \alpha : \blacksquare s_{\geq \gamma} : E \end{array}}$$

Expl.: $E[\nabla/s]$ holds for *all* subsequent states – i.e., for α, for all unknown states between α and γ, and for all states $\geq \gamma$.

$$\frac{\begin{array}{c} \alpha : \blacklozenge s_{\geq \beta} : E \\ [..., \beta, L, \gamma, ...] \end{array}}{\alpha : E[\beta/s] \;\Bigg|\; \begin{array}{r} [..., \beta, L \wedge \alpha : E[\nabla/s] \rightsquigarrow \bot, \\ \hat{\delta}(\mathsf{free}(T)), L, \gamma, ...] \\ L[\hat{\delta}(\mathsf{free}(T))/\nabla] \\ \alpha : (E[\beta/s] \rightsquigarrow \bot) \\ \alpha : E[\hat{\delta}(\mathsf{free}(T))/s] \end{array} \;\Bigg|\; \begin{array}{c} \text{if } \gamma \neq \infty\text{:} \\ [..., \beta, L \wedge \alpha : E[\nabla/s] \rightsquigarrow \bot, \gamma, ...] \\ \alpha : E[\beta/s] \rightsquigarrow \bot \\ \alpha : \blacklozenge s_{\geq \gamma} : E \end{array}}$$

Expl.: $E[\nabla/s]$ holds for *some* subsequent state – thus, this must be α, or some state between α and γ which becomes named in this case, or some state $\geq \gamma$.

Here, the second part of the consequence of the rule for $\blacklozenge s_{\geq \beta}$ names a state $\hat{\delta}(\mathsf{free}(T))$ which is considered to be relevant (since it is a possible instantiation of s). In this case, the list L in the path information formula states some requirements on all states on a path segment – thus, also on $\hat{\delta}(\mathsf{free}(T))$. These are made explicit by instantiating L with $\hat{\delta}(\mathsf{free}(T))/\nabla$.

Temporal Implication. When resolving constraints $E \leadsto F$, in the base case, E is a first-order formula or an action formula or a delay:

for E a first-order formula or an action formula:
$$\frac{\alpha : E \leadsto F}{\begin{array}{c|c} \alpha : \neg E & \alpha : E \\ & \hat{0} : F \end{array}} \qquad \frac{\alpha : \partial \leadsto F}{\hat{0} : F}$$

By applying the following rules, constraints are rewritten until the antecedent consists only of a first-order formula or an action formula:

$$\frac{\alpha : (\beta \rhd E) \leadsto F}{\begin{array}{c|c} \alpha \equiv \beta & \alpha \not\equiv \beta \\ \alpha : E \leadsto F & \end{array}} \qquad \frac{\alpha : (E{+}F) \leadsto G}{\begin{array}{c} \alpha : E \leadsto G \\ \alpha : F \leadsto G \end{array}} \qquad \frac{\alpha : (\blacklozenge s : E) \leadsto F}{\alpha : \blacksquare s_{\geq \alpha} : (E \leadsto F)} \qquad \frac{\alpha : (E \leadsto F) \leadsto G}{\begin{array}{c|c} \alpha : E & \alpha : E \leadsto F \\ \hat{0} : (F \leadsto \bot) & \hat{0} : G \end{array}}$$

$$\frac{\alpha : (E \otimes F) \leadsto G}{\alpha : \blacksquare s_{\geq \alpha} : ((E \lhd s) \leadsto (\partial \otimes s \rhd F \leadsto G))}$$

$$\frac{\alpha : ((E \times F) \leadsto G)}{\alpha : \blacksquare s_{\geq \alpha} : ((\alpha \rhd E \lhd s) \leadsto (\partial \otimes \alpha \rhd F \lhd s \leadsto G))}$$

$\triangle$ Expl.: if E implies F then G holds, if either $E \leadsto F$ does not hold – i.e, E is detected and F cannot be detected, or $E \leadsto F$ hold and G can be detected.

Postfixed event formulas require additional attention: base cases can be resolved immediately, non-base cases have to be rewritten:

$$\frac{\alpha : (E \lhd \beta) \leadsto F\ ,\ \mathsf{len}(E) = \{0\}}{\begin{array}{c|c} \beta \not\equiv \alpha & \beta \equiv \alpha \\ & \alpha : E \leadsto F \end{array}} \qquad \frac{\alpha : (\partial \lhd \alpha) \leadsto F}{\hat{0} : F}$$

$$\frac{\begin{array}{c} \alpha : (E \lhd \beta) \leadsto F\ ,\ \mathsf{len}(E) = \{1\} \\ [..., \alpha, L, \gamma, ...] \end{array}}{\begin{array}{c|c|c} \beta \not\equiv \gamma & [..., \alpha, \mathsf{false}, \hat{\delta}(\mathsf{free}(T)), L, \gamma, ...] & [..., \alpha, \mathsf{false}, \gamma, ...] \\ & L[\hat{\delta}(\mathsf{free}(T))/\nabla] & \beta \equiv \gamma \\ & \beta \equiv \gamma & \alpha : E \leadsto F \end{array}}$$

Expl.: First case: $\gamma \not\equiv$ is the next known state – thus, β is later than $\alpha{+}1$, then $E \lhd \beta$ cannot be detected in α.
Second case: $\beta = \gamma$ is the next known state, but not the successor state.

$$\frac{\begin{array}{c} \alpha : (\partial \lhd \beta) \leadsto F \\ [..., \alpha, ..., \beta, ...] \end{array}}{\hat{0} : F} \qquad \frac{\begin{array}{c} \alpha : (\partial \lhd \beta) \leadsto F \\ [..., \beta, ..., \alpha, ...] \end{array}}{\mathsf{close}} \qquad \frac{\begin{array}{c} \alpha : (E \lhd \beta) \leadsto F \\ \mathsf{len}(E) \cap \{2, 3, ...\} \neq \emptyset \end{array}}{\alpha : \Theta(E \lhd \beta) \leadsto F}$$

Some constraints show a special behavior: Since $E^\star$ has trivial occurrences, $E^\star \leadsto F$ reduces to $0 : F$:

$$\frac{\alpha : E^\star \leadsto F}{\hat{0} : F}$$

Events of the form $\blacksquare s : E$ cannot be finitely detected, thus, implications containing them in the antecedent have to be resolved in a different way. $\alpha : (\blacksquare s : E) \leadsto F$ is equivalent to the fact that either there is a state β later than α such that $\alpha : E[\beta/s]$ does *not* occur, or $\boldsymbol{K}$ satisfies F:

$$\frac{\alpha : (\blacksquare s : E) \leadsto F}{\begin{array}{c|c} \alpha : \blacklozenge s : (E \leadsto \bot) & \hat{0} : F \end{array}}$$

Remark 3 (Properties of $\mathcal{TE}$). $\mathcal{TE}$ has some special properties which can easily be verified when carefully looking at the rules:

- every prefix symbol is introduced exactly once, with a given arity and the current free variables of the branch as arguments. Thus, for every prefix symbol, at every time, there is exactly one prefix which is built from it.
- every prefix which occurs as prefix or postfix in some formula (i.e., as $\gamma \rhd \mathrm{E}$ or $\mathrm{E} \lhd \gamma$) of a branch occurs also in the most recent path information formula of the branch.
- if a branch of the tableau contains a formula of the form $\alpha : \blacksquare_{\geq \beta}$ or $\alpha : \blacklozenge_{\geq \beta}{:}P$, $\alpha \neq \beta$, the most recent path information formula on this branch is of the form $[\ldots, \alpha, \ldots, \beta, \ldots]$.
- there are no free state variables in the calculus: Whereas first-order variables are replaced by free variables or Skolem terms, state variables are always replaced by prefixes (see the rules for $\blacksquare_{\geq \gamma}$ and $\blacklozenge_{\geq \gamma}$).

Theorem 1 (Correctness of $\mathcal{TE}$).

(a) If a tableau $\mathcal{T}$ is satisfiable and $\mathcal{T}'$ is created from $\mathcal{T}$ by an application of any of the rules mentioned above, then $\mathcal{T}'$ is also satisfiable.
(b) If there is any closed tableau for $\mathcal{F}$, then $\mathcal{F}$ is unsatisfiable.

The proof (see [May98]) of (a) is done by case-splitting separately for each of the rules. By assumption, there is a Kripke structure $\boldsymbol{K}$ with a transition oracle and a prefix interpretation Π such that for every variable assignment χ there is a branch T_χ in $\mathcal{T}$ with $(\boldsymbol{K}, \Pi, \chi) \models\!\models T_\chi$. In all cases apart from the atomic closure rule, $\boldsymbol{K}$ and Π are extended such that they witness the satisfiability of $\mathcal{T}'$. In case of the atomic closure rule, a Substitution Lemma guarantees the existence of a satisfying branch for every variable assignment to free($\mathcal{T}'$). (b) follows directly from (a).

Since first-order ECL is not compact, no calculus for it can be complete. The calculus is complete modulo inductive properties. For such cases, induction rules for temporal properties and well-founded data structures have to be included. In this setting, the notion of completeness has to be relativized to that any proof done in a mathematical way can be completely redone formally.

6 Conclusion

This paper presents a tableau calculus for a linear time temporal logic which is based on *temporal connectives* instead of *modal operators*. The underlying Kripke semantics is explicitely encoded into the tableau, based on the ideas of the tableau representation of branching-time structures in [MS96,May97]. In both calculi, exactly those states which are required to construct a potential model of the given formula are named explicitly, all states in-between are characterized intensionally within the path information. From the conceptual point of view, the contribution of the paper is that this tableau representation is both suitable for *modal temporal logics* and for logics using *temporal connectives* and *explicit temporal quantification*.

Focusing on temporal connectives, the logic and the calculus show how temporal connections between events can be modeled explicitly by synchronization points. The calculus integrates this synchronization smoothly into the tableau semantics via the introduction of state variables. With the ■ and ♦ operators, the handling of state variables is closely related to the strategy for resolving the CTL modalities □ and ◇, making up one more connection between the calculus presented here and the CTL calculus.

Due to its path-orientation, the language is significantly different from CTL which is based on state-formulas. Although, the tableau semantics and calculus shares its basic ideas with the CTL calculus, allowing a potential integration of both calculi.

References

BK94. A. J. Bonner and M. Kifer. An Overview of Transaction Logic. *Theoretical Computer Science*, 133(2):205–265, 1994.

BT98. H. Bowman and S. Thompson. A Tableau Method for Interval Temporal Logic with Projection. In TABLEAUX'98, LNCS 1397, pp. 108–123, Springer, 1998.

CT98. J. Chomicki and D. Toman. Temporal Logic in Information Systems. In *Logics for Databases and Information Systems*, Ch. 3, pp. 31–70. Kluwer, 1998.

Fit90. M. Fitting. *First Order Logic and Automated Theorem Proving*. Springer,1990.

Jab94. S. Jablonski. Functional and Behavioural Aspects of Process Modelling in Workflow Management Systems. *Proc. CON '94: Workflow Management*,1994.

May97. W. May. Proving Correctness of Labeled Transition Systems by Semantic Tableaux. In TABLEAUX'97, LNCS 1227, pp. 261–275. Springer, 1997.

May98. W. May. *Integrated Static and Dynamic Modeling of Processes*. PhD thesis, Institut für Informatik, Universität Freiburg, Logos Verlag, 1998.

Mos86. B. Moszkowski. *Executing Temporal Logic Programs*. Cambridge University Press, 1986.

MP95. Z. Manna and A. Pnueli. *The Temporal Logic of Reactive and Concurrent Systems: Safety*. Springer, 1995.

MS96. W. May and P. H. Schmitt. A Tableau Calculus for First-Order Branching Time Logic. In *Intl. Conf. on Formal and Applied Practical Reasoning, FAPR'96*, LNCS 1085, pp. 399–413. Springer, 1996.

Pra90. V. R. Pratt. Action Logic and Pure Induction. In *Logics in AI: Europ. Workshop Jelia 90*, LNCS 478, pp. 97–120, 1990.

SGL97. P. H. Schmitt and J. Goubault-Larrecq. A Tableau System for Linear-Time Temporal Logic. In *Tools and Algorithms for the Construction and Analysis of Systems*, LNCS 1217, Springer, pp. 130–144, 1997.

Sin95. M. P. Singh. Semantical Considerations on Workflows: An Algebra for Intertask Dependencies. In *Intl. Workshop on Database Programming Languages*, Electronic Workshops in Computing, Gubbio, Italy, 1995. Springer.

TN96. D. Toman and D. Niwinski. First-Order Queries over Temporal Databases Inexpressible in Temporal Logic. In *Proc. Int. Conf. on Extending Database Technology*, LNCS 1057, pp. 307–324. Springer, 1996.

Wol85. P. Wolper. The Tableau Method for Temporal Logic. *Logique et Analyse*, 28:110–111, 1985.

A Tableau Calculus for Pronoun Resolution

Christof Monz[1,2] and Maarten de Rijke[2]

[1] Institute for Computational Linguistics (IMS), University of Stuttgart, Azenbergstr. 12, 70174 Stuttgart, Germany. E-mail: christof@ims.uni-stuttgart.de
[2] ILLC, University of Amsterdam, Plantage Muidergracht 24, 1018 TV Amsterdam, The Netherlands. E-mail: {christof, mdr}@wins.uva.nl

Abstract. We present a tableau calculus for reasoning in fragments of natural language. We focus on the problem of pronoun resolution and the way in which it complicates automated theorem proving for natural language processing. A method for explicitly manipulating contextual information during deduction is proposed, where pronouns are resolved against this context during deduction. As a result, pronoun resolution and deduction can be interleaved in such a way that pronouns are only resolved if this is licensed by a deduction rule; this helps us to avoid the combinatorial complexity of total pronoun disambiguation.

1 Introduction

The general aim of Natural Language Processing (NLP) is to analyze and understand human language using computational tools. In computational semantics, one of the subdisciplines of NLP, two specific tasks arise. First, what is the semantic value, the meaning, of a natural language utterance and how can we determine it. And, second, given the semantics of a natural language utterance, how can we use it to deduce further information? In practice, these questions are interdependent: to properly represent an utterance, one has to access contextual information and check what can be derived from it, and to perform derivations in the first place we obviously need to represent our information.

It is probably fair to say that developing inference methods for natural language is one of the most pressing tasks in computational semantics, and the present paper tries to contribute to this area. More specifically, we develop a tableau calculus in which deduction and pronoun resolution are interleaved. Before diving into the details in later sections, let us give a simple example of the natural language phenomenon that we are focusing on. Briefly, we are dealing with so-called *anaphoric expressions* or *anaphora*; typical examples of anaphora are pronouns such as 'she', 'he,' or 'it'. Anaphora are *resolved to* or *identified with* other terms, usually occurring earlier on in an utterance or discourse; such terms are called *antecedents*. Here's an example:

(1) A woman found a cat on a playground. She liked it.

What should 'it' in the second sentence in (1) refer back to—'a cat' or 'a playground'? As a rule, we, the human language users, don't have a problems resolving such ambiguities; in the case at hand 'a cat' would probably be selected as antecedent for 'it.' But how can a theorem prover that receives (1) as one of its premises use it to derive conclusions? As long as the pronoun 'it' has not been resolved, this question introduces the problem of ambiguity to the task of deduction with natural language semantics. Can we conclude either of the following from (1)?

(2) a. $\models$ A woman liked a cat.
    b. $\models$ A woman liked a playground.[1]

One way to tackle this problem is by assuming that anaphoric expressions have to be resolved before deductive methods are applied. This assumption is common in several approaches to the semantics of natural language, but in practice it seems to be too strong and highly implausible, since resolution of pronouns may in fact require deductive processing to be completed successfully [All94]. Here, we propose a different approach. We interleave disambiguation and deduction steps, where a pronoun is resolved only if this is needed by a deduction rule, and where deductive information is used to steer the resolution process.

In this paper, we assume that the semantic representations for natural language sentences are already given. Of course, this is not a trivial task, and it would be far beyond the scope of this paper to discuss this. [Als92] gives an overview of the Core Language Engine, an implementation builds (underspecified) semantic representations for natural language discourses.

The rest of the paper is organized as follows. In Section 2 we provide further examples and some linguistic background; this section may be skipped by anyone familiar with pronoun resolution. Then, in Section 3 we briefly introduce our formal language, and formalize the notion of context that we will need to model pronoun resolution interleaved with deduction. In Section 4 the semantics of our formal language is defined, and in Section 5 we provide it with a tableau calculus. Finally, Section 6 summarizes our results, and in Section 7 we draw some conclusions and formulate further challenges.

2 Some Linguistic Background

In this section we quickly review some basic facts and intuitions from natural language semantics as they pertain to pronoun resolution. Refer to [KR93] for further details.

If a sentence contains a pronoun, the hearer has to identify it with some person or thing that has been mentioned earlier to understand this sentence. Roughly, one can identify context with what has been said earlier. Of course, this blends out other contextual information like world knowledge, gestures, etc., but as these non-linguistic sources of context are hard to formalize, in general, we will restrict ourselves to the notion of context as linguistic context.

Saying that a pronoun has to be resolved to something that appears in the context does not mean that it can be identified with just anything in the context:

[1] To keep things simple, we do not employ any preference order of the readings, although this may be desirable in the long run.

there are some clear constraints. To illustrate these, we give some examples (the asterisk (*), indicates that a discourse is not well-formed).

The discourse in (3) below is not well-formed, because the pronoun 'She' and 'a man', which is the only thing that could function as an antecedent, do not agree on gender.

(3) * A man sleeps. She snores.

In (4), it is not possible to bind 'it' to 'a car', because although 'a car' was mentioned before, its existence has not been claimed, on the contrary, it was said that there is no such car. In other words, 'it' cannot refer to something which is not existing.

(4) * Buk doesn't have a car. It is red.

Conditionals are another interesting case. The if-clause in (5.a) introduces two antecedents 'a linguist' and 'a car' which can both serve as antecedents for pronouns in the then-clause. But they cannot serve as antecedents for pronouns occurring in later sentences as in (5.b). Roughly, objects that are introduced in an if-clause are just assumed to exist, and the then-clauses expresses what has to hold, under this assumption. Clauses that follow the conditional sentence are not uttered within the context of this assumption, and therefore, their pronouns cannot access things occurring inside the assumption. One can say, that the assumption expressed by the if-clause is a local context, which is only accessible to the then-clause.

(5) a. If a linguist has a car, then it didn't cost much.
b. * If a linguist has a car, then it didn't cost much. It is very old.

Universal quantification, as in (6), does not talk about particular individuals and it is not possible to refer back to 'every poet' with the pronoun 'he'. The same holds for indefinite noun phrases that occur in the scope of the universal quantifier. As they depend on each instantiation of the universally quantified variable, it does not mean that there has to be a particular individual which can be referred to by a singular pronoun.

(6) Every poet who has published a book likes it. { *He is arrogant. / *But it is really bad. }

Summarizing the important points of the above examples, pronouns need to agree with their antecedents a number of features, and some information within a discourse may be inaccessible to pronouns that occur later in the discourse. These two points will play an important role in our tableau calculus below.

3 Towards Context-Based Reasoning

This section provides a formal account of context and the way it is dealt with in deduction. It will become obvious that deduction with natural semantics is much more structure-sensitive than for instance classical first-order logics. Here, we restrict ourselves to those kinds of structural information that is needed in order to allow pronoun resolution, but see [MdR98a] for a more general overview on this topic.

3.1 Formalizing Context

In the preceding section we provided some intuitions about pronoun-antecedent relations and the role structural information played in this setting. We will now formalize the way in which contextual information flows within a discourse. As a first step we introduce the formal language that we will be using.

Definition 1 (The Language $\mathcal{L}^{pro}$). Assuming that φ_1 and φ_2 are in $\mathcal{L}^{pro}$, we say that φ is in $\mathcal{L}^{pro}$, if:

$$\begin{aligned}\varphi ::= {} & R(x_{1_g}, \ldots, x_{n_{g'n}}) \mid \neg\varphi \mid \varphi_1 \wedge \varphi_2 \mid \varphi_1 \vee \varphi_2 \mid \varphi_1 \rightarrow \varphi_2 \mid \\ & \forall x_g\, \varphi_1 \mid \exists x_g\, \varphi_1 \mid\ ?x_g\, \varphi_1\end{aligned}$$

where $g, g' \in \{he, she, it\}$.

Thus, besides the usual logical connectives, $\neg$, $\wedge$, $\rightarrow$, $\vee$, $\forall$, $\exists$, we introduce a new operator ? that binds pronoun variables.

Contrary to approaches like Dynamic Predicate Logic (DPL, [GS91]) it is not assumed that pronouns are already resolved when constructing the semantic representation of a discourse. Given a formula φ, we say that $[\varphi]$ is a function from subsets of VAR (the set of variables) to subsets of VAR, where the argument is the *input context* and the value denotes the *output context* or *context contribution*. The contextual contribution of a formula φ is the set of variables that φ adds to the input context.

Definition 2 (Contextual Contribution). The *contextual contribution* of a formula φ in $\mathcal{L}^{pro}$, $[\varphi]$, is defined recursively, as specified below. There, i is a subset of VAR. Note that $[\cdot]$ is partial, where $[\varphi](i)$ is undefined whenever φ contains pronouns that cannot be resolved against i.

$$\begin{array}{rrcl}
\text{(i)} & [R(x_{1_g}, \ldots, x_{n_{g'}})](i) & = & \emptyset \\
\text{(ii)} & [\neg\varphi](i) & = & \emptyset, \text{ if } [\varphi](i) \text{ is defined} \\
\text{(iii)} & [\varphi \wedge \psi](i) & = & [\varphi](i) \cup [\psi](i \cup [\varphi](i)) \\
\text{(iv)} & [\varphi \rightarrow \psi](i) & = & \emptyset, \text{ if } [\varphi](i) \text{ and } [\psi](i \cup [\varphi](i)) \text{ are defined} \\
\text{(v)} & [\varphi \vee \psi](i) & = & \emptyset, \text{ if } [\varphi](i) \text{ and } [\psi](i) \text{ are defined} \\
\text{(vi)} & [\exists x_g\, \varphi](i) & = & \{x_g\} \cup [\varphi](i \cup \{x_g\}) \\
\text{(vii)} & [\forall x_g\, \varphi] & = & \emptyset, \text{ if } [\varphi](i \cup \{x_g\}) \text{ is defined} \\
\text{(viii)} & [?x_g\, \varphi](i) & = & [\varphi](i), \text{ if } \exists y_g \in i
\end{array}$$

Here g, $g' \in \{she, he, it\}$, and $[\varphi](i)$ is undefined, i.e., there is no o such that $[\varphi](i) = o$, if the condition on the right hand side is not fulfilled. Undefinedness is preserved by set union: if $[\varphi](i)$ is undefined, then $[\varphi](i) \cup i'$ is not defined either, for any input i'.

Let us briefly discuss the above definition. Atomic formulas do not add variables to the input context and the output context is the empty set. Negation behaves as a *barrier*. In (ii), the output context is $\emptyset$, no matter what the output context of the formula in the scope of the negation is. Conjunction is totally dynamic: things introduced in the first conjunct can serve as antecedents for the second conjunct as well as for any later formula, and the output of the first conjunct contributes to the input of the second conjunct while the output of the second conjunct contributes to the output of the whole formula. The existential quantifier in (vi) adds the variable that it binds to the input context of its scope, but unlike the universal quantifier, it also adds the variable to the output context. In (viii), the pronoun operator is treated. It assumes that there is a variable y in the input context that agrees with x on gender.

3.2 Contextual Information and Deduction

Definition 2 explains how context flows through a sequence of formulas. As deductive methods such as the tableau method manipulate the structure of formulas, we have to guarantee that the flow of contextual information is preserved by these manipulations. Our informal discussion below explains how we achieve this by introducing suitable labels on formulas; the formal details are postponed until Section 5.

Threading Context. To resolve pronouns during deduction, it is necessary to keep track of the context against which a particular pronoun can be resolved. The context is not a global parameter because it can change while processing a sequence of formulas. To implement this idea, formulas will be annotated with contextual information of the form $(i, o) : \varphi$, where i is the input context and o is the output context.

Structure Preservation. One of the major differences between dynamic semantics and classical logics is the structural sensitivity of the former. As an example, whereas $\neg\neg\varphi$ is classically equivalent to φ, this does not hold in dynamic semantics, because the output contexts of the formulas $\neg\neg\varphi$ and φ are not the same since negation functions as a kind of barrier. Consider (7):

(7)
$$\frac{(i, \emptyset) : \varphi \to \psi}{(i, o) : \neg\varphi \quad \Big| \quad (i \cup o, o') : \psi} \; (\to)$$

Neglecting labels, (7) is the regular tableau expansion rule for implication. Compare this to the definition of the contextual contribution of the implication in Definition 2, where the input context of the consequent ψ consists of the union of the input context of the formula as a whole, $\varphi \to \psi$, *and* the set of contribution of the antecedent φ. Now in (7), $[\neg\varphi](i)$ will always equal $\emptyset$, simply because negation functions as a barrier; as explained in Section 2. Therefore, the implication rule $(\to)$ has it was stated in (7) gives the wrong results. Of course, the problem is that a negation sign has been introduced by a tableau rule, which is a violation of one of the major principles of deduction methods for natural language semantics, viz. preservation of structure. But this can easily be remedied by using signed tableaux, where each formula is adorned with its polarity. Reconsidering the tableau expansion rule for implication, we have to distinguish two cases: implication under positive and implication under negative polarity.

(8) $$\frac{(i,\emptyset,+):\varphi\rightarrow\psi}{(i,o,-):\varphi \quad | \quad (i\cup o,o',+):\psi}\ (+:\rightarrow) \qquad \frac{(i,\emptyset,-):\varphi\rightarrow\psi}{\begin{array}{c}(i,o,+):\varphi\\ (i\cup o,o',-):\psi\end{array}}\ (-:\rightarrow)$$

Now, we can clearly distinguish between the truth-functional and contextual behavior of negation. Note, that both rules in (8) thread the context in a similar fashion even though their truth-functional behavior is different.

The order in which we process sentences is important, as they may contain anaphoric expressions that are only meaningful if the context provides an appropriate antecedent. This is also mirrored in the tableau rules where the input context of some node depends on the output of another node. For instance, $(i\cup o,o',-):\psi$ depends on $(i,o,+):\varphi$. Observe that dependency does not only hold between formulas on the same branch, but can also occur between formulas on different branches, as exemplified by the rule $(+:\rightarrow)$.

A Note on Unification. In Definition 2 contexts are defined as sets of variables. Below we will be using a free-variable tableau method (cf. [Fit96]), and we have to think about the double role of variables in a deduction: they are carriers of a value and possible antecedent for pronouns. Recall that in free-variable tableaux, universally quantified variables are substituted by a free variable and existentially quantified variables are substituted by a skolem function that depends on the free variables of the existentially quantified formula.

Consider the following situation. In a tableau, there are two nodes of the form $(i,o,p):\varphi(x)$ and $(\{x\}\cup i',o',p'):\psi$, where p, $p'\in\{+,-\}$ and x is a free variable in φ. If x is instantiated to a term t, then we have to substitute t for x in all formulas. But do we also have to substitute t for x in all context parameters? In our calculus presented in Section 5 below, the following solution is adopted: If t unifies with t', then t and t' denote the same entity in the model that we are implicitly building while constructing a tableau. If t is a possible antecedent for a pronoun z, then t' has to be a possible antecedent for z, too, since t and t' simply denote the same entity. Therefore, term substitution is applied to both formulas and contexts.

Introducing Goodness. Up to now, labels adorning formulas carry two kinds of information: contextual information (i, o) and polarity information ($+$, $-$). These parameters reflect the dynamic behavior of natural language utterances and the way in which context is threaded through a sequence of sentences. In addition, we have to account for a more general restriction on natural language utterances. In the set-up that we have so far, if a pronoun x_g occurs in a context i, all variables that are members of i and agree on gender with x_g can serve as antecedents. Unfortunately, this is too liberal, as the following example shows.

(9) A man sees a friend of his. He doesn't see him or he is in a rush.

The pronoun 'he' in (9) cannot refer to 'a man'. Intuitively, this would seem violate some kind of consistency constraint. To put it differently, a pronoun x_g cannot be resolved to an antecedent y_g if they carry contradictory information. Following [vD98], we call this restriction on possible pronoun resolutions *goodness*. Observe that goodness is a special case of a more general pragmatic principle like Grice's *maxim of quality*, cf. [Gri89].

How do we implement the notion of goodness in our calculus? The premises and the conclusion themselves should be consistent, as we assume that native speakers do not utter inconsistent sentences. In our calculus we will implement this idea by making an explicit distinction between the (original) premises and (original) conclusions of a tableau proof; we will mark the former with p and the latter with c.[2]

Summing up, then, the nodes in our tableau calculus will be labeled formulas of the form $(i, o, \varrho, p) : \varphi$. Here, i is the input context, o is the context contribution of φ, $\varrho \in \{\mathsf{p}, \mathsf{c}\}$ indicates whether φ occurs as part of the premises or the conclusion, and $p \in \{+, -\}$ carries the polarity of φ.

4 The Semantics of Pronoun Ambiguity

Before we introduce our tableau calculus for $\mathcal{L}^{pro}$, we present its semantics and a notion of entailment for it. Starting with the latter, there are various possibilities. Following our discussion in Section 2, we opt for an entailment relation $\models_a$ where ψ follows from $\varphi_1, \ldots, \varphi_n$ if there is a disambiguation θ of $\varphi_1, \ldots, \varphi_n$ and a disambiguation θ' of ψ such that $\theta(\varphi_1, \ldots, \varphi_n) \models \theta'(\psi)$. This choice might lead to overdefinedness of some formula φ, since it might be the case that $M, h, i \models \theta(\varphi)$, for some disambiguation θ, but $M, h, i \not\models \theta'(\varphi)$, for another disambiguation θ'.

To be able to deal with this, we distinguish between *verification* ($\models_a$) and *falsification* ($=\!\!|_a$). To motivate this distinction, compare the sentences in (10).

(10)a. It is not the case that he sleeps.
b. He doesn't sleep.

Their semantic representations are formulas of the form $\neg ?x_g\, \varphi$ and $?x_g\, \neg\varphi$, respectively. Intuitively, (10.a) and (10.b) have the same meaning, therefore it should be the case that $\neg ?x_g\, \varphi$ and $?x_g\, \neg\varphi$ are logically equivalent. If we would try to set up a semantics for $\mathcal{L}^{pro}$ by simply using $\models_a$, we would not get the desired equivalence of $\neg ?x_g\, \varphi$ and $?x_g\, \neg\varphi$:

[2] Readers familiar with abduction may find it helpful to compare this distinction to the one where, in abduction, one requires that explanations preserve the consistency of the premises; see [CMP93].

(11)a. $M, h, i \models_a \neg ?x_g \varphi$ iff $M, h, i \not\models_a ?x_g \varphi$
iff $M, h[x_g/h(y_g)], i \not\models_a \varphi$ for all $y_g \in i$

b. $M, h, i \models_a ?x_g \neg\varphi$ iff $M, h[x_g/h(y_g)], i \models_a \neg\varphi$ for some $y_g \in i$
iff $M, h[x_g/h(y_g)], i \not\models_a \varphi$ for some $y_g \in i$

The problem is that a semantics built up by using $\models_a$ interprets the ?-operator as a quantifier, which it is not. On the other hand, if we distinguish between verification and falsification, we get the desired equivalence:

(12)a. $M, h, i \models_a \neg ?x_g \varphi$ iff $M, h, i \dashv_a ?x_g \varphi$
iff $M, h[x_g/h(y_g)], i \dashv_a \varphi$ for some $y_g \in i$

b. $M, h, i \models_a ?x_g \neg\varphi$ iff $M, h[x_g/h(y_g)], i \models_a \neg\varphi$ for some $y_g \in i$
iff $M, h[x_g/h(y_g)], i \dashv_a \varphi$ for some $y_g \in i$

In the following definition verification and falsification for the other boolean connectives are defined.

Definition 3 (Semantics of $\mathcal{L}^{pro}$). Verification and falsification are defined, given a model M, a variable assignment h and a context i. As usual, a model $M = \langle \mathcal{U}, \mathcal{I} \rangle$ consists of two parts: a universe $\mathcal{U}$ and an interpretation $\mathcal{I}$ of the non-logical constants. First, we are going to define the semantics of the terms of $\mathcal{L}^{pro}$. x_g is a variable (possibly a pronoun) with gender g, c_g is a constant with gender g, and f_g is a function with gender g, where $g \in \{he, she, it\}$

(a) $[\![x_g]\!]^{M,h,i} = h(x_g)$
(b) $[\![c_g]\!]^{M,h,i} = \mathcal{I}(c_g)$
(c) $[\![f_g(t_1 \ldots t_n)]\!]^{M,h,i} = f_g^{\mathcal{I}}([\![t_1]\!]^{M,h,i} \ldots [\![t_n]\!]^{M,h,i})$

For formulas, $\models_a$ and $\dashv_a$ can be defined recursively:

(i) $M, h, i \models_a R(t_1, \ldots, t_n)$ iff $\langle [\![t_1]\!]^{M,h,i}, \ldots, [\![t_n]\!]^{M,h,i} \rangle \in \mathcal{I}(R)$
$M, h, i \dashv_a R(t_1, \ldots, t_n)$ iff $\langle [\![t_1]\!]^{M,h,i}, \ldots, [\![t_n]\!]^{M,h,i} \rangle \notin \mathcal{I}(R)$
(ii) $M, h, i \models_a \neg\varphi$ iff $M, h, i \dashv_a \varphi$
$M, h, i \dashv_a \neg\varphi$ iff $M, h, i \models_a \varphi$
(iii) $M, h, i \models_a \varphi \wedge \psi$ iff $M, h, i \models_a \varphi$ and $M, h, i \cup [\varphi](i) \models_a \psi$
$M, h, i \dashv_a \varphi \wedge \psi$ iff $M, h, i \dashv_a \varphi$ or $M, h, i \cup [\varphi](i) \dashv_a \psi$
(iv) $M, h, i \models_a \varphi \rightarrow \psi$ iff $M, h, i \dashv_a \varphi$ or $M, h, i \cup [\varphi](i) \models_a \psi$
$M, h, i \dashv_a \varphi \rightarrow \psi$ iff $M, h, i \models_a \varphi$ and $M, h, i \cup [\varphi](i) \dashv_a \psi$
(v) $M, h, i \models_a \varphi \vee \psi$ iff $M, h, i \models_a \varphi$ or $M, h, i \models_a \psi$
$M, h, i \dashv_a \varphi \vee \psi$ iff $M, h, i \dashv_a \varphi$ and $M, h, i \dashv_a \psi$
(vi) $M, h, i \models_a \exists x_g \varphi$ iff $\exists d \in \mathcal{U} : M, h[x_g/d], i \models_a \varphi$
$M, h, i \dashv_a \exists x_g \varphi$ iff $\forall d \in \mathcal{U} : M, h[x_g/d], i \dashv_a \varphi$
(vii) $M, h, i \models_a \forall x_g \varphi$ iff $\forall d \in \mathcal{U} : M, h[x_g/d], i \models_a \varphi$
$M, h, i \dashv_a \forall x_g \varphi$ iff $\exists d \in \mathcal{U} : M, h[x_g/d], i \dashv_a \varphi$
(viii) $M, h, i \models_a ?x_g \varphi$ iff $\exists y_g \in i : M, h[x_g/h(y_g)], i \models_a \varphi$
$M, h, i \dashv_a ?x_g \varphi$ iff $\exists y_g \in i : M, h[x_g/h(y_g)], i \dashv_a \varphi$

Overdefinedness is induced by the ?-operator. It is possible that a formula containing a pronoun can be verified *and* falsified by a model M; i.e., $M, h, i \models_a ?x_g\, \varphi$ and $M, h, i \Dashv_a ?x_g\, \varphi$. In addition, it might also happen that the semantic value of a formula φ is undefined. This is also due to (viii), where undefinedness results if there is no accessible variable in the context to which the pronoun could be resolved. In this case it holds that $M, h, i \not\models_a ?x_g\, \varphi$ and $M, h, i \not\Dashv_a ?x_g\, \varphi$.

Thus, the resulting logic is four-valued containing besides truth (1) and falsity (0), overdefinedness and underdefinedness. This can be illustrated by a Hasse diagram, as in (13).

(13)

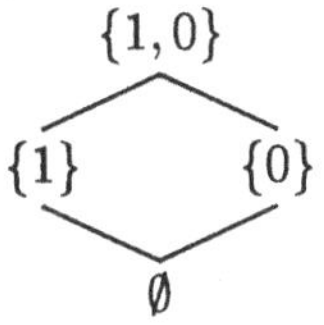

The sets denote the truth values that can be assigned to a formula. The singletons $\{1\}$ and $\{0\}$ denote the classical truth values, $\emptyset$ denotes undefinedness, and $\{1, 0\}$ denotes overdefinedness.

Finally, we define a notion of entailment for sequences of formals that possibly contain unresolved pronouns.

Definition 4 (Entailment in $\mathcal{L}^{pro}$). Let $\varphi_1, \ldots, \varphi_n, \psi$ be in $\mathcal{L}^{pro}$, h an arbitrary variable assignment, and i an arbitrary context. We say that $\varphi_1, \ldots, \varphi_n$ *ambiguously entail* ψ, written as $\varphi_1, \ldots, \varphi_n \models_a \psi$, if for all M:

if for all $j \in \{1, \ldots, n\}$: $M, h, [\varphi_1 \wedge \cdots \wedge \varphi_{j-1}](i) \models_a \varphi_j$
then $M, h, i \models_a \psi$

Pronouns occurring in ψ are resolved against the context i which is also the context of the premises. Thereby, ψ cannot pick antecedents introduced in the premises. Note, that there are several ways to define dynamic entailment relations and the one proposed is just one of them. [vB96, Chapter 7] classifies the entailment relation defined above as *update-to-update consequence.* Observe, by the way, that our notion of entailment is nonmonotonic, as most entailment relations in dynamic frameworks.

5 A Tableau Calculus for Pronoun Resolution

This section introduces our tableau calculus for reasoning with unresolved pronouns. The calculus consists of two components, a set of tableau expansion rules, and contextual parameters that allow us to interleave pronoun resolution and deduction steps. We first discuss the rules and then provide a short example.

5.1 The Tableau Expansion Rules

To reason with pronoun ambiguities we use a tableau calculus that is both free-variable and signed. The first property is simply to avoid the inefficiency of ground tableaux. Free-variable tableaux are fairly standard and we will not say much about them here; the reader is referred to [Fit96] instead. Signed tableaux are not new either, but here the signs are employed for a novel purpose. In Section 3, we motivated the distinction between negation in the object language ($\neg$) and polarities of tableau nodes ($+$, $-$). This was necessary because $\neg$ has an impact on the flow of contextual information, and to guarantee structure preservation we do not want to allow tableau rules to introduce additional negations. In addition, a distinction between verification and falsification is important to assign the right semantic values to formulas containing pronouns. An occurrence of a node of the form $+ : \varphi$ means that φ is verifiable, which corresponds to $\models_a$, and an occurrence of the form $- : \varphi$ means that φ is falsifiable, corresponding to $=\!|_a$.

Table 1. The tableau rules for $\mathcal{T}^{pro}$

$$\frac{(i,o,\varrho,+) : \varphi \wedge \psi}{\begin{array}{c}(i,o',\varrho,+) : \varphi \\ (i \cup o', o, \varrho, +) : \psi\end{array}}\ (+:\wedge) \qquad \frac{(i,o,\varrho,-) : \varphi \wedge \psi}{(i,o',\varrho,-) : \varphi \ \mid\ (i \cup o', o, \varrho, -) : \psi}\ (-:\wedge)$$

$$\frac{(i,\emptyset,\varrho,+) : \varphi \vee \psi}{(i,o,\varrho,+) : \varphi \ \mid\ (i,o',\varrho,+) : \psi}\ (+:\vee) \qquad \frac{(i,\emptyset,\varrho,-) : \varphi \vee \psi}{\begin{array}{c}(i,o,\varrho,-) : \varphi \\ (i,o',\varrho,-) : \psi\end{array}}\ (-:\vee)$$

$$\frac{(i,\emptyset,\varrho,+) : \varphi \rightarrow \psi}{(i,o,\varrho,-) : \varphi \ \mid\ (i \cup o, o', \varrho, +) : \psi}\ (+:\rightarrow) \qquad \frac{(i,\emptyset,\varrho,-) : \varphi \rightarrow \psi}{\begin{array}{c}(i,o,\varrho,+) : \varphi \\ (i \cup o, o', \varrho, -) : \psi\end{array}}\ (-:\rightarrow)$$

$$\frac{(i,\emptyset,\varrho,+) : \neg\varphi}{(i,o,\varrho,-) : \varphi}\ (+:\neg) \qquad \frac{(i,\emptyset,\varrho,-) : \neg\varphi}{(i,o,\varrho,+) : \varphi}\ (-:\neg)$$

$$\frac{(i,\emptyset,\varrho,+) : \forall x_g\, \varphi}{(i \cup \{x_g\}, o, \varrho, +) : \varphi[x_g/X_g]}\ (+:\forall) \qquad \frac{(i,\emptyset,\varrho,-) : \forall x_g\, \varphi}{(i \cup \{x_g\}, o, \varrho, -) : \varphi[x_g/f_g(X_1 \dots X_n)]}\ (-:\forall)^{\dagger}$$

$$\frac{(i, o \cup \{x_g\}, \varrho, +) : \exists x_g \varphi}{(i \cup \{x_g\}, o, \varrho, +) : \varphi[x_g/f_g(X_1 \dots X_n)]}\ (+:\exists)^{\dagger} \qquad \frac{(i, o \cup \{x_g\}, \varrho, -) : \exists x_g\, \varphi}{(i \cup \{x_g\}, o, \varrho, -) : \varphi[x_g/X_g]}\ (-:\exists)$$

$$\frac{(i \cup \{t_g\}, o, \varrho, +) : ?x_g\, \varphi}{(i \cup \{t_g\}, o, \varrho, +) : \varphi[x_g/t_g^{pro}]}\ (+:?) \qquad \frac{(i \cup \{t_g\}, o, \varrho, -) : ?x_g\, \varphi}{(i \cup \{t_g\}, o, \varrho, -) : \varphi[x_g/t_g^{pro}]}\ (-:?)$$

$$\frac{\begin{array}{c}(i,o,\varrho,+) : R(s_1, \dots, s_n) \\ (i',o',\varrho',-) : R(t_1, \dots, t_n)\end{array}}{\bot}\ (\bot)^{\ddagger}$$

†Where $X_1 \dots X_n$ are the free variables in φ and i.
‡If $\varrho \neq \varrho'$ then $\{s_1, \dots, s_n, t_1, \dots, t_n\} \cap PRO = \emptyset$

The complete set of tableau rules constituting our calculus for pronoun ambiguity, $\mathcal{T}^{pro}$, is given in Table 1. The rules may seem somewhat overwhelming, but most of them are familiar ones. Remember that nodes are annotated by labels and are of the form $(i, o, \varrho, p) : \varphi$, where i is the input context, o is the output context, which is computed by $[\varphi](i)$. ϱ indicates the origin of the formula, whether it occurred as a premise (p) or a conclusion (c). Polarity is simply expressed by p, $p \in \{+, -\}$. The way in which context is threaded through the tableau corresponds to the definition of contextual contribution, cf. Definition 2. Polarity assignment is done as defined in Definition 3.

Given our earlier discussions, the expansion rules should be obvious, but some rules deserve special attention. Let us first discuss the pronoun rules $(+ : ?)$ and $(- : ?)$. First, the ?-operator is simply dropped, and the variable it binds is substituted by one of its accessible terms that agrees with the pronoun on gender. These instantiations are marked as *pro*, in order to distinguish them from argument positions that are no instantiations of a pronoun. The set *PRO* is the set of all marked terms. The superscript has no influence on unification of terms, it is just needed to constrain the closure of a branch to cases that obey goodness.

Next, we consider the rules $(+ : \exists)$ and $(- : \forall)$. Both rules involve skolemization, and the question is which influence pronoun variables have on skolem terms. Consider the node in (14).

(14) $(i, o, \varrho, +) : \exists x_g \, ?y_{g'} \, \varphi$

In (14), applying the tableau expansion rule $(+ : \exists)$ will substitute x_g by a skolem function $f_g(X_1 \ldots X_n)$, where $X_1, \ldots, X_n$ are the free variables in φ. But what about $y_{g'}$? It does not occur free in φ, because it is bound by the ?-operator, but it could be resolved to some t_n in the context, which contains free variables. This dilemma is due to the order of application. First, skolemization is carried out, and then pronoun resolution. This leads to incorrectness. For instance, from $\forall x_g \, \exists y_{g'} \, ?z_g \, R(z_g, y_{g'})$ we can now derive $\exists y_{g'} \, \forall x_g \, ?z_g \, R(z_g, y_{g'})$, which is clearly not a valid derivation. Here, x_g does not occur overtly in $R(z_g, y_{g'})$, but z_g can be resolved to x_g. To fix this, skolemization does not only have to depend on the free variables occurring in formulas, but also on the free variables occurring in the terms of the input context since pronouns can be resolved to these terms.

Finally, $(\perp)$ carries the proviso that two literals of distinct polarity, where both originate from the premises (marked p) or both originate from the conclusion (marked c), do not allow to close a tableau branch if they contain pronoun instantiations. This allows us to encode goodness into the tableau calculus, saying that pronouns can only be resolved to antecedents that do not carry contradictory information, as exemplified by (9). It ensures that the premises themselves and the conclusion on its own are interpreted consistently. But of course, it is still possible to derive a contradiction from the combination of the former with the negation of the latter.

5.2 An Example

Given a two-sentence sequence *A man sees a boy. He whistles*, we want to see whether we can derive *A man whistles*. The semantic representation of the premises is given by the first two nodes, and the negation of the conclusion is given by the third node. The corresponding proof is displayed in Table 2.

Table 2. A Sample Proof in $\mathcal{T}^{pro}$

$$(\emptyset, o_1, \mathsf{p}, +) : \exists x_{he}\,(man(x_{he}) \wedge \exists y_{he}\,(boy(y_{he}) \wedge see(x_{he}, y_{he})))$$

$$(o_1, o_2, \mathsf{p}, +) : ?z_{he}\; whistle(z_{he})$$

$$(\emptyset, o_3, \mathsf{c}, -) : \exists u_{he}\,(man(u_{he}) \wedge whistle(u_{he}))$$

$$o_1 := \{f_{he}\}$$

$$(\{f_{he}\}, o_1, \mathsf{p}, +) : man(f_{he}) \wedge \exists y_{he}\,(boy(y_{he}) \wedge see(f_{he}, y_{he}))$$

$$(\{f_{he}\}, \{f_{he}\}, \mathsf{p}, +) : man(f_{he})$$

$$(\{f_{he}\}, o_1, \mathsf{p}, +) : \exists y_{he}\,(boy(y_{he}) \wedge see(f_{he}, y_{he}))$$

$$o_1 := o_1 \cup \{g_{he}\}$$

$$(\{f_{he}, g_{he}\}, o_4, \mathsf{p}, +) : boy(g_{he}) \wedge see(f_{he}, g_{he})$$

$$(\{f_{he}, g_{he}\}, \emptyset, \mathsf{p}, +) : boy(g_{he})$$

$$(\{f_{he}, g_{he}\}, \emptyset, \mathsf{p}, +) : see(f_{he}, g_{he})$$

$$(\{f_{he}, g_{he}\}, \emptyset, \mathsf{p}, +) : whistle(g_{he})$$

$$o_3 := \{U_{he}\}$$

$$(\{U_{he}\}, o_3, \mathsf{c}, -) : man(U_{he}) \wedge whistle(U_{he})$$

$$(\{U_{he}\}, \emptyset, \mathsf{c}, -) : man(U_{he}) \qquad (\{U_{he}\}, \emptyset, \mathsf{c}, -) : whistle(U_{he})$$

$$(\{f_{he}, g_{he}\}, \emptyset, \mathsf{p}, +) : whistle(f_{he}) \qquad \perp \{U_{he}/g_{he}\}$$

$$o_3 := o_3 \cup \{V_{he}\}$$

$$(\{V_{he}\}, o_3, \mathsf{c}, -) : man(V_{he}) \wedge whistle(V_{he})$$

$$(\{V_{he}\}, \emptyset, \mathsf{c}, -) : man(V_{he}) \qquad (\{V_{he}\}, \emptyset, \mathsf{c}, -) : whistle(V_{he})$$

$$\perp \{V_{he}/f_{he}\} \qquad \perp \{V_{he}/f_{he}\}$$

First, we try to resolve the pronoun to g_{he}. This allows us to close the rightmost branch, with mgu $\{U_{he}/g_{he}\}$. But then there is no contradictory node for $(\{g_{he}\}, \emptyset, \mathsf{c}, -) : man(g_{he})$. Hence, we apply pronoun resolution again, and this time resolve it to f_{he}. Next, universal instantiation is applied with the new free variable V_{he}. Now, all remaining branches can be closed by the mgu $\{V_{he}/f_{he}\}$. In Table 2, the pairs that allow to close a branch are connected by a dashed line.

The threading of contextual information may seem a bit confusing, but it is hard to display the dynamics of the instantiation of the context variables on 'static' paper. It may be helpful to read the tableau rules in Table 1 as PROLOG clauses, where the context variables of the parent of a rule unify with the context variables of the node the rule is applied to.

6 Results

The tableau calculus $\mathcal{T}^{pro}$ has a number of advantages over a resolution-based approach to pronoun resolution, as provided in [MdR98b]. First of all, it is possible to interleave the computation of accessible variables with deduction, since preservation of structure is guaranteed in our signed tableau method. This is not possible in resolution, because it is assumed that the input is in conjunctive normal form, which destroys all structural information needed for pronoun binding. Accessible antecedents can only be computed by a preprocessing step, cf. [MdR98b].

But the major advantage is that no backtracking is needed if the choice of an antecedent for a pronoun does not allow us to close all open branches; we simply apply pronoun resolution again, choosing a different antecedent. Of course, more has to be said about controlling proof construction than we have room for here. For instance, one would like to prevent the proof method from choosing again an antecedent for a pronoun that did not allow to close some branches. This can be accomplished by some simple book keeping about the antecedents that have been used before.

$\mathcal{T}^{pro}$ has been implemented in PROLOG, and is based on lean$T^{A}P$ [BP95,PSar], a well-known depth-first theorem prover for classical first-order logic. It is slightly adapted for our purposes, where we dispense with the assumption that the input is in negation normal form as this violates the principle of structure preservation. Of course, this adaption results in a less lean, but still rather efficient theorem prover. The PROLOG implementation of $\mathcal{T}^{pro}$ is available online at `http://www.wins.uva.nl/~christof/implementations.html`.

To conclude this section, let us turn to a brief discussion of soundness and completeness of $\mathcal{T}^{pro}$. There are at least two strategies for establishing soundness and completeness. Of course, one can follow a *direct* strategy: prove soundness by in the traditional manner, and prove completeness by using the 'classical' completeness proof for free variable tableaux based on Hintikka sets is adapted. Here, we sketch an *indirect* strategy that consists in reducing the soundness and completeness of $\mathcal{T}^{pro}$ to the soundness and completeness of a traditional free-variable tableau calculi for first-order logic, $\mathcal{T}^{class}$. The basic intuition is the following: by analyzing tableaux for $\mathcal{T}^{pro}$ one can extract pronoun resolutions that can be used to help preprocess ambiguous $\mathcal{L}^{pro}$ formulas and turn them into traditional first-order formulas, while preserving enough information about satisfiability.

Theorem 5 (Soundness of $\mathcal{T}^{pro}$). *If a closed tableau can be generated from* $\Gamma = \{(\emptyset, o, \mathsf{p}, +) : \bigwedge_{k=1}^{n} \varphi_k, (\emptyset, o'', \mathsf{c}, -) : \psi\}$, *where* $\varphi_1, \dots, \varphi_n, \psi \in \mathcal{L}^{pro}$, *then* $\varphi_1, \dots, \varphi_n \models_a \psi$.

Proof. Given a closed tableau T for Γ, the pronoun instantiations $\{t_1^{pro} \dots t_m^{pro}\}$ that led to the closure of the branches of T are collected. Then, we relate the instantiations to the pronoun variables $\{x_1 \dots x_m\}$ that introduced them by an application of $(+ : ?)$ or $(- : ?)$. As $\{t_1 \dots t_m\}$ are free variables or skolem terms, we identify the quantifier variables $\{y_1 \dots y_m\}$ that introduced $\{t_1 \dots t_m\}$. This yields two substitution of the form $\theta = \{x_1/y_1 \dots x_j/y_j\}$ and $\theta' = \{x_{j+1}/y_{j+1} \dots x_m/y_m\}$, where θ disambiguates the pronouns occurring in the premises, and θ' disambiguates the pronouns occurring in the conclusion. To ensure that substituted variables are classically bound, we apply a re-bracketing algorithm which is used in dynamic semantics, in order to relate dynamic semantics to classical logic, cf. [GS91]. To illustrate the process of re-bracketing, it allows us to replace a dynamic formula such as $\exists x\, \varphi(x) \wedge \psi(x)$ by its classical counterpart $\exists x\, (\varphi(x) \wedge \psi(x))$. More generally the re-bracketing algorithm may be specified as follows:

Definition 6 (Re-bracketing). Every dynamic formula can be translated to a formula of classical first-order logic. In [GS91] a function $\mathbf{b}$ is defined that accomplishes this. $\mathbf{b}$ is defined recursively:

1. $\mathbf{b}R(t_1 \dots t_n) = R(t_1 \dots t_n)$
2. $\mathbf{b}\neg\varphi = \neg\mathbf{b}\varphi$
3. $\mathbf{b}(\varphi_1 \vee \varphi_2) = \mathbf{b}\varphi_1 \vee \mathbf{b}\varphi_2$
4. $\mathbf{b}\exists x\, \varphi = \exists x\, \mathbf{b}\varphi$
5. $\mathbf{b}\forall x\, \varphi = \forall x\, \mathbf{b}\varphi$
6. $\mathbf{b}(\varphi_1 \wedge \varphi_2) =$
   (a) $\mathbf{b}(\psi_1 \wedge (\psi_2 \wedge \varphi_2))$ if $\varphi_1 = \psi_1 \wedge \psi_2$
   (b) $\exists x\, \mathbf{b}(\psi \wedge \varphi_2)$ if $\varphi_1 = \exists x\, \psi$
   (c) $\mathbf{b}\varphi_1 \wedge \mathbf{b}\varphi_2$ otherwise
7. $\mathbf{b}(\varphi_1 \rightarrow \varphi_2) =$
   (a) $\mathbf{b}(\psi_1 \rightarrow (\psi_2 \rightarrow \varphi_2))$ if $\varphi_1 = \psi_1 \wedge \psi_2$
   (b) $\forall x\, \mathbf{b}(\psi \rightarrow \varphi_2)$ if $\varphi_1 = \exists x\, \psi$
   (c) $\mathbf{b}\varphi_1 \rightarrow \mathbf{b}\varphi_2$ otherwise

Re-bracketing can be applied, because pronoun variables are always substituted by quantified variables that are accessible in the sense of Definition 2, which is based on the notion of accessibility in dynamic semantics, see e.g., [KR93,GS91].

Then, a closed tableau for $\varphi_1, \dots, \varphi_n, \neg\psi$ in $\mathcal{T}^{pro}$ gives rise to a closed tableau for $\varphi'_1, \dots, \varphi'_n, \neg\psi'$ in $\mathcal{T}^{class}$, by the soundness of $\mathcal{T}^{class}$, where $\varphi'_1, \dots, \varphi'_n$ is the result of applying θ and re-bracketing to $\varphi_1, \dots, \varphi_n$, and $\neg\psi'$ results from applying θ' and re-bracketing to $\neg\psi$ □

Theorem 7 (Completeness of $\mathcal{T}^{pro}$). *If an open tableau can be generated from* $\Gamma = \{(\emptyset, o, \mathsf{p}, +) : \bigwedge_{k=1}^{n} \varphi_k, (\emptyset, o'', \mathsf{c}, -) : \psi\}$, *where* $\varphi_1, \ldots, \varphi_n, \psi \in \mathcal{L}^{pro}$, *then* $\varphi_1, \ldots, \varphi_n \not\models_a \psi$.

Proof. If Γ is consistent in $\mathcal{T}^{pro}$, then it may be shown that for all admissible pronoun resolutions θ, θ', the set $\theta\varphi_1, \ldots, \theta\varphi_n, \theta'\neg\psi$ is consistent in $\mathcal{T}^{class}$. Obviously, we neeed to get rid of ambiguous formulas involving the ?-operator. when moving from $\mathcal{T}^{pro}$ to $\mathcal{T}^{class}$, but this is what the admissible pronoun resolution does for us. By the completeness of $\mathcal{T}^{class}$ (see [Fit96]), we get that $\theta\varphi_1, \ldots, \theta\varphi_n, \theta'\neg\psi$ is (classically) satisfiable, for any admissible θ, θ'. Hence, $\varphi_1, \ldots, \varphi_n, \neg\psi$ is satisfiable according to $\models_a$, as required. □

7 Conclusions

In this paper, we have proposed a tableau calculus that tries to tackle an instance of a particularly important and difficult task in computational semantics: automated reasoning with ambiguity. A tableau calculus that allows one to interleave disambiguation and deduction has been proposed to overcome the problem of state explosion one inevitably runs into if theorem proving is applied to naïvely disambiguated semantic representations.

To enable on-the-fly disambiguation during proof development, it is necessary that enough structural information of the original representation is preserved. In the case of pronoun resolution this structural information is needed to define which variables can serve as antecedents for pronouns. The nodes in the tableau were adorned with labels containing this additional contextual information.

It turned out that tableau methods are especially well-suited for reasoning with natural language semantics, since they are analytic (in contrast to Natural Deduction), and they allow for a more sensitive manipulation of the syntactic structures of the formulas (in contrast to resolution methods). See, for instance, [KK98,MdR98c] for other applications of tableau methods in the area of computational semantics.

Future work will be devoted to extending our tableau calculus to more complex cases of anaphora resolution, like presuppositions, or plural pronouns, where contextual information has to contain more structure than just lists of accessible terms. At the same time, it has to be investigated how a more comprehensive framework that allows to reason with different kinds of ambiguity can be set up. We plan to combine our tableau calculus for pronoun resolution with some of our earlier work on reasoning with quantificational ambiguity, cf. [MdR98c].

Acknowledgments. We want to thank the referees for their helful comments. Christof Monz was supported by the Physical Sciences Council with financial support from the Netherlands Organisation for Scientific Research (NWO), project 612-13-001. Maarten de Rijke was supported by the Spinoza Project 'Logic in Action' at ILLC, the University of Amsterdam.

References

[All94] J.F. Allen. *Natural Language Understanding.* Benjamin Cummings, second edition, 1994.

[Als92] H. Alshawi, editor. *The Core Language Engine.* MIT Press, Cambridge, Massachusetts, 1992.

[BP95] B. Beckert and J. Posegga. Lean, tableau-based deduction. *Journal of Automated Reasoning*, 15(3):339–358, 1995.

[vB96] J. van Benthem. *Exploring Logical Dynamics.* Studies in Logic, Language and Information. CSLI Publications, 1996.

[CMP93] M. Cialdea Meyer and F. Pirri. First order abduction via tableau and sequent calculi. *Bulletin of the IGPL*, 1(1):99–117, 1993.

[vD98] K. van Deemter. Ambiguity and the principle of idiosyncratic interpretation. Submitted for publication, 1998.

[Fit96] M. Fitting. *First-Order Logic and Automated Theorem Proving.* Springer-Verlag New York, 2nd edition, 1996.

[Gri89] H.P. Grice. *Studies in the Way of Words.* Harvard Univ Press, 1989.

[GS91] J. Groenendijk and M. Stokhof. Dynamic Predicate Logic. *Linguistics and Philosophy*, 14:39–100, 1991.

[KK98] M. Kohlhase and K. Konrad. Higher-order automated theorem proving for natural language semantics. SEKI-Report SR-98-04, Universität des Saarlandes, 1998.

[KR93] H. Kamp and U. Reyle. *From Discourse to Logic.* Kluwer Academic Publishers, 1993.

[MdR98a] C. Monz and M. de Rijke. Inference and natural language semantics. In *Proceedings of Logical Aspects in Computational Linguistics (LACL'98)*, 1998.

[MdR98b] C. Monz and M. de Rijke. A resolution calculus for dynamic semantics. In J. Dix, L. Fariñas del Cerro, and U. Fuhrbach, editors, *Logics in Artificial Intelligence (JELIA'98)*, Lecture Notes in Artificial Intelligence 1489, pages 184–198. Springer, 1998.

[MdR98c] C. Monz and M. de Rijke. A tableaux calculus for ambiguous quantification. In H. de Swart, editor, *Automated Reasoning with Analytic Tableaux and Related Methods,* TABLEAUX'98, Lecture Notes in Artificial Intelligence 1397, pages 232–246. Springer, 1998.

[PSar] J. Posegga and P.H. Schmitt. Implementing semantic tableaux. In *Handbook of Tableau-Based Methods in Automated Deduction.* Kluwer Academic Publishers, to appear.

Generating Minimal Herbrand Models Step by Step

Heribert Schütz

Institut für Informatik, Universität München, Germany
Heribert.Schuetz@informatik.uni-muenchen.de

Abstract. This paper presents a way to improve minimal model generation for clausal theories. It works by breaking up the model generation process into several steps according to several parts of the given theory. It is shown that elimination of non-minimal or duplicate models can be performed after each step, which reduces the overall search space. An even stronger reduction of the search space is possible if we are interested only in certain parts of the models to be generated.
The techniques are applicable to any method for the generation of minimal Herbrand models. The paper goes into some detail how they can be integrated tightly into the PUHR tableau method.

1 Introduction

Various methods for generating models of logic theories have been developed and described in the literature. Some of these methods (e.g., [7, 4, 9]) actually generate Herbrand models for clausal theories. Herbrand models are known to exist for a clausal theory if the theory is satisfiable at all. The restriction to Herbrand models has the advantage that the interpretation of the function symbols is fixed and thus only the interpretation of the predicate symbols needs to be determined.

Frequently it is desirable that the generated Herbrand models are minimal, i.e., there should not be another Herbrand model that satisfies only a subset of the ground atoms satisfied by some generated Herbrand model. Non-monotonic reasoning is one important application of minimal models. Another reason for dealing with minimal models is that further processing steps applied to the generated models are typically more efficient for smaller models. This is especially important if these processing steps are carried out by humans. In diagnosis applications a generated model should be as small as possible so that it represents a diagnosis as precise as possible [8].

This paper introduces two refinements that can be applied to various methods for generating minimal Herbrand models of clausal theories. For the first of these refinements we divide a clausal theory Th into parts $Th_1, Th_2, \ldots, Th_n$. Now we generate minimal Herbrand models step by step. First we generate the minimal Herbrand models of Th_1. Then we try to extend each such model yielding Herbrand models of Th_2 and we select the minimal ones. This procedure is repeated until we reach Th_n. Under certain conditions the models that we have finally generated are just the minimal models of Th. Model generation methods like the PUHR-tableau calculus and its variants [7,4] do not only generate the minimal Herbrand models of a theory but also some non-minimal ones. A model may also be generated more than once. Special measures (which are sometimes considered part of the model generation method) have to be taken in order to remove non-minimal models and duplicates. The first refinement has the advantage that it allows to apply these measures early and frequently, namely after each step dealing with a Th_i. This reduces the number of intermediate results and thus makes the further process more efficient.

For the second refinement note that we are usually not interested in an entire model, but only in its "relevant" parts. That is, we want to know how certain ground atoms are interpreted, but we don't care about others. We also want to minimize models w.r.t. the relevant atoms. That is, we are interested in models that satisfy as few as possible of the relevant ground atoms. Diagnosis applications are important examples here: We are interested in and want to minimize w.r.t. only those atoms that describe the diagnosis itself, but not those atoms that describe other details of a system state. It turns out to be possible to perform a restriction to the relevant parts of generated models after each step, i.e., after model generation for one of the Th_i has been performed. Two models that are not comparable (i.e., none is a subset of the other) may become comparable or even equal after the restriction to relevant parts, which then allows to eliminate one of them. So the second refinement allows us to prune the search space even more.

In order to get a better intutitive understanding of these ideas consider a clausal theory Th consisting of the clauses

$$
\begin{array}{ll}
p_1 & \\
p_i \rightarrow q_{i,1} \vee \ldots \vee q_{i,m} & \text{for } i \in \{1, \ldots, n\} \\
q_{i,j} \rightarrow p_{i+1} & \text{for } i \in \{1, \ldots, n\} \text{ and } j \in \{1, \ldots, m\}
\end{array}
$$

and assume that we are interested only in p_{n+1}.

A naive method would generate m^n minimal Herbrand models, each of which satisfies all the p_i for $i \in \{1, \ldots, n+1\}$ and some q_{i,j_i} for every $i \in \{1, \ldots, n\}$. In particular, every generated model satisfies p_{n+1}, which we were interested in.

Now we divide Th into subsets $Th_1, \ldots, Th_n$ in such a way that every Th_i contains the clauses of the form $p_i \rightarrow q_{i,1} \vee \ldots \vee q_{i,m}$ and $q_{i,j} \rightarrow p_{i+1}$ with the respective value of i. In addition, Th_1 contains p_1. The step-by-step model generation proceeds as follows: For Th_1 we get several models of which those m models that satisfy only p_1, p_2 and one of the $q_{1,j}$ are minimal. For our further computation we are only interested in p_2, which is satisfied by all generated models. We now generate models of Th_2 which also satisfy p_2. We do this only once and need not repeat it for all generated models of Th_1. Among the generated models there are again m minimal ones, namely those that satisfy only p_2, p_3 and one of the $q_{2,j}$. We perform similar steps for Th_3 to Th_n. In the last step we get again m models, each of which satisfies p_{n+1}. The number of minimal models generated in all steps is now only $n * m$. Furthermore the models are a lot smaller than the ones generated by the naive method.

The rest of the paper is organized as follows. The next section introduces terminology and notation and also recalls results about the structure of the set of Herbrand models of a clausal theory. In Section 3 the main result of this paper is derived, namely that step-by-step model generation is correct under certain conditions. We will see how these results can be applied to the PUHR tableau calculus in Section 4. Section 5 concludes the paper with some considerations about related and possible future work as well as a practical application area.

2 Preliminaries

Even though the reader is expected to be familiar with basic notions of set theory, first order logic, and logic programming, this section repeats some definitions in order to introduce the notation of this paper and to fix some notions that are not always used with the same meaning. It also introduces some simple notions that are not in general use.

2.1 Partial Orders

We will need some properties of the subset relation when we compare Herbrand interpretations. These properties actually hold and are formulated here for an arbitrary partial order $\sqsubseteq$.

Definition 1. *Let $\sqsubseteq$ be a binary relation on a set M and let $H \subseteq M$. Then*

$$\min_{\sqsubseteq}(H) := \{m \in H \mid h \sqsubseteq m \text{ implies } h = m \text{ for all } h \in H\}$$
$$\exp_{\sqsubseteq}(H) := \{x \in M \mid h \sqsubseteq x \text{ for some } h \in H\}$$

If $\sqsubseteq$ is a partial order, then the elements of $\min_{\sqsubseteq}(H)$ are the minimal *elements of H w.r.t. $\sqsubseteq$. If $\sqsubseteq$ is at least reflexive, then $\exp_{\sqsubseteq}(H)$ is a superset of H, which gave rise to the operation name "exp" for* expansion. ◇

The following two lemmas about the operations $\min_{\sqsubseteq}$ and $\exp_{\sqsubseteq}$ hold trivially:

Lemma 2. *Let $\sqsubseteq$ be a partial order on a set M and let H be a subset of M. Then $\min_{\sqsubseteq}(\exp_{\sqsubseteq}(H)) = \min_{\sqsubseteq}(H)$.*

Lemma 3. *Let $\sqsubseteq$ be a partial order on a set M and let H be a subset of M such that for every $h \in H$ there is a minimal element m of H with $m \sqsubseteq h$. Then $\exp_{\sqsubseteq}(\min_{\sqsubseteq}(H)) = \exp_{\sqsubseteq}(H)$.*

Definition 4. *Let $\sqsubseteq$ be a partial order on a set M.*

- *A subset K of M is a* chain *w.r.t. $\sqsubseteq$ if $k \sqsubseteq k'$ or $k' \sqsubseteq k$ holds for all $k, k' \in K$.*

- *A subset H of M is* chain-complete *w.r.t.* $\sqsubseteq$ *if for every non-empty chain* $K \subseteq H$ *w.r.t.* $\sqsubseteq$ *the greatest lower bound* $\inf_{\sqsubseteq} K$ *exists and is an element of H.* ◇

Notice that without the restriction to *non-empty* chains, chain-completeness would have been dual to the notion of a complete partial order as it is used in domain theory. We will use the following variant of Zorn's Lemma:

Lemma 5. *Let* $\sqsubseteq$ *be a partial order on a set M and let* $H \subseteq M$ *be chain-complete w.r.t.* $\sqsubseteq$. *Then for every* $h \in H$ *there is a minimal element m of H with* $m \sqsubseteq h$.

2.2 First Order Logic, Clauses, and Herbrand Interpretations

Disjunction and conjunction will be considered to be associative, commutative, idempotent, and with neutral elements. Conjunctions and disjunctions bind stronger than implications. Ground clauses will be denoted equivalently in *disjunctive form*, i.e., as a disjunction of literals (atoms or negations of atoms) or in *implication form*, i.e., as an implication with a conjunction of atoms as its antecedent (the *body*) and a disjunction of atoms as its consequent (the *head*). A *unit clause* consists of a single literal. The *empty clause* is the neutral element $\perp$ of the disjunction, i.e., the falsity.

We will assume a first order language to be given with some fixed set of predicate and function symbols that does not depend on the set of symbols actually used in some theory. The *Herbrand base*, i.e., the set of all ground atoms of this language is denoted as $\mathcal{HB}$. As usual in logic programming, an Herbrand interpretation is identified with the set of ground atoms it satisfies. The set of Herbrand models of a theory Th is denoted as $\mathcal{M}(Th)$. The set of minimal Herbrand models is $\mathcal{M}_{min}(Th)$. We will implicitly rely on the fact that an Herbrand interpretation satisfies a set C of clauses iff it satisfies all ground instances of clauses in C.

We will also use some properties of ground resolution [12]. Let $C = A \vee R$ and $C' = \neg A \vee R'$ be ground clauses with an atom A. Then C and C' are *resolvable* and the result of a *ground resolution* step applied to C and C' is the *resolvent* $R \vee R'$. Ground resolution is known to be sound and refutation-complete, i.e.

- If an interpretation M satisfies two resolvable ground clauses C and C', then M also satisfies the resolvent of C and C'.
- If a set C of ground clauses is unsatisfiable, then the empty clause can be derived from clauses in C by a finite number of ground resolution steps.

Corollary 7 below has been shown by Seipel et al. [13]. The central step of the proof is presented separately here as Lemma 6 because it will also be used for another result.

Lemma 6. *Let Th be a clausal theory. Then* $\mathcal{M}(Th)$ *is chain-complete w.r.t. the subset relation.*

By applying Lemma 5 to Lemma 6 we get:

Corollary 7 (Existence of Minimal Herbrand Models). *Let M be an Herbrand model of a clausal theory Th. Then there is a minimal Herbrand model M' of Th with $M' \subseteq M$.*

3 Step-by-Step Model Generation

In this section we see how model-generation procedures can be refined in such a way that they generate models step by step along a sequence of subsets of the given theory. For most of this section, however, we consider only two steps. Theorem 19, the central result of this paper, will say how a model generation process for a theory $Th_1 \cup Th_2$ can be divided into two steps corresponding to the two theories Th_1 and Th_2. The restriction to relevant atoms is propagated to the individual steps. This result is then easily extended to the general case by induction. Proofs for some of the simpler lemmas have been omitted for space reasons.

The division of a theory into parts must have the property that earlier steps do not depend on later steps. This can be formulated as a syntactic criterion as follows:

Definition 8. *Let Th_1 and Th_2 be clausal theories. Th_1 is* independent *from Th_2, written $Th_1 \not\leftarrow Th_2$, if no body atom from Th_1 is unifiable with a head atom from Th_2.* ◇

The following two lemmas are related to the notion of independence. Lemma 10 will be used in a chain of equations in the proof of Theorem 19.

Lemma 9. *Let M be a minimal Herbrand model of the clausal theory Th. Then every atom $A \in M$ is a ground instance of a head atom from Th.*

Proof. Assume there were an atom $A \in M$ that is not a ground instance of a head atom in Th. This contradicts the minimality property for M, because $M \setminus \{A\}$, which is a proper subset of M, would then also be a model of Th: Consider an arbitrary ground instance $\bigwedge_i B_i \rightarrow \bigvee_j H_j$ of a clause in Th such that all the B_i occur in $M \setminus \{A\}$. So the B_i also occur in M. Since M is a model of Th and thus of our clause instance, some H_j occurs in M. Since A is not a ground instance of a head atom in Th, we get $H_j \in M \setminus \{A\}$. □

Lemma 10. *Let Th_1 and Th_2 be clausal theories with $Th_1 \not\leftarrow Th_2$. Then*

$$\exp_{\subseteq}(\exp_{\subseteq}(\mathcal{M}(Th_1)) \cap \mathcal{M}(Th_2)) = \exp_{\subseteq}(\mathcal{M}(Th_1) \cap \mathcal{M}(Th_2)).$$

Proof. An Herbrand interpretation I is an element of the left hand side of the equation iff (L) there are Herbrand interpretations L_1 and L_2 such that (L1) $L_1 \models Th_1$, (L2) $L_1 \subseteq L_2$, (L3) $L_2 \models Th_2$, and (L4) $L_2 \subseteq I$. I is an element of the right hand side iff (R) there is an Herbrand interpretation R such that (R1) $R \models Th_1$, (R2) $R \models Th_2$, and (R3) $R \subseteq I$.

"(L) $\Rightarrow$ (R)": Note that we can consider L_1 not only as an Herbrand interpretation but also as a (ground positive unit) clausal theory, and that by (L2) L_2 is a model of L_1. With (L3) we get that $L_2 \models Th_2 \cup L_1$. By Corollary 7 there is a minimal Herbrand model $L_{1,2}$ of $Th_2 \cup L_1$ with $L_{1,2} \subseteq L_2$. We choose $R := L_{1,2}$. Now (R3) holds immediately and (R2) follows with (L4). (R1) is shown as follows. Consider an arbitrary ground instance $\bigwedge_i B_i \rightarrow \bigvee_j H_j$ of a clause in Th_1 with $B_i \in L_{1,2}$ for all i. Because $Th_1 \not\leftarrow Th_2$, none of the B_i occurs as a head atom in Th_2. So by Lemma 9 all the B_i must occur in L_1. Since by (L1) L_1 is a model of our clause instance, it must also contain one of the H_j. So this H_j is also an element of $L_{1,2}$.

"(R) $\Rightarrow$ (L)": We choose $L_1 := R$ and $L_2 := R$. Now (L1), (L3), and (L4) hold by (R1) to (R3). (L2) holds trivially. □

Before we deal with the second refinement of model generation procedures, namely the restriction of models to a set Q of relevant atoms (which may be considered a *query* to the theory), a syntactic counterpart to this restriction is introduced, namely the restriction of ground clauses to relevant atoms.

Definition 11. *Let C be a ground clause and Q a set of ground atoms. Then C_Q denotes the clause that we get from C by removing all literals with atoms not occurring in Q.* ◇

So obviously $C = C_Q \vee C_{\mathcal{HB}\setminus Q}$ for every ground clause C. Furthermore $C = C_Q$ if and only if $C_{\mathcal{HB}\setminus Q}$ is the empty clause. Definition 11 is actually only needed within the proof of the following proposition, which is a central step in the argumentation of this paper:

Proposition 12. *Let Th be a clausal theory and let Q be a set of ground atoms. Then there is a ground clausal theory Th_Q such that*

1. *all atoms in the clauses of Th_Q are elements of Q,*
2. *Th_Q is a logical consequence of Th, and*
3. *for every Herbrand model M of Th_Q there is an Herbrand model M' of Th such that $M' \cap Q = M \cap Q$.*

Proof. Define Th_Q and an auxiliary theory Th^+ as:

$$\begin{aligned} Th^+ := \{C \mid\ & C \text{ can be derived from ground instances of clauses in } Th \\ & \text{by a finite number (possibly zero) of resolution steps.}\} \end{aligned}$$

$$Th_Q := \{C \mid C \in Th^+ \text{ and } C = C_Q\}.$$

Obviously item 1 of the proposition holds. Item 2 is an immediate consequence of the soundness of ground resolution. For the proof of item 3 consider some Herbrand model M of Th_Q. We need two more auxiliary theories:

$$\begin{aligned} \text{enforce}_Q(M) &:= (M \cap Q) \cup \{A \rightarrow \bot \mid A \in Q \setminus M\} \\ Th_{M,Q} &:= \text{enforce}_Q(M) \ \cup \ \{C_{\mathcal{HB}\setminus Q} \mid C \in Th^+ \text{ and } M \not\models C_Q\} \end{aligned}$$

We will see below that $Th_{M,Q}$ is satisfiable. Since an Herbrand model is known to exist for any satisfiable clausal theory, there is an Herbrand model M' of $Th_{M,Q}$. It has the required properties:

- $M' \cap Q = M \cap Q$: This is an immediate consequence of $M' \models \text{enforce}_Q(M)$.
- $M' \models Th$: Consider some ground instance C of a clause in Th. If C_Q is satisfied by M, then C_Q is also satisfied by M' because of $M' \cap Q = M \cap Q$. Otherwise $C_{\mathcal{HB}\setminus Q}$ is an element of $Th_{M,Q}$ and is therefore satisfied by M'. So in either case $C = C_Q \vee C_{\mathcal{HB}\setminus Q}$ is satisfied by M'.

The satisfiability of $Th_{M,Q}$ follows by the refutation completeness of ground resolution from the facts that (a) $Th_{M,Q}$ does not contain the empty clause and (b) $Th_{M,Q}$ is saturated w.r.t. ground resolution:

(a) Assume the empty clause were in $Th_{M,Q}$. It cannot be an element of $\text{enforce}_Q(M)$ because this set consists entirely of unit clauses. So there must be some clause $C \in Th^+$ such that $M \not\models C_Q$ and $C_{\mathcal{HB}\setminus Q}$ is the empty clause. The latter condition means that $C = C_Q$. Therefore $C \in Th_Q$ and thus $M \models C$. Using the fact $C = C_Q$ again we get $M \models C_Q$, which contradicts the above condition $M \not\models C_Q$.

(b) Consider two resolvable clauses $A \vee R$ and $\neg A \vee R'$ in $Th_{M,Q}$, where A is a ground atom and R and R' are disjunctions of ground literals. We will see that $R \vee R'$ is in $Th_{M,Q}$.
A cannot be an element of Q because in $Th_{M,Q}$ the atoms from $M \cap Q$ do not occur in negative literals and the atoms from $Q \setminus M$ do not occur in positive literals. Therefore the two clauses are not in $\text{enforce}_Q(M)$.
So there are clauses $C, C' \in Th^+$ with $C_{\mathcal{HB}\setminus Q} = A \vee R$, $C'_{\mathcal{HB}\setminus Q} = \neg A \vee R'$, $M \not\models C_Q$, and $M \not\models C'_Q$. The clauses $C = A \vee R \vee C_Q$ and $C' = \neg A \vee R' \vee C'_Q$ can be resolved to $C^r := R \vee C_Q \vee R' \vee C'_Q$. This resolvent is in Th^+ because Th^+ is saturated w.r.t. resolution. Since none of the atoms of R and R' are in Q, we get $C^r_Q = C_Q \vee C'_Q$. From $M \not\models C_Q$ and $M \not\models C'_Q$ we conclude $M \not\models C^r_Q$. Therefore $Th_{M,Q}$ contains $C^r_{\mathcal{HB}\setminus Q} = R \vee R'$. □

It is not intended to actually compute Th_Q, which will frequently be infinite even for finite Th. Its existence is needed only for theoretical purposes.

Now we come to the semantic aspects of the notion of relevant atoms. In the following definition a parameter Q providing the set of relevant atoms is added to $\mathcal{M}$ and $\mathcal{M}_{min}$. Another parameter $\mathcal{I}$ is intended to provide the set of minimal models (or their relevant parts) generated by the previous model generation step.

Definition 13. *Let $\mathcal{I}$ be a set of Herbrand interpretations, Q a set of ground atoms, and Th a theory. Then*

$$\begin{aligned}
\text{restr}_Q(\mathcal{I}) &:= \{I \cap Q \mid I \in \mathcal{I}\} \\
\mathcal{M}(Th, Q) &:= \text{restr}_Q(\mathcal{M}(Th)) \\
\mathcal{M}(\mathcal{I}, Th, Q) &:= \text{restr}_Q(\exp_{\subseteq}(\mathcal{I}) \cap \mathcal{M}(Th)) \\
\mathcal{M}_{min}(Th, Q) &:= \min_{\subseteq}(\mathcal{M}(Th, Q)) \\
\mathcal{M}_{min}(\mathcal{I}, Th, Q) &:= \min_{\subseteq}(\mathcal{M}(\mathcal{I}, Th, Q))
\end{aligned}$$

An element of $\mathcal{M}(Th, Q)$ is an answer *to the* query *Q w.r.t. Th. An element of $\mathcal{M}_{min}(Th, Q)$ is a* minimal answer *to Q w.r.t. Th.* ◇

From an operational perspective, we might generate $\mathcal{M}_{min}(\mathcal{I}, Th, Q)$ as follows. We start with the elements of $\mathcal{I}$ and extend them to models of Th. Among all the possible models we generate only those that are minimal w.r.t. Q and we actually restrict them to Q.

The following lemma helps to transfer properties of sets of Herbrand models to sets of answers.

Lemma 14. *For a clausal theory Th and a set Q of ground atoms there is a ground clausal theory Th_Q with all atoms in Q such that*

$$\mathcal{M}(Th, Q) = \mathcal{M}(Th_Q, Q).$$

Proof. Let Th_Q be as given by Proposition 12. □

The property that we actually want to transfer from sets of Herbrand models to sets of answers is the chain-completeness property from Lemma 6:

Lemma 15. *For a clausal theory Th and a set Q of ground atoms the set $\mathcal{M}(Th, Q)$ is chain-complete.*

Proof. We may assume that Th is a ground clausal theory all atoms of which are in Q, because otherwise we can replace Th by an appropriate theory Th_Q according to Lemma 14.

For every $I \in \mathcal{M}(Th, Q)$ there is a model M_I of Th with $M_I \cap Q = I$. Consider an arbitrary ground clause $\bigwedge_i B_i \to \bigvee_j H_j$ in Th with all B_i in I. Thus all B_i are in M_I and since M_I is a model of Th, some H_j must also be in M_I. Since all the atoms of Th are in Q, H_j is in $M_I \cap Q = I$. Thus every $I \in \mathcal{M}(Th, Q)$ is a model of Th, and therefore $\mathcal{M}(Th, Q) \subseteq \mathcal{M}(Th)$.

Now consider a non-empty chain $\mathcal{K} \subseteq \mathcal{M}(Th, Q)$. By our considerations above $\mathcal{K}$ is also a non-empty chain in $\mathcal{M}(Th)$. So by Lemma 6 the greatest lower bound $\bigcap \mathcal{K}$ of $\mathcal{K}$ is in $\mathcal{M}(Th)$. Thus $\mathcal{M}(Th, Q)$ contains $\bigcap \mathcal{K} \cap Q$, which is equal to $\bigcap \mathcal{K}$ because $\mathcal{K}$ has at least one element, which is a subset of Q. □

In a way similar to Corollary 7 we can now apply Lemma 5 to Lemma 15 and get the following corollary:

Corollary 16 (Existence of Minimal Answers). *Let I be an answer to a query Q w.r.t. a clausal theory Th. Then there is a minimal answer I' to Q w.r.t. Th with $I' \subseteq I$.*

For the chain of equations in the proof of Theorem 19 we need two more lemmas, which can be proved in a style similar to Lemma 10, but without refering to any of the results above.

Lemma 17. *Let $\mathcal{I}$ be a set of Herbrand interpretations, Th a clausal theory, and Q_1 and Q_2 sets of ground atoms such that $Q_2 \subseteq Q_1$ and every body atom of Th is in Q_1. Then*

$$\mathrm{restr}_{Q_2}(\exp_{\subseteq}(\mathcal{I}) \cap \mathcal{M}(Th)) = \mathrm{restr}_{Q_2}(\exp_{\subseteq}(\mathrm{restr}_{Q_1}(\mathcal{I})) \cap \mathcal{M}(Th)).$$

Lemma 18. *Let $\mathcal{I}$ be a set of Herbrand interpretations and Q a set of ground atoms. Then*

$$\mathbf{exp}_{\subseteq}(\mathbf{restr}_Q(\mathbf{exp}_{\subseteq}(\mathcal{I}))) = \mathbf{exp}_{\subseteq}(\mathbf{restr}_Q(\mathcal{I})).$$

Now we have all the auxiliary results necessary to prove the main result for model generation in two steps:

Theorem 19 (Compositionality). *Let Th_1 and Th_2 be clausal theories with $Th_1 \not\leftarrow Th_2$ and let Q_1 and Q_2 be sets of ground atoms such that $Q_1 \supseteq Q_2$ and Q_1 contains all the body atoms of Th_2. Then*

$$\mathcal{M}_{min}(Th_1 \cup Th_2, Q_2) = \mathcal{M}_{min}(\mathcal{M}_{min}(Th_1, Q_1), Th_2, Q_2)$$

Proof.

$$\begin{aligned}
&\mathcal{M}_{min}(Th_1 \cup Th_2, Q_2) \\
&= \mathbf{min}_{\subseteq}(\mathbf{restr}_{Q_2}(\mathcal{M}(Th_1 \cup Th_2))) \\
&= \mathbf{min}_{\subseteq}(\mathbf{restr}_{Q_2}(\mathcal{M}(Th_1) \cap \mathcal{M}(Th_2))) \\
\text{(Lemma 2)} &= \mathbf{min}_{\subseteq}(\mathbf{exp}_{\subseteq}(\mathbf{restr}_{Q_2}(\mathcal{M}(Th_1) \cap \mathcal{M}(Th_2)))) \\
\text{(Lemma 18)} &= \mathbf{min}_{\subseteq}(\mathbf{exp}_{\subseteq}(\mathbf{restr}_{Q_2}(\mathbf{exp}_{\subseteq}(\mathcal{M}(Th_1) \cap \mathcal{M}(Th_2))))) \\
\text{(Lemma 10)} &= \mathbf{min}_{\subseteq}(\mathbf{exp}_{\subseteq}(\mathbf{restr}_{Q_2}(\mathbf{exp}_{\subseteq}(\mathbf{exp}_{\subseteq}(\mathcal{M}(Th_1)) \cap \mathcal{M}(Th_2))))) \\
\text{(Lemma 18)} &= \mathbf{min}_{\subseteq}(\mathbf{exp}_{\subseteq}(\mathbf{restr}_{Q_2}(\mathbf{exp}_{\subseteq}(\mathcal{M}(Th_1)) \cap \mathcal{M}(Th_2)))) \\
\text{(Lemma 2)} &= \mathbf{min}_{\subseteq}(\mathbf{restr}_{Q_2}(\mathbf{exp}_{\subseteq}(\mathcal{M}(Th_1)) \cap \mathcal{M}(Th_2))) \\
\text{(Lemma 17)} &= \mathbf{min}_{\subseteq}(\mathbf{restr}_{Q_2}(\mathbf{exp}_{\subseteq}(\mathbf{restr}_{Q_1}(\mathcal{M}(Th_1))) \cap \mathcal{M}(Th_2))) \\
&= \mathbf{min}_{\subseteq}(\mathbf{restr}_{Q_2}(\mathbf{exp}_{\subseteq}(\mathcal{M}(Th_1, Q_1)) \cap \mathcal{M}(Th_2))) \\
\text{(Lemma 3)} &= \mathbf{min}_{\subseteq}(\mathbf{restr}_{Q_2}(\mathbf{exp}_{\subseteq}(\mathbf{min}_{\subseteq}(\mathcal{M}(Th_1, Q_1))) \cap \mathcal{M}(Th_2))) \\
&= \mathcal{M}_{min}(\mathcal{M}_{min}(Th_1, Q_1), Th_2, Q_2)
\end{aligned}$$

Lemma 3 may be applied here because its condition is satisfied according to Corollary 16. □

By induction with Theorem 19 we immediately get the main result for model generation in an arbitrary finite number of steps:

Corollary 20. *Let $Th_1, \ldots, Th_n$ $(n \geq 1)$ be clausal theories with $Th_i \not\leftarrow Th_j$ for $i < j$ and let $Q_1, \ldots, Q_n$ be sets of ground atoms such that $Q_i \supseteq Q_{i+1}$ and Q_i contains all the body atoms of $Th_{i+1} \cup \ldots \cup Th_n$. Then*

$$\begin{aligned}
&\mathcal{M}_{min}(Th_1 \cup \ldots \cup Th_n, Q_n) = \\
&\quad \mathcal{M}_{min}(\ldots \mathcal{M}_{min}(\mathcal{M}_{min}(Th_1, Q_1), Th_2, Q_2) \ldots, Th_n, Q_n)
\end{aligned}$$

4 Integration into the PUHR tableau calculus

After a brief revision of the PUHR tableau calculus in Section 4.1, Section 4.2 will explain informally how this calculus can be improved by applying it in a step-by-step manner.

4.1 PUHR Tableaux

PUHR tableaux [4] for a clausal theory Th are constructed from an initial tableau consisting of a single empty branch by repeated application of the inference rule[1]

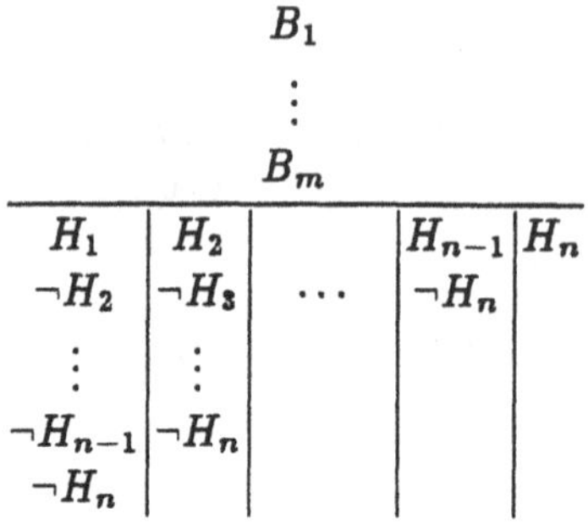

$B_1 \wedge \ldots \wedge B_m \rightarrow H_1 \vee \ldots \vee H_n$ is a ground instance of a clause in Th.

That is, if a branch Br contains all the body atoms of some ground instance C of a clause in Th with n head atoms, then Br may be split into n branches, each of which is extended by one of the head atoms H_i of C. In addition, an extended branch also contains the complements of the head atoms H_j with $j > i$. If C has no head atoms (i.e., $n = 0$), then the branch is *closed*. A branch is also considered *closed* if it contains an atom and its complement. PUHR tableaux satisfy a regularity condition that forbids the application of a ground clause C to a branch Br if Br already contains some head atom of C. A branch that is not closed is *open*. An open branch Br is *saturated* if for every ground instance C of a clause either some body atom of C does not occur in Br or some head atom of C does occur. A PUHR tableau is *saturated* if every open branch is saturated.

Example 21. A saturated PUHR tableau for the theory $\{a \vee b \vee c \vee d \vee e,\ a \rightarrow f,\ b \rightarrow c,\ c \rightarrow f,\ d \rightarrow c,\ e \rightarrow f\}$ is

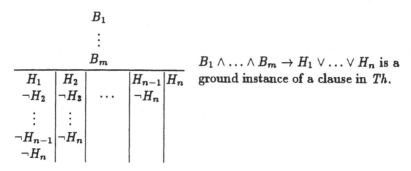

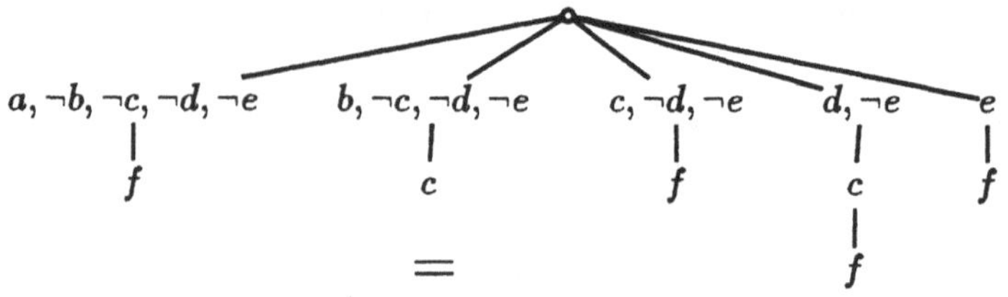

where "$=$" marks a closed branch. ◇

A branch of a PUHR tableau is frequently identified with the set of positive ground atoms along the branch, and thus with an Herbrand interpretation. A saturated PUHR tableau T for a theory Th has, among others, the following properties [4]:

1. Every open branch of T is an Herbrand model of Th.
2. Every minimal Herbrand model of Th appears as an open branch of T.

[1] We use the variant of PUHR tableaux with "complement splitting".

3. If two models M and M' with $M \subseteq M'$ are represented by branches, then the branch for M appears to the left of the branch for M'.

According to properties 1 and 2, PUHR tableaux can be used as a method for generating the set of minimal models if non-minimal models are eliminated. In order to eliminate all non-minimal or duplicate models we traverse a saturated tableau in depth-first left-to-right order and, according to property 3, we only need to check for every generated model that it is not a superset of some minimal model *already generated before*. In fact, one may close a branch as soon as the set of atoms along the branch becomes a superset of a minimal model generated before, even if the branch is not yet saturated. The procedure which does exactly this is called MM-Satchmo [4].

Example 22. In the tableau given in Example 21 MM-Satchmo closes the fourth branch because $\{d, c, f\}$ is a superset of the model $\{c, f\}$ represented by the third branch. ◇

4.2 Step-by-Step PUHR Tableaux

We will now see how PUHR tableaux can be made more efficient by handling parts of the given theory step by step. For simplicity we assume a division of the given theory in two parts. The extension to the general case with n parts is as simple as in Section 3.

Let the given theory be $Th := Th_1 \cup Th_2$ such that $Th_1 \not\leftarrow Th_2$. We construct a saturated PUHR tableau for Th in two steps as follows: In the first step we generate a saturated PUHR tableau T_1 for Th_1. In the second step we apply ground instances of clauses from Th_2 to the open branches of T_1 up to saturation. Notice that after the second step the tableau is still saturated w.r.t. Th_1 because we have required Th_1 not to depend on Th_2. So we have in fact constructed a saturated PUHR tableau for Th.

Up to now we have not gained anything compared to a straight-forward application of the PUHR tableau calculus to Th. However, we may prune (i.e., close) branches earlier and more frequently with the step-by-step approach. To get an intuition for the pruning possibilities, consider an example.

Example 23. Let Th_1 be the theory $\{a \vee b \vee c \vee d \vee e, a \rightarrow f, b \rightarrow c, c \rightarrow f, d \rightarrow c, e \rightarrow f\}$ from Example 21. Let $Q_1 := \{a, f\}$ be the set of atoms that are relevant in the first step because they are either body atoms in Th_2 or elements of Q_2 because they are relevant for the application. We do not care about details of Th_2 and Q_2. Let Th be $Th_1 \cup Th_2$. Then for Th_1 we get the tableau from Example 21, which we call T_1. Each of the open branches of this tableau is extended by some subtree for Th_2, yielding a tableau T for Th.

Notice that MM-Satchmo does not close the fourth branch $\{d, c, f\}$ of T_1 as in Example 22 unless the third branch $\{c, f\}$ happens to be immediately saturated w.r.t. Th_2. However, according to the results of Section 3 we may eliminate non-minimal models already for Th_1. So we may close the fourth branch of T_1 no matter what effect Th_2 will have on the third branch.

Since we are only interested in the atoms of Q_1 in the first step, we may close even more branches:

- We may close the fifth branch of T_1 because $\{e, f\} \cap Q_1 = \{f\}$ is a superset of (actually equal to) $\{c, f\} \cap Q_1 = \{f\}$ and thus any answer generated from the fifth branch will be a superset of some answer generated from the third branch.
- We may close the first branch of T_1 because $\{a, f\} \cap Q_1 = \{a, f\}$ is a proper superset of $\{c, f\} \cap Q_1 = \{f\}$ and thus any answer generated from the first branch will be a proper superset of some answer generated from the third branch.

So the only remaining open branch is the third branch. We may not close it using the fifth branch as a justification, because that one is already closed. In other words, we may not perform mutual subsumption between branches. ◇

Now we come to the general case. With $Th_1, \ldots, Th_n$ and $Q_1, \ldots, Q_n$ given as in Corollary 20 the possible pruning steps are given by the following two rules:

- A branch Br is closed within the ith step if $Br \cap Q_i \supseteq Br' \cap Q_i$ for some branch Br' to the left of Br that is saturated w.r.t. $Th_1 \cup \ldots \cup Th_i$.
- A branch Br is closed within the ith step if $Br \cap Q_i \supsetneq Br' \cap Q_i$ for some branch Br' to the right of Br that is saturated w.r.t. $Th_1 \cup \ldots \cup Th_i$.

The first of these rules is more powerful than the minimization rule of MM-Satchmo in two ways:

- It does not require Br' to be saturated w.r.t. $Th_1 \cup \ldots \cup Th_n$ but only w.r.t. $Th_1 \cup \ldots \cup Th_i$.
- It does not require Br' to be a subset of Br but only $Br' \cap Q_i$ to be a subset of $Br \cap Q_i$.

The second rule has no counterpart in MM-Satchmo, because such a weaker counterpart (checking for a proper subset relation between entire branches without a restriction to Q_i) would never be applicable according to property 3 above. A proper superset relation is required in this rule in order to avoid that two branches that are equal w.r.t. Q_i mutually eliminate each other. Notice that the second rule cannot be applied in a depth-first left-to-right traversal of the overall tableau. We rather have to complete the tableau after every step. If, however, we insist in a depth-first traversal of the overall tableau, then we still have an improved pruning of branches from the strengthened first rule.

5 Conclusion

A formal framework has been presented for (1) step-by-step generation of minimal models and (2) ignoring irrelevant parts of models early. The results such as Theorem 19 are simple and plausible. However the proofs are not that simple, in particular because they also cover the case where there is an infinite number of Herbrand models or answers, in which the existence of minimal models or answers is not trivial. Also the case of infinite clausal theories has been covered, even though this was more implicit. The treatment of the infinite case was necessary in particular to cover proper first-order clausal theories rather than only ones that are essentially equivalent to finite propositional theories.

It has also been demonstrated how the idea of step-by-step model generation can be used to refine the PUHR tableau method. But a similar refinement can be applied to any method that generates minimal models or answers because Theorem 19 does not depend on any particular method.

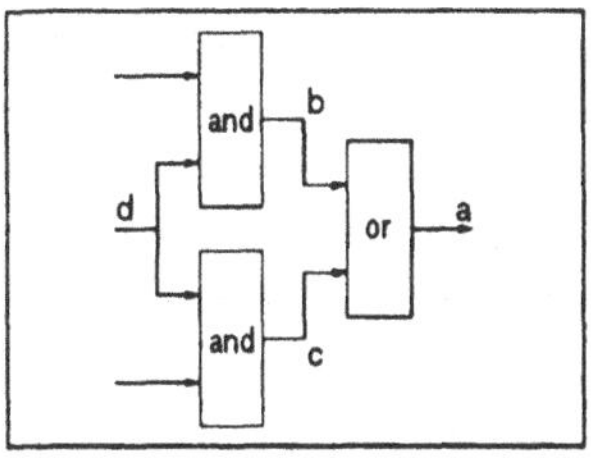

Fig. 1. A digital circuit.

Practical applications for the techniques described in this paper appear for example in model-based diagnosis for digital circuits [8, 3, 2]. Consider a circuit containing the part given in Figure 1. Assume that we already know that signal a is 1, and (for the sake of simplicity) that the gates in the figure are already known to work correctly. The circuit can be described by several clauses, including $a = 1 \rightarrow b = 1 \vee c = 1$ and $b = 1 \rightarrow d = 1$ and $c = 1 \rightarrow d = 1$. In order to determine the broken gate(s), assume that we need to know signal d, but we do not care about b and c. We can conclude that at least one of the inputs of the *or* gate (b or c) must also be 1. In either case the common input d of the two *and* gates must be 1. In a straight-forward application of a model generation method we would have to separately consider two cases: one in which $b = 1$ and $d = 1$ holds, and one with $c = 1$ and again $d = 1$. The refinements presented in this paper allow us to replace the two cases by a single case with just $d = 1$. We get a strong optimization effect as in the example given in the introduction if several parts of this kind are connected serially in a circuit. Examples like this have actually been the motivation for the work presented here. Nevertheless, a more detailed discussion of this application is beyond the scope of this paper. It should also be investigated whether and how the optimization from the current paper can be combined with other application-specific optimizations, as they are implemented, e.g., in the DRUM-II algorithm [8].

For many optimization techniques it is possible to construct examples for which the "optimized" treatment is actually less efficient than the straight-forward treatment. This is also true for the optimization presented in this paper. Consider the theory $Th := Th_1 \cup Th_2$ with $Th_1 := \{p(a), \forall X(p(X) \rightarrow q(X) \vee p(f(X))\}$ and $Th_2 := \{p(f(a)) \rightarrow \bot\}$ and let the entire Herbrand base be relevant. Then Th has only a finite number of minimal Herbrand models, each of which satisfies only a finite number of ground atoms and may actually be computed in finite time. In contrast to this, Th_1 has an infinite number of minimal Herbrand models, even including one that satisfies an infinite number of ground atoms. So unless we have a sophisticated way to represent infinite Herbrand models and infinite sets of Herbrand models, the first step of a step-by-step model generation procedure will not terminate. Unfavorable cases of this kind should be avoided when the theory is divided into steps. This paper does not provide a mechanism for dividing a theory into parts automatically. It is rather expected that appropriate divisions can be derived from knowledge about the application. So for example in model-based diagnosis for digital circuits the division might be derived from the structure of the given circuit. This fits with the general experience that the efficiency of automated deduction systems can be (and usually must be) improved by taking into account knowledge from the application domain. Nevertheless general guidelines for partitioning theories would be useful.

Given a theory Th and a set Q_n of relevant atoms, we need not only find appropriate components $Th_1, \dots, Th_n$ of Th, but we also have to find sets $Q_1, \dots, Q_{n-1}$ such that the conditions of Corollary 20 are satisfied. This is essentially a sort of backward propagation of relevancy for atoms, i.e., propagation in the direction opposite to the implication arrows. Notice that backward propagation of relevancy for atoms is also performed by Satchmore [6] and by the non-Horn magic-sets transformation [5, 10], even in a more sophisticated way than in the present paper. However, these techniques are intended for refutational theorem proving rather than for model generation. In particular, they do not deal with the elimination of non-minimal or duplicate models or answers. The non-Horn magic-sets transformation can probably be adapted in such a way that it works for model generation and preserves answers to queries. It would then be interesting to investigate how this method can be combined with the step-by-step approach.

The division of a theory into steps is similar to the notion of stratification for non-disjunctive logic programs with default negation in clause bodies [1]. Several refinements to the notion of stratification have been proposed, most prominently the notion of local stratification [11]. The granularity of steps as presented in this paper is finer than plain stratification but coarser than local stratification: We may assign two atoms with the same predicate symbol to different steps, but we cannot assign different ground instances of a clause to different steps. However, the fine granularity of local stratification can be achieved by a preprocessing step which replaces some clauses by an essentially equivalent set of instances of these clauses. So for example in the theory Th above the clause $\forall X(p(X) \rightarrow q(X) \vee p(f(X)))$ can be replaced by the clauses $p(a) \rightarrow q(a) \vee p(f(a))$ and $\forall X'(p(f(X')) \rightarrow q(f(X')) \vee p(f(f(X'))))$. After that transformation we are more flexible in dividing the theory into steps.

If a clausal theory can be divided into parts that are *mutually* independent, then minimal models or answers can be generated independently for all the parts and combined in the style of a cross product afterwards. In practical applications there will frequently be the situation that some parts of the theory are mutually independent while there are dependencies between others. Therefore it would be interesting to investigate a combination of step-by-step model generation with a technique for mutually independent parts.

Acknowledgements

The author thanks Norbert Eisinger, Tim Geisler, and Thomas Rudlof for helpful discussions and comments on an earlier version of this paper.

References

1. Krzysztof R. Apt, Howard A. Blair, and Adrian Walker. Towards a theory of declarative knowledge. In Jack Minker, editor, *Foundations of Deductive Databases and Logic Programming*, chapter 2, pages 89–148. Morgan Kaufmann, 1988.
2. Peter Baumgartner, Peter Fröhlich, Ulrich Furbach, and Wolfgang Nejdl. Semantically guided theorem proving for diagnosis applications. In *15th International Joint Conference on Artificial Intelligence (IJCAI 97)*, Nagoya, 1997.
3. Peter Baumgartner, Peter Fröhlich, Ulrich Furbach, and Wolfgang Nejdl. Tableaux for diagnosis applications. In *Automated Reasoning with Analytic Tableaux and Related Methods, International Conference (TABLEAUX '97)*, Springer LNCS 1227, pages 76–90, Pont-à-Mousson, France, May 13–16 1997.
4. François Bry and Adnan H. Yahya. Minimal model generation with positive unit hyper-resolution tableaux. In *Theorem Proving with Analytic Tableaux and Related Methods, 5th International Workshop (TABLEAUX '96)*, Springer LNCS 1071, Terrasini, Palermo, Italy, May 15–17 1996.
5. Ryuzo Hasegawa, Katsumi Inoue, Yoshihiko Ohta, and Miyuki Koshimura. Non-Horn magic sets to incorporate top-down inference into bottom-up theorem proving. In *14th International Conference on Automated Deduction (CADE-14)*, Springer LNCS 1249, pages 176–190, Townsville, North Queensland, Australia, July 13–17 1997.
6. Donald W. Loveland, David W. Reed, and Debra Sue Wilson. SATCHMORE: SATCHMO with relevancy. *Journal of Automated Reasoning*, 14(2):325–351, 1995.
7. Rainer Manthey and François Bry. Satchmo: A theorem prover implemented in Prolog. In *9th International Conference on Automated Deduction (CADE-9)*, Springer LNCS 310, pages 415–434, Argonne, Illinois, USA, 1988.
8. Wolfgang Nejdl and Peter Fröhlich. Minimal model semantics for diagnosis – techniques and first benchmarks. In *7th International Workshop on Principles of Diagnosis*, Val Morin, 1996.
9. Ilkka Niemelä. A tableau calculus for minimal model reasoning. In *Theorem Proving with Analytic Tableaux and Related Methods, 5th International Workshop (TABLEAUX '96)*, Springer LNCS 1071, pages 278–294, Terrasini, Palermo, Italy, May 15–17 1996.
10. Yoshihiko Ohta, Katsumi Inoue, and Ryuzo Hasegawa. On the relationship between non-Horn magic sets and relevancy testing. In *15th International Conference on Automated Deduction (CADE-15)*, Springer LNCS 1421, pages 333–348, Lindau, Germany, July 5–10 1998.
11. Teodor C. Przymusinski. On the declarative semantics of deductive databases and logic programs. In Jack Minker, editor, *Foundations of Deductive Databases and Logic Programming*, chapter 5, pages 193–216. Morgan Kaufmann, 1988.
12. J. A. Robinson. A machine-oriented logic based on the resolution principle. *Journal of the ACM*, 12(1):23–41, January 1965.
13. Dietmar Seipel, Jack Minker, and Carolina Ruiz. Model generation and state generation for disjunctive logic programs. *Journal of Logic Programming*, 32(1):48–69, 1997.

Tableau Calculi for Hybrid Logics

Miroslava Tzakova *

Max-Planck-Institut für Informatik

Abstract. Hybrid logics were proposed in [15] as a way of boosting the expressivity of modal logics via a novel mechanism: adding labels for states in Kripke models and viewing these labels as formulae. In addition, hybrid logics may contain quantifiers to bind the labels. Thus, hybrid logics have both Kripke semantics and a first-order binding apparatus. We present prefixed tableau calculi for weak hybrid logics (proper fragments of classical logic) as well as for hybrid logics having full first-order expressive power, and give a general method for proving completeness. For the weak quantifier-free logics we present a tableau-based decision procedure.

1 Introduction

Hybrid logics are extensions of modal logics with labels for states in Kripke models. The labels and the ordinary propositional symbols are treated in a uniform way to construct formulae of these logics. For example, given a label c, where labels are special sort of formulae, $c \wedge \neg\Diamond p$ is a well-formed formula of the hybrid logics. In addition, hybrid logics allow quantification over the set of states in Kripke models. For example, in the formula $\forall x \neg\Diamond x$, the quantifier $\forall x$ should be read as 'for all states'.

As the examples suggest, hybrid logics have a rather novel syntax and semantics. By viewing labels as formulae, they incorporate both Kripke semantics and first-order binding. Hybrid logics greatly increase the expressivity of modal logics, for example, they can express irreflexivity, the *Until* operator and counting modalities; for a discussion on the relevance of hybrid logics for temporal logic and AI, we refer to [12, 7, 6]. In fact, hybrid logics can be seen as fragments of classical logic ranging from strictly weaker systems to systems having full first-order expressive power (see [3, 4] for a hierarchy).

So far, the work on proof systems for hybrid logics has been mostly concerned with Hilbert-style systems (see, for example, [11, 8, 12, 5, 7, 14]), and a better deductive apparatus can be found only in [17, 18, 2]. The latter papers discuss sequent calculi and natural deduction systems for both weak quantifier-free hybrid languages and systems having full first-order expressive power.

In this paper we investigate tableau proof systems for such languages as well as for a variety of weak languages containing powerful quantifiers. Tableau proof

* Max-Planck-Institut für Informatik, Im Stadtwald, 66123 Saarbrücken, Germany. E-mail: tzakova@mpi-sb.mpg.de. Phone: +49 681 9325 226.

systems have been designed for a variety of modal logics and widely used for proving interpolation and other results (see, for example, [10, 16, 13]). However, tableau methods proved important not only from a theoretical point of view, but also they are nowadays successfully used for automated deduction (for an extensive overview we refer to [9]).

We present tableau systems for weak hybrid languages as well as for very expressive languages containing powerful binders, and thus show that hybrid logics behave proof-theoretically well. Tableau systems are important especially for weak systems with quantifiers for which the only known Hilbert-style axiomatizations contain infinite collections of rules of proof (see [5]). Completeness of the proposed calculi is proved in a uniform way using a systematic-tableau-construction argument. Our systematic procedure is based on the procedures in [19, 10], and constructs certain saturated sets that can be satisfied on *hybrid* Kripke models, namely on models in which labels are true at unique states.

For the weak quantifier-free (and decidable) hybrid languages we give a new tableau-based proof procedure that terminates and thus decides the binder-free languages (Section 5).

2 Hybrid logics

We begin by recalling the syntax of propositional modal logic. Given a denumerably infinite set PROP $= \{p, q, r, \ldots\}$ of *propositional symbols*, the well-formed formulae of propositional modal logic (PML) are defined as follows: $\varphi \;:=\; p \mid \neg\varphi \mid \varphi \wedge \psi \mid \Box\varphi$. The dual of the $\Box$ operator is $\Diamond\varphi := \neg\Box\neg\varphi$. Other Boolean operators are defined in the standard way.

To define hybrid logics we extend PML in two steps. First, we add two sets of new symbols: a countably infinite set SVAR $= \{x, y, z, \ldots\}$, called *state variables* and a countably infinite set NOM $= \{c, c_1, \ldots\}$, called *nominals.* (In what follows we assume that PROP, SVAR and NOM are fixed.) Second, we introduce operators. In this paper we consider two binding operators (binders): $\forall$ and $\downarrow$, and the operator @. Both state variables and nominals will be interpreted as singletons and thus, will act as 'labels' for the unique states they are satisfied at. The difference is that whereas state variables can be bound by the binders, nominals cannot. We call PROP $\cup$ SVAR $\cup$ NOM the set of *atoms*. The operator $@_l$ allows us to retrieve the information at the state labeled l.

Let $\mathcal{O} \subseteq \{\forall, \downarrow, @\}$ be a set of operators. We define $\mathcal{L}(\mathcal{O})$, the hybrid language over the operators in $\mathcal{O}$, to be the smallest set of formulae containing: (1) each atom a, (2) $\varphi \wedge \psi$ for each φ and ψ in $\mathcal{L}(\mathcal{O})$, (3) $\neg\varphi$ for each φ in $\mathcal{L}(\mathcal{O})$, (4) $\Box\varphi$ for each φ in $\mathcal{L}(\mathcal{O})$, (5) $Ox\varphi$, for each $x \in$ SVAR and each $\varphi \in \mathcal{L}(\mathcal{O})$ if $O \in \mathcal{O} \cap \{\forall, \downarrow\}$, and (6) $@_l\varphi$, for each $l \in$ SVAR $\cup$ NOM and each $\varphi \in \mathcal{L}(\mathcal{O})$ if $@ \in \mathcal{O}$. (Thus, we have eight hybrid languages: one for each choice of $\mathcal{O}$. Whenever $\mathcal{O}$ is clear from the context, we will write $\mathcal{L}$ instead of $\mathcal{L}(\mathcal{O})$.) We denote the simplest language containing no operator from $\mathcal{O}$ by $\mathcal{L}_o$.

The dual of $\forall$ is $\exists x\varphi := \neg\forall x\neg\varphi$. The binder $\downarrow$ will be self-dual.

Note that the definition of the hybrid languages treats *all* atoms as *formulae*. For example, $x \wedge \forall x((p \wedge \Diamond c) \rightarrow \neg\Diamond x)$ is a well-formed formula. Free and bound state variables, substitution and other syntactic concepts, are defined as in classical logic (for definitions see [5]). A formula φ is called a *sentence* iff φ does not contain any free occurrence of a state variable. Given a formula φ and state variables x and y, $\varphi[y/x]$ will denote the formula obtained from φ by substituting y for all free occurrences of x.

Now for the semantics. Let $\mathcal{L}$ be any of the hybrid languages defined above. A (Kripke) model $\mathcal{M}$ for $\mathcal{L}$ is a triple (S, R, V) such that S is a non-empty set of states, R a binary relation on S, called *the accessibility relation*, and $V : \mathrm{PROP} \cup \mathrm{NOM} \longrightarrow Pow(S)$. A valuation V is called *hybrid* iff for all nominals $c \in \mathrm{NOM}$, $V(c)$ is a singleton subset of S. A model $\mathcal{M}$ is called *hybrid* iff its valuation is hybrid. (That is: hybrid models treat nominals as labels.)

To bind state variables we will make use of the Tarskian idea of assignment functions. An assignment for $\mathcal{L}$ on $\mathcal{M}$ is a mapping $g : \mathrm{SVAR} \longrightarrow Pow(S)$ such that for all state variables $x \in \mathrm{SVAR}$, $g(x)$ is a singleton subset of S. (That is: assignments treat state variables as labels.) The notation $g' \stackrel{x}{\sim} g$ (g' is an x-variant of g) means that g' and g are assignments (on some model $\mathcal{M}$) such that g' agrees with g on all arguments save possibly x.

Let $\mathcal{M} = (S, R, V)$ be a hybrid model, g an assignment on $\mathcal{M}$ and $s \in S$ a state in $\mathcal{M}$. For any atom a, let $[V, g](a) = g(a)$ if a is a state variable, and $V(a)$ otherwise. Then the interpretation of the common fragment of all hybrid languages is carried out using the following definition:

$$\begin{array}{lll}
\mathcal{M}, g, s \models a & \text{iff} & s \in [V, g](a), \text{ where } a \text{ is an atom} \\
\mathcal{M}, g, s \models \neg\varphi & \text{iff} & M, g, s \not\models \varphi \\
\mathcal{M}, g, s \models \varphi \wedge \psi & \text{iff} & \mathcal{M}, g, s \models \varphi \;\&\; \mathcal{M}, g, s \models \psi \\
\mathcal{M}, g, s \models \Box\varphi & \text{iff} & \forall s'(sRs' \Rightarrow \mathcal{M}, g, s' \models \varphi).
\end{array}$$

Note that the clauses for state variables are just like those for propositional symbols, save that state variables make use of the assignment, whereas propositional symbols use the valuation. Here is the satisfaction definition for the binders:

$$\begin{array}{lll}
\mathcal{M}, g, s \models \forall x\varphi & \text{iff} & \mathcal{M}, g', s \models \varphi, \text{ for all } g' \stackrel{x}{\sim} g \\
\mathcal{M}, g, s \models \downarrow x\varphi & \text{iff} & \mathcal{M}, g', s \models \varphi, \text{ where } g' \stackrel{x}{\sim} g \\
 & & \text{and } g'(x) = \{s\}.
\end{array}$$

$\forall$ works globally: it binds state variables to arbitrary states in models, while $\downarrow$ binds locally: it binds a variable to the current state, and thus creates a label for here-and-now. Note that $\downarrow$ is self-dual: $\mathcal{M}, g, s \models \downarrow x\varphi$ iff $\mathcal{M}, g, s \models \neg\downarrow x\neg\varphi$.

For each $l \in \mathrm{SVAR} \cup \mathrm{NOM}$, the interpretation of the operator $@_l$ is given by:

$$\mathcal{M}, g, s \models @_l\varphi \text{ iff } \mathcal{M}, g, t \models \varphi \text{ where } [V, g](l) = \{t\}.$$

$@_l$ jumps to the state labeled l and evaluates its argument there.

A formula φ is *satisfiable* iff for some hybrid model $\mathcal{M}$, some assignment g on $\mathcal{M}$, and some state s in $\mathcal{M}$, $\mathcal{M}, g, s \models \varphi$. A formula φ is *valid* iff for all hybrid models $\mathcal{M}$, all assignments g on $\mathcal{M}$, and all states s in $\mathcal{M}$, $\mathcal{M}, g, s \models \varphi$. We write $\mathcal{M}, s \models \varphi$ iff $\mathcal{M}, g, s \models \varphi$ for all assignments g. Note that for every sentence φ, $\mathcal{M}, g, s \models \varphi$ iff $\mathcal{M}, s \models \varphi$.

Let $\mathcal{L}$ be any of the hybrid languages defined above. The hybrid logic of $\mathcal{L}$ is defined to be the set of all valid $\mathcal{L}$-formulae. Hybrid languages greatly increase the expressivity of PML. For example, the weakest hybrid language $\mathcal{L}_o$ is more expressive than PML, since $\mathcal{L}_o$ can express irreflexivity by $c \to \neg\Diamond c$. Here are two examples of properties that are not definable in PML while definable in hybrid languages.

Example 1. Counting modalities are definable. For example:

$$\textit{At-least-2}(\varphi) \;:=\; \exists x \exists y(\Diamond(x \wedge \neg y \wedge \varphi) \wedge \Diamond(y \wedge \neg x \wedge \varphi)).$$

At-least-2(φ) is satisfied at a state s iff φ is satisfied in at least two *distinct* successors of s. Read this definition as follows: it is possible to bind the variables x and y to two states in such a way that x is a successor of s and φ is true but y is false at x, and y is a successor of s and φ is true but x is false at y.

Example 2. Until is definable.

$$\textit{Until}(\varphi, \psi) \;:=\; {\downarrow} x \Diamond {\downarrow} y @_x (\Diamond(y \wedge \varphi) \wedge \Box(\Diamond y \wedge \neg y \to \psi)).$$

Note how this works: we label the current state with x, use $\Diamond$ to move to an accessible state, which we label y, and then use @ to jump us back to x. We then use the modalities to insist that (1) φ holds at the state labeled y, and (2) ψ holds at all successors of the current state that precede this y-labeled state.

In fact, hybrid languages can be seen as fragments of classical logic ranging from strictly weaker systems, like $\mathcal{L}(\downarrow)$, to systems with full first-order expressive power, like $\mathcal{L}(\forall, @)$. For further discussion on expressivity we refer to [3, 4].

Lemma 1 (Substitution Lemma). *Let $\mathcal{M}$ be a hybrid model, let g be an assignment on $\mathcal{M}$, and let φ be a formula of any of the hybrid languages defined above. Then, for every state s in $\mathcal{M}$, if y is a variable that is substitutable for x in φ and c is a nominal then:*

1. *$\mathcal{M}, g, s \models \varphi[y/x]$ iff $\mathcal{M}, g', s \models \varphi$, where $g' \stackrel{x}{\sim} g$ and $g'(x) = g(y)$.*
2. *$\mathcal{M}, g, s \models \varphi[c/x]$ iff $\mathcal{M}, g', s \models \varphi$, where $g' \stackrel{x}{\sim} g$ and $g'(x) = V(c)$.*

Proof. By induction on the complexity of φ.

3 Prefixed tableaux

Prefixed tableau systems have been designed for a variety of modal logics (see [10]). The idea is to use prefixes to 'label' states in Kripke models. In contrast to the branch 'modification' techniques, prefixes allow us to keep the information about the past. This is crucial to the hybrid languages as nominals and state variables should be satisfied at unique states. We follow the notation in [10].

Let $\mathcal{L}$ be any of the hybrid languages defined in Section 2. It suffices to construct tableau proofs for sentences in $\mathcal{L}$, since validity of arbitrary formulae can be reduced to that of sentences. As a consequence, tableau proofs will contain only sentences of $\mathcal{L}$ (and not arbitrary formulae). More precisely, tableau proofs will contain two types of formulae: prefixed sentences and accessibility sentences.

Prefixed sentences in $\mathcal{L}$ (prefixed $\mathcal{L}$-sentences) consist of a prefix followed by an $\mathcal{L}$-sentence. More formally, given a countably infinite set of prefixes PREF $= \{\tau, \sigma, \sigma', \ldots\}$, a prefixed sentence has the form $\sigma\varphi$, where $\sigma \in$ PREF and φ is an $\mathcal{L}$-sentence. A prefixed sentence $\sigma\varphi$ is typically read 'φ is true at σ'. We refer to prefixed sentences as *atomic* if they are of the form σa or $\sigma\neg a$, where σ is a prefix and a an atom in $\mathcal{L}$.

Recall that nominals are also used to label states in models. Thus, prefixed sentences contain two kinds of labels: nominals and prefixes. The difference is that nominals label states internally, that is, we refer to them in formulae in the object language, whereas prefixes label externally: they are used in the meta-language to keep the information about all states that have been created in the course of the tableau construction.

Accessibility sentences are of the form $\sigma < \sigma'$, where σ and σ' are prefixes.

As it was mentioned before prefixes will later be interpreted as states in models while accessibility sentences will define pairs of states that are in the accessibility relation.

Let Γ be a set of prefixed sentences and accessibility sentences. We use PREF(Γ) (resp. NOM(Γ) and PROP(Γ)) to denote the set of all prefixes (resp. nominals and propositional symbols) that occur in some prefixed or accessibility sentence in Γ.

A *tableau rule in* $\mathcal{L}$ consists of a premiss $\mathcal{P}$ and a (finite) set of conclusions $\mathcal{C}_1, \ldots, \mathcal{C}_n$, where $n \in \omega$: $\frac{\mathcal{P}}{\mathcal{C}_1 \mid \ldots \mid \mathcal{C}_n}$. The *premiss* and the *conclusions* are (finite) sets consisting of accessibility sentences and prefixed $\mathcal{L}$-sentences. The tableau rules can be read as follows: 'if all formulae in the premiss $\mathcal{P}$ of a rule are simultaneously satisfiable then so are all formulae in at least one of the conclusions'.

Let $\mathcal{O} \subseteq \{\forall, \downarrow, @\}$ be some set of operators and $\mathcal{L}$ the hybrid language over $\mathcal{O}$. A *tableau calculus* $\mathcal{TC}(\mathcal{O})$ for $\mathcal{L}$ is a finite collection of tableau rules in $\mathcal{L}$. Tableau calculi for the hybrid languages will be defined in the next section.

The definition of prefixed tableaux that we use is standard and can be found in [10]. Throughout the definition both prefixed $\mathcal{L}$-sentences and accessibility sentences are referred to as sentences.

A $\mathcal{TC}(\mathcal{O})$*-prefixed tableau* for $\sigma\varphi$ is a finite tree with root $\sigma\varphi$ each node of which carries either a prefixed $\mathcal{L}$-sentence or an accessibility sentence. We say that a $\mathcal{TC}(\mathcal{O})$-rule is *applicable* to a branch if the branch contains all sentences that occur in the premiss of the rule. The steps for extending the tableau are: (1) choose a branch θ and a rule ρ that is applicable to θ, (2) if ρ has n conclusions, split the end of θ to n branches and for all $k \leq n$, add $\mathcal{C}_k$ to the k-th branch. (That is, for all $k \leq n$ we add as many nodes to the k-th branch as there are sentences in $\mathcal{C}_k$.) All tableaux are constructed in this way.

The left-hand-side tableau in Example 3 below motivates the following:

Definition 1 (Closed branches and tableaux). *Let $\mathcal{T}$ be a prefixed tableau and θ a branch in $\mathcal{T}$. θ is* closed *if either (1) θ contains both $\sigma\varphi$ and $\sigma\neg\varphi$ or, (2) θ contains the following four prefixed sentences σc, $\sigma' c$, $\sigma\varphi$ and $\sigma'\neg\varphi$, where φ is an $\mathcal{L}$-sentence, σ, σ' prefixes and c a nominal. If a branch is not closed it is* open. *The tableau $\mathcal{T}$ is* closed *if all its branches are closed, otherwise $\mathcal{T}$ is* open.

Let $\mathcal{T}$ be a tableau and θ a branch in $\mathcal{T}$. Define a binary relation $<_\theta$, *the accessibility relation*, on the set PREF(θ) as follows: $\sigma <_\theta \sigma'$ iff $\sigma < \sigma'$ is on θ.

Let Γ be a set of prefixed sentences, $<_\Gamma$ a binary relation on PREF(Γ), and $\mathcal{M} = (S, R, V)$ a hybrid model for $\mathcal{L}$. A mapping $\mathcal{I}$: PREF $\longrightarrow S$ is called an *interpretation of* (Γ,$<_\Gamma$) if for all prefixes σ and σ' in Γ such that $\sigma <_\Gamma \sigma'$ we have $\mathcal{I}(\sigma)R\mathcal{I}(\sigma')$. In particular, if Γ is the set of all prefixed sentences that occur on a branch θ and $<_\Gamma$ is the accessibility relation $<_\theta$, we say that $\mathcal{I}$ is an *interpretation of* θ.

Definition 2 (Satisfiability of branches). *Let Γ be a set of prefixed sentences and $<_\Gamma$ a binary relation on* PREF(Γ). *Further, let $\mathcal{M}$ be a hybrid model for $\mathcal{L}$ and $\mathcal{I}$ an interpretation of $(\Gamma, <_\Gamma)$. We say that $(\Gamma, <_\Gamma)$ is* satisfiable in $\mathcal{M}$ under $\mathcal{I}$ *if for all $\sigma\varphi \in \Gamma$ we have $\mathcal{M}, \mathcal{I}(\sigma) \models \varphi$. A branch θ is* satisfiable in $\mathcal{M}$ under $\mathcal{I}$ *if $(\Gamma, <_\Gamma)$ is satisfiable in $\mathcal{M}$ under $\mathcal{I}$, where Γ is the set of all prefixed sentences that occur on θ and $<_\Gamma$ is the accessibility relation $<_\theta$. $(\Gamma, <_\Gamma)$ is* satisfiable *if there is a hybrid model $\mathcal{M}$ and an interpretation $\mathcal{I}$ such that $(\Gamma, <_\Gamma)$ is satisfiable in $\mathcal{M}$ under $\mathcal{I}$. A branch θ is* satisfiable *if there is a model $\mathcal{M}$ and an interpretation $\mathcal{I}$ such that θ is satisfiable in $\mathcal{M}$ under $\mathcal{I}$.*

It is easy to see that a closed branch θ cannot be satisfiable. A tableau is called *satisfiable* if it has a satisfiable branch. Let $\mathcal{O} \subseteq \{\forall, \downarrow, @\}$ be a set of operators, $\mathcal{L}$ the hybrid language over $\mathcal{O}$ and φ an $\mathcal{L}$-sentence. We say that φ is *provable* in a tableau calculus $\mathcal{TC}(\mathcal{O})$ iff there is a closed tableau for $\sigma\neg\varphi$ where σ is some prefix. In this case, the tableau is called a proof of φ in $\mathcal{TC}(\mathcal{O})$.

4 Tableau calculi for hybrid logics

In this section we define tableau calculi for hybrid languages and prove them complete. The collection of rules $\mathcal{TC}$ below defines a tableau calculus for the weakest hybrid language $\mathcal{L}_o$ that contains no operators from $\{\forall, \downarrow, @\}$. We use c and c_1 to denote nominals, and σ, τ and σ' to denote prefixes.

$(\alpha)\ \dfrac{\sigma\neg\neg\varphi}{\sigma\varphi};\ \dfrac{\sigma\varphi\wedge\psi}{\sigma\varphi,\ \sigma\psi} \qquad (\beta)\ \dfrac{\sigma\neg(\varphi\wedge\psi)}{\sigma\neg\varphi \mid \sigma\neg\psi} \qquad (\nu)\ \dfrac{\sigma\Box\varphi,\ \sigma{<}\sigma'}{\sigma'\varphi}$

$(\pi)\ \dfrac{\sigma\neg\Box\varphi}{\sigma'\neg\varphi,\ \sigma{<}\sigma'}$ σ' is not on the branch

(Labeling) $\dfrac{\sigma\varphi}{\sigma c}$ c is not on the branch

(S-Identifying) $\dfrac{\sigma c,\ \tau c,\ \tau{<}\sigma'}{\sigma{<}\sigma'}$

(L-Identifying) $\dfrac{\sigma c,\ \tau c,\ \sigma_1 c_1,\ \tau c_1}{\sigma c_1,\ \sigma_1 c}$

The rules α, β, ν and π are known from tableau calculi for modal logics and apply to hybrid languages as well. The *Labeling* and both *Identifying* rules reflect the hybrid languages. The *Labeling* rule says that whenever we have an external label σ for a state, we can introduce an internal label c for that state. The *S-Identifying* rule allows us to identify the successors of two states if the two states have a common internal label. More precisely, if two states are internally labelled by a label c then, we identify the successors of the first state with those of the second. The *L-Identifying* rule says that we can identify the internal labels of a state σ with those of a state σ_1, if σ and σ_1 share a comon external label, namely τ. The rules for the operators $\forall, \downarrow$ and @ are defined as follows:

$$(\forall 1)\quad \frac{\sigma \forall x \varphi}{\sigma \varphi[c/x]} \text{ } c \text{ is on the branch} \qquad (\forall 2)\quad \frac{\sigma \neg \forall x \varphi}{\sigma \neg \varphi[c/x]} \text{ } c \text{ is not on the branch}$$

$$(\downarrow 1)\quad \frac{\sigma {\downarrow} x \varphi,\ \sigma c}{\sigma \varphi[c/x]} \qquad (\downarrow 2)\quad \frac{\sigma \neg {\downarrow} x \varphi,\ \sigma c}{\sigma \neg \varphi[c/x]}$$

$$(@1)\quad \frac{\sigma @_c \varphi}{\sigma' c,\ \sigma' \varphi} \qquad (@2)\quad \frac{\sigma \neg @_c \varphi}{\sigma' c,\ \sigma' \neg \varphi}$$

(In the @-rules above, if σc is on the branch, $\sigma' = \sigma$, else σ' is not on the branch.) Let $\mathcal{O} \subseteq \{\forall, \downarrow, @\}$ be any set of operators and $\mathcal{L}$ be the hybrid language over $\mathcal{O}$. We define a *tableau calculus* $\mathcal{TC}(\mathcal{O})$ *for* $\mathcal{L}$ to be the following collection of rules in $\mathcal{L}$: $\mathcal{TC} \cup \{O\text{-rules} \mid O \in \mathcal{O}\}$. (For example, $\mathcal{TC} \cup \{\downarrow 1, \downarrow 2\} \cup \{@1, @2\}$ is the tableau calculus for $\mathcal{L}(\downarrow, @)$.) One can see that if a single tableau rule is applied to a satisfiable tableau, the resulting tableau will be satisfiable too. Therefore, $\mathcal{TC}(\mathcal{O})$ is sound: if an $\mathcal{L}$-sentence φ is provable in $\mathcal{TC}(\mathcal{O})$, then φ is valid.

Before turning to completeness, we consider three examples of tableau proofs. To simplify the presentation, we use finite sequences of natural numbers as prefixes, and assume that two prefixes $\sigma = k_1 \ldots k_i$ and $\tau = l_1 \ldots l_j$ are in the accessibility relation of a branch θ iff either $j = i + 1$ and for all $m \leq i$, $k_m = l_m$ or, θ contains $\sigma < \tau$.

Example 3. The tableau on the left-hand-side below is closed because of Definition 1. The tableau proof on the right-hand-side below uses the *Labeling* rule.

$1.\neg(\Diamond\Diamond(c \wedge \varphi) \rightarrow \Box(c \rightarrow \varphi))$
$1.\Diamond\Diamond(c \wedge \varphi)$
$1.\neg\Box(c \rightarrow \varphi)$
$1.1.\Diamond(c \wedge \varphi)$
$1.2.\neg(c \rightarrow \varphi)$
$1.1.1.c$
$1.1.1.\varphi$
$1.2.c$
$1.2.\neg\varphi$
$\bot$

$1.\neg(\Diamond p \rightarrow {\downarrow} x \Diamond {\downarrow} y @_x @_y p)$	
$1.\Diamond p$	*1*, α
$1.\neg{\downarrow} x \Diamond {\downarrow} y @_x @_y p$	*1*, α
$1.1.p$	*2*, π
$1.c_1$	*Labeling*
$1.\neg\Diamond{\downarrow} y @_{c_1} @_y p$	*3*, $\downarrow 2$
$1.1.\neg{\downarrow} y @_{c_1} @_y p$	*6*, ν
$1.1.c_{11}$	*Labeling*
$1.1.\neg @_{c_1} @_{c_{11}} p$	*7*, $\downarrow 2$
$1.\neg @_{c_{11}} p$	*9*, @2
$1.1.\neg p$	*10*, @2
$\bot$	

Example 4. The following tableau proof uses the *S-Identifying* rule.

$1.\neg(\Diamond(c \wedge \Box(c_1 \rightarrow p)) \rightarrow \neg\Diamond(c \wedge \Diamond(c_1 \wedge \neg p)))$	
$1.\Diamond(c \wedge \Box(c_1 \rightarrow p))$	*1*, α
$1.\Diamond(c \wedge \Diamond(c_1 \wedge \neg p))$	*1*, α
$1.1.c$	*2*, π, α
$1.1.\Box(c_1 \rightarrow p)$	*2*, π, α
$1.2.c$	*3*, π, α
$1.2.\Diamond(c_1 \wedge \neg p)$	*3*, π, α
$1.2.1.c_1$	*7*, π, α
$1.2.1.\neg p$	*7*, π, α
$1.1 < 1.2.1$	*4*, *6*, *S-Identifying*
$1.2.1.c_1 \rightarrow p$	*5*, *10*, ν
$1.2.1.\neg c_1$ | $1.2.1.p$ (branches)	*11*, β, α
$\bot$ | $\bot$	

4.1 A proof procedure

To prove that the tableau calculi defined above are complete we will use a systematic-tableau-construction argument (see [19, 10]). Given a sentence φ, we will describe a systematic procedure such that if φ is valid, the procedure on input $\neg\varphi$ will construct a tableau proof for φ, otherwise, the procedure will construct a counter-model for φ. Note that in the case of hybrid logics the counter-model should be a hybrid (Kripke) model.

The procedure will closely follow the systematic procedures in [19, 10]. We will work with each occurrence of a prefixed sentence in a tableau exactly once, after which we declare this occurrence finished. We fix an enumeration $E_{nom} = \{c_1, c_2, \ldots\}$ of all nominals in NOM and an enumeration $E_{pref} = \{\sigma_1, \sigma_2, \ldots\}$ of all prefixes in PREF.

The proof procedure. On input $\chi = \neg\varphi$ perform the following steps:

Step 1. Place $\sigma_1\neg\varphi$ at the origin and then add $\sigma_1 c$. (Here c is the first nominal in E_{nom} that is not in χ.) This completes *Step 1*.

Suppose that n steps of the procedure have been completed and the tableau that has been constructed is $\mathcal{T}_n$. Denote by (a) the condition that all occurrences of prefixed sentences in $\mathcal{T}_n$ are finished and by (b) the condition that there is an open branch θ in $\mathcal{T}_n$ such that for all prefixes σ and τ on θ if θ contains σc and τc for some nominal c then, σ and τ have the same $<_\theta$-successors, and for all prefixes σ, τ and σ_1 on θ, if for some nominals c and c_1, $\sigma c, \tau c, \sigma_1 c_1, \tau c_1$ are on θ, then $\sigma c_1, \sigma_1 c$ are on θ. Then, if either $\mathcal{T}_n$ is closed, or both (a) and (b) hold, then stop. Otherwise perform the next step.

Step n+1. This step consists of two substeps, namely of (A) and (B):

(A) For all open branches θ and:

(1) for all prefixes σ and τ on θ, if σc and τc on θ, where c is a nominal then, identify $<_\theta$-successors of σ with $<_\theta$-successors of τ by adding to the end of θ accessibility sentences as follows: for all τ' such that $\tau <_\theta \tau'$ add $\sigma < \tau'$, and for all σ' such that $\sigma <_\theta \sigma'$ add $\tau <_\theta \sigma'$.

(2) for all prefixes σ, τ and σ_1 on θ; if $\sigma c, \tau c, \sigma_1 c_1, \tau c_1$ are on θ where c and c_1 are nominals, add $\sigma c_1, \sigma_1 c$ to the end of θ.

Having done this for all open branches θ, all nominals and all prefixes on θ, go on to:

(B) Choose an occurrence of a prefixed sentence as high up in the tree as possible (as close to the origin as possible) that has not been finished, say this is $\sigma\gamma$. If $\sigma\gamma$ is atomic, declare $\sigma\gamma$ finished and complete *Step n+1*.

Otherwise, extend the tableau as follows. For each open branch θ through this occurrence of $\sigma\gamma$, do the following:
(1) If $\sigma\gamma$ is $\sigma\neg\neg\psi$ (resp. $\sigma\psi_1 \wedge \psi_2$), add $\sigma\psi$ (resp. $\sigma\psi_1$ and $\sigma\psi_2$) to θ.
(2) If $\sigma\gamma$ is $\sigma\neg(\psi_1 \wedge \psi_2)$, split θ to two branches and add $\sigma\neg\psi_1$ to the one branch and $\sigma\neg\psi_2$ to the other.
(3) If $\sigma\gamma$ is of the form $\sigma\Box\psi$, then for each prefix σ' such that σ' appears on θ and $\sigma < \sigma'$, add $\sigma'\psi$ to θ, after which add a fresh occurrence of $\sigma\Box\psi$ to θ.
(4) If $\sigma\gamma$ is of the form $\sigma\neg\Box\psi$, then add $\sigma'\neg\psi$, $\sigma < \sigma'$ and $\sigma' c$ to θ. (Here σ' is the first prefix in the enumeration E_{pref} that is not on θ and c is the first nominal in the enumeration E_{nom} that is not on θ.)
(5) If $\sigma\gamma$ is of the form $\sigma\forall x\psi$, then for all nominals c on θ, add $\sigma\psi[c/x]$ to θ, followed by a fresh occurrence of $\sigma\forall x\psi$.
(6) If $\sigma\gamma$ is of the form $\sigma\neg\forall x\psi$, then add $\sigma\neg\psi[c/x]$ to θ, where c is the first nominal in the enumeration E_{nom} that is not on θ.
(7) If $\sigma\gamma$ is $\sigma{\downarrow}x\psi$, add $\sigma\psi[c/x]$ to θ. Here c is a nominal such that σc is on θ.
(8) If $\sigma\gamma$ is $\sigma\neg{\downarrow}x\psi$, add $\sigma\neg\psi[c/x]$ to θ. Here c is a nominal such that σc is on θ.
(9) If $\sigma\gamma$ is $\sigma@_c\psi$, then add $\sigma'\psi$ and $\sigma' c$ to θ, where $\sigma' = \sigma$ if σc is on θ, and σ' is the first prefix in the enumeration E_{pref} that is not on θ otherwise.
(10) If $\sigma\gamma$ is $\sigma\neg@_c\psi$, then add $\sigma'\neg\psi$ and $\sigma' c$ to θ, where $\sigma' = \sigma$ if σc is on θ, and σ' is the first prefix in the enumeration E_{pref} that is not on θ otherwise.

Having done this for all open branches through the current occurrence of $\sigma\gamma$, declare this occurrence finished. This completes *Step n+1*.

End of the procedure.

Clearly, the procedure does not always terminate; for example, on input $\chi = \Diamond(c \wedge \Diamond c \wedge \Box\Diamond c)$. Termination will be discussed at the end of Section 4 as well as in Section 5.

4.2 Completeness

Note that if the procedure on input $\chi = \neg\varphi$ does not produce a closed tableau for $\neg\varphi$ then, it constructs an open branch θ having the properties listed in the following definition. More precisely, if Γ is the set of all prefixed sentences on θ and $<_\Gamma$ is the accessibility relation on θ, then $(\Gamma, <_\Gamma)$ is downward saturated.

Definition 3 (Downward saturated sets). *Let $\mathcal{O} \subseteq \{\forall, \downarrow, @\}$ be a set of operators and $\mathcal{L}$ be the hybrid language over $\mathcal{O}$. Further, let Γ be a non-empty set of prefixed sentences in $\mathcal{L}$ and $<_\Gamma$ a binary relation on the prefixes in Γ. $(\Gamma, <_\Gamma)$ is called* $\mathcal{O}$-downward saturated *iff the following properties from the list* *below hold: for all $n \leq 7$, property (n) and for every operator $O \in \mathcal{O}$, properties (O') and (O'').*

(1) *there is no atom a and no prefix σ in Γ such that both $\sigma a \in \Gamma$ and $\sigma\neg a \in \Gamma$; and, there are no prefixes σ and τ in Γ such that for some $c \in \mathrm{NOM}(\Gamma)$ and some atom a, Γ contains $\sigma c, \tau c, \sigma\neg a, \tau a$.*
(2) *for all nominals c and c_1 and all prefixes σ, τ and σ_1, if $\sigma c, \tau c, \sigma_1 c_1, \tau c_1 \in \Gamma$ then, $\sigma_1 c, \sigma c_1 \in \Gamma$*
(3) *for all nominals c and for all prefixes σ and τ, if $\sigma c, \tau c \in \Gamma$ then, σ and τ have the same $<_\Gamma$-successors*
(4) *if $\sigma\varphi \wedge \psi \in \Gamma$ (resp. $\sigma\neg\neg\varphi \in \Gamma$) then, $\sigma\varphi \in \Gamma$ and $\sigma\psi \in \Gamma$ (resp. $\sigma\varphi \in \Gamma$)*
(5) *if $\sigma\neg(\varphi \wedge \psi) \in \Gamma$ then, either $\sigma\neg\varphi \in \Gamma$ or $\sigma\neg\psi \in \Gamma$*
(6) *if $\sigma\Box\varphi \in \Gamma$ then, for all σ' in Γ, $\sigma <_\Gamma \sigma'$ implies $\sigma'\varphi \in \Gamma$*
(7) *if $\sigma\neg\Box\varphi \in \Gamma$ then, $\sigma'\neg\varphi \in \Gamma$ for some σ' in Γ such that $\sigma <_\Gamma \sigma'$*
($\forall'$) *if $\sigma\forall x\varphi \in \Gamma$, then $\sigma\varphi[c/x] \in \Gamma$ for every nominal c in Γ*
($\forall''$) *if $\sigma\neg\forall x\varphi \in \Gamma$, then $\sigma\neg\varphi[c/x] \in \Gamma$ for some nominal c in Γ*
($\downarrow'$) *if $\sigma\downarrow x\varphi \in \Gamma$, then $\sigma c, \sigma\varphi[c/x] \in \Gamma$ for some nominal c in Γ*
($\downarrow''$) *if $\sigma\neg\downarrow x\psi \in \Gamma$, then $\sigma c, \sigma\neg\varphi[c/x] \in \Gamma$ for some nominal c in Γ*
($@'$) *if $\sigma@_c\varphi \in \Gamma$ where c is a nominal, then $\sigma' c, \sigma'\varphi \in \Gamma$ for some prefix σ'*
($@''$) *if $\sigma\neg@_c\varphi \in \Gamma$ where c is a nominal, then $\sigma' c, \sigma'\neg\varphi \in \Gamma$ for some prefix σ'*

To cope with the binders when proving satisfiability of downward saturated sets we need the concept of a labeled model.

Definition 4 (Labeled Models). *Let $\mathcal{M}$ be a hybrid model in a hybrid language $\mathcal{L}$. We say that $\mathcal{M}$ is* labeled *if for all states $s \in \mathcal{M}$, there is a nominal c such that $\mathcal{M}, s \models c$.*

To state the next lemma we fix notation: a set of prefixed sentences Γ is called *labeled* iff for all prefixes σ in Γ, there is a nominal c such that σc is in Γ.

Lemma 2 (Satisfiability of Downward saturated sets). *Let $\mathcal{O} \subseteq \{\forall, \downarrow, @\}$ be a set of operators and $\mathcal{L}$ be the hybrid language over $\mathcal{O}$. Further, let Γ be a set of prefixed sentences in $\mathcal{L}$ and $<_\Gamma$ a binary relation on the prefixes in Γ. If $(\Gamma, <_\Gamma)$ is $\mathcal{O}$-downward saturated and Γ is labeled, then $(\Gamma, <_\Gamma)$ is satisfiable.*

Proof. Let $\sim$ be a binary relation on the set $\mathrm{PREF}(\Gamma)$ defined as follows: $\sigma \sim \tau$ iff there is a nominal c such that $\sigma c, \tau c$ are in Γ. Since Γ is labeled and (2) of Definition 3 holds, $\sim$ is an equivalence relation on $\mathrm{PREF}(\Gamma)$; let S be the set of the equivalence classes. Define $f : \mathrm{PREF}(\Gamma) \longrightarrow S$ to be a function that maps each prefix $\sigma \in \mathrm{PREF}(\Gamma)$ to its equivalence class.

Our model $\mathcal{M}$ is a triple (S^+, R, V), where $S^+ = S$ if for all $c \in \mathrm{NOM}(\Gamma)$ there is σ such the $\sigma c \in \Gamma$, and $S^+ = S \cup \{*\}$ otherwise. (Here $*$ is an entity that is not an equivalence class.) For every two states $s_1, s_2 \in S^+$, $s_1 R s_2$ iff there are $\sigma_1, \sigma_2 \in \mathrm{PREF}(\Gamma)$ such that $\sigma_1 <_\Gamma \sigma_2$, $f(\sigma_1) = s_1$ and $f(\sigma_2) = s_2$; for all $p \in \mathrm{PROP}(\Gamma)$, $V(p) = \{s \mid \exists\sigma : \ f(\sigma) = s \ \& \ \sigma p \in \Gamma\}$, for all $c \in \mathrm{NOM}(\Gamma)$, $V(c) = \{s \mid \exists\sigma : \ f(\sigma) = s \ \& \ \sigma c \in \Gamma\}$ if this set is non-empty and $V(c) = \{*\}$

otherwise; for all $p \in \mathrm{PROP}$ such that $p \notin \mathrm{PROP}(\Gamma)$ and all $c \in \mathrm{NOM}$ such that $c \notin \mathrm{NOM}(\Gamma)$, $V(p) = V(c) = \{*\}$.

First, note that $\mathcal{M}$ is a hybrid model, that is, for all $c \in \mathrm{NOM}$, $V(c)$ is a singleton set. If $c \notin \mathrm{NOM}(\Gamma)$ this is obvious, so let $c \in \mathrm{NOM}(\Gamma)$ and suppose that there are $s_1, s_2 \in S^+$ and $\{s_1, s_2\} \subseteq V(c)$. Then, there exist σ_1, σ_2 such that $f(\sigma_1) = s_1, f(\sigma_2) = s_2, \sigma_1 c \in \Gamma$ and $\sigma_2 c \in \Gamma$, hence $s_1 = s_2$.

Second, $\mathcal{M}$ is a labeled model, as the set Γ is labeled and if $\mathcal{M}$ contains the state $*$ then, $\mathcal{M}, * \models c$ for some nominal c in Γ.

Third, consider an interpretation $\mathcal{I} : \mathrm{PREF} \longrightarrow S^+$ which is an arbitrary extension of the function $f : \mathrm{PREF}(\Gamma) \longrightarrow S^+$ to PREF. To show that $(\Gamma, <_\Gamma)$ is satisfiable in $\mathcal{M}$ under $\mathcal{I}$, we will prove by induction on the complexity of φ, that for every prefixed sentence $\sigma\varphi$, if $\sigma\varphi \in \Gamma$ then $\mathcal{M}, f(\sigma) \models \varphi$.

The base case, that is, for φ an atom a or $\neg a$, follows from the definition of $\mathcal{M}$ and property (1) of Definition 3.

Now, assume that $\sigma\varphi \in \Gamma$ and for all prefixed sentences $\sigma\psi \in \Gamma$ if ψ has lower complexity than φ then $\mathcal{M}, f(\sigma) \models \psi$. We consider different cases for φ.

If φ is $\neg\neg\psi$, $\psi \wedge \chi$, $\neg(\psi \wedge \chi)$ or $\neg\Box\psi$ we use (4), (5) and (7) of Definition 3.

Let φ be $\Box\psi$ and $\sigma\varphi \in \Gamma$. We have to prove that for all $s \in S^+$, $f(\sigma)Rs$ implies $\mathcal{M}, s \models \psi$. So, suppose that $f(\sigma)Rs$ for some $s \in S^+$. Note that, by the definition of $\mathcal{M}$, $f(\sigma) \in S$ and, since $*$ is not a successor of any state in S, s cannot be $*$, and so $s \in S$ too.

Then, there are σ_1, σ_2 such that $\sigma_1 <_\Gamma \sigma_2$, $f(\sigma_1) = f(\sigma)$ and $f(\sigma_2) = s$. Hence $\sigma <_\Gamma \sigma_2$. (If $\sigma \neq \sigma_1$, this follows from the fact that, since $f(\sigma_1) = f(\sigma)$, there is $c \in \mathrm{NOM}(\Gamma)$ such that $\sigma_1 c, \sigma c \in \Gamma$, and by (3) of Definition 3, σ_1 and σ have the same set of successors.) Now, as $\sigma\Box\psi \in \Gamma$ and $\sigma <_\Gamma \sigma_2$, by (6) of Definition 3, $\sigma_2\psi \in \Gamma$. By the inductive hypothesis, $\mathcal{M}, f(\sigma_2) \models \psi$ and hence equivalently, $\mathcal{M}, s \models \psi$. We have shown that for all states $s \in S^+$, $f(\sigma)Rs$ implies $\mathcal{M}, s \models \psi$, and hence $\mathcal{M}, f(\sigma) \models \Box\psi$.

Let φ be $\forall x\psi$ and $\sigma\varphi \in \Gamma$. We have to show that $\mathcal{M}, f(\sigma) \models \forall x\psi$, that is, for all states $s \in S^+$, if g is an assignment such that $g(x) = \{s\}$ then, $\mathcal{M}, g, f(\sigma) \models \psi$. Since $\mathcal{M}$ is a labeled model, s is labeled by some nominal c. Moreover, as $\sigma\forall x\psi \in \Gamma$ and $(\Gamma, <_\Gamma)$ is downward saturated (see $(\forall')$ of Definition 3), $\sigma\psi[c/x] \in \Gamma$ and hence, by the inductive hypothesis, $\mathcal{M}, f(\sigma) \models \psi[c/x]$. Therefore, by Substitution Lemma, $\mathcal{M}, g, f(\sigma) \models \psi$ for all $s \in S^+$.

Let φ be $\downarrow x\psi$ and $\sigma\varphi \in \Gamma$. We have to show that $\mathcal{M}, f(\sigma) \models \downarrow x\psi$, that is $\mathcal{M}, g, f(\sigma) \models \psi$ where g is an assignment such that $g(x) = \{f(\sigma)\}$. As $(\Gamma, <_\Gamma)$ is downward saturated (see $(\downarrow')$ of Definition 3) and $\sigma\downarrow x\psi \in \Gamma$, for some nominal c in Γ we have $\sigma c, \sigma\psi[c/x] \in \Gamma$. Then, by the inductive hypothesis, $\mathcal{M}, f(\sigma) \models c$ and $\mathcal{M}, f(\sigma) \models \psi[c/x]$. Hence $V(c) = \{f(\sigma)\}$. Therefore, by Substitution Lemma, $\mathcal{M}, g, f(\sigma) \models \psi$.

Suppose that φ is $@_c\psi$ and $\sigma\varphi \in \Gamma$. We have to show that $\mathcal{M}, f(\sigma) \models @_c\psi$. Since $\sigma @_c\psi \in \Gamma$, by $(@')$ of Definition 3, there is σ' such that $\sigma' c, \sigma'\psi \in \Gamma$. Hence, by the inductive hypothesis, $\mathcal{M}, f(\sigma') \models c$ and $\mathcal{M}, f(\sigma') \models \psi$, and therefore $\mathcal{M}, f(\sigma') \models @_c\psi$.

The cases when φ is $\neg\forall x\psi$, $\neg{\downarrow}x\psi$ and $\neg@_c\psi$ can be proved similarly using ($\forall''$), ($\downarrow''$) and ($@''$) of Definition 3.

Theorem 1 (Completeness). *Let $\mathcal{O} \subseteq \{\forall, \downarrow, @\}$ be a set of operators and $\mathcal{L}$ be the hybrid language over $\mathcal{O}$. If an $\mathcal{L}$-sentence φ is valid, then φ has a systematic tableau proof in $\mathcal{TC}(\mathcal{O})$.*

Proof. The proof is standard. If φ is not provable, a systematic attempt at proving φ will produce an open branch θ, such that the set Γ of all prefixed sentences on θ will be labeled and $(\Gamma, <_\theta)$ will be $\mathcal{O}$-downward saturated. Hence, by Lemma 2, $(\Gamma, <_\theta)$ will be satisfiable, and therefore φ cannot be valid.

Soundness and completeness imply that the systematic procedure is a proof procedure for the hybrid languages:

Corollary 1. *Let $\mathcal{O} \subseteq \{\forall, \downarrow, @\}$ be a set of operators and $\mathcal{L}$ be the hybrid language over $\mathcal{O}$. Then, for every $\mathcal{L}$-sentence φ, if φ is provable in $\mathcal{TC}(\mathcal{O})$, then φ has a systematic tableau proof in $\mathcal{TC}(\mathcal{O})$.*

Any hybrid language that contains either the binder $\forall$ or the binder $\downarrow$ is undecidable (see [3, 4]).[1] There are only two binder-free languages: $\mathcal{L}_o$ and $\mathcal{L}(@)$. Both languages are decidable, since they can be embedded into the guarded fragment defined in [1]. However, the proof procedure we introduced in Section 4.1 does not terminate for these two decidable languages; $\chi = \Diamond(c \wedge \Diamond c \wedge \Box\Diamond c)$ is an example of non-termination. The reason for the non-termination here is the occurrence of an infinite alternation of the π and the *S-Identifying* rule.

In the next section, we define a procedure that uses a new rule called the *S-Identifying$'$* rule instead of the previously introduced *S-Identifying* rule. Moreover, we allow applying the π rule only with proviso. As a result, the new procedure we will be able to prove termination and moreover, that it is in fact a decision procedure for $\mathcal{L}_o$ and $\mathcal{L}(@)$.

5 A terminating proof procedure

The proof procedure we define in this section will use only the following rules: α, β, ν, π, *L-Identifying* and @-rules from Section 4, and in addition the rule:

$$(\textit{S-Identifying}')\qquad \frac{\sigma c,\ \tau c,\ \sigma\Box\varphi\quad \tau{<}\tau'}{\tau'\varphi}$$

(Here c is a nominal and σ, τ and τ' are prefixes.) Obviously, the latter rule is correct.

In the tableau construction below when the π-rule is applied, the prefix that is introduced is new to the entire tableau. As a consequence, for each prefix τ in the tableau there is a unique sequence of prefixes $\tau_1, \ldots, \tau_n$ such that $\tau_n = \tau$,

[1] Decidable hybrid logics containing binders exist and can be obtained by restricting the classes of models (see [4]).

for each $i < n$, $\tau_i < \tau_{i+1}$ is on the tableau and, there is no prefix σ such that $\sigma < \tau_1$ is on the tableau. We call n the *depth of the prefix* τ. As before we will work with each occurrence of a prefixed sentence that is not of the form $\sigma\Box\varphi$ exactly once, after which we declare this occurrence finished. No prefixed sentence should be added to a branch if the sentence is already on the branch. Let $E_{pref} = \{\sigma_1, \sigma_2, \ldots\}$ and $E_{nom} = \{c_1, c_2, \ldots\}$ be enumerations of respectively all prefixes in PREF and all nominals in NOM.

The terminating procedure. On input χ perform the following steps:

Step 1. Place $\sigma_1\chi$ at the origin and add $\sigma_1 c$, where c is the first nominal in E_{nom} that is not in χ. While there is an unfinished occurrence of a prefixed sentence $\sigma\varphi$ that is not of the form $\tau\neg\Box\gamma$ and $\tau\Box\gamma$, do the following:
For all branches θ throughout $\sigma\varphi$, if φ is:

- atomic, do not extend θ;
- $\neg\neg\psi$ (resp. $\psi_1 \wedge \psi_2$), add $\sigma\psi$ (resp. $\sigma\psi_1$ and $\sigma\psi_2$) to θ;
- $\neg(\psi_1 \wedge \psi_2)$, split θ to two branches and add $\sigma\neg\psi_1$ and $\sigma\neg\psi_2$ respectively to the first and to the second branch;
- $@_c\psi$ (resp. $\neg @_c\psi$) then, if there is a prefix τ such that τc is on θ, add $\tau\psi$ (resp. $\tau\neg\psi$) to θ; else, add τc and $\tau\psi$ (resp. τc and $\tau\neg\psi$) to θ; (Here τ is the first prefix in the enumeration E_{pref} that is not on the tableau.)

Declare $\sigma\varphi$ finished.
For all open branches θ, if c and c_1 are nominals and σ, τ and σ_1 prefixes such that $\sigma c, \tau c, \sigma_1 c_1, \tau c_1$ are on θ, add $\sigma_1 c, \sigma c_1$ to θ, and declare them finished.

Complete *Step 1.* Denote the tableau that has been constructed by $\mathcal{T}_1$.

Suppose that n steps of the procedure have been completed, and the tableau that has been constructed is denoted by $\mathcal{T}_n$. If $\mathcal{T}_n$ is a closed tableau or all occurrences of prefixed sentences of the form $\tau\neg\Box\gamma$ are finished, stop. Otherwise:

Step $n+1$. Consider the following three conditions:
(A) There is an unfinished occurrence of a prefixed sentence that is not of the form $\tau\Box\gamma$ or $\tau'\neg\Box\gamma$, where τ' has depth $n+1$;
(B) There is a branch θ, a prefixed sentence $\sigma\Box\varphi$ and a prefix σ' such that both $\sigma\Box\varphi$ and $\sigma < \sigma'$ are on θ, but $\sigma'\varphi$ is not on θ;
(C) There is a branch θ such that the *S-Identifying*$'$ rule is applicable to θ. (That is, there is a branch θ such that θ contains σc, τc, $\sigma\Box\varphi$, and $\tau < \tau'$ and θ does not contain $\tau'\varphi$.)
(D) There is a branch θ such that for some nominals c and c_1 and some prefixes σ, τ and σ_1, $\sigma c, \tau c, \sigma_1 c_1, \tau c_1$ are on θ but $\sigma_1 c, \sigma c_1$ are not on θ.

While at least one of (A), (B), (C) or (D) holds do the following:
(1) If $\sigma\varphi$ is an unfinished occurrence of a prefixed sentence such that $\sigma\varphi$ is not of the form $\tau\Box\gamma$ and $\tau'\neg\Box\gamma$, where τ' has depth $n+1$ then, for all branches θ throughout $\sigma\varphi$, if φ is of the form:

- atomic, do not extend θ;
- $\neg\neg\psi$ (resp. $\psi_1 \wedge \psi_2$), add $\sigma\psi$ (resp. $\sigma\psi_1$ and $\sigma\psi_2$) to θ;
- $\neg(\psi_1 \wedge \psi_2)$, split θ to two branches and add $\sigma\neg\psi_1$ and $\sigma\neg\psi_2$ respectively to the first and to the second branch;
- $\neg\Box\psi$ and there are no τ and c such that σc, τc and $\tau\neg\Box\psi$ are on θ and

$\tau\neg\Box\psi$ is finished, add $\sigma < \sigma'$, $\sigma'\neg\psi$ and $\sigma' c$ to θ. (Here σ' is the first prefix in E_{pref} that is not on the tableau and c is the first nominal in E_{nom} that is not on the tableau.)

– $@_c\psi$ (resp. $\neg @_c\psi$) then, if there is a prefix τ such that τc is on θ, add $\tau\psi$ (resp. $\tau\neg\psi$) to θ; else, add $\tau' c$ and $\tau'\psi$ (resp. $\tau' c$ and $\tau'\neg\psi$) to θ; (Here τ' is the first prefix in the enumeration E_{pref} that is not on the tableau.)

Declare $\sigma\varphi$ finished.

(2) If $\sigma\Box\varphi$ is an occurrence of a prefixed sentence then, for all branches θ throughout $\sigma\Box\varphi$, if σ' is such that $\sigma < \sigma'$ is on θ, but $\sigma'\varphi$ is not on θ, add $\sigma'\varphi$ to θ.

(3) If θ is a branch such that the *S-Identifying'* rule is applicable to θ, apply the rule. (That is, if θ contains σc, τc, $\sigma\Box\varphi$ and $\tau < \tau'$ and, θ does not contain $\tau'\varphi$, add $\tau'\varphi$ to θ.)

(4) If θ is an open branch such that for some nominals c and c_1 and some prefixes σ, τ and σ_1, $\sigma c, \tau c, \sigma_1 c_1, \tau c_1$ are on θ, add $\sigma_1 c, \sigma c_1$ to θ.

Complete *Step* $n+1$. Denote the tableau that has been constructed by $\mathcal{T}_{n+1}$.

End of the procedure.

Theorem 2. *The above procedure terminates and is a decision procedure for the languages* $\mathcal{L}_o$ *and* $\mathcal{L}(@)$.

Proof. First, for the sake of a contradiction suppose that there is a sentence χ such that on input χ the procedure will not terminate. Then, by König's lemma (cf. [10]), there will be an infinite branch, say θ. Let θ^n be the part of θ constructed in *Step n*, that is θ^n is $\theta \cap \mathcal{T}_n$. Note that all prefixes that occur on θ^n have depth at most n. Define $c(\theta^n) = \max_\varphi\{c(\varphi) \mid \sigma\varphi \text{ on } \theta^n \;\&\; \sigma \text{ has depth } n\}$ to be the maximal complexity of a sentence φ that occurs on θ^n prefixed by some σ of depth n. (Complexity $c(\varphi)$ of a sentence φ is the number of occurrences of Boolean connectives and operators in φ.) Define $b(\theta^n)$ and $d(\theta^n)$ to be the cardinality of respectively $\bigcup_{c \text{ in } \chi}\{\Box\psi \mid \exists\sigma : \sigma c \text{ and } \sigma\Box\psi \text{ are on } \theta^n\}$ and $\bigcup_{c \text{ in } \chi}\{\neg\Box\psi \mid \exists\sigma : \sigma c \text{ and } \sigma\neg\Box\psi \text{ are on } \theta^n \;\&\; \sigma\neg\Box\psi \text{ is finished on } \theta^n\}$. Let $s(\theta^n) = b(\theta^n) + d(\theta^n)$.

For all n, $s(\theta^n) \leq s(\theta^{n-1})$. Moreover, if in Step n no *S-Identifying'* rule that results in extending θ^{n-1} has been applied, then $c(\theta^n) = c(\theta^{n-1}) - 1$. Otherwise, it is possible that $c(\theta^n) \geq c(\theta^{n-1})$. However, if in Step n, the *S-Identifying'* rule has been applied at least once, then $s(\theta^n) \leq s(\theta^{n-1}) - 1$. This contradicts the assumption that θ is infinite.

Second, let χ be an arbitrary sentence of either $\mathcal{L}_o$ or $\mathcal{L}(@)$. From the above we know that the procedure on input χ will terminate, say after completing *Step n*. Then, the tableau $\mathcal{T}_n$ that has been constructed is either closed, or contains an open branch, say θ. Note that the set of all prefixed sentences on θ is labeled. Moreover, θ is saturated in the following sense: θ satisfies conditions (1), (2), (4), (5), (6), ($@'$) and ($@''$) of Definition 3 as well as conditions (3)$'$ and (7)$'$ defined below:

(3)$'$ for all nominals c, all prefixes σ, τ and τ', if σc, τc, $\sigma\Box\varphi$ and $\tau < \tau'$ are on θ, then $\tau'\varphi$ is on θ too;

(7)′ if $\sigma\neg\Box\psi$ is on θ then, there are prefixes τ and τ', and a nominal c such that σc, τc, $\tau < \tau'$ and $\tau'\neg\psi$ are on θ.
Then, similarly to the proof of Lemma 2, we can show that θ is satisfiable.

Acknowledgments

I would like to thank the referees and Andreas Nonnengart for their comments and suggestions.

References

1. H. Andréka, J. van Benthem, and I. Németi. Modal languages and bounded fragments of predicate logic. *Journal of Philosophical Logic*, 27(3):217–274, 1998.
2. P. Blackburn. Internalizing labeled deduction. Manuscript, 1998.
3. P. Blackburn and J. Seligman. Hybrid languages. *Journal of Logic, Language and Information*, 4:251–272, 1995.
4. P. Blackburn and J. Seligman. What are hybrid languages? In M. Kracht, M. de Rijke, H. Wansing, and M. Zakharyaschev, editors, *Advances in Modal Logic, vol. 1*, pages 41–62. CSLI Publications, Stanford University, 1998.
5. P. Blackburn and M. Tzakova. Hybrid completeness. *Logic Journal of the IGPL*, 6(4):625–650, 1998.
6. P. Blackburn and M. Tzakova. Hybridizing concept languages. *Annals of Mathematics and Artificial Intelligence*, 24(1–4):23–49, 1998.
7. P. Blackburn and M. Tzakova. Hybrid languages and temporal logic. *Logic Journal of the IGPL*, 7(1):27–54, 1999.
8. R. Bull. An approach to tense logic. *Theoria*, 36:282–300, 1970.
9. M. D'Agostino, D. Gabbay, R. Hähnle, and J. Possega, editors. *Handbook of Tableau Methods*. Kluwer, Dordrecht, 1998. To appear.
10. M. Fitting. *Proof methods for modal and intuitionistic logic*. Synthese Library. Reidel, Dordrecht, 1983.
11. G. Gargov and V. Goranko. Modal logic with names. *Journal of Philosophical Logic*, 22(6):607–636, 1993.
12. V. Goranko. Hierarchies of modal and temporal logics with reference pointers. *Journal of Logic, Language and Information*, 5(1):1–24, 1996.
13. R. Goré. Tableau methods for modal and temporal logics. Technical Report TR-ARP-15-95, ARP, Australian National University, 1995.
14. S. Passy and T. Tinchev. An essay in combinatory dynamic logic. *Information and Computation*, 93:263–332, 1991.
15. A. Prior. *Past, present and future*. Oxford University Press, Oxford, 1967.
16. W. Rautenberg. Modal tableau calculi and interpolation. *Journal of Philosophical Logic Vol. 12 No. 4*, 12(4):403–424, 1983.
17. J. Seligman. A cut-free sequent calculus for elementary situated reasoning. Technical Report HCRC-RP 22, HCRC, University of Edinburgh, 1991.
18. J. Seligman. The logic of correct description. In M. de Rijke, editor, *Advances in Intensional Logic*, Applied Logic Series. Kluwer, Dordrecht, 1997.
19. R. M. Smullyan. *First-order logic*. Dover Publications, New York, 2nd edition, 1995.

Full First-Order Free Variable Sequents and Tableaux in Implicit Induction

Claus-Peter Wirth

Informatik 5, Universität Dortmund, D-44221, Germany
wirth@LS5.cs.uni-dortmund.de

Abstract. We show how to integrate implicit inductive theorem proving into free variable sequent and tableau calculi and compare the appropriateness of tableau calculi for this integration with that of sequent calculi.

When first-order validity is introduced to students it comes with some complete calculus. If this calculus happens to be an analytic calculus augmented with a Cut rule like a sequent or tableau calculus the students can compare the formal proofs with the informal ones they are hopefully acquainted with. This is because these calculi can mirror the human proof search process better than others. While knowing a complete calculus does not mean to know much about first-order theorem proving, the interrelation of a human-oriented calculus and the informal proof search of the students will turn out to be fruitful for their later mathematical work. It is a pity that—while nearly all proofs of a working mathematician include induction—nothing comparable for *inductive* first-order validity is offered to the students. Some may argue that this is generally impossible because not even the theory of the Peano algebra of natural numbers is recursively enumerable, cf. e.g. Enderton (1973). Nevertheless, there really is some general way a working mathematician searches for an informal proof, may it be inductive or not. The inductive version of this proof search method goes back to the ancient Greeks and was rediscovered under the name "descente infinie" by Pierre de Fermat (1601-1665). If you want to prove a conjecture, this method requires that you show, for each assumed counterexample of the conjecture, the existence of another counterexample of the conjecture that is strictly smaller in some wellfounded ordering. The working mathematician applies it in the following fashion. He (who may be female!) starts with the conjecture and simplifies it in case analyses which can be described as steps in a sequent or tableau calculus with Cut. When he realizes that the goals become similar to a different instance of the conjecture, he applies the conjecture just like a lemma, but keeps in mind that he actually has applied some induction hypothesis. Finally, he searches for some wellfounded ordering in which all the instances of the conjecture that he has applied as induction hypotheses are smaller than the original conjecture itself. Looking for a formal inductive calculus for mirroring this style of human inductive theorem proving (*ITP*), the "implicit induction" of Bachmair (1988) was a starting point because it included hypothesis application, although it was restricted to universally quantified pure equations and was not human-oriented. In Wirth (1997) we have presented a human-oriented inductive calculus for universally quantified clausal logic. In Kühler (1999)—implemented as the QuodLibet system—this calculus is extended with some necessary and important concretion for reasoning on the induction ordering and with a tactic-based concept for proof guidance that is intended to partially automate the construction of proofs. Extending this approach to full first-order logic turned out to be more difficult than expected (cf., however, Padawitz (1996) for the extension to another interesting sub-class): The state-of-the-art free variable analytic first-order calculi were not suited for the integration of "implicit induction" because they confused the Herbrand universes with their Skolem functions and did not preserve solutions (i.e. closing substitutions) (like Prolog does), thereby destroying the wellfoundedness of "descente infinie". In Wirth (1998) we have developed sequent and tableau calculi for full first-order formulas that do not Skolemize but do preserve solutions. These new calculi come in two versions. The *weak* version is simple, but cannot model liberalized versions of the δ-rule, which the *strong* version can. Since the strong version is much more complicated, the space is limited here, and many researchers today are quite unacquainted with "descente infinie", in this paper we will use the weak version only and concentrate on the inductive aspects (i.e. induction hypothesis application) and not on the deductive ones (i.e. α-, β-, γ-, and δ-steps, cf. Smullyan (1968)). Even for the experts in *implicit* ITP each of the following aspects will be new: Tableau presentation, full first-order formulas, and free variables.

We use '$\uplus$' for the union of disjoint classes and 'id' for the identity function. For a class R we define *domain*, *range*, *restriction to*, *image* and *reverse-image of a class A* by $\mathrm{dom}(R) := \{\, a \mid \exists b\colon (a,b)\in R \,\}$; $\mathrm{ran}(R) := \{\, b \mid \exists a\colon (a,b)\in R \,\}$; ${}_A|R := \{\, (a,b)\in R \mid a\in A \,\}$; $\langle A\rangle R := \{\, b \mid \exists a\in A\colon (a,b)\in R \}$; $R\langle B\rangle := \{\, a \mid \exists b\in B\colon (a,b)\in R \}$. '$\mathbb{N}$' denotes the set of and '$\prec$' the ordering on natural numbers. We use '$\emptyset$' to denote the empty set as well as the empty function or empty word. A *quasi-ordering* '$\lesssim$' *on* A is an A-reflexive and transitive (binary) relation on A. As with all our asymmetric relation symbols we define $a \gtrsim b$ if $b \lesssim a$. By an (irreflexive) *ordering* '$<$' (on A) we mean an irreflexive and transitive relation (on A). The *ordering* $<$ *of a quasi-ordering* $\lesssim$ is $\lesssim\setminus\gtrsim$. A quasi-ordering $\lesssim$ is called *total on* C if $C\times C \subseteq {\lesssim} \cup {\gtrsim}$. A $\lesssim$*-chain* is some subclass $C \subseteq A$ such that $\lesssim$ is total on C. $\lesssim$ is called *wellfounded* if each $\lesssim$-chain C has a least element, i.e. $\exists a\in C\colon \forall b\in C\colon a \lesssim b$. The *class of total functions from A to B* is denoted with $A \to B$. The *class of (possibly) partial functions from A to B* is denoted with $A \rightsquigarrow B$.

We define a *sequent* to be a list of formulas. The *conjugate* of a formula A (written: $\overline{A}$) is the formula B if A is of the form $\neg B$, and the formula $\neg A$ otherwise. In the tradition of Gentzen (1935) we assume the symbols for *free existential variables* (i.e. the free variables of Fitting (1996)), *free universal variables* (i.e. nullary parameters), *bound variables* (i.e. variables for quantified use only), and the *constants* (i.e. the function (and predicate) symbols from the signature) to come from four disjoint sets $\mathrm{V}_\exists$, $\mathrm{V}_\forall$, $\mathrm{V}_{\mathrm{bound}}$, and Σ. We assume each of $\mathrm{V}_\exists$, $\mathrm{V}_\forall$, $\mathrm{V}_{\mathrm{bound}}$ to be infinite (for each sort) and set $\mathrm{V}_{\mathrm{free}} := \mathrm{V}_\exists \uplus \mathrm{V}_\forall$. For a term, formula, sequent Γ etc., '$\mathcal{V}_\exists(\Gamma)$', '$\mathcal{V}_\forall(\Gamma)$', '$\mathcal{V}_{\mathrm{bound}}(\Gamma)$', '$\mathcal{V}_{\mathrm{free}}(\Gamma)$' denote the sets of variables from $\mathrm{V}_\exists$, $\mathrm{V}_\forall$, $\mathrm{V}_{\mathrm{bound}}$, $\mathrm{V}_{\mathrm{free}}$ occurring in Γ, resp.. For a substitution σ we denote with '$\Gamma\sigma$' the result of replacing in Γ each variable x in $\mathrm{dom}(\sigma)$ with $\sigma(x)$. We tacitly assume that each substitution σ satisfies $\mathcal{V}_{\mathrm{bound}}(\mathrm{dom}(\sigma) \cup \mathrm{ran}(\sigma))$

$= \emptyset$, such that no bound variables can be replaced and no additional variables become bound (i.e. captured) when applying σ.

A *variable-condition* R is a subset of $V_\exists \times V_\forall$. Roughly speaking, $(x^\exists, y^\forall) \in R$ says that $x^\exists$ is older than $y^\forall$, so that we must not instantiate the free existential variable $x^\exists$ with a term containing $y^\forall$.

Validity is expected to be given with respect to some Σ-structure (Σ-algebra) $\mathcal{A}$, assigning a universe (to each sort) and an appropriate function to each symbol in Σ. For $X \subseteq V_{free}$ we denote the set of total $\mathcal{A}$-valuations of X (i.e. functions mapping free variables to objects of the universe of $\mathcal{A}$ (respecting sorts)) with $X \to \mathcal{A}$ and the set of (possibly) partial $\mathcal{A}$-valuations of X with $X \rightsquigarrow \mathcal{A}$. For $\pi \in X \to \mathcal{A}$ we denote with '$\mathcal{A} \uplus \pi$' the extension of $\mathcal{A}$ to the variables of X which are then treated as nullary constants. More precisely, we assume the existence of some evaluation function 'eval' such that $\mathrm{eval}(\mathcal{A} \uplus \pi)$ maps any term over $\Sigma \uplus X$ into the universe of $\mathcal{A}$ (respecting sorts) such that for all $x \in X$: $\mathrm{eval}(\mathcal{A} \uplus \pi)(x) = \pi(x)$. Moreover, $\mathrm{eval}(\mathcal{A} \uplus \pi)$ maps any formula B over $\Sigma \uplus X$ to TRUE or FALSE, such that B is valid in $\mathcal{A} \uplus \pi$ iff $\mathrm{eval}(\mathcal{A} \uplus \pi)(B) = \mathsf{TRUE}$. We assume that the *Substitution-Lemma* holds in the sense that, for any substitution σ, Σ-structure $\mathcal{A}$, and valuation $\pi \in V_{free} \to \mathcal{A}$, validity of a formula B in $\mathcal{A} \uplus ((\sigma \uplus {}_{V_{free} \setminus \mathrm{dom}(\sigma)}|\mathrm{id}) \circ \mathrm{eval}(\mathcal{A} \uplus \pi))$ is logically equivalent to validity of $B\sigma$ in $\mathcal{A} \uplus \pi$. Finally, we assume that the value of the evaluation function on a term or formula B does not depend on the free variables that do not occur in B: $\mathrm{eval}(\mathcal{A} \uplus \pi)(B) = \mathrm{eval}(\mathcal{A} \uplus {}_{\mathcal{V}_{free}(B)}|\pi)(B)$. Further properties of validity or evaluation are definitely not needed.

We are now going to briefly recapitulate the notions from the weak version of Wirth (1998) which we need in what follows. Several binary relations on free variables will be introduced. The overall idea is that when (x, y) occurs in such a relation this means something like "x is older than y" or "the value of y depends on or is described in terms of x".

Definition 0.1 (E_σ, U_σ, Existential R-Substitution, σ-Update)
For a substitution σ with $\mathrm{dom}(\sigma) = V_\exists$ we define the *existential relation* to be $E_\sigma := \{ (x', x) \mid x' \in \mathcal{V}_\exists(\sigma(x)) \wedge x \in V_\exists \}$ and the *universal relation* to be $U_\sigma := \{ (y, x) \mid y \in \mathcal{V}_\forall(\sigma(x)) \wedge x \in V_\exists \}$.
Let R be a variable-condition. σ is an *existential R-substitution* if σ is a substitution with $\mathrm{dom}(\sigma) = V_\exists$ for which $U_\sigma \circ R$ is irreflexive.
Let σ be an existential R-substitution. The *σ-update of R* is $E_\sigma \circ R$.

Note that, regarding syntax, $(x^\exists, y^\forall) \in R$ is intended to mean that an existential R-substitution σ may not replace $x^\exists$ with a term in which $y^\forall$ occurs, i.e. $(y^\forall, x^\exists) \in U_\sigma$ must be disallowed, i.e. $U_\sigma \circ R$ must be irreflexive.

After application of an existential R-substitution σ, in case of $(x^\exists, y^\forall) \in R$, we have to ensure that $x^\exists$ is not replaced with $y^\forall$ via a future application of another existential R-substitution that replaces a free existential variable $u^\exists$ occurring in $\sigma(x^\exists)$ with $y^\forall$. In this case, the new variable-condition has to contain $(u^\exists, y^\forall)$. This means that $E_\sigma \circ R$ must be a subset of the updated variable-condition.

Let $\mathcal{A}$ be some Σ-structure. We now define a semantic counterpart of our existential R-substitutions, which we will call "existential $(\mathcal{A}, R)$-valuation". Suppose that e maps each free existential variable not directly to an object of $\mathcal{A}$ (of the same sort), but can additionally read the values of some free universal variables under an $\mathcal{A}$-valuation $\pi \in \mathrm{V}_\forall \to \mathcal{A}$, i.e. e gets some $\pi' \in \mathrm{V}_\forall \leadsto \mathcal{A}$ with $\pi' \subseteq \pi$ as a second argument; short: $e\colon \mathrm{V}_\exists \to ((\mathrm{V}_\forall \leadsto \mathcal{A}) \to \mathcal{A})$. Moreover, for each free existential variable x, we require the set of read free universal variables (i.e. $\mathrm{dom}(\pi')$) to be identical for all π; i.e. there has to be some "semantic relation" $S_e \subseteq \mathrm{V}_\forall \times \mathrm{V}_\exists$ such that for all $x \in \mathrm{V}_\exists$: $e(x)\colon (S_e\langle\!\{x\}\!\rangle \to \mathcal{A}) \to \mathcal{A}$. Note that, for each e, at most one semantic relation exists, namely

$$S_e := \{ (y, x) \mid y \in \mathrm{dom}(\bigcup(\mathrm{dom}(e(x)))) \wedge x \in \mathrm{V}_\exists \}.$$

Definition 0.2 (S_e, Existential $(\mathcal{A}, R)$-Valuation, ϵ)
Let R be a variable-condition, $\mathcal{A}$ a Σ-structure, and $e\colon \mathrm{V}_\exists \to ((\mathrm{V}_\forall \leadsto \mathcal{A}) \to \mathcal{A})$.
The *semantic relation of* e is $S_e := \{ (y, x) \mid y \in \mathrm{dom}(\bigcup(\mathrm{dom}(e(x)))) \wedge x \in \mathrm{V}_\exists \}$.
e is an *existential* $(\mathcal{A}, R)$*-valuation* if $S_e \circ R$ is irreflexive and, for all $x \in \mathrm{V}_\exists$,

$$e(x)\colon (S_e\langle\!\{x\}\!\rangle \to \mathcal{A}) \to \mathcal{A}.$$

Finally, for applying existential $(\mathcal{A}, R)$-valuations in a uniform manner, we define the function $\epsilon\colon \ (\mathrm{V}_\exists \to ((\mathrm{V}_\forall \leadsto \mathcal{A}) \to \mathcal{A})) \ \to \ ((\mathrm{V}_\forall \to \mathcal{A}) \to (\mathrm{V}_\exists \to \mathcal{A}))$ by ($e \in \mathrm{V}_\exists \to ((\mathrm{V}_\forall \leadsto \mathcal{A}) \to \mathcal{A})$, $\pi \in \mathrm{V}_\forall \to \mathcal{A}$, $x \in \mathrm{V}_\exists$)

$$\epsilon(e)(\pi)(x) := e(x)({}_{S_e\langle\!\{x\}\!\rangle}|\pi).$$

Lemma 0.3 *Let R be a variable-condition.*

1. *Let R' be a variable-condition with $R \subseteq R'$. For each existential $(\mathcal{A}, R')$-valuation e' there is some existential $(\mathcal{A}, R)$-valuation e such that $\epsilon(e) = \epsilon(e')$.*
2. *Let σ be an existential R-substitution and R' the σ-update of R. For each existential $(\mathcal{A}, R')$-valuation e' there is some existential $(\mathcal{A}, R)$-valuation e such that for all $\pi \in \mathrm{V}_\forall \to \mathcal{A}$:*

$$\epsilon(e)(\pi) \quad = \quad \sigma \circ \mathrm{eval}(\mathcal{A} \uplus \epsilon(e')(\pi) \uplus \pi).$$

We now define R-validity of a set of sequents with free variables, in terms of validity of a formula (where the free variables are treated as nullary constants).

Definition 0.4 (Validity)
Let R be a variable-condition, $\mathcal{A}$ a Σ-structure, and G a set of sequents.
G is *R-valid in $\mathcal{A}$* if there is an existential $(\mathcal{A}, R)$-valuation e such that G is $(e, \mathcal{A})$-valid.
G is *$(e, \mathcal{A})$-valid* if G is $(\pi, e, \mathcal{A})$-valid for all $\pi \in \mathrm{V}_\forall \to \mathcal{A}$.
G is *$(\pi, e, \mathcal{A})$-valid* if G is valid in $\mathcal{A} \uplus \epsilon(e)(\pi) \uplus \pi$.
G is valid in $\mathcal{A}$ if for all $\Gamma \in G$: Γ is valid in $\mathcal{A}$.
A *sequent Γ is valid in $\mathcal{A}$* if there is some formula listed in Γ that is valid in $\mathcal{A}$.
Validity in a class of Σ-structures is understood as validity in each of the Σ-structures of that class. If we omit the reference to a special Σ-structure we mean validity in some fixed class K of Σ-structures, e.g. the class of all Σ-structures (Σ-algebras) or the class of Herbrand Σ-structures (term-generated Σ-algebras), cf. Wirth (1997), Wirth & Gramlich (1994) for more interesting classes for establishing inductive validities.

Lemma 0.5 (Anti-Monotonicity of Validity in R)
Let G be a set of sequents and R and R' variable-conditions with $R \subseteq R'$. Now: If G is R'-valid in $\mathcal{A}$, then G is R-valid in $\mathcal{A}$.

Example 0.6 (Validity)
For $x^{\exists} \in \mathrm{V}_{\exists}$, $y^{\forall} \in \mathrm{V}_{\forall}$, the sequent $x^{\exists}{=}y^{\forall}$ is $\emptyset$-valid in any $\mathcal{A}$ because we can choose $S_e := \mathrm{V}_{\forall}{\times}\mathrm{V}_{\exists}$ and $e(x^{\exists})(\pi) := \pi(y^{\forall})$ resulting in $\epsilon(e)(\pi)(x^{\exists}) = e(x^{\exists})(s_{S_e\langle\{x^{\exists}\}\rangle}|\pi) = e(x^{\exists})(\mathrm{v}_{\mathrm{V}_{\forall}}|\pi) = \pi(y^{\forall})$. This means that $\emptyset$-validity of $x^{\exists}{=}y^{\forall}$ is the same as validity of $\forall y\colon \exists x\colon x{=}y$. Moreover, note that $\epsilon(e)(\pi)$ has access to the π-value of $y^{\forall}$ just as a raising function f for x in the raised (i.e. dually Skolemized) version $f(y^{\forall}){=}y^{\forall}$ of $\forall y\colon \exists x\colon x{=}y$.

Contrary to this, for $R := \mathrm{V}_{\exists}{\times}\mathrm{V}_{\forall}$, the same formula $x^{\exists}{=}y^{\forall}$ is not R-valid in general because then the required irreflexivity of $S_e{\circ}R$ implies $S_e = \emptyset$ and $e(x^{\exists})(s_{S_e\langle\{x^{\exists}\}\rangle}|\pi) = e(x^{\exists})(\emptyset|\pi) = e(x^{\exists})(\emptyset)$ cannot depend on $\pi(y^{\forall})$ anymore. This means that $(\mathrm{V}_{\exists}{\times}\mathrm{V}_{\forall})$-validity of $x^{\exists}{=}y^{\forall}$ is the same as validity of $\exists x\colon \forall y\colon x{=}y$. Moreover, note that $\epsilon(e)(\pi)$ has no access to the π-value of $y^{\forall}$ just as a raising function c for x in the raised version $c{=}y^{\forall}$ of $\exists x\colon \forall y\colon x{=}y$.

For a more general example let $G = \{\, A_{i,0} \ldots A_{i,n_i-1} \mid i{\in}I \,\}$, where for $j{\prec}n_i$ and $i \in I$ the $A_{i,j}$ are formulas with free existential variables from $\vec{x}$ and free universal variables from $\vec{y}$. Then $(\mathrm{V}_{\exists}{\times}\mathrm{V}_{\forall})$-validity of G means validity of $\exists\vec{x}\colon \forall\vec{y}\colon \forall i{\in}I\colon \exists j{\prec}n_i\colon A_{i,j}$; whereas $\emptyset$-validity of G means validity of $\forall\vec{y}\colon \exists\vec{x}\colon \forall i{\in}I\colon \exists j{\prec}n_i\colon A_{i,j}$.

1 Weights, Syntactic Constructs, and Counterexamples

A proposition Γ can be proved by induction as follows:

> *Show that for each counterexample of Γ there is another counterexample of Γ that is strictly smaller in a quasi-ordering $\lesssim$ in that each $\lesssim$-chain [of counterexamples] has a least element!*

Now by the Principle of Dependent Choice (cf. Rubin & Rubin (1985)) a class without minimal elements contains a chain without a least element. Thus, if we can show the above, we know that Γ cannot have any counterexamples at all and must be valid.

This paradigm of ITP was already used by the ancient Greeks, rediscovered by Pierre de Fermat under the name "descente infinie", and is in our time sometimes called "implicit induction", cf. Wirth & Becker (1995). Moreover note that theoretically it is also possible to use the strictly stronger Axiom of Choice instead but require only that each $\lesssim$-chain [of counterexamples] has a lower bound [being a counterexample], cf. Geser (1995).

In order to measure our sequents in our *induction ordering* (i.e. the above quasi-ordering for avoiding non-termination in the inductive argumentation), we supply them with weights from some set 'Weight'. Why these explicit weights are so important in implicit induction is explained in Wirth & Becker (1995) and more detailed in Wirth (1997), section 12. A weight $\aleph$ together with a sequent Γ forms a *syntactic construct* $(\Gamma, \aleph)$. For practical purposes a weight initially is a term $w(y_0,\ldots,y_{n-1})$ where the y_i are the free universal variables of Γ and w is similar to a global (rigid) free existential variable in that it can be chosen during the induction proof appropriately, e.g. when the goal is $w(t_1,t_2) < w(t_2,\mathsf{s}(t_1))$ for natural number terms t_i a good idea might be to choose w to be the addition on natural numbers, or when in another proof we have the goals $w(t_1,(t_1+t_2)) < w(\mathsf{s}(t_1),t_1)$ and $w(t_1,t_2) < w(t_1,\mathsf{s}(t_2))$ a good idea might be to choose w to be the lexicographic combination of length up to 2. While in principle also the induction ordering could be chosen for each proof differently, in practice it has shown to be sufficient and adequate to use a fixed wellfounded quasi-ordering (depending on the Σ-structures). E.g. in QuodLibet, a tactic-based ITP system for clausal logic, we essentially use the size of a uniquely denoting constructor ground term in the standard ordering on natural numbers, cf. Kühler (1999). Therefore, we assume that for each Σ-structure $\mathcal{A} \in \mathrm{K}$ there is some wellfounded quasi-ordering $\precsim_{\mathcal{A}}$. Furthermore, we assume that Σ contains the binary constant predicate symbol '$<$' which is interpreted by $\mathcal{A}$ as $<_{\mathcal{A}}$, i.e. the ordering of $\precsim_{\mathcal{A}}$. Furthermore, $\mathcal{A}$ should be able to interpret the functions constructing the weight terms (lexicographic combination etc.) as functions into $\mathrm{dom}(\precsim_{\mathcal{A}})$.

Syntactic constructs are the basic data structure for ITP, just like sequents or formulas are for the deductive case. The set of all syntactic constructs is denoted by 'SynCons'. The function 'logic' extracts the *logic part* (here: the sequents) of a set G of syntactic constructs: $\mathrm{logic}(G) := \mathrm{dom}(G)$.

For powerful ITP we have to be able to restrict the test of whether the weight of a hypothesis is smaller than the weight of a goal (which has to be satisfied for the permission to apply the hypothesis to the goal) to the special case semantically described by their logic parts. This can be achieved by considering only such instances of their weights that result from those valuations that describe invalid instances of their logic parts. A syntactic construct augmented with such a valuation providing extra information on the invalidity of its logic part in some Σ-structure $\mathcal{A}$ is called a "counterexample". More precisely, for an existential $(\mathcal{A},R)$-valuation e we define: (S,π) is an *$(e,\mathcal{A})$-counterexample (for S)* if S is a syntactic construct, $\pi \in \mathrm{V}_\forall \to \mathcal{A}$, and $\mathrm{logic}(\{S\})$ is not $(\pi,e,\mathcal{A})$-valid. Thus, the logic part of a syntactic construct S is $(e,\mathcal{A})$-valid iff S has no $(e,\mathcal{A})$-counterexamples. Furthermore, our induction ordering is not simply a wellfounded quasi-ordering on 'Weight' but actually the function mapping each $(e,\mathcal{A})$, where $\mathcal{A}$ is a Σ-structure from K and e an existential $(\mathcal{A},R)$-valuation, to the wellfounded quasi-ordering on $\mathrm{Weight} \times (\mathrm{V}_\forall \to \mathcal{A})$ given by $(\aleph,\pi) \precsim_{(e,\mathcal{A})} (\beth,\pi')$ if $\mathrm{eval}(\mathcal{A} \uplus \epsilon(e)(\pi) \uplus \pi)(\aleph) \precsim_{\mathcal{A}} \mathrm{eval}(\mathcal{A} \uplus \epsilon(e)(\pi') \uplus \pi')(\beth)$. Finally, we extend the induction ordering to $\mathrm{SynCons} \times (\mathrm{V}_\forall \to \mathcal{A})$ by defining

$$((\Gamma,\aleph),\pi) \precsim_{(e,\mathcal{A})} ((\Delta,\beth),\pi') \quad \text{if} \quad (\aleph,\pi) \precsim_{(e,\mathcal{A})} (\beth,\pi').$$

Note that our induction ordering $\precsim_{(e,\mathcal{A})}$ is semantic in the sense of Definition 13.7 of Wirth (1997) because it cannot depend on the syntactic term structure of a weight $\aleph$ but only on the value of $\aleph$ under the evaluation function. In Wirth (1997) we have rigorously investigated the price one has to pay for the possibility to have induction orderings also depending on the syntax of weights. For powerful concrete inference systems this price is surprisingly high. Furthermore, after improving the ordering information in implicit induction by our introduction of explicit weights, the former necessity of sophisticated induction orderings that exploit the term structure does not seem to exist anymore.

Definition 1.1 (Foundedness) *(Cf. Wirth & Becker (1995))*
Let R be a variable-condition. Let '$\searrow\!\!/\!\!\curvearrowright_R$' be a symbol for a single relation. Let $G_0, G_1, H \subseteq \mathrm{SynCons}$. Now G_0 is *R-strict/quasi-founded* on (H, G_1) (denoted by $G_0 \searrow\!\!/\!\!\curvearrowright_R (H, G_1)$) if
$\forall \mathcal{A} \in \mathrm{K}$: $\forall e$ existential $(\mathcal{A}, R)$-valuation: $\forall S \in G_0$: $\forall \pi$:

$$\left(\begin{array}{l} ((S,\pi) \text{ is an } (e,\mathcal{A})\text{-counterexample}) \;\Rightarrow \\ \exists S'\colon \exists \pi'\colon \left(\begin{array}{l} ((S',\pi') \text{ is an } (e,\mathcal{A})\text{-counterexample}) \\ \wedge \left(\begin{array}{l} \left(\begin{array}{l} S' \in H \\ \wedge\, (S',\pi') <_{(e,\mathcal{A})} (S,\pi) \end{array}\right) \\ \vee \left(\begin{array}{l} S' \in G_1 \\ \wedge\, (S',\pi') \precsim_{(e,\mathcal{A})} (S,\pi) \end{array}\right) \end{array}\right) \end{array}\right) \end{array}\right)$$

G_0 is *strictly R-founded on H* (denoted by $G_0 \searrow_R H$) if $G_0 \searrow\!\!/\!\!\curvearrowright_R (H, \emptyset)$.
G_0 is (quasi-) *R-founded on G_1* (denoted by $G_0 \curvearrowright_R G_1$) if $G_0 \searrow\!\!/\!\!\curvearrowright_R (\emptyset, G_1)$.

Note that the expressive power of $\searrow\!\!/\!\!\curvearrowright_R$ is higher than that of $\searrow_R$ and $\curvearrowright_R$ together: ($\{S\} \searrow_R H \vee \{S\} \curvearrowright_R G_1$) implies $\{S\} \searrow\!\!/\!\!\curvearrowright_R (H, G_1)$ for $S \in$ SynCons, but the converse does not hold in general. For an informal but quite imaginative introduction to foundedness cf. Wirth (1997).

Lemma 1.2
Let R, R' be variable-conditions; $G_0, G_1, G_2, G_3, H_1, H_2, H_3 \subseteq \mathrm{SynCons}$.

1. *If* $G_0 \curvearrowright_R G_1$ *and* logic(G_1) *is R-valid, then* logic(G_0) *is R-valid, too.*
2. *If* $G_0 \subseteq G_1$, *then* $G_0 \curvearrowright_R G_1$.
3. *If* $G_0 \curvearrowright_R G_1 \searrow\!\!/\!\!\curvearrowright_R (H_2, G_2)$, *then* $G_0 \searrow\!\!/\!\!\curvearrowright_R (H_2, G_2)$.
4. *If* $G_0 \searrow\!\!/\!\!\curvearrowright_R (H_1, G_1)$ *and* $G_2 \searrow\!\!/\!\!\curvearrowright_R (H_3, G_3)$, *then* $G_1 \cup G_2 \searrow\!\!/\!\!\curvearrowright_R (H_1 \cup H_3, G_1 \cup G_3)$.
5. *In case of* $R \subseteq R'$: *If* $G_0 \curvearrowright_R G_1$, *then* $G_0 \curvearrowright_{R'} G_1$.
6. *In case of R' being the σ-update of R for an existential R-substitution σ: If* $G_0 \curvearrowright_R G_1$, *then* $G_0\sigma \curvearrowright_{R'} G_1\sigma$.
7. *If* $H_1 \searrow\!\!/\!\!\curvearrowright_R (H_1, G_1)$, *then* $H_1 \curvearrowright_R G_1$.

Proof of Lemma 1.2: (1), (2), (3), and (4) are trivial. (5) follows from part (1) of Lemma 0.3, (6) follows from part (2) of Lemma 0.3. (7) relies on the wellfoundedness of $\precsim_{(e,\mathcal{A})}$. □

2 Abstract Inductive Calculi

Now we are going to abstractly describe inductive sequent and tableau calculi. In Wirth (1998) we have shown that the usual deductive first-order calculi are instances of the deductive version of our abstract calculi. This will still be the case for the abstract calculi below, but in this paper we have to concentrate on the inductive part. The main difference to the deductive case is that the sequents are replaced with syntactic constructs, i.e. to each sequent a weight is added for controlling the loops in ITP. The benefit of the abstract version is that every instance is automatically sound. Due to the small number of inference rules in deductive first-order calculi and the locality of soundness, this abstract version is not really necessary for deductive calculi. For inductive calculi, however, due to a bigger number of inference rules (which usually have to be improved now and then) and the globality of soundness, such an abstract version is very helpful, cf. Wirth & Becker (1995), Wirth (1997).

Definition 2.1 (Inductive Proof Forest)
An *inductive proof forest in a sequent* (or else: *tableau*) *calculus* is a pair (F, R) where R is a variable-condition and F is a set of pairs (S, t), where S is a syntactic construct and t is a tree whose nodes are labeled with syntactic constructs (or else: whose root is labeled with a weight and whose other nodes are labeled with formulas).

Note that the tree t is intended to represent a proof attempt for S. In case of a tableau calculus the nodes of t are labeled with formulas (the root, however, with a weight). In case of a sequent calculus the nodes are labeled with syntactic constructs. While the syntactic constructs at the nodes of a tree in a sequent calculus stand for themselves, in a tableau calculus all the ancestors have to be included to make up a syntactic construct and, moreover, the formulas at the labels are in negated form:

Definition 2.2 (Goals(), $\mathcal{AX}$, **Closedness)**
'Goals(T)' denotes the set of syntactic constructs labeling the leaves of the trees in the set T (or else: the set of syntactic constructs $(\Delta, \beth)$ with Δ resulting from listing the conjugates of the formulas labeling a branch from a leaf to the root (exclusively) in a tree t in T and $\beth$ being the label of the root of the tree t).
In what follows, we assume $\mathcal{AX}$ to be some set of *axioms*. By this we mean that $\mathcal{AX}$ is $\mathrm{V}_\exists \times \mathrm{V}_\forall$-valid. (Cf. the last sentence in Def. 0.4.)
The tree t is *closed* if $\mathrm{logic}(\mathrm{Goals}(\{t\})) \subseteq \mathcal{AX}$.

The readers may ask themselves why we consider a forest instead of a single tree only. If we have two trees (S, t), $(S', t') \in F$ we can apply S as a lemma or induction hypothesis in the tree t' of S', provided that the lemma application relation is acyclic and the application of the hypothesis produces a goal that expresses that the instance of the hypothesis is smaller than S' in the induction ordering.

Definition 2.3 (Inductive Invariant Condition)
The *inductive invariant condition* on (F, R) is $H \curvearrowright_R \mathrm{Goals}(\mathrm{ran}(F))$ for the set of hypotheses $H := \mathrm{dom}(F)$.

From Lemma 0.5 and Lemma 1.2(1) we immediately get:

Theorem 2.4 *Let the inductive proof forest* (F, R) *satisfy the above inductive invariant condition and set* $H := \mathrm{dom}(F)$.
If all trees in $\mathrm{ran}(F)$ *are closed, then* $\mathrm{logic}(H)$ *is R-valid.*

Note that, contrary to the deductive case, local argumentation on a single tree is not possible: If $(S,t) \in F$, (F,R) satisfies the inductive invariant condition, and t is closed, we do not know that logic($\{S\}$) is R-valid because we may have applied some induction hypothesis $S' \in H \setminus \{S\}$ when constructing the proof tree t of S and the proof tree of S' is not closed. In other words, all trees in the forest must be closed before we know that any hypothesis in logic(H) is R-valid.

Theorem 2.5 *The inductive invariant condition is always satisfied when we start with an empty inductive proof forest* $(F,R) := (\emptyset,\emptyset)$ *and then iterate only the following kinds of modifications of* (F,R) *(resulting in* (F',R')*):*

Hypothesizing: *Let* R' *be a variable-condition with* $R \subseteq R'$. *Let Let* $(\Gamma,\aleph)$ *be a syntactic construct. Let* t *be the tree with a single node only, which is labeled with* $(\Gamma,\aleph)$ *(or else: with a single branch only, such that* Γ *is the list of the conjugates of the formulas labeling the branch from the leaf to the root (exclusively) and* $\aleph$ *is the label of the root). Then we may set* $F' := F \cup \{((\Gamma,\aleph),t)\}$.

Expansion: *Let* R' *be a variable-condition with* $R \subseteq R'$. *Let* $(S,t) \in F$ *and* $H := \mathrm{dom}(F)$. *Let* l *be a leaf in* t. *Let* $(\Delta,\beth)$ *be the label of* l *(or else:* Δ *result from listing the conjugates of the formulas labeling the branch from* l *to the root (exclusively) and* $\beth$ *be the label of the root of* t*). Let* G *be a finite set of syntactic constructs (or else: let* M *be a finite set of sequents and set* $G := \{\ (\Pi\Delta,\beth) \mid \Pi \in M\ \}$*). Now if* $\{(\Delta,\beth)\} \searrow\!/\!\curvearrowright_{R'} (H,G)$ *then we may set* $F' := (F \setminus \{(S,t)\}) \cup \{(S,t')\}$ *where* t' *results from* t *by adding to the former leaf* l*, exactly for each syntactic construct* S' *in* G*, a new child node labeled with* S' *(or else: exactly for each sequent* Π *in* M *a new child branch such that* Π *is the list of the conjugates of the formulas labeling the branch from the leaf to the new child node of* l*).*

Instantiation: *Let* σ *be an existential* R*-substitution. Let* R' *be the* σ*-update of* R*. Then we may set* $F' := F\sigma$.

Proof of Theorem 2.5: The empty proof forest satisfies the inductive invariant condition by Lemma 1.2(2). Hypothesizing: From $H \curvearrowright_R \mathrm{Goals}(\mathrm{ran}(F))$ we get $H \curvearrowright_{R'} \mathrm{Goals}(\mathrm{ran}(F))$ by Lemma 1.2(5) for $H := \mathrm{dom}(F)$. Thus, from $\{(\Gamma,\aleph)\} \curvearrowright_{R'} \{(\Gamma,\aleph)\}$ (by Lemma 1.2(2)) we get $H \cup \{(\Gamma,\aleph)\} \curvearrowright_{R'} \mathrm{Goals}(\mathrm{ran}(F)) \cup \{(\Gamma,\aleph)\}$ by Lemma 1.2(4), i.e. $H' \curvearrowright_{R'} \mathrm{Goals}(\mathrm{ran}(F'))$ for $H' := \mathrm{dom}(F')$. Expansion: $\{(\Delta,\beth)\} \searrow\!/\!\curvearrowright_{R'} (H,G)$ and $(\mathrm{Goals}(\mathrm{ran}(F))) \setminus \{(\Delta,\beth)\} \curvearrowright_{R'} (\mathrm{Goals}(\mathrm{ran}(F))) \setminus \{(\Delta,\beth)\}$ (by Lemma 1.2(2)) give $\mathrm{Goals}(\mathrm{ran}(F)) \searrow\!/\!\curvearrowright_{R'} (H,G')$ for $G' := (\mathrm{Goals}(\mathrm{ran}(F)) \setminus \{(\Delta,\beth)\}) \cup G$ by Lemma 1.2(4). From the old invariant condition $H \curvearrowright_R \mathrm{Goals}(\mathrm{ran}(F))$ we get $H \curvearrowright_{R'} \mathrm{Goals}(\mathrm{ran}(F))$ by Lemma 1.2(5), and then by Lemma 1.2(3) conclude $H \searrow\!/\!\curvearrowright_{R'} (H,G')$. Thus, by Lemma 1.2(7) we have $H \curvearrowright_{R'} G'$, and then from $G' \curvearrowright_{R'} \mathrm{Goals}(\mathrm{ran}(F'))$ (due to Lemma 1.2(2)) we get $H \curvearrowright_{R'} \mathrm{Goals}(\mathrm{ran}(F'))$ due to Lemma 1.2(3), which is the new invariant condition on (F',R') due to $H = \mathrm{dom}(F) = \mathrm{dom}(F')$. Instantiation: From the old invariant condition $H \curvearrowright_R \mathrm{Goals}(\mathrm{ran}(F))$ for $H := \mathrm{dom}(F)$ we get $H\sigma \curvearrowright_{R'} \mathrm{Goals}(\mathrm{ran}(F\sigma))$ by Lemma 1.2(6), which is the new invariant condition on (F',R') due to $\mathrm{dom}(F') = \mathrm{dom}(F)\sigma = H\sigma$. □

Now the crucial step of implicit induction (i.e. the application of an induction hypothesis $(\Gamma, \aleph)$ instantiated with a substitution ϱ to expand a goal $(\Delta, \beth)$) can be formulated as an Expansion step in the tableau calculus (sequent calculus analogously) as follows.

Theorem 2.6 *Let (F, R) be an inductive proof forest in a tableau calculus. We want to apply $(\Gamma, \aleph) \in H := \mathrm{dom}(F)$ as an induction hypothesis to expand the goal $(\Delta, \beth)$ that results from listing the conjugates of the formulas and the weight labeling the branch from a leaf l to the root of a tree $t \in \mathrm{ran}(F)$. Set $\mathrm{X} := \mathcal{V}_{\exists}((\Gamma, \aleph))$ and $\mathrm{Y} := \{\, y \in \mathcal{V}_{\forall}((\Gamma, \aleph)) \mid \mathrm{X} \times \{y\} \subseteq R \,\}$. Let $\varrho \in \mathrm{Y} \to (\mathrm{V}_{\exists} \setminus \mathcal{V}_{\exists}(F))$ be an injective substitution. Now the following instantiation of R' and M describes a sub-rule of the Expansion rule of the tableau calculus of Theorem 2.5: Set $R' := R$ and set M to be the set containing the sequents $\aleph\varrho < \beth$ and $\overline{B\varrho}$ for each formula B listed in the sequent Γ.*

Note that Y contains exactly those free universal variables of $(\Gamma, \aleph)$ that have no free existential variables in their scopes when imagining any list of quantifiers for all free variables of $(\Gamma, \aleph)$ that represents (a superset of) R. The variables in Y are those on which no solution for the free existential variables in X depends. Therefore, the variables in Y are those which we can instantiate when applying the induction hypothesis $(\Gamma, \aleph)$. Although it does not seem impossible to use more variables for induction, this does not seem to be necessary; especially because we can extend R with $\mathrm{X} \times \{y\}$ in order to instantiate y when applying the induction hypothesis. Moreover, I do not known any more general approach in the literature. E.g., in Baaz & al. (1997), the inductive part of theorem proving is triggered by application of a δ-rule and the variable y of the quantifier removed by the δ-rule becomes the induction variable. In our approach, the δ-rule application would replace y with a new free universal variable $y^{\forall}$ and extend the variable-condition with $\mathrm{X} \times \{y^{\forall}\}$ such that $y^{\forall} \in \mathrm{Y}$ would hold.

Proof of Theorem 2.6: According to the definition of an Expansion step in the tableau calculus of Theorem 2.5 we have to show $\{(\Delta, \beth)\} \searrow/\!\curvearrowright_R (H, \{\, (A\Delta, \beth) \mid A \in M \,\})$. Thus, for $\mathcal{A} \in \mathrm{K}$, e an existential $(\mathcal{A}, R)$-valuation, $\pi \in \mathrm{V}_{\forall} \to \mathcal{A}$, assume $((\Delta, \beth), \pi)$ to be an $(e, \mathcal{A})$-counterexample. If some formula $A \in M$ is not $(\pi, e, \mathcal{A})$-valid then also $((A\Delta, \beth), \pi)$ is an $(e, \mathcal{A})$-counterexample with $((A\Delta, \beth), \pi) \precsim_{(e, \mathcal{A})} ((\Delta, \beth), \pi)$. Otherwise, $\aleph\varrho < \beth$ is but $\Gamma\varrho$ is not $(\pi, e, \mathcal{A})$-valid. Define $\pi' \in \mathrm{V}_{\forall} \to \mathcal{A}$ by

$$\pi'(y) := \epsilon(e)(\pi)(\varrho(y)) \text{ for } y \in \mathrm{Y} \qquad \text{and} \qquad \pi'(y) := \pi(y) \text{ for } y \in \mathrm{V}_{\forall} \setminus \mathrm{Y}.$$

Claim 1: For $x^{\exists} \in \mathcal{V}_{\exists}((\Gamma, \aleph))$ we have $\epsilon(e)(\pi)(x^{\exists}) = \epsilon(e)(\pi')(x^{\exists})$.

Proof of Claim 1: Otherwise there must be some $y^{\forall} \in \mathrm{Y}$ with $y^{\forall}\ S_e\ x^{\exists}$. Since $x^{\exists} \in \mathrm{X}$ we have $x^{\exists}\ R\ y^{\forall}$ by definition of Y. But then $S_e \circ R$ is not irreflexive, which contradicts e being an existential $(R, \mathcal{A})$-valuation. Q.e.d. (Claim 1)

Hence, the values of Γ and $\aleph$ under $\mathrm{eval}(\mathcal{A} \uplus \epsilon(e)(\pi') \uplus \pi')$ are the same as the values of Γ and $\aleph$ under $\mathrm{eval}(\mathcal{A} \uplus \epsilon(e)(\pi) \uplus \pi')$ which again are the same as the values of $\Gamma\varrho$ and $\aleph\varrho$ under $\mathrm{eval}(\mathcal{A} \uplus \epsilon(e)(\pi) \uplus \pi)$ by the Substitution-Lemma. Thus, on the one hand from the $(\pi, e, \mathcal{A})$-validity of $\aleph\varrho < \beth$ we get $((\Gamma, \aleph), \pi') <_{(e, \mathcal{A})} ((\Delta, \beth), \pi)$, and on the other hand from $\Gamma\varrho$ not being $(\pi, e, \mathcal{A})$-valid we know that $((\Gamma, \aleph), \pi')$ is an $(e, \mathcal{A})$-counterexample. □

3 An Example

Due to limited space we are not able to show the usefulness of our integration of free existential variables and full first-order formulas into implicit induction with a sophisticated example. Instead, we will sketch a simplified toy example with mutual induction that will give the reader a concrete idea on how proofs look like. Note, however, that (due to mutual induction and non-trivial weights) even this toy example has no straightforward proofs in the ITP calculus of Baaz & al. (1997) or any known ITP system with the exception of QUODLIBET, cf. Kühler (1999).

In order not to require even more prerequisites, we do not explicitly refer to our inductive specification techniques described in Kühler & Wirth (1996), but use a standard (order-sorted) first-order specification style.

Signature: Sorts: $\mathsf{nat} \subseteq \mathsf{ORD}$. Here nat is the sort of natural numbers and ORD the sort for the induction ordering. We use zero $0\colon \to \mathsf{nat}$ and successor $\mathsf{s}\colon \mathsf{nat} \to \mathsf{nat}$ as constructors for the sort nat. Moreover, $\mathsf{P}\colon \mathsf{nat}$ and $\mathsf{Q}\colon \mathsf{nat},\mathsf{nat}$ are two defined predicates on the natural numbers. Furthermore, $<\colon \mathsf{ORD},\mathsf{ORD}$ is the induction ordering and $\mathsf{lex}\colon \mathsf{nat},\mathsf{nat},\mathsf{nat} \to \mathsf{ORD}$ is the lexicographic combination of length 0, 1, or 2 as indicated by the first argument, e.g. $\mathsf{lex}(\mathsf{s}(0), x, y)$ models the 1-tuple (x) while $\mathsf{lex}(0, x, y)$ models the 0-tuple or empty word $()$. We use x, y, z for variables of the sort nat where superscripts like $x^{\exists}$, $x^{\forall}$ indicate free existential and free universal variables. Axioms:

$$\begin{array}{llr} (\mathsf{lex0}) & \forall x_1, y_0, y_1, z_0, z_1\colon & \mathsf{lex}(0, y_0, z_0) < \mathsf{lex}(\mathsf{s}(x_1), y_1, z_1) \\ (\mathsf{lex1}) & \forall x_0, x_1, y_0, y_1, z_0, z_1\colon & \left(\mathsf{lex}(\mathsf{s}(x_0), y_0, z_0) < \mathsf{lex}(\mathsf{s}(x_1), y_1, z_1) \Leftarrow y_0 < y_1 \right) \\ (\mathsf{lex2}) & \forall x_0, x_1, y, z_0, z_1\colon & \left(\begin{array}{l} \mathsf{lex}(\mathsf{s}(x_0), y, z_0) < \mathsf{lex}(\mathsf{s}(x_1), y, z_1) \\ \quad \Leftarrow \mathsf{lex}(x_0, z_0, 0) < \mathsf{lex}(x_1, z_1, 0) \end{array} \right) \\ (\mathsf{nat0}) & \forall x\colon & \left(x = 0 \vee \exists y\colon\ x = \mathsf{s}(y) \right) \end{array}$$

(lex0) says that the empty tuple is the smallest, (lex1) implements a comparison of the first tuple elements, and (lex2) discards identical first tuple elements. (nat0) says that any natural number is zero or the successor of another natural number. The following axioms define the special predicates of our example.

$$\begin{array}{lll} (\mathsf{P0}) & & \mathsf{P}(0) \\ (\mathsf{P1}) & \forall x\colon & \left(\mathsf{P}(\mathsf{s}(x)) \Leftarrow \left(\mathsf{P}(x) \wedge \mathsf{Q}(x, \mathsf{s}(x)) \right) \right) \\ (\mathsf{Q0}) & \forall x\colon & \mathsf{Q}(x, 0) \\ (\mathsf{Q1}) & \forall x, y\colon & \left(\mathsf{Q}(x, \mathsf{s}(y)) \Leftarrow \left(\mathsf{Q}(x, y) \wedge \mathsf{P}(x) \right) \right) \end{array}$$

We want to show $\forall x\colon\ \mathsf{P}(x)$ and $\forall y, z\colon\ \mathsf{Q}(y, z)$. We first do a tableau calculus proof. We start with the empty forest. Two Hypothesizing steps provide us with the hypotheses $(\mathsf{P}(x_0^{\forall}); \mathsf{w}_0(x_0^{\forall}))$ with single-branch tree (1) $\mathsf{w}_0(x_0^{\forall})$, (1.1) $\neg\mathsf{P}(x_0^{\forall})$; and $(\mathsf{Q}(y_0^{\forall}, z_0^{\forall}); \mathsf{w}_1(y_0^{\forall}, z_0^{\forall}))$ with single-branch tree (2) $\mathsf{w}_1(y_0^{\forall}, z_0^{\forall})$, (2.1) $\neg\mathsf{Q}(y_0^{\forall}, z_0^{\forall})$. Note that the first number in the preceding list is the number of the proof tree (indicating its root node) and a suffix "$.i$" denotes the step to the ith child node. Since the formulas of the specification are implicitly on all branches, we can use (nat0) to add to (1.1) the children $x_0^{\exists} = 0$ and $x_0^{\exists} = \mathsf{s}(x_1^{\forall})$ in an Expansion step with variable restriction $(x_0^{\exists}, x_1^{\forall})$. An Instantiation step with $\{x_0^{\exists} \mapsto x_0^{\forall}\}$ (which a concrete inference system should do immediately together with the preceding Expansion step) gives us the new tree (1.1.1) $x_0^{\forall}=0$, (1.1.2) $x_0^{\forall}=\mathsf{s}(x_1^{\forall})$. Rewriting copies of (1.1) with these children in two Expansion steps yields (1.1.1.1) $\neg\mathsf{P}(0)$, (1.1.2.1) $\neg\mathsf{P}(\mathsf{s}(x_1^{\forall}))$. By (P0) we can close the first branch with (1.1.1.1.1) $\mathsf{P}(0)$. By (P1) we can add (1.1.2.1.1) $\mathsf{P}(\mathsf{s}(x_1^{\forall}))$ (closed), (1.1.2.1.2) $\neg\mathsf{P}(x_1^{\forall})$, (1.1.2.1.3) $\neg\mathsf{Q}(x_1^{\forall},\mathsf{s}(x_1^{\forall}))$. Now, after these standard first-order tableau steps we do an induction hypothesis application step as described in the previous section. We apply the hypothesis $(\mathsf{P}(x_0^{\forall});\mathsf{w}_0(x_0^{\forall}))$ with substitution $\varrho := \{x_0^{\forall}\mapsto x_1^{\exists}\}$ to (1.1.2.1.2), resulting in the new children $\mathsf{P}(x_1^{\exists})$ and $\mathsf{w}_0(x_1^{\exists})\not<\mathsf{w}_0(x_0^{\forall})$, where $\mathsf{w}_0(x_0^{\forall})$ comes from the root (1) and $\not<$ is the negation of $<$. After instantiating $\{x_1^{\exists}\mapsto x_1^{\forall}\}$ we get (1.1.2.1.2.1) $\mathsf{P}(x_1^{\forall})$ (closed) and (1.1.2.1.2.2) $\mathsf{w}_0(x_1^{\forall})\not<\mathsf{w}_0(x_0^{\forall})$. Note that the only difference to an Extension step in Model Elimination tableaux (cf. Baumgartner & al. (1997)) lies with the additional child (1.1.2.1.2.2), which asks us to show that the instance of the hypothesis is smaller than the weight of our proof tree. Indeed: Hypothesis application differs from the standard lemma (or axiom) application only in producing an additional $\not<$-goal. This makes hypothesis application a little more expensive than lemma application. Similarly, we apply the induction hypothesis $(\mathsf{Q}(y_0^{\forall},z_0^{\forall});\mathsf{w}_1(y_0^{\forall},z_0^{\forall}))$ with substitution $\varrho := \{y_0^{\forall}\mapsto y_0^{\exists}, z_0^{\forall}\mapsto z_0^{\exists}\}$ to (1.1.2.1.3), which after instantiation with $\{y_0^{\exists}\mapsto x_1^{\forall}, z_0^{\exists}\mapsto \mathsf{s}(x_1^{\forall})\}$ results in (1.1.2.1.3.1) $\mathsf{Q}(x_1^{\forall},\mathsf{s}(x_1^{\forall}))$ (closed) and (1.1.2.1.3.2) $\mathsf{w}_1(x_1^{\forall},\mathsf{s}(x_1^{\forall}))\not<\mathsf{w}_0(x_0^{\forall})$. Rewriting the leaves of the open branches in place with (1.1.2) we get (1.1.2.1.2.2) $\mathsf{w}_0(x_1^{\forall})\not<\mathsf{w}_0(\mathsf{s}(x_1^{\forall}))$ and (1.1.2.1.3.2) $\mathsf{w}_1(x_1^{\forall},\mathsf{s}(x_1^{\forall}))\not<\mathsf{w}_0(\mathsf{s}(x_1^{\forall}))$. Expanding the tree (2) analogously to the tree (1) we get as leaves of the open branches (2.1.2.1.2.2) $\mathsf{w}_1(y_0^{\forall},z_1^{\forall})\not<\mathsf{w}_1(y_0^{\forall},\mathsf{s}(z_1^{\forall}))$ and (2.1.2.1.3.2) $\mathsf{w}_0(y_0^{\forall})\not<\mathsf{w}_1(y_0^{\forall},\mathsf{s}(z_1^{\forall}))$. Now both hypotheses have been applied in both trees. Next, we choose our weight functions in such a way that we can close both trees: $\mathsf{w}_0(x) := \mathsf{lex}(\mathsf{s}(0),x,0)$ and $\mathsf{w}_1(y,z) := \mathsf{lex}(\mathsf{s}(\mathsf{s}(0)),y,z)$. Applying (lex0), (lex1), (lex2) to the resulting leaves in the standard fashion results in $x_1^{\forall}\not<\mathsf{s}(x_1^{\forall})$ and $z_1^{\forall}\not<\mathsf{s}(z_1^{\forall})$ as the leaves of the only open branches. Finally, these branches are closed by comparing the size of a uniquely denoting constructor ground term: A branch containing a literal of the form $t_0\not<t_1$ is closed if the number of occurrences of each free variable in t_0 is not bigger than the number of occurrences of that variable in t_1, the size of t_0 is strictly smaller than the size of t_1, and t_0, t_1 are pure constructor terms. Cf. Kühler & Wirth (1996) for the notion of "constructor term" and for the models where our induction ordering is wellfounded indeed.

We may ask: Which steps in this proof were typical for ITP in the sense that their soundness relies on notions of inductive validity instead of the stronger notion of deductive (first-order) validity? Besides the four induction hypothesis applications, the final branch closure rules are typical for induction because they require that, in all models in K, the successor of each natural number is different from that natural number and each natural number is built-up from zero by a finite number of successor steps (i.e. there are neither cycles nor $\mathbb{Z}$-chains in the models, cf. Enderton (1973)). Other steps typical for induction but not applied in this example are narrowing steps to solve equality literals. Their soundness relies on the freeness of the models in K. (Note that narrowing in ITP relies on confluence but *not* on termination of the reduction relation of the specification, cf. Wirth (1997).) Moreover, ITP often is only successful when one tries to show theorems that are more general than the ones one initially intended to show. This is because an inductive theorem is not only a task (as goal) but also a tool (as induction hypothesis) for ITP. This generalization is *unsafe* in the sense that it may transform a valid hypothesis into an invalid one (*over-generalization*). Therefore, generalization should not be modeled in Expansion steps within a tree. Instead, the generalized sequent should start a new tree (Hypothesizing step) and be later applied to the original tree as an induction hypothesis or lemma. Since a valid input theorem may result in an invalid goal due to over-generalization, the ability of an ITP system to detect invalid goals is important under a practical aspect. When all Expansion and Instantiation steps in a tree are known to be safe, the detection of an invalid goal in the tree implies invalidity of the hypothesis of this tree, which then should be completely removed from the proof forest.

Now we are going to compare the above tableau calculus proof with a corresponding sequent calculus proof of the same hypotheses. Of course, we could simply transform the tableau trees into sequent trees by bottom-up replacing the label of each node with the syntactic construct listing the conjugates of the formulas and the weight labeling the (partial) branch from this node to the root, and finally removing the root part of the tree where the nodes are ancestors of a node of the initial Hypothesizing steps (here: removing the root nodes). This, however, would mean to pay the price for sequent calculi (i.e. multiplying the number of formulas labeling each proof tree with at most nearly the depth of that tree) without using the advantages of sequent calculi. Thus, let us start again with the hypotheses $(\mathsf{P}(x^{\vee}_0); \mathsf{w}_0(x^{\vee}_0))$ and $(\mathsf{Q}(y^{\vee}_0, z^{\vee}_0); \mathsf{w}_1(y^{\vee}_0, z^{\vee}_0))$. The single-node tree for the former is (1) $\mathsf{P}(x^{\vee}_0);\ \mathsf{w}_0(x^{\vee}_0)$. Note that the goal in the tree is identical to the hypothesis, contrary to the tableau version where the two differ in duality and locality. While this is not a hindrance for completely automatic ITP systems, it poses considerable practical problems in systems where user-guidance is possible: The primitive process of switching duality is a typical source of errors for human beings (or me at least). Perfectly analogous to the tableau proof we get the children $x^{\vee}_0 \neq 0,\ \mathsf{P}(x^{\vee}_0);\ \mathsf{w}_0(x^{\vee}_0)$ and $x^{\vee}_0 \neq \mathsf{s}(x^{\vee}_1),\ \mathsf{P}(x^{\vee}_0);\ \mathsf{w}_0(x^{\vee}_0)$. Contrary to the tableau proof we are now able to rewrite the literal inherited from the parent node in place without copying it. Note that in tableau proofs an equality literal can be used to rewrite formulas of its offspring in place, whereas it must copy ancestor formulas beforehand down to its offspring because the ancestor is also part of other branches that do not include the equality literal. Moreover, the weight term can be rewritten as well, which again is not possible in the tableau version where the weight is at the root node. After rewriting we get $x^{\vee}_0 \neq 0,\ \mathsf{P}(0);\ \mathsf{w}_0(0)$ and $x^{\vee}_0 \neq \mathsf{s}(x^{\vee}_1),\ \mathsf{P}(\mathsf{s}(x^{\vee}_1));\ \mathsf{w}_0(\mathsf{s}(x^{\vee}_1))$. Since the equality literals are in solved form for the variable $x^{\vee}_0$ that does not occur elsewhere in the syntactic constructs, we know that validity cannot rely on this literal. This means that we can safely remove both equality literals resulting in (1.1) $\mathsf{P}(0);\ \mathsf{w}_0(0)$ and (1.2) $\mathsf{P}(\mathsf{s}(x^{\vee}_1));\ \mathsf{w}_0(\mathsf{s}(x^{\vee}_1))$. Removing redundant formulas is the most important simplification step besides contextual rewriting. It seems to be impossible in tableau trees unless the redundancy of the formula is due to the ancestor nodes only, which only is the case for useless formulas that should not have been added at all. In Wirth (1997) and in QuodLibet (cf. Kühler (1999)) the Expansion from (1) into (1.1) and (1.2) is done by a single inference step applying a so-called "covering set of substitutions". Note that the present state of the sequent proof is much simpler than the corresponding state of the tableau proof. The former consists of the nodes (1.1) and (1.2) and has two formulas and one variable. The latter consists of a six node tree with five formulas and two variables. This is of practical importance because tactics for proof search are more easily confused with less concise proof state representations. The rest of the whole sequent proof is analogous to the tableau proof with the exception that all rewrite steps are omitted since there are no equality literals to rewrite with and the terms are already in normal form.

Another possibility restricted to sequent calculi is that each syntactic construct labeling a node in the trees can be applied as an induction hypothesis. We do not see a real advantage in this because splitting the tree in two above such an induction hypothesis results in a better structure of the proof forest and in more successful proofs because we can adjust the syntactic construct appropriately: Suppose we had not started a new proof tree for the hypothesis for Q but instead kept the hypothesis for Q down in the tree (1) at position (1.2.3). Several unsafe generalization steps would have been necessary before $\mathsf{Q}(x^{\forall}_1, \mathsf{s}(x^{\forall}_1)),\ \mathsf{P}(\mathsf{s}(x^{\forall}_1));\ \mathsf{w}_0(\mathsf{s}(x^{\forall}_1))$ would have become useful as an induction hypothesis, namely removing the second formula, generalizing $\mathsf{s}(x^{\forall}_1)$ to a new variable, and switching to a weight that measures also this new variable. Moreover, in practice one should not apply the hypothesis for Q in the tree for P before it is obvious that the tree for Q mutually needs the hypothesis for P: Most of the time a proof for Q can be completed in a proof forest not containing the tree for P. In this case, not only the number of trees in the proof forest for Q gets smaller, but also the tree for P because $\forall y, z\colon\ \mathsf{Q}(y, z)$ can then be applied as a lemma and not as an induction hypothesis, which cuts off the $\not<$-branch of the proof tree of P.

4 Conclusion

We have shown how to integrate implicit ITP into first-order sequent and tableau calculi. The following aspects are novel compared to the concrete implicit induction calculus of Wirth (1997): The tableau presentation, the possibility to use full first-order formulas instead of literals only, and the important addition of free existential variables, i.e. the "dummies" of Prawitz (1960), making the major difference between the free variable calculi of Fitting (1996) and the calculi of Smullyan (1968). Contrary to Baaz & al. (1997) we really integrate *implicit* induction: When we start an inductive proof we do not restrict the applicable induction hypotheses. We can do mutual induction and invent completely new induction hypotheses, which can be full first-order sequents instead of literals only. Moreover, we can also generate induction hypotheses eagerly in the style of explicit induction, which enables goal-directedness w.r.t. induction hypotheses. All this is not possible in the calculus of Baaz & al. (1997).

Furthermore, we exemplified that although tableau calculi may save repetition of formulas, sequent calculi have substantial advantages: Rewriting of formulas in place is always possible, and we can remove formulas that are redundant w.r.t. the other formulas in a sequent. Note that formulas like (nat0) make equality omnipresent in induction and that these simplification steps are even more important in inductive than in deductive theorem proving: Not only do they play a role in the generation of appropriate induction hypotheses; they are an essential part of the failure detection process that has to compensate for over-generalization of induction hypotheses in addition to the detection of invalid input theorems. Finally, the presence of two dual versions of each hypothesis in inductive tableau calculi makes proof guidance by human users more difficult.

References

Matthias Baaz, Uwe Egly, Christian G. Fermüller (1997). *Lean Induction Principles for Tableaux.* 6thTABLEAUX 1997, LNAI 1227, pp. 62-75, Springer.

Leo Bachmair (1988). *Proof By Consistency in Equational Theories.* 3rd IEEE symposium on Logic In Computer Sci., pp. 228-233, IEEE Press.

Peter Baumgartner, Ulrich Furbach, Frieder Stolzenburg (1997). *Computing Answers with Model Elimination.* Artificial Intelligence **90**, pp. 135-176.

Herbert B. Enderton (1973). *A Mathematical Introduction to Logic.* Academic Press.

Melvin Fitting (1996). *First-Order Logic and Automated Theorem Proving.* 2nd extd. ed., Springer.

Gerhard Gentzen (1935). *Untersuchungen über das logische Schließen.* Mathematische Zeitschrift **39**, pp. 176-210, 405-431.

Alfons Geser (1995). *A Principle of Non-Wellfounded Induction.* In: Tiziana Margaria (ed.): Kolloquium Programmiersprachen und Grundlagen der Programmierung, MIP-9519, pp. 117-124, Univ. Passau.

Ulrich Kühler (1999). *A Tactic-Based Inductive Theorem Prover for Data Types with Partial Operations.* Dissertation (Ph.D. thesis), Univ. Kaiserslautern, to appear.

Ulrich Kühler, Claus-Peter Wirth (1996). *Conditional Equational Specifications of Data Types with Partial Operations for Inductive Theorem Proving.* SEKI-Report SR-96-11, FB Informatik, Univ. Kaiserslautern. Short version in: 8th RTA 1997, LNCS 1232, pp. 38-52, Springer.

Peter Padawitz (1996). *Inductive Theorem Proving for Design Specifications.* J. Symbolic Computation **21**, pp. 41-99, Academic Press.

Dag Prawitz (1960). *An Improved Proof Procedure.* In: Siekmann & Wrightson (1983), Vol. 1, pp. 159-199.

Herman Rubin, Jean E. Rubin (1985). *Equivalents of the Axiom of Choice.* Elsevier.

Jörg Siekmann, G. Wrightson (eds.) (1983). *Automation of Reasoning.* Springer.

Raymond M. Smullyan (1968). *First-Order Logic.* Springer.

Claus-Peter Wirth (1997). *Positive/Negative-Conditional Equations: A Constructor-Based Framework for Specification and Inductive Theorem Proving.* Dissertation (Ph.D. thesis), Verlag Dr. Kovač, Hamburg.

Claus-Peter Wirth (1998). *Full First-Order Sequent and Tableau Calculi With Preservation of Solutions and the Liberalized δ-Rule but Without Skolemization.* Report 698/1998, FB Informatik, Univ. Dortmund. Short version in: Gernot Salzer, Ricardo Caferra (eds.). Proc. 2nd Int. Workshop on First-Order Theorem Proving (FTP), pp. 244-255, Vienna, 1998. Also submitted for LNCS version, Springer, 1999.

Claus-Peter Wirth, Klaus Becker (1995). *Abstract Notions and Inference Systems for Proofs by Mathematical Induction.* 4thCTRS 1994, LNCS 968, pp. 353-373, Springer.

Claus-Peter Wirth, Bernhard Gramlich (1994). *On Notions of Inductive Validity for First-Order Equational Clauses.* 12th CADE 1994, LNAI 814, pp. 162-176, Springer.

WWW-home-page: http://LS5.cs.uni-dortmund.de/~wirth/welcome.html

Acknowledgements: I would like to thank Ulrich Furbach and his whole group for all they taught me on tableau calculi and Paul Howard for a short private E-mail communication on the Principle of Dependent Choice that was very helpful to me.

An Interactive Theorem Proving Assistant

Ulrich Endriss

Department of Computer Science, King's College London,
Strand, London WC2R 2LS, UK, Email: endriss@dcs.kcl.ac.uk
URL: http://www.dcs.kcl.ac.uk/~endriss/WinKE/

Abstract. This paper describes WinKE, an interactive proof assistant, which is based on the KE calculus. The software has been designed to serve as a tutoring system supporting the teaching of logic and theorem proving through KE.

1 Introduction

The KE calculus [4] is a refutation system close to the common method of semantic tableaux. The main difference between the two is, that KE is explicitly *not* cut-free. Its analytic cut rule, *PB*, is the only branching rule of the system. Elsewhere [3] it has been argued that KE might be better suited for teaching elementary classical logic than for instance Tableau. The first logic textbook based on KE has been published recently [5].

Even though KE proofs are essentially shorter than Tableau proofs [3, 4], the traditional way of manually building up such trees is – within the teaching context – hardly feasible for examples exceeding, say, five branches, and is in general very time consuming and error-prone. The use of a proof assistant with a strong graphical user interface can help to overcome such problems. It may be used for demonstration purposes during classes or as an interactive learning environment for students working on their coursework. WinKE has been designed to meet those requirements. First of all, it serves as a 'drawing board' for constructing KE proof trees. On top of that various levels of user support are provided, ranging from basic bookkeeping facilities to a fully automated theorem prover for propositional and first order logic. WinKE's design was strongly inspired by the work described in [6]. The program runs under Windows and has been implemented in LPA WinProlog.

In the sequel WinKE's interface and its most important features are described. The last section briefly compares WinKE with other programs of similar objectives.

2 Interface and Graphic Tools

WinKE's interface consists of four windows (see Fig. 1), all of which are opened after the program has been started. The large window is used to display the currently active proof tree. Whenever a particular action requires a specific formula

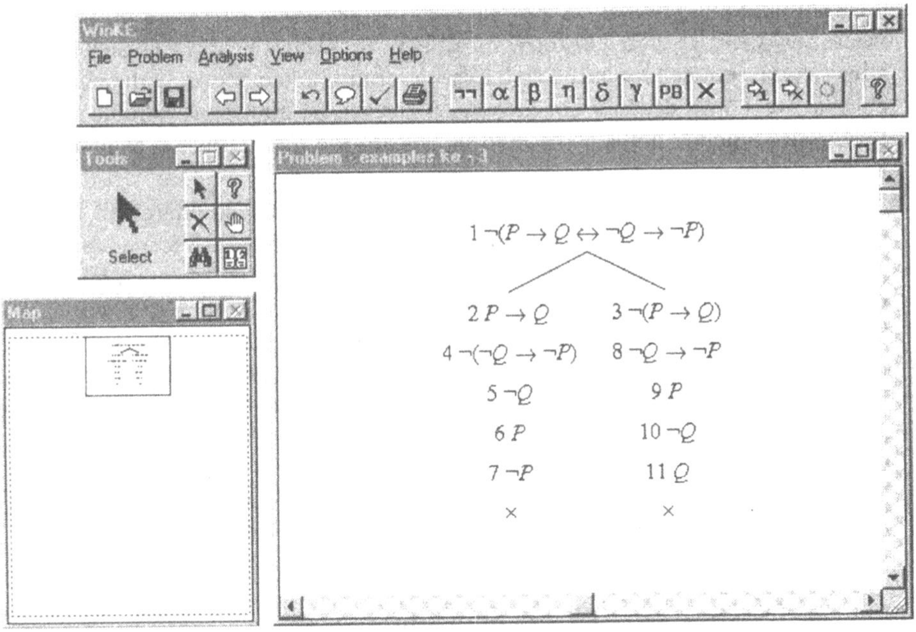

Fig. 1. The WinKE Interface

to be selected, this is done by clicking on that formula on the tree using the mouse. In what way the system will react on such a selection depends on the graphic tool chosen. A graphic tool can be selected from the graphic tool box, just as in any standard graphics software for Windows. The main window contains all the menus to call dialogues for the user's interaction with the program. The buttons on that window provide shortcuts to menu options likely to be used frequently. Finally, the window in the lower left-hand corner can be used as a viewer to navigate around large proof trees that do not fit onto a single screen.

Proof trees displayed in the graphic window consist of graphical objects, which are either formulae or so-called branch markers used to refer to a certain branch of a tree. A branch marker is either represented as a circle (for open branches) or as a cross (for closed branches), placed below the last formula of that branch. Every formula is associated with a certain number, which can be used to refer to parent formulae.

The default graphic tool is the select tool. Clicking on a formula or a branch marker with the select tool will highlight that object. The user may then choose a particular action (by choosing a menu option) to be applied to the selected objects. This will typically be an application of a KE rule. Where necessary the user is prompted for further input (via a dialogue), e.g. the conclusion of a rule application. Then the tree is expanded accordingly. The formulae on a tree are automatically grouped in a space-saving and 'aesthetic' way, thus making sure the user can concentrate on the semantics of a proof tree, instead of its layout.

Two different graphic tools to delete formulae from a tree are provided, the delete and a retract tool. The former simply prunes the tree at the clicked formula, whereas the retract tool only deletes those formulae that logically depend on the clicked one, i.e. that could not have been derived without that formula being on the same branch. This is completed by a standard 'undo' option available from the menus.

The hint tool applied to an open branch marker will highlight all formulae that have not yet been analysed on the associated branch. Vice versa clicking a formula will highlight all open branch markers denoting a branch which that formula has not yet been analysed on. Finally, the bookkeeping tool will display the bookkeeping information available for each node. If that node is a formula, the bookkeeping information consists of the KE rule used to derive it, the parent formula(e), and possibly the sibling formula. In addition, formulae that are either analysed or subsumed on all open branches are marked. If the node clicked on is a closed branch marker, the bookkeeping tool reveals which pair of formulae has been used to close that branch. The button showing a question mark can be used to enter the WinKE help system directly at the section on graphic tools.

3 Deduction and Countermodels

Typically WinKE is used to perform a step-by-step deduction. The system provides three different modes, namely the supervisor, the pedagogue, and the assistant mode. In supervisor mode within the rule application dialogues (for an example see Fig. 2) any (syntactically correct) input is accepted, whereas in pedagogue mode the correctness of the rule applications is checked on-line. The same is true for the assistant, but here the user's input is reduced to a minimum. That means, for the simple rules (the propositional ones apart from *PB*), no input of the conclusion(s) is required as their derivation is straightforward given the premise(s). For the other rules the system gives a list of possible inputs to choose from (alternatively, the user may also type in a formula). In case the supervisor mode has been used, WinKE also provides off-line proof checking. This will display all errors on a tree in turn and allow to retract the wrong formulae directly. For novice users the pedagogue mode will be the most useful one. After some training, possibly in an exam-like context, the supervisor mode may be used. Once a student is familiar with the basics, the assistant mode provides a comfortable way for studying KE more profoundly, for example by comparing different ways of proving the same theorem.

For the on- as well as for the off-line checking the user may choose the level of error reporting. Only the very basic KE rules are checked in any case, in addition you may or may not add checking for beta simplification (subsumption), analytic application of *PB*, and/or checking of the order of rule applications (like for example: analyse an alpha formula before you split a branch using *PB*, etc.).

In particular to make the system a more convenient assistant, but also to be able to demonstrate proofs to novice users, the option to automatically derive (parts of) proofs has been added. You can either ask WinKE to perform the next

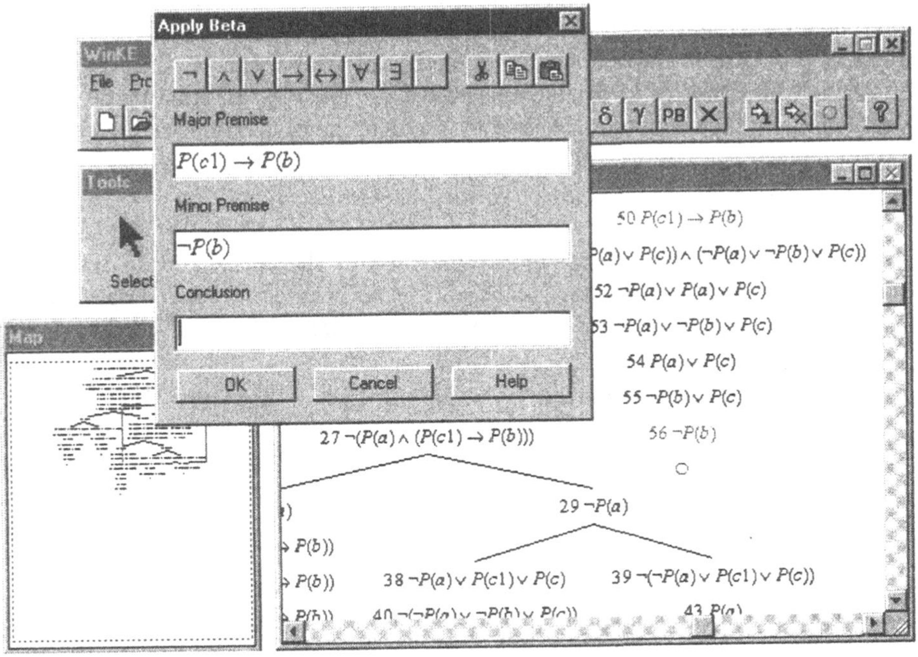

Fig. 2. Applying a Beta Rule

proof step on a selected branch automatically, to finish a branch, or to complete an entire proof.

For consistent sets of formulae, i.e. if there are open branches that cannot be closed, WinKE can automatically derive the description of a countermodel. Moreover, for certain classes of problems a graphical visualization of a countermodel may be displayed. If for instance the countermodel just contains a single 2-ary predicate and the number of terms appearing is limited, the positive atoms in the model can be represented as edges in a graph. Another example where visualization is possible is the class of (simple) 'pigeon hole' problems.

4 Additional Features

KE problems are saved in files, either as problems, proofs, or incomplete proofs. Within the program you can jump between different problems of the same file. Problem files are edited in the same environment as they are worked on. You have the option to cut and paste from existing problems when defining new ones. This offers a comfortable way for teachers to write up and test new exercises. Students could be encouraged to make their own experiments trying different sets of formulae.

Every problem is associated with a text of arbitrary length. Also that text can be edited and read directly within WinKE. In the context of a student exercise it might contain hints for finding a solution or a reference to a page of a textbook. Other features available include printing and generating LaTeX descriptions of proof trees. Parts of the functionality of WinKE can be made password protected, for example to disable automated proving, the assistant mode, or the proof checker. The tool is completed by a comprehensive on-line help system.

5 Conclusion

WinKE's principal task is to support teaching in the context of an introductory course on elementary classical logic. The software is complementary to the logic textbook [5], which is based on KE. Evaluation copies of the software are available on request.

Other logic tutors include popular programs like Tarski's World [1] and Hyperproof [2]. Using Tarski's World students are asked to verify first order formulae stating propositions about simple worlds inhabited by geometric objects, but unlike WinKE the program does not deploy a systematic proof procedure. Hyperproof is used to construct proofs of statements about that same geometric world applying a natural deduction like calculus. As it is restricted to examples of that particular domain it is difficult to be compared with WinKE. WinKE has been designed to simulate an existing proof procedure. In that sense it is supportive of the teaching process. For Hyperproof, on the contrary, teaching is more likely to be centered around the software.

The Tableau II program [7] is based on semantic tableaux and therefore much closer to WinKE than the other two systems. As far as interface and usability are concerned WinKE clearly offers noticeable advantages over Tableau II.

Acknowledgments. This work has partly been supported by CARID (Centro di Ateneo per la Ricerca e l'Innovazione Didattica) at the University of Ferrara. The author would like to thank Jeremy Pitt, Marcello D'Agostino, Marco Mondadori, and Dov Gabbay for their help and support, and two anonymous referees for their valuable comments.

References

1. J. Barwise and J. Etchemendy. *Tarski's World.* CSLI Publications, Stanford, 1991.
2. J. Barwise and J. Etchemendy. *Hyperproof.* CSLI Publications, Stanford, 1994.
3. K. Broda, M. D'Agostino, and M. Mondadori. A solution to a problem of Popper. In *The Epistemology of Karl Popper.* Kluwer Academic Publishers. To appear.
4. M. D'Agostino and M. Mondadori. The taming of the cut. Classical refutations with analytic cut. *Journal of Logic and Computation*, 3:285–319, 1994.
5. M. Mondadori and M. D'Agostino. *Logica.* Edizioni Scolastiche Bruno Mondadori, Milan, 1997. English translation in preparation.
6. J. Pitt. MacKE: Yet another proof assistant & automated pedagogic tool. In P. Baumgärtner *et al.*, editors, *Theorem Proving with Analytic Tableaux and Related Methods (TABLEAUX'95)*, vol. 918 of *LNAI*, pages 324–337. Springer-Verlag, 1995.
7. M. Potter and D. Watt. Tableau II: A logic teaching program. Technical report, Oxford University Computing Services, Learning and Resource Centre, Oxford, 1988.

A Time Efficient KE Based Theorem Prover

Ulrich Endriss

Department of Computer Science, King's College London,
Strand, London WC2R 2LS, UK, Email: endriss@dcs.kcl.ac.uk
URL: http://www.dcs.kcl.ac.uk/~endriss/

Abstract. We present a proof procedure based on the KE calculus for propositional logic and its implementation as a short Prolog program. The procedure's time complexity is discussed and compared to that of an efficient Tableau based prover.

1 Introduction

The KE calculus [2] is a refutation system close to Tableau. The crucial feature that distinguishes the former from the latter is the integration of an analytic cut rule (*PB*). Even though some sort of 'superiority' of KE over Tableau in terms of proof size has been stated in the literature, until now no *implemented* KE based proof procedure can compete with state-of-the-art Tableau provers as far as runtimes are concerned.

The aim of this work has been to close that gap, at least for the case of classical propositional logic. As a benchmark we take leanTAP [1], a 'lean' Tableau based theorem prover implemented in Prolog, which is simple and efficient. As leanTAP was build for first order logic we will first reduce it to a propositional prover in order to guarantee a 'fair competition'. Then a KE based proof procedure is designed in a similar fashion. The problems naturally arising during such a transformation are addressed and – where possible – solved. We conclude with an experimental comparison of the two procedures.

2 Space and Time

In [2] it has been shown that KE linearly simulates the Tableau method, whereas the latter cannot p-simulate KE, in other words: *KE proofs are basically shorter than Tableau proofs.* This is in fact true – with respect to space – for 'ideal' (again, with respect to space) proof procedures.

But, from that observation alone, we *cannot* conclude, that for a specific problem the KE deduction is also *faster* than the Tableau deduction. Apart from the space complexity results also the following points need to be considered:

- The time taken by a proof procedure depends on the number of derived formulae *and* on the time required to derive one such formula. In a KE based procedure an application of a beta rule takes much more time than any step (apart from closing a branch) in a Tableau prover.

- KE has more rules than Tableau. A proof procedure has to check which rule to apply to a given formula. As there are fewer possibilities in Tableau, the checking will be faster in that setting.
- A fast prover is not necessarily ideal with respect to space. leanTAP for instance does not build up a minimal proof tree, but still is very time efficient.

3 A Tableau Procedure for Propositional Logic

The Prolog program leanTAP as defined in [1] implements a small theorem prover for first order logic, based on free-variable semantic tableaux. Table 1 shows an adaptation for propositional logic, which we call `tap`.[1] Like the original, `tap` is restricted to negation normal form (*NNF*), i.e. negation has to be pushed down to the atomic level before deduction starts.

```
tap( (A,B), Fmls, Lits) :- !,       % apply alpha
    tap( A, [B|Fmls], Lits).

tap( (A;B), Fmls, Lits) :- !,       % apply beta
    tap( A, Fmls, Lits), !,
    tap( B, Fmls, Lits).

tap( Lit, _, Lits) :-               % close branch
    (Lit = -(C) ; -(Lit) = C) -> member( C, Lits).

tap( Lit, [Fml|Fmls], Lits) :-      % next formula
    tap( Fml, Fmls, [Lit|Lits]).
```

Table 1. leanTAP for propositional logic

To obtain `tap` from leanTAP the clauses handling quantified formulae have been omitted and the clause for closing branches has been simplified as no occur check is necessary. Due to the nature of these simplifications, it is clear that `tap` will be slightly faster than leanTAP for propositional logic.

4 Designing the KE Proof Procedure

In KE proof trees are constructed in a similar way to the Tableau method. Alpha rules and the notion of a closed branch are identical for both calculi. KE beta rules are linear and take two premises. For example from $A \vee B$ and $\neg A$ we can infer B. Unlike Tableau, KE is not cut-free. Following the principle of bivalence (*PB*) a branch may be split adding a formula A to the left and its negation $\neg A$ to the right branch. For analytic KE the choice for such *PB*-formulae is restricted to subformulae of beta formulae that are already on the branch to be split [2].

[1] The provers described in this paper can handle conjunction, disjunction, and negation, which have been represented in Prolog as ',', ';', and '-', respectively.

When trying to follow the lines of `tap`'s design to construct a KE based theorem prover (for propositional formulae in *NNF*) we encounter the following problems:

- If *PB* is applied to a non-atomic subformula, its negation will not be in *NNF*. On the other hand we cannot simply restrict *PB* to literals, as the remaining calculus would not be complete.
- The most time consuming steps during proof search are those where you have to search a list for a matching formula, i.e. closure (both calculi) and KE's beta rules. For closing branches it is possible to restrict this search to complementary literals. It would be nice to have a similar restriction for the search of complements of minor premises for beta formulae. Unfortunately, KE is not complete if beta rules can only be applied to literals as minor premises.

To overcome those difficulties we introduce an adaptation of KE, which we will call KE*. Informally we obtain KE* from KE by restricting the application of beta rules to literals as minor premises, with one exception: directly after every application of *PB* the next (obvious) application of beta is performed in any case. For example, if *PB* is applied to A, the left subformula of $A \vee B$, then write A on the left branch, and $\neg A$ *and* B on the right one (whether A is a literal or not). KE* is restricted to formulae in *NNF*. The problem addressed before, namely that *PB* can produce non-*NNF* formulae is solved by immediately transforming the negated *PB*-formula into *NNF*. KE* is easily shown to be sound and complete (via a 'reduction' to KE and Tableau, respectively).

The simplest transformation of `tap` into a KE* proof procedure would only involve replacing the Tableau beta rule with the *two* beta rules for KE* (one for the left and one for the right subformula) and the new *PB* rule. This procedure can be improved by holding back beta formulae unless there are no more unexpanded alpha formulae on the branch.

A Prolog implementation of this procedure, which we call `kep`, is shown in Table 2. The alpha rule is the same as for `tap`. So is the clause which moves the active literal into the lists `Lits` and puts the next unexpanded formula into focus ('next formula'). The second clause does the 'storing' of beta formulae: they are temporarily stored in the list `Betas` and the next formula is tackled. The last clause takes the first element of that list of beta formulae and puts it into focus, if there are no more unexpanded formulae left in the main list `Fmls`. Also the implementation of the beta rule for the left subformula is straightforward. An attempt to apply beta is only made if the left subformula `A` is a literal. For the second beta rule things are more complicated. If the left subformula `A` is also a literal, we already know that the complement of `A` is *not* on the branch (i.e. in `Lits`). Otherwise beta would have been applied to it before. Because the conclusion of the beta rule is `A`, the next step would be to try to close the branch using `A`, i.e. to search `Lits` again. As we do not want to repeat this time consuming search, which is bound to fail anyway, that step can be omitted; `A` can be added to the list of literals directly, and the next formula can be addressed. If there is no such formula left, the procedure fails, because the branch cannot

```
kep( (A,B), Fmls, Betas, Lits) :- !,           % alpha
  kep( A, [B|Fmls], Betas, Lits).

kep( (A;B), [Fml|Fmls], Betas, Lits) :- !, % store beta
  kep( Fml, Fmls, [(A;B)|Betas], Lits).

kep( (A;B), [], Betas, Lits) :-               % apply beta: left
  (literal( A) -> ((A = -(C); -(A) = C) -> member( C, Lits))), !,
  kep( B, [], Betas, Lits).

kep( (A;B), [], Betas, Lits) :-               % apply beta: right
  (literal( B) -> ((B = -(C); -(B) = C) -> member( C, Lits))), !,
  (literal( A)
  -> Betas = [Beta|Rest], kep( Beta, [], Rest, [A|Lits])
  ;  kep( A, [], Betas, Lits)).

kep( (A;B), [], Betas, Lits) :- !,            % apply pb
  (literal( A)
  -> Betas = [Beta|Rest], kep( Beta, [], Rest, [A|Lits])
  ;  kep( A, [], Betas, Lits)),
  nnf( -(A), NNF), !,
  (literal( B)
  -> kep( NNF, [], Betas, [B|Lits])
  ;  kep( NNF, [B], Betas, Lits)).

kep( Lit, _, _, Lits) :-                      % close branch
  (Lit = -(C); -(Lit) = C) -> member( C, Lits).

kep( Lit, [Fml|Fmls], Betas, Lits) :- !,     % next formula
  kep( Fml, Fmls, Betas, [Lit|Lits]).

kep( Lit, [], [Beta|Betas], Lits) :-         % next beta formula
  kep( Beta, [], Betas, [Lit|Lits]).
```

Table 2. The KE based theorem prover `kep` for propositional logic

be closed. Similarly, when applying *PB* we already know, that, if one of the subformulae is a literal, its complement will not be found in `Lits`. So again, time can be saved. Note that the negated *PB*-formula is directly transformed into *NNF*.

5 Performance: Tableau v. KE

Applying a beta rule in KE reduces the number of branches compared to Tableau, but in Tableau such additional branches can be closed directly after having applied beta. For the given procedures those two actions have the same time complexity. In `tap` we have one basic step for the application of beta and one search through the list of literals for the closure. For `kep` we first search the list for the complement of the literal subformula and then we have the basic step of the actual rule application. What remains are four major differences between the two procedures that determine which of them will perform better when trying to refute a set of formulae.

- As **kep** has more clauses than **tap**, for every formula on the tree more checks of which clause applies have to be made.
- As in Prolog it is easier to insert an element at the beginning of a list than at the end, the storing of beta formulae in **kep** changes the order in which the two procedures analyse those formulae. What impact this has on the proof size is not clear and depends very much on the specific example.
- *PB* introduces a new formula on the right branch, the negated *PB*-formula, which Tableau does not do. This may help closing a branch earlier, but could also distract from applying the 'right' rules.
- For **kep** the transformation into *NNF* during an application of *PB* will require additional time.

	tap			kep		
No.	Time (*msecs*)	Formulae Derived	Branches Closed	Time (*msecs*)	Formulae Derived	Branches Closed
1	4	16	4	4	13	2
2	2	6	2	2	7	2
3	2	6	1	2	6	1
4	4	16	4	4	13	2
5	4	18	3	4	12	2
6	1	2	1	1	2	1
7	1	2	1	1	2	1
8	2	6	2	2	5	1
9	4	22	9	4	16	3
10	6	38	9	8	42	7
11	2	6	2	2	7	2
12	26	138	24	41	185	32
13	6	36	9	7	28	3
14	8	42	10	13	52	9
15	4	16	4	4	13	2
16	2	6	1	2	6	1
17	10	64	14	12	39	3

Table 3. Performances of **tap** and **kep** on the Pelletier Problems 1–17

Table 3 shows results for the runtimes of **tap** and **kep** on the Pelletier Problems for propositional logic [4]. Both programs have been tested on a Sun Sparc 10 running SWI-Prolog 2.1. The times given (average runtime for 100 tests) include the search for a *NNF*. While **kep** derives slightly fewer formulae and requires about three quarters of the branches,[2] it is on average around 10% slower than tap.

In [3] the KE based prover leanKE is compared with leanTAP (both for first order logic). It derives slightly fewer formulae than kep and closes slightly fewer branches. The average runtime compared to leanTAP on the same set of problems is around 350%. That leanTAP is that much faster than leanKE is partly due to the size of the latter: leanKE has many more clauses, which means that for every formula to be analysed the time to find the right clause is longer. Moreover, leanKE, unlike kep, does not implement a strategy preventing it from searching for the complement of a formula a second time after a beta rule or *PB* has been applied.

Acknowledgements. The author would like to thank Marco Mondadori, Marcello D'Agostino, and Bernhard Beckert for many inspiring discussions, and two anonymous referees for their helpful comments.

References

1. B. Beckert and J. Posegga. leanTAP: Lean Tableau-based deduction. *Journal of Automated Reasoning*, 15(3):339–358, 1995.
2. M. D'Agostino and M. Mondadori. The taming of the cut. Classical refutations with analytic cut. *Journal of Logic and Computation*, 4(3):285–319, 1994.
3. J. Pitt and J. Cunningham. Theorem proving and model building with the calculus KE. *Bulletin of the IGPL*, 4:129–150, 1995.
4. F. Pelletier. Seventy-five problems for testing automatic theorem provers. *Journal of Automated Reasoning*, 2:191–216, 1986.

[2] Remember that both procedures have not been designed for minimal space requirements. The smallest possible proof trees are smaller for most of the examples.

Strategy Parallel Use of Model Elimination with Lemmata
– System Abstract –

Andreas Wolf & Joachim Draeger

Institut für Informatik der Technischen Universität München, D–80290 München
{wolfa,draeger}@in.tum.de

Abstract. Automated Deduction offers no unique strategy which is uniformly successful on all problems. Hence a parallel combination of strategies increases the chances of success. Our approach is made even more efficient by the exchange of suitable intermediate results. We present in this paper the model of a cooperative parallel model elimination prover which combines different lemma selection strategies in a strategy parallel prover environment. We assess the results of first experiments and give an outline of the future work.

Introduction. Up to now, sequential automated theorem provers (ATPs) have set a high standard. But when dealing with difficult problems, ATPs are still inferior to a skilled human mathematician. An important technique to increase the performance is to employ parallelism. Another promising technique is the use of lemmata for reducing the search space which has to be processed for obtaining a solution. We want to show that both parallelism and lemmatization can profit from the combination of several lemma selection strategies in a competitive manner. Thus our aim is the realization of such a combination.

Our prover system is based on model elimination [Lov68]; all sub-provers are instances of the SETHEO [MIL+97] prover.

Several approaches for cooperation have been discussed in the literature like the resolution based DARES [CMM90] or the model elimination provers METEOR [AL97] and DELTA [Sch94], which use lemmata.

The system abstract is organized as follows. The three main sections deal with the topics lemma generation and evaluation, lemma selection, and combination of lemma generation techniques. We conclude with a short assessment of first experimental results and with an outlook.

Lemma Evaluation. Lemmata have the potential to reduce the search space to be processed. By separating parts of an original proof p one can achieve a modularization of both the proof and the search process. Technically a simple version of such a modularization can be realized as a procedure which generates unit-lemmata and uses them for constructing a proof p' of the actual problem. The new proof p' is smaller and hence easier to find than p. The restriction of the generation procedure to lemmata, which are 'useful' with respect to the modularization of the actual proof task performs the desired restriction of the search space. Which lemmata can be considered to be useful? The lemmatization has to reduce the necessary effort for finding a proof by modularization. Consequently, a lemma is considered to be useful only if it enables a separation of a ***significant part*** of the original proof. This is only possible, if the lemma itself requires a significantly complex proof. A suitable way to measure the proof complexity of a lemma f is the *minimal proof length* $p(f)$, the number of inferences contained in the smallest proof of f. Due to practical reasons, we assume the first proof of a certain lemma l generated by the applied proof procedure to be the minimal one (it is the proof generated consuming minimal resources). A comparatively large value of this parameter will be our first selection criterion.

To use the proof length as the only criterion is not sufficient for an efficient lemma selection. In most cases an overwhelming number of lemmata requiring non-trivial proofs exist. Hence an additional selection criterion is needed. This criterion can be based on the observation that the *potential* of separating a significant part of *some* proofs is not sufficient; the separation must actually *happen* in a proof of the *actual* problem. Consequently, we choose the *relevancy* $r(f)$ of a lemma f with respect to the actual proof task as a second selection criterion. Many different methods for the relevancy estimation are possible. Each one leads to a specific selection strategy. In the experiments, we evaluate some of these criteria.

The *information measure I* described in [Dra98a] evaluates a lemma f with respect to the two criteria given above. This is done by using the product $I(f)=p(f)\cdot r(f)$ of the proof complexity $p(f)$ and the relevancy $r(f)$. A lemma f is considered to be suitable if $I(f)$ has a large value. So both, uninteresting lemmata with a small relevance value, and trivialities with a small complexity, are excluded. These considerations establish an argument for the naming of information measure, too. The value of $I(f)$ is large, if f seems to be of great value for the construction of the final proof.

Dynamic Lemma Selection. In this section, we present a prover model, which allows a dynamic selection of sets of high value lemmata to enrich the original proof task. Our prover is based on the cooperation in a *cooperative cell*, which is a triple (RG,LG,LS) consisting of a *request generation component* (RG), a *lemma generation component* (LG), and a *lemma selection component* (LS). In our implementation, both generators use SETHEO. LG produces unit lemmata similar to DELTA and uses the evaluation strategies given in the previous section. RG tries to prove the set of input clauses and generates proof requests (subgoals which fail because of the lack of resources during the proof attempt). To achieve cooperation between RG and LG, LS repeatedly chooses a subset of the lemmata generated by LG. Each time such a set of lemmata has been selected, a new *dependent sub-prover* is started. In detail, our implementation works as follows. LG sends a data stream of generated lemmata to LS accompanied with the value of the information measure of this lemma. In order to support the lemma selection RG adds data on the information measure to the generated proof requests and sends the requests to LS. If a lemma l is more general than the request r, it may be useful for the proof search. When additionally using l in the original proof task, the RG would succeed at the generation position of r and possibly complete the proof attempt. In LS the received data is ranked with respect to the attached evaluation value. At any time, the best k lemmata of the lemma pool in LS represent possibly well-suited lemmata and form a lemma-set $\mathcal{L}$. Every time $\mathcal{L}$ has "significantly" changed, a new dependent sub-prover is started. This prover tries to refute the original input clauses augmented with $\mathcal{L}$.

In the following figure, the data flow of a cooperative cell is illustrated. The width of the arrows indicates the amount of data transmitted between the components. The scheme additionally shows that not all generated lemmata and requests will be transmitted. Those formulae which get a very low evaluation value do not enter LS.

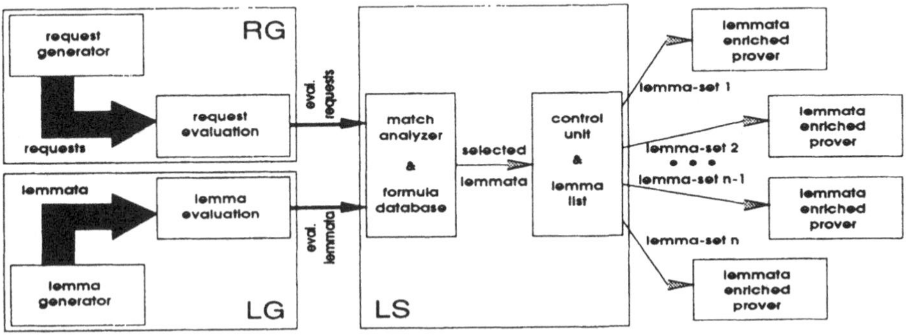

Strategy Parallelism. A search problem is typically solved by applying a *uniform* search procedure. In automated deduction, different search strategies may have a strongly different behavior on a given problem. This especially holds considering cooperative strategies. In general, it cannot be decided in advance which strategy is the best for a given problem. This motivates the *competitive* use of different strategies. In our approach, we employ the paradigm of *strategy parallelism* [WL98]. Strategy parallelism is, roughly spoken, the selection of more than one search strategy in combination with techniques to partition the available resources depending on the actual task.

When trying to determine an optimal selection of strategies for a given set of problems, we are faced with the *strategy allocation problem*. For details on this problem see [WL98]. It was shown that this problem is strongly NP-complete. Therefore, in practice the determination of an optimal solution is not possible, at least not on larger sets and with classical methods. One reasonable possibility is to use a gradient procedure [Wol98b] as we do it in our implementation. This procedure has been used to determine the schedule for the following experiments.

Experiments. To determine the influence of the cooperation on the proof process, we compare the results of our lemma selection strategies with a successful conventional prover strategy of SETHEO. The considered lemma selection strategies can be divided into two different approaches. In *strategy 1* we define the relevancy of a lemma f as reciprocal value of its *syntactic complexity*. A special version of this strategy is discussed in [Dra98b]. Here, we measure the syntactic complexity of a unit-lemma f in two variants. The *symbol size*

$sc_1(f)$ counts the number of constant and function symbols contained in the assertion of f. The *symbol depth* $sc_2(f)$ describes the length of the longest path in the assertion of f represented as a symbol tree. *Strategy 2* defines the relevancy of a lemma f in terms of its *similarity to the query* q. The main idea of this strategy is the identification of lemmata, which are useful with respect to a step-by-step construction of the query q [Dra98a]. The first version of strategy 2 sets the relevancy to be the *structural similarity* $sq_1(f)$, the second version uses the *signature similarity* $sq_2(f)$. Let $w_1, \ldots, w_n$ be the maximal subterms contained both in f and q. Then the function $qs_1(f)$ is defined to be $qs_1(f) = sc_1(q) + sc_1(f) - 2 \cdot sc_1(w_1) - \ldots - 2 \cdot sc_1(w_n)$. Similarly, the function $sq_2(f)$ counts the numbers $n_q(a_i)$,$n_f(a_i)$ of occurrences of each function, constant, and predicate symbol $a_1, \ldots, a_m$ contained in q and f. The value of $g_q(f)$ is determined by $g_q(f) = |n_q(a_1) - n_f(a_1)| + \ldots + |n_q(a_m) - n_f(a_m)|$.

In the first table we depict the time needed using each lemma evaluation strategy and a conventional reference strategy for some selected problems from the TPTP library. The time limit in this experiment was 300 seconds. The table shows by some examples, how strong the computational behavior of the considered strategies differs.

strategy	conventional strategy	strategy 1 sc_1 (size)	strategy 1 sc_2 (depth)	strategy 2 sq_1 (structure)	strategy 2 sq_2 (signature)
CAT008-1	-	-	13s	7s	28s
GEO004-1	-	66s	108s	-	-
GRP048-2	-	14s	-	20s	-
HEN006-3	-	-	-	138s	44s
LCL090-1	-	27s	68s	67s	151s
PUZ010-1	-	-	122s	137s	127s
RNG038-1	-	-	178s	3s	-
ROB016-1	92s	-	-	16s	17s
SYN310-1	187s	202s	55s	202s	51s

The next table shows the summarized results on a subset of 92 problems (all problems not solvable by the conventional strategy in 20 seconds but solvable by one of the five strategies) taken from the 547 eligibles of the CADE-15 Automated Theorem Prover Competition.

	proofs	%	time (s)	%	time/proof (s)	%
strategy 1 size sc_1	46	65	15825	102	344	156
strategy 1 depth sc_2	41	62	16416	105	400	182
strategy 2 structure sq_1	53	75	14217	96	268	122
strategy 2 signature sq_2	40	56	17923	115	448	204
conventional	34	48	21181	136	622	283
strategy parallel	71	100	15589	100	220	100

We measure the time needed by our four lemma evaluation strategies to treat all problems and count the proofs. Then we do the same with the conventional reference strategy and the strategy parallel system p-SETHEO [Wol98a] (on one processor) which integrates the four cooperative strategies and the conventional one. The maximal amount of time spent to each proof attempt (even the strategy parallel) is 300 seconds. This experiment shows that the cooperative strategies are able to prove much more problems than the conventional strategy. But the sets of problems solved by different lemma selection strategies differ greatly. This makes lemma generation strategies very convenient for strategy parallelism (lemma selection strategies tend to have a low ***overlap value***, i. e., the non trivial problems solved by these strategies differ significantly, see [WL98]). The strategy parallel combination of conventional and lemma selection based strategies combines the high number of solvable problems with comparatively low response times.

Assessment and Future Work. The experimental results show that the combination of cooperating strategies can achieve very high speed-ups. Our lemma evaluation and selection techniques were successful in order to solve problems which have been unreachable with conventional search methods. Nevertheless, the methods and techniques for information assessment and selection still need further research. Note that our cooperation approach can be combined with other parallelization paradigms like search space partitioning [SS94]. Thus, the good scalability of these models can easily be incorporated into our prover.

A second advantage of our model is the adaptability of the underlying approach to the difficulty of the actual proof task. The lemmata are generated step by step, and so we get new sets of selected lemmata during the whole run time of the generators. So a simple proof task may be proved even without starting a sub-prover with a lemma enriched clause set, and difficult problems with a long run-time will employ a large amount of these sub-provers.

References

[AL97] O. Astrachan and D. Loveland. The Use of Lemmas in the Model Elimination Procedure. *JAR*, 19(1):117–141, 1997.

[CMM90] S. Conry, et al. DARES: A Distributed Automated Reasoning System. In *AAAI-8*, pages 78–85, 1990.

[Dra98a] J. Draeger. Modularisierte Suche in Theorembeweisern. PhD thesis, Munich University of Technology, 1998.

[Dra98b] J. Draeger. Acquisition of Useful Lemma Knowledge in Automated Reasoning. In *AIMSA-98*, LNAI 1480, pages 230–239, 1998.

[Lov68] D. Loveland. Mechanical Theorem-Proving by Model Elimination. *JACM*, 15(2), 1968.

[MIL+97] M. Moser, et al. SETHEO and E-SETHEO. The CADE-13 Systems. *JAR*, 18(2):237–246, 1997.

[Sch94] J. Schumann. DELTA - A Bottom-Up Preprocessor for Top-Down Theorem Provers. In *CADE-12*, LNAI 814, pages 774–777, 1994.

[SS94] C. Suttner and J. Schumann. Parallel Automated Theorem Proving. In *PPAI*, pages 209–257, 1994.

[WL98] A. Wolf and R. Letz. Strategy Parallelism in Automated Theorem Proving. *IJPRAI*, 13(2): to appear, 1998. AAAI Press.

[Wol98a] A. Wolf. p-SETHEO: Strategy Parallelism in Automated Theorem Proving. In *Tableaux'98*, LNAI 1397, pages 320–324, 1998.

[Wol98b] A. Wolf. Strategy Selection for Automated Theorem Proving. In *AIMSA-98*, LNAI 1480, pages 452–465, 1998.

Author Index

Lecture Notes in Artificial Intelligence (LNAI)

Vol. 1458: V.O. Mittal, H.A. Yanco, J. Aronis, R. Simpson (Eds.), Assistive Technology in Artificial Intelligence. X, 273 pages. 1998.

Vol. 1471: J. Dix, L. Moniz Pereira, T.C. Przymusinski (Eds.), Logic Programming and Knowledge Representation. Proceedings, 1997. IX, 246 pages. 1998.

Vol. 1476: J. Calmet, J. Plaza (Eds.), Artificial Intelligence and Symbolic Computation. Proceedings, 1998. XI, 309 pages. 1998.

Vol. 1480: F. Giunchiglia (Ed.), Artificial Intelligence: Methodology, Systems, and Applications. Proceedings, 1998. IX, 502 pages. 1998.

Vol. 1484: H. Coelho (Ed.), Progress in Artificial Intelligence – IBERAMIA 98. Proceedings, 1998. XIII, 421 pages. 1998.

Vol. 1488: B. Smyth, P. Cunningham (Eds.), Advances in Case-Based Reasoning. Proceedings, 1998. XI, 482 pages. 1998.

Vol. 1489: J. Dix, L. Fariñas del Cerro, U. Furbach (Eds.), Logics in Artificial Intelligence. Proceedings, 1998. X, 391 pages. 1998.

Vol. 1495: T. Andreasen, H. Christiansen, H.L. Larsen (Eds.), Flexible Query Answering Systems. Proceedings, 1998. IX, 393 pages. 1998.

Vol. 1501: M.M. Richter, C.H. Smith, R. Wiehagen, T. Zeugmann (Eds.), Algorithmic Learning Theory. Proceedings, 1998. XI, 439 pages. 1998.

Vol. 1502: G. Antoniou, J. Slaney (Eds.), Advanced Topics in Artificial Intelligence. Proceedings, 1998. XI, 333 pages. 1998.

Vol. 1504: O. Herzog, A. Günter (Eds.), KI-98: Advances in Artificial Intelligence. Proceedings, 1998. XI, 355 pages. 1998.

Vol. 1510: J.M. Zytkow, M. Quafafou (Eds.), Principles of Data Mining and Knowledge Discovery. Proceedings, 1998. XI, 482 pages. 1998.

Vol. 1515: F. Moreira de Oliveira (Ed.), Advances in Artificial Intelligence. Proceedings, 1998. X, 259 pages. 1998.

Vol. 1527: P. Baumgartner, Theory Reasoning in Connection Calculi. IX, 283 pages. 1999.

Vol. 1529: D. Farwell, L. Gerber, E. Hovy (Eds.), Machine Translation and the Information Soup. Proceedings, 1998. XIX, 532 pages. 1998.

Vol. 1531: H.-Y. Lee, H. Motoda (Eds.), PRICAI'98: Topics in Artificial Intelligence. XIX, 646 pages. 1998.

Vol. 1532: S. Arikawa, H. Motoda (Eds.), Discovery Science. Proceedings, 1998. XI, 456 pages. 1998.

Vol. 1534: J.S. Sichman, R. Conte, N. Gilbert (Eds.), Multi-Agent Systems and Agent-Based Simulation. Proceedings, 1998. VIII, 237 pages. 1998.

Vol. 1535: S. Ossowski, Co-ordination in Artificial Agent Societies. XVI, 221 pages. 1999.

Vol. 1537: N. Magnenat-Thalmann, D. Thalmann (Eds.), Modelling and Motion Capture Techniques for Virtual Environments. Proceedings, 1998. IX, 273 pages. 1998.

Vol. 1544: C. Zhang, D. Lukose (Eds.), Multi-Agent Systems. Proceedings, 1998. VII, 195 pages. 1998.

Vol. 1545: A. Birk, J. Demiris (Eds.), Learning Robots. Proceedings, 1996. IX, 188 pages. 1998.

Vol. 1555: J.P. Müller, M.P. Singh, A.S. Rao (Eds.), Intelligent Agents V. Proceedings, 1998. XXIV, 455 pages. 1999.

Vol. 1562: C.L. Nehaniv (Ed.), Computation for Metaphors, Analogy, and Agents. X, 389 pages. 1999.

Vol. 1570: F. Puppe (Ed.), XPS-99: Knowledge-Based Systems. VIII, 227 pages. 1999.

Vol. 1571: P. Noriega, C. Sierra (Eds.), Agent Mediated Electronic Commerce. Proceedings, 1998. IX, 207 pages. 1999.

Vol. 1572: P. Fischer, H.U. Simon (Eds.), Computational Learning Theory. Proceedings, 1999. X, 301 pages. 1999.

Vol. 1574: N. Zhong, L. Zhou (Eds.), Methodologies for Knowledge Discovery and Data Mining. Proceedings, 1999. XV, 533 pages. 1999.

Vol. 1582: A. Lecomte, F. Lamarche, G. Perrier (Eds.), Logical Aspects of Computational Linguistics. Proceedings, 1997. XI, 251 pages. 1999.

Vol. 1585: B. McKay, X. Yao, C.S. Newton, J.-H. Kim, T. Furuhashi (Eds.), Simulated Evolution and Learning. Proceedings, 1998. XIII, 472 pages. 1999.

Vol. 1599: T. Ishida (Ed.), Multiagent Platforms. Proceedings, 1998. VIII, 187 pages. 1999.

Vol. 1609: Z. W. Raś, A. Skowron (Eds.), Foundations of Intelligent Systems. Proceedings, 1999. XII, 676 pages. 1999.

Vol. 1611: I. Imam, Y. Kodratoff, A. El-Dessouki, M. Ali (Eds.), Multiple Approaches to Intelligent Systems. Proceedings, 1999. XIX, 899 pages. 1999.

Vol. 1617: N.V. Murray (Ed.), Automated Reasoning with Analytic Tableaux and Related Methods. Proceedings, 1999. X, 325 pages. 1999.

Vol. 1621: D. Fensel, R. Studer (Eds.), Knowledge Acquisition Modeling and Management. Proceedings, 1999. XI, 404 pages. 1999.

Vol. 1634: S. Džeroski, P. Flach (Eds.), Inductive Logic Programming. Proceedings, 1999. VIII, 303 pages. 1999.

Lecture Notes in Computer Science

Vol. 1577: J.-P. Finance (Ed.), Fundamental Approaches to Software Engineering. Proceedings, 1999. X, 245 pages. 1999.

Vol. 1578: W. Thomas (Ed.), Foundations of Software Science and Computation Structures. Proceedings, 1999. X, 323 pages. 1999.

Vol. 1579: W.R. Cleaveland (Ed.), Tools and Algorithms for the Construction and Analysis of Systems. Proceedings, 1999. XI, 445 pages. 1999.

Vol. 1580: A. Včkovski, K.E. Brassel, H.-J. Schek (Eds.), Interoperating Geographic Information Systems. Proceedings, 1999. XI, 329 pages. 1999.

Vol. 1581: J.-Y. Girard (Ed.), Typed Lambda Calculi and Applications. Proceedings, 1999. VIII, 397 pages. 1999.

Vol. 1582: A. Lecomte, F. Lamarche, G. Perrier (Eds.), Logical Aspects of Computational Linguistics. Proceedings, 1997. XI, 251 pages. 1999. (Subseries LNAI).

Vol. 1584: G. Gottlob, E. Grandjean, K. Seyr (Eds.), Computer Science Logic. Proceedings, 1998. X, 431 pages. 1999.

Vol. 1585: B. McKay, X. Yao, C.S. Newton, J.-H. Kim, T. Furuhashi (Eds.), Simulated Evolution and Learning. Proceedings, 1998. XIII, 472 pages. 1999. (Subseries LNAI).

Vol. 1586: J. Rolim et al. (Eds.), Parallel and Distributed Processing. Proceedings, 1999. XVII, 1443 pages. 1999.

Vol. 1587: J. Pieprzyk, R. Safavi-Naini, J. Seberry (Eds.), Information Security and Privacy. Proceedings, 1999. XI, 327 pages. 1999.

Vol. 1590: P. Atzeni, A. Mendelzon, G. Mecca (Eds.), The World Wide Web and Databases. Proceedings, 1998. VIII, 213 pages. 1999.

Vol. 1592: J. Stern (Ed.), Advances in Cryptology – EUROCRYPT '99. Proceedings, 1999. XII, 475 pages. 1999.

Vol. 1593: P. Sloot, M. Bubak, A. Hoekstra, B. Hertzberger (Eds.), High-Performance Computing and Networking. Proceedings, 1999. XXIII, 1318 pages. 1999.

Vol. 1594: P. Ciancarini, A.L. Wolf (Eds.), Coordination Languages and Models. Proceedings, 1999. IX, 420 pages. 1999.

Vol. 1596: R. Poli, H.-M. Voigt, S. Cagnoni, D. Corne, G.D. Smith, T.C. Fogarty (Eds.), Evolutionary Image Analysis, Signal Processing and Telecommunications. Proceedings, 1999. X, 225 pages. 1999.

Vol. 1597: H. Zuidweg, M. Campolargo, J. Delgado, A. Mullery (Eds.), Intelligence in Services and Networks. Proceedings, 1999. XII, 552 pages. 1999.

Vol. 1598: R. Poli, P. Nordin, W.B. Langdon, T.C. Fogarty (Eds.), Genetic Programming. Proceedings, 1999. X, 283 pages. 1999.

Vol. 1599: T. Ishida (Ed.), Multiagent Platforms. Proceedings, 1998. VIII, 187 pages. 1999. (Subseries LNAI).

Vol. 1601: J.-P. Katoen (Ed.), Formal Methods for Real-Time and Probabilistic Systems. Proceedings, 1999. X, 355 pages. 1999.

Vol. 1602: A. Sivasubramaniam, M. Lauria (Eds.), Network-Based Parallel Computing. Proceedings, 1999. VIII, 225 pages. 1999.

Vol. 1605: J. Billington, M. Diaz, G. Rozenberg (Eds.), Application of Petri Nets to Communication Networks. IX, 303 pages. 1999.

Vol. 1606: J. Mira, J.V. Sánchez-Andrés (Eds.), Foundations and Tools for Neural Modeling. Proceedings, Vol. I, 1999. XXIII, 865 pages. 1999.

Vol. 1607: J. Mira, J.V. Sánchez-Andrés (Eds.), Engineering Applications of Bio-Inspired Artificial Neural Networks. Proceedings, Vol. II, 1999. XXIII, 907 pages. 1999.

Vol. 1609: Z. W. Raś, A. Skowron (Eds.), Foundations of Intelligent Systems. Proceedings, 1999. XII, 676 pages. 1999. (Subseries LNAI).

Vol. 1610: G. Cornuéjols, R.E. Burkard, G.J. Woeginger (Eds.), Integer Programming and Combinatorial Optimization. Proceedings, 1999. IX, 453 pages. 1999.

Vol. 1611: I. Imam, Y. Kodratoff, A. El-Dessouki, M. Ali (Eds.), Multiple Approaches to Intelligent Systems. Proceedings, 1999. XIX, 899 pages. 1999. (Subseries LNAI).

Vol. 1614: D.P. Huijsmans, A.W.M. Smeulders (Eds.), Visual Information and Information Systems. Proceedings, 1999. XVII, 827 pages. 1999.

Vol. 1615: C. Polychronopoulos, K. Joe, A. Fukuda, S. Tomita (Eds.), High Performance Computing. Proceedings, 1999. XIV, 408 pages. 1999.

Vol. 1617: N.V. Murray (Ed.), Automated Reasoning with Analytic Tableaux and Related Methods. Proceedings, 1999. X, 325 pages. 1999. (Subseries LNAI).

Vol. 1621: D. Fensel, R. Studer (Eds.), Knowledge Acquisition Modeling and Management. Proceedings, 1999. XI, 404 pages. 1999. (Subseries LNAI).

Vol. 1622: M. González Harbour, J.A. de la Puente (Eds.), Reliable Software Technologies – Ada-Europe'99. Proceedings, 1999. XIII, 451 pages. 1999.

Vol. 1625: B. Reusch (Ed.), Computational Intelligence. Proceedings, 1999. XIV, 710 pages. 1999.

Vol. 1629: H. Leopold, N. García (Eds.), Multimedia Applications, Services and Techniques - ECMAST'99. Proceedings, 1999. XV, 574 pages. 1999.

Vol. 1634: S. Džeroski, P. Flach (Eds.), Inductive Logic Programming. Proceedings, 1999. VIII, 303 pages. 1999. (Subseries LNAI).